# A History of India

# A
# History of India

UNDER

THE TWO FIRST SOVEREIGNS

OF

# THE HOUSE OF TAIMUR,

BÁBER AND HUMÁYUN

**WILLIAM ERSKINE,** ESQ.

(TRANSLATOR OF "MEMOIRS OF THE EMPEROR BABER)

IN TWO VOLUMES.

VOL. II

GYAN

*Published by*

GYAN

Gyan Publishing House
5, Ansari Road
Daryaganj, New Delhi-110002
Phone: 011-47034999, 9811692060
E-mail: books@gyanbooks.com

*Distribution Network*
gyanbooks.com
India, USA, Canada, UK, Australia, France



ISBN : 978-81-212-9701-1 (Set)
ISBN : 978-81-212-9699-1 (PB)
First Published, 1854

2nd Impression 2023

*Printed at:* Gyan Press, Delhi.



**A HISTORY OF INDIA (VOL. II)**
Translator: WILLIAM ERSKINE

A

# HISTORY OF INDIA

UNDER

THE TWO FIRST SOVEREIGNS

OF

# THE HOUSE OF TAIMUR,

BABER AND HUMÁYUN.

BY WILLIAM ERSKINE, ESQ.,

TRANSLATOR OF "MEMOIRS OF THE EMPEROR BÁBER.

IN TWO VOLUMES.

VOL. II.

# CONTENTS

OF

# THE SECOND VOLUME.

---

## HISTORY OF HUMÁYUN.

---

## BOOK FOURTH.

### FROM HUMÁYUN'S ACCESSION TO HIS EXPULSION FROM INDIA.

### CHAPTER I.

#### AFFAIRS OF HUMÁYUN FROM HIS ACCESSION TO HIS INVASION OF MALWA AND GUJRÁT.

## CHAPTER II.

### AFFAIRS OF GUJRÁT AND MALWA.

---

## SECTION I.

### EARLY HISTORY OF THOSE KINGDOMS.—PROGRESS OF BEHÁDER SHAH.

## SECTION II.

### CONQUEST OF MALWA BY HUMÁYUN.



## SECTION III.

### CONQUEST OF GUJRÁT BY HUMÁYUN.

## SECTION IV.

### LOSS OF GUJRÁT AND MALWA.

## CHAPTER III.

### AFFAIRS OF KHORÁSÁN AND KANDAHÁR.



## CHAPTER IV.

### AFFAIRS OF BENGAL.

### SECTION I.

#### STATE OF BENGAL.—HISTORY OF SHÍR KHAN.

## SECTION II.

### CONQUEST AND LOSS OF BENGAL BY HUMAYUN.

## CHAPTER V.

### HUMÁYUN'S EXPULSION FROM HINDUSTÁN.

# BOOK FIFTH.

## HUMÁYUN IN EXILE.

## CHAPTER I.

### HUMÁYUN'S RESIDENCE IN SIND.

### SECTION I.

#### FIRST RESIDENCE IN SIND.

## SECTION II.

### HUMÁYUN IN THE DESERTS OF MÁRWÁR AND IN SIND, A SECOND TIME.

## SECTION III.

### HUMÁYUN'S ROUTE FROM SIND TO SÍSTÁN.



## CHAPTER II.

### HUMÁYUN IN PERSIA.

## CHAPTER III.

### HUMÁYUN IN AFGHÁNISTÁN.

---

### SECTION I.

#### HUMAYUN'S CONQUEST OF KANDAHÁR AND KÁBUL.—EXPEDITION TO BADAKHSHÁN.

## SECTION II.

### CAPTURE AND LOSS OF KÁBUL BY KÁMRÁN.—HIS SUBMISSION.



## SECTION III.

### STATE OF KASHMÍR.—EXPEDITION TOWARDS BÁLKH.—REVOLT AND DEFEAT OF KÁMRÁN.

## SECTION IV.

SUBSEQUENT HISTORY OF KÁMRÁN. — DETERMINATION OF HUMÁYUN TO RECOVER INDIA.

---

## BOOK SIXTH.

### THE SÚR DYNASTY IN INDIA.

## CHAPTER I.

### SULTAN SHÍR SHAH SÚR.

## CHAPTER II.

### SULTAN ISLÁM (OR SELÍM) SHAH SÚR.

## CHAPTER III.

### SULTAN FIRÚZ SHAH SÚR.



## CHAPTER IV.

### SULTAN MUHAMMED SHAH ADEL SÚR.

---

# BOOK SEVENTH.

## HUMÁYUN'S RECONQUEST OF INDIA; AND DEATH.

---

## SUPPLEMENTARY REMARKS

ON THE STATE OF GOVERNMENT AND MANNERS IN KÁBŪL AND THE SURROUNDING COUNTRIES DURING THE REIGNS OF BÁBER AND HUMÁYUN.

# HISTORY OF INDIA.

## BOOK FOURTH.

FROM HUMÁYUN'S ACCESSION TO HIS EXPULSION FROM INDIA.

### CHAPTER I.

AFFAIRS OF HUMÁYUN FROM HIS ACCESSION TO HIS INVASION OF MALWA AND GUJRÁT.

HUMÁYUN'S ACCESSION. — DIFFICULTIES OF HIS SITUATION. — COMPETITORS FOR THE THRONE. — UNSETTLED STATE OF THE EMPIRE — AND OF FOREIGN RELATIONS. — CHARACTER OF HUMÁYUN. — PROVISION FOR HIS BROTHERS. — PRETENSIONS OF KÁMRÁN. — HIS ADVANCE TOWARDS HINDUSTÁN. — CAPTURES LAHÚR — AND OCCUPIES THE PENJÁB. — CONCESSIONS OF HUMÁYUN. — CAMPAIGN AGAINST KALINJER — AND TO THE EASTWARD. — HUMÁYUN RETURNS TO AGRA. — CAMPAIGN AGAINST CHUNÁR — INTERRUPTED BY THE PROGRESS OF BEHÁDER SHAH. — NOMINAL CAPITULATION OF SHÍR KHAN. EMBASSY FROM BEHÁDER SHAH. — MUHAMMED ZEMÁN MÍRZA — IS IMPRISONED, AND ESCAPES TO GUJRÁT. — MUHAMMED SULTAN MÍRZA, AND HIS SONS. — PROGRESS OF BEHÁDER SHAH. — MEASURES OF HUMÁYUN AGAINST THE AFGHÁNS OF BEHÁR — ARRESTED BY THE ADVANCE OF BEHÁDER SHAH — AND TÁTÁR KHAN LODI.

CHAP. I. A.D. 1530.

WHEN Nasír-ed-dín Muhammed Humáyun succeeded his father, he was in the twenty-third year of his age.*

* He was born in the citadel of Kábul, A. H. 913, Zikáda 4, (A. D. 1508, March 6) and mounted the throne A. H. 937, Jemádi I. 9. (A. D.

BOOK IV.

A. D. 1530.

Humáyun's accession, A. H. 937, A. D. 1530, Jemádi I. 9. Dec. 29.

He ascended the throne in the city of Agra, on the 29th of December, A. D. 1530, three days after the late Emperor's death. The usual solemnities followed; the chief nobility presented themselves at the Derbár, and tendered their allegiance, and money was scattered among the populace. The public prayers were read, and coin struck, in name of the new prince.

Difficulties of his situation.

But, though the son of the great Báber thus mounted the throne of Agra, his situation was not free from danger and difficulty. Even in his own court, and in the army, all was not sound. In that age, the right of succession to the crown was very unsettled. Though the claim of the eldest son to succeed his father was acknowledged in a general way, the order of succession was not in practice rigidly adhered to. The public feeling was little hurt when any other of the sons, or an aspiring uncle, made his way to the throne. The sword was the grand arbiter of right; and every son was prepared to try his fortune against his brothers. The custom of granting large governments or appanages to the younger princes, gave them the means of asserting their ambitious pretensions by force, at the head of armies. In the present instance, other principles unfavourable to the regular succession were in operation. The conquest of Hindustán had been begun only five years before, and was still in progress. Humáyun had not latterly been employed in any military command in that country. The government was still, of course, military. The army was not a national one, connected by common language and country, but a mixed body of adventurers, Chaghatái, Uzbek, Moghul, Persian, Afghán and Indian. Even the Chaghatái chiefs, who had enjoyed most of the Emperor's confidence and favour, were not perfectly unanimous. Though

1530, Dec. 29). His mother was Máham Begum, a relative of Sultan Husein Mírza of Khorásán. Akbernama, f. 35. v. Was Máh-am, "My Moon," a term of endearment converted into a name?

CHAP. I.

A.D. 1530.

attached to the family of Báber, as the representatives of that revered prince and of the great Taimúr, yet no eminent chief or head of a tribe considered the crown itself as beyond the range of his ambition. It was the age of revolution; and the kingdoms on every side,—Persia, Samarkand, Bokhára, Hissár, Balkh, and Hindustán itself,—saw the throne occupied by adventurers, or the immediate descendants of adventurers, not more distinguished than themselves. The length of time during which the late Emperor's health had been declining, had given time for parties and intrigues to be formed among them, which his talents and respected name had hitherto prevented from bursting out, but which were not the less dangerous on that account.

Competitors for the throne.

We have seen by what a minute accident a plan of the prime minister himself, for setting aside Báber's son altogether, had been defeated. Syed Mehdi Khwája, the candidate in whose favour he had acted, seems to have been of a religious family, was a son-in-law of Báber, and known to the army, a division of which he had often led. Muhammed Zemán Mírza, another great lord of the court, and a descendant of Taimúr, being a grandson of the celebrated Sultan Husein Mírza Baikra of Khorásán, and who had also married a daughter of Báber, was supposed to have in his interest a formidable party, consisting of many of the most powerful men in the army. He was a man of talent, and had been employed by the late Emperor in many important commands. Muhammed Sultan Mírza, also a descendant of Taimúr and grandson of the late Sultan of Khorásán by a daughter, was a third nobleman, who, from his royal birth and high station, was thought worthy to aspire to the throne. All had their followers and adherents. The very supposition that such men might be placed in hostility to the legal heir, rendered their position dangerous; and it might in some circumstances seem safer to incur the immediate

BOOK IV.

A. D. 1530.

risks of revolt than to endure the lingering annoyances and real dangers of suspicion. Under such circumstances, a thousand unforeseen accidents might occur to blow the smouldering embers of intrigue and faction into a flame.

Unsettled state of the Empire.

Nor was it only in the court and in the camp that dangers were to be apprehended. The Empire was far from being yet consolidated, when Báber died. It was only five years since that able prince had entered India; and, during that period, his life had been too busily employed, in military expeditions, to admit of his devoting the needful time to settling the details of the internal administration of the kingdoms that he had conquered. He had entered the country as a stranger and a spoiler; he had defeated the armies and broken the power of the reigning dynasty; but the only hold which he, or his race, yet had upon the people of India was military force. Of the two great classes of which the population of India was composed, the Hindus could have little unity of feeling with their Muhammedan conquerors. Both religions are, in their particular ways, exclusive. The Hindus admit of no proselytes; regard all strangers, even their rulers, as not only far behind them in the road to final happiness, but as, at best, only successful barbarians, many of whose habits they view with disgust and abhorrence. The Musulman, too, though eager for proselytism, is an exclusive religion, which looks with hatred or contempt on every other, and is very unfavourable to the existence of much sympathy between the believing lord and the infidel subject; especially where that subject adds to his other crimes that of idolatry. But the difficulty was not less, even with the old Muhammedans. India, for centuries, had been governed by Muhammedan dynasties of foreign descent. The last of these had been the Afghán; and chiefs of that race, with their followers, were scattered all over the kingdom, and held the most important offices and the most valuable

Formidable power of the Afgháns.

CHAP. I.

A.D. 1530.

jágírs. These they considered as their birth-right; and they were indignant that so noble a prize, so long enjoyed as an inheritance, should be wrested from them. Though repeatedly defeated in the field, they were still numerous and powerful, ripe for revolt, and ready on the first signal to fly to arms, in what was a personal as well as a national cause. They had also the advantage of possessing a rallying point. The cause of Sultan Mahmúd Lodi, the brother and successor of the late Sultan Ibráhím, was still supported by Baban and Bayezíd, the old heads of the Afghán nobility; who, though lately driven into the recesses of the eastern provinces and of Behár, were only waiting for a fit opportunity to return, and re-occupy the kingdom from which they had been expelled; and their countryman Shír Khan, one of the ablest men of the age, had already taken up arms in Behár and Bengal, about the close of Báber's reign.

Foreign relations.

Of the princes and states beyond the limits of the Empire, the King of Bengal was friendly to the Afgháns and had given protection to Sultan Mahmúd Lodi, whose daughter he afterwards married. The Rájpúts, though stunned by their late discomfiture, were powerful still; and, though the kingdom of Málwa at that moment possessed little strength,—being in a state of deplorable confusion from the intestine factions that had long torn it to pieces, and made it a prey to its neighbours,—yet, in Gujrát, Behádar Shah was fast rising into power, had added to his territories on every side, and, from the mere extension of his conquests, was likely soon to come into direct collision with the Emperor of Delhi.*

Character of Humáyun.

At such a crisis, the personal character of the prince was a matter of deep importance. If we remove the glare of eulogy thrown over the actions of all Asiatic

* Abulfazl, in the Akbernáma; Báber's Memoirs, *passim*. Taríkh-e Kháfi Khan; Ferishta;

BOOK IV. A.D. 1530.

sovereigns by the historians who wrote in their own time, or in that of their immediate descendants, we shall find that Humáyun, though a prince of lively parts and elegant accomplishments, brave, and on the whole of a humane temper, was volatile, fond of pleasure, and deficient in those enlarged views so necessary for conducting the affairs of an extensive Empire; as well as in that decision and spirit of command, without which no prince can secure the respect and confidence of his subjects.

Provision for his brothers.

One of Humáyun's first acts was to assign jágírs to be held by his brothers. Kámrán he confirmed in the kingdoms of Kábul and Kandahár, which seem to have been bestowed on him by his father. To Askeri Mírza he allotted the province of Sambhal; and that of Alwar or Mewát to Hindal Mírza. He confirmed his cousin Suleimán Mírza in the government of the little kingdom of Badakhshán. His nobles, and the army, he conciliated, as is usual with Asiatic princes at the commencement of a new reign, by conferring on them titles, khiláts, and other marks of honour, and by munificent largesses.

Pretensions of Kámrán,

But the want of union among the brothers was not long of showing itself. No sooner did Kámrán, who was at Kábul, hear of his father's death, than, disdaining the ample dominions he had enjoyed under his father, and in the possession of which his brother had consented to confirm him, he consigned Kandahár to Askeri, collected an army, and, in the true spirit of brotherhood among Asiatic princes, marched for Hindustán; under pretence of congratulating Humáyun on his accession, but in reality to try the strength of his sword, and to see whether his own good fortune might not raise him to the throne of Delhi itself. Humáyun, alarmed at the news of his motions, and harassed by the dangers that surrounded him, despatched an envoy to meet the Mírza, and to announce to him his intention of adding

Who advances towards Hindustán, A.H. 938, A.D. 1531.

the countries of Pesháwer and Lamghán to the territories which he already enjoyed. But Kámrán's views were too extensive to be satisfied even with that concession. He crossed the Indus; and, having traversed the greater part of the Penjáb, drew near to Lahúr, the capital. CHAP. I. A.D. 1531.

There he found that Mír Yúnis Ali, who had been the governor under Báber, was faithful to his trust, and adhered to Humáyun. To have bestowed the time necessary for reducing the capital of the Penjáb by regular military operations, might have been fatal to his enterprise. To gain possession of it without delay therefore, Kámrán resorted to stratagem. Having arranged his plan, he one night affected to be violently offended with Kerácha Beg, one of his chief Amírs, and publicly, in the Derbár, reviled him in the most harsh and unmeasured terms. Next night the Beg fled from the camp with all his followers, and sought refuge in Lahúr. In those days of versatile and unstable allegiance, such a defection had in it nothing uncommon. Mír Yúnis Ali, delighted to have gained a man of so much consequence, went out of the city with an honorary procession to meet and welcome him. He afterwards treated the Beg not merely as a political, but as a personal, friend; gave him constant invitations to partake of the hospitality of his table, and made several social and friendly parties for his amusement. Kerácha Beg coolly watched his time; till, one night, after a convivial entertainment at the Mír's palace, where, in consequence of the lateness of the hour, the soldiers had been allowed to go home to their quarters, he seized his opportunity, perfidiously took his host into custody, got possession of one of the gates, and despatched messengers to Kámrán to announce his success. The Mírza, who had been waiting with much anxiety, no sooner learned the result of the stratagem, than he hastened to the gate with a strong force and entered Lahúr Captures Lahúr.

BOOK IV. A.D. 1531.

without resistance. Mír Yúnis Ali was then relieved from custody, and Kámrán, who wished to give the whole proceeding the air, not of a conquest, but of an ordinary assumption of the government, apologising to Yúnis Ali for the violence he unwillingly employed, asked him to enter his service, and to retain the office he had held. This the Mír declined, and was allowed to leave the city and to join Humáyun.

And occupies the Penjáb. A. H. 938, A. D. 1531-2.

After this first success, Kámrán took possession of all the neighbouring provinces; so that, in a short time, the whole of the Penjáb, as far as the Sutlej, acknowledged his authority.

Concessions of Humáyun.

Still, however, as if nothing uncommon had occurred, and as if he had been acting all along like a faithful subject, he continued, by his ambassadors, to assure Humáyun of his attachment and fidelity; and, at the same time, petitioned, in the humblest terms, to be allowed to hold the territory of which he had thus become possessed. The Emperor, who, before these transactions were brought to a conclusion, had become involved in troubles and difficulties on every hand, affected to accede cheerfully to a request, which he could not without danger refuse. He signified his assent; and, to save appearances, ascribed his large concessions to the ties of kindred which united them, and the wishes expressed by their late father. After some delay, a firmán was accordingly issued, bestowing on Kámrán the government of Kábul, Kandahár, and the Penjáb; a grant which exalted that prince to the possession of dominions and power nearly equal to his own. Kámrán, who had a turn for poetry, delighted with the success of his schemes of ambition, in the fulness of his joy, addressed several odes to Humáyun, in which he exhausted all the powers of song to express his gratitude. The Emperor, either flattered by his high-flown praises, or to gain time and to confirm him in his pacific dispositions, farther rewarded the royal poet by bestowing on him, what seems a most imprudent grant, the rich province of Hissár-Firóza; an acquisition the more acceptable to the Mírza as it lay nearly on the high road between his possessions in the Penjáb and Delhi. Each probably attempted to deceive the other. At all events, a friendship founded on such a basis could be neither sincere nor lasting. These transactions with Kámrán*, which occupied a considerable part of two years, have been recorded in this place, to avoid interrupting the future course of the narrative.

CHAP. I. A.D. 1531. A. H. 937–9, A. D. 1531–2.

Before his relations with Kámrán began to bear a threatening aspect, Humáyun, about five or six months after his accession, had set out to besiege the strong fort of Kalinjer, in Bandélkand†, the possession of which was necessary at once to strengthen his frontier, and to open an easier communication between Malwa and his dominions on the Jamna and the Ganges. The Raja of Kalinjer was probably in the interest of the Afgháns. When Humáyun had blockaded the fort about a month, and had made some progress in his advances, he was alarmed by the information that Sultan Mahmúd Lodi, supported by Biban Khan Jilwáni and Sheikh Bayezíd, the most eminent leaders of the Afgháns, had again invaded the provinces east of the Ganges, had taken Juánpúr, and was overrunning the country in great force. Eager to meet the invaders, he proposed a treaty to the Raja of Kalinjer, who gladly gave a large sum of money to hasten his retreat.‡

Campaign against Kalinjer, A. H. 937. Shawal or Zilkader, A. D. 1531, May or June.

Humáyun, on leaving Kalinjer, directed his course to the eastward, crossed the Ganges, and reached the

And to the Eastward.

* Akbernáma, f. 35—37.; Kháfi Khan. Some specimens of Kámrán's verses may be found in the Akbernáma, f. 37.

† The siege of Kalinjer, according to the Akbernáma, occurred in A. H. 937; according to Ferishta, A. H. 938. As Humáyun seems to have left Agra in the last months of 937, had afterwards to march to Bandélkand, and lay a month before the fort, he must have raised the siege in A. H. 938.

‡ Akbernáma; Tabakát-i-Akberi, f. 173, 174.; Kholáset-ul-Towáríkh, f. 255.; Kháfi Khan; Abulfazl, f. 35, says twelve máns of gold and other valuable considerations.

BOOK IV. A.D.1531-2. town of Doura, when he was met by the Afgháns in great force. A battle ensued, in which Sheikh Bayezíd was slain, and Sultan Mahmúd and his Afgháns completely dispersed, as his friends affirmed, by the treachery of Shír Khan. Mahmúd was soon after expelled from the province of Juánpúr, and fled to Patna and Bengal, whence he never returned, and where he died a natural death.*

Humáyun returns to Agra.

The Emperor, having defeated this invasion, settled the country, and reinstated Sultan Juneid Birlás as his lieutenant in the government, returned to Agra, where, on the anniversary of his accession, he gave a grand entertainment, in the course of which, besides rich presents and other gratifications to his nobles, in elephants, jewels, &c., he is said to have distributed among the officers of his court and army no less than twelve thousand khiláts, or honorary dresses, two thousand of which were richly embroidered and ornamented with precious stones.†

A. H. 938, Jemádi I. 9. A. D. 1531, Dec. 19.

Campaign against Chunár.

The most important object of policy for the Emperor of Delhi at this moment, next to that of crushing the seeds of rebellion in his own family and court, was undoubtedly to break in pieces the power still possessed by the Afgháns throughout India, and to become master, if possible, of the course of the Ganges. To secure these objects, the Emperor soon afterwards again took the field, and marched towards the fort of Chunár, in the province of Behár, a place of extraordinary strength, and one of the most important positions on that river. It was now held by the celebrated Shír Khan, who, since the defeat and flight of Sultan Mahmúd Lodi, had risen to the first distinction

A. H. 938, A. D. 1532.

* Kholáset-ul-Towáríkh, f. 255. In the translation of Jouher, the battle is said to have been fought on the banks of the Goompty. Mem. of Humáyun, p. 3. In the original, it is said to have been at "Daurch on the river Sini," probably an error of the transcriber for Gumti. No date is given, nor are Kalinjer or Juánpúr mentioned.

† Tabakát-i-Akberi, f. 144.; Ferishta, ii. 72.

among the Afgháns. Formerly it had belonged to Sultan Ibráhím, but soon after his defeat and death had submitted to Báber, as we have seen, and, by a series of events to be afterwards mentioned, had very recently passed into the hands of its present master. Humáyun, desirous both to possess the fort and to humble the owner, had sent a large force in advance to invest it, and now himself followed and laid close siege to it, at the head of a formidable army. At his approach, Shír Khan, leaving his son, Jilál Khan, in the fortress with a strong garrison of trusty adherents, retired to the higher grounds, and hovered round the imperial camp, for the double purpose of harassing it and of succouring the besieged. After the blockade had lasted three or four months, Humáyun, who, fortunately for the Afghán chiefs, was surrounded by enemies, received intelligence, with some alarm, of the rapid progress made by Behåder Shah, the King of Gujrát, in Málwa and Nagór. Shír Khan, seizing the favourable moment, sent ambassadors to the Emperor to sue for peace, to express the Khan's gratitude to the Emperor and his illustrious father, by whose patronage he had attained his present rank; to make professions of submission, and such offers as, while they saved the dignity of the sovereign, left the Khan in possession of his stronghold. Humáyun, little disposed to protract a siege which might be drawn out to a very inconvenient length, and had already interfered with most important objects, concluded a capitulation with Shír Khan, who was perfectly willing to make ample promises, flattering himself, that when the imperial troops were withdrawn, it would cost him nothing to act as he pleased, and to pursue his own policy, unfettered by any flimsy treaty that had been forced upon him. A peace was, therefore, concluded, by the terms of which he agreed, that his son, Kutb Khan, should join the Emperor's army, with a body

*Interrupted by the progress of Beháder Shah.*

*Nominal capitulation of Shír Khan.*

BOOK IV. A.D. 1532-3.

of Afgháns; and the young prince, accordingly, along with Isa Khan Hijáb Sirwáni, his vizier, did wait upon Humáyun, and accompany him on his march into Gujrát. While there, Shír Khan having found the time favourable for revolt, and Humáyun being busy reducing that province, Kutb Khan contrived to make his escape, and rejoined his father.*

Embassy from Beháder Shah, A. H. 939, A. D. 1532-3.

On relinquishing the siege of Chunár, Humáyun returned to Agra, where he gave audience to an embassy that Beháder Shah had sent, for the purpose of quieting any apprehensions which he might entertain in consequence of the rapid progress that prince was making in Málwa, and in the Rájpút territories. This mission he received with much pleasure, as circumstances rendered it important that his declared enemies should be as few as possible. He dismissed the ambassadors with every mark of distinction, and with assurances of his own pacific intentions, and turned himself to averting the dangers which threatened him in his own court and in the heart of his dominions.

Muhammed Zemán Mírza.

The Emperor had long entertained a jealousy of Muhammed Zemán Mírza's ambitious projects, and now resolved to take away from him all means of carrying them into execution. It has been mentioned that he was the son of Badi-ez-zemán Mírza, and grandson of the famous Sultan Husein Mírza Baihra, of Khorásán. After his father's kingdom had passed into the hands of the Uzbeks, he had resided at the court of Báber, with whom he is said to have been a particular favourite, and had married one of his daughters. He

* Akbernáma, f. 42.; Ferishta, ii. pp. 110—113.; Jouher, c. 2.; Tar. Kháfi Khan; Tabakát-i-Akberi, f. 174.; Tar. Nizámi, f. 213.; Nisábnáma Afgh. f. 88.; Tar. Bed. f. 147. The Tabakát, Nisábnáma, Ferishta, Kháfi Khan, and the original text of Jouher, call this young prince Kutb Khan. Abulfazl calls him Abdal Reshíd; and is followed in the translation of Jouher. The Kholáset-ul-Towáríkh, f. 275., solves the mystery, calling him "Kutb Khan, generally known as Abdal-Reshíd."

CHAP. I. A.D. 1533-4.

had been honoured with the most important commands. Many of the northern Chaghatái chiefs, who formed the Emperor's great strength, had much influence in his court and filled the chief offices in the country, were attached to this prince. We have seen that, in the late reign, he held the government of Behár. The events that preceded his imprisonment are not known with much certainty. Abulfazl affirms, that he formed a party and carried on intrigues in conjunction with his cousin, Muhammed Sultan Mírza, also a grandson of Sultan Husein Mírza, but by a daughter, as well as with Muhammed's son, Ulugh Mírza, with whom at this crisis he rose in rebellion a second time, after having been once pardoned; that, to check this revolt, Humáyun led an army down the Ganges, and, when opposite to Bhujpúr, sent a strong detachment across to the right bank of the river, under the command of his cousin, Yádgár Násir Mírza, who defeated the rebels, and made Muhammed Zemán, Muhammed Sultan, and Wáli Khub Mírza, prisoners.* The narrative of other historians makes it more probable that the Emperor, acting on his belief or suspicion of their treasonable designs, had arrested the first of these princes, in his government of Behár, by means of an armed force, before any rising took place, and afterwards seized the others as his accomplices. Muhammed Zemán, on his earnest professions of fidelity, was pardoned, and sent under the custody of Yádgár Taghái Beg to be imprisoned in Biána; but he had not been long there before he wrought upon his keeper not only to allow him to escape, but to accompany him in his flight. He reached the court of Behάder Shah, where he was well received. Muhammed Sultan Mírza, with his sons, Ulugh and Shah Mírzas, when thrown into prison, were ordered to be blinded by the fire-pencil,

A.H. 940, A.D. 1533-4.

Suspected and imprisoned,

escapes to Guzrat.

Muhammed Sultan Mírza and his sons.

* Akbernáma, f. 36.

BOOK IV. A.D. 1534.

that so an end might be put to their public life; but, from the indulgence of the operator, it was so lightly applied that the structure of their eyes remained unimpaired. They, too, effected their escape from prison, about the same time, and hastened to Kanaúj, where Muhammed Sultan soon saw himself at the head of a respectable army of six thousand men,—Chaghatáis, Afgháns, and Rájpúts.*

Progress of Behádor Shah, A.H. 941, A.D. 1534.

While Humáyun was occupied at home in dreamy speculations of false science, and by dangers within and without his court, which he found it difficult to avert, the King of Gujrát was pursuing his victorious career. So decisive were the advantages which he gained over the Rána of Cheitúr, whom, after overrunning Malwa, he now attacked in his own dominions, that he was emboldened to advance and lay siege to Cheitúr itself, the capital of the Rájpút. The Rána, in his distress, despatched an envoy to ask succour from Humáyun, who could not see with indifference the rapid progress of a rival rendered more odious to him by the protection which he ostentatiously afforded to the refugees from Delhi. Humáyun, thus invited, moved forward with a considerable army, as far as Gualiár; as if to assist the Rána. There he encamped

* Briggs's Ferishta, ii. p. 73.; Kháfi Khan, f. 40.; Tabakát-i-Akberi, f. 145. Abulfazl and Ferishta do not mention that Muhammed Zemán was ordered to be blinded; which the author of the Tabakát-i-Akberi, and of the Taríkh-i-Bedáuni do. The former says, that they did not injure the organisation of the iris of his eye, so that he soon recovered his sight (f. 145.); and is followed by the Kholáset-ul-Towárikh, f. 255. There were two modes at that time employed in blinding princes, who were the objects of jealousy. By the one, the eye itself was cut with a lancet: by the other, a heated plate, or sometimes a heated pencil of brass or iron was applied to it, till the sight was destroyed. The latter was often preferred in the case of princes, since, the form of the eyeball not being destroyed, the appearance of the countenance was less injured. There is some disagreement among historians as to the chronology of these events. I have followed the leading authorities in the way that seems to me best fitted to reconcile this difference.

for about two months, and despatched an ambassador to Behåder, to demand that he should desist from his enterprise against Cheitúr; and, at the same time, deliver up the traitors who had fled from the Emperor's dominions. Neither demand was complied with; and the Emperor, with some loss of reputation, soon after decamped, being compelled by the necessity of his affairs to march toward Juánpúr and the Behár provinces, to repress new disturbances which had arisen in that quarter. The Ráua, upon this, despairing of any effectual assistance, was glad to purchase the temporary retreat of Behåder Shah, by consenting to pay a large sum of money, and by sending him as a propitiatory offering, a celebrated crown and belt adorned with jewels of immense value *, and other costly presents.

Measures against the Afgháns of Behár.

Humáyun determined to employ the interval of quiet, which this pacification promised to afford, in putting an end to the perpetual invasions and insurrections of the Afgháns of Behár, and in punishing his own rebel-

* These are said to have been the crown and regalia which Sultan Mahmúd of Malwa carried off from the tent of Kutb-Shah of Gujrát (A. H. 856, Sefer 1, A. D. 1452, Feb. 23), and which fell into the hands of Rána Sánga of Cheitúr, on the defeat of Sultan Mahmúd II. of Malwa, about A. H. 925 (A. D. 1519). Ferishta, iv. pp. 39. 263. It will be afterwards seen that, from Behåder Shah, they were said to have passed to Soliman the Magnificent, Emperor of Constantinople.

There seems some difficulty, however, in the transmission of these regalia. "When Rána Sánga defeated Sultan Mahmúd, and made him prisoner," says Báber, (Mem. p. 385.), "the Sultan had on a splendid crown-cap and golden girdle, which fell into the hands of the pagan, who, when he set Sultan Mahmúd at liberty, retained them. They were now with Bikermájít. His elder brother, Ruttonsi, who had succeeded his father as Rána, and who was now in possession of Cheitúr, had sent to desire his younger brother to deliver them up to him, which he refused to do. By the envoys, who came from him to wait on me, he now sent me" (Qy. tendered?) "this crown and golden girdle, and asked Biána in exchange for Rantambór," &c. We nowhere hear of their being regained from Báber or his successor. Yet the Mirát-e Ahmedi, agreeing with or following Ferishta, makes Bikermájít's mother give this very "waistband and jewelled crown, which had been captured from Mahmúd Khilji I., of Malwa, when the Rána defeated him" to Behåder Shah, to induce him to raise the siege. Bird's transl. p. 244.

BOOK IV. A. D. 1534.

lious nobles. For this purpose, having collected a large army, he once more marched from Agra, and had reached Kinár, in the district of Kalpi, on the Jamna, when his progress was arrested by the intelligence that Behâder Shah had again laid siege to Cheitúr; and that, supported by him, Tátár Khan, the son of Sultan Alá-ed-dín Lodi, the uncle and rival of the late Sultan Ibráhím Lodi, was advancing, at the head of a formidable army, to assert his father's claim to the throne of Delhi itself. He hastened back to Agra, and took immediate measures for repelling the aggression, and for hurling back the danger on the head of Behâder Shah *, whose success seemed now to threaten ruin to the house of Taimúr. But, as Malwa and Gujrát are soon to become the scene of important operations, it becomes necessary to interrupt for a while the course of the narrative, in order to give some idea of the political state of these countries at this period.

Arrested by the advance of Behâder Shah and Tátár Khan Lodi.

* Tabakát-i-Akberi, f. 145.; Ferishta, ii. 72—74. The Akbernáma, f. 35—37. does not mention the two months' encampment at Gualiár.

# CHAPTER II.

## AFFAIRS OF GUJRÁT AND MALWA.

---

## SECTION I.

### EARLY HISTORY OF THOSE KINGDOMS. — PROGRESS OF BEHÁDER SHAH.

DISRUPTION OF THE EMPIRE UNDER SULTAN MUHAMMED TOGHLAK. — KINGDOM OF GUJRÁT. — KINGDOM OF MALWA. — PROSPERITY OF GUJRÁT — ITS IMPORTANCE. — STATE OF MALWA. — POSITION OF THE EARLY MUSULMÁNS IN INDIA. — PRINCES OF MALWA. — MAHMÚD II. — INTRIGUES OF MOHÁFEZ KHAN. — INTERPOSITION OF MEDÍNI RAO. — RÁJPÚT LEAGUE, AT THE COURT OF MALWA. — KINGS OF DELHI AND GUJRÁT INTERFERE. — DEFENSIVE MEASURES OF MEDÍNI RAO. — THE RÁJPÚTS ALL-POWERFUL IN MALWA. — MAHMÚD ATTEMPTS THEIR DISMISSAL — IS DISCOMFITED — ESCAPES TO GUJRÁT — HIS RESTORATION. — EXPEDITION AGAINST THE REFRACTORY RÁJPÚTS, AND DEFEAT. — DISMEMBERMENT OF MALWA. — BEHÁDER SHAH IN GUJRÁT. — RÁNA RUTTONSI AND BEHÁDER SHAH IN MALWA. — MÁNDU TAKEN. — BEHÁDER SHAH PROCLAIMED KING. — PARTITION OF MALWA. — CAPTURE OF SILÁH-ED-DÍN BY BEHÁDER. — CATASTROPHE OF RAISEN. — FURTHER SUCCESSES OF BEHÁDER SHAH.

CHAP. II. SECT. I.

Disruption of the empire, under Sultan Muhammed Toghlak.

THE kingdoms both of Malwa and Gujrát, at a former period, nearly a century and a half before the time of Humáyun, had been included in the kingdom of Delhi. About the close of the fourteenth century, on the decline of the Toghlak dynasty, when the empire fell to pieces, many of the provinces, and among others Gujrát and Malwa, became independent sovereignties. The insane violence and brutal cruelty of Sultan Muhammed

BOOK IV. Toghlak of Delhi had spread universal alarm over his dominions. Having, by his profusion, exhausted the treasury, he imposed taxes beyond what his subjects could bear. He rigidly enforced them; and the landholders and peasantry, to escape from his tyranny, fled to the woods and wastes. He tampered with the coin; and the distress and ruin, which in all circumstances follow an injudicious meddling with the currency, were soon experienced. He attempted to remove the population and city of Delhi to Doulatábád in the Dekhan; and thousands of the wretched inhabitants perished on the road and after their arrival, of fatigue, want and misery in every shape. Famine, civil war, robbery, murder, and anarchy, all over his dominions, marked the close of his reign. Driven to desperation by misgovernment, each district and province was forced to provide separately for its own safety; so that, from the mere necessity of substituting some kind of government for the misrule and rapine that prevailed, several new dynasties arose in the principal provinces of the empire.

Kingdom of Gujrát. A.H. 793, A.D. 1391.

The nobleman who at that crisis rose to be King of Gujrát was Mozeffer Khan. His origin is uncertain. While some describe him as having been the son of a low spirit-distiller, or water-carrier; others, with more probability, represent him as the son of a Hindu chief converted to Muhammedanism.* The menial office, which he is said to have filled in the palace, argues little; as men of rank in all countries have been eager to fill offices nominally menial, about the person of the sovereign; and Báber †, a judicious and careful reader of history, describes the employment to have been that of cup-bearer. The disorders which at that period pervaded India, and the consequent confusion and indistinctness in the narrative of the historians of the time,

* Ferishta, vol. iv. p. 3.

† Mem. p. 311.

leave us rather uncertain as to the extent of Gujrát, when its governor assumed the symbols of royalty. His capital was Nehrwála or Patan; but what now forms the southern part of the province did not then belong to it. The new King, however, an active and able man, speedily compelled the various Rajas of Kattiawár, and the western peninsula, to acknowledge his authority, and to pay tribute. He, likewise, turned his arms against the Raja of Eder, and expelled him from his dominions. CHAP. II. SECT. I.

Kingdom of Malwa.

Emboldened by this success, he ventured at a future time to invade Malwa. That country had also recently undergone a revolution, similar to what had occurred in Gujrát, and from the same causes. Diláwer Khan, a Ghúri Afghán, from governor had become king; and his son Hosheng now reigned. A strong party, however, opposed his government, and called in to their assistance Mozeffer Shah of Gujrát, who readily marched to their aid. The hostile armies met near the ancient town of Dhár in Malwa; and, after a desperate battle, in which Mozeffer was wounded and Hosheng unhorsed, victory declared for the invader; and Hosheng was forced to take refuge in Dhár, where he was besieged, and soon after compelled to surrender. Mozeffer, leaving a part of his army in Malwa, to retain it in subjection, returned with his prisoner to Gujrát. But he had hardly turned his back on his new conquest, when, the officers whom he had left in command having made some burdensome exactions on the inhabitants, the party that had called him in, who wanted an ally not a master, rose and expelled his troops, setting up a king of their own. This change of affairs induced him to release Sultan Hosheng from confinement, and to send him, accompanied by a strong force, to assert his rights; and the different internal parties, tired of the evils which civil war had brought on their country,

A.H. 810, A.D. 1407.

A.H. 811, A.D. 1408.

BOOK IV. soon after united, and once more acknowledged Hosheng as King of Malwa.

Prosperity of Gujrát. A. H. 815–847, A. D. 1412–1443. After the death of Mozeffer Shah, several of his descendants increased the territory of Gujrát. His grandson, Ahmed Shah, a very distinguished prince, and the founder of Ahmedábád, reduced under his power nearly the whole country that forms the present Gujrát, including the low lands to the south below the Gháts, the Northern Kokan, and the island of Bombay; he forced the Rajas of the western peninsula, and other chiefs bordering on his dominions, especially the Raja of Champanír, who, it is affirmed*, could at that time bring sixty thousand men into the field, to pay tribute; and he carried his victorious arms in different campaigns into Khándesh, and Málwa, the capital of which he besieged. Under him, and his immediate successors, Gujrát obtained a high degree of prosperity.

A. H. 863–917, A. D. 1459–1511. One of them, Mahmúd Shah Bigara, was particularly successful. He besieged and took the strong and, in the opinion of the natives, impregnable hill-forts of Girnál or Júnagar, and of Champanír†; he did much to consolidate the kingdom within; and without, he extended his marches in different expeditions, as far as the Indus on one side, and Doulatábád in the Dekhan on the other; at the same time that he carried on an active war, by sea and land, with the Portuguese.

A. H. 917–932, A. D. 1511–1526. His son, Mozeffer Shah II. maintained the glory of his arms. He restored the King of Malwa to the throne of that kingdom, from which he had been expelled by a combination of Rájpút chiefs, taking Mándu from them by storm. A. H. 932. Ramzán 26. A. D. 1526. July 6. To this prince, with the intervention of the short reigns of two of his brothers, Sultan Be-

* Ferishta, iv. p. 66.

† It is pretended that the reduction of these two strong hill-forts gave rise to Mahmúd's appellation of Bigara (from *ba*, two, and *gur*, a fort). Ferishta mentions another and more probable origin, namely, the colour of his mustachios.

háder Shah had succeeded, and now swayed the sceptre of Gujrát.

Its importance.

That kingdom had always an extraordinary influence over the neighbouring states; and could raise armies, and subsidise troops, with a facility apparently disproportioned to its extent. But few countries in the world are more blest in a fertile soil and a favourable climate; and the possession of the great emporia of Cambay, Diu, and Surat, besides other convenient harbours, had enriched it with the most active commerce of any portion of India. The greater part of the trade of that country with Persia, Arabia, Africa, the Red Sea, and Europe, besides an active coasting trade, passed through its harbours; and the various commodities imported from these regions were conveyed over Hindustán, and the north of the Dekhan, through its provinces, and by its merchants. The benefit of this trade overflowed upon the country, which became a garden, and enriched the treasury of the prince. The noble mosques, colleges, palaces and tombs, the remains of which still adorn Ahmedábád, and its other cities, to this day, while they excite the admiration of the traveller, prove both the wealth and the taste of the founders.

State of Malwa.

The same circumstances which, on the decline of the Toghlak dynasty of Delhi, induced the governor of Gujrát to assert his independence, had, as has been noticed, a similar effect on Diláwer Khan, the governor of Malwa; who also assumed the sovereign power in his capital of Dhár. We have seen his son Hosheng defeated and made prisoner, and again restored to his kingdom by the Sultan of Gujrát. Hosheng Ghúri was the founder of Mándu. After his death, the intrigues in his court led to the murder of his successor; and the son of his prime minister was raised to the throne, under the title of Sultan Mahmúd Khilji.* He was an

A. H. 804, A. D. 1401.

* Have the *Khilji* monarchs any connection with the *Ghilji* Afgháns? They are generally described as Túrks.

BOOK IV. A. H. 839, A. D. 1436.

able prince; but the country, in consequence of the dissensions that always attend a change of dynasty, was harassed for some time by civil wars. The weakness of the kings of Delhi, at this period, enabled Sultan Mahmúd to extend his dominions on different sides; and he reduced the important forts and districts of Bhílsa, Chándéri, and Hoshengábád in Malwa. He carried his arms into the centre of the Rájpút states, reduced Kambelmér in Mewár, and besieged the mountain capital of Cheitúr. He even aspired to the throne of Delhi, and engaged in war, not only with the King of Gujrát, but with the kings of the Dekhan, of Khándesh, and of Juánpúr; with which last he had quarreled about the possession of Kalpi on the Jamna. He levied contributions on Kota and Biána, and added Mandsúr, Mandelgar, Búndi and Rantambór to his dominions. At one time, he overran Gujrát; but was finally defeated, near Ahmedábád, and compelled to retreat from that country. He was one of the most distinguished princes of his age; and, in his reign, Malwa attained the summit of its power and glory.

Position of the early Musulmans in India.

Much of the time of all the Musulman kings of India, and among others of the Sultans of Malwa, seems to have been employed in reducing to subjection the half-independent Hindu chiefs in or bordering on their states. The Musulmans had no hold of the country, but by military force. Their capital was a camp; and the different towns and forts that they occupied, were posts in an enemy's country. The great mass of the population had no sympathy with them, either in religion or civil policy. The popular religion was considered by their conquerors as a guilty idolatry, which it was, to a certain degree, sinful even to tolerate; and pious or bigoted princes were often led to persecute their pagan subjects. They had no general system for conducting their internal government. The will of the ruler, capricious and uncertain at best, but to which there was no check, was the acknowledged rule.* Fortunately, the old inhabitants were strongly attached to their own system of village and district government, which remedied many of the evils of political neglect and oppression to which they were exposed; and they continued to be warmly devoted to such of their native chiefs as still maintained their authority in their hereditary states. As the Musulmans extended their power, first by arms, and afterwards gradually by colonisation and proselytism, the range of territory enjoyed by these little Hindu chieftains was gradually diminished, and the power of many of them was, in the end, altogether extinguished. The superiority of the Musulmans increased every day. The causes of this were various. They were strangers, and felt that their power, and in some degree their existence, in India, depended upon their mutually supporting each other. They were bigots to their religion, and this bigotry, which was increased by their being placed among infidels and heathens, whom they regarded as the enemies of God, and whose lands and wealth they willingly imagined were unjustly withheld from the true believer, whose natural portion they were, formed another bond of union. They had also a burning zeal for making proselytes, indifferent whether by argument or force; and their great power was naturally attended with great success. The Hindus, on the contrary, long divided, even under their own great monarchies, into petty principalities that had little intercourse with each other, but in the way of quarrel or hostility, had no principle of union, except in cases of intolerable oppression; and that only against the immediate tyrant of the hour. Their principles of quietism led them to acquiesce in any govern-

CHAP. II. SECT. I.

Extension of their influence.

Its causes and character.

* See General Vans Kennedy's admirable little "Abstract of Muhammedan Law," (Journal of the Royal Asiatic Society, vol. ii.) especially his additional remarks on the *Urf*, or customary law, p. 157.

BOOK IV. ment once established; and though they might lose they could not gain by proselytism, since with them religion was a matter of birth, and every one was held to be bound for life to the class and faith in which he was born; so that, by their tenets, no converts could be received. In war, too, the Muhammedans, who were not always braver than their Hindu enemies, owed their superiority to the same causes that have ensured success to the Europeans in modern times. They had more active energy of character, were more intelligent, were more ready to change their policy and their tactics as experience required; and had the unspeakable advantage of being constantly joined by new crowds of adventurers from Tartary, Persia, Arabia, and Afghánistán. These adventurers flocked to support them, inspired with all the ardour, activity, and enterprise natural to men who had still their fortune to make, and whose minds and bodies were still unenervated by the impatience of exertion, and the habit of self-indulgence which in India are almost inevitably generated by the physical and moral influences that surround those educated in the country. It is to be remembered, too, that though the great majority were bold, hardy, ignorant, and unpolished adventurers, many of them were men of no mean class, gentlemen and scholars, some of whom had served in the wars of different countries; while others had their minds enriched with all the literature, both of the Túrki nations and of Persia and Arabia. This literature, which we are too apt to despise, while totally ignorant of its nature and extent, however defective in some of its branches, if measured by the standard of modern Europe, was yet extremely valuable; not only as affording some acquaintance with the positive sciences and arts, but as, to a certain degree, counteracting the harsh bigotry of the Muhammedan religion. It had a tendency to open and refine the reason and imagination by the ample stores of history, as well as of moral truth and ingenious speculation, which it possessed; while its poetry, enriched and animated by the genius of such writers as Ferdausi, Háfez, Sádi, and Jámi,—names that fall dead on a western ear—displayed an enthusiasm, a sublimity, and a grace, to which the west, since the most favoured ages of Greece and Rome, had nothing to compare. These new comers constantly infused a fresh spirit of ardour and enterprise into the descendants of their countrymen, whom they found in India; they generally occupied the higher offices; and, in several instances, on a change of dynasty, were elevated to the throne. The Musulmans, inflamed by the spirit of political and military adventure, were generally on the offensive, an invaluable advantage; the Hindus, with the inertia common to their character and cherished by their religion, and with the passiveness often found in old establishments, acted merely on the defensive. Of these foreigners, in Hindustán in general, the Túrks and Moghuls, the Afgháns and Persians, were most numerous; while, in Gujrát and the Dekhan, the adventurers of these races were often counterbalanced by the Abyssinians and Arabs. These observations may serve to account for the nearly uniform success and progress of the Muhammedan arms, with a few remarkable exceptions to be afterwards noticed. In Malwa, nearly all the great chiefs were Hindús; many of them Rájpúts, the bravest of the Hindús, who have more feeling of common origin than usually belongs to their countrymen.

Princes of Malwa. A. H. 873–916. A. D. 1469–1510. Mahmúd II.

The reigns of the son and grandson of Sultan Mahmúd Khilji were chiefly remarkable for the disgusting sensuality and wanton cruelty of these princes. That of Sultán Mahmúd II. was more important. The valour and activity that characterise usurpers had now, after several generations of regular succession, given way to the incapacity and ignorance of life and

BOOK IV. business, that are the lot of hereditary princes, when educated under ambitious ministers, and confined to the pleasures and amusements of the haram. Sultan Mahmúd, a weak prince, but personally brave, was A. H. 916, A. D. 1510, raised to the throne by his father's will and the influence of the minister, Moháfez Khan; though he had two elder brothers. The Sultan soon felt that he was a mere puppet in the hands of a party, who sought to govern in his name. He had ambition enough to wish to deliver himself from this thraldom, and to assert his authority. For that purpose, he fled from the palace; and thus, for a time, escaped from the personal re-

Intrigues of Moháfez Khan.

straint to which he had been subjected. Alarmed at this manifestation of an unexpected spirit, Moháfez Khan attempted to throw down the idol he had raised; and placed Mahmúd's immediate elder brother on the throne, under the name of Muhammed Shah. Sultan Mahmúd was, at first, supported in asserting his authority only by the Persians, Arabs, and Abyssinians immediately about the court; but, as these foreigners, though numerous and personally brave, had not been long enough settled in Malwa to establish any extensive influence among the natives, and so depended chiefly on their individual numbers and vigour, he must have sunk under the power of his rival, had he

Interposition of Medíni Rao.

not been opportunely joined by Medíni Rao or Rai, a powerful Rájpút chief, who brought over to his cause not only the force of his own tribe, but the support of the great body of the Hindu population; the example of so eminent a leader being followed by many other men of rank and consequence. Moháfez, and his king, A. H. 917, A. D. 1511. Muhammed Shah, were in the end driven out of Malwa; and took refuge, first in Gujrát, and next in Berár. But this did not restore the country to repose; for, on the death of the eldest brother of Mahmúd, a party declared his son Mahsós king, under the title of Hosheng. This prince, however, seeing no prospect of success, soon gave himself up to Sultan Mahmúd, who had thus the satisfaction of having one of his rivals in his power, while the other was driven into exile. These events were passing, between that important period of Báber's life when he was driven from Ferghána, and that when he once more attempted the conquest of Transoxiana, after the defeat and death of Sheibáni Khan.

Rájpút league at the court of Malwa.

But though Mahmúd thus became the only sovereign in Malwa, his throne was far from being secure; for while Medíni Rao, his prime minister, managed everything with absolute authority, the jealousy which always subsisted between the Rájpút and Musulman lords was not abated. The former, — from meeting together at court, instead of residing as formerly detached in their little principalities; and from their reliance upon, and pride in, the talents of the minister, — had gained more of that principle of cohesion, which is as necessary for the permanence of political as of physical bodies, than is usually attained among Hindu chiefs. The Muhammedan lords, on the other hand, mourned to see their king and the country directed by Pagans. To remove this grievance, a confederacy was formed among them, under Bohjat Khan, then the chief of Chándéri; in which the pagan Rais of Gondevána were induced to join. Medíni Rao, however, who did not slumber, was successful in detaching from the league Sekander Khan of Bhilsa, one of the principal confederates. Alarmed at this defection, the Musulman lords invited the exiled Muhammed Shah Chándéri, that they might once more oppose him to his younger brother, Sultan Mahmúd. But still, even with the assistance of his name, finding themselves unable to cope with Medíni Rao, they called in Sultan Sekander Lodi of Delhi, and Mozeffer Shah of Gujrát *, resolved, at any cost, to check this Hindu

* Ferishta, vol. iv. pp. 252, 253.

BOOK IV.

influence, and to defend the Muhammedans, now overborne by the power of the Rájpúts.

The Kings of Delhi and Gujrát interfere.

The King of Delhi, Sultan Sekander Lodi, glad of so favourable an opportunity of extending his influence over the kingdom of Malwa, sent a body of twelve thousand cavalry, under Imád-ul-mulk Lodi, to assist Muhammed Shah; while, on the side of Gujrát, Mozeffer Shah, at the head of an army, entered the country, and advanced as far as Dhár. At the same time, Sekander Khan of Bhílsa, who had lately joined the Sultan, once more revolted and sided with the confederates.

Defensive measures of Medíni Rao.

Medíni Rao, undismayed by the dangers that encompassed him on every hand, resolved to bend his chief force, in the first place, against him whom he regarded as the most formidable opponent. While he despatched an army against Sekander Khan, to keep him in check, he himself marched to meet Mozeffer Shah, who had now approached Mándu; engaged and defeated him, and drove him back into his own country. Against Sekander of Bhílsa, his arms were less fortunate; for the general sent to oppose him having fallen at the close of a successful action, Sekander rallied his broken troops, and totally defeated Mahmúd's army, thus deprived of its leader.*

Medíni Rao, on his return from his campaigns against the troops of Gujrát, neglecting, for the present, Sekander Khan, who after his victory had retired to Sivás, advanced to meet the more important invasion that threatened him from Chándéri. The force there collected was led by his rival Moháfez Khan, accompanied by Muhammed Shah; and was composed of the disaffected nobles of Málwa, and the Delhi auxiliaries. The hostile armies approached, and lay opposite to each other, neither party being in haste to bring the contest to a final issue, by hazarding a decisive battle. At this

* Ferishta, vol. iv. pp. 253, 254.

crisis, the prince, Mahsós (Hosheng II.), who was in Sultan Mahmúd's camp, and Sadr Khan, an officer of great rank and consideration, deserted and joined the invaders; carrying along with them a large body of cavalry. By this defection the affairs of Sultan Mahmúd seemed to be brought to the brink of ruin. Fortunately for him, however, the general in command of the auxiliaries of Delhi, presuming too much upon the value of his services, and mistaking the feelings of those whom he came to succour, insisted with Bohjat Khan of Chándéri, the chief of most influence among the insurgents, and the real leader of the revolt, that the public prayers should be read in the name of Sultan Sekander Lodi, as the supreme sovereign. This he absolutely refused to admit. Besides such attachment as he may have had to Muhammed Shah, for whom he was fighting, his own power, and that of the other confederate nobles, rested on the weakness of their King; and they were little disposed, by acknowledging a more powerful prince, to resign all their own importance. This produced a coolness, which was followed by Bohjat Khan's withdrawing himself from the camp of the allies. Sultan Sekander probably discovered that Malwa was not yet ready to fall into his hands, and the Delhi auxiliaries were soon after recalled. In the extremity to which he, in his turn, was reduced by these losses, Muhammed Shah, resolving to strike a bold *coup-de-main*, despatched a strong body of his troops, by a circuitous route, to surprise Mándu. But this detachment was overtaken and defeated; and Moháfez Khan, who conducted it in person, was slain. In spite of this disaster, however, Muhammed Shah and Bohjat Khan, who had again joined him on the retreat of the Delhi troops, succeeded, by the intervention of Sheikh Oulía, a holy man, in concluding a peace with Sultan Mahmúd; by which Raisen, Bhílsa, and Dhamoni were assigned to Muhammed Shah, as a provision for his support, at the

Their success.

BOOK IV.

same time that a general amnesty was granted to all his followers; and Medíni Rao was glad thus to be able to put an end to hostilities, which exhausted the kingdom and endangered its independent existence.

Subsequent history.

To conclude the history of this little kingdom, some years after these transactions, Muhammed Shah died, leaving a son Ahmed Shah. Sultan Ibráhím Lodi, who had now succeeded his father in the throne of Delhi, and who professed to be the ally and protector of the prince, carried him off, and committed the charge of his forts to such persons as he supposed to be in his own interest. When Rána Sánga, the head of the Hindu interest, advanced to attack Sultan Ibráhím, the governor of these strongholds, being much more attached to the Rájpúts than to Delhi, revolted; and all these places, with Chándéri and many other towns, fell into the hands of the Rána, who bestowed them on his allies, the leading Rájpút chiefs of Malwa. Raisen and Bhilsa he gave to Siláh-ed-dín; and Chandérí to Medíni Rao.*

The Rájpúts all-powerful in Malwa.

The conclusion of a peace, and the discomfiture of the Musulman cc .federacy, had left Medíni Rao and the Rájpúts all-ŗ werful at the court of Malwa. They filled the princ' pal offices with their dependents; the royal guards ᵛ ere composed entirely of Rájpúts. An unsuccessful ·.ttempt made to secure Mándu for the Muhammedan interest by revolt, gave a colour for removing the few Moslems who still continued to hold any charge of importance. Except the personal servants of the king, about twenty in number†, few were

Mahmúd attempts their dismissal.

left in any situation of trust. The king either taking an alarm at these proceedings, or wrought upon by the complaints and representations of the discontented Musulmans about his person, resolved for once to act with vigour and to dismiss his Rájpút troops. This

* Ferishta, vol. iv. p. 256.

† Tabakát-i-Akberi. Ferishta says, two hundred.

would have been no easy task even for the ablest prince. The mode of doing it adopted by Mahmúd, proved only his weakness and ignorance. It is usual, in many parts of India, when a master discharges a servant of some consideration, with whom he wishes to part on friendly terms, to present him, as a mark of his good will, a little betel-nut and lime wrapped up in a leaf *, as is done to a guest when taking leave. As the Rájpút troops amounted to forty thousand, the king ordered that number of packets of *pán* to be prepared, and sent in baskets to Medíni Rao, that he might present them to the troops, and at once dismiss the whole army. The Rajpúts, inflamed at the indignity, called upon Medíni Rao to depose Mahmúd, and at once to elevate his own son, the Rái-Ráian †, to the throne. The minister, by his influence, contrived to suppress this mutiny; but Mahmúd, tired of the restraint under which he felt himself, and too pusillanimous to resort to any politic or manly measure,—with dastardly imbecility attempted, by means of his household servants, to assassinate Medíni Rao and Salbhan, his principal ministers. Salbhan fell murdered under their blows; but Medíni Rao escaped, severely wounded. No sooner did the troops hear of this violent outrage, than they rushed to the palace, which they attacked; but were repulsed by the personal bravery of the king and his immediate attendants; and were once more appeased by Medíni Rao, who was, to appearance, again received into favour.‡ Mahmúd, however, not long after, contrived to escape from the palace, with but a few attendants; and made good his way into Gujrát.

Is discomfited.

Escapes to Gujrát.

From Gujrát, he soon returned, accompanied by Mozeffer Shah, then king of the country, at the head of a powerful army. Medíni Rao, though deprived of that authority which in monarchical countries attends

A. H. 923. A. D. 1517.

* Pán-supári.

† Rai of Rais.

‡ Tabakát-i-Akberi, f. 453.; Ferishta, vol. iv. p. 257.

BOOK IV. the name of king, took active measures to sustain his cause. He left his son to defend Mándu, and himself hastened to meet the invaders in the field; but, soon finding himself too weak to oppose the army of the two kings, with any hopes of success, he retreated; and, having reinforced the garrison of Mándu, proceeded to Cheitúr, to solicit succour from Rána Sánga, at that period the chief of the Rájpút race. The allied sovereigns, advancing, took Dhár; and then besieged Mándu, which, in the course of a few days, surrendered on terms; but the terms were broken by the besiegers, the place attacked and carried by surprise, and nineteen thousand Rájpúts, without discrimination of age or sex, are said to have perished,—numbers falling in the *jóhar* or voluntary massacre, by which the sack of the place was accompanied.* Mozeffer Shah, having reinstated Sultan Mahmúd in his capital, returned to Gujrát, leaving an auxiliary force behind him under Asof Khan.

His restoration.

A. H. 924. Sefer 3. A. D. 1518. Feb. 24.

But though Sultan Mahmúd was thus restored to his capital and the adjoining provinces, a large portion of Malwa was still hostile to him. Medíni Rao possessed Chándéri and Gagrown; while Siláh-ed-dín held Bhílsa, Raisen, and Sarangpút, some of the most important forts and districts of Malwa. While these chiefs were nearly independent, or dependant rather on the Rána than on Mahmúd, their extensive territories could hardly be reckoned parts of his kingdom. Sultan Mahmúd resolved, therefore, to reduce them to obedience; and led his own troops and his Gujrát auxiliaries against Gagrown, which he besieged.

Expedition against the refractory Rájpúts.

Medíni Rai, having been joined by Rána Sánga from Cheitúr, advanced with a formidable army to its assistance. On hearing of this movement, Mahmúd raised the siege, and made several days' march to meet him. On the last of these days, the Sultan, after a long

* Ferishta makes the siege last some months, and says nothing of the treachery, the particulars of which are detailed in the Tabakát-i-Akberi, ff. 455, 456.

march, came to his ground about seven kos from the enemy. Rána Sánga, however, who had heard of his approach, and who was determined to attack him while his troops were fatigued and in disorder, mounted and moved forward. As he approached the camp, he came upon scattered parties of Mahmúd's men; but, even when he had reached the main army, found all in disorder, and no regular opposition was attempted. It could hardly be called a battle. Thirty-two of the chief nobles of Malwa fell in the contest and rout that ensued; as did Asof Khan, and hundreds of the Gujrát auxiliaries. Sultan Mahmúd himself was taken prisoner, after an obstinate resistance, in which he received several wounds. He was, as we have seen, generously treated by Rána Sánga, and restored to his kingdom; partly, perhaps, by the influence of Medíni Rao. But, as Medíni Rao, Siláh-ed-dín, and Sekander Khan of Sivás, besides a number of small chiefs, retained their possessions; and, as Rána Sánga had himself seized upon many districts, insomuch that not above a tenth part of the kingdom of Malwa remained in the Sultan's hands, the revenues of the state were miserably impaired. Indeed, it was generally believed that the Rána was restrained from occupying the whole kingdom only by respect for the power and influence of Mozeffer Shah.*

Defeat of Mahmúd,

and dismemberment of Malwa.

But the imprudence of Sultan Mahmúd soon involved him in new dangers. On the death of Mozeffer Shah, Beháder Shah, after two reigns of only a few months' duration, succeeded to the throne of Gujrát; and Chand Khan, his younger brother, fled to Mándu, where he was entertained by Mahmúd. Attempts were made to engage in his cause the Emperor Báber, who, by this time, had gained possession of the throne of Delhi; and a correspondence was carried on between

Behâder Shah in Gujrát. A. H. 932, A. D. 1526.

* Tab. Akb. f. 457.; Ferishta, iv. p. 262.

BOOK IV. Delhi and Mándu, for that purpose. Information of this reached Behåder, who smothered his resentment for the moment, but resolved to take the earliest opportunity to revenge the injury.

Báber in Rájputána. A. H. 934, A. D. 1528. About two years afterwards, Báber himself appeared on the stage of Malwa. After he had defeated Rána Sánga, he turned his arms against Medíni Rao, the chief supporter of the Rájpút interest in Malwa; and took by storm Chándéri, the seat of his power, with the slaughter of all its defenders, and of that eminent man himself. He restored it to Ahmed Shah, Muhammed Shah's son, whose cause he affected to espouse, leaving a "governor over him." It was the Emperor's intention to have followed up his success by reducing Bhílsa, Raisen and Sarangpúr, the Chiefship of Siláh-ed-dín, and then to have marched to Cheitúr to attack the Rána in his capital; but this plan he was forced to abandon, by insurrections, which made his presence necessary in the eastern provinces.*

Rána Ruttonsi and Behåder Shah in Malwa. At this period, Rána Sánga died, and was succeeded by his son Rána Ruttonsi. Sultan Mahmúd, thinking this a favourable opportunity to recover what he had lost, with that spirit of restless incapacity which marked his character, sent an army to attack and plunder the new Rána's territories. Ruttonsi, in revenge of this injury, marched into his dominions; upon which the Sultan advanced from Sarangpúr to oppose him. Here he summoned to his standard Siláh-ed-dín (with whom A. H. 926, A. D. 1520. he had, a few years before, been at war; and whom he had even deprived of Sarangpúr) and Moyín Khan, the adopted son of the late Sekander Khan of Sivás. He now, when too late, attempted to conciliate these chiefs. On Moyín Khan he conferred the title of Masnad Khan, and presented him with a scarlet pavilion; to Siláh-ed-dín he gave some additional villages, near his various

* Báber's Mem. p. 377, 378.

jágírs. But the Sultan had ceased to command their confidence; and these noblemen, — believing that the favours conferred upon them were intended to serve a present purpose, while his hatred was in nothing abated, and that they had every thing to apprehend from his intrigues,—soon after left his camp and joined the Rána. Meanwhile, Behàder Shah, seizing the opportunity for which he had been in wait, of prosecuting his revenge, had also entered Malwa. The Rána, with the Malwa chiefs who had joined him, marched towards the King of Gujrát, that all might act in concert. Sultan Mahmúd, filled with alarm at this revolt and double invasion, sent to Behàder Shah, professing his readiness to wait upon him; but, under various frivolous pretexts, constantly put off the time of meeting. Behàder, at length, aware of his insincerity, pushed on to Mándu, his capital, into which the Sultan had thrown himself; and, after a short siege, took it by escalade. Mahmúd fell into his hands, and was at first treated with respect; but three days afterwards, on some offence, real or pretended, Behàder Shah proclaimed himself King of Malwa; and next day sent off the Sultan, in chains, with twenty of his sons, under an escort of an hundred horse, to be confined in the hill-fort of Champanír. But the escort that attended him being attacked, near Dokad, during the night by a party of Bhíls, he was put to death by his guard, to prevent a rescue. This event occurred only three months after Humáyun had mounted the throne.*

CHAP. II. SECT. I.

A. H. 937. Shábán 9. A. D. 1531. March 8. Mándu taken.

Shábán 12.

Shábán 13. Behàder Shah proclaimed King.

Shábán 15.

* Ferishta, in the History of Malwa, (vol. iv. p. 368.) fixes the date of the storming of Mándu, on the 9 Shábán, A. H. 932, (22 May, A. D. 1526). This can hardly be correct, as Báber, (Mem. p. 376.) in Moharrem 934, (Jan. 1528), speaks of Sultan Mahmúd as still in Mándu. The real date is probably A. H. 937, Shábán 9, (A. D. 1531, March 8), that assigned in the Tabakáte Akberi, and by Ferishta in the History of Gujrát (vol. iv. p. 115.). In the History of Kándesh (vol. iv. p. 310.), Ferishta seems to place the reduction of Mándu, and, consequently, the death of Sultan Mahmúd, in A. H. 939 (A. D. 1532-3). The Mirát-i-Ahmedi (Bird's transl. p. 238.) makes the escalade of Mándu take place

BOOK IV.

Partition of Malwa.

Behåder Shah and Rána Ruttonsi now overran all Malwa. The capital, with the western and northern provinces, Behåder added to his dominions. The Rána, on the other hand, seems to have added little to his own immediate territories; but the Malwa lords, who had espoused his interest, and who, for some time before, had acknowledged his authority, he confirmed in the possession of Ráisen, Rantambór, Sarangpúr, and several other extensive districts.

Capture of Siláh ed-dín by Behåder. A. H. 938, A. D. 1531.

The ambition of Behåder, nourished by success, was not to be restrained by conventions and treaties. Siláh-ed-dín or Silhádi was too powerful a subject not to be viewed with jealousy; and he determined to ruin him. That chieftain's son, who was in Behåder's camp, was sent to invite his father to wait upon the King, who wished to consult with him before returning to Gujrát.* The Rájpút, leaving his son in Ujein, met Behåder Shah near Dhár. That prince entered the fort, accompanied only by Silhádi, whom he there treacherously seized, with the two Rájpúts by whom the chief was attended. One of them, laying his hand on his dagger, drew it, and prepared for resistance. "Forbear," said the chief, "it is me whom you are killing." "'Twas in your defence it was drawn," said his faithful follower; "but, since my act endangers you, thus I slay myself, and escape the misery of seeing you a prisoner." With these words, he inflicted on himself several mortal wounds, "and so," says the Musulman historian, "went to hell." Behåder's pretext for this outrage, and for his quarrel with Siláh-ed-dín, was that the pagan had in his seraglio several Muhammedan women, and even some ladies of the haram of a deceased Sultan.

20 Shábán, (A. H. 937) and the surrender of Mahmúd Shah follow, 12 Moharrem. A. H. 938, (26 Aug. 1531). Ferishta makes him killed five days after the escalade (14 Shábán). The Tabakáte Akberi makes his death occur on the Sheb-e-Berát (15 Shábán) one day later, f. 459. Instead of twenty sons, Ferishta gives him seven.

* Tabakáte Akberi, ff 391. 459.; Báber's Mem. pp. 312. 376.

CHAP. II. SECT. I.

The King, after getting Siláh-ed-dín into his power, entered his dominions, and, with little opposition, gained possession of Ujein, Sarangpúr, and Bhilsa. He finally besieged the brother and one of the sons of that chief in the strong fort of Ráisen, which contained also his wives and family, and, after a long siege, reduced it to the greatest distress.

Catastrophe of Ráisen.

Silhádi, though in captivity, and even, it is said, compelled to renounce his own religion for the Moslem creed, most keenly sympathised with his afflicted subjects. Seeing no prospect of relief from an army sent to his assistance by Rána Ruttonsi, a prince far inferior in all respects to his illustrious father, and in which his own son Bhopat served with the shattered remains of his force, was compelled to seek relief in submission or despair. A capitulation was at length entered into, on condition that the fort was to be given up, but that the lives, liberties, and honour of all who were in it should be respected, and that Siláh-ed-dín was to be set at large. That chieftain asked permission to enter the fort for the purpose of bringing out the females of his household, in terms of the treaty. Here he had to sustain the reproaches of his wife, Durgáwati, a daughter of Rána Sánga, who, distrusting any Moslem promises, declared her resolution to die free and unblemished, and concluded her invectives by setting fire to a pile that she had reared, which consumed in its flames the palace and seven hundred beautiful females that were in the haram. Siláh-ed-dín himself, stung to madness, put on his armour, and, accompanied by his brother, rushed out with their devoted followers, and died the death of Rájpúts. Behader bestowed Ráisen, with Bhílsa and Chándéri, on Alem Khan Jilál-Khan Jigat*, a noble-

* The Miráte Ahmedi calls him Sultan Alem Lodi. He seems to have been the son of a Sultan Jilál-khan, who aspired to the throne in the beginning of his brother Sultan Ibráhím's reign. See also Baber's Mem. pp. 349. 335.

BOOK IV.

man, who had lately held the government of Kalpi, under Báber; but who had subsequently fled from that place, and renounced his allegiance.* Having thus strengthened his power in Malwa, Behàder returned in triumph to his hereditary dominions.

Further successes of Beháder Shah. A. H. 936. A. D. 1529.

Besides his conquests in Malwa, Beháder Shah had extraordinary success in other quarters. He marched through the territories of his nephew, Miran Muhammed Khan, the prince of Kandesh, to succour Imád-ul-Mulk, the King of Berár, when attacked by the kings of Beder and Ahmednagar†; and, driving the invaders before him, advanced by Jálna to Doulalábád. He compelled Burhán Nizám Shah to acknowledge him as King of Ahmednagar, as well as Gujrát; and to read the public prayers in his name. He gained some important advantages over the Portuguese, who infested his dominions. He was fond of state, and affected much pomp and splendour, both in his court and camp. His armies were numerous, and the Prince of Kandesh, and the King of Berár, served in them with their auxiliaries; as did the legitimate Prince of Malwa, who was allowed or compelled to attend his court.‡

A. H. 939. A. D. 1532-3.

* Báber's Mem. p. 378.; Ferishta, vol. iv. pp. 270. 118.

† Briggs's Ferishta, vol. iii. p. 489.; vol. iv. p. 112.

‡ The greater part of the preceding narrative is from the Tabakáte Akberi, ff. 389—392.* Ferishta, Hist. of Gujrát, vol. iv. pp. 1—123.; Hist. of Malwa, Ibid. pp. 167—269.; Hist. of Kandesh, Ibid. p. 310., corrected by a few short notices in Báber's Memoirs.

It may be remarked, that the different histories of Ferishta vary from each other in several particulars, especially in the chronology. In each, he probably followed the historian of the particular dynasty whose annals he was writing.

# CHAPTER II.

## AFFAIRS OF GUJRÁT AND MALWA.

---

## SECTION II.

### CONQUEST OF MALWA BY HUMÁYUN.

RELATIONS OF GUJRÁT AND CHEITÚR. — SUCCESSES OF BEHÁDER SHAH IN MALWA AND RÁJPUTÁNA. — HE FORMS A LEAGUE AGAINST HUMÁYUN. — JOINED BY SULTAN ALÁ-ED-DÍN LODI AND HIS SON, TÁTÁR KHAN LODI — AND BY MUHAMMED ZEMÁN MÍRZA. — HUMÁYUN REMONSTRATES WITHOUT EFFECT. — OPERATIONS OF THE ALLIES. — THEIR ENTIRE DEFEAT. — HUMÁYUN INVADES MALWA. — STORM AND SACK OF CHEITÚR BY BEHÁDER SHAH. — THE ARMIES OF HUMÁYUN AND BEHÁDER MEET AT MANDSÚR. — THE LATTER ENTRENCH THEMSELVES. — DISTRESS IN BEHÁDER'S CAMP. — FLIGHT OF THE KING — HIS TROOPS PLUNDERED AND PURSUED. — INVESTMENT OF MÁNDU. — DESCRIPTION OF THAT CAPITAL. — OVERTURES OF BEHÁDER. — MÁNDU ESCALADED. — BEHÁDER ESCAPES TO GUJRÁT. — MÁNDU PLUNDERED BY THE IMPERIALISTS. — HUMÁYUN SUPREME IN MALWA.



*Relations of Gujrát and Cheitúr.*

THE destruction of the kingdom of Malwa, as an independent state, entirely changed the political relations which had subsisted between the rulers of Gujrát and Cheitúr. Formerly, they were often allies; henceforward, they of necessity became direct rivals. The spoils and provinces of that extensive country were the prize for which both contended. In this contest, the means which they employed to attain their objects were different. The King endeavoured to occupy the country directly by his own troops; the Rána, to secure an ascendency by the intervention of chieftains of great

BOOK IV.

local influence. The wealth and commercial prosperity of Gujrát enabled Behâder Shah to bring into the field a large regular army and a powerful artillery; the Rána's gallant followers were ever prepared to sacrifice their lives for their chief or their tribe, in the day of battle, but they had no means of keeping the field for any great length of time, or of securing permanently such conquests as they made. A battle being gained, or a city stormed and pillaged, they were eager to return to their homes, with their glory and their plunder. The constitution of the Rájpút states, a confederacy of tribes or of little chieftains, was little suited for retaining distant possessions.

Successes of Behâder Shah.

The attack of Behâder Shah on Siláh-ed-dín had brought the Rána into the field, in his defence. But the Rájpút army were no longer directed by a warrior like Rána Sánga. Rána Ruttonsi, after a short reign, had yielded the sword of command to his brother Bikermájít.* This impolitic prince, having disgusted the chiefs, who formed the strength of his armies, could offer but an imperfect resistance to the attack of Behâder; who now, flushed with victory, invaded his territories, year after year. In the summer after the death of Siláh-ed-dín, following up his success, he reduced the important fortress of Gágrown, and sent an army to besiege Rantambór. Though compelled to hasten back to Diu, to check the encroachments of the Portuguese on his coasts, he next season returned to Malwa; marched victorious through its provinces; and, not only wrested from his rival the conquests made by Rána Sánga in that kingdom, but even advanced into the Rána's hereditary dominions, and besieged him in

A. H. 939, A. D. 1532-3.

A. H. 940. in Malwa and Rájputána.

* The period of the death of Ruttonsi, and accession of Bikermájít, is not well known. The Musulman historians do not fix it, and the chronology of the Rájpúts themselves is in general extremely erroneous. As Colonel Tod allows Ruttonsi a reign of five years, and as he ascended the masnad in A. H. 934, his death may be placed A. H. 939.

Cheitúr itself. We have seen, that, in spite of the march of the Emperor Humáyun, as far as Guáliár, to his assistance, the Rána was compelled ignominiously to purchase, at a high price, the retreat of the King of Gujrát. CHAP. II. SECT. II.

He forms a league against Humáyun.

These continued successes added fuel to the naturally ambitious temper of Behádor. He and Humáyun had now become neighbours, and the events of the last campaign had shown that they must inevitably soon come to a collision. The King of Gujrát, indignant that his prey should have been wrested from him, looked round for means to occupy and injure the Emperor; and they were not wanting.

Many Afghán Amírs, and other refugees from Delhi and the eastern provinces, who had been driven into exile by the successes of Báber, had fled to his court for shelter. Sultan Behádor, who had himself been a fugitive from Gujrát at the time of Báber's invasion, and who had spent some time in exile at the court of Sultan Ibráhím Lodi, as well as at Juánpúr, stood in too great awe of the late Emperor to hazard any hostile proceedings during his lifetime. But after the succession of Humáyun, he was incessantly urged by Tátár Khan Lodi, and other fugitives from what had been the Afghán, and were now the imperial, dominions, to lend them even a moderate aid; as they boasted, with that, to be able, if not to exterminate the Chaghatái invaders, at least to drive them back beyond the Indus. We have seen that Sultan Alá-ed-dín Lodi, the father of Tátár Khan, the uncle of the late Sultan Ibráhím, and twice an unsuccessful competitor for the throne of Delhi, had been sent by Báber to be imprisoned in the distant fort of Kila-Zefer, in Badakhshán*, for reasons unknown, but probably for the crime of being dangerous from his birth and his pretensions. Having escaped

Joined by Sultan Alá-ed-dín Lodi, and his son Tátár Khan Lodi.

* Akbernáma, I. 37. MS. B. f. 74.

BOOK IV.

from custody, by the assistance of some Afghán merchants, he found his way in disguise, through many perils, across the Afghán country and Baluchistán, to the court of Gujrát. Behádcr, who had long resisted the solicitations of the exiles, at last, prompted by what he regarded as his own wrongs, yielded to their importunity; and, entering into their views, began to make preparations for an attack on Humáyun. He secretly employed considerable sums in drawing off the adherents of his rival, and received, with distinguished favour, the refugees from Agra, who flocked to his court.

and by Muhammed Zemán Mírza.

It was about this period that Muhammed Zemán Mírza, having escaped from Biána, arrived in his camp*, with his keeper, Yádgár Taghái Beg, whom he had seduced to accompany him in his flight. Behåder Shah, situated as he was, and indulging the plans which he did, regarded the arrival of a prince of his rank and talents as a fortunate occurrence, and warmly entered into his animosities. The fugitive confirmed the opinion given by Tátár Khan, of the ease with which the Emperor might be expelled. He represented the discipline of the army as relaxed since the late Emperor's death; the troops, as giving themselves up to ease and luxury; the nobles, as discontented; and both the native and Afghán chiefs and officers, as only waiting for an opportunity to revolt.

Humáyun remonstrates without effect.

These proceedings could not escape the notice of Humáyun, who called upon Behádcr Shah to dismiss Muhammed Zemán Mírza†, and the other rebels and

* An instance of Behåder's luxurious and ostentatious magnificence is mentioned on this occasion. When Muhammed Zemán reached Behåder's camp, before Cheitúr, he was suffering from the heat of the weather. His physicians recommended Gúl-kend (candied conserve of roses) to allay the heat. The Mírza sent to ask Behåder for a small quantity, and received forthwith twenty cart-loads. The King had been accustomed to have a spirit distilled from it. Tárikhe-Bedáuni, f. 129.

† No mention is made of any

fugitives from the imperial dominions, who were entertained in his court. This the King of Gujrát declined, on the general ground of that hospitality which all princes are accustomed to extend to the distressed. He adduced the precedent of Sultan Alá-ed-dín himself, Sultan Sekander Lodi's brother, who, as well as several other princes of the blood, in circumstances resembling the present, had found refuge with his predecessor, Mozeffer Shah, without giving offence to the sovereigns of Delhi.

Humáyun, in return, maintained, that the reception afforded to the fugitive enemies of his government was inconsistent with the relations of amity that subsisted between them, and must lead to dangerous consequences. He denied that the case of Alá-ed-dín, referred to, had any similarity to the present; he reminded the King, with something of a menace, that, unwilling as the great Taimúr had long been to attack Beyezíd* Ilderim, while he was engaged in war with the infidels of Europe, and many as were the injuries which on that account he long bore, yet that his patience was finally exhausted, when that monarch refused to withdraw his protection from Kara Yúsef Túrkomán, and Sultan Ahmed Jeláir, Taimúr's rebellious subjects, who had taken refuge with him. That the consequences were sufficiently well known. And he insisted, that Behâder Shah should either deliver up Muhammed Zemán Mírza, or at least expel him from his dominions. Behâder obstinately persisted in his refusal.

Preparations for hostilities.

The demonstration which Humáyun made on the side of Gualiár, during the siege of Cheitúr, was a suf-

demand to deliver up Sultan Alá-ed-dín Lodi; either, because he had not then arrived; or, as is more probable, because his situation was different from that of Muhammed Zemán, and did not in the same degree justify the Emperor's demand. The former, though a claimant of the throne of Delhi, was an Afghán of the race of Lodi; the latter, a Chaghatái prince of the race of Taimúr, who had been long in the imperial service, and had married a sister of the Emperor.

* Called Bajazet by our historians.

BOOK IV. A.D. 1534. ficiently intelligible indication of what he would have attempted, had the internal disorders, which occupied him at home, admitted of his marching beyond the limits of his own dominions. Behάder, offended at the tone of his rival's remonstrances, now entered heartily into the views of the exiles, and lent every assistance in his power to the claims of Sultan Alá-ed-dín or Alim Lodi, who once more put forward his pretensions to the throne of Delhi. Tátár Khan, Alim's son, who managed the affairs of his father, urged the King to declare for him openly; contending, that the Emperor's army, in its present state, would not dare to meet that of Gujrát. But Behάder was still anxious not to come prominently forward; and it was, therefore, arranged, that the intended attack should have only the air of an unauthorised irruption of the Afghán refugees, for the recovery of their former empire; and that the King himself should not appear to take any share in it. He privately, however, supplied them with large sums of money, to enable them to put their army on an effective footing. The amount stated, probably with some exaggeration, to have been not less than a million sterling*, was sent to Rantbór, to be employed by Tátár Khan. Adventurers and exiles flocked to his standard, from every quarter; and a formidable force was soon ready to take the field.

A. H. 941, A. D. 1534-5. An extensive plan of operations was formed, and vigorously acted upon. Sultan Alá-ed-dín Lodi, Tátár Khan's father, led a considerable force † to Kalinger,

* Twenty krór of old Gujrát gold coin, which Abulfazl (Akbernama, f. 37.) estimates at double the currency of his time, or forty krórs. This, if reckoned in rupees, would give forty millions sterling, which cannot be admitted. If reckoned in dáms, the current mode of Treasury computation, it would amount to one million sterling; if in double dáms, to two millions. Briggs's Ferishta calls the sum three krórs of rupees, or about three millions sterling.

† I have been sometimes tempted to believe that this army was commanded by Alá-ed-dín or Alim Khan Jilál Khan Jigat, who, we have seen, now held Raisen, Bhílsa, and Chánderi. Abulfazl, however, says

CHAP. II. SECT. II.

in Bandelkand, to encourage the hostile spirit already existing in that quarter, and to threaten, or in case of success, to invade Behár and the neighbouring provinces. Burhán-el-mulk Sistáni, with a body of Gujrátis, was directed to march through the northern Rájpút territory of Nagór, to make a feint of attacking the Penjáb; and thus to distract attention, and, by spreading alarm, to prevent any assistance being rendered from that province. The real attack, under Tátár Khan, was to be made in the line of Agra. Meanwhile, Behàder Shah himself, under cover of these different forces, proceeded with the army of Gujrát, as if uninterested in what was going on around him, to lay siege once more to the Rájpút capital, Cheitúr, where he would be at hand to assist and take advantage of the invasion, should it succeed. Many able men in Behàder's council blamed, we are told, this disjointed plan of operations; giving it as their opinion, that it would be much better to keep the army in a concentrated state; and expressed their apprehension that the whole proceedings would be regarded as a breach of peace. But their advice was not listened to; the King having persuaded himself that, since the Lodis had undoubted pretensions to the throne of Delhi, their asserting such claims would be held to be a matter of their own, and could lead to no inferences unfavourable to himself. The different armies were soon put in motion. Tátár Khan, who had increased his troops to forty thousand horse, Afgháns and others, advanced towards Agra *; and, having by the way attacked and carried Biána, his plundering parties extended their ravages to the very suburbs of the capital.

*Operations of the allies.*

Humáyun, on receiving intelligence of these transactions, gave up, for the present, his expedition against

*Their entire defeat.*

expressly, that it was Sultan Alá-ed-dín, Tátár Khan's father; and the Tárikhe Bedáuni calls him the son of Sekander, f. 139.

* Akbernáma, f. 37.; Tabakáte Akberi, f. 145.

BOOK IV.
A.D. 1534.

Bengál and Behár, and hastened back to Agra. Meanwhile, however, he ordered his brothers, Hindal and Askeri, his cousin, Yádgár Násir Mírza, the son of his late uncle, Násir Mírza, and Kásim Husein Sultan, Uzbek, with eighteen thousand horse, to proceed without delay to check the invaders; rightly judging, that, if their grand army was defeated, the others could do little mischief. When the approach of the imperialists, inferior as they were in number, became known, the invading troops were seized with a sudden panic, and large bodies of them deserted every day and returned home; insomuch that, in a short time, of this great army, collected with so much parade and expence, not more than three thousand * horse remained with Tátár Khan. That nobleman, indignant at the treachery of his mercenaries, stung with shame at the result of his high promises, and defeated in his long-cherished schemes of ambition, when they seemed on the very eve of being accomplished, hesitated for some time whether he should fight or retreat. Impelled, however, by indignation and despair, he came to a conflict with the enemy at Mandráel, where the brave followers who still adhered to him were routed with great slaughter, and himself and three hundred of his officers slain. Biána was soon recovered, without a blow; and the other two invading armies, on hearing of these calamitous events, retreated into the territories of Gujrát.†

Humáyun invades Malwa.

Eager as Humáyun was to repress the disorders that were arising in his dominions on the Ganges, and in Behár, he saw clearly that he could not with safety leave behind him a victorious prince so formidable as Beháder Shah, who had shown the worst dispositions, and whose dominions now approached so near to his capital. It was evident that, should he proceed to Bengal, and should Beháder, after reducing Cheitúr,

* Ferishta says, ten thousand.

† Akbernáma, f. 37, 38.; Ferishta, vol. ii. pp. 73, 74.

avail himself of his absence to occupy Agra, the communication between the northern and southern parts of the imperial dominions would be cut off, and himself and his army exposed to the danger of being totally destroyed. He determined, therefore, at once to attack his enemy in the centre of his power; and, in the middle of November, A. D. 1534 *, set out for a vigorous campaign. Marching in the direction of Malwa, he soon arrived near the strong fort of Raisen, on the Betwa. The governor sent a deputation to meet him, and, in the Asiatic style, to represent that he and the fortress were his Majesty's. Humáyun did not lose time in endeavouring to reduce the place; but, accepting the proffered submission, such as it was, pushed forward, and was soon encamped at Sarangpúr, an important town on the Kali-Sind, in the very heart of Malwa.

Behâder Shah at Cheitúr.

This rapid advance disconcerted Behâder Shah, who was still busily, and not unsuccessfully, employed in the siege of Cheitúr. He saw the thin mask, with which he had sought to cover his hostile intentions, rudely torn away; and an offended enemy in the centre of his dominions. His most experienced councillors differed as to the course proper to be pursued. Some advised him at once to abandon the siege, which could be resumed at any time, and march to repel the invading army. On the other hand, Sadr Khan, the most eminent man of his court, and equally distinguished for his rank and for his political and military talents, was of a different opinion. He urged, that Cheitúr was reduced to the last extremity, and must soon fall; that, to quit the siege now, was not only to lose all the labour which had been bestowed on it, but to injure the reputation of their arms; that besides, the Emperor, sensible of the

* A. H. 941. beginning of Jemádi I. (A. D. Nov. 1534). It seems not very clear whether this is the date of his giving up his campaign against the Purebis, or of marching from Agra. Akbernáma, MS. B. f. 73. and 5 r.

BOOK IV.

A.D. 1535.

odium which would attend such an interference, would not attempt directly to interrupt the operations of Musulmans, engaged in a holy war against infidels. This opinion prevailed; the operations of the siege were pushed on with redoubled fury; the defences were battered by the cannon of Rúmi Khan, a Turkish engineer, who was assisted by Portuguese and other European artillerymen; and finally, a mine was sprung, which left a broad and accessible breach. A storm followed, on the 8th of March, A.D. 1535, when the fort was carried by assault, in spite of every effort made by the courage and despair of the Rájpúts. The garrison, seeing that all hope was gone, proceeded to put to death their wives and women, who, on their part, voluntarily presented their bosoms to the sword, or rushed into the blazing pyre, to avoid the defilements of slavery, and to maintain untarnished the honour of their tribe.* The remaining Rájpúts, then, clothing themselves in their yellow-died garments, the well-known sign of despair and death, sallied out to meet their assailants, and were cut off to a man. The victors, on entering the city, found only a heap of ruins and a lifeless solitude. The booty, which was great, was divided among the victorious troops.

Storm and sack of that place.

A.D. 941. Ramzán 3. A.D. 1535. March 8.

The armies of Humáyun and Beháder meet at Mandsúr.

Beháder Shah had now nothing to detain him from marching to chastise the invader of his dominions. To account for the inaction of Humáyun, at this important crisis, we are told, that, on reaching Sarangpúr, and being informed that it was the opinion of Beháder's councillors that, as a faithful believer, he would not attack a prince engaged in a holy war, he declared that they only did him justice; and immediately ceased

* Akbernáma, as above; Tabakáte Akberi, ff. 145. 146.; Tod's Rajasthán, vol. i. pp. 311, 312. From native authorities, Col. Tod estimates the number of women, who perished in this johár, at thirteen thousand; the loss of the Rájpúts, in the siege and storm, at thirty-two thousand, the flower of their tribe.

CHAP. II. SECT. II.

from all offensive operations. There was now, however, an end of this point of honour. On hearing of the fall of the Rájpút capital, Humáyun left Ujein, where he then was, and moved to the northward; while Behâder Shah, marching to meet him, the two armies soon came in sight of each other, on the banks of a large tank, near the town of Mandsúr.*

The latter intrench themselves.

The tents of the army of Gujrát were not all pitched, and the army itself had not yet come to its ground, when its advanced pickets were attacked and driven in upon their centre with some slaughter, by a body of the imperial horse. This little incident had an effect on the spirits of the troops on both sides. Táj Khan and Sadr Khan, two of Behâder's most distinguished officers, strongly urged him, while his troops were still flushed with their success at Cheitúr, and before they had tried the discipline and vigour of the Túrki warriors, to lead his men at once to battle, in which they would assuredly exert themselves gallantly. Rúmi Khan, however, who commanded the artillery, and who had much influence with the king†, was of a different opinion. He had with him about three hundred Turkish artillerymen, besides eighty Portuguese and Franks commanded by a native Portuguese, named San Jago, who had received the title of Feringi Khan. Rúmi Khan was an Ottoman Turk, who had been honoured with the title of Khodáwend Khan. He had learned his art in the Turkish service, which, about this period, was distinguished for superiority in the management of heavy artillery. The

* Akbernáma, f. 38.; Tabak. Akberi, ff. 146. 395. Jouher, (in the original) chap. ii. says, that the imperial army halted near Tálwar (or Tilúr, or Tisúr); that Behâder, after taking Cheitúr, had directed his march for Gujrát, but was intercepted by the Emperor, near Mori, a town dependent on Burhánpúr. Jouher does not appear to give a very distinct account of any campaign before that of Bengal; though, as he tells Kámrán Mírza, in Rámzán, A. H. 960, that he had been nineteen years in the Emperor's service, he was probably with him at this time. The Tabakát calls the place Sirsúr.

† Lafitau, Hist. des Découvertes des Portugais, vol. i. p. 209. 4to.

BOOK IV.

A. D. 1535.

trade of the sea-coast, and the capture of several Portuguese ships, had furnished the king with an excellent train, which Rúmi Khan pronounced to be second only to that of the "Kaisar of Rúm." He said, that it would be foolish to throw away their superiority, by renouncing the use of the force in which they most excelled; that it would be better to cover themselves by trenches on all sides; to strengthen their lines by their cars, waggons and carriages, and to plant their guns so as to make their position impregnable to the enemy; that the Moghuls, as they called the imperialists, with their usual daring and impetuosity, would soon be seen to gallop up to the lines, within range of their shot, when they would be swept off in crowds; that, when they saw themselves unable to make any impression and beginning to suffer from scarcity, they must, in the end, be compelled to retreat; that, then was the time for the royal horse to follow, and cut them off in detail, in their long retreat, when exhausted and broken as they would be. Rúmi Khan's success at Cheitúr, and previously at Raisen, under circumstances very different from the present, gave perhaps an undue weight to his opinion; which prevailed, and was acted upon. For a time, skirmishes daily ensued, in which the invaders, from the quality of their troops, had uniformly the advantage; when, however, they followed the flying foe close to the trenches, they were soon made aware of the risk; and, as might have been foreseen, ceased to approach them.*

Become disheartened.

The fortified camp of Behåder was, indeed, unassailable; but it was in danger of becoming his prison. The Chaghatái army had all the advantage of daring and activity. They soon taught their enemies to dread them, and showed a decided superiority, not only in discipline and in close combat, but in more distant

* Tabak. Akberi, ff. 395, 396.

fighting, from the use of the bow. The Gujrátis, whose defensive armour could not resist their powerful arrows, after some experience of their energy and skill, did not willingly meet them in the field, and became dispirited; while the ardour and enterprise of their invaders daily increased.* At this crisis Behâder was strengthened by the arrival of Sultan Alim, of Kalpi, with the troops of Raisen and Chándéri. CHAP. II. SECT. II.

While the armies thus lay facing each other, it happened one night that some young officers, who had met at a drinking party in the Emperor's camp, having indulged in liberal libations, began to vaunt their prowess, and to exalt themselves, as nowise inferior to the heroes of former days. Warmed with their own boasting, and with the effects of the wine, they armed, mounted, and, in spite of the efforts made by their soberer comrades to prevent them, sallied forth, to the number of about two hundred, to have a dash at the enemy, and rode right for the hostile camp. When they had nearly reached it, they chanced to fall in with a division, under one of the Gujráti generals, who, on seeing them approach, drew up his men, about four thousand in number, to receive them. The young enthusiasts, not deterred by this disparity of force, charged in amongst them without hesitation. The Gujrátis, astonished as they were, nevertheless at first stood their ground, and a short but sharp conflict ensued; but, being confounded and daunted by the unusual energy of the assailants, and numbers of them falling, they finally gave way, and fled back to their camp in confusion. In Humáyun's army this "Combat of Friends," as it was called, was loudly celebrated, and an official report† published, in a lofty strain, to make it generally known; while, in the camp of Behâder, it spread equal dismay, so that afterwards few The "Combat of Friends."

* Tabak. Akberi, f. 396.

† Kárnáma.

BOOK IV.

A.D. 1535. Sháwál 1. April 4.

of his troops willingly ventured beyond the protection of their field works and batteries. On one occasion, indeed, on the day of the rejoicings for the close of the Rámzán, Muhammed Zemán Mírza, anxious to distinguish himself among his new allies, advanced out of the trenches with about five or six hundred men, as if to challenge a combat, and was met by a party from the opposite side. His followers, after shooting a few arrows, retreated, and contrived to draw their pursuers within the range of the artillery, which poured in its fire upon them with terrible effect.

Distress in Behá-der's camp.

To act upon a plan of operations altogether defensive and passive, in an entrenched camp, is always dangerous, but, above all, in an open country. It places every advantage of daring and enterprise in the hands of an active enemy, and seldom fails to terminate in the discouragement of the troops who are placed on the defensive, and in their being cut off from all their resources. The Chaghatái Túrks, having established their ascendency in the field, and not choosing to shatter their force by throwing themselves on the lowering barricades of the enemy, scoured the country on every side, cut off all foraging parties, intercepted all supplies of grain, provisions, and stores, and nearly succeeded in blocking up the Gujrátis in their position, which was thus impregnable to no purpose. All the grain and provender in the neighbourhood was exhausted, and the Gujráti troops did not venture out to bring them from a distance. Scarcity was soon followed by famine. They were glad to subsist on horse-flesh, and on the vilest foods. Multitudes of men, as well as horses and camels, perished from hunger*; and, in the end, the army of Beháder found themselves nearly in the same condition in which, rather more than two centuries

* Jouher says, that grain sold for four and five rupees the sír, and was not to be had even at that price.

later, the Mahrattas were placed previous to the famous battle of Panipát. CHAP. II. SECT. II.

Flight of the King and a portion of his followers.

Extreme as the distress of the Gujrátis had now become, it was not easy to adopt any new plan of operations. On the other hand, it being announced to the Emperor that a fortunate day was at hand, he resolved to attempt a general assault. But the misery of the enemy had already reached its height. Behâder, in despair of being able, by any active exertion of his dispirited troops, to extricate himself from his unhappy situation, resolved to break up his camp, and to consult his safety by flight. On the 24th and 25th of April, accompanied by his nephew, Mirán Muhammed Khan, prince of Kandesh, and afterwards for a short time King of Gujrát*, Malu Khan, then governor, and afterwards King of Malwa, under the title of Káder Shah, and three or four other confidential friends, in the last watch of the night, making his way through a rent in the royal tent, he left the camp unnoticed; and, first taking the road to Agra, to elude observation, soon after turned round towards Mándu. Sadr Khan, and Imád-ul-mulk Khaseh-khail, with twenty thousand cavalry, set out at the same time for that place by the direct road, while Muhammed Zemán Mírza, with another body of men, took the road of Lahúr, to attempt to excite revolt in that quarter. The heavy artillery, having been loaded and crammed with powder, were burst.

Sunday, Shawál 21. April 24–5.

Humáyun, who had intended early next morning to make his attack, hearing a continued noise, accompanied with an occasional discharge as of great guns in the enemy's lines during the night, and ignorant of the cause, thought it probable that a general attack upon his camp was intended. He stood, with a body

* Briggs's Ferishta, vol. iv. pp. 127, 128. The same author, vol. ii. p. 76., calls the ruler of Kandesh, Mobárck Khan. (Did he afterwards assume that name?)

BOOK IV.

A. D. 1535.

of thirty thousand cavalry, mounted and in arms, ready for battle. All night long the alarm, confusion, shouting, and uproar in the Gujráti camp, mixed with discharge of artillery, continued. When at length the departure of the King became known to his army, it immediately broke up and dispersed; but it was only in the course of the first morning watch that the Emperor learned the real state of things, accompanied with the information that Behâder Shah had disappeared. Upon this the imperial army burst into the deserted camp, and a general pillage ensued. Property of every description, baggage, horses, and elephants, fell into the hands of the soldiers. Many, of all ranks, were made prisoners. Humáyun, pursuing his advantage, not only dispatched a large force, under Yádgár Násir Mirza, to follow the flying enemy, but himself set out soon after with a body of horse, and hotly urged the pursuit. The Gujráti cavalry, under Sadr Khan and Imád-ul-mulk, seem to have made good their retreat, bravely fighting and closely followed by the Emperor, with three or four thousand horse, all the way to the very gates of Mándu, which they succeeded in entering, though not without great loss. Behâder Shah, by taking bye-roads, and passing through a wild and unfrequented country, also reached Mándu.*

Pillage of the camp.

Pursuit of the fugitives.

* Akbernáma, f. 38.; Tabak. Akb. ff. 146. 395, 396.; Ferishta, vol. ii. p. 76.; vol. iv. p. 127.; Kháfi Khan, &c. There are some differences among historians regarding the flight of Behâder. Ferishta, ii. 76. says, that Sadr Jehán Khan was one of the *five* who accompanied him. The Tabakáte Akberi also says, that he was attended by *five* Amirs *of note*. The Muntekhib-ul-Towárikh (ap. Briggs, iv. p. 128. note) says, that he was accompanied by a guard of an hundred officers. Kháfi Khan makes him attended, in his retreat, by Sadr Khan and four thousand horse; and, after the surrender of Mándu, introduces Humáyun complimenting Sadr Khan upon the gallantry with which, in the flight, he had twice extricated his sovereign from his pursuers, by his personal exertions; on one of which occasions, Humáyun himself had nearly engaged the King hand to hand. Ferishta, too, alludes to the same circumstance, vol. ii. p. 77. This supposes that Behâder, after leaving the camp, joined Sadr Khan's force, which is probable. The Ak-

**Investment of Mándu.**

The place was closely invested by the Emperor, who fixed his head-quarters at the adjoining village of Nálcha.*

**Desertion of Rúmi Khan.**

Among the numbers who entered the imperial service after the victory of Mándsúr, one of the first was Rúmi Khan, who, probably on no better grounds than the want of success that had attended his advice, was accused of having betrayed his master, in the late operations, by a secret understanding with the enemy. According to one account, Behåder, before setting out from Mándsúr, ordered one of his officers to put him to death; but the man, who had formerly received some favours from the Khan, gave him private notice of his danger, so that he escaped to the hostile camp, where he was well received, and immediately employed.†

**Description of that capital.**

Mándu, at that time the capital of Malwa, is a place of great strength. "The site of Mándu," says Sir John Malcolm, "was very inviting. The space chosen by Hosheng Shah for his future capital is thirty-seven miles in circumference. It extends along the crest of the Vindhya range about eight miles, and is parted from the table-land of Malwa, with which it is upon a level, by an abrupt and rugged valley of unequal depth, but nowhere less than two hundred feet, and generally from three to four hundred yards in breadth. On the brink of this valley"——"and on the summit of the ridge of the Vindhya mountains, which form the southern face of Mándu, a wall of considerable height was built, which, added to the natural strength of the ground, made it unassailable by any but a regular attack.‡

**Overtures of Behader.**

After Behåder Shah had been a few days in the place, he proposed a conference, offering, as the basis of a treaty, to give up Mándu, with all its depen-

bernáma and Tabakát are chiefly followed in the text.

* Khafi Khan, MS. A. f. 43.

† Lafitau, Hist. &c. vol. i. p. 212.

‡ Malcolm's Central India, vol. i. p. 29.

BOOK IV. A.D. 1535.

dencies,—that is, the kingdom of Malwa,—reserving to himself Gujrát and Cheitúr. The proposal was accepted; and Sadr Khan, on the part of Behúder, and Mouláná Muhammed Bergholi, on the part of Humáyun, accordingly met*, and proceeded to arrange the definitive articles. Meanwhile, the garrison being thrown off their guard, relaxed in their watchfulness. Late at night, about two hundred of the imperial troops, taking advantage of the circumstance, applied scaling-ladders to a remote part of the walls, which they mounted. Having assisted their comrades by ropes to gain the top of the works, they next let themselves down into the town, and took possession of the nearest gate, which they opened to their countrymen, who rushed in in considerable numbers.

Mándu escaladed.

Behúder escapes to Gujrát.

No sooner did the news of this irruption reach Milu Khan, who had charge of the works †, than, mounting the first horse he could find, he galloped off to give the alarm to Behúder Shah, then fast asleep. The King, starting up at the sound of Milu Khan's voice, between sleeping and waking, took to flight, with only two or three attendants. As he proceeded through the town, he was joined by Bhopat Rai, the son of the late Silhádi, and one of the leading chieftains of Malwa, who overtook him, with about twenty horse. They had reached the Esplanade gate ‡, which seems to have led into the citadel, when they met about two hundred of Humáyun's cavalry. Behúder Shah, without hesitation, bravely charged into the midst of them, and was followed by all his little party. He succeeded in breaking through; and, accompanied by Milu Khan and one other attendant, entered the fort of Sóngar, the citadel of

* The conferences were held at a place called *Nili Sabil* (the blue road).

† It is not perfectly clear what character Milu Khan bore, in the court of Behúder. He is sometimes called governor of Malwa; but there seems reason to believe that he was nominally prince or Wáli of Malwa, under the overbearing protection of Behúder.

‡ Derwazeh, Sire Meidán.

Mándu. He did not venture, however, to prolong his stay there. Having had his horses, with much difficulty, hoisted by ropes over the wall, during the night, and himself descending the precipice that surrounds it, he finally, with excessive toil and danger, gained the high road to Gujrát. An Uzbek, formerly in his service, who had deserted to the enemy, and was stationed near the fort, recognised him in his flight*; and informed the officer in command that he had certainly seen the King; but this information was not believed, or acted upon; so that Behåder was not pursued; and, before he reached the fort of Champanír, about fifteen hundred men had joined him.

Mándu plundered by the imperialists.

The escalade of Mándu by Humáyun's troops being wholly unexpected on both sides, no intelligence of it reached the Emperor at Nalcha that night, nor till near eight o'clock next morning. When informed of what was going forward, he flew to the Delhi gate†, by which he entered. Here he found the combat still maintained, in the streets; and Sadr Khan, though wounded, gallantly keeping his ground near the gate of his house. In this obstinate defence he persisted, till some of his officers, seeing the hopeless nature of his resistance, seized the reins of his horse and led him away to Sóngar, into which many of the troops that had escaped from Mándu also threw themselves. For three whole days, the victorious army was incessantly employed in plundering the houses of this fine town, before a stop was put to their rapacity.

Humáyun supreme in Malwa.

The Emperor, eager to pursue his flying enemy, in-

* Jouher says, that he escaped through the trenches of Hindu Beg, by his connivance. But, as Hindu Beg afterwards quarrelled with Biram Khan and his party, the occasional charges made against him, by their adherents, are to be received with caution. Abulfazl, with more probability, affirms that the Uzbek made his report to his superior, Kásim Husein Khan, who who was himself an Uzbek, and who commanded in that quarter.

† The gate by which Behåder entered was the Choli-Mheisur gate.

BOOK IV. A.D. 1535.

vited the garrison of the citadel to surrender. Sadr Khan and Alim Khan* of Kalpi were the principal officers in the place; and, from necessity, entered into a negotiation. After some delay, arising chiefly from apprehension of the Emperor's resentment, a capitulation was concluded, and the fort surrendered, on condition of quarter to the garrison. Sadr Khan was received with much courtesy, applauded for his fidelity to his sovereign in his reverse of fortune, and for his distinguished gallantry, and honoured with the Emperor's friendship; while Alim Khan was treated with great severity, being mutilated, by having his foot cut off, as a deserter from the imperial service. The reduction of Mándu put Humáyun in possession of the whole open country of Malwa, which he thus in some measure conquered, by a single blow.

* There were two Alim Khans, Alim Khan Lodi, the brother of Sultan Sekander Lodi, and Alim Khan Jigat of Kalpi, apparently the son of Jilál Khan, the brother and rival of Sultan Ibráhím Lodi. The person taken in Mándu, I suppose to have been the latter. Yet there is considerable uncertainty. Abulfazl, in Akbernáma, ff. 38, 39., and the Tabakáte Akberi, ff. 146. 396., call this person Sultan Alim Khan. The Tárikhe Bedáuni, f. 140., calls him Sultan Alim Khan Lodi. The Mirát-e Ahmedi says expressly, that he was the brother of Sultan Sekander Lodi, who had been driven from Kalpi by Humáyun, and, accompanied by twelve thousand horse, sought an asylum with Sultan Behádor. The greatness of the jágír bestowed on him proves him to have been a man of no small note.

The expressions used in describing his punishment are *pai kirdeh riha* and *pai buridend.* Ferishta tells us, that he suffered capitally, vol. iv. p. 128.

We afterwards find a Sultan Alim Khan, commanding the Gujráti left, at the battle of Mahmúdábád; and in possession of the jágír of Dandúka.

# CHAPTER II.

## AFFAIRS OF GUJRÁT AND MALWA.

---

## SECTION III.

### CONQUEST OF GUJRÁT BY HUMÁYUN.

HUMÁYUN ADVANCES TO GUJRÁT.—BEHÁDER FLIES TO DIU.—NIGHT ATTACK ON THE IMPERIAL CAMP.—HUMÁYUN GIVES OVER CAMBAY TO PILLAGE.—DESCRIPTION OF CHAMPANÍR.—IT IS CAPTURED BY ESCALADE.—THE GOVERNOR, EKHTIÁR KHAN.—MASSACRE OF THE GARRISON—AND IMMENSE BOOTY.—INDOLENCE AND REVELS OF HUMÁYUN—AND THEIR CONSEQUENCES.—DEMONSTRATION IN HUMÁYUN'S FAVOUR FROM SIND.—SHAH HASAN ADVANCES TOWARDS PATAN AND MAHMÚDÁBÁD.—HE RETREATS.—BEHÁDER SHAH AT DIU.—NEGOTIATES WITH THE PORTUGUESE.—ANARCHY IN GUJRÁT.—BEHÁDER DEPUTES IMÁD-UL-MÚLK TO COLLECT THE REVENUES.—RAPID INCREASE OF IMÁD'S FORCE.—HUMÁYUN MARCHES AGAINST HIM.—HIS ADVANCED GUARD SURPRISED.—HE DEFEATS IMÁD.—HUMÁYUN AT AHMEDÁBÁD.—ARRANGEMENTS FOR THE GOVERNMENT OF GUJRÁT.—ADVICE OF HINDÚ BEG.—ALARMING INTELLIGENCE FROM AGRA—AND FROM MALWA.—HUMÁYUN RETURNS TO MÍNDU.—TRANQUILLIZATION OF MALWA.

CHAP. II. SECT. III.

A.D. 1535. Humáyun sets out for Gujrát.

THE destruction of the combined armies of Gujrát and Malwa, in the trenches of Mandsúr; the possession of Mándu; and the disappearance of every armed force that could oppose him in Malwa, encouraged Humáyun to pursue his success, and to follow Behúder Shah into his own country. Only three days after the fall of the citadel, the Emperor, with ten thousand cavalry, hastened by forced marches towards Gujrát, ordering the rest of his army to follow without delay.

BOOK IV. A.D. 1535. Arrives at Champanír.

When he arrived at Champanír, he encamped at Imád-ul-mulk's tank, opposite the Pipli gate. Behâder, who had put the fort in a condition to stand a long siege, and had sent away the crown and state jewels with a quantity of treasure to Diu, no sooner heard of his arrival, than, giving his final instructions for its defence, he left the town by another gate near the Leshker Taláo, and fled for Cambay.* Before setting out, however, the large town of Muhammedábád-Champanír, situated under the hill on which the fort stands, was set on fire by his orders or with his connivance. Humáyun's troops entered in time to assist in extinguishing the flames. The Emperor, eager to have Behâder Shah in his power, leaving Mír Hindú Beg with the bulk of his force to invest the citadel, himself set out, attended only by a thousand horse, in pursuit of the flying prince. Behâder no sooner reached Cambay, where a hundred war-grabs, which he had built for the purpose of combating the Portuguese, were stationed, than, setting them all on fire to prevent their falling into the hands of his enemies, he renewed his flight, proceeding towards Diu. The same day on which he left Cambay, Humáyun arrived; and then, says his historian, for the first time, "encamped on the shore of the salt sea," which none of his ancestors had ever seen. He sent on a party to overtake the Sultan; who, however, made good his entrance into Diu. His pursuers returned back with a rich booty, collected in the neighbourhood of that city †; and thus, says Abulfazl, was the conquest of Mándu and Gujrát accomplished, in the course of this year.

Behâder flies to Diu.

A. H. 942, which begins 2nd July, A. D. 1535.

* Kambáit.

† The Akbernáma, f. 39.; Tabakáte Akberi, f. 146.; Táríkhe Bedáuni, f. 140.; and Kháfi Khan, make Behâder fly, and Humáyun follow, to Ahmedábád; the Tabakát adds, that that city was entered and plundered by the Emperor's troops. It is more probable that Behâder, as reported in the Tab. Akb. f. 396., and by Ferishta, fled directly to Cambay, where the Tabakát says, that he only staid long enough to get fresh horses, ff. 146. 396. v.

CHAP. II. SECT. III.

Night attack on the imperial camp.

While Humáyun lay encamped near Cambay, with the diminutive force that he had brought along with him, Malek Ahmed Lád and Rakn Daúd,—chiefs subject to Behâder Shah, and who possessed the greatest influence in the adjoining districts of Kolwára,—seeing that the Emperor was attended by so inconsiderable a number of troops, and was not apprehensive of any attack, pointed out to the rude Kóli and Gowár chiefs in the neighbourhood, how favourable the moment was for surprising and plundering his camp; and easily induced them to concert measures for a night attack. This could hardly have failed of success, but for an unforeseen accident. An old woman of one of the tribes, who became acquainted with the plan, resolved to turn this knowledge to account. Repairing to the imperial tent, she told a servant of the household, that she had some information of most urgent importance, which she could communicate only to the Emperor's private ear. As the woman was steady in her asseverations, and seemed to be an honest and decent person, her apparently extravagant request was complied with; and, being brought before the Emperor, she gave a clear and detailed account of the plan of an attack, which was that night to be made upon him. Surprised, yet doubtful, he questioned her, what motive could have led her to make a disclosure so injurious to her tribesmen. The woman told him in reply, that her son had been seized, and was detained as a slave, by one of his servants; and that all she wished, in return for the service she was now doing his Majesty, was to be able to deliver her child from captivity; adding, that if her information was found false, he might inflict any punishment he pleased both on herself and her son. The lad was sought for and found, and both were placed in custody. The troops were ordered to be on the alert; and the Emperor withdrew to a rising ground at a little distance, to watch the event.

BOOK IV.

A. D. 1535.

It is defeated.

All was quiet during the night; but just before the day began to dawn, the Bhíls and Gowárs, to the number of five or six thousand, suddenly burst into the camp *; and rushed towards the imperial tents, which they completely plundered; putting to death all whom they met. Having succeeded in this, their first object, they next spread themselves on every side, bearing down all before them. As soon as the light appeared, the Emperor led down the troops that were with him, against the disorderly assailants, whom they found dispersed and plundering in every quarter of the camp. They were soon routed, and pursued in their flight with much slaughter. Humáyun, enraged at this attack, in which many of his followers fell, issued orders for setting fire to the neighbouring, and probably innocent, town of Cambay, which he gave up to be pillaged by his followers.

Humáyun gives over Cambay to pillage.

Description of Champanír.

From Cambay, Humáyun returned back to Champanír, which he found still blockaded. This important fortress occupies the upper part of a hill that rises towering out of the level plain, in the south-eastern portion of Gujrát; and is visible over a great part of

* Akbernáma, f. 39.; Tabakáte Akberi, f. 147.

This surprise seems to have been more complete, and the loss sustained in it greater, than Abulfazl acknowledges; for, not only was the camp plundered, but several men of eminence fell. Jám Firózeh, the chief of Tatta, who, when driven from his dominions by the Arghúns, had joined Behárder Shah, at Baróda, in A. H. 935, (A. D. 1528), and whose daughter Behárder had married, (Ferishta, iv. 110.) was in the Emperor's camp, having been made prisoner at the rout of Mandsúr. He was put to death, on this occasion, by the persons in whose custody he was, to prevent his being rescued. The famous Sadr Khan Gujráti, who had followed Humáyun, was also slain.—Akbernáma and Tabakát, as above. In the plunder of the Emperor's baggage, a number of books, which the Emperor always carried with him as the companions of his leisure, were destroyed or lost. Among these, Abulfazl particularly notices a splendid copy of the Taimúr-náma, or History of the great Taimúr, written by the pen of Múlla Sultan Ali, and illuminated by Ustád Behzád, a famous painter, "which," he adds, "having been recovered, is now in the imperial library." It was probably the Zefer-náma of Sherf-ed-dín Ali Yezdi.

that rich and populous country.* The fortress is surrounded on several of its sides by steep and nearly perpendicular rocks, which, among the natives of India, have gained it the reputation of being impregnable to active operations. It had an upper and a lower fort, the one rising above the other; while the extensive, and at that time magnificent town of Muhammedábád-Champanír, extended on one side along its base. Humáyun, who had caused the place to be invested on his first arrival there, on his return from Cambay planted his battering cannon against it, and continued the siege and blockade; but without apparent effect. The fort was bravely defended by Ekhtiár Khan, the son of a Kázi of Neriád, one of the finest districts of the kingdom. The Khan, an officer of great resolution and intelligence, and faithful to his prince, vigorously defended the towers and works that were attacked, and nightly annoyed the besiegers by the fire from his wall-pieces, and by throwing showers of rockets into their batteries and camp. He had established a secret understanding with the wood-cutters and some of the villagers of the surrounding country, who, tempted by the high prices given for their supplies, penetrated through the ravines of the hill, which, being covered by jungle and thorny plants, were nearly inaccessible to persons on foot, and totally impervious to horsemen. These peasants, however, by their acquaintance with the by-paths of the hill, and by forcing themselves through the thickets, continued to carry quantities of grain and oil to the foot of the fort wall †; when the



* See Lieut. (now Col.) Wm. Miles's account of this fort in the Transactions of the Literary Society of Bombay, vol. i.

† Ferishta says (vol. ii. p. 78.) that this was a needless precaution on the part of the governor, as the fort was provisioned for a siege of some years. Kháfi Khan, the historian, who afterwards, in the reign of Sultan Alim Beháder, was himself governor and collector of the fort and district of Champanír, and who consequently knew the place well, says, that the fort is by no means of such strength as to enable it to stand out against the attack of an imperial army; and he ascribes

BOOK IV. A.D. 1535-6. garrison, letting down the price from above by means of ropes, drew up in exchange such provisions as were thus supplied.

Its capture by escalade.

After the blockade had been thus protracted for upwards of four months, Humáyun, who had become impatient of the delay, while making the circuit of the place, in order to discover some spot where it might be possible to attempt an escalade, in passing near the gardens of the Kábul suburb, observed a party of these peasants issue from the wood. Riding up, he began to question them about their employment in such a place. They affirmed that they were wood-cutters occupied with their trade; but as they could produce neither hatchets nor any other implements of that calling, reasonable suspicions were excited. The Emperor, according to the fashion of the country, instantly commanded them to be seized and beaten; assuring them that the punishment should not cease, till they had declared the whole truth. Seeing no remedy, they confessed everything; and, acting as guides, conducted the Emperor's party back through the paths by which they had gained the foot of the fortifications.

The rock, and wall by which it was surmounted, were found to be sixty or seventy cubits high, and so steep and smooth, that it was impossible to climb them. Humáyun, who saw that the garrison entertained no apprehension of an attack in this quarter, fixed upon it as a fit place for attempting an escalade. For this purpose, he ordered seventy or eighty iron spikes to

A. H. 943, A. D. 1536.

be made; and, one moonlight night, repairing with a chosen band of followers to the ground, he caused the spikes to be driven in to right and left, at the distance of a cubit above each other, in the face of the hill wall. This being effected without observation, some of the

the merit of the long resistance which it made, to the skill and gallantry of Ekhtiár Khan. In the time of Humáyun, however, the attack of fortified places was very imperfectly understood.

bravest of the warriors, eager to distinguish themselves under the eye of the Emperor, mounted, to the number of thirty-nine. The Emperor was next about to ascend, when Biram Khan besought him to wait till those who were mounting should be higher up, when the road would be clear. The Khan himself then began to ascend; the Emperor followed, and was the forty-first* on the top of the wall. About three hundred men mounted by this iron ladder, in safety, before daybreak.

While this was going forward, the troops which were stationed in the batteries before the place, had been ordered to open a cannonade, and to make assaults on the other side of the fort, so as to draw off the attention of the enemy. In this they succeeded; the garrison, ignorant of what was passing behind, were intent only upon repelling the open and visible attack in front; and, as the morning dawned, suddenly found themselves assailed in rear by a shower of arrows. While yet stunned by this unlooked-for occurrence, the sound of the kettle-drum and trumpet from behind, announced that the Emperor himself was among the assailants. Confounded by the advantage thus unexpectedly gained over them, and ignorant of the numbers of the enemy who had effected an entrance, they were struck with terror, and the escaladers succeeded in seizing a gate †, by which they admitted the rest of the besiegers. Ekhtiár Khan, with some of his troops, escaped to the upper fort, or Ark, where he was again invested; but the whole magazines of grain, oil, and other necessaries being in the lower fort, which had been taken, he was next day compelled to surrender on promise of quarter. Besides being a brave soldier, Ekhtiár Khan was eminent for his acquirements in science, especially in geometry and astrology, and was also a poet, and a

Governor Ekhtiár Khan.

First week of Sefer, July 20–26.

* According to some the fortieth.

† Called Mouliah, (Akbernáma and Tabakát), Múlba (Ferishta).

BOOK IV. A. D. 1536.

man of letters; qualities, we are told, which had favoured his rise at the court of Behâder, and afterwards recommended him to the special favour of the Emperor.* The whole garrison, the governor and his family excepted, were barbarously put to the sword.

Massacre of the garrison.

The treasure and property found in Champanír are said to have been immense. Being, from its situation, regarded as impregnable, great quantities of jewels, precious stuffs, and bales of rich goods of every description, which had been laid up in it as a place of security, besides arms, armour, provisions, and warlike stores fell into the hands of the victors. Much gold and treasure of former kings of Gujrát were also dug out of the ground, where they had been hid. "Humáyun," says Ferishta, "gave to his officers and soldiers as much gold, silver, and jewels as could be heaped on their respective shields, proportioning the value to their rank and merit; and the merchandises and rich cloths of Rúm, Khita and Ferang †, which had been there collected to a vast amount, were at the same time plundered by the captors." ‡

Immense booty.

* Akbernáma, MS. f. 40, B. ff. 78, 79.; Tabakáte Akberi, ff. 147. 396. I know not whether "*Amán*" always means an offer of quarter. In its consequences, it is often a surrender at discretion.

† Turkey, China, and Europe.

‡ Ferishta, vol. ii. p. 80., copied, adding what regards the shields, from the Tabakáte Akberi, which Ferishta often follows, f. 146. See also, f. 386.

A lively idea of the manner in which valuable property was sometimes hid, in India, may be gained from the account given by Jouher in his Memoirs of Humáyan, chap. ii., of the discovery of part of the treasures of Champanír. A few days after the fall of the fort, one of Behâder Shah's officers, named Alem Khan, came and made his submission to Humáyun. As he was supposed to be in the Sultan's confidence, several of the Emperor's advisers recommended that he should be seized and put to the torture, to make him discover where the treasures were concealed; but this the Emperor would not suffer, as Alem Khan had come in of his own accord; but he allowed him to be invited to a banquet, and there plied with wine, and interrogated on the subject. A banquet, accordingly, was prepared; and when the good cheer had produced its natural effects upon the Khan, he was asked about the treasure. Alem Khan, gratified by his reception, replied, that his Majesty had only to make the water of a certain large reservoir be drawn

CHAP. II. SECT. III.

Indolence and revels of Humáyun.

After this event, Humáyun, instead of prosecuting the decisive advantages he had gained, and which placed the whole kingdom of Gujrát at his mercy, spent his time near Champanír, on the banks of the Douríah tank, in celebrating his successes by sumptuous entertainments, and enjoying the immense wealth that had fallen into his hands. The long succession of these festivities withdrew his attention, for a time, from the cares of state, and the discipline of his troops, which was gradually relaxed. Neglecting their military duties, they gave themselves up to those excesses in which rich and idle soldiers are wont to indulge. His affairs fell into confusion; the government of the provinces was neglected; and, even his own camp became a scene of uproar and insubordination.

Injurious results.

A striking instance of this spirit soon appeared. A party composed principally of the secretaries, librarians, armour-bearers, clerks, and others, in the service of the Emperor and his chief nobles, imitating the example of their lords, were enjoying themselves in a grand banquet at the gardens of Halál, in the vicinity of the city. When heated with wine the story recorded of Taimúr in the Zefer-náma, but borrowed from a much more ancient fable, was read to them. The great conqueror, near the beginning of his career, and in his days of difficulty, is said to have taken, from each of his forty companions, two arrows; which, tying in a bundle, he offered to them to be broken. Each, in suc-

off, when treasure would be found enough to satisfy the whole army. This being reported to the Emperor, he caused a number of buckets and other vessels to be collected, to empty the tank. While the people were thus employed, the Khan remarked, that there was a much more expeditious mode of doing it. He made them dig under the tank, where an outlet or drain was found, which, being opened, the water quickly ran off. An immense quantity of treasure was discovered, and immediately divided among the army. The Khan afterwards pointed out a well, that was found to be filled with gold and silver, which had been melted into bars. No part of this last treasure was given to the troops.

BOOK IV. A.D. 1536.

cession, tried in vain. He then presented their own two to each, who broke them with ease. Whereupon, with a voice of authority, he drew the moral, and told them, that, if they remained united and assisted each other faithfully, making common cause, no enterprise was too arduous for them to achieve.

The revellers, as they listened, applied the incident to their own situation. They counted their party, which was found to consist, not of forty, but of four hundred. Flushed with the recent successes and with wine, they magnanimously resolved to imitate the great Taimúr,—to set up for themselves, and to attempt no less than the conquest of the Dekhan, at that moment the grand resort of adventurers. Hurried away by this heroic resolution, they instantly set out for the south. Nothing could be more wild than such an attempt, made by men in their circumstances, in a body, and by one effort; though many of them were probably persons who, individually, might have successfully aspired to high eminence. They lived in an age and country of revolutions; they seem to have been men of some education; and every day proved the wonderful superiority of the hardy and enterprising men of the north over the natives of India. Even in the Dekhan, the principal offices were filled by their countrymen, of a rank originally not much superior to their own. But such an enterprize as was in this instance attempted, was an act of madness, and should have been punished only as a drunken frolic.

Next morning, when the heroes who composed this chivalrous band were wanted in their various offices, not one of them was to be found. The cause and direction of their flight, however, became speedily known; a thousand men were sent in pursuit; they were overtaken, and brought back in bonds to the imperial presence.

The day of the week happened to be a Tuesday,

when the Emperor, according to the fantastic astrological fancies, on which at this period of his age he acted, clothed in red robes, the colour suited to Mars, the guardian planet of the day, was sitting in state on the throne of wrath and vengeance. He, too, though the judge, was probably still labouring under the effects of his previous excesses. The deserters were brought it, in small parties *, and sentence pronounced on them with a capricious cruelty, embittered by the levity with which it was accompanied. Some were trampled to death by elephants, some were beheaded, some had their ears and noses cut off, some their fingers pared away. In the evening, the Imám, or leader of the religious service in the mosque, who was a man of no great understanding, read, according to custom, a portion of the Korán, after the first genuflexion. The chapter that he chose was that which alludes to the destruction, by the divine wrath, of the masters of the elephant, who impiously attempted to destroy the temple of Mekka. It displeased the Emperor, as if chosen with some allusion to his own recent employment †;

* The details of this judgment, as given by Abulfazl (Akbernáma, f. 40.) are very disgusting; and exhibit the wretched punning propensity of our James I., but on an occasion when it is not ridiculous, but revolting. The sentences pronounced depend on idiomatic Persian phrases, hardly translateable. "Some of the culprits," says he, "having *stretched their head* beyond the *line of duty*, had their bodies relieved altogether of the burden of the head; some, who, *not knowing hand from foot*, (*i. e.* foolishly) had *struck their hand* in rebellion, were deprived of both *hand and foot;* a band, who, from *self-conceit* (khúd-*bíni*), had not *lent their ears* to the imperial commands, could find neither *ears nor nose* (*bíni*) in their usual place. Others, who had touched the limits of revolt with the tips of their fingers, were unable any longer to discover the figure of their fingers on their fists," &c.

† This Chapter, CV., entituled "The Elephant," is a very short one, and does not seem to contain much matter of offence. Humáyun probably referred to himself the expression of "Master of the Elephant," and believed that allusion was made to such as had recently been trodden to death.

"In the name of the most merciful God!

"Hast thou not seen how the Lord dealt with the Masters of the Elephant? Did he not make their treacherous design an occasion of drawing them into error; and send

BOOK IV.

A.D. 1536.

and, when the service was over, he ordered the Imám to be trodden to death by an elephant, for charging him, by insinuation, with tyranny. Moulána Muhammed Bergholi, a learned and saintly personage, high in the Emperor's favour, interceded for the Imám, and pleaded that, being an ignorant man, he did not understand the Koran, and meant no ill. But this interference only further enraged the Emperor, who vented the passion, with which he was still inflamed, in reproaches directed against the intercessor himself; and the sentence was carried into effect. When, however, Humáyun's rage had somewhat evaporated, and when he had leisure for cool reflection, he was seized with the deepest sorrow and remorse, and spent the ensuing night in tears and lamentations.*

Demonstration in Humáyun's favour from Sind.

It was, probably, about this time that a demonstration, for the purpose of favouring Humáyun's invasion of Behâder's territories, was made on the side of Sind. The Emperor, when he marched to attack Gujrát, wishing to create a diversion in his favour by a formidable inroad into that kingdom from the north and west, wrote to Shah Hasan, the ruler of Sind, inviting him to lead his army towards Patan, there to await farther orders. With this requisition Shah Hasan complied, and marched, with a considerable force, from Nasirpúr on the Indus, by way of Idphal, towards Patan in Gujrát. Khizer Khan, who was governor of Patan-Nehrwála, for Behâder, on hearing of his approach, being resolved to make a vigorous defence, directed all the neighbouring cattle to be driven within the inclosure of the town. As soon as Sultan Mahmúd Khan Bhekeri, who commanded the advance of the Sind army, and plundered the country and the villages as he marched along, had arrived, with five hundred cavalry, within about seven kos of the town, he encamped. At the

Shah Hasan advances towards Patan.

against them flocks of birds, which cast down upon them stones of baked clay; and rendered them like the leaves of corn, eaten by cattle?"

* Akbernáma, f. 40.

same time, he sent a message to the governor, inviting him to surrender to Shah Hasan, who was on his route to attack him, with a large army; and offered to allow him and his family to leave the town unmolested, and to retire in safety, wherever they might wish to go. Khizr Khan returned for answer, that Behâder Shah was safe in Girnâl; and that he, as a faithful subject, would defend to the last extremity the city entrusted to his care. The envoys, who were of the Jháreja tribe, desirous that their mission should not be altogether fruitless, then waited on the governor's mother, to whom they held out the policy of sending some propitiatory offering to the invaders; and prevailed upon her to present the sum of a lak of Firúzsháhis to Shah Hasan, and thirty thousand to Sultan Mahmúd, to induce and enable them to leave the Patan territory, and to march on.



Next morning, Shah Hasan arrived with the main body of his army, near Patan. Sultan Mahmúd, a man of impetuous courage, was eager to be allowed to push forward into Gujrát; but Shah Hasan halted, and sent on messengers to the Emperor to announce his arrival, and to ask farther orders. Meanwhile, Khizr Khan's people arrived with the presents, which seem to have secured the city of Patan from molestation. Sultan Mahmúd, however, extended his plundering excursions to the close vicinity of Mahmúdábád, in Gujrát; and his followers were enriched by the plunder of that wealthy and flourishing country.

His troops plunder on to Mahmúdábád.

Here, the diversion from Sind terminated; Shah Farakh, one of Sultan Hasan's principal generals, having represented to him, that, should Humáyun order the Sind army to join his own, the Arghúns and Terkháns of Sind, who were at present satisfied with their condition,—if they once witnessed the luxury in which the Chaghatáis lived, and the wealth gained by the imperial army, in consequence of the division of the royal

BOOK IV. A. D. 1536.

treasure,—would certainly become discontented; and that many of them would exchange his service for that of the Emperor. Shah Hasan acquiesced in the justice of this representation. He, therefore, dispatched messengers to report to Humáyun, that he had received information that the Kilmiti and Jitwi tribes, invited by the Zemindars of Sind, had entered that country, during his absence, and threatened to throw every thing into confusion; so that his immediate return was indispensable. Without waiting for an answer, he led back his army, by way of Radhanpúr; inflicting severe chastisement on the Jháreja and Sodha tribes, as he went along.*

He retreats.

Behader Shah at Diu.

When Sultan Behader fled from Champanír, he took refuge in the island of Diu, on which stood a rich and populous seaport town, as well as a royal palace. It was the great emporium of the coasting trade of that part of India; since it possessed a safe harbour, which saved the necessity of encountering the banks and shallows of the Gulph of Cambay; and Surat had not yet absorbed the commerce of Gujrát. The Portuguese, who, since the discovery of the route to the East by the Cape of Good Hope, aimed at a monopoly of the Indian trade, and had become the tyrants of the west coast, from Ceylon to the Red Sea, were eager to establish themselves at Diu; not only in order to have the command of the Gulph of Cambay,—and of the coast of Gujrát Proper, and of the Kókan on the one side, and of the peninsula of Gujrát and the coast of Kach and Sind on the other,—but to be enabled to intercept the trade of the Persian and Arabian Gulphs with India. Beháder had been, for some time, at war with the Portuguese; but, latterly, had entered into an accommodation with them. In his distress, he was now

Negotiates with the Portuguese.

* Taríkhe Sind, ff. 149—151. This incursion evidently occurred while the Emperor's army lay at Champanír, A. H. 942-3 (A. D. 1536).

urged by those about him to apply to them for succour. To this he consented, as a measure of temporary relief; though, at the same time, he privately dispatched an embassy to Soliman the Magnificent, the Sultan of Constantinople, with rich presents for the Sultan, valued at six hundred thousand pieces of gold *, besides large sums of money to pay the auxiliary force that might be sent. Nuño d'Acuña, the Portuguese viceroy, thus called upon, agreed to furnish assistance; but only on condition that he should be allowed to erect a fortification at Diu, for the protection of his fleet, and put in possession of the sea-tower which commanded the entrance of the harbour. These demands he represented as made solely for the necessary security of his troops and shipping; and undertook that his countrymen should levy no duties or customs on ships, whether entering or sailing from the port; and should exercise no act of sovereignty. The King, in his distress, acceded to these terms; and no sooner was his consent given, than the Portuguese, who had long sought in vain to settle at Diu, set to work, and in forty days erected a fortress, which was impregnable, at least to their enemies, and made them in reality masters of the island, and of the trade of the whole coast. The Portuguese affirm, that, in return for this concession, they afforded Behádcr Shah the aid of five hundred Europeans, of whom fifty were men of note. †



Anarchy in Gujrát.

After the fall of Champanír, the whole country of Gujrát, as far north as the river Myhi or Mehindri, had come into the Emperor's hands, and was occupied by his orders; but so much does he seem to have been engaged in discovering and enjoying the rich treasures of Champanír, that nobody was appointed to conduct the government, or to collect the revenues of the provinces beyond that river ‡, though, in the universal

* Lafitau, vol. i. p. 213.

† Briggs's Ferishta, vol. iv. p. 134.

‡ Tab. Akberi, f. 386.

BOOK IV.

A. D. 1536.

panic that prevailed, they had been altogether abandoned by the officers of Behâder, civil and military. The landholders and raiats in that quarter, left in this singular predicament, wrote to Sultan Behâder, to whom they were still attached, to represent, that the revenues of the country were now due; but that there were no collectors to receive them; and that, if his Majesty would appoint a proper person, they should be paid to him as usual.

Behâder deputes Imád-ul-mulk to collect the revenues.

We are told that Behâder Shah, sitting in council, mentioned the tenor of these letters; and asked, who would repair to Ahmedábâd, and undertake the management of this business. All were silent, till Imád-ul-mulk, a distinguished nobleman, who had been a slave of the King's *, boldly offered himself for the enterprise; but required, as an indispensable condition, that, in consideration of the perturbed state of the country, and of the peculiar exigency of affairs, he should have the sole and absolute power to demand or remit the revenue, to make grants of land, or pay away money, as he judged expedient; without being liable to be called to account at any future time. This being assented to, he set out on his mission, with only two hundred horse; and marched for Ahmedábâd. As he went along, he appointed officers to collect the revenues of the province; wrote and delivered grants of land or of pensions to different persons, in whom he could confide, and who had weight in the country; and was

Rapid increase of his force.

joined by them and their followers in such numbers, (especially by the zemindars of Sorath or Kattiawár,) that his force growing as he advanced, by the time he reached Ahmedábâd, which he occupied, he found himself at the head of not less than ten thousand horse. He now expended, with open-handed liberality, the revenues which he collected; and, the cause being

* Ferishta (iv. p. 80.) calls him a Circassian; the Tabakát, a slave, f. 148.

popular, his army speedily increased to thirty thousand men.* Mujáhid Khan, the chief of Júnagar, joined him with ten thousand followers; and the army received a valuable reinforcement by the arrival of Behádcr's European soldiers.† CHAP. II. SECT. III.

Humáyun marches against Imád.

When the news of these transactions reached Humáyun, they roused him from the trance of pleasure in which he had too long indulged. Leaving Terdi Beg in charge of Champanír, and having made a second division among his troops of the plunder that had been collected, he marched straight for Ahmedábád, and crossed the Mehindri; Askeri Mírza, with Yádgár Násir Mírza, and Hindú Beg, being ordered to keep one march in advance of the army. Imád-ul-mulk, emboldened by the success that had hitherto attended his exertions, set out from Ahmedábád with his army, now amounting to fifty thousand men; and prepared to meet him. By a forced march, he suddenly, about mid-day, when the heat was most oppressive, and no attack was apprehended, came by surprise upon Askeri Mírza, who was lying, with the advance of the imperial army, between the town of Neriád and Mahmúdábád,—now a heap of ruins, at that time a flourishing city. Yádgár Násir Mírza had taken his ground about a mile to the right; and Hindú Beg his, as much to the left. The Gujráti army came upon Askeri with such expedition, that he had not time to form his troops, which were scattered in all directions; but he retired, with such as were at hand, into a thicket of thorny milk-bush, that was hard by; and there took up a position. The Gujrátis, without following the Mírza or attempting to improve their victory, dispersed to plunder the

Imád surprises his advanced guard.

* The Tabakát, ff. 147. 397. says fifty thousand. He is said to have given all who joined him with two horse, one lak Gujráti, 2,500 rupees, according to price. Mahomedan Hist. vol. iii. p. 739.

† Akbernáma, f. 40.; Tabakáte Akberi, as above, Ferishta, ii. 80.; iv. 128.; Kháfi Khan.

BOOK IV.

A.D. 1536.

camp. They gained, indeed, a rich booty; but fell into inextricable disorder. The two wings of the imperial army soon came in sight, marching in battle order. At their approach, the enemy at once abandoned the camp; and Askeri Mírza, at the same time, issuing again from the jungle, reared his standard, beat his kettle-drums, and pressed upon them in their retreat.

Is routed by the main army.

The Gujrátis were broken and defeated; and were pursued, as far as Ahmedábád, leaving more than two thousand dead on the field. When the Emperor reached the scene of action, he is said to have inquired of Khodáwend Khan*, who had been in the service of Beháder, and was well acquainted with the composition of his armies, if he should have another battle to fight, or if the business was over. The Khan answered, that, if Imád-ul-mulk was himself in the battle, the business was over; but, if not, that his Majesty might expect another bloody bout. Humáyun sought eagerly to discover how the fact stood; and, from two men, who were lying wounded, he ascertained, with pleasure, that that nobleman had himself commanded in the fight.†

Humáyun at Ahmedábád.

Next day, the imperial army marched forward; Askeri Mírza commanding the advance, as before. When the army reached Kankaria ‡ tank, close by Ahmedábád, where it encamped, the Mírza, to whom the Emperor had given the government of that city and the surrounding districts, preferred a request, that the troops should not be allowed indiscriminately to enter the town, as it would be the certain ruin of the place.

* Khodáwend Khan was the title of Rúmi Khan, now in Humáyun's service.

† Tabakáte Akberi, f. 148.; Akbernáma, f. 40. The only intelligible account of the action is that of Nizám-ed-dín, the author of the Tabakáte Akberi, or Tárikhe Nizámi, who had it from his father, Muhammed Mokím Hirvi (of Herát), who was then Mírza Askeri's vazír. Abulfazl estimates the loss of the Gujrátis at three or four thousand men. He mentions Alim Khan Lodi, as commanding the Gujráti left. The accounts of Ferishta and Kháfi Khan are evidently incorrect.

‡ Or, Kúkaria.—Hamilton.

Orders were in consequence issued, to station guards at every gate of the city, and that none but Askeri Mírza and his people should be permitted to enter. The more effectually to preserve the inhabitants from injury, the Emperor led his army across the Sabramati, so as to interpose that river between his camp and the city; and took post at the beautiful village of Sirkích, still an object of interest, from the splendid tombs of the kings of Gujrát, which it contains. From his head-quarters there, accompanied by his principal officers, he visited the magnificent palaces, mosques, and colleges of his new capital, which was then certainly one of the richest and noblest in the world.

CHAP. II. SECT. III.

His arrangements for the government of Gujrát.

The conquest of Gujrát being now nearly complete, the Emperor turned his thoughts to the settlement of the country and the preservation of what he had gained. Askeri Mírza retained Ahmedábád, and was raised to the dignity of viceroy. The veteran Hindú Beg, with a large force, was to act as minister and commander-in-chief, and to send or carry assistance wherever the exigencies of the service required. Terdi Beg retained Champanír; Yádgár Násir Mírza had the district of Patan-Nehrwála; Kásim Husein Sultan, Uzbek, had Barúch and Nousári, with the port of Surat; Dost Beg Ishekágha* had Cambay and Baróda; and Mír Bochak Behádar, Mahmúdábád.†

Advice of Hindú Beg.

It appears to have been at this crisis that the Emperor was urged by some of his counsellors, especially by Hindú Beg, to make some permanent settlement of the affairs of Gujrát, so as to enable him to march back, with the great body of his army, to the provinces of the Ganges, which, while he was overrunning Malwa and Gujrát, were already suffering deeply from the miseries of invasion and revolt. Their advice was, to

* Chamberlain.

† The Tabakát makes a different allotment of some of these places, giving Barúch to Hindú Beg, and Baróda to Kásim Husein Sultan.

BOOK IV. A.D. 1536.

set apart a sum equal to one or two years' pay of his troops, to reserve the rest for future exigencies, and to restore Sultan Behâder, nominally, to the throne of Gujrât. This, they affirmed, would not only add to his reputation for generosity, but would enable him to govern that country in the easiest and most peaceful way, and at the same time to provide for the safety of his other dominions. The Emperor, however, could not bear the idea of appearing to give up kingdoms, on the conquest of which he valued himself so much. The future history of his reign proves that the advice was a sound one. It was impossible, with the force that he possessed, to maintain kingdoms so extensive and so scattered as he now occupied, especially as the natives of Gujrât showed a decided partiality for the old dynasty of their kings. Situated as he then was, Behâder would probably have consented to become his vassal, and to have left in his hands the principal forts of the kingdom.

Alarming intelligence from Agra,

Humâyun, after having divided the country among his Amírs, pushed on towards Diu in pursuit of Behâder Shah, who had taken refuge there. Scarcely, however, had he reached Dandúka, about thirty kos from Ahmedâbâd, when he was overtaken by expresses from Agra, bringing him the most alarming intelligence. His long absence from his capital, and the great distance to which he had marched with the main body of his army, so as to be almost lost sight of, had encouraged the disaffected to rise in several quarters. The Afghâns in Behar and in the East were again active. Muhammed Sultan Mírza, assisted by his sons, Ulugh and Shah Mírzas, had made himself master of the country from Kanauj to Juánpúr, and caused the Khútba to be read in his own name. Symptoms of commotion and revolt had begun to show themselves even in the provinces on the Jamna, and close around Agra. Dispatches of similar import followed in rapid

and from Malwa.

succession from different parts of Malwa, conveying information that Sekander Khan and Milu Khan, hereditary chieftains in that kingdom, recovering themselves from their discomfiture, had made an irruption into the territory of Hindia, on the Nerbáda, which they had plundered, and compelled Mehter Zambúr, his governor, to quit his capital for Ujein; that the imperial troops, who had been stationed in various parts of Malwa, unable to keep the field, had thrown themselves into Ujein, where they were besieged; and finally, that Derwísh Ali, the governor, having been killed by a musket shot, the garrison, in despair of not being able to hold out till they were relieved, had capitulated.

Humáyun returns to Mándu.

On receiving this unwelcome news, the Emperor determined to retrace his steps. His plan now was, to make Mándu, as being a centrical position, his permanent head-quarters, till he had cleared Malwa of invaders, reduced to order the kingdom of Gujrát, which he considered as substantially subdued, and suppressed the commotions and revolt in the vicinity of Agra. Setting out, on his return, therefore, he left Mírza Askeri, his brother, in the government of Gujrát, assisted by Hindú Beg and other experienced officers; and marched, by Cambay, Baróda, and Barúch, to the town of Surat. Thence, he proceeded to Malwa, taking a circuitous route by way of Búranpúr, where he staid eight days. The kings of Ahmednagar and Berár, on hearing of his march, sent him letters congratulating him on his successes. He proceeded on his route, passing close under the strong fort of Asír, and at length reached Mándu. The report of his approach had induced the invaders to hasten back to their former retreat; so that the country was soon restored to a

Tranquillization of Malwa.

* "It was during this march that Khondemí, the author of the Kabíl-us-Seir, died in his camp. The remains of this eminent person were conveyed to Delhi, and interred in the same vault with Amír Khosrou and Sheikh Nizam-ed-dim Oulia." Briggs's Ferishta, vol. ii. p. 81.

BOOK IV. A.D. 1536.

state of tranquillity. He was fond of the climate of Malwa, and lingered there with pleasure. He established several of his most confidential servants in the province, by bestowing on them estates and jágírs; and his affairs once more seemed to assume a promising aspect.

# CHAPTER II.

## AFFAIRS OF GUJRÁT AND MALWA.

---

## SECTION IV.

### LOSS OF GUJRÁT AND MALWA.

REACTION IN GUJRÁT, IN FAVOUR OF BEHÁDER. — SURAT OCCUPIED IN HIS NAME — AND BARÚCH — AND CAMBAY — AND PATAN. — INDECISION OF THE IMPERIAL GENERALS — GHÁZANFER DESERTS. — BEHÁDER ADVANCES TOWARDS AHMEDÁBÁD.—DANGER OF THE IMPERIAL ARMY.—DISAFFECTION OF MÍRZA ASKERI — AND THE CHIEFS. — PRECIPITATE RETREAT FROM AHMEDÁBÁD. — PURSUIT BY BEHÁDER. — THE MÍRZA AND HIS ARMY AT CHAMPANÍR. — TERDI BEG REFUSES TO ADMIT THEM. — THEY MARCH TOWARDS AGRA. — BEHÁDER TAKES CHAMPANÍR — AND RECOVERS ALL GUJRÁT. — HUMÁYUN INTERCEPTS ASKERI, IN RÁJPUTÁNA. — THEY RETURN TO AGRA. — STATE OF THE GANGETIC PROVINCES. — SUCCESSFUL CAMPAIGN OF HINDAL MÍRZA. — LOSS OF MALWA. — BEHÁDER SHAH AND THE PORTUGUESE. — DEATH OF BEHÁDER. — FATE OF DIU. — ALLEGED REAPPEARANCE OF BEHÁDER. — HIS ADHERENTS RETIRE TO AHMEDÁBÁD. — HIS IMMEDIATE SUCCESSORS.

CHAP. II. SECT. IV.

Reaction in Gujrát in favour of Behader.

But this was only a transient gleam of prosperity. Gujrát had been overrun, indeed, but it was far from being settled. The conquerors were still considered in the light of strangers and marauders. Hardly had Humáyun turned his back on the province, when revolt began to show itself. Behader Shah had succeeded in concluding a treaty with the Portuguese, by which they agreed to furnish him an auxiliary force. He was also busy in raising a body of five or six thousand Habshi or

BOOK IV.

A.D. 1536.

Surat occupied in his name;

Abyssinian slaves.* His partizans, within the country, were not idle. Rúm Khan Sefer, the engineer who had conducted the building of Surat castle †, seems to have shut himself up in it; and another officer established a fortified position near Nousári, at the mouth of the Tapti ‡; and they maintained themselves against the invaders, by the aid of the Gujráti fleet. These officers, being joined by Khan Jehán Shirázi, now ventured to act in concert, on the offensive; drove Abdalla Khan, a relation of Kásim Husein Sultan Uzbek, the governor of the district, from the Nousári territory, after he had held it little more than three months; and seized the city of Surat. Abdalla Khan retreated to Barúch, the seat of Kásim Husein's government; while, following up their success, Khan Jehán marched his troops by land towards Barúch, at the same time that Rúmi Khan, with the ships §, in which were embarked the heavy baggage and artillery, sailed round the coast and ascended the Nerbáda to that town. Kásim Husein, not prepared for such an attack, abandoned the place, and retired towards Champanír, whence he proceeded to Ahmedábád, to solicit assistance from Askeri Mírza, the viceroy, and Hindú Beg, the commander-in-chief.

and Barúch;

But these were not the only enemies whom the partizans of Humáyun had to encounter. Syed Ishák, who received from Beháder Shah the title of Shitáb

* The Habshis are properly Abyssinians; but negroes of all descriptions are often, in common speech, so called.

† General Briggs, Ferishta, (as well as Major Price, Retrospect of Mahomedan History, vol. iii. p. 726. note) supposes that Surat castle was built by Rúmi Khan Khodáwend Khan, who was Beháder's engineer at the siege of Cheitúr, and who afterwards conducted the siege of Chunár for Humáyun. But Rúmi Khan was a common name for chief engineers, who were frequently Rúmis or Osmanli Turks. The builder of Surat castle, buried near the Mírza Shámi mosque at Surat, is not Khodáwend Khan, (who died at Chunár, after the fall of that place, a deserter from the Gujrát service,) but Rúmi Khan Sefer (Akbernáma, f. 41.) who was with Beháder Shah at the time of his death, and who, as here mentioned in the text, retook Surat and Barúch.

‡ Or, Tápi.

§ Grabs.

Khan, had recovered Cambay; and all Gujrát was soon in arms and hostile. Askeri Mírza, seeing the danger approach so near, summoned Yádgár Násir Mírza, who held Patan-Nehrwála, to attend him at Ahmedábád. The Mírza obeyed the call; but, in the meanwhile, the troops* which Beháder had left behind in the north and east, at Raisen, Rantambór, Ajmír, and Cheitúr, — at the time of his discomfiture and precipitate flight from Malwa, — and the followers of some native chiefs, who still adhered to his interest, having formed a junction, advanced in great force, by a circuitous route on the north, through the Rájpút country, to meet Beháder at Diu; and, hearing that the town of Patan was left without a garrison, took possession of it. They now sent to inform Beháder Shah of their approach, their numbers, and success; and offered to attack Yádgár Násir Mírza. The Sultan, however, ordered them to engage in no offensive operations till he joined them, which he did soon after.

and Cambay; and Patan.

Indecision of the imperial generals.

There appears, at this time, a great want of decision among those who conducted the Emperor's affairs in Gujrát; but as many of the generals were veterans of undoubted talent, and as the same want of success appears in other quarters, the blame probably lay on Humayún, and on the ministers who concerted the general plan of operations, by which the force of the Empire was frittered down, and dispersed over situations very remote from each other. Want of success was speedily followed by its inseparable attendant, want of union. The discontent at head-quarters, at Ahmedábád, came to a great height; it even reached the length of a partial defection. The immediate cause was trifling. Mírza Askeri, sitting late one night at a party of pleasure, and being heated with wine, happened boastfully to exclaim, "I am a king, and the shadow of

* The Miráte Ahmedi makes their numbers amount to forty thousand. Bird's transl. p. 249.

BOOK IV. A. D. 1536.

God." Gházanfer*, a nobleman of rank, and his own foster-brother, whispered to one who sat by him, "That may well be, for he is not himself." † The person to whom the words were addressed, smiled; which the Mírza observing, insisted on knowing the cause; and, when told, was extremely incensed, and placed Gházanfer in confinement. In a few days that officer made his escape, or was released, and deserted, with three hundred horse, to Sultan Beháder, whom he strongly incited to march upon Ahmedábád, assuring him that he was well acquainted with the counsels of the enemy, who were all most anxious to retreat, and were only looking for a pretext. "If you have any doubts," said he, "put me in confinement; march against the Moghuls; and, if they meet you in the field, then punish me as you please." Many invitations coming to Behåder, at the same time, from his numerous adherents in the districts, all urging him to march to their relief, he was finally induced to move upon Ahmedábád. Everywhere he was received by the people with tumultuous acclamations of joy; his army swelled as he moved along; and he soon encamped at the town of Sirkech, nearly opposite to the capital.

Desertion of Gházanfer.

Behåder advances towards Ahmedábád.

Danger of the imperial army.

The situation of the imperial army, at this time, was one of considerable danger. It was in the midst of a hostile, and probably incensed country. Humáyun's troops had been forced to abandon all the principal towns, except Champanír. They had now, however, been concentrated; and Mírza Askeri, — the viceroy, with Hindú Beg, Yádgár Násir Mírza, and Kasim Husein Sultan Uzbek, his principal officers, — encamped at Sirganj, near Asáwel, a suburb of Ahmedábád, on the left bank of the Sabramati, with nearly twenty thousand horse, facing Behåder Shah. It is alleged, that, at this momentous crisis, Hindú Beg strongly

Disaffection of Mírza Askeri and the chiefs.

* He was the brother of Kásim Khan.

† Or, "but he is not an autocrat," (self-governed).

advised Askeri Mírza, as the only way of preserving Gujrát, to assume the ensigns of royalty, and to declare himself independent; arguing, that not only would this declaration encourage the inhabitants to join him, by the hope of more effectual protection, but that his own soldiers, having their king among them, would be elevated to much higher exertion and daring, and would more cheerfully devote themselves to his service. Askeri Mírza hesitated; but finally rejected the advice, at least in the form in which it was offered.

It does, however, appear that, at a council in which were met Askeri, Yádgár, Hindú Beg, and all the principal Amírs then in Gujrát, Terdi Beg excepted, it was the general opinion that, as Humáyun persisted in remaining at Mándu, and sent them no assistance, it was vain, as matters stood, to think of resisting Behâder Shah in the field; and, acting under the influence of the discontent and disaffection * produced by existing circumstances, they resolved to march to Champanír; to seize upon the treasure; to proceed to Agra; and there declare Askeri Mírza Emperor, and Hindú Beg visír; assigning, at the same time, suitable appointments to all the other Mírzas and officers who joined them. A retreat was accordingly resolved upon, only three days after they had encamped at Sirganj, over against Behâder.

Precipitate retreat from Ahmedábád.

It happened, on the last of these days, that a shot from one of the Mírza's guns struck the audience-tent of the Sultan, and threw it down. Enraged at the occurrence he sent for Ghâzanfer, that he might deal with him in terms of his own agreement. Ghâzanfer entreated that the sentence might be deferred till the armies were fairly drawn out; adding, that he still maintained his former opinion, and had sure information that the Mírza was to retreat in the course of the night.

* Tabakáte Akberi, f. 397.

BOOK IV. A.D. 1536.

And, accordingly, the Mírza and his Amírs did retreat, without fighting, and with such precipitation and confusion that they left behind them, not only their stores and heavy baggage, but even their private baggage and wearing apparel; and made a forced march of ten kos, on the road to Champanír. A retreat, under such circumstances, while it emboldened the enemy, disheartened their own adherents, and threatened irretrievable ruin to their affairs.

Pursuit by Behâder.

This sudden change roused the activity of Behâder Shah, who had entered upon the campaign with many uneasy forebodings. He now pursued the retreating foe. His advanced body, commanded by Syed Mobárek Bokhári, came up with the imperial rear, under Yádgár Násir Mírza. Yádgár halted his troops, wheeled round, and met the pursuers bravely. A severe action ensued. The Mírza's troops displayed great gallantry; many of the advance were slain, and others fell wounded into the Mírza's hands. The enemy did not follow beyond Mahmúdábád; and Yádgár, unmolested, rejoined the main body of his own army. Askeri Mírza continued his retreat in a state of discouragement and alarm, and with such confusion that many of his soldiery were drowned in crossing the Mehindri, which lay in his route. Behâder Shah advanced as far as that river, and halted.*

The Mírza and his army at Champanír.

When the Mírza reached Champanír in his disastrous retreat, Terdi Beg, the governor, who had heard of the plans of defection that had been debated in his council, and had communicated them to the Emperor, received him with caution; and, while he gave the troops all the assistance in his power, did not suffer them to enter the fort. The day after their arrival, the Mírzas sent to inform the Beg, that they and the army under their command were in a state of the most complete destitu-

Terdi Beg refuses to admit them.

* For the preceding events, consult the Akbernáma, f. 41.; Tabakát-e Akberi, f. 148. 397.; Ferishta, vol. ii. p. 81.; Bird's Miráte Ahmedi, pp. 248—250.; Jouher, c. 2.

tion; and, therefore, called upon him to supply them with some part of the public treasure preserved in the fort, that the troops might be put in a condition to take the field. When the governor declined to touch the treasure, without his Majesty's express commands, they insisted that, as an express sent to the Emperor at Mándu would reach him in six days, and as there could be no doubt of his Majesty's sanctioning an appropriation of such indispensable necessity for his affairs, he should in the meanwhile make the advance on his own authority. But Terdi Beg, who had no desire to put the Mírza's army into a condition that would have enabled it more effectually to injure the Emperor, refused to consent. In this extremity, Askeri's chief Amírs determined to seize Terdi Beg, to take possession of the fort and the whole treasure, and at once openly to raise the Mírza to the throne. Should their attempt upon Champanír fail, they agreed to push on nevertheless for Agra, which was left defenceless; and trusted that they could reach it before Humáyun. While these consultations were going on, Terdi Beg had been prevailed upon to come out of the fort, to meet the Mírzas; but, getting some accidental intimation of a plan to seize his person and the fort, he turned back and sent to announce to them, that he could no longer suffer the army to remain where it was, and summoned them to remove it beyond range of his guns. They promised to comply, but asked for a previous conference on the present urgent state of affairs. Aware of their intentions, he absolutely declined any interview; and, as they did not move their camp, he next morning did fire upon them, as he had threatened. The Mírzas, thus disappointed, made their troops defile by the Kerji Ghat, and took the road to Agra, — abandoning Gujrát, after it had been occupied little more than nine months.

They march towards Agra. A. H. 943, A. D. 1536.

As long as the imperial army halted at Champanír,

BOOK IV.

A.D. 1536-7.

Behader Shah did not venture to cross the Mahendri, which is only fifteen kos distant; but no sooner did it march in the direction of Agra, than he moved forward and advanced to Champanír. In spite of the strength of the fort, and of its being, it is said, amply supplied with provisions and stores to support a siege, Terdi Beg abandoned the place, and withdrew on capitulation, taking along with him as much of the treasure as he had the means of transporting. He may in this have followed the orders of Humáyun; and, indeed, in the present state of affairs, and with the prospect of retreating from Malwa, the only effect of resistance would be the inevitable destruction of the garrison, and the loss of the whole treasure. The town and fort were immediately occupied by Behader Shah, who thus saw himself once more in possession of the whole kingdom of Gujrát.

Behader takes Champanír; and recovers all Gujrát.

Terdi Beg, on leaving Champanír, repaired directly to Mándu, where he was received with distinction by the Emperor, to whom he had acted a faithful part. To prevent the conspirators from executing their new purpose, Humáyun pushed forward by forced marches for Agra, taking the route of Cheitúr. By a fortunate accident, the two armies met in the Cheitúr territory, while on their march. The Mírzas, taken by surprise, saw no remedy but to feign submission and obedience. The Emperor, being in many respects in equal difficulties with themselves, shut his eyes to the past, affected to be satisfied with their explanations, and bestowed upon them princely presents. The united army then marched towards Agra, where its presence was imperiously required.*

Humáyun intercepts Askeri in Rájputana.

They return to Agra.

* Akbernáma, f. 41.; Tabakát-e Akberi, ff. 149. 397.; Ferishta, v. ii. pp. 82, 83.; Tar. Bedáuni, f. 140.; Jouher, c. 2. Jouher, in the original, does not affirm that Yádgár went *privately* to the governor, or that he alleged *the King's orders*, as in transl. p. 7. His words are, "Násir Mírza comes into the fort of Champanír, and says to Terdi Beg, 'Give me the treasures.' Terdi Beg answers,

CHAP. II. SECT. IV.

State of the Gangetic provinces.

One of the chief reasons that had drawn Humáyun from Gujrát was the state of Behár, and the eastern provinces. Since Muhammed Shah Loháni and Sultan Mahmúd Lodi had both been driven out of them, and disappeared from the theatre of public affairs, new candidates for royalty had started up, and collected the discontented Afgháns, who were still numerous and powerful. Shír Khan Súr, had gradually overrun all the countries on the southern or Behar side of the Ganges; and Muhammed Sultan Mírza, after his escape from prison, had raised the standard of revolt in the upper provinces. The long absence of the Emperor had latterly encouraged them to act with the greater boldness and security. Muhammed Sultan, having gained possession of a great portion of the countries on the left bank of the Ganges, had fixed the seat of his government at Belgrám, opposite to Kanauj, and had gained sufficient strength to send his son, Ulugh Mírza, with a large force to besiege Juánpúr; while Shah Mírza, another of his sons, reduced Karra-Mánikpúr. Kanauj too had fallen into his hands.

Shír Khan.

Successful campaign of Hindal Mírza.

Hindal Mírza,[1] whom the Emperor had left in command at Agra, marched to quell this revolt, and soon retook Kanauj. As soon as Muhammed Sultan Mírza heard of his approach, he called in all his detachments, and was joined by Shah Mírza, while Ulugh Mírza wrote to say, that he would hasten with all possible speed to meet him; at the same time urging him not to hazard a battle till his arrival. Muhammed Sultan and Shah Mírza, encamping on the left bank of the river, used every exertion to obstruct the passage of the imperial army. Hindál, however, eager to engage the enemy before Ulugh Mírza could join them, having discovered a ford ten miles* above Kanauj, left his camp standing, and effected a passage, unobserved,

'Without the Emperor's orders I cannot give them,' and he sent off an express to His Majesty," &c.

* Five kos.

BOOK IV. A.D. 1537. with all his troops. The two armies soon met face to face; but when they were on the point of engaging, a strong north-wester* rising, blew such clouds of dust right in the eyes of the insurgents that they could not keep their position. The imperial troops, who had the wind on their backs, availing themselves of their advantage, pressed hard upon the enemy, whose retreat was soon converted into a flight. Hindal, after taking possession of Belgrám and the surrounding country, pursued the remainder of their army, as they marched to form a junction with Ulugh Mírza. He overtook them at Oud, where Muhammed Sultan and his sons, having concentrated all their force, halted to check his advance. The two armies lay opposed to each other for nearly two months, when news arrived, that Humáyun had left Mándu, and was on his way back to Agra. This decided Muhammed Sultan to bring on an action, as his only chance of safety. He marched out of his trenches; an engagement ensued, in which the imperial troops had the advantage. The insurgents, dispirited by their continued want of success, began to despair, and soon after dispersed. Muhammed Sultan Mírza, and three of his sons, fled to Kuch-Behár†; while Mírza Hindal, following up his advantage, went on to Juánpúr. Having soon after heard of Humáyun's arrival at the capital, he left the army and joined his brother there.‡

Loss of Malwa. Meanwhile, the Emperor was less fortunate on the side of Malwa. No sooner was it known in the surrounding countries that he was on his march back to Agra, than Bhopal Rai, the chief of Bijagar, a district that lies to the east of Malwa, finding that no garrison was left in Mándu, entered and occupied the place. There he was speedily joined by Milu Khan, who

* Bád-e-kibla.

† Jouher has Koh-Khanda Behár near Parnián (or, Parbatián).

‡ Akbernáma, f. 41.; Jouher, c. 2.

CHAP. II. SECT. IV.

aspired to the throne, which he ascended under the title of Káder Shah; and by Mirán Muhammed Fárúki of Kandesh. As the Emperor's troops appear to have been entirely withdrawn, they met with no opposition anywhere, and soon took possession of the whole country; and thus the kingdom of Malwa, as well as that of Gujrát, slipped from the unsteady grasp of Humáyun.*

Transactions between Beháder Shah and the Portuguese.

But while the course of events was thus once more so favourable to Beháder Shah, that monarch was not doomed long to enjoy his prosperity. Fourteen days after the fall of Champanír, he hastened back to Diu. His negociations with the Portuguese had become complicated. When his fortunes were at the lowest ebb, he had received some assistance from them, as has been mentioned; and, at the same time, had sent rich presents to the Portuguese Viceroy of Goa, inviting him to come to his aid with a more powerful force. The Viceroy, Nuño d'Acuña, had accordingly obeyed his call, and set sail from Goa and Chewel, with a large fleet and army. But when he reached the coast of Gujrát, understanding that the Emperor of Delhi's troops had in the interval been driven out of the country, he began to apprehend, that, as his services were no longer necessary, he might not gain those advantages to himself and his followers, and that increase of territory to his country, which he had anticipated. Some quarrels had arisen before the King's arrival, between the Portuguese and his officers, in consequence of the insulting pretensions and encroaching spirit of the former. Beháder would gladly have seen his troublesome allies removed from Diu, where the building of the new fort was hurried on upon a plan infinitely more extensive than had been reckoned upon. Both parties, however, dissembled their feelings.

A. H. 943. A. D. 1537.

* Akbernáma, ut supra.

BOOK IV. A. D. 1537. Death of Behâder.

Behâder Shah, on his arrival in the neighbourhood of Diu, attempted to restore confidence by acting with the utmost frankness, putting himself boldly in the power of the governor of the castle, and visiting him in his fort. The Viceroy, who arrived off Diu about this time, appears to have blamed the governor for not availing himself of the opportunity thus offered to seize the King, for the purpose of extorting from him the cession of some towns and sea-ports which he was anxious to possess. To repair this oversight, D'Acuña feigned sickness, and sent a message to inform Behâder, who had spent some days in the vicinity in hunting, that he was come, at his call, with powerful succours, and would wait upon him as soon as his health allowed. The Sultan, thrown off his guard, or perhaps suspecting no ill as intending none, laid ceremony aside, and towards the close of the day rowed off from the shore, with only a few attendants and went aboard the admiral's ship, to visit him, and to inquire after his health. No sooner, however, did he see the Viceroy, than he plainly perceived that his illness was a mere pretence, and felt vexed that he had gone. The Viceroy, on his part, had probably been taken unprepared by Behâder's sudden and unexpected appearance. During the conversation that ensued, a page came in and whispered something in his ear. In the state of mind in which the King then was, this little incident increased his uneasiness and excited his suspicion. He continued to sit, however, though the intercourse was forced and constrained; till the Viceroy, rising, requested to be excused for a few moments, as he wished to show his Majesty some presents that were intended for his acceptance, and left the cabin. This confirmed the suspicions of the King, who hurriedly intimating a desire that they might be sent after him, started up and hastened to his boat. He reached it and put off; when Emanuel de Souza, the governor of Diu castle,

Ramzán 3, Feb. 13.

coming up in his barge *, invited him to visit the new fortifications. Rúmi Khan Sefer, who was in the boat with the King, advised him to decline the invitation, as treachery was probably intended; but the King desired de Souza to come into the boat. De Souza, in attempting to step from his own barge into the King's, fell into the sea, but was taken up by Behàder's attendants. This occasioned considerable bustle and confusion; the cause was unknown, but the act of dragging de Souza into the boat, was observed by the Portuguese in the numerous vessels that lay on every side. Hastily concluding that an attempt was made upon their countrymen's life, in their eagerness to succour him, they closed round the King's boat, into which some of them leaped. The instant consequence was uproar and menace; blows speedily succeeded. Behàder, totally unprepared for such an occurrence, and now confirmed in his suspicions of treachery, threw himself into the sea, and was followed by Rúmi Khan. After swimming for some time towards the shore, as he approached a Portuguese vessel, one of the officers held out an oar to assist him in getting in; when a soldier who stood by, struck him on the face with a halbert, and his example was imitated by others of his comrades, who repeated their blows, till Behàder sank dead in the water. Rúmi Khan was saved by a Portuguese to whom, on some former occasion, he had shown kindness. De Souza, the governor, was struck and fell overboard, during the scuffle in the King's boat. Neither his body nor that of the King could be found.†

Fate of Diu.

This scene passed before the eyes of the inhabitants

* Abulfazl's account is, that a Feringi magistrate, (Kazi Fering) by which, I suppose, the governor de Souza is meant) having stept before him as he left the Viceroy, insisted on his remaining; upon which the Sultan, drawing his sabre, cut him down, and leapt into his own boat; seeing this, the Portuguese boats that were around closed in, and Behàder and Rúmi leaped into the sea.

† Akbernáma, ff. 41, 42.; Tabakát-e Akberi, ff. 397, 398.; Ferishta, and General Briggs's note, vol. iv. pp. 130—141.

BOOK IV.

A.D. 1537.

of Diu. They were filled with alarm at the sight; and, as they concluded that their town would be instantly plundered by the Portuguese, leaving their houses, and abandoning all their property, they rushed in such numbers to escape from the place, that many were crushed to death in the crowds that overflowed at the gates; while numbers were drowned in crossing the narrow channel that separates the island from the mainland. The Viceroy left no effort untried to quiet the fears of the survivors, and to bring back the rich traders and other inhabitants of the town; but at the same time he took possession of the King's palace, the arsenals, and all the public magazines. Only a small sum in money was said to have been found by the officers commissioned to take possession of the treasury *; which gave rise to the belief, that they, as well as the Viceroy himself, were guilty of extensive embezzlement; but the jewels, furniture, artillery and stores certainly seized, are said to have been of immense value; besides an hundred and twenty ships, which also fell into their hands.† Each party charged the other with treachery

* Lafitau, vol. i. pp. 256, 257.

† Behâder Shah was the most magnificent, and for some time the most fortunate, prince of his age. When first driven from Champanír, in his despair, he had resolved to abdicate the throne and pass the rest of his life at Mekka. The Turkish historian, Ferdi, according to Chevalier de Hammer, "relates," says General Briggs, "that when Behâder Shah was compelled to retreat to Diu, he sent his family and the royal jewels to Medina. They consisted of three hundred iron chests, the accumulated wealth acquired from the Hindu princes of Junagar, Champanír, Abugar, and Cheitúr, and also the property of the kings of Malwa. These gorgeous treasures never returned to India, but fell into the hands of the Grand Signior of Constantinople, who, from their possession, became entitled to the appellation of Soliman the Magnificent. The celebrated waist-belt, valued at three millions of aspers, which had been three times taken and retaken in the wars of India, was sent to Soliman, by the ambassador whom Behâder Shah deputed to Constantinople to solicit the aid of the Grand Signior against Humáyun." Briggs's Ferishta, vol. iv. p. 141.

The original accounts of the death of the Sultan, as given by the principal Indian and Portuguese authorities, have been extracted at considerable length by Gen. Briggs, (iv. pp. 131—141.) who concludes, that Behâder and the Viceroy "were in this melancholy affair. That Behâder, if actuated by evil intentions, should have put himself unattended in the power of his enemy, seems hardly credible. The Viceroy, without desiring his death, would probably have willingly seen him his prisoner. The catastrophe was evidently brought on prematurely, by accidental circumstances. The conduct of the Portuguese after the event, may be held as the best proof of their disposition before it. The spirit which in that age regulated the proceedings of Europeans towards the princes of America or of Asia and their subjects, was that of the most unprincipled cruelty and rapacity; in no degree superior to that of the buccaneers of a later period. The Portuguese have kept possession of Diu, thus acquired, from that time to the present day.

Alleged re-appearance of Behâder.

Sultan Behâder was only about thirty years of age, and had reigned between eleven and twelve years, when he was cut off. The internal confusion and misery which followed made his subjects long look back with regret to the splendid, and, in general, tranquil period of his reign; while the deplorable circumstances attending his death, which deprived him of all funeral honours, produced a belief, in this as in several similar instances fondly indulged by the common people, that the King

resolved each to seize the other, that the followers of both knew the intentions of their respective masters, and suspected the opposite party; so that nothing was wanting to bring about bloodshed but such an affray as arose, originating entirely out of an accident, which blew the embers of suspicion and mistrust into a blaze, and produced the melancholy result which has been related." *Ibid.* p. 141. I have taken rather a different view of the subject. I see no evidence that Behâder had formed any design against the person of the Viceroy. In case of need he probably would not have been very scrupulous as to the means he employed to defeat the aims of the Portuguese; but, in fact, his whole conduct was conciliatory. He put himself unarmed and defenceless into the power of his enemy. He was passive in the whole affair. No overt act of treachery on his part appears. He had little to gain by seizing the Viceroy; it would only have transferred the command to the next in rank. The case was different had the Viceroy got the King into his power. The Portuguese, by their conduct after the event, threw light on their intentions before it.

BOOK IV. A.D. 1537.

was not really dead, and would one day return to govern his dominions with glory. Many pretended that he reached the shore; and there were various reports of his reappearance, on different occasions, both in Gujrát and the Dekkan. It was, in particular, currently reported and believed that a person appeared in Nizám-ul-múlk's territory, whom that prince acknowledged as Behàder Shah, and as such played with him at chougán*; that, a crowd gathering about him, the concourse of people was marked by the Nizam with some uneasiness; and the same night the stranger disappeared from his tent, having been put to death, as was conjectured, by that prince. It is added, that Múlla Kútb-ed-dín, of Shiráz, who had been Beháder's preceptor, was then in the Dekhan, and conversed with the stranger, and that he affirmed, with the most solemn asseverations, that it was Beháder, and that he reminded the Mírza of many incidents of which they alone were cognizant.†

His mother and nobles retire to Ahmedábád.

As soon as the death of Beháder was ascertained, the Portuguese viceroy sent to Makhdúma Jehan, the King's mother, at once to condole with her on the melancholy event, and to remove all blame from himself. He ascribed the whole unfortunate affair to unpremeditated and unforeseen accident, and offered to lend her any assistance which it might be in his power to afford at the present juncture. But she rejected his offers with indignation, considering him as the murderer of her son; and, accompanied by the Prince of Asír, and the principal nobles, set out for Ahmedábád.

His immediate successors.

While they were on the road, and while all Beháder's household and family were overwhelmed with sorrow, Múhammed Zemán Mírza, who had returned from the fruitless expedition against Lahúr, on which he had been sent by the late king after the dispersion at Mandsúr, fell in with them, and professing the deepest distress, joined the camp, under pretence of assisting in the usual rites

* Horse-shinty.

† Akbernáma, f. 42.

of mourning. By his show of sympathy, and his soothing attentions, he so far insinuated himself into the queen-mother's favour, that she is said to have been prevailed upon to adopt him as her son. He succeeded in seizing a large portion of the public treasures of Gujrát from those who had charge of them; though, of the royal treasure and stores in Diu, part had been plundered during the confusion, and the rest had fallen into the hands of d'Acuña. He at first made a show of revenging the murder of Beháder on the Portuguese; but soon after, observing the extent of their power, he altered his plan, courted their support, and sought, by large sums of money, to induce them to proclaim him Sultan. In this he at last succeeded, the khutba being read in his name in the Sefa Mosque, at Diu, under their authority. He collected an army of twelve thousand men, Moghuls and Hindustánis, and for some time maintained the style of a sovereign prince. But Imád-ul-múlk, supported by the nobles of Gujrát, having proclaimed Mirán Muhammed Shah Farúki, of Khándesh, a sister's son of Beháder's, who was at that time driving the imperial troops from Malwa, to be King of Gujrát, marched against Muhammed Zemán, attacked and dispersed his forces, and compelled him to fly to Sind. Muhammed Zemán did not remain long there, as his presence was far from being agreeable to Shah Hasan, the ruler of that country; so that he, at last, found himself under the necessity of once more returning to Hindustán, and of throwing himself on the clemency of the offended Humáyun. The new king, Mirán Muhammed Shah, reigned only six weeks, and was succeeded by Mahmúd Khan, another nephew of Beháder Shah, who reigned several years under the name of Mahmúd Shah. He was a son of Beháder's brother, Latíf Khan, who was at that time a prisoner in Burhánpúr.*

CHAP. II. SECT. IV.

A.H. 944, A.D. 1538.

* Akbernáma, f. 42.; Briggs's Ferishta, vol. iv. pp. 142—144.

## CHAPTER III.

### AFFAIRS OF KHORÁSÁN AND KANDAHÁR.

STATE OF KHORÁSÁN. — INROADS OF OBEID KHAN, AND THE UZBEKS. — THEY ARE EXPELLED FROM KHORÁSÁN. — AGAIN OVERRUN IT — AND BESIEGE HERÁT — WHICH IS RELIEVED BY SHAH TAHMASP. — THE UZBEKS ONCE MORE EXPELLED. — JÁM MÍRZA IN HERÁT AND KANDAHÁR. — SIEGE OF THE LATTER PLACE. — RAISED BY KÁMRÁN — WHO ROUTS THE INVADERS. — ATTEMPTS ON LÁHÚR, BY MUHAMMED ZEMÁN MÍRZA. — NEW INVASION OF KHORÁSÁN BY THE UZBEKS. — OBEID KHAN BESIEGES MESHHÍD — AND HERÁT — WHICH IS PILLAGED. — ADVANCE OF SHAH TAHMASP — AND RETREAT OF THE UZBEKS. — TAHMASP OCCUPIES KANDAHÁR — WHICH IS RETAKEN BY KÁMRÁN.

BOOK IV.

State of Khorásán, A.H. 935, A.D. 1529.

WHILE these events were passing in Malwa and Gujrát, Khorásán and the Persian frontier were the scene of important transactions. After the great defeat which the Uzbeks sustained at Jám, about nine years before this time, it was expected that Khorásán would, for a long period, have been delivered from their inroads and invasions. But they were an enemy not easily daunted.

Inroads of Obeid Khan and the Uzbeks.

That same year, as soon as Shah Tahmasp had quitted the province, Obeid Khan again collected an army, crossed the Amu, and marched against Meshhíd, which he took possession of, after a blockade of two months. Thence he proceeded to Herát, besieged it for seven months, and took it by capitulation. His Sunni zeal is said, by the Persian writers, to have led him to retaliate the Shía persecutions of Shah Ismael and his successor, and even to put to death many of the opposite sect, as Shías and heretics.

They are expelled from Khorásán;

Next year, the victorious Uzbek advanced to Farra, which he beleagured for some time, but without success, so that he was compelled to raise the seige; and, on hearing of the march of Shah Tahmasp into Khorásán, at the head of seventy thousand men, he hastily abandoned Herát, and retreated to Merv. He summoned all the force of the Uzbeks to join him there; and the Sultans, from beyond the Amu, obeyed his call. But when met, their opinions differed. Kuchum Khan, of Samarkand, the Grand Khan, dying, was succeeded by his son Abusaíd, who set his face against the war, declaring his resolution not to join in it, and advising Obeid to desist. His views were supported by some other chiefs; and Obeid, seeing himself thus deserted, and hearing of the Shah's near approach, turned his back, with an indignant heart, upon Khorásán. Shah Tahmasp, having expelled the enemy, marched to Herát; and the fish-standard of Persia again gleamed over the whole province. Having established his brother Behrám Mírza as viceroy, with Ghází Khan, of the Taklu tribe, as his Protector and Amír-ul-omra, he returned to Irák.

CHAP. III. A.H. 936. A.D. 1530.

Again overrun it: A.H. 937. A.D. 1531.

Obeid Khan, though unsupported by the Uzbek confederacy, next year sent a detachment into Khorásán, who marched as far as Meshhíd, but were driven back by the local force. Nothing dismayed, however, by this repulse, he, the following season, again entered the country with a powerful host, having induced the other Uzbeks to join him, and marched straight for the capital, while divisions of his troops overran the provinces of Meshhíd, Asterábád, Sebzáwár and Bostám with various success. For a year and a half, the country was plundered in all directions, and Obeid continued to push on the siege of Herát. Shah Tahmasp, completely and painfully occupied by the rebellion of Aláma Taklu in Azerbáiján, who had called in the Osmanli Turks to his assistance, was unable to succour them. At length, famine began to rage in the besieged capital. The inhabitants were expelled, their provisions, money and property seized by the domineering Taklus, and the floors of their houses dug up to discover hidden trea-

A.H. 938. A.D. 1532.

and besiege Herát;

BOOK IV. sure. Cats and dogs, and food deemed the most impure, were eagerly eaten. The strength of the troops, who suffered alike from want and fatigue, began to fail. An offer was made to give up the place, provided Obeid would withdraw his troops a march or two, so as to let the garrison quit the city unmolested. He, on the other hand, haughtily insisted that they should march out and defile under his tent-ropes.* This condition Behrám Mírza and his Taklu allies rejected, and the operations of the siege were continued.

which is relieved by Shah Tahmasp;

Meanwhile, however, Tahmasp, having quelled the rebellion of Aláma, was proceeding by forced marches to the relief of Herát. A party that he sent out surprised the Uzbeks who were in Asterábád, one morning when most of them were in the bath, put them to death with little resistance, and sent him five hundred heads. The Uzbeks, who held Sebzáwár, were in like manner attacked, but retired fighting bravely, first to Nishapúr, and then to Meshhíd. Abdal-azíz, who was near that city, hurried to Herát with seven thousand horse, to support his father. Obeid did not venture to meet the Shah in the field, and retired to Bokhára, while Shah Tahmasp once more entered Herát, to the great joy of the inhabitants, and spent the winter in the neighbourhood.

and the Uzbeks once more repelled. Jemádi II. 2. A.D. 1532, Dec. 30.

A. H. 939, A.D. 1533.

In the spring, he sent a division of his troops to reduce the adjoining province of Ghurjistán among the mountains, and was preparing to retaliate upon the Uzbeks by invading Máwer-al-neher, when the news that his grand enemy, Soliman the magnificent, was on his march to attack his dominions in the west, compelled him to relinquish his intention. As the Taklu Turks had been guilty of great oppression during the government of their chief, and were very unpopular, he named his brother, Sám Mírza, to be Viceroy; ap-

* Tenáb-e-Khíma.

pointing Aghziwár Khan, of the Shamlu tribe, his Protector and Amír-al-omra of Khorásán; then entrusting the defence of the city to the townspeople*, he set out for Irák. CHAP. III.

Sám Mírza in Herát and Kandahár.

For rather more than two years, Khorásán enjoyed quiet under Sám Mírza and Aghziwár Khan, as the Uzbeks did not renew their ravages. But, when news reached Herát, of the death of Husein Khan Shamlu, and the destruction of his tribe under the royal indignation, the Mírza, and still more Aghziwár Khan, himself a Shamlu, began to look to rebellion for safety. Collecting money, by extortion and violence in every shape, they raised an army, and resolved to attack Kandahár; proposing, according to the Persian authorities, to erect it, along with Herát, into an independent sovereignty.

A. H. 941, A. D. 1535.

We have seen that Humáyun, on the death of his father, had given up the countries from the Satlej to Khorásán, to his brother Kámrán Mírza. Early in the summer of 1535, Sám Mírza and his protector Aghziwár Khan, being joined by Sultan Murád Afshár of Farra, advanced with a considerable army, crossed the Helmend, and laid siege to Kandahár. The place was bravely defended for eight months by Khwája Kilán, the governor, who had succeeded Askeri Mírza in the management of the province. Kámrán Mírza, when apprised of the invasion, marched from Láhúr, and led an army of twenty thousand men to its relief. On his approach, the besiegers retired one march, and encamped. They were attacked, however, in their new position, on the 25th of January, 1536, and defeated with great slaughter, principally by the military skill and bravery of Khwája Kilán. Aghziwár Khan Shamlu, the young prince's Atálík, or Protector, having been thrown from his horse, was taken prisoner and put to

Siege of the latter place; raised by Kámrán Mírza;

A. H. 942, Shábán 1, A. D. 1536, Jan. 25, who routs the invaders.

* Shahr-zadegan. Alem-arái Abási, ff. 24—27.

BOOK IV.

death. The Mírza effected his escape to the Germsír, whence he soon after proceeded to Tabas. Having by this exploit secured the western part of his dominions, Kámrán returned back to Láhúr.

Unsuccessful attempt on Lahúr by Muhammed Zemán Mírza.

It was while he was absent on this expedition, that Muhammed Zemán Mírza, who, it will be recollected, after the rout of Beháder Shah at Mandsúr, had set out to try his fortune, or to make a diversion on the side of the Penjáb, reached the borders of Sind. Shah Husein, the son of Shah Shuja Beg Arghún, the sovereign of Sind, unwilling that an ambitious prince of such pretensions should enter his dominions, encouraged him to proceed to the conquest of Láhúr, which he represented as a tempting and practicable object, since Kámrán was absent with the army in Kandahár, so that that fertile and populous country was left comparatively defenceless. The Mírza accordingly went on to the Penjáb and laid siege to Láhúr. But unfortunately for his views, Kámrán Mírza returned victorious at that very crisis, and the invader saw himself forced to retire with precipitation, and to return to Gujrát, which he reached with a few followers in the utmost want and misery. We have seen that he there enjoyed a short-lived sovereignty, before he was compelled to flee once more to Sind, and finally to Hindustán.

New invasion of Khorásán by the Uzbeks; A. H. 941, A. D. 1535.

The march of Sám Mírza to attack Kandahár, was a signal for the Uzbeks to renew their inroads. In the north, a body of five or six thousand entered and laid waste Khorásán. Sufián Khalífa, the governor of Meshhíd, an undaunted but hot-headed soldier, was successful in coming up with, and defeating them. To the eastward, another inroad was made from Ghurjistán. Khalífa Sultan Shamlu, whom the Protector had left governor of Herát, having marched to repel them, with a motley and ill-assorted body of troops, collected in haste, in absence of the regular forces, was attacked, defeated and slain. The inhabitants of Herát, thus left

CHAP. III.

without a head, sent to invite Sufián to take charge of the capital, his success in desultory warfare having gained him great reputation all over the province. Leaving his son in Meshhíd, he obeyed their call.

Obeid Khan besieges Meshhíd; A. H. 942, A. D. 1536;

Obeid Khan, finding that Khorásán continued without troops, and without a governor, once more crossed the Amu at the head of an immense army, and besieged Meshhíd. Despatches were sent to recal Sufián, who promised soon to be at the holy city, when he would slay Obeid, and send his skin to the King, stuffed with straw. Setting out from Herát with only three thousand horse, he, on the road, filled a bag with hay, and ostentatiously carried it along with him, lest the Uzbeks, by not leaving a blade of grass around Meshhíd, might defeat his boast. The first detachment that he met, he dispersed; but getting nearer the town in his insane career, he was hard pressed and compelled to take shelter in an old ruin, where he obstinately defended himself several days, subsisting his followers on the flesh of their horses; but was in the end taken and put to death.

and Herát, which is taken and pillaged.

The unfortunate city of Herát was now again in imminent hazard. The lieutenant whom Sufián had left in charge of it, used his endeavours to make the people of the town and country join in its defence. But the severities that he exercised for that purpose disgusted and enraged them, so that they sent to call even the Uzbeks to their relief. Obeid, arriving, besieged the city for five months, while the inhabitants endured all the miseries of war and famine. At length, three hundred Uzbeks, having gained entrance by night into a bastion, it is said by treachery, the city was taken, the garrison flying into the citadel of Ekhtiár-ed-dín. All the horrors of a city taken by storm ensued. Obeid afterwards gained possession of the citadel by a treaty *,

* Alem-arái-Abási, f. 28.

BOOK IV.

in which it was stipulated that the garrison were to be allowed to march out with all their property. But, as they left the fort, they were all stripped naked and marched for Bokhára, the greater part of them perishing miserably by the way.

Advance of Shah Tahmasp; A. H. 943, A. D. 1537;

During four months, Obeid held possession of Herát, and the Sunni persecution of the Shías was renewed. At length, Shah Tahmasp, compassionating the sufferings of his subjects, seized an interval of comparative peace, and set out for Khorásán. As he approached, Obeid Khan, eager to keep permanent possession of that province, proposed to meet him in the field. The other Uzbek chiefs, however, preferred a retreat; and, though it was then winter, the invading army set out to regain their own country by the route of Balkh. Tahmasp reached Herát unopposed, and sent to Tabas to bring Sám Mírza, who had shut himself up in that town after his flight from Kandahár. He was pardoned for his rebellious designs, and for the invasion he had made, as was pretended, without the royal authority; and some of his servants were put to death, as being his evil advisers. Khorásán was now committed to Sultan Muhammed Mírza, another young prince; and Muhammed Khan Sherf-ed-dín Ughli Taklu, was placed beside him in Herát, as Protector, and Amír-ul-omra.

and retreat of the Uzbeks.

Tahmasp occupies Kandahár;

Having cleared Khorásán of enemies, and provided for its safety and the proper administration of affairs, Shah Tahmasp now turned his eyes to the side of Kandahár. That province had been dependent on Herát in the days of its prosperity; and the Shah, though he had pretended to be ignorant, and to disapprove, of Sám Mírza's attack on it, now entered it himself with a powerful army. The capital does not seem to have been placed in a sufficiently defensible state, after the late siege. Khwája Kilán, from the want of provisions and scarcity of military stores, seeing no hopes of being able to stand a siege, resolved to shun an ineffectual contest; put in order his palace, which was magnificently furnished; and arranged all its rich carpets and sumptuous gold and silver plate, to be ready for the reception of the Shah. He then left orders with his deputy, Kanji Khwája, that, on his Majesty's approach, he should present him with the keys of the fort and public offices, and deliver a message in his name; that, as the Khwája, from want of warlike stores, had not the means of either defending the place, or of meeting him in the field,—as, if able, he would have done,—he thought that the next most honourable course he could pursue, was to put his house in order, and, in that condition, leave it for the guest whom he could not entertain in person. He then withdrew, and retired, by way of Sind and Uch, to Láhúr. Mírza Kámrán was much offended at this conduct, and did not admit him to his presence for a whole month after his arrival; complaining, that the Khwája had not held out even for a short time so as to admit of his being relieved. The Khwája's valour, judgment and fidelity were indisputable; and this attempt to soften the asperity of war may, perhaps, be regarded not only as a proof of the refinement of the man, the friend of Báber, and of the politeness that originated in the liberal studies so successfully cultivated in the Court of that prince; but, perhaps, as a symptom of the growing civilisation of the age so rudely checked by the confusion and turmoil that followed.

CHAP. III.

Kámrán lost no time in preparing a force for another expedition against Kandahár. Leaving his cousin, Mírza Haider Doghlat, who had lately arrived from Káshghar by way of Badakhshán, to conduct the government of Láhúr in his absence, he sat out. But before Kámrán's arrival, Shah Tahmasp had quitted Kandahár, which he left under the charge of Bidágh*

which is retaken by Kámrán.

* Or, Budák.

BOOK IV. Khan Kajar, a great noble of his Court, and of the tribe of the present royal family of Persia. The fort sustained a siege of some length, when Bidágh Khan
A.H. 944, capitulated and surrendered it, on condition of being
A.D. 1538. allowed to return home with his troops. Kámrán, having put the place in a state of defence, marched back to Láhúr.

Though two or three inroads were made into Khorásán by the Uzbeks, during the life of Obeid Khan, who died AH. 949, no great invasion was attempted, and that province remained in possession of the Persians during that period, and enjoyed comparative tranquillity.*

* For the events in Khorásán and Kandahár, see the Alem-arái-Abási, ff. 24—28.; Akbernáma, MS. A. f. 39.; MS. B. f. 77.; Tabakát-e Akberi, ff. 146—149.; Taríkh-e Bedáuni, f. 140.

# CHAPTER IV.

## AFFAIRS OF BENGAL.

---

## SECTION I.

### STATE OF BENGAL.—HISTORY OF SHÍR KHAN.

STATE OF THE EMPIRE.—SHÍR KHAN IN BEHÁR AND BENGAL.—INDOLENCE OF THE EMPEROR AT AGRA.—SHÍR KHAN, HIS CHARACTER, FAMILY, AND HISTORY—REPAIRS TO THE COURT OF SULTAN IBRÁHÍM LODI.—SUCCEEDS TO HIS FATHER'S JÁGÍRS.—OVERTHROW OF THE AFGHÁN DYNASTY BY BÁBER.—SHÍR KHAN FAVOURED BY THE AFGHÁN KING OF BEHÁR—HIS ELEVATION.—INTRIGUES OF HIS ENEMIES.—DIVISION OF HIS JÁGÍRS ORDERED.—HE REFUSES TO DIVIDE THEM—AND IS EXPELLED.—REINSTATED BY AID FROM ONE OF BÁBER'S GOVERNORS.—INCREASES HIS RESOURCES.—VISITS BÁBER AT AGRA.—MEDITATES A RESTORATION OF THE AFGHÁN EMPIRE.—WITHDRAWS SUDDENLY FROM THE COURT.—IS RECONCILED TO THE KING OF BEHÁR.—BECOMES PRIME MINISTER—AND REPELS AN INVASION.—A CONSPIRACY FORMED AGAINST HIM.—THE KING FLIES FROM BEHÁR—WHICH IS INVADED FROM BENGAL.—THE INVASION DEFEATED BY SHÍR KHAN.—RIVAL CLAIMANTS OF THE CROWN.—SULTAN MAHMÚD LODI ACKNOWLEDGED.—EXPELLED BY BÁBER, WHO OCCUPIES BEHÁR.—SHÍR KHAN EXTENDS HIS JÁGÍRS AND POWER.—ACQUIRES CHUNÁR.—SULTAN MAHMÚD RENEWS HIS PRETENSIONS.—IS JOINED BY SHÍR KHAN.—ADVANCE OF HUMÁYUN.—TREACHERY OF SHÍR KHAN, AND DISPERSION OF THE AFGHÁN FORCES.—SHÍR KHAN RETAINS CHUNÁR AND HIS JÁGÍRS.—CONSOLIDATES HIS RESOURCES.—PLUNDERS TO THE NORTH OF THE GANGES.—TAKES POSSESSION OF SOUTHERN BEHÁR—AND INVADES BENGAL.

WHEN Humáyun reached Agra, on his return from Gujrát and Malwa, he found the affairs of the empire in CHAP. Sect.

BOOK IV.

A.D. 1536.

State of the Empire on Humáyun's return from Malwa.

A.H. 943, A.D. 1536.

great disorder. We have seen that, from the time of his accession, there were dangers to his government, which it required a strong and steady hand to avert. Even in his own court, the fidelity of several of his great Amírs, some of them the most distinguished among the Túrki and Chaghatái nobles who had accompanied Báber in his wars, was tottering and had failed. Muhammed Zemán Mírza, as well as Muhammed Sultan Mírza and his sons, had broken out in open rebellion; and, though defeated, the latter of them were still in arms. The situation of the country itself favoured such attempts. It was but recently subdued, and the emperor's followers were strangers to the inhabitants. A great proportion of the kingdom of Delhi was composed of little states, more or less independent, and not easily reduced to order. Even in the Doáb, and in the vicinity of Agra itself, there had for ages been a set of refractory chieftains, who willingly seized every opportunity, when the power or attention of the government was relaxed, to indulge in plundering depredations; and while Humáyun was absent in Malwa and Gujrát, these freebooters had carried their inroads to the very gates of the capital. Such petty and unsettled states were ever ready to join a bold adventurer.

Shír Khan in Behár and Bengal.

But the most concentrated opposition to his arms was presented in the eastern provinces of Juánpúr and Behár. These countries had, at no distant time, been the seat of an independent kingdom, which, though it had been subdued by Sultan Sekander Lodi, had revived under a new dynasty, the Loháni, in the time of his son Sultan Ibráhím, and had only recently been again subdued by Báber. A bold attempt made by the Afgháns to renew, in that kingdom, the Lodi Dynasty of Delhi, under Sultan Mahmúd Lodi, Ibráhím's brother, had been defeated only by the energy of that illustrious prince. All the materials of revolt and resistance, however, were amply scattered over the

Eastern provinces. They had for many years been the theatre of war; the minds of the inhabitants were unsettled, had become familiarised to change, and were almost strangers to regular government. Though the old Sherki, and the more recent Loháni dynasty had disappeared, and though the attempts of Sultan Mahmúd Lodi, and of Muhammed Sultan Mírza, to revive the kingdom had failed, Shír Khan Súr, a new candidate for distinction and power, though as yet in an humbler form, had started up; was extending and consolidating his influence, gradually but with consummate skill, in Behár and on the side of Bengal; and by his valour in the field and the equity of his financial administration, was gaining the admiration and the affection of his subjects. The Afgháns, in every part of India, began to turn their eyes to him, as the leader, who, at some future time, might be destined to restore to them that proud ascendency of their nation, the loss of which every man of them so deeply deplored.

As Humáyun, in his expedition to the westward, had necessarily been attended by a large proportion of his best troops, some of the provinces on the Jamna and Ganges were held by very scanty detachments. This circumstance, the long absence of the Emperor from his capital, and latterly his losses and want of success, had encouraged the discontented and turbulent; so that, though Hindal Mírza had been successful in quelling the revolt of Muhammed Sultan in Juánpúr, a great part of the country was in a very unquiet state.

**Indolence of the Emperor at Agra.**

Humáyun, for some time after his return, fixed his residence at Agra. The loss of the kingdoms which he had subdued with so much glory, and the generally unfavourable posture of his affairs, preyed upon his mind, and affected his spirits and his health. He sought relief in the habitual use of opium, which, if for a time it deadened his uneasy feelings, soon affected both his judgment and his temper. For about a year,

BOOK IV. A.D. 1536-7.

he passed most of his time in his private apartments, and rarely held any councils. He could not, however, overlook the disorders that disturbed the immediate neighbourhood of his capital. They were soon quelled, and heavy contributions raised on the offending zemíndárs, in punishment of their rebellious or predatory inroads.* It had been his resolution that his first expedition, when he again took the field, should have for its object to wipe off the stain upon his glory, by once more conquering Malwa and Gujrát. But there were soon demands for his presence much nearer at hand.

Shír Khan, A. H. 944, A. D. 1537.

About the end of this period, Sultan Juneid Birlás died, a veteran of great eminence, who for some years had governed Juánpúr and the eastern provinces, and who, by his talents and the weight of his character, had restrained the ambitious attempts of Shír Khan, now decidedly at the head of the Afgháns in India, both in genius and reputation. No sooner, however, was that restraint removed by his death, than Shír Khan, who already possessed a great part of Behár, ventured to launch out into bolder enterprises, and to turn his undivided force against the province of Bengal; and his success in that quarter was such as speedily to break even the slumbers of Humáyun.

His character,

Shír Khan, who afterwards became king of Delhi under the title of Shír Shah, was one of the most extraordinary men whose name appears in the history of India. His character has been represented in very different lights by different authors. As he was long the grand enemy of the house of Taimur, whom for a time he drove out of India, by their partisans he has been drawn in very unfavourable colours. But the evidence of less prejudiced writers, and of facts, must restore to him the high praise and honourable distinction that,

* Akbernáma, f. 42.; Ferishta, iv. 83.; Kháfi Khan, 45.

with all the imperfections of his character, are justly his due. CHAP. IV. SECT. I.

His original name was Feríd; he was the son of Hasan and grandson of Ibráhím *, an Afghán of the tribe of Súr, who dwelt near Pesháwer. The family claimed descent from the ancient kings of Ghúr, who reigned in the mountains that lie between Kábul and Herát; and Ferishta, on the supposition that the Súr family had established this claim, holds it to be the most illustrious of the Afgháns. † The marriages which they formed in that part of the Afghán country to which they removed ‡, prove them to have been of what was deemed an honourable race; though Abulfazl relates that Ibráhím was originally a horse-dealer. It is by no means improbable that even a well-born Afghán may have engaged in that occupation, or that, when leaving his own country for India, he may have invested his little fortune in a venture of horses, as is often done at this day. Ibráhím arrived in India in the reign of Sultan Behlúl Lodi, in search of military service, which he procured; served under some Amírs of distinction; and remained for a time, first at Hissár Firúza and after-

and family.

* The Akbernáma, f. 41., calls Ibráhím the grandfather, Shiber-kheil, or according to Col. Price's reading, Shirakhíl. The Nisáb-náma-e Afghánán, f. 81., makes Hasan Khan, the father, to be of the tribe (táifa) of Mati, and family or clan (gabíla) of Súr.

† Vol. ii. p. 99. The Tar. Bed. f. 145., describes him as being *az deh keh ibárat az Afghán est,*" the town that takes its name from the Afghán." Can this be Deh-Afghánán, a suburb of Kábul?

‡ When Sultan Behlúl was seated on the throne, he invited a number of his countrymen from Roh, a district inhabited by the Afgháns. "Roh," continues the author of the Tabakát-e Akberi, "has the same meaning as Koh (a hill). The country comprehended under that name extends in length from Swát and Bajour to the township of Síwí, which is dependent on Bheker; and in breadth from Hasan-Abdal to Kábul and Kandahár. It is bounded by the Daman-koh." Tab. Akb. ff. 35. 169. A similar passage occurs in Ferishta. This extent of country includes nearly the whole of Afghánistán-Proper. Instead of the words following "Hasan Abdal to Kábul," the Taríkh-e Nizámi, f. 207. reads, "Kandahár lies on the confines of this hill-country."

BOOK IV.

wards at Shámlu, or Simla, a district in the province of Agra.*

Ibráhím's son, Hasan, who was born in Hissár, early in life entered the employment of Rái-mal, a Hindu (the grandfather of Rái-Sál, an officer of eminence in Akber's court), under whom he probably gained some insight into revenue concerns. He afterwards went to Juna, in the district of Sahsarám, in Behár, to Nasír Khan Loháni, one of Sekander Lodi's most powerful nobles, in whose employment he remained some time; and having, by his faithful service and intelligence, distinguished himself among his equals, was admitted into his master's confidence. On Nasír Khan's death, Hasan entered into the service of that nobleman's brother, Doulat Khan; and from his passed into that of Baban Khan Jilwáni, a distinguished Afghán chief, in which he advanced himself, was actively employed in much business of importance, and became his principal adviser. His reputation finally became such that when Jemál Khan was appointed to the government of Juánpúr, he was taken into his service, in which he spent the rest of his life; received from him in jágír the valuable districts of Sahsarám and Kháwáspúr-Tánda, places dependent on Rhotas in Behár, and was sent to take possession of them with five hundred horse.†

And history.

Hasan's eldest son was Feríd, afterwards known with so much distinction as Shír Shah. Omens seldom fail to attend the birth of every eminent man, and they were not wanting to Feríd's. His mother, when with

* The Akbernáma has Simla in the district of Narnúl. The Tab. Akb., f. 169., Narnúl; the Tar. Bedáuni, f. 145., Nárnul, in Hissár-Firúza; the Kholúset-al-Towáríkh, f. 271.; and Nisábnáma, f. 81.; Nímla, in Nárnúl.

† Akbernáma, f. 42.; Tabakát-e Akberi, f. 169.; Tar. Niz. f. 207.; Tar. Bedáuni, f. 145.; Ferishta, vol. ii. p. 95. et seq.; Kholáset-ul-Towáríkh, f. 271.; Kháfi Khan, f. 50.; Nisábnáma-e Afghánán, f. 81. The Tabakát, Ferishta, and Nisábnáma, do not mention any circumstances of Hasan's life, till he entered the service of Jemál Khan. in Sultan Sekander Lodi's time.

child of him, dreamed that the moon, in its full brightness descending from heaven, entered her womb. Waking her husband, she communicated to him her dream; upon which he struck her several blows. Surprised, she angrily asked him what he meant; and was told, that the sages of former times had advised that one who had a fortunate dream ought not, by dreaming again the same night, to run the risk of counteracting its happy influence; and that his blows were intended to prevent her again falling asleep. In like manner, we are told of Feríd, that when he was about four years old, as he was one day childishly whining to his father to give him a dirhem, a wise and holy derwísh who was near, exclaimed aloud, "Great God! the Emperor of Hindustán is crying for a dirhem."* This expression filled his father with delight, as confirming his wife's dream, and inspired him with high hopes of his son's future eminence; hopes which the boy's opening talents seemed early to justify.

Hasan had eight sons; two of them, Feríd and Nizám, by his wife, a noble Afghán lady; the other six by different slaves or concubines, three of them, Suleimán, Ahmed and Mádár being by one mother. It is hardly necessary to remark that while, by the Musulman law, the number of wives is limited to four, that of concubines is left unlimited; but that, as all of them live in the master's house like the wives, under the same superintendence, and liable to the same punishment for infidelity, and as consequently no more doubt exists in the one case than in the other as to paternity, the children of both classes are acknowledged by the law, and entitled to a share in the paternal succession; much as, for the same reasons, was customary among the patriarchs and Jews in ancient times. Hasan was not partial to his Afghán wife; and his fondness for

* Khol. al-Tow. f. 271.

BOOK IV. Suleimán's mother, who had acquired a great ascendency over him, led him to show more favour to her sons than to his other children. Feríd, who, even when little more than a boy, evinced a proud and decided temper, unable to brook this preference, left his father's house, and repaired to Juánpúr, where he placed himself under the protection of Jemál Khan, his father's patron. Hasan wrote to his son to return, and to Jemál to send him back, that he might be instructed in learning, and trained up in the accomplishments suited to his station; but Feríd resisted every solicitation of the friendly Khan, saying that Juánpúr, which was a large city and abounded with learned men, was a much better place for instruction than such a village as Sahsarám. He, however, applied himself ardently to the pursuit of knowledge. He is said to have studied the Arabic and Persian languages, and the religious and civil code of the Musulman law, as contained in the Koran and the commentaries upon it; and such was his delight in the beautiful poets of Persia, that he was able to repeat by heart the whole poems of the celebrated moralist and poet Sádi.* With such acquirements, it is not wonderful that he soon came to be considered as a great scholar among his countrymen, the Afgháns; who, though distinguished in arms, have always been noted for their dulness in letters and the arts. Besides this, he took pleasure in frequenting the monasteries and colleges of the Derwíshes and other religious orders; and courted the society of the Ulema, or Muhammedan lawyers and

* The author of the Tabakát-e Akberi, (ff. 169. 35.) himself a man of letters and versed in Persian literature, speaks doubtfully of Feríd's scholarship. He mentions his reading the Káfia (or, Arabic Grammar) with the commentaries and other books, "such," says he, "as the Gulistán, Bostán, and Sekandernáma, which were then generally read by the people of Hind, and made himself acquainted with the principles of morals and with some books of history." This would suppose but a limited course of study, and such it probably was. The Nisábnáma mentions, as part of his reading, history and the Akhláqi-Súri, f. 81. *bis*.

doctors, as well as of the Sheikhs and men of saintly reputation, studied their manners and habits of thinking, and secured their favour, which he retained through life, and which was often of singular advantage to him in his plans of ambition. His father heard of the young man's reputation, when he visited Juánpúr a few years after. Their relations interfered to make up their quarrel, and to prevail upon the son to return home.

Appointed to manage his father's jágírs.

As Hasan was himself about to attend the governor of Juánpúr with his troops, he offered Feríd the management of both his jágírs, during his absence; a burden which the youth consented to undertake, on the express understanding that, though many of the officers in the jágírs were his own near friends and relations, he was to have the absolute direction of all, so as to be able, he said, to govern the raiats with impartiality, by gentleness and justice, and to relieve them from the ignorant oppression which he saw exercised over them by his countrymen.

His judicious and bold measures.

Feríd accordingly repaired to the jágírs to act as Sheikhdár or military collector; and soon gained the confidence of the inhabitants, by the kindness with which he treated them, and his invariable regard to justice, from which neither the calls of interest nor the claims of relationship could divert him. Soon after his arrival, he also showed the bold decision of his character. The head men of some villages in the jágír, who had been refractory, refused to wait upon him, which was equivalent to withdrawing from his authority. These he determined to punish, and consulted the officers of the jágír as to the best means of effecting his object. He was told that, as all the troops had gone with his father, it was necessary to put off any operations till their return. But this dilatory conduct, and passive acquiescence in injury, were little suited to the energetic character of Feríd. He gave orders to make two hundred saddles, borrowed one horse from the head-

BOOK IV.

man of every village in his Perganas, and selecting the most active of the men who had seen service and lived scattered about in the jágír, supplied them with money and clothes, animated their zeal by his example and promises, mounted them on the borrowed horses, and led them against the rebels. With unexpected speed he destroyed the houses and property of the refractory, and made some of them prisoners; at the same time seizing a number of their wives and children, whom he retained as hostages.

Having quelled all opposition in the interior of his little territory, he next proceeded to punish some turbulent neighbours, who, from the woods and hills on the limits of the jágír, trusting to their inaccessible fastnesses, made frequent inroads, plundering and harassing the cultivators. As they refused to meet him or to give suitable redress, he marched such a force as he could collect into their country, till he came near their chief town, which they had fortified as a castle or fastness. There he halted; drew a trench round his camp; and, cutting down, day after day, a portion of the jungle by which the enemy's fort was surrounded and defended, he at length reached their stronghold, which he regularly attacked and finally stormed, killing numbers of the defenders, and making the rest prisoners. These early acts of resolute determination inspired his rude neighbours on every side with such alarm, that they never after troubled him, but remained quiet and inoffensive, paying him regularly an annual tribute.

Prosperity of his districts.

The freedom from internal and external oppression enjoyed in his villages, soon drew to them an influx of cultivators from all the districts around, so that he was enabled to bring into cultivation nearly the whole of the waste lands within their limits. He relieved the inhabitants from many burdensome exactions, neither molesting them himself, nor suffering others to molest them; insomuch that the produce of the jágír was soon amazingly increased; the villages flourished; the inhabitants pursued their industry in quiet, and he himself was extremely beloved. Hasan, who some time after paid a visit to his jágírs, was delighted with the order, populousness, and general prosperity which he everywhere witnessed.*

Jealousy of his step-mother.

But, says the native historian, as the love of gold and woman are the great disturbers of human society and of private families, so the mother of Suleimán, jealous of the reputation and importance which Feríd was daily acquiring, and anxious that her son should have the management of the jágírs, exerted the influence which she possessed over Hasan's mind, and had succeeded in extracting from him a promise to transfer to her sons, when they came of age, the management of the Perganas. Hasan was, however, well aware of the heart-burning in his family, and the injury to his estate, that such a change would occasion; and, having every reason to be satisfied with Feríd's conduct, put off from time to time the performance of his promise. But Feríd, whose observation the intrigues that were carrying on and the perplexity of his father could not escape, put an end to his difficulties by resigning, in disgust, the charge of the jágírs, to which his brothers Suleimán and Ahmed were immediately appointed.

He resigns.

Though Hasan used every endeavour to soothe the injured feelings of Feríd, by representing the appointment of his brothers as made merely with a view to initiate them into business, while he was still to be the heir, the young man once more resolved to leave his father's house. Sultan Ibráhím Lodi had now become king at Agra, whither Feríd repaired, with his brother Nizám, and entered into the service of Doulat Khan Lodi, one of the great Amírs of the court. Feríd, by his talents and assiduity, gained the esteem and

Repairs to the camp of Sultan Ibráhím Lodi.

* Tab. Akb. f. 170.; Tar. Níz. ff. 272, 273.; Ferishta, vol. ii. ff. 207, 208.; Khol. al-Towárikh, pp. 99, 100.

BOOK IV.

patronage of that chief, who, having on some occasion asked in what way he could serve him, Ferid seized the opportunity of informing him how he was situated; that, though the son of Hasan by a noble Afghán lady, his father, now in his dotage, bewitched by the arts of a favourite Hindu concubine, who had gained unlimited power over his mind, had set him aside from the management of his jágír, and had bestowed it on her sons; he represented both the revenue and military force of the districts as falling into decay, and the soldiers as discontented; but added that, if he and his brother were put in possession of the jágírs, he would undertake that, while one of the two brothers remained in the perganas to manage them and to take care of their aged father, the other should at all times attend the Sultan with a body of five hundred horse.

When Doulat Khan took an opportunity of representing these circumstances to Sultan Ibráhím, the king coldly remarked, that he must be a bad man who could depreciate and undermine his own father. Doulat informed Feríd of this repulse, but at the same time kept up his spirits by increasing his allowance, and by assuring him that he would neglect no opportunity of still effecting his object. Feríd, by his liberality and generous qualities, gained the heart of his patron, to whom he still continued attached, and whom he accompanied in his daily attendance at the derbár. A short time afterwards, Feríd's father having died, Doulat Khan, once more waiting on the king, renewed his application under more favourable circumstances, and secured for his follower a grant of the jágírs of Sahasrám and Kháwáspúr-Tánda; in consequence of which, Feríd returned to Sahasrám with a strong retinue, and took possession of the jágírs, which he again governed with his former moderation and justice.*

Appointed to succeed his father in the jágírs.

* Taríkh-e-Nizámi, f. 208. followed by Ferishta, vol. ii. pp. 101, 102.; and by Tar. Bedáuni, f. 145.

Suleimán, unable to oppose his brother thus supported by the royal authority, repaired to Muhammed Khan Súr, a relation of the family, who then held the government of Junda and Baksár, with fifteen hundred horse. By this time the invasion of Báber had begun, and a decisive battle was daily expected. Suleimán's patron promised that, if the Sultan was successful, he would carry him to court and secure for him his jágírs. The impatience of Suleimán, however, who complained that, while he was waiting, his mother and family were without house and home, induced Muhammed Súr to send a confidential person to attempt to bring Feríd to an accommodation. The reply was that Feríd was perfectly willing to share with his brothers whatever belonged to the private inheritance and estate of his father, but would part with none of the military or political power entrusted to him by his prince; observing, in the words of a well-known saying, that one scabbard could not hold two swords, nor one city contain two rulers. To this arrangement Suleimán would not accede, insisting on having a share in the government of the jágírs; and Muhammed Khan was preparing to restore him by force, when news arrived of the defeat and death of Sultan Ibráhím.

Overthrow of the Afghán dynasty by Báber. A. H. 932, A. D. 1526.

In the disorders and wars that followed the overthrow of the Afghán kingdom of Delhi, Feríd was not inactive.* He remained attached to the interests of his tribe, and joined Behár Khan, the son of Deria Khan Lohâni, when, supported by the Afgháns of India, he occupied Behár,

Shír Khan favoured by the Afghán

* It does not appear what part Hasan took in the Lohâni rebellion; but, from his connection with Násir Khan Lohâni and Baban Khan Jilwáni, who were so active in the revolt, we may conjecture that he sided with the insurgents. When Ferid went to Sultan Ibráhím, was it resorting to his father's enemies? while Suleimán sided with the rebels.

It may perhaps be suspected that the whole of Hasan's service with Násir, Doulat, and Baban was in the reign of Ibráhím, and during their revolt, not in Sekander's time: the chronology is very confused.

BOOK IV.

King of Behár.

and assumed the ensigns of royalty as king of the Eastern provinces of Behár and Juánpúr, under the name of Sultan Muhammed. Ferid's bravery, his knowledge of affairs, and his assiduity speedily gave him a high reputation in the council and camp of the Afgháns. He was much employed in business of importance, and became a personal favourite of the king.

His prowess and elevation.

An accidental occurrence raised him to still higher distinction. It happened that, the king being one day on a hunting party, a tiger unexpectedly made its appearance. Feríd, who was present, bravely pushed forward, and was fortunate enough to attack and slay the ferocious animal with his sabre. The King loaded him with praises, and honoured him with the title of Shír-Khan (lion lord). He rapidly rose from one office of trust to another, until he was at last appointed Atálik, or Governor, of Jilál Khan, the Sultan's son and heir, an office which implied the highest degree of rank and confidence.*

Intrigues of his enemies.

This proud elevation could not be attained without exciting the envy of his compeers. Shír Khan, having some time after obtained leave of absence, went to visit his jágírs, where he seems to have remained beyond the prescribed period. The occasion of injuring him, thus offered, was not lost on his enemies. The King one day took notice of the circumstance, and spoke of it with some appearance of dissatisfaction. Muhammed Khan Súr, the governor of Junda, Suleimán's patron, who was present, seized the occasion to throw suspicions on the fidelity of Shír Khan, insinuating that his delay was owing to his desire to wait the arrival of Sultan Muhammed Lodi, a brother of the late Sultan Ibráhím, who was at this time a candidate for the throne of Behár as well as Delhi. The King, irritated at the moment, and moved by these insinuations, threw out

* Tar. Nizámi, f. 209.; Khol. f. 145.; Ferishta, vol. ii. p. 103. al-Tow. f. 273.; Tar. Bedáuni,

some angry expressions against Shír Khan; upon which Muhammed Khan suggested, that the most effectual way to keep him in order was to bestow his jágír on his half-brother and rival, Suleimán, who had managed it in their father's lifetime, and had been fixed on by him as his successor. Suleimán was at that time living under Muhammed Khan's protection. Though this was rejected, as being too strong a measure against one who had been guilty of no active or overt offence, yet the party hostile to Shír Khan succeeded in procuring from the Sultan an order for dividing the jágír among the brothers.

The division of his jágírs ordered.

But Shír Khan had become too strong to be removed at will, in such turbulent times. A firmán was indeed issued, that an account of Hasan's estate should be taken, for the purpose of making an equal division between his sons; and this duty was entrusted to Shír Khan's enemy, Muhammed Khan Súr. To a demand sent by that officer, that Shír Khan should divide with his brothers the jágír which he had so long unjustly withheld from them, a reply was returned, that they were not now in the Roh (or Afghán mountains), where all the sons shared in the father's lands; that here the land was the king's, granted for the support of troops, and followed his pleasure; that he held his land by a special grant of Sultan Ibráhím, and that his brothers had no concern whatever with it; but that he had already declared his readiness to grant his brothers their due share of their father's private property, which was all that in law they were entitled to demand.*

He refuses to divide them.

On receiving this answer, the governor of Junda, glad of an opportunity to enforce his demand by arms,

Is expelled.

* Tar. Niz. f. 209.; Nisábnáma, f. 83. The Roh is the Afghán Highlands. This argument of Ferid's is precisely that of the feudal system. It marks the difference between allodial and feudal lands. The tenure by military service affords the best explanation of the origin of primogeniture.

BOOK IV. immediately despatched his slave, Shadi, with a large body of troops, to put Suleimán in possession of Kháwáspúr-Tánda; with orders, if Shír Khan made any resistance or opposition, to seize Sahasrám, and all the rest of the jágír also. Shír Khan, who did not anticipate such active measures, was taken by surprise. He wrote, however, to his deputy in Kháwáspúr,—who was Malek Saka, a slave, the father of the celebrated Khowás Khan,—to harass and delay the invading troops on their route by every means in his power, but on no account to engage in a general action * till he himself arrived. Unfortunately Malek Saka, hurried on by his impetuosity, or by a desire of distinguishing himself, rashly met the invaders as they approached Kháwáspúr, was defeated, and slain.

This deranged all Shír Khan's plans, and deprived him of those means of resistance on which he had depended. The enemy, pursuing their advantage, advanced to Sahsarám; and he was forced to abandon the jágír. Some of his friends now advised him to repair to the court of Sultan Muhammed; but, dreading the influence of Mohammed Khan Súr with that monarch, he preferred throwing off his allegiance to the king of Behár, and entered into a correspondence with Sultan Juneid Birlás †, who was then governor of the province of Karra-Manikpúr on the part of Báber, and who agreed to receive and protect him. He waited upon Juneid with rich offerings, submitted to him his claims and his means of enforcing them, and in the end obtained from him a body of troops to assist in recovering his country. With these he advanced, and Muhammed Khan Súr, unable to resist him, fled to the Rhotas hills. Shír Khan now, not only regained his

Reinstated by aid from one of Báber's governors.

* The Tar. Nizámi rather intimates that Saka had power to engage.

† Sultan Juneid Birlás, an amír of an illustrious family, is said to have married a sister of Báber's. Khol. al-Tow. f. 273.

own jágírs, but seized Junda and several other adjoining districts that belonged to Muhammed Khan himself. Having liberally rewarded the auxiliary troops that had accompanied him, he sent them home, with suitable presents for Sultan Juneid.

Increases his territory and forces.

His scattered family and clansmen now returned. He recruited his forces, took again into his service many inhabitants of the country who had fled to the hills, and speedily became very formidable. With the foresight and sound judgment which formed so remarkable a part of his character, he now wrote to his late enemy Muhammed Khan, begging him to pardon the steps which necessity alone had compelled him to take, that he might secure his own possessions, from the usurpation of his brothers; assured him that while he was determined to retain his own jágír, he had no desire to interfere with the possessions of one whom he honoured as an uncle; and invited him to return from the hills, and resume possession of Junda and his other districts. He, at the same time, sent him the whole amount of the revenue that had been collected from the perganas during his occupation of them; besides a large sum of arrears, which the former managers had returned in their accounts as irrecoverable, but which Shír Khan, from his thorough knowledge of revenue concerns, had been able to realise. This act of generosity ever after attached Muhammed Khan to his interests.*

His generous policy.

As soon as the state of his affairs at Sahsarám permitted, Shír Khan, leaving his brother Nizám in charge of his jágírs, again visited Sultan Juneid Birlás at Karra, and accompanied him to Agra, where he was

He visits

* The preceding narrative is from the Tabakát-e Akberi, ff. 171, 172.; Tar. Nizámi, ff. 207—209., which Ferishta, vol. ii. pp. 98—103.; and Tar. Bed. ff. 145, 146., have followed; and is modified by the Akbernáma, f. 42.; the Nisábnáma-e Afgh. ff. 81—84.; the Kholáset-al-Towáríkh, ff. 171—173.; Kháfi Khan, ff. 50—52.; and Stewart's History of Bengal.

BOOK IV.

Báber at Agra. A. H. 934, A. D. 1528.

presented to the Emperor Báber, whom he attended in his expedition against Chandéri.

Shír Khan remained for some time in Báber's camp, where he had the best opportunity of observing the manners and policy of that prince, and of his ministers. His keen eye saw defects, even where to others all seemed to be sound. One day, in conversing with some of his Afghán friends, he happened to remark, that, from all the observations he had made, he thought it by no means an impracticable thing to drive these foreigners out of Hindustán. To their inquiries, on what he founded this opinion, he answered, that the Emperor, great as were his talents, applied but little to business, so that everything was left to his ministers, who, being selfish and corrupt, did not attend to the interest of the state; that the Afgháns unfortunately were divided, constantly at enmity with each other, and consequently powerless; but that, could they be brought to lay aside their mutual animosities and support him heartily, he did not doubt that he could himself accomplish the business. His friends laughed at the idea, and jeered him on his wild and impracticable fancies.

Meditates a restoration of the Afghán empire.

About the same time, he was one day invited to an entertainment at the Emperor's, where some solid dish* was placed before him, and only a spoon with which to eat it. Having in vain asked for a knife, he at length drew his hanger, and, cutting up the meat into small pieces, proceeded to complete his meal with the spoon, perfectly indifferent to the smiles and remarks of those who were diverted with his Afghán rusticity. Báber, when the incident was pointed out to him, turning to Mír Khalífa, his prime minister, quietly remarked, "this Afghán is a man of sense and spirit;" and, being informed of his conduct towards Muhammed Khan, he did not hesitate to predict his rise to future greatness.

* Máhcheh.

Shír Khan got notice of this conversation of the Emperor and his minister, and understanding that his own observations to his friends had been repeated to him, apprehensive that he was viewed with suspicion, fled from the camp the same night, and returned to his jágír. To excuse this step he wrote to his patron Sultan Juneid, that he must not regard this precipitate retreat as owing in the slightest degree to disaffection; that having learned that his old enemy Muhammed Khan had urged Sultan Muhammed to send an army to occupy his jágírs while he was absent in the Chaghatái camp, and knowing how much delay must necessarily occur, before he could in the regular way obtain permission to leave the camp, being hard pressed, he had ventured to depart at once without loss of time; and begged Juneid to assure his Majesty how faithfully he continued to be attached to his service. Sultan Juneid saw plainly that these were mere professions, and was much offended. But, while Shír Khan thus attempted to excuse his flight, seeing no prospect of succeeding at the Emperor's court, he sought to be reconciled to Sultan Muhammed. This he easily effected; and soon after, accompanied by his brother Nizám, repaired to the court at Patna, where he was joyfully welcomed by the king and restored to the office of Atálik, or protector, to his son Jilál Khan.*

Withdraws suddenly from the Court.

Is reconciled to the king of Behár.

It was not long after his return to the court of Sultan Muhammed Loháni that that prince died, and was succeeded by Jilál Khan, his son, still a minor, who was proclaimed king under the name of Sultan Jilál-ed-dín. Affairs were for some time conducted by the young king's mother, Bíbí Dúdú, in conjunction with Shír Khan, who became prime minister. His usual ability did not forsake him upon this elevation. He strenuously exerted himself to maintain the prosperity and

Becomes prime minister.

* Tar. Niz. ff. 210, 211.; Tab. Akb. f. 172.; Tar. Bed. f. 146.; Ferishta, v. ii. pp. 106, 107.; Kháfi Khan, f. 53.

BOOK IV.

reputation of the kingdom, which was still in its infancy. Makhdúm Alim Khan was the governor of Hájípúr, an important province on the north of the Ganges, at that time belonging to Bengal. He had for some time cultivated Shír Khan's friendship, and having quarrelled with his master, Nasret Shah, now entered into a close alliance with the Khan. Enraged at this injury, Nasret sent Kutb Khan, the governor of Mongeir, with a large force to invade Behár, to punish the regent, and to seize the country; and afterwards to root out his own rebellious subject from Hájípúr. Shír Khan, who was able to bring only a very inferior army to meet the invaders, tried every art to effect an accommodation, but in vain. He therefore resolved to hazard the issue of a battle, marched against the enemy, whom he boldy attacked, and, by his superior skill and hardihood, totally defeated, with the loss of their leader, — the whole elephants and camp equipage, as well as the military chest of the army of Bengal, falling into his hands.*

Repels an invasion.

A conspiracy is formed against him.

His success on this occasion, added to the high reputation he had already obtained, only increased the envy and dislike with which he had previously been regarded by the Loháni Afgháns, the young king's relations, who now formed a conspiracy for the purpose of cutting him off, and engaged the king himself in it. They alleged, probably not without foundation, that his ambition extended beyond the mere office of regent, and did not stop short of the crown itself. Though his vigilance, and some quarrels among themselves, enabled him to discover and to defeat the schemes of the conspirators, he failed in the attempts which he made to cut them off. But he waited on the young King, Sultan Jilál-ed-dín, to whom he represented the implacable hostility of the conspirators, and the guilty

* Tar. Akb. f. 172.; Tar. Niz. f. 311.; Tar. Bed. f. 146. The Lohánis are also called Nuhánis.

plans they had formed; he added, that if his Majesty did not actively second his views, he himself must of necessity retire from his service, which he was prepared to do at a single word; that his Majesty must choose between his regent and those who were combined for his ruin. The King, confused, overawed, and quite unprepared for such an offer, protested his ignorance of the plot, and put himself into his minister's hands. Shír Khan, thus invested with absolute power, took means to separate and divide the confederated lords. One portion of them he sent to collect the revenues of the perganas; another, to face the King of Bengal, who was again in arms. Though the conspirators were thus thwarted for the time, yet, as they consisted of the king's nearest relations, and of the officers immediately about his person, they continued to fill his mind with suspicion and distrust; and as Shír Khan, who was at this time engaged in facing the Emperor's troops, persisted in carrying everything with a high hand, the King was at length prevailed upon to make his escape by night, accompanied by a few officers, and to take refuge in the territory of Nasret Shah, of Bengal; imploring his assistance to remove an overbearing minister, who had now in reality usurped all the powers of the government; and offering to hold his kingdom of Behár as dependent on Nasret Shah.

The king flies from Behár.

Nasret Shah, happy to find an opportunity of revenging at once his own wrongs and those of the King of Behár, ordered Ibráhím Khan, the son of the Kutb Khan, of Mongeir, whom Shír Khan had defeated and slain, to accompany Jilál-ed-dín into Behár, at the head of a large army, for the purpose of revenging his father's death, and of replacing him on the throne. Shír Khan avoided meeting so superior a force* in the field, and retired into an entrenched camp which he had formerly

Invasion from Bengal.

* Kháfi Khan intimates that he had met with a defeat before entering the camp, f. 53.

BOOK IV.

fortified, and in which he was soon besieged. Here the two armies lay for some time opposed to each other, and had daily skirmishes. In these affairs, and from the constrained situation in which he was, in a hostile country, Ibráhím Khan suffered so much, that he was at last obliged to send to his master to solicit reinforcements. Shír Khan, discovering this, and finding his army in high spirits, led them out to offer battle to the enemy. It was joyfully accepted. Ibráhím drew out his army, which was strong in artillery and elephants, and marched to meet them. Shír Khan added stratagem to bravery. The battle began with great ardour on both sides; but while Ibráhím was engaged in front, in keen pursuit of a party of the retreating enemy, he was attacked in the rear by a body of chosen troops, who had been posted in ambush behind an eminence, under the personal command of Shír Khan. Ibráhím was defeated and slain, with the flower of his troops. All his artillery, elephants and baggage, fell into the hands of Shír Khan; and the young King, Sultan Jilál-ed-dín, escaping with difficulty from the field of slaughter, sought refuge in Bengal.* This decisive success freed the dominions of Behár from foreign enemies.†

Is entirely defeated by Shír Khan.

Rival claimants of the crown.

But these were not the only rivals who contended for the possession of the eastern provinces, so miserably distracted by war and faction. There were three rival princes who aspired to Behár. Sultan Jilál-ed-dín Sherki, the representative of the older Sherki dynasty of Juánpúr, which for a long time had nearly disappeared from the stage, but still possessed Benáres and other districts, and who had placed himself under the

* Tab. Akb. ff. 172, 173.; Tar. Nizámi, f. 211.; Tar. Bedáuni, f. 146.; Nisábnáma-e Afg. ff. 184—186.; Ferishta, vol. iv. pp. 98—109.; Kháfi Khan, ff. 52, 53.; Khol. al-Towár. ff. 273, 274.

† The acquisition of Chunár is placed at this time by most historians. Tab. Akb.; Akbernáma; Nisábnáma, &c. But Báber's Memoirs prove that Táj Khan was still alive, and in possession of the place, at the close of the ensuing campaign, pp. 431, 432.

CHAP. IV. SECT. I.

protection of Báber, to whom he submitted: Sultan Jilál-ed-dín Loháni, the son of Behár Khan, who, when driven from his kingdom of Behár, had fled to the territory of Bengal, where he now was; and a third competitor, Sultan Mahmúd Lodi, the brother of the late Sultan Ibráhím Lodi, also appeared in the field.*

Sultan Mahmúd Lodi.

After the ruin of his hopes on the side of Delhi, by the defeat of Rána Sánga and the death of Hasan Khan of Mewát, he had remained for some time in the territories of Cheitúr, but being at this time invited by several powerful Lodi chiefs and some zemíndárs of the country, who had assembled at Pana, he now joined them. His pretensions were favoured by various classes, as well as by the numerous friends of the Lodi family. Indeed, he had with him the good wishes of the Afgháns in general, who, whatever party feuds existed among them, would gladly have seen the race of Lodi restored to the throne of Delhi. The recent destruction of the Loháni dynasty of Behár, by the flight of the King to Bengal, had made it clear to the inhabitants of the eastern provinces, even of such as had formerly revolted from the Lodis and opposed them, that, unless the Afgháns of every tribe united under some new chief, their reign was over, and that no individual was so likely to unite the whole Afghán population of India in a steady union as a member of the royal race of Lodi. This feeling produced a temporary union. Sultan Mahmúd was universally acknowledged. He entered

Is universally acknowledged.

* There seems to be considerable confusion, in many instances, in the native historians, or their transcribers, between Patna, Panah, Pateh, and Tehia, which differ only by the points. Sultan Mahmúd is made by Ferishta to come down from Patna, upon Shír Khan. The Tar. Nizámi, f. 212., has Tirhatch. The Tar. Bed. f. 147. has Patna, but immediately after mentions his *going into Behár*. The Nisábnáma-e Afgh. f. 87. has *viláet-e Patch*; Mahmúd is invited to that country, and thence enters Behár. It seems to have been the district of Panah (or Pateh or Tehia) in Bundélkand, where the Afgháns assembled before marching into Behár. It is often, probably by the fault of the copyists, confounded with Patna, which is better known.

BOOK IV.

A. H. 935, A. D. 1529. End of February.

Behár at the head of a few troops, rapidly made himself master of the town of that name, and of the greater part of the province, and was proclaimed King. He soon found himself at the head of a large army, amounting, according to the reports brought to Báber, of no less than a hundred thousand men. Shír Khan, who saw the tide strongly running in Mahmúd's favour, however willing he might have been to maintain his own pretensions, saw that he did not possess the means of stemming the torrent, waited upon Sultan Mahmúd and acknowledged him. The territories of Behár were parcelled out by the Sultan among the leaders of the insurrection, little probably beyond his own jágír being left to Shír Khan; but, at the same time, the Sultan granted him a written agreement, by which he stipulated that, as soon as he was in possession of Juánpúr, he would resign Behár to Shír Khan, in full dominion.*

Is expelled by Báber;

Sultan Mahmúd Lodi, having sent Baban and Bayezíd across the Ganges to the province of Sirwar, with a strong army, himself advanced up the river and laid siege to Chunár; while Shír Khan crossed over and occupied Benáres. The advance of Báber, from Agra, soon put an end to the hopes of Mahmúd. On his approach, Benáres was hastily abandoned, and the siege of Chunár raised. Sultan Mahmúd retreated in confusion towards the Són, his army broke up, and he was soon after obliged to pass to the left bank of the Ganges, where he too, like his rival Jilál-ed-dín Loháni, sought refuge with the army of Bengal. Upon this dispersion, Shír Khan sent to Báber his submission, which was accepted; and Jelál-ed-dín Loháni, making his escape from the Bengal army, where he felt himself a prisoner, also submitted. Báber, as we have seen, defeated the army of Bengal, as well as that of Baban and Bayezíd, who were pursued across the Ganges and Jamna, into

* Báber's Mem. p. 405.

the territory of Bandelkand, whence, at a future time, they once more entered Behár. Báber assigned a jágír to Jilál-ed-dín Loháni, the late sovereign of Behár, and made provision for several thousands of the Loháni troops, who had followed that prince's fortune.

CHAP. IV. SECT. I.

who occupies Behár.

At the conclusion of the campaign, the Emperor returned to Agra, leaving Muhammed Zemán Mírza governor of Juánpúr, and entrusting the government of Chunár and other districts of Behár to Sultan Juneid Birlás, the governor of Karra-Mánikpúr, under whom Táj Khan Sarangkhani had the immediate command in that fortress. Báber did not visit the eastern provinces for the two last years of his life. Shír Khan, being now a dependent on the empire, seems to have been left in full possession of his jágír. The country, after so many wars and revolutions, was in a very distracted state.*

Shír Khan extends his jágírs and power;

This interval, and the confusion that prevailed over all the eastern provinces, afforded Shír Khan a favourable opportunity of extending his influence, his reputation with his tribe, and even his territories.† Nor did he neglect it. Among other important acquisitions, he became master of Chunár, about the end of Báber's reign, or the beginning of that of Humáyun.‡ That celebrated fort lies on the banks of the Ganges, above Benáres; and, from its strength and position, commands the country around, and especially the course of the river. It had been held under the late Sultan Ibráhím Lodi, by Táj Khan §, who afterwards continued to hold it in Báber's name. Táj Khan was much under the influence of his wife, Lád Malek, a high-spirited lady,

acquires Chunár.

* Báber's Memoirs, pp. 405—432.

† Ibid. p. 407.

‡ Stewart, Hist. of Bengal, p. 120., makes the event take place A. H. 943; but this date is much too late. From many authorities it appears that it was in Shír Khan's possession as early as A. H. 937.

§ Táj-Khan was the son of Jilál-Khan Sarangkhani, one of Sultan Ibráhím Lodi's great Amírs.

BOOK IV. of Túrkomán extraction, of great beauty and accomplishments, who, though childless, entirely possessed his affection. This inevitably excited the jealousy and hatred of his other wives, whose sons resolved to put her to death. One of them, the eldest, assaulted her one night with a sword; but the wounds which he inflicted were not mortal, though the cry spread over the harem that they were murdering Lád Malek. On hearing the alarm, Táj Khan, with a naked sword in his hand, hastened to attack the assassin, who, seeing that he could not escape from his father, turned upon him, and laid him dead upon the spot. As all Táj Khan's sons, except the murderer, were too young to be able to conduct the government, Lád Malek, who had the affection of the garrison, became mistress of the fort; and by her address induced the chiefs and zemindars of the districts subject to Chunár to acquiesce in her assuming the management of the whole jágír. Shír Khan, who was not far off, finding how matters stood, entered into an understanding with Mír Ahmed Túrkomán, Lád Malek's uncle, seized and confined the delinquent, who had fled into his territory, and, after some negotiation, it was arranged that he should marry Lád Malek, which he did; and by that means gained possession of the valuable country of Chunár, with the fort, which is the key of that part of the province, with all the treasures that had been accumulated in it, as a place of safety.*

Sultan Mahmúd renews his pretensions. A. H. 937, A. D. 1531.

In spite of his late discomfiture, Sultan Mahmúd Lodi, soon after the death of Báber, had found means to collect another army of Afgháns, and resolved to march against Juánpúr. He summoned Shír Khan, who still in secret professed attachment to his cause,

* Akbernáma, f. 35.; Tabak. Akb. f. 173., followed by Ferishta, ii. p. 110.; Tar. Niz. f. 212.; Nisábnáma-e Afgh. f. 86.; Kholáset-al-Tow. f. 274.; Kháfi Khan, ff. 33, 34. A statement of the treasures found in Chunár is given in the Nisábnáma, f. 87.

to join his army. Shír Khan was in reality little disposed to render him any active assistance, and made so many delays that Sultan Mahmúd, by the advice of his Amírs, who were not unaware of his character and views, contrived, in marching for Juánpúr, to take his route through Shír Khan's jágír of Sahsarám. This quickened the lukewarm diligence of the crafty Afghán, who, as the Sultan approached, came out to receive him with every mark of honour, gave him a splendid reception, and joined him in prosecuting the campaign. On the approach of the Afghán army, the troops of Humáyun, under Sultan Juneid Birlás, abandoned Juánpúr *; and Sultan Mahmúd was soon master of the country, as far as Karra-Mánikpúr and Laknau.

CHAP. IV. SECT. I.

Is joined by Shír Khan.

Humáyun was at that time, as we have seen, occupied with the siege of Kalinjer, which, on hearing of the irruption of the army of Behár into his territory, he raised, and marched straight to meet them. On hearing of his approach, Sultan Mahmúd concentrated his force. When the two armies were encamped, facing each other, and ready to engage, Shír Khan, offended that Baban Khan Jilwáni†, and Bayezíd Khan Fermuli, two old and distinguished leaders of the Afgháns, had been preferred to him in the command of the army, to which he aspired, sent a secret message to Mír Hindu Beg Kochín, a veteran Moghul chief, who was at this time Humáyun's Amír-ul-omra and commander-in-chief, to assure him that he continued a hearty friend to the house of his patron, Báber, which he would prove by his deeds; and proposed that, when the two armies were engaged, he should draw off his own division and retreat, so that the defeat of the pretender would be certain. Accordingly, in the battle that ensued, while the two armies were engaged, he retreated with all his troops. A general panic

Advance of Humáyun.

Treachery of Shír Khan, and dispersion of the Afghán force.

* Tab. Akb. ff. 173—174.; Tar. Niz. f. 212.; Ferishta; Nisábnáma, f. 87.

† The Nisábnáma calls Baban, "valad Ata Lodi," f. 88.

BOOK IV. ensued. Sultan Mahmúd was entirely defeated, with the loss of his whole camp and of the symbols of sovereignty. He fled to Patna,* disgusted with the world, and believing that he was persecuted by fate, renounced public life, gave himself up to devotion, and some years after†, died in Orissa.

Shír Khan retains Chunár and his jágírs.

Humáyun, after this victory, having replaced his governors, hastened back to Agra. Hindu Beg was sent to receive possession of Chunár, and to garrison the castle with imperial troops. But Shír Khan's purpose had been served, and he delayed from time to time, under various pretexts, to surrender the place; so that, in the end, Hindu Beg returned to court, without having effected his object.

A. H. 938, A. D. 1532.

We have already seen that, in the following year, the Emperor, determined to break the power of Shír Khan and of the Afgháns in Behár, laid siege to Chunár; but that, being called away by the rapid progress of Behåder Shah in the west, he found himself obliged to enter into an agreement with Shír Khan, by which he allowed him to retain Chunár and his other territories.‡

And consolidates his resources.

For nearly five years after this period, the disturbed state of the provinces on the Ganges, and the Emperor's absence from his dominions, while engaged in the conquest of Malwa and Gujrát, left Shír Khan an invaluable opportunity, which he did not neglect, for extending his dominions and his power. It is said that when Behåder Shah, the king of Gujrát, found himself hard pressed by the powerful invasion of the Emperor, anxious to create a diversion that might draw off the whole or a part of his troops, he sent envoys to Shír Khan with large sums of money, to induce him to

* The Tar. Niz. f. 213. calls it *Bateh*; Tar. Bed. f. 147. *Tehiat*.

† According to Ferishta, he died that same year; the Tar. Niz. f. 213. places his death in A. H. 949; so does the Tar. Bedáuni, f. 147. The Kholás. al-Tow. f. 275. places it in A. H. 945. The Nisábnáma in A. H. 944.

‡ Tabak. Akb. ff. 173, 174.; Akbernáma, f. 42.; Ferishta, vol. ii. pp. 110—113.; Nisábnáma Afgh. ff. 88, 89.; Kháfi Khan, f. 35.

march to his assistance. Shír Khan, it is said, having got the treasure into his hands, pretending that his difficulties at home prevented his marching to a distance, proceeded to accomplish his own plans of aggrandisement, and left Behâder to his fate. CHAP. IV. SECT. I.

Shír Khan's success was much assisted by the revolt of Muhammed Sultan Mírza and his sons, on the side of Laknau and Juánpúr, which threw that portion of the eastern provinces into confusion. He profited by this occurrence to make excursions into the provinces north of the river, and to seize immense booty, not probably paying any very scrupulous attention to the rights or interests of either of the contending parties. While returning from one of these predatory inroads to the north of the Ganges, he found means to come unexpectedly on Ulugh Mírza, Muhammed Sultan's son, who was then lying on the Siru or Gogra, defeated him by a stratagem, and, turning round, plundered Benáres. Plunders to the north of the Ganges. A. H. 941, A. D. 1535. A. H. 942.

Enriched and emboldened by this success, he soon after turned his arms against the Sultan of Bengal. Having marched across Behár with a large force, he reduced Patna * and the neighbouring territory, which Takes possession of Southern Behár.

* At this period, when going with some friends through the bazaar of Patna, a religious mendicant, who was sitting in a corner silent and buried in meditation, suddenly burst out, as if inspired, exclaiming, "Behold the king of Delhi walking on foot." Shír Khan accepted the omen, which was the stronger, as the man was regarded as a simpleton; took his handkerchief, tied a knot in the corner of it to hold firm the response, and resolved, to follow his fortune up to the throne itself. Nisábn. f. 89. This anecdote might have been published to influence his followers, but one recorded by Abulfazl in the Akbernáma, and which occurred soon after, serves to illustrate not only the habits of thinking of the time, but of the individual. When Shír Khan entered Bengal, being desirous of knowing what was to be the event of his enterprise, he invited to his court a famous astrologer, who was then with the Raja of Orissa, informing him that, as he had strange notions and unusual plans in his head, he wished for his presence that he might have the benefit of his skill. The Raja, who, like some European princes not long before, kept his astrologer shut up as a kind of state-prisoner, refused to let him go. The astrologer, however, wrote to Shír Khan, that for a year to come he would not be completely master of Bengal, but

BOOK IV. A.D. 1537.

had for some time been occupied by that potentate. Not content with this, he proceeded downwards to the farthest limits of Southern Behár, and at Surajpúr, above Mongeir, engaged and defeated the Bengal army, and improving this advantage, took possession of the whole country. His ambition and his success did not stop short here; he entered the kingdom of Bengal itself. That country had not been free from the convulsions that had afflicted the kingdoms around. On the death of Nasret Shah, which happened some time before this invasion, he was succeeded by his son Firúz Shah, who, after a short reign of three months, was murdered by his uncle Sultan Mahmúd Shah. Against this prince, Shír Khan now carried on a successful warfare, defeated him in several actions, driving him before him, and at last shut him up in his magnificent capital of Gour, to which he laid siege. An insurrection of some zemindars of Behár called off Shír Khan for a time, but the siege was conducted in his absence by Jilál Khan, his son, under the guidance of Khowás Khan, the ablest of his generals.*

A. H. 943. And invades Bengal.

that he would become so on a date which he mentioned; and that, moreover, on that very day the river Ganges would be fordable for one hour; and, says Abulfazl, himself an adept in astrology, as he predicted, so it happened.

* Akbernáma, ff. 42, 43.; Ferishta, vol. ii. pp. 109—113.; vol. iv. p. 350. Stewart's Hist. of Bengal, p. 118. The exact time of the death of Nasret (or Nasíb) Shah is uncertain. Ferishta, in the Hist. of Bengal, vol. iv. p. 352., tells us that he never could ascertain whether Nasíb died a natural death, or was murdered; but that he died A. H. 945, after a reign of eighteen years. In this there is some mistake. His predecessor, Alá-ed-dín, is stated to have died A. H. 930 (vol. iv. p. 350.), so that, if Nasíb died in A. H. 945, his reign was only of fifteen years. In Ferishta, General History, vol. ii. pp. 108, 109—113., the actions elsewhere ascribed to Nasíb in the last part of his reign, are given to Mahmúd in the early part of his. Stewart, Hist. of Bengal, p. 117., says that Nasret was murdered A. H. 940, after a reign of thirteen years, though some historians, he thinks inaccurately, make him die A. H. 943, after a reign of sixteen years. Abulfazl (Akbernáma, f. 43. v.) calls the king of Bengal defeated by Shír Khan, Nasíb Shah. The second siege of Chunár occurred in A. H. 945. It is possible that Nasíb may have died during the siege of Gour, which was in the same year; though not

The report of these rapid successes had alarmed Humáyun, during his residence in Gujrát and Malwa; and now, after his return to Agra, made him march with his grand army to re-establish his authority in Behár. The events that followed, it is now time to detail.

CHAP. IV. SECT. I.

A. H. 944, A. D. 1537.

probable, as Stewart makes Mahmúd die in A. H. 945, the same year, which would allow only a few months for his reign. I should be inclined to fix upon the early part of A. H. 943 as the time of his death.

# CHAPTER IV.

## AFFAIRS OF BENGAL.

---

## SECTION II.

### CONQUEST AND LOSS OF BENGAL BY HUMÁYUN.

HUMÁYUN AT AGRA.—PREPARES TO ATTACK SHÍR KHAN.—LAYS SIEGE TO CHUNÁR; WHICH SURRENDERS, AFTER SIX MONTHS.—SHÍR KHAN IN BENGAL.—HUMÁYUN ADVANCES TO BENÁRES.—CAPTURE OF GOUR, AND REDUCTION OF BENGAL AND BEHÁR, BY SHÍR KHAN. —HUMÁYUN SUMMONS HIM TO SUBMIT; HE REFUSES.—HUMÁYUN TRAVERSES BEHÁR, AND APPROACHES THE TERIA-GARHI PASS.—PLANS OF SHÍR KHAN.—SURPRISE AND ROUT OF THE IMPERIAL ADVANCED GUARD.—RETREAT OF THE ENEMY.—SHÍR KHAN GAINS RHOTAS BY TREACHERY.—HUMÁYUN ENTERS BENGAL, OCCUPIES GOUR, AND SUBDUES THE WHOLE PROVINCE.—INDOLENCE OF THE EMPEROR, AND COURT.—SHÍR KHAN RE-OCCUPIES BEHÁR, AND THE PASSES.—LAYS SIEGE TO JUÁNPÚR AND CHUNÁR.—REVOLT OF HINDAL MÍRZA, AT AGRA.—HUMÁYUN RETREATS FROM BENGAL; HIS DANGEROUS SITUATION.—MÍRZA ASKERI FORCES THE PASSES INTO BEHÁR.—SHÍR KHAN PROCLAIMED KING.—THE TWO ARMIES APPROACH.—SHÍR SHAH'S TACTICS; OPERATIONS AT CHONSA.—DISTRESS OF THE IMPERIAL ARMY.—REBELLIONS IN HINDUSTAN.—TREASONABLE CONDUCT AND VACILLATIONS OF HINDAL MÍRZA.—HE ATTACKS DELHI.—KÁMRÁN MÍRZA CALLED IN TO RELIEVE IT. —HINDAL RETREATS TO AGRA.—KÁMRÁN ALSO REVOLTS.—PURSUES HINDAL, AND RECEIVES HIS SUBMISSION.—MARCHES AGAINST SHÍR SHAH; BUT RETURNS WITHOUT FIGHTING.—CONTINUED DISTRESS OF HUMÁYUN AT CHONSA.—HE SENDS AN ENVOY TO SHÍR SHAH; NEGOTIATIONS AND ARMISTICE.—NEGLIGENCE OF HUMÁYUN.—ATTACK BY SHÍR SHAH.—SLAUGHTER OF THE IMPERIALISTS.—DANGER AND WOUND OF HUMÁYUN.—HIS ARMY ANNIHILATED.—PROCEEDINGS OF SHÍR SHAH.—HUMÁYUN MAKES HIS WAY TO AGRA. —SHÍR SHAH SUPREME ON THE LOWER GANGES.

BOOK IV.

A.D. 1537.

THOUGH Humáyun's return to Agra had been hurried

on by the reports that had reached him of the alarming progress of Shír Khan in Bengal, and by the recent death of Sultan Juneíd Birlás, which had added still farther to the disturbed state of the eastern provinces; he, however, wasted a twelvemonth, after his arrival in the capital, in pleasure and inactivity, before he seriously resolved on taking the field. The first wish of his heart was to have again marched into Málwa and Gujrát, and to have retrieved his affairs in these provinces. Burhán Nizám Shah, of Ahmednagar, who was assailed by his neighbours in the Dekkan, as well as from Gujrát, sent an embassy, offering to assist Humáyun in a new invasion of that country.* But the danger from Shír Khan's unexpected progress drew off the Emperor in another direction. Sensible, at last, of the danger of any farther delay in seeking out and combating his indefatigable enemy, he made every preparation for an active campaign. He despatched his Amírs to their different jágírs to expedite the march of their contingents, while he committed the government of the principal provinces of the crown to his most eminent nobles. Delhi, he entrusted to Mír Fakr Ali; Agra, to Mír Muhammed Bakhshi; Kalpi, to Yádgár Násir Mírza, his cousin and brother-in-law; and Kanáuj, and the adjoining country, to Núr-ed-dín Muhammed Mírza, who also had married a daughter of Báber. Having concentrated the whole moveable force that he could command, the Emperor set out, and proceeded down the Jamna, sometimes by land, sometimes by water, accompanied by his brothers, Askeri and Hindal, and taking with him a part of his harem. On the way, Muhammed Zemán Mírza, whose pardon had been negotiated by his wife, a sister of Humáyun's, met him, with a body of troops, who still accompanied him, after all his elevations and misfortunes, and was honourably

CHAP. IV. SECT. II.

Humáyun at Agra.

A. H. 944. A. D. 1537.

Prepares to attack Shír Khan.

Sefer 8. July 17.

* Briggs's Ferishta, vol. iii. pp. 228, 229.

BOOK IV. A.D. 1537-8.

received. Chunár was the first object of the campaign. Shír Khan, being still absent in Bengal, the moment was regarded as favourable for an attack. Before the army reached Chunár, Kutb Khan, his second son, whom he had left in charge of it, retired * to the neighbouring hills of Bharkanda, to observe and harass the besiegers from without, leaving Gházi Khan Súr†, the father of the future king, Ibráhím Shah Súr, to conduct the defence within.

Lays siege to Chunár.

The place was strong, well provided with stores and ammunition, and defended by a brave and numerous garrison. In spite of every effort on the part of the assailants, little progress was made. Rúmi Khan, Beháder Shah's celebrated engineer, who had left him after the disastrous discomfiture of Mandsúr, was now Humáyun's Mír-Atesh, or Grand-Master of Ordnance, and directed the operations of the siege. When it had lasted several months‡, seeing that his battering guns

* According to Jouher, this was on the Sheb-e-Berát, 16 Shábán, which would be the 18 Jan. A. D. 1538. Six months, between Agra and Chunár, is a long time.

† Bedáuni, f. 141., says that it was Jilál-Khan, and that he retired in a boat during the siege.

‡ Rúmi Khan, when he found that his batteries did not produce the desired effect, and desirous to ascertain on what part of the fortifications an impression could most successfully be made, is said by Jouher to have resorted to an artifice not altogether singular in barbarous warfare. Having caused a faithful and intelligent Abyssinian slave, with whom he had a perfect understanding, to be severely flogged, the slave made his escape by night, and found admittance into the fort. There, with imprecations against the injustice and cruelty of his master, he exhibited his limbs still flagrant from the scourge, explained with truth in whose service he had been; spoke of the skill, as an engineer, that he had gained under so able a teacher; and professed his readiness, in revenge of the injurious treatment he had received, to point out the spots, from which the camp of the besiegers could be most effectually annoyed. To evince at once his skill and his sincerity, he showed some defects in the fortifications that required to be remedied. The officers who had charge of the defences, the better to avail themselves of his remarks, carried him to the most important parts of the works, on which he silently made his observations; and, having gained his object, in the course of a few days he found means to escape and return to the camp, where he communicated his remarks to his master, who acted upon them in his future operations. Jouher, c. 3.

did not make the impression which he expected, he made a more scrutinising survey; and, having discovered that the defences were weakest on the side of the river, besides running some works to cut off the communication of the garrison with the country, and a mine or two on the land side, in furtherance of his previous operations, Rúmi Khan constructed a battery near the Ganges, in which he placed a huge piece of cannon, to bear on the walls by the river side. But soon, finding that, from its distance and position, it did not produce the desired effect, he resolved to attack the river face directly, where the works were weakest. For this purpose he constructed a large platform upon boats in the river, on which he raised a battery, surmounted by a high tower that overtopped the fortifications. This floating battery he moved across the river by night, and anchored close to the fort. This movement was supported by a general attack on every side. A furious cannonade ensued, and soon threw down a portion of the wall, by which the besiegers attempted to enter*; but so well did the garrison defend themselves, that seven hundred of the assailants were killed, and the floating battery was half-destroyed by the shot. Next morning, artificers were set to work to repair the battery for a fresh attack, when such of the garrison as had not already escaped, seeing that the Emperor was resolved to take the place at any expense, and that there was no prospect of relief, capitulated on condition that their lives should be spared. After the surrender, Moveiid Beg Duldi, a favourite of Humáyun's, under pretence of an order from the Emperor, caused the hands of three hundred artillerymen to be struck off; a breach of faith for which, on the indignant complaint of Rúmi Khan, he was sharply rebuked by Humáyun. The command of the place was conferred

**Which surrenders after six months.**

* Jouher says that no breach was made.

BOOK IV.

A.D. 1538.

on Rúmi Khan, who held it but a few days, when he died, it was strongly suspected of poison administered by some of the nobles with whom he was unpopular. He was succeeded in the government of Chunár by Beg Mírak, whom he had pointed out as most fit for the office.*

Shír Khan in Bengal.

The six months during which Humáyun was detained by the siege of Chunár afforded a most valuable breathing time for Shír Khan, who employed it in the reduction of Bengal, and especially in pushing on the siege of Gour, where his troops were directed, sometimes by himself, and sometimes by his son, Jilál Khan, and his great general, Khowás Khan, the son of the late Malek Saka.

Humáyun advances to Benáres.

After the fall of Chunár, the Emperor moved down to Benáres, where he learned that Shír Khan was actively occupied in the siege of Gour, and had the prospect of being soon master of the whole kingdom. On this, he resolved to prosecute his march into Bengal, that he might check his progress, and had reached the river Són, when news arrived that Gour had fallen.

Capture of Gour, and reduction of Bengal and Behár by Shír Khan.

It appears that after a siege of many months, a scarcity of food began to prevail in the city, upon which the king, Syed Mahmúd Shah, seeing no hopes of successful resistance, and that the place must soon fall, effected his escape in a swift rowing boat, and reached Hájípúr. He was afterwards pursued and attacked by a party of Shír Khan's troops, his followers dispersed,

* Jouher's Mem. c. 3.; Akbernáma, f. 43.; Tabakát-e Akberi, ff. 149, 150. 175.; Tar. Niz. f. 213.; Ferishta, vol. ii. pp. 83, 84. 113.; Nisábnáma, f. 89.; Kháfi Khan, f. 45. The Tabakát, f. 150., says that the artillerymen were mutilated *bahukm* (q. *bihukm*) *Ashraf*, and that their left hand was cut off. Abulfazl seems to extend this to all the garrison of two thousand. The Tab. Akberi, f. 175.; Tar. Niz. f. 213. call Rúmi's successor, Dost Beg, as does the Nisábnáma. Ferishta, following the Tabakát, makes the siege last six months (vol. ii. p. 114.) as does the Nisábnáma. Jouher allows six months for the construction of the floating battery and tower. There is a good deal of diversity in the various accounts of the siege, which it is needless to attempt to reconcile.

and himself wounded; so that he was soon after compelled entirely to abandon his kingdom, and to seek refuge in the camp of the Emperor.* Shír Khan, after his victory, hastened back to Gour, which fell into his hands; and the greater part of the dependent provinces of Bengal and Behár followed the fate of the capital.

CHAP. IV. SECT. II.

Humáyun calls upon him to submit,

This intelligence induced Humáyun to follow a more vigorous plan of operations. He saw the necessity of preventing the Afghán from having time to confirm his power in the wealthy and populous kingdom of Bengal. He therefore despatched an envoy to Shír Khan, commanding him, without delay, to resign to him the throne, the umbrella, and other ensigns of royalty, with the royal treasures which had fallen into his hands; and, at the same time, to surrender all the territory that he had recently seized; offering to assign to him, in jágír, the fort of Chunár, the city of Juánpúr, or any other place that he might choose. Shír Khan received the message with every mark of deference, but declined the offer, saying that the conquest of Bengal had been achieved by years of toil, and the lives of many of his bravest followers, and that he was therefore by no means disposed to part with what had cost him so much. The envoy, who was detained some time in Shír Khan's camp, on his return, besides reporting as to his mission, informed the Emperor that the Khan had already set out on his way from Ghour to Rhotas and the hill country, carrying with him the immense treasure that he had taken, and which he intended to secure in the fastnesses among the hills.

which he declines.

Humáyun traverses Behár.

Meanwhile Humáyun, leaving Mír Hindu Beg Kochín, his Amír-al-omra, as governor of Juánpúr, with directions for the general management of affairs in that

* Mahmúd, in his distress, made application for assistance to Nuño d'Acuña, the Portuguese Governor-General of India, who sent nine ships, but they did not arrive till the town was taken. Hist. Faria de Souza, quoted by Stewart, Hist. of Bengal, p. 121.

BOOK IV. A.D. 1538. A. H. 945.

quarter, marched forward for Bengal. At Moníah, a small town between Arra and Dinapúr, near the confluence of the Són with the Ganges, he was met by Syed Mahmúd Shah*, the expelled king of Bengal, who was still suffering severely from his wounds. As the rainy season had now commenced, many of the Emperor's officers were of opinion that it would be better to suspend operations till its close, since the movement of troops, especially of cavalry, must be attended with extreme difficulty during that season in the low country of Bengal. But Mahmúd Shah contended, that the earliest moment was the best; that Shír Khan was still unconfirmed in the possession of the country, and, if attacked without delay, could easily be expelled. He added, that there was no danger of suffering from want of supplies, as was apprehended by some, since there were granaries in Bengal adequate to the support of many armies. Humáyun, persuaded by these reasons, in which there was great weight, and dazzled with the prospect of conquering another kingdom to make up for those he had lost, willingly adopted the views of the exiled monarch.

Approaches the Teria-garhi pass.

The army continued its march, and before it had quitted the territory of Mongeir, information arrived that Jilál Khan, Shír Khan's second son, and Khowás Khan, his ablest general, had occupied the narrow defile near the village of Teria-garhi†,—the grand pass that leads from Behár to Bengal,—and fortified a strong position in the heart of it, for the purpose of checking the advance of the imperial army. On reaching Bhágilpúr, between the town of Mongeir and the pass, Mírza Hindal was detached across the river‡, with a

* The Akbernáma and Tar. Bed. f. 141. call him Nasíb Shah, which must be erroneous.

† Tiliagulley. Rennell.

‡ Jouher, c. 4., speaks of Hindal, and Yádgár Násir Mírza's being sent back from the Són, to look after Agra and Delhi. The Tabakát-e Akberi and Tar. Bedáuni say that Hindal Mírza was sent from Mongeir to Agra, to check and chastise Muhammed Sultan Mírza, and his sons,

body of five or six thousand men, to act on the opposite bank; and, soon after, Jehángír-Kuli Beg and Biram Khan, with a detachment of about the same strength, were sent forward to clear the road by the Teria-garhi and Sikria-garhi pass. CHAP. IV. SECT. II.

The defile which Shír Khan had ordered his son to occupy, is the long and narrow passage lying between the Ganges and the termination of the Rájamahl hills, where, on the east-side, the narrow space is, for some distance, washed by that river. The ground on the west rises abruptly into the Rájamahl hills *, here precipitous, and rendered impassable by jungle and thorny shrubs. It is the great natural highway through the hills from Behár into Bengal. Shír Khan, seeing no probability of defending Bengal against the formidable army commanded by the Emperor, by resistance in the open field, had given his son a body of about fifteen thousand men, with instructions to defend the upper, or Teria-garhi, pass as long as he safely could, but charging him on no account to involve himself in offensive opperations, and, as soon as the main body of the enemy's army approached, and it was known that he, Shír Khan, had reached Shírpúr, to abandon his ground, and hasten by forced marches to join him.

Plans of Shír Khan.

Shír Khan's plan of operations was to allow Humáyun's army to take possession of Bengal; to move by the road of the hill-country of Jharkend †, towards Rhotas, and secure his treasure and spoil in the difficult recesses of the hills, or in that fort, if he could have access to it; and then to operate on the Emperor's rear

Ulugh and Shah Mírza, who had fled at Humáyun's approach, and were still exciting commotions. Ferishta, v. ii. p. 85., agrees that Hindal was sent to suppress the revolt of Muhammed Sultan Mírza, at Kanáuj. Abulfazl, Akbernáma, f. 43. v., merely makes him sent across the Ganges with five or six thousand men, to co-operate with the grand army.

* See Rennell's Atlas of Bengal, Plate, No. 15.

† Jharkend and Bharkend.

BOOK IV.

A. D. 1538.

and communications as he advanced into Bengal, seizing upon Behár behind him, and cutting off all intercourse with his dominions, both in the north and west.

Surprise and rout of the Imperial advanced guard.

When the imperial detachment, under Jehángír-Kuli, approached the défile, they found it strongly fortified. This forced them to halt, in order to examine if the enemy could be dislodged by an attack, or if any other practicable pass could be found, by which their position could be turned, and they taken in the rear. Jilál Khan, seeing the imperial troops encamped so near, and learning that they lay carelessly on their ground, less occupied with securing their own camp than with devising means for assailing their opponents, seized the favourable opportunity for cutting them off, fell upon them by surprise with great fury, wounded Jehángír-Kuli himself, and put numbers to the sword. The detachment was saved chiefly by the valour and conduct of Biram Khan, who had a command in it. Collecting some of his troops, he attempted by his gallant resistance to give the imperialists time to rally. But, though he made several desperate charges, and even broke through the enemy, yet, as Jehángir's force had been pushed greatly too much in advance, and was consequently left unsupported*, they were overborne by superior numbers; and, unable to recover their ground, were compelled to fall back on the grand army at Kohlgám, between Bhágilpúr † and the pass. Many officers of rank fell in this affair. A violent storm which sank the Emperor's barge at the moorings, attended by a heavy fall of rain,

* Jouher, c. 3., makes no mention of any sally, but represents them as being overpowered, while on their march in the narrow defile, by Jilál Khan's men, who were placed in ambush in the overhanging heights.

† The Colgong and Bogilpoor of Rennell. Jouher calls it Kahlgram. One account makes the Emperor here allow his brother Hindal to proceed to the provinces of Tírhut and Purnía, which were given him in jágír, with directions to settle them, and return with stores and necessaries for the expedition.

which flooded the surrounding country, prevented the Emperor from moving on for several days after. When he was able, however, to send forward reconnoitring parties to examine the passes, it was found that the Afghâns, who had received notice that Shír Khan with his whole plunder and artillery had reached Rhotas, having thus attained their object, had already abandoned their works and retreated.* CHAP. IV. SECT. II. Retreat of the enemy.

It was at this moment of danger that Shir Khan succeeded in gaining possession of the hill-fort of Rhotas. Having lost Chunár, to which he had formerly trusted as a secure retreat for his family and his treasures, he had now no commanding fortress in which he could deposit them in the moment of need. His own country was overrun, and he found it necessary to withdraw his troops from the open country of Bengal. In such circumstances, the possession of Rhotas would be of unspeakable advantage to him. It lies high up, in a strong country, on the upper course of the Són; was reckoned impregnable; and had never submitted to the Kings of Delhi. It would not only be a place of security for his family and treasure, but a most important military post in the warfare he anticipated. With caution and secrecy he proposed to the Raja, Hari Kishen Birkís†, to be allowed, in this pressing exigency, to send his harem and family, with his treasure and a few attendants, into the fort, as a place in which they might be safe from all the accidents of war. This was at first refused. But Shír Khan employed an able agent, who gained the Raja's favourite wife and his minister by rich presents, and who represented to the Raja, that, Shír Khan gains Rhotas by treachery.

* Akbernáma, f. 43.; Tabakát-e Akberi, f. 150.; Tar. Bedáuni, f. 141.

† Abulfazl calls the Raja, Chintáman. Akbern., f. 43.; the Kholáset-ul-Towárikh, f. 275., describes him as Raja Chintáman, a Brahman. The Nisábnáma, apparently on good authority, makes Chintáman a Brahman and the Rajah's minister.

BOOK IV. A. D. 1538.

in the doubtful enterprises in which Shír Khan was engaged, it would be an unspeakable relief to his mind to know, that, even should he be deprived of life, his harem and his honour would be safe; and that his wealth, such as it was, the treasures and the plunder of Bengal, instead of falling into the hands of his inveterate enemies, would enrich a friend who had ever been faithful to him. And the Raja, thus strongly urged, whatever were his motives, whether friendship or avarice, was finally persuaded to comply with Shír Khan's request.

The plan said to have been adopted by him was not altogether novel, and was founded on the severe and jealous delicacy with which, in the East, women of rank are treated. A thousand dolis *, or covered litters, were provided, in each of which was placed a chosen Afghán warrior, in armour, and sent up to the fort. In some of the first, ladies were seated, to cover the deceit; in others were arms. When the persons in charge of the gates stopped the dolies at the head of the procession, and began examining them, Shír Khan despatched a messenger to the Raja, to remonstrate with him on the unspeakable disgrace he would incur, were his females exposed to view; and the Raja sent orders to let them pass without examination. As soon as all the dolis were within the fort, the armed men issued from them; the bearers and attendants supplied themselves with arms from the dolis; one party advanced to seize the palace, another took possession of the gates, and admitted Shír Khan and his troops. Hari Kishen effected his escape by a private passage. "Thus," says Ferishta, "fell one of the strongest fortresses in the world into the hands of Shír Khan, together with much treasure, that had been accumulated for ages. Although the author, Muhammed Kásim Ferishta, has

* The authorities differ as to the number of the dolis, as well as in many other particulars, making them 300, 1000, and 1200.

seen many hill-forts in India, he has seen none to compare with that of Rhotas. It is situated on a table-land, on the top of a mountain more than five kos (seven miles) square. It has only one entrance, by a very narrow road, along a steep ascent of two miles from the foot of the hill to the gates; and water is found everywhere in abundance, by digging a few feet below the surface." *

Humáyun enters Bengal, and occupies Gour;

As soon as Humáyun found that the passes were clear, he left Kohlgám, and continued his march into Bengal. At the same time he allowed his brother Hindal, at his own request, to proceed to the provinces of Tírhut and Purnía, which he had given him in jágír, enjoining him to bring from thence to Bengal such stores and necessaries as might assist the invasion. In the course of a few days, Humáyum took possession of Gour, the capital of Bengal, which, as well as the neighbouring country, he found wasted and ruined by the ravages of war, and the inhabitants in extreme misery and wretchedness. In Gour†, dead bodies were still lying everywhere in the streets and bazars, which were covered with rubbish. These marks of war and desolation were soon removed. Humáyun met with little opposition in completing the conquest of the whole province, which submitted to him in the course of the year, and, with the restoration of order, it was speedily restored to comparative prosperity.

and subdues the whole province.

* Briggs's Ferishta, vol. ii. pp. 114, 115. See Tabak. Akb. f. 175.; Tar. Niz. ff. 213, 214.; Abulfazl Akbern., f. 43.; Tar. Bedáuni, f. 141.; Nisábn. Afgh. f. 89.; Kholáset-ul-Tow. p. 275.; Jouher's Mem. c. 3.; Kháfi Khan, ff. 55, 56. There is some discrepancy as to the date of the taking of Rhotas. Jouher, who accompanied Humáyun on his expedition to Bengal, mentions his hearing of Shír Shah's being in Rhotas before he left Agra, and even makes the Emperor march against it, while Shír Shah was employed in Bengal. But his Memoirs were written from memory, at the distance of many years after the events, and, in this, as in several other instances, are probably erroneous.

† The old name of Gour was Laknouti; Humáyun, who was very partial to it, called it Jinnetábád (Paradise). After residing in it three months, he was forced to leave it, the troops finding it unhealthy.

BOOK IV.

A.D. 1538.

Indolence of the Emperor and Court.

Humáyun, thus far successful, was fully alive to all the enjoyments of his new situation. He soon portioned out the whole country into jágírs, which he divided among his principal officers. He was delighted with the fertility, and with all the novelties and luxuries of that rich province. Giving way to the habitual improvidence of his temper, he shut himself up in his private apartments, and resigned himself wholly to frivolous indulgences, and to idle pleasures. He was faithfully imitated by his court and his officers, who, in like manner, devoted themselves to jollity and sensual pursuits. Nothing was done to conciliate the inhabitants, to improve their condition, to strengthen the government, or to secure the possession of the new conquest.

Unsatisfactory state of his affairs.

Some time elapsed in this manner, while Humáyun and his court enjoyed themselves*, without thoughts of the past, and with little care about the future. By degrees, the intelligence from the north became less frequent. Hindal Mírza did not forward the expected convoys. On the contrary, news full of suspicion were brought; first, that without leave, and in spite of the rains which then prevailed, he had marched straight for Agra; and next, that he was comporting himself in a manner not consistent with his fidelity to his brother. Humáyun immediately despatched Sheihk Bhúl, to bring back the Mírza to his duty. Meanwhile, no reinforcements or supplies arrived from any quarter. The little news that did arrive became daily less; and gradually all routes of communication were completely blocked up. This state of things might have roused the most unthinking. But the inconveniences experienced were only negative; there was no positive and active annoyance pressing close at hand; and the victors thought-

* The length of Humáyun's residence in Bengal is not well defined. The Tar. Nizámi, f. 214., Tar. Akb. f. 175., Nisábnáma-e Afgh. f. 90., make him spend three months in Gour, in pleasure; as does the Tar. Bedáuni, f. 141. The Tab. Akb. allows six months for his residence in Bengal, in all; the original of Jouher, nine months.

lessly pursued their career of enjoyment. Such rumours of what was going on at a distance as reached Gour, being seldom of a favourable description, were carefully concealed from the Emperor by those about his person, as of too disagreeable a nature for royal ears; so that he was on the brink of a precipice, before he suspected that there was any danger.

Shír Khan re-occupies Behár and the passes.

At length news the most alarming, and which could no longer be concealed from the Emperor, arrived in rapid succession. It was discovered, that not only was Shír Khan in possession of the passes, but that the country through which they had recently marched was rapidly falling into his power. As long as Humáyun pursued his route through Behár, the Khan had shunned meeting him. He, for a moment, stopped his progress on the confines of Bengal, to gain time to remove his booty, from Gour and the conquered country, to the mountains of Jharkend, and to Rhotas, where he deposited it in safety. While the Emperor, having fairly passed the defiles, entered Bengal to the south of the hills on the one side, the Afghán descended from his mountain recesses into Behár on the other, and spread his forces once more to the north of the hills, where his own strength lay. He was speedily master of the whole province, and had occupied every road by which troops or couriers could pass down to Bengal, so that the Emperor was totally excluded from all co-operation, or even communication, with the rest of his dominions. Availing himself of the absence of the imperial army, he passed the Ganges, took the city of Benáres after a short siege, and slew the governor Mír Fazli, and seven hundred Chaghatáis. Thence he proceeded to Juánpúr, which he prepared to besiege. It was defended by Bába Beg Jiláir, who had succeeded to that command by the recent death of Hindu Beg. The governor had just been joined by Yúsef Beg from Oud, who had got so far with a body of five thousand men, that he was

Lays siege to Juánpúr,

BOOK IV. A. D. 1538.

attempting to carry to Bengal, to reinforce the Emperor. Yúsef Beg* joined the governor to assist in defending the place, and indulged his fondness for action in constant sallies and skirmishes. Jilál Khan, Shír Khan's eldest son, taking with him a few thousand men, succeeded in coming up with him while on one of these excursions near Juánpúr. Yúsef's officers advised an instant retreat, his numbers being far inferior to the Khan's. But, hurried on by the ardour of his courage, he engaged, was defeated and slain, and his troops dispersed. Next day, Jilál laid siege to Juánpúr. Shír Khan's joy at this victory, the first considerable one gained by his troops in the open field against the Emperor's, was very great. He regarded it as a happy omen and pledge of future success; observing in homely phrase, that a cock, when once soundly beaten, is not easily brought again to the scratch. Bába Beg made a brave and skilful defence of Juánpúr; and despatched expresses to the Emperor and the neighbouring governors of provinces, to ask assistance. Meanwhile, Shír Khan blockaded Chunár also. He seized the families of the principal zemíndárs of Behár and Juánpúr, as hostages, and sent them in custody to Rhotas. His army was now very strong, and his operations, planned and conducted with consummate sagacity, had in all quarters been crowned with success. No less alarming were the reports received, at the same time, from Agra, where Hindal Mírza had put to death Sheikh Bhúl, soon after his arrival; had thrown off his allegiance; had assumed all the ensigns of sovereignty; and caused himself to be proclaimed Emperor.†

*and Chunár.*

*Revolt of Hindal Mírza at Agra.*

* The Nisábnáma (f. 91.) asserts that Biram Khan, who had not then attained the rank he afterwards did, held a command in Yúsef Beg's army.

† Akbernáma, ff. 43, 44.; Tabakát Akb. f. 175.; Tar. Niz. f. 214.; Ferishta, v. ii. pp. 83, 84.; Jouher, c. 4.; Kháfi Khan, ff. 45—47.; Nisábnáma-e Afgh. ff. 89—91.; Taríkhe Reshídi, ff. 365, 366.; Tar. Bedáuni, ff. 141, 142.

CHAP. IV. SECT. II.

Humáyun retreats from Bengal.

For some time, Humáyun affected to treat the news as unfounded and impossible; but he soon found that it was no time to linger where he was. He summoned a council, to make arrangements, both for his return, and for leaving an adequate force to preserve his conquest. Some difficulty arising, as to a proper person to be entrusted with the future command of the province, Humáyun proposed to appoint Záhid Beg to be governor of Bengal; and to leave him behind, with a competent number of officers and troops, for the protection of the province. That nobleman had married the sister of Baiké Begum, one of the Emperor's favourite ladies, who had often importuned his Majesty to confer some appointment on him. The Beg, being present when the nomination was made, asked the Emperor, with some petulance, if his Majesty could find no place but Bengal, in which to make away with him. Humáyun, enraged at this unseasonable and insolent speech, vowed that he should put him to death. Záhid Beg, however, escaped from the Council, and sent a message to the Begum, entreating her to intercede for his pardon. This she did, but in vain. He was, therefore, obliged to fly privately from the camp, and, along with Háji Muhammed Koka and Zíndár Beg, two officers of distinction, succeeded in reaching the upper provinces. The government of Bengal was committed to Jehángír-Kuli Beg, a gallant veteran, who was left behind with a body of five thousand horse.

Humáyun, when about to retrace his steps, sent forward Khan Khánán Lodi with the advanced guard of the army, ordering him to occupy Mongeir in Behár, and to hold it till his arrival. He himself followed; but from the heavy rains, which rendered the roads deep and nearly impassable with mud*,

* This of the rains and mud deserves attention. For the months, see Tar. Niz. p. 214.

BOOK IV. A.D. 1538.

much of the baggage of the army was soon lost, many horses perished, and the troops began to endure great hardship. To add to their distress, before the Emperor had quitted Bengal, he learned that a strong body of Shír Khan's troops, under Khowás Khan, had destroyed the gates of Mongeir by fire, entered the town, and carried off Khan Khánán.*

His dangerous situation.

The danger was now more urgent than ever. The difficult straits that separate Bengal from Behár were still to be passed; the troops were worn out and dispirited, and numbers of them suffering from sickness. Humáyun, sending for Askeri Mírza, whose division was reckoned the most efficient in the army, offered to reward him to any extent, or, as he expressed himself, to grant any four demands he should make, provided he could extricate him from his present situation. Askeri called a meeting of his principal officers, and explained what had passed. They asked him, what boon he thought of requiring. His answer is a melancholy symptom of the degradation of the court and times of Humáyun. "It is my intention," said he, "to ask a round sum of money, a supply of the most costly manufactures of Bengal, some handsome slaves, and a few eunuchs." His officers, filled with surprise and indignation at his short-sighted selfishness, told him without hesitation, that the crisis was one of great difficulty and danger, from which nothing but their strenuous exertions could relieve him or the Emperor; that they would expect, therefore, to share in some reward proportioned to the extent of the benefit conferred; and proposed, that all of them should be raised to a higher military rank, should receive an increase of pay for their followers, and a large dona-

* Akbernáma, ff. 43, 44.; Tabakát-e Akberi, f. 175.; Tar. Niz. f. 214.; Jouher, c. 4. This Khan-Khánán was Diláwer-Khan, son of Doulat Khan. He had been made Khan-Khánán by Báber.. He died in prison in Shír Shah's reign.

tion in ready money for themselves. On these conditions they hoped to be able to extricate the army from its present distress. The Emperor complied with their demands, paid down the money, and added rich presents to gratify his mercenary warriors. Having received a reinforcement of the best troops in the camp, the Mírza advanced, made his way through the passes, and reached Kohlgám, where he halted. From that place he sent back to inform the Emperor of his success, and to communicate intelligence, the truth of which he had been able to ascertain. His report was, that Shír Khan was busy besieging both Chunár and Juánpúr; was in possession of Behár and the country as far as Kanáuj; had been encouraged by his success to declare his independence, by assuming the title of Shah, or King *; and was now collecting a large force at Rhotas.

Mírza Askeri forces the passes into Behár.

Shír Khan proclaimed King.

This intelligence seems to have induced the Emperor to march up the left bank of the Ganges, till he came opposite to Mongeir, where he found Askeri and the advance. Here Muhammed Zemán Mírza communicated undoubted information which he had procured, that Shír Khan was not far off, and was secretly, but carefully, watching every motion of the army. Instead of proceeding onwards by the same bank to Juánpúr, by which route he would have been less liable to meet with interruption, and could have collected reinforcements from various quarters, the Emperor,— from some false point of honour, as is alleged, lest Shír Shah should boast that he had given up the ordinary high road, which lay to the south of the river, and taken that on the north, to avoid facing him, — was induced to recross to the right bank. This movement he is said to have made by the advice of his favourite, Moveiíd Beg, in opposition to the remonstrances of his ablest officers,

The two armies approach.

* He probably at this time assumed the style of King of Behár.

BOOK IV. A.D. 1538.

who represented the miserably unprepared state of the army for active service, worn out, as they were, by a long and difficult march through heavy roads, and nearly destitute of baggage and warlike stores. Having crossed over to the right bank, Humáyun resumed his march upwards, past Patna, till he reached Moníah, at the confluence of the Són with the Ganges.*

At Moníah, the enemy, who, though hovering at no great distance, had hitherto hardly shown themselves, were discovered to be at hand in great force. Orders were issued to the troops to arm and prepare for action; and, next day, a body of the Afgháns appeared in sight.

The day following, just as the army was about to march, news arrived that the Afgháns had seized the boat which carried a huge piece of ordnance † that had been used at the siege of Chunár. The army, however, crossed the Són; and, on the fourth day, with some skirmishing, reached Chonsa‡, near which the Karamnassa flows into the Ganges.

Shír Shah's tactics.

On hearing of the Emperor's march from Gour, Shír Khan had raised the siege of Juánpúr, and concentrated his force. His plan of campaign was laid with great coolness and skill. If the enemy pushed forward, for the purpose of bringing on a pitched battle, he resolved not to face them in the open field, nor to hazard the fate of the war on a single great action, in which the imperialists, from the quality of their force, were likely to have the advantage. On the contrary, in that case, he proposed to give them the slip, and to re-enter Bengal, as he had formerly left it, by the Jharkend

* Abulfazl makes Muhammed Zemán Mírza join the army before the siege of Chunár (Akbernáma, f. 43.). Jouher makes him and Muhammed Sultan Mírza join during the siege, c. 3.; the Tabakát makes him arrive at this time with a considerable party, f. 150.; and Ferishta, v. ii. p. 85. follows that authority.

† Díg Koh-shikan, the hill-breaker.

‡ Chonsar. Rennell.

hills. If, on the other hand, the Emperor, instead of marching to attack him, pushed on straight for Agra, then he was to hang on his flanks and rear, cut off his supplies, and harass him on the line of march; and even, if occasion offered, to attempt a surprise. The accounts which soon reached him, of the broken and disabled state of the imperial army, induced him, however, to deviate from this plan; and, adopting a bolder system of operations, to march down and meet his enemy face to face.*



Operations at Chonsa. End of A. H. 945, April 1539.

Accordingly, when the Emperor's army reached Chonsa, about nine in the morning, before they had dismounted, an immense cloud of dust was seen in the east. The Emperor gave orders to ascertain whence it proceeded, and soon learned that it was Shír Khan, whose army had arrived by a forced march. A consultation was held. Kásim Husein Sultan proposed an instant attack, observing that Shír Khan must have come that day eighteen or nineteen kos, and that his horses must be worn out and fatigued, while theirs were comparatively fresh. The Emperor was inclined to fall into his opinion, but was induced by Moveiíd Khan to defer the attack till next day. A bridge was thrown across the Karamnassa, and the army passed and encamped without fighting, which disheartened both Amírs and soldiers. Shír Khan, who had placed himself in the direct line of his march, fortified his camp on every side with strong entrenchments.

Distress of the Imperial army.

Humáyun's further advance was now checked. The army, brought into this trying situation, was already much weakened by sickness and disease, as well as by the casualties of a long march through bad roads. The greater proportion of the draught cattle had perished on the march, the rest were worn out and emaciated; numbers of the cavalry, having lost their horses, were

* Akbernáma, f. 43.

BOOK IV.

A. D. 1539.

dismounted, and forced to accompany the army on foot. Even the cavalry horses left were in a wretched condition. The troops were dispirited. These evils were not likely to be remedied by their present position, cooped up in their camp under the eye of a vigilant enemy. The Emperor had lost the power of moving. Daily skirmishes ensued, bravely contested, and generally terminating in favour of Humáyun's troops, but in which many lives were lost on both sides. Any onward movement must be through the enemy's lines; yet, such was now the reduced and disheartened condition of the imperial army, that it would have been imprudent to hazard such an attack; and without an action of some kind, it was impossible even to change their ground. In this situation the two armies remained, facing each other for about two months.* During this

* The Tabakát-e Akberi; the Tar. Bed., and Ferishta, say three months. The chronology of Humáyun's expedition to Bengal is not very distinctly marked by historians, but some of the leading points may be ascertained. He left Agra, A. H. 944, Sefer 8. (A. D. 1537, July 17.). According to Jouher, the army reached Chunár on the Sheb-e-Berát, Shábán 16.[1] (A. D. 1538, Jan. 18.) Six months between Agra and Chunár is a long time; and, as it is agreed that the siege lasted six months, we may suppose that the blockade had begun before the arrival of Humáyun. The rains had begun before the Emperor reached Moníah. At Patna, he was advised to halt, because the rains had come on. Shír Khan is said to have taken Gour on the 12th of Ferverdin (Zikádeh, A. H. 944, A. D. 1538, April); Humáyun remained three months at Gour; and, according to different accounts, from six to nine months in Bengal altogether; the Tabakát, f. 150., and Bedáuni, f. 141., allow six; Jouher, who was on the expedition, nine.[2] All Bengal, we are told, was conquered in the course of A. H. 945, which ends May 29. A. D. 1539. The month, in which Humáyun commenced his return from Bengal, is not specified; but he remained two months at Chonsa, probably, April and May, 1539, before the rains set in, and his final discomfiture occurred A. H. 946, Sefer 5. (A. D. 1539, June 23.) when he had been nearly three months at Chonsa. On these data, I have attempted to arrange the chronology of the events.

[1] Major Stewart, in his translation of Jouher, p. 9., makes this occur A. H. 945; but there is no date of any year in the original, and it is clear that it is A. H. 944. The Sheb-e-Berát of A.H. 945 would bring it down to A. H. 1539, Jan. 7.

[2] Stewart's Jouher, p. 13., has *several* months, but the original has *nine*.

time some of those who had lost their horses or their health in the Bengal expedition, and found their way to Juánpúr and Chunár, contrived to rejoin the Emperor, whose situation, cooped up as he was, grew daily worse. Messenger after messenger was despatched to Hindal, and afterwards to Kámrán, whose arrival at Agra became known, beseeching them to turn their arms against Shír Khan, and to march to the relief of the Emperor and his army; but not a symptom of succour appeared.*

Rebellions in Hindustan. A. H. 945, A. D. 1538.

Indeed, it was not on the side of Bengal and Behár alone that the affairs of Humáyun were in a dangerous state. Revolt and rebellion were raging in his capital, and in his own family. Situated as he now was, Humáyun, in ordinary circumstances, might have looked for assistance from his brothers, and the provinces around his capital. But no consolatory ray of hope gleamed upon him from that quarter. Instead of ready succour, all there was procrastination, intrigue, and treason. When Humáyun entered Bengal and proceeded to Gour, Hindal Mírza, instead of remaining to keep the rebels in check, and maintain the communications with the grand army, taking advantage of the season, abandoned his post, and set out for Agra, without leave. His absence, and the death of Hindu Beg, had encouraged and enabled Shír Khan to pass the Ganges, and, as we have seen, to take Benáres, defeat Yúsef Beg, and lay siege to Juánpúr; besides cutting off all the communications of Humáyun's army. Hindal, who was now in his twentieth year, misled by the evil counsellors who so often surround an aspiring prince, and incite him to sacrifice every duty at the shrine of ambition, on his arrival at Agra, entered the city, took possession of the Emperor's palace, issued his orders as if vested with absolute power, and seemed to direct his views to the throne itself.†

Treasonable conduct and vacillation of Hindal Mírza.

* Akbernáma, f. 43.; Tabak. Akb. f. 150.; Jouher, c. iv.; Ferishta.

BOOK IV. A.D. 1538.

The great officers, whom Humáyun had left in situations of trust, could not witness such proceedings with unconcern. The man who, at this moment of danger and turmoil, seems to have exerted himself above all others, was Mír Fakhr Ali*, an old and distinguished officer of Báber's, whom Humáyun had left as military governor of Delhi, under Yádgár Násir Mírza. Alarmed at the course which Hindal was pursuing, he hastened down to Agra to meet the young prince; and represented to him, in the strongest terms, the danger to which he was exposing the power and the very existence of the Chaghatái race in India; he pointed out, that it was a moment when, instead of destroying everything by discord and disunion, it was most necessary that every friend of the family of Taimur should exert himself, to break the rapidly increasing power of Shír Khan and the Afgháns. By such remonstrances, he prevailed upon Hindal to leave the city, to cross over the Jamna into the Doáb, and there collect whatever forces could be brought together, to march and raise the siege of Juánpúr. Muhammed Bakhshi, Humáyun's military governor of Agra, readily furnished every assistance in his power from the arsenal and magazines, to equip the troops, and enable them to take the field. Mír Fakhr Ali, thus far successful, next hastened to Kalpi, to induce Yádgár Násir Mírza, the Emperor's cousin and brother-in-law, who commanded there, and whose jágír Kalpi was, to put his troops in motion, so as to form a junction with those of Hindal in the territory of Karra, that they might thence proceed in concert to Juánpúr.

It happened, unfortunately, that at this time Záhid Beg, Khosrou Beg Kokiltash, Háji Muhammed Bába Kushke, and other discontented and turbulent nobles, who had fled from Bengal, arrived, and had secret

* Or, Mír Fakr Ali.

communications with Núr-ed-dín Muhammed Mírza, the governor of Kanáuj, who had married Gulreng Begum, Humáyun's sister, and who seems to have been privy to Hindal's designs. Núr-ed-dín wrote to Hindal Mírza, announcing the arrival of these noblemen, and at the same time forwarded to him a petition from them, asking his favour and protection, and proffering their own duty and services. To this address the Mírza, who, in spite of his change of conduct, had still a strong leaning to his treasonable purposes, returned a gracious answer, which he gave to Muhammed Ghází Tagháí, one of his trusty adherents, by whom he at the same time wrote to inform Yádgár Násir Mírza, and Mír Fakhr Ali, of the arrival of the Amírs. The Amírs did not wait at Kanáuj for his answer, but proceeded to Kol, a jágír of Záhid Beg's. Hindal's envoy, hearing of this movement, instead of going first to Yádgár, went straight to meet them. The conspirators, finding that Hindal was irresolute or insincere, and being themselves desperate, told the envoy, explicitly, that their mind was made up; that they had for ever shaken off their allegiance to the Emperor; that, if Hindal would assume the imperial dignity, and read the Khutba in his own name, they were ready to be his most faithful subjects; but if not, that they would straightway repair to Kámrán Mírza, and make him the same offer, which would not be refused. The envoy, returning to Hindal, reported what had passed, and added his own opinion; that the Mírza was so far committed as to have only one of two measures to adopt; he must either at once call in the Amírs, accede to their advice, and declare himself Emperor; or get them into his power, cast them into prison, and treat them as rebels. Hindal, whose mind was misled by high and dazzling projects, was not long of coming to a decision on this

BOOK IV. A.D. 1538.

alternative.* He agreed to accept the proposal of the fugitive nobles, and to raise the standard of rebellion.

It was at this very juncture that Sheikh Bhúl or Behlúl, who had been sent by Humáyun from Gour, on a mission to the Mírza, arrived near Agra. He was the elder brother of Sheikh Muhammed Ghous, who had gained Guáliár for Báber, and who was one of the most eminent saintly men then in India. The possession of the mysterious names of God, by the secret use of which it was devoutly believed that the most wonderful and miraculous effects could be produced, added awe to his character. He was revered by Humáyun as his religious teacher and spiritual guide, and had acted as a councillor to Hindal himself, in his campaign against Muhammed Sultan Mírza and his sons, beyond the Ganges. Hindal, on hearing of his approach, went out and received him with every mark of honour. He had been sent from Bengal, as we have seen, by the Emperor, when he first heard of the Mírza's defection, to reason with him on the folly of his proceedings, that could only serve to elevate the Afgháns on the ruins of the imperial family and race. He brought with him assurances from Humáyun, not only of forgiveness for his past misconduct, but of every favour and exaltation for the future, that the affection and generosity of a prince and a brother could bestow. The weak and wavering mind of Hindal was shaken by these remonstrances of duty and wisdom. He had not yet made any irrevocable manifestation of his rebellious intentions, and was once more persuaded to return to his allegiance, and to join in an active effort to drive the common enemy out of the field, and free his sovereign from his distress and peril. The very next day, he sent to make fresh requisitions from Muhammed Bakhshi, the governor, of such a quantity of

* Akbernáma, ff. 43—45.; Tab. Akb. 150, 151.; Jouher, c. 4.; Nisábnáma-e Afgh. ff. 90, 91.; Tar. Bed. f. 142.

warlike stores and equipments, arms, cattle and money, as would enable him to put his army instantly in motion, and to proceed to the relief of Juánpúr. With all his demands, the governor, influenced by the Sheikh, professed his readiness instantly to comply, except as to money; all that was in the treasury having already, he affirmed, been disbursed among the troops.

Only four or five days had gone on, in this course of vigorous preparation, when Núr-ed-dín Mírza, who had entered entirely into the views of the fugitive lords, arrived from Kanáuj. He came, intending to carry into effect the plan that had so lately been concerted and settled between them and Hindal. Finding the course things had taken, he, by the weight of his authority, once more produced a change in the vacillating mind of the Mírza. Muhammed Gházi was again sent to renew the agreement with them. To this they consented, but only on condition that Sheikh Bhúl, who was the acknowledged agent of the Emperor in Hindal's camp, and had been the means of breaking the first agreement, should be publicly put to death; an act, they said, necessary to prove at once the sincerity of the Mírza's return to their views, and his fixed determination to enter into no terms with his brother. These conditions were acceded to by the prince; and Sheikh Bhúl, who suspected no change of policy, and every moment of whose time was actively employed in superintending the despatch of arms and stores to the camp, and in removing any impediments to the immediate march of the troops, was seized in his own house by Núr-ed-dín Muhammed Mírza, carried across the Jamna, and beheaded on a sandy down* near the gardens of Báber's palace, under the shallow pretence that he carried on a secret correspondence with the Afgháns.

* Registán.

BOOK IV.

A.D. 1538.

The compact of the confederates being thus sealed in holy blood, the rebellious Amírs now moved to Agra, and waited on Hindal, who was proclaimed Emperor; and the public prayers were read, and money coined in his name. The troops were immediately put in motion, but it was towards Delhi, not Juánpúr. Muhammed Bakhshi, deeply shocked at the murder of the Sheikh, waited on the Mírza: "You have slain the Sheikh," said he, "why am I spared?" But blood enough had been shed. He tried to pacify the faithful Amír, and sent him to the camp. The most earnest remonstrances on his cruel proceedings, came from the ladies of his father's Harem. When Hindal went to the palace of his mother, Dildár Aghácheh, he found her attired in deep mourning. On his reproaching her for assuming the garb of sorrow, at a moment when his accession to the throne called only for joy and festivity, that lady, whose affections made her far-sighted, with tears assured her son, that, far from participating in his delight, she saw, in all that was passing around her, matter only of profound regret and condolence; that she seemed already to be mourning over his bier; that, young and inexperienced as he was, he had given himself up to the guidance of evil counsellors, who had engaged him in a course that could lead only to ruin. "And," continued she, "to your other guilt, you have added the stain of innocent blood. You have murdered the holy Sheikh. Away! and do not defile my palace with your presence." * The prince used every means he could devise to soothe her resentment and sorrow, and insisted on carrying her along with him in his march to Delhi.

The news of these procedings at Agra soon reached Yádgár Násir Mírza and Mír Fakhr Ali, who were still at Kalpi, preparing to join Hindal on his march to

* Akbernáma, ff. 43, 44.; Tabak. Akb.; Ferishta, ii. 85, 86.; Jouher, c. 4.; Tar. Bedáuni, f. 142.; Kháfi Khan, f. 47.

the eastward. Perceiving at once that nothing could be done to prevent the intended revolt, they instantly resolved to strain every nerve to secure Delhi; and accordingly, proceeding by forced marches, and by a circuitous route, that they might escape observation, they succeeded in throwing themselves into that ancient capital. Hindal Mírza, on leaving Agra, had marched straight for Delhi, expecting to get possession of it with little resistance, in the absence of the governor. When he arrived at Hamídpúr, near Firúzábád, he got notice of their rapid march; and, seeing himself anticipated, hesitated whether or not to go on. Finally, however, he resolved to push forward, and besiege the town. On his march, he was joined by many of the smaller zemíndárs of the neighbourhood.

He attacks Delhi.

The faithful noblemen, who had thrown themselves into Delhi, used every exertion to strengthen the works and the garrison; and did all that activity and valour could effect to repulse the besiegers. They despatched messenger after messenger to Kámrán Mírza, to call him to their aid. That prince was then at the height of his reputation. He had made two successful expeditions from Láhúr to Kandahár, in the first of which he had relieved, and in the second, re-taken that important town. His dominions stretched from Hissár-Firúza to Zemín-dáwer on the one side, and to Badakhshán on the other. On hearing of the distracted state of the empire, the danger of Humáyun in Bengal, the increasing power of Shír Khan, and the rebellion of Hindal, Kámrán Mírza had determined to advance into Hindustán, and had set out at the head of ten thousand horse. He met the messengers on the road, received their despatches, and moved forward with increased speed; so that ere long news arrived in the camp of the besiegers that he was near at hand, and had reached Sonpat, which lies between Pánipat and Delhi. Upon

Kámrán Mírza is called in to relieve it.

BOOK IV. A. D. 1539. this, Hindal, seeing all hope gone of gaining the town, abandoned the siege, and hastened back to Agra.

Hindal retires to Agra. Kámrán also in revolt. The part that Kámrán Mírza was to act, in the present state of affairs, was a matter of the deepest importance. In his hand was placed the fate of the house of Báber. It soon appeared that he pursued a short-sighted policy; and that, while he professed to serve his brother Humáyun, he in reality looked only A. H. 946. A. D. 1539. to his own supposed advantage. As he approached Delhi, the governor came out to meet him. Mír Fakhr Ali, having easily penetrated the prince's designs, ventured to offer him his advice. He told him that Yádgár Násir Mírza was in the place, determined to hold it for Humáyun, which he certainly would do, if attacked at that moment; that it was Kámrán's best policy, whatever were his ultimate views, to follow Hindal to Agra, so as to prevent his gaining a decided influence there; that, if Agra, the capital, fell, Yádgár Násir would no longer have the same inducement to hold out, and Delhi would then submit without a struggle. In the end, he had sufficient address to persuade Kámrán to march on to Agra; and Yádgár, thus left undisturbed, employed the leisure afforded him in strengthening the defences, and adding to the garrison.

Pursues Hindal; As Kámrán approached Agra, Hindal, who had been joined by none of the jágírdárs of note, finding himself unequal to maintain a contest with his brother, fled with five thousand horse to Alwar, the capital of Mewát, his government. His mother remained behind; and, influenced by the representations of Kámrán Mírza, who became responsible for his safety, soon after prevailed upon him to make his submission to that prince, receives his submission; and to return to Agra. In this submission he was joined by the refractory Amírs, who had espoused his cause; and the whole confederates, now apparently united in a common cause, met; and, having crossed the Jamna, formed an army on its left bank for the professed purpose of marching against Shír Khan. Kámrán Mírza held the chief command. The army moved slowly forward a few marches. The general confidence began to revive, insomuch that traders ventured to carry stores and other supplies, which they attempted to introduce into the Emperor's camp at Chonsa. But Kámrán was the slave of a guilty ambition, and swayed by bad advisers, among whom appear to have been the fugitive Amírs, who sought to widen the breach between the brothers. They sought to convince him that to destroy the enemy, and so release the Emperor, was only laying a snare for his own destruction. Influenced by such counsellors, the advance, slow at first, afterwards ceased; and by and by he was persuaded that the season for doing any thing was past; that it was better to return, preserve the stores and munitions of war, and husband his resources, that the troops might be allowed to return home, and make every thing ready for a new campaign; that, meanwhile, should Shír Khan defeat the Emperor, they would be prepared to face him; and should Humáyun destroy Shír Khan, they would possess the means of making terms with arms in their hands. Lending a ready ear to such false and shallow reasoning, Kámrán led his army back to Agra about the beginning of the rains, abandoning his brother to his fate.*

marches against Shír Khan.

But returns without engaging him.

Humáyun had now been for two months cooped up in his camp at Chonsa, and suffering many privations. He could not bring his wary antagonist, whose camp was deeply entrenched and defended by artillery, to leave it and engage in the open plain; nor was he able,

Continued distress of Humáyun at Chonsa.

* *Akbernáma, ff. 43, 44.; Tar. Akb.; Jouher, c. 4.; Ferishta, vol. ii. pp. 85—87.; Kháfi Khan, f. 47.; Tar. Reshídi, ff. 365, 366.* Several historians, *Nizám-ed-dín* Ahmed, the author of the Tabakát-e Akberi, Ferishta, and Kháfi Khan, make Kámrán assume the title of Emperor. From the narrative of Abulfazl and of Jouher, c. 5., and still more from that of Haider Mírza, I think it probable that he assumed the authority, but not the name.

BOOK IV. A.D. 1539.

in face of the enemy, to effect the passage of the Ganges, though he lay close to that river. The superiority which his troops maintained in partial skirmishes was of no avail. He lay in an enemy's country; and the opposite bank, as far as Kanáuj, was overrun by the Afgháns. His only hope of relief was from his brothers, who possessed the means of collecting an army, and marching to succour him; but the news which reached him from Agra, first of the treason of Hindal, and afterwards of the arrival and unworthy conduct of Kámrán, at length convinced him that, while his danger was daily increasing, he had nothing to expect from them. To add to his misfortunes, the periodical rains, which set in with great violence, increased the difficulty of moving, or of receiving supplies or reinforcements. Part of the camp of Shír Shah was laid under water, which forced him to move, with the greatest part of his troops, to the higher ground, two or three kos off, leaving his cannon and fortified position under the guard of a portion of his army. But the skirmishing continued, and no prospect of relief appeared.

A. H. 946, Moharrem. A. D. 1539, June.

He sends an envoy to Shír Shah.

At length Humáyun, compelled by the necessity of his situation, sent one Múlla Muhammed Barghíz, who was known to Shír Shah, to treat of a pacification. He found the new king busy with his spade, in the heat of the day, among his soldiers, who were employed in digging a trench. On seeing the ambassador, the King washed his hands, a temporary awning was spread, and he sat down under it on the ground, without ceremony, and received the envoy. To the observations which the Múlla made, when he communicated the Emperor's message, the King only replied, "Go, and tell your Emperor this from me: he is desirous of war, his troops are not; I do not wish for war, my troops do." He, however, gave instructions to Sheikh Khalíl, whom he called his Murshid, or spiritual father, an eminent and pious divine, descended from the famous saint, Sheikh Ferid Shakerganj; and, having sent him to Humáyun, a negotiation was entered into.

Negotiations and armistice.

An intercourse of messengers between the camps now took place; the conditions of the treaty were discussed, and were supposed to be nearly arranged. An armistice seems to have followed; the men of the two armies met on friendly terms, and even amused themselves by making pleasure parties to visit the opposite camps. Shír Shah took advantage of this calm to despatch Khowás Khan, with some thousand horse, to chastise Raja Mharta, who had assisted Humáyun, not only with his troops, both horse and foot, but by cutting off the supplies of Shír Shah's army; and who had resisted every offer of reward and threat of vengeance that had been made to secure his neutrality. The Khan prevailed, after an obstinate encounter, defeated and slew the Raja, and brought back his head, which he laid at the feet of his sovereign.

Proposed terms of treaty.

The treaty was meanwhile in progress*, and the conditions at last settled between the envoys were, that all Bengal, and his old jágír in Behár, should be conceded to Shír Shah, who was to acknowledge Humáyun as his lord paramount, and to read the Khutba in his name. But Shír Shah insisted that, in addition to this, Chunár should be restored to him; and, after some

* As to the supposed treaty of peace, Abulfazl says little, but declaims against the cunning and treachery of Shír Khan, Akbern. f. 45. The Tar. Nizámi, f. 214.; Tabak. Akb. f. 150., and Tar. Bed. f. 142., make peace concluded, on condition that Humáyun was to be allowed to return home in safety, Shír Khan retaining Bengal as far as Garhi, the khutba to be read in the Emperor's name. Jouher makes him insist on Chunár being given up, to which Humáyun was compelled to assent. The Nisábnáma makes Bengal given up as far as Garhi. Ferishta makes Bengal and Behár be ceded to Shír Khan for the payment of a trifling tribute, and adds that the treaty was signed and ratified by mutual oaths. Briggs's Ferishta, vol. ii. p. 87. The Kholáset-ul-Towáríkh, f. 276., also supposes a peace to have been concluded.

BOOK IV.

A.D. 1539.

delay, Humáyun, though reluctantly, was obliged to consent.

Negligence of Humáyun.

Some affirm that this treaty was mutually agreed to, and confirmed by oath; but perhaps no definitive treaty was signed. Preparations were made for breaking up both camps. Shír Shah, having constructed a bridge over the Karamnása, had sent his best men two or three days' march to Behár, on their way to Bengal. The Emperor seems to have withdrawn his outposts. His troops dispersed carelessly about the camp, and all were busy in packing up their baggage and the public stores, and in finishing a bridge of boats, which they were constructing over the Ganges for their return home. The camp was a scene of bustle and rejoicing.

Attack by Shír Shah.

Shír Shah, seeing that Humáyun and his generals were thrown off their guard, believed that the wished-for moment was at hand for striking a blow, which should at once avenge the wrongs of the Afgháns, and destroy the Emperor, his army, and the House of Báber. The most atrocious breach of faith cost his mind nothing; it was the very basis of his policy. He directed the troops that had marched, to countermarch secretly and with speed. He divided the force intended for the enterprise into three columns; taking one himself*, giving another to his son, Jilál Khan, and the third to his general, Khowás Khan. He ordered Khowás Khan to take a circuit with his division, and as the day dawned, to surprise the enemy by the river side, to seize the boats and other craft in the river, and to put to the sword all who came in his way. The other two columns were to co-operate by attacking on different quarters. It is asserted that Sheikh Khalíl, who was in Shír Shah's camp, sent to desire the Emperor to be on his guard against a surprise, as Khowás Khan had marched, about afternoon prayers†, with a

* "Having his back to the Kibleh," says Jouher, which looks as if he had come from the west.

† Namáz-diger. Jouher.

strong body of men; but that no attention was paid to the intimation. CHAP. IV. SECT. II.

Slaughter of the Imperialists.

The watch, which that night was under Muhammed Zemán Mírza, was but negligently kept. Before the morning twilight appeared, an uproar was heard in the rear toward the river. Soon after was seen a crowd of women and camp-followers, flying in confusion over the whole camp. The Afgháns were found to have entered, and were slaying all they met, without mercy or distinction. The surprise was complete. To numbers their sleep became the sleep of death. The troops in general had not time to arm, to saddle their horses, or to form in order, before the Afgháns poured in on every side. Humáyun started from sleep* on the first alarm. The imperial kettle-drums were beaten, and about three hundred horse soon gathered around him. Just as he was mounting his horse, Bába Jeláir and Terdi Beg Kuch Beg joined him. He besought them to spare no exertion to bring off the empress, Háji Begum. These devoted servants, while zealously attempting to execute his orders, were slain fighting at the entrance of the private tents. Mír Pehlewan Badakhshi, another officer of distinction, and a considerable number of men, shared the same fate, in attempting the same achievement. They failed in their purpose, and the princess fell into the hands of the Afgháns. At this crisis, Shír Shah himself happened to arrive. He ordered his eunuchs and most trusty servants, with a party of armed men, to keep watch round the harem, and to suffer none to be injured. The wives and families of the officers and men of the vanquished army fled, and took refuge in this asylum, where they were safe. While Humáyun was attempting to collect his troops, a party of the enemy, with an elephant, came down upon him. He made a sign to some of his household, who were by, to

Danger of Humáyun.

* The Nisábnáma says that he was reading the Koran.

BOOK IV. A.D. 1539.

He is wounded;

attack it. As they hesitated, he snatched his spear from the officer who carried it, spurred on his horse, and struck the animal on the head with such force, that he was unable to draw the spear out again. Meanwhile, an archer who sat on the howdah, wounded him on the arm with an arrow. This compelled the Emperor to retire, leaving his spear in the wound. He now called out to those who were near him to join him in a charge, but was not seconded. All was disorder. One of his followers, seizing his reins, exclaimed, in Oriental phrase, "This is no time for dallying: the feast is over, why linger near the food?" and led him towards the river. On reaching the bank, he found the bridge broken down. At once he spurred his horse, and plunged into the stream, but was soon dismounted.* At this moment of danger, a water-carrier swam up to him, presented him with his water-bag, which he had filled with air, and made a sign to the sinking monarch to lay hold of it. He did so, and made his way across, the water-carrier swimming by him and assisting him. On reaching the opposite bank, the Emperor asked his deliverer what was his name. He said it was Nìzám. "To me," said the Emperor, in the exuberance of his gratitude, "thou art as Nizám Aulía, and thou shalt be placed on my throne."†

swims the river.

His army annihilated.

The defeat was complete. Shír Shah had left nothing to accident. The camp had been attacked on every side, as soon as it was entered on the rear. On the river, the bridge was broken down, and boats were in

* "The Emperor came to the banks of the river," says Jouher, c. v. "An elephant, Girdbáz by name, accompanied him. He ordered the driver to break down the bridge, which he did. His Majesty drove his horse into the river, but lost his seat," &c. The Akbernáma, f. 45. and Nisábnáma, ff. 91, 92., represent the bridge as being broken down by the Afgháns.

† Nizám-ed-dín Aulía is a celebrated saint. Some writers make the promise to Nizám to be, that he should occupy the throne for half a day; others, till noon. The Tabakát calls Nizám, Muhammed Sakka, Muhammed the water-carrier. See Akbernáma, f. 45.; Jouher, c. 5.; Tar. Bed. ff. 142, 143.

readiness, which sailed up and down, filled with men armed with matchlocks and spears, who killed all they could reach in the water. The whole tents, camp-equipage, baggage, artillery, stores, and what remained of the treasure, fell into the hands of the conqueror. Muhammed Zemán Mírza, Mouláná Muhammed Ali, Mouláná Kásim Ali, the Sadr, or Head of the Law, many other officers of distinction, and eight thousand of the Emperor's best Tartar troops, perished on this disastrous day, besides numbers of inferior note and camp followers. This memorable event occurred at the Chúpah Ghat, on the banks of the Ganges, on the 27th day of June, A. D. 1539.*

CHAP. IV. SECT. II.

A. H. 946. A. D. 1539.

Sefer 9, June 27.

Proceedings of Shír Shah.

When Shír Shah, after the final discomfiture and dispersion of the enemy, returned to the imperial tents, he dismounted in the Hall of Audience, and humbly prostrated himself in prayer to the Giver of all victory. He did not now hesitate to declare a dream which he had on the preceding night. He thought that he and Humáyun were both carried into the presence of the prophet of God, who was sitting in state on a throne, and who, addressing the Emperor, told him, that the Almighty had bestowed his kingdom on Shír Shah; and at the same time, taking the crown and cap of authority from his head, placed them on that of his rival, commanding him to rule with justice. This dream, he said, he had not published before the battle, lest it should be regarded as a device to inspire courage into the Afgháns. He sent a courteous message to the captive Empress, condoling with her on the deceitfulness of fortune; but adding that, in former

* In this account of the campaign of Bengal and Behár, and its disastrous close, the authorities chiefly followed have been, Akbern. ff. 44, 45.; Tab. Akb. ff. 150. 175.; Tar. Nizámi, ff. 213, 214.; Jouher's Mem. c. 4, 5.; Nisábnáma-e Afgh. ff. 90—92.; Tar. Bedáuni, f. 142.; Briggs's Ferishta, vol. ii. pp. 81—88.; Kháfi Khan, f. 47. The Taríkh-e Bedáuni gives some lines which Shír Shah wrote on the memorable victory which closed the campaign.

BOOK IV.

A.D. 1539.

days he had been protected and cherished by the imperial house, and regarded himself as a child of the family, and he promised to send her back, with all the Harem, to Agra, as soon as the Emperor was known to have reached it,—a promise which he faithfully performed. He ordered the same allowances to be issued to all who were in the Harem, that they had previously been accustomed to receive; and commanded that all the other women and children of the vanquished army, who had been made prisoners, should be protected, and allowed to return home, at their own pleasure.*

Humáyun makes his way to Agra.

The Emperor remained but a short time on the left bank of the Ganges, to collect such of his troops as, by the strength of their horses, or in any other manner, had been able to get across the river. Having been joined by his brother Askeri and some other chiefs, they soon after rode off for Agra. He had not advanced far, when he found that he had not yet escaped all danger; as it appeared that Mír Feríd Gúr, an Afghán officer, was following him in the rear; while Shah Muhammed Afghán had taken post in front, to arrest his farther progress. This news so much disheartened the troops, already worn out with fatigue, that fears were entertained lest they should desert their standards. In this emergency, Raja Prabhan, a Rájpút chief, volunteered with his followers to check the advance of Mír Feríd, so as to allow his Majesty to bend the whole force of his arms against the enemy, who shut up the road by which they were to advance. The offer was accepted, and the Emperor with his followers marched straight against the Afgháns in front, who, intimidated by their determined appearance, abandoned their ground and left the road open. The

* Nisábnáma-e Afgh. f. 92.

Emperor proceeded by way of Kalpi; and, after a rapid and laborious march, reached Agra.* CHAP. IV. SECT. II.

Shír Shah supreme in Bengal and Behár.

Meanwhile Shír Shah lost no time in improving his victory. Besides the force which he despatched in pursuit of the fugitives, he hastened back into Bengal with a strong body of troops, accompanied by his son Jilál Khan; and attacked Jehángír-kuli, the Emperor's general, whom he defeated in several successive actions. That brave officer, unable to keep the field, was compelled to retreat into the territory of some native zemíndárs, where he maintained an obstinate struggle for some time; but, in the end, he and most of his troops were overtaken and slain by the overpowering superiority of the Afgháns; so that, of his whole army, Derwísh Maksúd Bengáli † was the only man of note who ever re-joined the Emperor. Shír Shah was now proclaimed King, without opposition, in Bengal also; and, though he was soon obliged to leave the country ‡, to attend in person to his affairs in the north, he directed his attention unremittingly, for the next two years, to complete the reduction of that kingdom, and to place its revenue and internal affairs on a satisfactory footing.

And all the lower Gangetic provinces.

The effects of the great victory at Chonsa were not confined to Bengal; they extended in every direction.

* Jouher, c. 5. The Raja, who behaved with so much spirit, is said to be of Arîl or Aráil. There are two Aráils. One opposite Allahábád, across the Jamna; and one eleven miles S. by E. from Kanáuj. (See Hamilton's Hindustan, vol. i. pp. 301. 374.).

† He was of the Ziáret-gáh near Herát, and consequently of a religious family. Akbern. f. 61. Ferishta states, vol. ii. p. 88., that Jehángír Beg was expelled from Bengal, and rejoined Humáyun; which is certainly a mistake, as he himself mentions, vol. ii. p. 117., that he was defeated and slain in Bengal.

‡ Tar. Nizám-i. f. 214.; Tab. Akh. f. 160.; Akbernáma, f. 45.; Taríkh. Bedáuni, f. 143.; Nisábnáma, ff. 91—93. The Nizábnáma says that, after many actions, Jehángír was besieged and slain in Garohi. Is this the Garrows? Abulfazl makes Shír Shah halt on the borders of Behár, and send his son, Jilál Khan, to complete the destruction of Jehángír-Kuli's force.

BOOK IV.

A.D. 1539.

Shír Shah was soon undisputed master of Behár. He crossed the Ganges to renew the siege of Juánpúr, which, with the whole territory dependent on it, surrendered with little resistance. In like manner he overran the rest of the country, east of the Ganges, as far as Kanáuj. Not content with this success, he sent his son Kutb Khan across that river, and through the Doáb, with a large detachment, for the purpose of reducing the important towns of Kalpi and Etáwa on the Jamna. The wide dominions of Humáyun seemed now to have shrunk into the narrow space circumscribed by the walls of Agra and Delhi; and his tenure, even of these cities, was far from being secure.

# CHAPTER V.

## HUMÁYUN'S EXPULSION FROM HINDUSTÁN.

HUMÁYUN JOINS KÁMRÁN AT AGRA.—HUMILIATION OF HINDAL.—HUMÁYUN PREPARES AGAIN TO ATTACK SHÍR SHAH.—ILLNESS AND RETREAT OF KÁMRÁN.—DEFEAT OF SHÍR SHAH'S ADVANCED ARMY. HAIDER MÍRZA DOGHLAT IN HUMÁYUN'S CAMP.—HIS CHARACTER OF THE EMPEROR—AND ACCOUNT OF THE CAMPAIGN—AND OF THE BATTLE OF KANÁUJ.—OTHER ACCOUNTS OF THAT DISASTER.—FLIGHT OF HUMÁYUN.—HE ARRIVES AT AGRA.—PROCEEDS TOWARDS DELHI—AND ONWARDS TO THE PENJÁB.—SHÍR SHAH AT DELHI.—HIS PARTIES PURSUE HUMÁYUN ACROSS THE SATLEJ.—SELFISH CONDUCT OF KÁMRÁN.—TREATY AMONG THE IMPERIAL BROTHERS.—THEIR WANT OF UNION.—TREACHERY OF KÁMRÁN.—SHÍR SHAH RECEIVES HIS OVERTURES.—ENTERS THE PENJÁB.—THE IMPERIAL FAMILY QUIT LÁHÚR.—KÁMRÁN DEPARTS FOR KÁBUL.—HINDAL FOR SIND AND GUJRÁT.—HUMÁYUN MEDITATES AN EXPEDITION TO KASHMÍR.—RECENT EVENTS THERE.—KÁMRÁN THWARTS THE PLANS OF HUMÁYUN—WHO PROCEEDS TOWARDS SIND.—HINDAL REJOINS HIM AT GUL-BALÚCH.—THEY PASS THE TERRITORIES OF BAKHSHUI LANGA—AND REACH SIND.—RECENT STATE, AND PAST CAREER OF HUMÁYUN.—THE AFGHÁN SUPREMACY RESTORED IN INDIA, UNDER SHÍR SHAH.

CHAP. V.

A. H. 946, A. D. 1539.

Humáyun joins Kámrán at Agra.

HUMÁYUN, on his arrival near Agra after his disastrous expedition, found his brother Kámrán, who, about a month after his impolitic and inglorious retreat, was encamped at the Zirefshán gardens. When the Mírzas, Kámrán and Hindal, received intelligence of the Emperor's discomfiture, followed by certain information that Shír Shah was taking possession of the country on every side, they perceived, too late, that, circumstanced as things were, it was in vain to think of dethroning the Emperor, with any hope of establishing themselves in his stead; and that the only safety of the brothers lay in their union. Nor would it have been politic, on the

BOOK IV. A.D. 1539.

Emperor's part, with the small force that he had been able to save from the wreck of his army, to attempt to punish them for their late defection. As he came near Agra, he galloped forward and entered Kámrán's tent, before the Mírza was aware of his coming.* The brothers embraced each other affectionately, and with many tears. They afterwards went and sat down together, in a friendly manner, in the porch of the pavilion. Mutual explanations followed. The veil of silence was probably thrown over the offences of Kámrán, still chiefly secret and in embryo. Hindal's desertion and his open assumption of royalty were pardoned, at the intercession of his excellent mother, and of Kámrán; and he soon after arrived from Alwar, his jágír, and joined his brothers.

Humiliation of Hindal.

But as his offence was public, so was his humiliation. Humáyun, soon after his return, gave a grand feast in the palace of Báber's garden, to which all the Mírzas and the chief officers and Amírs were invited. In the midst of the entertainment, and in presence of the whole assembly, the Emperor, addressing Kámrán, asked him why Hindal Mírza had rebelled. Kámrán, turning to Hindal, who was present, inquired, what had induced him, instead of assisting his Majesty in his difficulties, to break out into revolt. The Mírza, covered with confusion, replied, that he was young and inexperienced, and that some Amírs, such as Záhid Beg, Khusrou Kokiltash, Háji Muhammed, and others, had misled him by bad advice, but entreated forgiveness of his offences, —an answer fatal to a man of ambition. "Well," said Humáyun, "at Kámrán Mírza's entreaty, I do forgive you and them; but correct your views, and amend your conduct; and above all, henceforward do not listen to my enemies." After some farther admonition, he

* Tab. Akb. f. 51. The author mentions that his father, Muhammed Mokim, was one of the few who attended the Emperor in this flight. See also Jouher, c. v.

added, "What is past is past. We must now all join manfully to repel the common enemy." The princes and Amírs, applauding his clemency, loudly joined in assuring him that, by his favour and the divine assistance, they would soon extirpate Shír Khan and his race. Solemn prayers and vows were repeated, and it was fixed that, as early as was practicable, the imperial tents should be pitched in the Zirefshán garden, ready for the field.* CHAP. V.

Humáyun rewards his deliverer at Chonsa.

Not long after the Emperor's return to Agra, the water-carrier, who had saved his life at Chonsa, presented himself at the public derbár. Humáyun, as soon as he saw the poor man from afar, mindful of his danger and his vow, descended from the throne, and, in strict compliance with the words of his promise, allowed him to mount "the throne of the world," and to occupy it for half a day. Whatever commands the new sovereign issued were literally and instantly fulfilled, even where the imperial decrees and usages happened to stand in the way; and the delighted monarch employed his power, during his short reign, to make several of his friends and family happy for the whole future course of their lives. This mummery did not escape the ridicule and scorn of Kámrán.†

Prepares again to attack Shír Shah;

Indeed, though policy and necessity united the brothers for a season, it was soon but too evident that there was little cordiality between them. Meanwhile, however, the levying of troops went on; many Amírs joined the Emperor with reinforcements from their jágírs; and among others, Muhammed Sultan Mírza

* Jouher, c. v.

† Abulfazl, Ferishta, and the author of the Kholáset-ul-Towáríkh, say that he filled the throne for half a-day: Jouher, for two hours (*do saat*). The author of the Kholáset adds that the report prevalent in his day was, that the water-carrier, to complete the semblance of imperial power, had his leathern *mashek*, or water-bag, cut into pieces of the size and shape of different coins, which were gilt or plated, and stamped with his name, and the date of his reign and of the Hejra, as a sovereign prince.

BOOK IV. A. D. 1539. and his sons, who had so long been in a state of rebellion, finding, probably, that no single branch of the divided house of Taimur could withstand the overwhelming superiority of the Afgháns, once more sought and gained the imperial pardon and protection. The army gradually swelled, but more perhaps in numbers than in effective strength.

A. D 1540. The brothers, after their reconciliation, held many long consultations on the course to be pursued, but, in the state of mutual feeling in which they were, to very little purpose. Nothing was concluded. Kámrán strongly urged Humáyun to remain in the capital, and to entrust to him the conduct of the campaign; undertaking, with his army of the Penjáb, which amounted to 20,000 men, still fresh and unbroken, to give a good account of Shír Shah. But to this the Emperor refused to consent, declaring that, as he had been treacherously defeated by the Afgháns, he was determined to have his revenge in person. During the delays that succeeded, Kámrán, who in no respect entered into the Emperor's views, showed the strongest desire to return to Láhúr, and repeatedly asked leave to go. Every wish of Kámrán's, but that alone, was readily granted. In vain did the Mírza urge that the government of his extensive territories required his presence. For seven months did he persist in his petitions and entreaties to be allowed to depart; when news arrived that Shír Shah, having cleared Bengal of the imperial troops, had collected a formidable army, and was on his march to attack the brothers.*

who advances to meet him. Ramzán, January.

Illness and retreat of Kámrán.

It might have been supposed that such a demonstration would have induced them to unite heartily against the common enemy. But Kámrán had no wish to add to his brother's power, which he still regarded as dangerous to his own independence: and his impatience

* Akbernáma, f. 46.; Tab. Akb. f. 151.; Tar. Niz. f. 214.; Tar. Bedáuni, f. 143.; Jouher, c. 5.; Ferishta, &c.

to return to the north was increased by a severe attack of illness, which ended in a complication of disorders. The climate of Hindustán was unfavourable to his constitution. His malady, in the course of two or three months, was aggravated by a slow fever attended with eruptions over his body, great emaciation and the partial loss of the use of his limbs. The power of medicine failed: it was insinuated that his complaints were the effect of poison, and he determined to return.

CHAP. V.

February to April.

"The retreat of Kámrán," says Haider Mírza *, "was the efficient cause of the rise of Shír Khan, and of the fall of the Chaghatái dynasty." The Emperor spared no entreaty to prevail upon him to leave some of the chief men of his army with their followers behind as auxiliaries; but, far from assenting to this, he perversely used his endeavours to seduce such of the Emperor's officers and troops as were in Agra, to accompany him. His minister, Amír Khwája Kilán, who never ceased urging him to quit Agra, was at last sent before with the mainbody of the army, and Kámrán himself prepared to follow.

Defeat of Shír Shah's advanced army.

Meanwhile Shír Shah advanced to the Ganges, which he crossed, and detached his younger son Kutb Khan across the Doáb to attack Kalpi and Etáwa, positions of importance from their vicinity to the capital. They were held by Yádgár Názir Mírza and Kásim Husein Sultan Uzbek; and a part of Kalpi had been given in jágír to Kámrán. The Amírs assembled their followers, and being joined by Sekander Sultan with a detachment of Kámrán's troops, marched out to check the progress of the invaders. They had no difficulty in bringing the enemy to an action, and completely routed them in a desperate battle, in which Kutb Khan was left dead on the field. His head was cut off, and sent with many others to Agra. The victorious generals strongly

* Taríkh-e-Reshídi, f. 367.

BOOK IV.

A.D. 1540.

advised the Emperor to follow up his success, and instantly to take the field in person. He accordingly marched from Agra towards the Ganges to meet and engage Shír Shah.*

Haider Mírza Doghlat in Humáyun's camp.

The efforts of Humáyun to detain his brother and his troops at this important and dangerous crisis were unsuccessful; but several of Kámrán's officers were prevailed upon to remain. Of these, the most eminent was his cousin, the celebrated Haider Mírza Doghlat †, who, in his own defence, states at some length the arguments used to influence him, and they are curious as showing the feelings of the brothers to each other. He was high in the Mírza's confidence, and we have seen that he was even left, for upwards of a year, in charge of the government of Láhúr, during Kámrán's last expedition for the recovery of Kandahár. Kámrán remonstrated with him on his proposed desertion; and reminded him that he had received him in his Court when an exile from his own country; that he had treated him all along as if he had been a brother, with the most distinguished confidence and consideration, and intrusted to him the chief conduct of his affairs; and that, in return for all this, to leave him, his cousin, at such a moment, when a powerful enemy threatened his kingdom, and his body was wasting under a dangerous disease, would be the height of unkindness and ingratitude. On the other hand, Haider tells us that he had become the Emperor's brother after the Moghul fashion, an engagement which bound them to each other by the strongest ties of honour: the Emperor never spoke to him nor addressed him, even in his public firmáns, by any other name than that of brother and friend, a distinction shown to none of the Sultans of the Court, nor even to his own brothers. Humáyun,

* Akbernáma and Tab. Akberi, as above.

† Haider was the son of Muhammed Husein Korkán Doghlat, by the sister of Báber's mother.

on his part also, remonstrated with Haider Mírza, and laid claim to his services. He said, that though Haider was in Kámrán's employment, he himself had really been latterly guided in every thing by his counsels; that as to his being Kámrán's cousin, he stood in exactly the same relation to him; and as for his illness, even if it were real, Haider was no physician: that the present was no ordinary time: that, on the issue of the approaching combat with Shír Shah, depended the fate, not of Humáyun merely, but of Kámrán himself, nay of the whole family of Báber, and of Hindustán itself: that if Shír Khan was successful, all was lost, and Kámrán would not find himself safe even in Láhúr: that, as a faithful and enlightened friend of their house, it was Haider's duty to consult the general good and remain behind: unless, indeed, he dreaded the issue of the contest, and was anxious to shelter himself from danger by getting to Láhúr as a place whence, in case of calamity, he could easily betake himself elsewhere at will. "This reasoning," says Haider Mírza, "was to me conclusive, and I made up my mind to remain. Being unable, by any entreaties, to obtain Kámrán's permission, I staid without it. Kámrán Mírza, leaving Iskander Mírza with about a thousand men as auxiliaries, and taking with him as many as he could *, set out for Láhúr: and this," continues he, "to the enemy was a victory, and to his friends a defeat."

His character of the Emperor.

The selfish and short-sighted policy of Kámrán was fatal to his family: and Humáyun, with many excellent and agreeable qualities, had not the talents required to support a sinking empire. We have a character of him, as he was at this time, drawn by an able hand, which

* Ferishta, vol. ii. p. 89., follows Haider in regard to the number of men left. The Akbernáma, f. 46., has three thousand under Abdalla Moghul; the Kholáset-ul-Towáríkh has the same number; the Tab. Akb. and Nisábnáma, f. 93., have two thousand. The number carried back is stated at twenty thousand. He must have been joined by reinforcements after leaving the Penjáb.

BOOK IV. A. D. 1540. bears every mark of truth and impartiality. "Humáyun," says Haider Mírza, "as he was the eldest, was the greatest and most distinguished of Báber's sons. I have seen few persons possessed of so much natural talent and excellence as he: but in consequence of his having dissolute and sensual men in his service, and of his intercourse with them, and with men of mean and profligate character, such as in particular Mouláua Muhammed Farghari, and others like him, he contracted some bad habits, as, for instance, the excessive use of opium*; and the business which, as a prince, he should himself have managed, he left to them. Nevertheless, he had many excellent qualities. In battle he was steady and brave; in conversation, ingenious and lively; and at the social board, full of wit. He was kind-hearted and generous. He was a dignified and magnificent prince, and observed much state; insomuch that, though I came into his service at Agra, in his broken fortunes, when people said his pomp and style were no longer what they had been, yet, when the army was arrayed for the Ganges campaign, at which time the superintendence devolved upon me, the number of artisans who accompanied him was seventeen thousand, from which the extent of the other branches of his establishment may be imagined."

State of the imperial army. End of Zikáda; beginning of April.

It was about the beginning of April when the imperial tents were pitched in the Zirefshán garden. The natural consequences of the Emperor's want of success in the preceding campaigns, and of the discord of the brothers, were visible in the bad spirit that prevailed in the camp and court. The higher Amírs, and especially the Chaghatái nobles, were discontented. The army consisted, in a great measure, of troops hastily raised, and who had seen no service. The great body of veterans had perished in the Bengal expedition. In

* Tarikh-e-Reshidi, f. 365.

the camp there was a general languor and disaffection. The officers showed little zeal, the troops little ardour; all was disorganised. Shír Shah appears to have recrossed the Ganges on the Emperor's approach, and to have baffled him in an attempt to cross the river, over which he had thrown a bridge. Humáyun then marched along the banks to Kanáuj. Some of the enemy's ships appearing in the river to dispute the passage, one of the largest was sunk by the fire from the imperial guns. The events that followed may be best understood from the narrative, somewhat abridged, of Haider Mírza, who held a high rank in his army, tinged though in some respects it may be by the colouring thrown upon them by his wounded feelings.

Haider Mírza's account of the campaign.

"The imperial army reached the banks of the Ganges in the best way that it could. There it encamped, and lay for about a month, the Emperor being on one side of the river, and Shír Khan on the other, facing each other. The armies may have amounted to more than two hundred thousand men.* Muhammed Sultan Mírza, and his sons Ulugh Mírza and Shah Mírza, were princes of the house of Taimur, who had been entertained with every mark of kindness and kingly favour by Báber, but after his death had more than once revolted, had been pardoned and received back into favour by Humáyun. They now once more deserted. This defection quite changed the face of things. Desertion became general in the army. The most surprising part of it was, that such as deserted did not go over to Shír Khan, and of course could expect nothing from him. The general cry was, 'Let us go and rest in our own homes.' A number even of Kámrán's auxiliary troops deserted, and fled to Láhúr.

"The Emperor had with him a formidable artillery;

* The Emperor's army is usually stated at 90,000, or 100,000; Shír Shah's, at 50,000.—Tar. Nizámi, f. 214.; Nisábnáma, f. 92.; Bedáuni, f. 143.

seven hundred carriages, each having a swivel, and drawn by four pair of bullocks; and sixty-one heavy guns, each drawn by sixty pair of bullocks, and supplied, not with stone, but with leaden bullets.

"As the army had begun to desert, it was judged better to risk a battle than to see it go to ruin without fighting. If the result was unfavourable, in that case we could not at least be accused of having abandoned an empire like Hindustán without striking a blow. Another consideration was, that if we passed the river, desertion would no longer be possible. We, therefore, crossed over.

"Both armies entrenched themselves. Every day, skirmishes occurred between the irregulars and the Hindus. At length, however, the monsoon rains came on, and there was a heavy fall which flooded the camp. To move was indispensable. Those about the Emperor told him that such another rain would ruin the army; and proposed to move to a rising ground, which the inundation could not reach, and which lay in front of the enemy. I went to reconnoitre, and found the place suitable for the purpose. They wished to march immediately. I represented that, when we did march, it would be desirable to divert the attention of the enemy by engaging them in skirmishes, as it would not do to be drawn into a general action, when the army was marching to change its ground: that next day was the tenth of Moharrem, when we could draw out our troops in battle array, without advancing on the Afghans, or courting an engagement, but that if they left their trenches to attack us, we should engage; that a battle we must have in the end; but that, in the first instance, it was best for us to draw up the army in battle array, and plant the heavy cannon and small guns in front; that there were nearly five thousand gunners, who could be stationed with the guns: that if the enemy did not come out that day, we should return back to the camp; and next day, having again drawn out the troops in the same order as before, we could keep our ground, while the baggage and stores were conveyed, covered by our lines, from the old camp to the new ground; and when that was accomplished, we might retire to our new quarters. CHAP. V.

"The plan was approved of, and, accordingly, next day* the army was drawn out to carry it into effect. The ranks were marshalled, but were unsteady: the guns and cannon, under the guidance of Muhammed Khan Rúmi, the son of Ustád-Kuli, Ustád Ahmed Rúmi and Hasan Khalífat, were moved forward to the appointed place, accompanied by the artillery men, and chains were extended between them, as is the practice. In the rest of the army were Amírs, — Amírs only in name, who enjoyed governments and rich jágírs, without the slightest tincture of prudence, or knowledge, or energy, or emulation, or nobleness of mind, or generosity, qualities from which nobility draws its name. The Emperor placed the author on his left side, so that his right was next the Emperor's left; on the Emperor's right was a chosen band of his tilándeh. On my left were placed my retainers, four hundred in number, all tried men, veterans who had experienced the changes of fortune, and were nurtured in hardships. On the day of the battle, they were all mounted on tipchák horses, and clad in mail. Between me and the extreme left of the centre stood seven and twenty Amírs, all having the horse-tail banner.† Beyond that was the left wing, the extent and nature of which may be judged of from the other. On the day of battle, when Shír Khan marched out with his army in columns, of the seven and twenty horse-tail standards that were with these great lords, there was not one that was not

And of the battle of Kanáuj. Moharrem 10. A.H. 947, May 17.

* Roz-e-Ashúr. Moharrem, 10.

† Or, more literally, the *túgh*, or banner of the tail of the Tibet, or mountain, cow. This was held only by Amírs of a high class.

BOOK IV. A.D. 1540.

hid, from fear lest the enemy might see and bear down upon it. The soldiership and bravery of the Amírs may be estimated from this trait of courage.

" Shír Khan led out his troops in five divisions of a thousand men each, having one of three thousand in advance. I reckoned his whole force at less than fifteen thousand, while I estimated the Chaghatái army at forty thousand, or thereabouts, all mounted on tipchák horses, and in armour. The noise of their movement was like the waves of the ocean; the courage of their Amírs and commanders such as has been said. When Shír Khan's army quitted their trenches, two of the columns drew up before the ditch, the other three advanced towards our army. On our side the centre was in motion, to take the ground I had marked out for it, but we were unable to reach it. In the Chaghatái army every man, Amír and Vazír, rich and poor, has his camp-followers (gholáms), so that an Amír of any note, if he has an hundred retainers *, will, for himself and them, have perhaps five hundred camp-followers, who, in the day of battle, do not attend their master, and are not masters of themselves, so that they wander at large; and as, when they have lost their master's control, they are under no other, however much they may be beaten back on face or head, with mace or stick, they are totally unmanageable. In a word, by the pressure of the masses of these men, the troops were quite unable to keep their ranks; the camp-followers, crowding behind, bore them so down that they were thrown into disorder; and the crowd continuing still to press on, some on one side, some on another, pushed the soldiers upon the chains of the carriages. Even then the camp-followers, who were behind, went on urging those before, till in many instances the chains burst, and every person who was

* Nouker.

stationed at the chain so broken, driven out beyond it, while the order, even of such as kept within, was totally broken and destroyed, and, from the pressure and confusion, not a man could act. CHAP. V.

"Such was the state of the centre, nor were matters more prosperous on the right. As Shír Khan's three columns approached, a cry of 'defeat' was heard, and that instant a panic seized the men; and before an arrow was shot from a bow, they fled like chaff before the wind. The fugitives ran towards the centre. Here they found all in disorder, the camp-followers, having pushed clear through the line, had disordered every thing, and separated the Mír from the men, and the men from the Mír. But when, to this confusion, the rush of the terrified men flying from the right was added, the defeat was sure, and the day irretrievable. The Chaghatái army, which counted forty thousand men in armour, besides camp-followers and artisans *, fled before ten thousand. It was not a fight, but a rout, for not a man, friend or foe, was even wounded. Shír Khan gained a great victory; the Chaghatáis suffered a ruinous defeat. Not a cannon was fired—not a gun. The artillery was totally useless.

"When the Chaghatáis took to flight, the distance from the field of battle to the banks of the river might be about a farsang.† Before a man was wounded, the whole army, Amírs, Beháders, and common men, fled, broken and dismayed, to the banks of the Ganges. The enemy's army followed, and overtook them. The Chaghatáis, not having time to take off their horse-armour or their own cuirasses ‡, plunged, accoutred as they were, into the stream. Its breadth might be about five bowshots. Many Amírs of illustrious name perished; and all from want of concert and control. Every one went, or came, at his own will. When we

* Shágird-pesheh.

† Nearly four miles.

‡ *Kichim* and *jaba*.

BOOK IV. A.D. 1540.

emerged from the river on the other bank, a monarch, who at noon had seventeen thousand artisans in his establishments, was mounted upon a wretched spavined horse, with both his head and feet bare. Permanence belongs to God alone, the King of kings. The author had nearly a thousand persons, retainers and servants, of whom only sixty escaped out of the river. All the rest were drowned. From this instance the general loss may be estimated." *

Other accounts of that disaster.

Such is the account of Haider Mírza, which, though it bears evident mark of the disappointment and chagrin which embittered his mind, is that of an able man, and an eyewitness who had the best means of information. From other authorities, even more disposed to cover the failures of the imperial arms, we may glean a few further particulars of this battle, which, for a season, was decisive of the fate of Hindustán. The rains appear to have commenced with unwonted violence, nearly a fortnight before the usual time. Humáyun commanded his own centre, Hindal the advance, Askeri the right, Yádgár Násir the left. On Shír Shah's side, Jilál Khan with his column, chiefly composed of Niázi Afgháns, advanced against Hindal, Mobárez Khan led his against Yádgár and Kásim Husein Sultan, while Khowás Khan was opposed to Askeri. The action is said to have commenced by a rencounter between Hindal's division and that of Jilál Khan, in which Jilál being thrown from his horse, his troops fell into disorder, and Yádgár, on the left, having gained some advantage over the force opposed to him, drove in the right of the Afgháns upon their centre. On observing this, we are told Shír Shah led up a body of his reserve, and checked the progress of the imperialists, while Khowás Khan, on his side, rode forward to attack Askeri, whose division instantly fled. Humáyun in

* Tar. Reshídi, ff. 368—371.

CHAP. V.

vain attempted to rally his troops, and to seize a rising ground. His personal exertions were unavailing. All agree that in a short time every thing was confusion and flight.*

Flight of Humáyun.

When he reached the Ganges, he found an old elephant, and mounted into the howdah, where he found an eunuch of his household, named Káfúr. He ordered the driver to cross the river, but the man told him that the animal was quite unequal to it, and would be drowned. Káfúr hinted to the Emperor that the man wished to carry over the elephant to the Afgháns, and that it was better to put him to death; that he would undertake to guide the animal. On this Humáyun drew his sword, and struck the driver, who fell wounded into the water. The eunuch then stepped down on the elephant's neck, and directed him across. As they gained the banks, which were very steep, the Emperor found it difficult to mount them, when a soldier, who had just gained the shore, presenting his hand to the Emperor, drew him up. Humáyun asked his deliverer's name, and was answered, Shems-ed-dín Muhammed of Ghazni, in the service of Mírza Kámrán. The Emperor made him high promises. At this moment he was recognised by Mokadam Beg, one of Kámrán's nobles, who came forward and presented his own horse.†

* Akbernáma, ff. 45, 46, 47.; Jouher, c. 5.; Ferishta, vol. ii. pp. 89, 90.; Kháfi Khan, ff. 48, 49. The Tab. Akb. ff. 151. 166., and Tar. Niz. f. 214., Tar. Bed. 143., with the Nisábnáma, f. 93., agree that the Chaghatái army fled with little or no fighting.

† Akbernáma, f. 47.; Nisábnáma, f. 93.; Jouher, c. 5.; Tar. Bedáuni, f. 144.; Kholáset-ul-Towáríkh, f. 260.

The narrative of Jouher, which he gives on the Emperor's own authority, differs from the account of the others in several particulars. "His Majesty further related," says he, "that when he arrived near the bank, it was so steep that he could not find a place to ascend. At length, some of the standard bearers (túgh-bárán), sons of Bába Jeláir, viz., Mírza Muhammed and Ters Beg, tied their turbans together, and throwing an end of the cloth to him, he, with some difficulty, climbed up; they then brought him a horse, on which he mounted and proceeded to Agra." — Stewart's Jouher, p. 22., corrected by the

BOOK IV. A. D. 1540.

Shems-ed-dín afterwards became one of the most distinguished noblemen of the empire, was made Khan Azim, and was the atkeh, or foster father, of Akber, in those days a connection of no small importance.

Humáyun was soon after joined by Askeri Mírza, and by Yádgár Násir Mírza, and they all, with the few attendants they could collect, pushed on for Agra. By the road they passed a walled village *, the inhabitants of which, probably accustomed to be plundered alike by the conquerors and the conquered, refused all intercourse with the fugitives, even in the way of buying and selling the necessaries of life; and, it was alleged, attempted to cut off and plunder the stragglers. Humáyun, when informed of this refusal, desired Askeri Mírza, Yádgár and Hindal, who had also joined him, to go and punish their insolence. If we believe Abulfazl, about thirty thousand of the neighbouring population had by this time risen to defend themselves, or attack the retiring troops. But the number on the spot was probably inconsiderable. Askeri declined

original. Stewart calls the *túghbárán*, "camp-colour men:" I suspect the word should be *túghdárán*, "nobles who had the túgh-banner," Bába Jeláir was a man of high rank.

* The name of this village is not very clear. Major Price (Mahom. Annals) calls it Bankapúr, or Behgánu; Major Stewart's Jouher has Bhyngang. My copy of the Akbernáma, No. 1. f. 47., reads Behkánu, or Behgánu; that No 2. f. 96., has Bingala. In the Memoirs of Jouher, the opposition made near this village is not treated as so formidable as it is by Abulfazl. It is said "that the peasants stopped the road, and one of them wounded Myrza Yádgár with an arrow: on which the Myrza said to the prince Askeri, 'Do you go on and punish these villagers, while I stop to dress my wound.' The prince was displeased at this request, and gave the Myrza some abuse: on which the other retorted in harsher language, when the prince struck him three times with his horsewhip. 'I will repay you after the fashion of kings,' said Yádgár, and struck him several successive blows with his whip, without intermission. When intelligence of this unpleasant fracas reached the Emperor, he said, 'They had better have vented their spite on the robbers than on each other. What has happened cannot be recalled; but let us hear no more of it.'"—Stewart's Mem. of Humáyun, p. 23., slightly modified from the original. Abulfazl makes the first blows proceed from Yádgár.

CHAP. V.

going. "It is from such want of co-operation among you," said Yádgár Násir Mírza indignantly, "that we are brought to the state in which we are; and still you are not corrected." These words produced an altercation, and some blows of a whip followed on both sides. Yádgár and Hindal Mírza then attacked the villagers, and put many of them to the sword. Mírza Askeri's conduct on this occasion gave great offence to the Emperor. From this place Humáyun posted on to Agra.*

He arrives at Agra.

At Agra, Humáyun found little to console him. The quarrels of the brothers and their mutual jealousies had thrown every thing into disorder. The whole government and army were disorganised. Kámrán, when he set out from Agra, had induced some of the officers of government, and a great portion of the garrison, to accompany him to the Penjáb. The country had been drained of troops to form the Emperor's army, the greater part of which had perished in the Ganges, or by the sword of the Afgháns, while the scanty remainder was dispersed in flight. There was, therefore, no considerable force in reserve to form the nucleus of a new army. Nor did any means exist of calling out, in this emergency, the national resources that were still left. The nobles were discontented; the peasantry, a prey to misrule and anarchy; the Afgháns hard in pursuit. The Emperor, without entering the city, alighted in the suburbs at the house† of Syed Rafía-ed-dín, a very learned and eminent Sufi doctor, who, like many of the distinguished divines of his time, had a high reputation for political sagacity. As circumstances were urgent, Hindal Mírza was sent with his followers into the fort to

* Akbernáma, f. 47.

† The Akbernáma (f. 47.) makes this visit take place the morning after Humáyun's arrival. The Nisábnáma (f. 94.) asserts that, in this conversation, Humáyun affirmed that in the late battle he saw a troop of derwishes attack his lines, and not desist till they had broken through them. This of course referred to something supernatural.

BOOK IV. A.D. 1540. bring off the Emperor's mother, sisters and family, with their domestics, and such part of their treasure and jewels as they were able to remove. The Syed, meanwhile, placed before the Emperor, bread, melons, and such homely fare as his house at the moment afforded, and soothed his mind by moral and religious reflections on the instability of fortune. Having breakfasted, the Emperor consulted him as to the practicability of defending Agra. From this attempt the Syed strongly dissuaded him, as being hopeless, and advised him to hasten forward to Láhúr, where his brother Kámrán's power was still unbroken. When the Emperor departed, he presented him with a horse richly caparisoned, and gave him his blessing. Humáyun, now abandoning his capital, rode off to Síkri.* He was soon after followed and joined by Hindal with the household.

Humáyun had not been long at Síkri, in his father Báber's garden, when an arrow discharged from an eminence by an unknown hand, fell close by his side. Haider Mírza and an officer, who were sent to discover whence the arrow proceeded, both returned wounded. Proceeds towards Delhi. Apprehensive of treachery, he proceeded on his route to Delhi. He seems to have been in an irritable state, and had but few Amírs left along with him. One of them, Mír Fakr Ali, happening to ride on before him on the road, Humáyun called out angrily, "It was by thy advice that I passed the Ganges. Better would it have been that thou hadst perished there than that this should happen. Go immediately, and leave me." Fakr Ali fell back.† The Emperor had not a more faithful or zealous servant than the Mír, who died soon after Sefer 20. June 26. on the road to Sirhend.

But the Emperor was not doomed to retreat in quiet. Hardly had he reached his ground at the first stage, at Bijúna on the banks of the Kanbír, when Askeri

* Jouher, c. 5.; Akbernáma, f. 47.

† Jouher, c. 6.; Akbernáma, f. 47.

arrived with information that Mír Feríd Gúr, who had been sent in pursuit of them by Shír Shah, was fast approaching. The Mírza, therefore, advised Humáyun to renew his march without losing a moment, offering, with the few troops still left, to cover his retreat. All was now unseemly trepidation. "In consequence of this advice," says Jouher, "the (Emperor) mounted his horse and set off, but the followers were thrown into the greatest alarm, not knowing what to do. No one attempted to assist another; the son paid no attention to his father, nor the father to the son, but each person endeavoured to conceal whatever valuables he had, and to make his escape; and, to add to their distress, a very heavy rain fell. In short, God preserve us from seeing such another day."* The Emperor, struck with the misery and dismay of his followers, seems at length to have thought of conducting his retreat with some degree of method. He ordered the troops to halt; divided them into different columns. He himself led the advance; Hindal had the right, Yádgár Násir the left, and the other Amírs brought up the rear. "It was ordered," continued Jouher †, "that if any person went before the Emperor, he should be punished, and his house plundered."

CHAP. V

And to the Penjáb. Moharrem 18. May 25.

Humáyun at length reached Delhi, where, on the 25th of May, he was joined by Kásim Husein Sultan Uzbek, and several other Amírs. Hindal and Askeri now took leave to proceed to their jágírs, the one to Alwar, the other to Sambhal, for the purpose of making some hasty arrangements on the spot. The Emperor did not venture to prolong his stay in the ancient capital of the kingdom, and on the 27th, only ten days after the decisive battle, he left it. On the 29th, Hindal Mírza and Haider Mírza rejoined him at the village of Rahtak, where he halted next day. Thence,

Moharrem 20. May 27.

* Stewart's Jouher's Memoirs, p. 24.

† Jouher, from the original.

BOOK IV. A. D. 1540. Beginning of Sefer.

by long marches of ten or twelve kos, they proceeded to Sirhend, which they reached before the middle of June. There Hindal was halted for a few days, while the Emperor proceeded to Máchíwára on the Satlej. As the river was swollen by the rains, and as no boats were to be found, they passed it as they best could, and marched on.

Shír Shah at Delhi.

Intelligence now arrived that Shír Shah had halted on reaching Delhi, but had sent forward detachments in pursuit, which were only forty or fifty kos off. The Afghán prince, during his whole life, whether from superstition or policy, had maintained a close intimacy with the leading devotees and holy men of his religion, and with the whole body of religious mendicants, whose influence often afforded him essential service in his various political enterprises. He seems to have been willing to have it believed that a supernatural power favoured all his designs, and among other means, led him on by dreams and visions of the night. The morning of the discomfiture of Humáyun near Kanáuj, he related that, the night before, he dreamed that he and Humáyun, alighting from their horses, had wrestled between the two armies; after long and keen struggling, the Emperor threw him upon the ground, and made strong efforts to lift him up again from it, but could not succeed; Shír Shah, clinging to the ground, baffled his attempts. He himself proceeded to interpret the dream, affirming that his aim and ambition had long been to take possession of the ground of Hindustán, which his dream portended that he would do, and that he would baffle Humáyun. Immediately after the battle he pushed after the fugitives, and took possession of Agra, where he got possession of the treasures and arsenals, and then hastened on to Delhi. Here he paused for some time to give the orders rendered necessary by his great success. No effectual resistance was now presented to him from any point of the Emperor's peculiar dominions. The hopes of the family of Báber

CHAP. V.

were turned to the Penjáb, and to Kábul. Shír Shah pushed on a strong force in pursuit of the flying monarch, which soon approached the Satlej. Upon this Hindal Mírza, with the Emperor's rear-guard, crossed that river, and joining the main body, the whole proceeded to Jalindher, between the Satlej and Bíah, where Hindal's division again halted, while Humáyun proceeded to Láhúr on the Rávi.* On his arrival at Láhúr, Mozeffer Beg was despatched with a body of troops to support Hindal, and encamped on the western bank of the Bíah. The Afgháns, who had passed through Sirhend, and crossed the Satlej in pursuit, soon appeared on the opposite bank. Askeri Mírza arriving about this time from Sambhal, all the four brothers met at Láhúr. Muhammed Sultan Mírza and his sons, who, it may be remembered, had deserted from the Emperor's army before it crossed the Ganges, and had gone to Láhúr, fled from that city, as soon as Humáyun approached it, and went down to Multán.† When the imperial princes held their consultations at Láhúr, it was still only the beginning of July, not two months since the grand discomfiture of Kanáuj.

His parties pursue Humáyun across the Satlej.

Rebi I. 1. July 5.

When Humáyun resolved to bend his flight towards the Penjáb, he had cherished a hope that Kámrán might still receive him cordially, and acknowledge and submit to him as his sovereign lord; or at least employ the whole force of his extensive dominions in repelling and humbling the Afgháns. He was disappointed in all these hopes. Kámrán was much more his rival than his subject, or even his ally. The Emperor was received with external honours, and suspicion that could not be disguised. At Láhúr he found nothing pre-

Selfish conduct of Kámrán.

* Called also Gandwál, or Goindwál.

† Akbernáma, f. 47.; Jouher, c. 6.; Tabakát-e Akberi, f. 151.; Tar. Niz. f. 188.; Nisábnáma-Afgh. ff. 93, 94. Shems-ed-dín Muhammed, the fortunate soldier who assisted Humáyun in mounting the banks of the Ganges at Kanáuj, also came to Láhúr, and was gratefully welcomed by the Emperor.

BOOK IV.

A. D. 1540.

pared to meet the common enemy. The conduct of Kámrán at this crisis was unkind to his brother, and ruinous to the family. His situation was certainly very trying. He was placed between two dangers, and hardly knew whether most to dread his brother or Shír Shah. He saw that the hereditary claims of the former might be employed to wrest from him the whole of his extensive dominions, which stretched from Persian Khorásán and the Helmend, to the Satlej and Hissár-Firóza. The utmost success of the former would be confined to the conquest of the Penjáb, leaving Kábul, Ghazni, and Kandahár untouched. Hence his energies appeared to be paralysed, and he was evidently more anxious to keep under his brother Humáyun and his dreaded pretensions, than to meet and repel the Afgháns. Could the brothers have trusted each other, and combined to act as their common interest required, much might still have been effected; but there was no sympathy among them, no mutual confidence. All was suspicion, jealousy, and distrust.

Treaty among the imperial brothers.

The Afgháns continued to advance. When their entrance into the Penjáb was known, the brothers, and such of the Amírs as had followed them, or were on the spot, held many consultations, to which the most eminent of the holy men, who then flourished in that country, were invited, that they might at once add solemnity to the council by their presence, and enlighten it by their wisdom. Terms were finally agreed to, after much discussion, and a regular treaty of alliance and concord concluded between the princes, and sealed and witnessed by all the assembly. But signatures and seals were vain, where confidence and unity of purpose were wanting. Neither adversity, nor the progress of events not to be mistaken, could teach them the most obvious lessons of prudence. Each still urged on a separate project of his own. Humáyun, who had been the greatest sufferer, enforced the necessity of unanimity, and the mischiefs of discord. But his past success and conduct were not such as to make them turn to him with much hope, as the leader of a confederacy. Kámrán Mírza, who, from the first, betrayed the general cause, and consulted only his own individual interest, was anxious chiefly for the speedy breaking up of the congress, that the princes might separate, and he himself be at liberty to proceed to Kábul. He, therefore, proposed to retreat from Láhúr, as soon as it was attacked, into the neighbouring hill-country; and he undertook to convey the families of his brothers and of their adherents into the highlands of Kábul, above the passes, where they would be safe; after which he engaged to return, and join his brothers. Hindal Mírza and Yádgár Násir Mírza had a plan of their own. They recommended an attack upon the fort and territory of Bheker on the Indus; after conquering which, they affirmed that it would be no difficult matter to invade and subdue Gujrát; and, aided by the wealth of that kingdom, to resume operations with a powerful force, in the very heart of Hindustán. The plan of Haider Mírza was different still. His thoughts were turned towards Kashmír, which he had once already overrun, and with which he was well acquainted. He advised the princes to occupy and fortify the skirts of the hill-country between Sirhend and Sarang, and undertook within two months to be in possession of Kashmír, whither their families could be sent as a place of safety, for which no situation could be better fitted. In support of his opinion he maintained that it would take Shír Shah at least four months to bring on to the hill-country his carriages and artillery, on which he chiefly relied; and that, should the Afgháns attempt to follow them among the mountains, their army, in a short time, would be completely ruined.*

CHAP. V.

Their want of union.

* Akbernáma, f. 47.

BOOK IV.

A.D. 1540.

All these deliberations, however, ended without leading to any combined plan of operation. Humáyun did not possess the qualities that command at once respect and confidence. Each of the princes was led to pursue schemes of his own, and became an adventurer on his own account. The genius of Báber had descended on none of his sons. Kámrán, on whom every thing depended, was resolved to admit of no competitor in his dominions; and, at the very moment when he signed the treaty with the other princes, and joined in their deliberations, regardless of his oaths, was carrying on an underhand correspondence with their inveterate enemy, Shír Shah. For that purpose he had secretly sent Kázi Abdalla, his Sadr or Chief Judge, to endeavour to enter into a treaty with the Afghán, hoping to confirm his own independence and power, by an alliance with the common enemy. He instructed his envoy to assure Shír Shah, that, if left in possession of the Penjáb, he was ready to evince his gratitude by rendering him the most important services.*

Treachery of Kámrán.

Shír Shah halted for some time at Delhi, highly delighted with his success, and unwilling, by an imprudent advance, to hazard any portion of what he had gained. He heard with some alarm of the assemblage at Láhúr, and was apprehensive of its consequences. The arrival of the Sadr was, therefore, to him a most pleasing occurrence. It relieved him from great anxiety. He gave him a gracious reception, learned with rapture the divisions that prevailed among the Mírzas, and readily promised Kámrán all that he asked. The Sadr, probably anxious to expel Humáyun from the Penjáb, pressed Shír Shah to advance without delay towards Láhúr; and the king soon sent him back, accompanied by an ambassador, who had instructions carefully to mark the real state of affairs, and to re-

Shír Shah receives his overtures,

* Akbernáma, f. 48.; Kholáset-ul-Towáríkh, f. 260. See also Jouher, c. 6.; Tar. Nizámi, f. 188.

turn and report what he saw. Kámrán made every thing be conducted as if this mission had been to the Emperor. The ambassador was introduced to a public audience of Humáyun, with much pomp, in a royal garden at Láhúr, when Kámrán entertained the Emperor and his brothers at a grand festival; the whole population of the city being called out to witness the entry and the reception. But the real business was transacted with Kámrán himself at a private nocturnal conference. The Sadr was once more sent back, with new instructions, and again meeting Shír Shah, who by this time had advanced to the banks of the Bíah river near Sultanpúr, encouraged him to cross it. Mozeffer Turkomán, who had been left to defend the passage, was unable to resist the force opposed to him, and soon after arrived at Láhúr, bringing information that Shír Shah had forced his way over, and secured a position on the right bank, in spite of all the opposition he could offer; was bringing the rest of his troops across, and might soon be expected to arrive in sight of Láhúr.

CHAP. V.

enters the Penjáb.

There was now no longer room for delay. Whether Kámrán was overreached by Shír Shah, or whether he had privately consented to surrender to him all the Penjáb, it is difficult to determine. The former supposition is most probable. At all events no attempt at resistance was made. The Emperor and the Mírzas instantly abandoned Láhúr, crossed the Rávi, which happened to be fordable, and hastened towards the Chenáb. Kámrán conveyed his followers and his property across in boats. The princes were at that moment on such bad terms with each other, that some of Humáyun's counsellors advised him, as the only way to render the army unanimous and efficient, to make away with Kámrán, who was evidently intriguing to depose him. But this proposal the Emperor at once rejected. "No," he replied, in the style of his country, "never, for the vanities of this perishable world, will I imbrue

The imperial family quits Láhúr.

Jemádi II. 29.
October 31.

BOOK IV. A.D. 1540.

my hands in the blood of a brother, but will for ever remember the dying words of our respected parent (Báber), who said to me, 'O, Humáyun! beware! beware! Do not quarrel with your brothers, nor even form any evil intentions towards them?' These words are engraved on my heart, never to be erased."

Humáyun, in the exigency in which he was placed, had resolved to adopt the plan proposed by Haider Mírza, and to attempt the conquest of Kashmír. After crossing the Rávi, he marched on to the town of Hazára, which he reached in the morning. Here he was informed that Kámrán, with his troops and followers all in arms, was marching right towards him. The Emperor's followers offered to arm also to repel any aggression, but he forbade them, and waited the issue. Kámrán, on coming up, sat down beside him, when they conversed for about an hour. The Mírza said, that from the instant he had last set out for Hindustán, so incessant had been his occupations, that he had enjoyed no interval of rest, and that his followers also were quite exhausted. He, therefore, found it necessary to use his endeavours to put his affairs on a proper footing, and to recruit his force, and asked the Emperor's leave to proceed to Kábul for that purpose, promising to return as soon as that object was effected. Humáyun assented, with prayers for his safety and success, after which the brothers separated. Humáyun then continued his march, and halted about four kos further on; when he got notice that Hindal Mírza, Yádgár Mírza, and Kásim Husein Sultan Uzbek, had been induced by Beg Mírak to set out on their proposed attempt on Gujrát. Many of the Emperor's followers, upon this, deserted and joined them. Hindal's party marched down the Penjáb towards the Balúch country.

Rejeb 1. Nov. 1.

Kámrán departs for Kábul;

Hindal, for Sind and Guzrát.

Humáyun meditates

Humáyun, thus abandoned by two of his brothers,

* Stewart's Jouher, p. 26.; Akbernáma, f. 48.

hastened forward to join his cousin, Haider Mírza*, in the projected expedition against Kashmír. CHAP. V.

an expedition to Kashmír. Recent events there.

It is necessary shortly to advert to the state of parties in that country. When Kámrán marched from the Penjáb for the purpose of recovering Kandahár from the Persians, it has been mentioned that he left Haider Mírza in charge of Láhúr. At that time several nobles of Kashmír, who were discontented with the reigning prince of that kingdom, waited on Haider Mírza, who had formerly commanded in Kashmír, and attempted, through his influence, to obtain from Kámrán a body of troops with which to dethrone the present ruler, and restore themselves to their country, from which they were exiled. Haider Mírza, who, from the incidents of his past life, took a lively interest in the affairs of Kashmír, entered warmly into their views; but, in spite of all his exertions, was, from various circumstances, always prevented from procuring for them the assistance they desired, while Kámrán remained at Láhúr.

Afterwards, when that prince was lying at Agra, Haider Mírza succeeded in prevailing upon him to send Bába Jujkeh, one of his officers, to attempt the adventure along with the exiled nobles. But so dilatory was the general in his motions that, before he reached the scene of action, the news of Humáyun's defeat at Chonsa arrived, an event which withdrew the attention of the Mírzas from distant expeditions, and turned it to providing for their immediate safety. The attempt on Kashmír was therefore suspended, and the exiled nobles were placed in the Noushehr and Rájwari † territory, in the opening of the mountains between the Penjáb and Kashmír, to wait better times.

The exiles, however, never ceased from urging Haider Mírza to support their interests; and after Haider

* Haider was the maternal cousin of Báber.

† Ráj ·ur.

BOOK IV. A.D. 1540.

changed Kámrán's service for that of Humáyun, he had regularly communicated their letters to the Emperor, who, in his present distress, seeing nothing better to be done, agreed, with their assistance, to attempt the conquest of Kashmír. He had, therefore, sent forward Haider Mírza, with such of his troops as were willing to join in the enterprise, to Noushehr, which was the most practicable road into the mountain-circled valley, and where he could see and confer with the exiled and the discontented Kashmírian nobles. Haider was to be joined by Sekander Topchi, who had a considerable jágír in that quarter, and by his followers; and in addition to these, Khwája Kilán Beg, one of Kámrán's principal Amírs, was to meet them with a reinforcement. On hearing of the Khwája's arrival at Noushehr, Humáyun himself was to join them, and the expedition was to enter the hills.

Kámrán thwarts the plans of Humáyun.

The accounts of what happened at this period of alarm are very uncertain and contradictory. It would appear, however, that Kámrán Mírza, who retired by way of Bhíra, contrived to thwart the plans of Humáyun. Khwája Kilán, who probably governed the Bhíra country, had written, both to Kámrán and to Humáyun, with assurances of his fidelity and attachment. On hearing of the advance of the Afgháns within thirty kos of Láhúr, and of the flight of the Emperor and Kámrán towards Bhíra, he had hastened from Siálkot, where he was, to meet them at Bhíra. Humáyun, on his part, had set out for that town, eager to meet the Khwája. It was about afternoon prayers when he reached the Jelem, which was much swollen. Anxious to cross, he desired Terdi Beg to lead the way, and to spur his horse into the river. The horse swam awhile, but turned round, and could not be made to go on. Determined to force his way, Humáyun caused an elephant to be driven into the stream, and then plunged in on horseback, and followed it across. He thus crossed with forty men about evening prayers. They rode all night without stopping, and arrived next morning at the town of Bhíra. Here he found that they had been anticipated by Kámrán, who had already seized Khwája Kilán in his house, and thus secured his services. While irritated by this sudden disappointment, and his brother's breach of faith, Jabar Kuli Korchi, an officer of his guard, offered to him to lay violent hands on Kámrán. "No," said Humáyun, among whose faults cruelty was not one: "No; I refused to slay him at Láhúr, and I will not do it here." He could not, however, remain where he was, nor could he perhaps, with safety, venture to push on to Noushehr. He resolved at once to turn back, and riding, without halt, down the banks of the river, by noon next day he reached Khusháb, where he was well received by Husein Sultan, the governor of the district.*

CHAP. V.

The Emperor, confounded and perplexed by these untoward events, renounced altogether the plan of proceeding to Kashmír, and resolved to join Hindal and Yádgár Mírza in their expedition again Bheker. Haider Mírza meanwhile, adhering to his original purpose, though deprived of the assistance of Sekander Topchi, who retired into the mountains of Sarang, as well as of Khwája Kilán's co-operation, penetrated the mountain passes of Kashmír, and, as will hereafter be mentioned, was, on the 22d November, less than three weeks after this time, acknowledged in the capital of Kashmír, as sole ruler of the kingdom, without a battle.

Rejeb 22. Nov. 22.

Humáyun left Khusháb the morning after his arrival, along with the governor, who agreed to accompany him, and had proceeded about six kos, when he reached a narrow pass beyond which the road divides, one branch leading to Multán, the other to Kábul. It

Who proceeds towards Sind.

* Jouher, c. 7. Compare Akbernáma, f. 48., and Tar. Nizámi, f. 188., Tabak. Akberi, f. 152.

BOOK IV. A.D. 1540.

happened that he and his brother Kámrán came to the entrance of the defile at the very same time. The Emperor wished to enter it first, but Kámrán, who now threw off the mask, refused to give way, saying he was determined to take the lead. Humáyun was much irritated, and the followers of the princes preparing to assert the right of their masters by force, the affair bore a threatening aspect, when Mír Abul-Baká, a man noted for his sanctity, who belonged to Kámrán's court, riding up to the Mírza, remonstrated with him on his conduct. The Mírza was brought to acquiesce, and the Emperor, passing on first, took the Multán road; after which Kámrán following, turned off for Kábul. It was observed that Kámrán was accompanied by his brother Askeri; and he was soon after joined by the restless Muhammed Sultan Mírza and his sons, Ulugh and Shah Mírzas, from Multán. The family had no sooner heard of the dispersion of the Emperor and his brothers, than they resolved to attach themselves to Kámrán, and overtook him on the banks of the Indus.

After some days' march down the desert that lies between the Chenáb and the Sind, the Emperor arrived at Gul-Balúch, where he received information that Hindal and Yádgár Násir Mírzas, who had preceded him in the same route, had been attacked and interrupted by the Balúches, a barbarous and hardy race spread over all that country, who would not suffer the Mírzas to proceed on their route. Here Humáyun halted his little force. It appears that the Mírzas, who had left Láhúr and crossed the Rávi along with the Emperor, after separating from him near Hazára, had marched down into the Multán territory. Their rangers* soon after fell in with a party of Afgháns who escorted Kázi Abdalla, the Sadr, Kámrán's envoy, to

* Keráwalán.

Shír Shah. The Sadr was then probably returning from a secret mission to the Afghán camp, and on his way to meet his master. They were all taken and brought to the camp of the Mírzas. The Afgháns were put to death; and the Kázi saved at the intercession of a friend.* The march of the Mírzas through the western desert lasted twenty days, during which period they were subject to the greatest fatigue, and to suffering and danger of every description. The Balúches already occupied these wastes, and were in possession of the few strong positions within their bounds, so that they were able to cut the wanderers off from water and provisions: and so determined was the opposition which they made to the progress of the Mírzas that, harassed and in despair at the increasing difficulties which they daily encountered, the princes were forced to retrace their steps, and were now actually on their way back. The Emperor, while at Gul-Balúch, hearing a kettle-drum in the desert, sent out to discover whence the sound proceeded, and found that it was from the camp of Hindal and Yádgár, which was pitched only two or three kos off. He sent forward the reverend Mír Abul-Baká, who had left Kámrán, and joined him, after the occurrence at the defile. The holy man, who had authority to invite the Mírzas to join the Emperor, was successful in his mission, and brought them back with their followers; after which, both the little bands, having once more united, advanced in conjunction on their march.

**Hindal rejoins him at Gul-Balúch.**

Before the Emperor, attended by the Mírzas, set out from Gul-Balúch, an alarming report reached them, that Khowás Khan, the Afghán general, had been sent in pursuit of the Emperor, and was only twenty kos distant. Humáyun prepared for battle, few as his numbers comparatively were, but was soon relieved by

* Mír Bába Dost.

BOOK IV. A. D. 1540. intelligence that Khowás Khan had halted, and seemed to have abandoned the pursuit. That distinguished officer, having pushed on to Multán, finding his enemy totally dispersed, and being unable to get any intelligence of the Emperor or the Mírzas, had retired for the purpose of rejoining the main body of the Afghán army. The belief of his vicinity, however, quickened the movements of the Emperor's army, who hastened along once more on their dreary and painful route towards Uch, over against which town, after many sufferings from hunger, thirst, and fatigue, they at length halted, on the banks of the Chenáb, which, after receiving the waters of the Satlej and Bíah, is known by the name of the Gára.

End of Shábán. End of December.

They pass the territories of Bakhshui Langa.

When Humáyun approached the territories of Bakhshui Langa, who was one of the great chieftains of the country, and whose tribe, in times not long past, had given sovereigns to Multán, he was anxious to avert opposition in passing through his country, and especially in crossing the Gára. For that purpose, he sent forward a mission, who bore a firmán conferring on the Langa the high title of Khan Jehán; and a khilát, composed, among other articles, of a dress of honour, a horse-tail standard, shield and kettle-drum, with four elephants. The Emperor required the Langa, on his part, to furnish grain for the supply of the camp, and boats for crossing the river. Bakhshui, who dreaded his uninvited guests, seems to have conducted himself with great caution and prudence; did not wait on the Emperor, but sent supplies for present use, accompanied by suitable presents. He, at the same time, encouraged merchants to proceed to the suffering camp with necessaries of all kinds for sale, and furnished boats by which the Emperor was enabled to pass the Gára. After accomplishing the passage of that river, near Uch, he moved down the left bank of the Indus to Bheker, the territory of which he reached in the end of January,

A. D. 1541, beginning of January.

Ramzán 28. January 26.

A. D. 1541. There he encamped at the town of Lohri, on the left bank of the river, near the city and fortress of Bheker, which filled the small island in the middle of the stream, the opposite bank being occupied by the town of Sakar.* CHAP. V.

and reach Sind.

Present state and past career of Humáyun.

Humáyun, for several years to come, does not re-appear on the theatre of India. He was now completely driven out of the empire left him by his father, and was not permitted to enter, even as a guest, the wide extent of dominions still enjoyed by his younger brother, and of which he was liege lord. His fortune, during the ten years that had elapsed since he mounted the throne, had been various. He had conquered the kingdoms of Malwa and of Gujrát, and had been expelled from them. He had conquered the kingdom of Bengal, and had been compelled to abandon it. These conquests, effected by the superior military skill, and the greater vigour of mind of his brave Túrki and Moghul troops, and their veteran leaders, seem to have been lost chiefly by the want of any well-combined general plan of operations. In his advance into Gujrát and Bengal, every obstacle gave way before the fury of his attack. But when in possession of the object of his ambition, he found that he had gained nothing. He totally failed in securing the fruits of his victory. No sufficient army of reserve, or of communication, supported the victorious troops. Wherever the imperial camp moved, all, at first, was conquest and glory. But as the government was essentially military, on the army all depended: any disaster to it was ruin to the government. The change of dynasty was still so recent, that a most wakeful and patient superintending policy would have

* The chief authorities for these transactions are the Akbernáma, ff. 47—49.; Jouher, c. 7.; Ferishta, vol. ii. pp. 90, 91.; Tarikh-e-Sind, ff. 151—154.; Kháfi Khan. The Tar. Sind. makes the army reach Bheker, Ramzán 26. Yádgár Násir Mírza led the advance of the imperial army, and perhaps arrived two days before the main body.

BOOK IV. A.D. 1541.

been indispensably requisite in every quarter. The empire had really, as yet, attained no unity, and it had little of what can be called political, or civil, organization; so that the government took its colour entirely from the character of the person at its head. The want of a grand superintending mind was soon felt. There was no adequate provision for the regular administration of affairs in the provinces; no effective system of mutual support among the officers of the empire. The head of the government had not the weight of character which inspired awe or reverence. Revolt early began to appear in different quarters; and that not merely among the Afgháns, burning to recover their lost greatness, but among the chief nobles of the imperial court itself. The empire of the great Báber was in danger of falling to pieces. The discord of the brothers completed the mischief; for the leading Amírs, seeing no hopes of retrieving affairs by adhering to the Emperor, who, brave and accomplished as he was, was regarded with no confidence, had lost heart, even before they were dispersed by the last decisive discomfiture. It was not yet fifteen years since the defeat and death of Ibráhím Shah, from which event the overthrow of the Afghán, and the rise of the Taimúrian, dynasty in India may be dated. Of these fifteen years, the vigorous government of Báber occupied only five; the other ten were filled by the indolent and thoughtless misrule of his son. There had not been much time to consolidate the influence of the new race. Their power still remained entirely military; so that, when the army of the Túrki monarch was dispersed, and his camp taken at Kanáuj, the authority of the family of Báber seemed to be rooted out from India for ever.

The Afghán supremacy restored in India under Shír Shah.

Shír Shah, whose success made him the representative of the Afghán race, and whose abilities rendered him worthy of the trust, lost no time in pursuing his advantage. Though the Afgháns had been routed in battle, and driven to the extremities of the empire by the great Báber; yet they had so long previously held power and sovereignty in India; they were so numerous there, as so many of their race had resorted to that country in pursuit of fortune and of subsistence, and settled in it: and so many of them, for several reigns, had held all the great offices of the kingdom, and numerous rich jágírs and estates in every part of the land, that their power and influence were much deeper rooted, and better established, than it was possible for the authority of their Túrki rivals to be, in the few years they had enjoyed it. The Afghán power, though broken for the moment, could still, by a skilful hand, be speedily repaired. The interest of a rich, powerful, and numerous class of brave men was at stake; and every arm was prepared to aid the hero, who was struggling to raise their nation once more to the eminence from which it had fallen, and to hurl destruction on the hated invaders, whose success must infallibly wrest from the whole Afghán population of India, not their political power only, but their very estates and property, and, what was equally dear to them, the importance individually enjoyed by the meanest Afghán, as belonging to the dominant race. All of these, delighted with the rising prospects of Shír Shah, now flocked to his standard, and hailed him as the restorer of their glory, of their power, and of the Afghán ascendency. CHAP. V.

# BOOK FIFTH.

## HUMÁYUN IN EXILE.

## CHAPTER I.

### HUMÁYUN'S RESIDENCE IN SIND.

### SECTION I.

#### FIRST RESIDENCE IN SIND.

STATE OF SIND ON THE ARRIVAL OF HUMÁYUN. — CONDUCT OF SHAH HUSEIN. — HUMÁYUN AT ROHRI. — HIS FOLLOWERS DETACHED OVER THE COUNTRY. — DISTRESS IN HIS CAMP. — HE SENDS ENVOYS TO SHAH HUSEIN — WHO PROCRASTINATES, AND ATTEMPTS TO INDUCE HUMÁYUN TO LEAVE SIND. — HUMÁYUN LAYS SIEGE TO BHEKER. — SCARCITY IN UPPER SIND. — HUMÁYUN AT THE CAMP OF HINDAL. — HIS MARRIAGE TO AKBER'S MOTHER. — HE RETURNS TO HIS CAMP. — INTENDED DESERTION OF HINDAL, PREVENTED BY THE EMPEROR'S CONCESSIONS. — DISMISSAL OF SHAH HUSEIN'S ENVOY. — HUMÁYUN ADVANCES TO SEHWÁN. — DESCRIPTION OF SEHWÁN, TO WHICH HE LAYS SIEGE. — APPROACH OF SHAH HUSEIN. — DIFFICULTIES OF THE SIEGE, AND DESERTIONS FROM THE IMPERIAL CAMP. — PROGRESS OF THE SIEGE OF BHEKER. — HUMÁYUN URGES HINDAL TO ACT AGAINST SHAH HUSEIN. — DEFECTION OF YÁDGÁR NÁSIR MÍRZA. — SHAH HUSEIN SEIZES THE EMPEROR'S FLOTILLA. — HUMÁYUN RETREATS FROM SEHWÁN WITH THE LOSS OF HIS BAGGAGE. — REACHES ROHRI, AND CROSSES THE INDUS. — CONDUCT OF YÁDGÁR. — DISORGANIZATION OF HUMÁYUN'S FORCES. — THREATENED ATTACK OF YÁDGÁR. — DESPONDENCY OF HUMÁYUN, WHO RETREATS TO THE DESERT OF MÁRWÁR.

BOOK V.

A. D. 1541,
A. H. 947.
State of

WHEN Humáyun, driven first from Hindustán, and afterwards from the Penjáb, resolved to try his fortune on the Lower Indus, he had not long left Uch, in his

Sind on the arrival of Humáyun.

disastrous flight, before he reached the dominions of Shah Husein Mírza, the ruler of Sind. That prince, though he had been forced to relinquish Multán, after having conquered it from the Langas, as has been mentioned, was still the undisputed ruler of Upper and Lower Sind, or of Bheker and Tatta, and his dominions extended along the Indus, from the sea nearly to Uch. To the east of the Indus, the country, wherever the waters of that river or its branches were found, was rich, and seems to have been fairly peopled. The more desert portions, as far as the borders of the Rájpút states, were inhabited by various tribes, chiefly Balúches. On the west of the river, and above Tatta, the Lakki hills and the Balúch mountains enclosed Sehwán, Bághbán, and Dádar with the present Shikárpúr, all of which acknowledged Shah Husein as their prince. Though he had professed to be dependent on Báber, the dependence was little more than nominal, and he governed his dominions uncontrolled, as an absolute sovereign.

Shah Husein was a man of great talent and sagacity, and the events that had been recently passing in Hindustán did not escape his attention. When Humáyun was at the height of his power, and had overrun Gujrát, Husein had sent Mír Anka Arghún, as his ambassador, to congratulate the Emperor on his conquests. The ambassador, who cast a keen eye on what was passing around him, reported to his master that such was the negligence of Humáyun, and such the arrogance of his officers, that it was impossible that affairs could continue long to go on, as they were doing.* Events justified the prediction. The defeat of Humáyun, however, and more especially his subsequent expulsion from his Indian dominions, filled Shah Husein with uneasy apprehensions, as he had just reason to look for a visit

Conduct of Shah Husein.

* Tar. Sind, f. 152.

BOOK V. A. D. 1541.

of at least some portion of the fugitives. He had committed the charge of Upper Sind, and of the island fortress of Bheker, to Sultan Mahmúd Bhekeri, with instructions, if invaded, to lay waste the country before the invaders, to leave them nothing but a desert on every side, and to defend himself in his castle to the last extremity. As Humáyun advanced, these orders were punctually executed. On both sides of the river, from Uch to Bheker, and, at a later time, from Bheker nearly to Sehwán, the cattle were driven away, the forage or grain removed or burnt, the inhabitants compelled to migrate, and the villages destroyed.

Humáyun at Rohri. Beginning of Ramzán. Ramzán 28. January 26.

Humáyun left Uch about the beginning of January, A. D. 1541, and on the 26th of the same mouth, in spite of the difficulties which he encountered, reached Lohri, and was waited upon by some individuals of the Darícha and Sefiáni tribes, who had remained in the town. Next day he moved to the Mírza's College, and the day after to the delightful garden, or Chárbágh, of Báberlú, which he made his head quarters while he remained in that vicinity.

Lohri, or Rohri *, is situated on a high flint rock on the left bank of the Indus, opposite to the celebrated fort of Bheker, which rises near it from a rocky island in the centre of the river. This island had, some years before, been strongly fortified by Shah Husein, and more recently had been supplied, not only with a strong garrison, but with provisions and warlike stores sufficient to enable it to maintain a long siege. "The island fortress of Bheker," says a late traveller †, "is built upon an oval flint rock, three quarters of a mile in circumference, which divides a stream eight hundred yards in width. The fort itself is strongly built, but it is overlooked by the bank, upon which stands the town

* The older writers in general call this town Lohri; in modern times it is always called Rohri.

† Conolly's Overland Journey, vol. ii. p. 260.

of Rohri. It commands the river, and all boats, that pass up and down the river, pay a toll." Still farther to secure his position, Sultan Mahmúd had ordered all the boats and other craft on the river to be seized, and moored under the walls of the fort. The gardens at which Humáyun encamped were about four miles from Rohri, and had been formed and ornamented at great expense, with all the skill and taste of the age. He and his household occupied the palace, with the garden in which it was situated; his chief nobles took possession of the rich houses that had been built by the Arghún chiefs in the immediate vicinity, while the rest of the troops were placed in the neighbourhood, and in the grounds, all the way to the town itself, where they gladly enjoyed some repose after their long sufferings.*

His followers detached over the country.

But the life of Humáyun was not doomed to be one of quiet. It was necessary to make provision for the support of his followers. In the course of a few days, Mírza Hindal moved with his division four or five kos farther down the river, where he halted, and soon after crossed over to the right bank. Yádgár Násir Mírza also crossed, and encamped near him. But soon after, for the purpose of extending their quarters, and securing a larger supply of provisions, Hindal marched down to Páter in the fertile province of Sehwán, and Yádgár to Dárbila; the former fifty, the latter twenty kos below Rohri.

Distress in his camp.

Immediately on his arrival †, the Emperor had lost no time in calling upon Sultan Mahmúd, the governor of Bheker, to repair to the presence, and to deliver up the fort to the imperial officers. Sultan Mahmúd replied, that he was only a servant of Shah Husein, and that, without orders from his master, his duty would not

* Akbernáma, f. 49.

† Akbernáma, f. 49.; Tab. Akb. f. 152.; Tar. Niz. f. 188.; Tar. Bed. f. 179. Jouher, 29., calls these towns Pát, in the district of Suhán (Sehwán), and Bhíla.

BOOK V. A. D. 1541.

permit him to comply with either request. As, however, a serious scarcity already prevailed in Humáyun's camp, Sultan Mahmúd was induced to send to him, out of the provisions laid up in store in the fort, five hundred loads of grain, besides other victuals.

He sends envoys to Shah Husein,

The answer of Sultan Mahmúd, from which he obstinately refused to depart, compelled Humáyun to refer directly to Shah Husein himself. Without delay he deputed* Mír Táher Sadr and Mír Samander, two of his confidential servants, to the Mírza, who was then at Tatta, desiring them, by every practicable means, to gain him to his purpose. He bade them represent that the Emperor's coming to Bheker had not been optional; that his object now was, not to interfere with Shah Husein in the government of Sind, but to proceed on to the conquest of Gujrát; and he called upon the Mírza to come and consult with him in person, on the best means of invading that country.

who procrastinates,

The Mírza received the envoys with every mark of honour, and even offered his Majesty the revenues of all the country † from Kalikanda to Betura for the support of his household: but, on the grand subject of their mission, he deferred, from time to time, giving them a definitive answer, though he kept their hopes alive by the most artful representations. After a delay of some months ‡, Humáyun, whose patience was exhausted, sent them instructions either to return at once, or to let him know distinctly what prospect they had of success. The envoys wrote in return, begging to be allowed to remain some little time longer, as they entertained fair hopes of bringing their negociation to

* Jouher, c. 8., calls the envoys Keber Beg Baríki, and Mír Táher Pír-záda.

† This seems to be the territory lying north-west of the Ran. It is doubtful if it really belonged to the Mírza.

‡ They seem to have been detained upwards of six months; Tar. Niz. f. 189. The Tarikh-e-Bedáuni says five or six months, f. 179.

a favourable issue. But a farther time having elapsed, during which no communication whatever was received from them, and the Emperor's difficulties increasing daily, he despatched orders, commanding the envoys, in case Shah Husein refused to accompany them to the presence, to return without him. CHAP. I. SECT. I.

On receiving these orders, Mír Samander, one of the envoys, prepared to return to Rohri. The Mírza, seeing that he was unable to create any farther delay, and that the Emperor's army had not been broken up by famine and disease, as he probably anticipated, now attempted to remove Humáyun from his territories in a different manner. Along with Mír Samander he sent, as his ambassador, Sheikh Mírak, a man descended of the holy Sheikh Puran, whose family was highly revered by all the Arghúns. This ambassador, who carried various presents to his Majesty, was desired to represent to him that the produce of Bheker was at all times but scanty, and, far from being adequate to support his Majesty and his troops, was hardly enough to maintain the inhabitants of the country; that, on the contrary, should he march his army to Cháchkán*, he would find a rich country, fertile and highly cultivated, which could furnish supplies of every kind, to recruit and refresh the army after its late marches and fatigue; that, if the imperial army moved to occupy that province, Shah Husein would himself be at hand to assist their operations; that Cháchkán, from its situation, was admirably suited as a *place d'armes* for an invasion of Gujrát, a kingdom which Humáyun could reduce with ease, and, aided by its wealth, gradually recover the whole of Hindustán.

and attempts to induce Humáyun to quit Sind.

These plans of conquest seem to have captivated the imagination of Humayún, who, at first, gave his assent

* Cháchkán lies east of Tatta and west of the Ran, on the eastern branch of the Indus. See James Burnes's Narrative of a Visit to Sind; and Map. Edin. 1831.

BOOK V. A. D. 1541.

to the ambassador's proposals. But his ministers viewed the matter in a different light. The country of Chách-kán, which lies to the east of Sind, was inhabited by some brave tribes, whom Shah Husein had been unable to subdue; and must be conquered by the Emperor from its present occupants. It had, indeed, rich fields and villages, and was watered by branches of the Indus, but it possessed no fortress, in which, when the army moved forward against Gujrát, the families and heavy baggage of the army could be deposited, so as to be in safety from the attacks of Shír Shah, of Shah Husein Mírza himself, or even of the neighbouring tribes. They considered the whole proposal as only an artifice of the crafty Mírza, to remove the Emperor from his territory. If Shah Husein was really as desirous as he pretended to be to serve the Emperor, why, they said, did he not give him admission into some one of his own strongholds? Mír Samander, who had studied the Mírza's character in his court, confirmed this view, by declaring that, in his opinion, Shah Husein had really no intention to join the Emperor.

Humáyun lays siege to Bheker.

Humayún having, at length, concurred in this opinion, the siege of Bheker was resolved upon, and immediately begun. When Shah Husein was told that the Emperor had laid siege to Bheker, which, as well as Sehwán, he had placed in the best posture of defence, he is said to have remarked, that he felt quite at ease on that subject; for that Humáyun would not give up the delicious garden in which he dwelt, to go to watch the operations of the siege in the camp over against Bheker; and that his amírs never would take the place; a prediction which was fully verified.*

Scarcity in Upper Sind.

From the time that the imperial camp reached Rohri, multitudes from different quarters seem to have flocked

* Akbernáma, f. 49.; Tab. Akb. 89.; Jouher, 2—9.; Tarikh-e-Sind, ff. 151, 152.; Tar. Niz. ff. 188, ff. 154, 155.

to join it. The contest in Hindustán had not been merely between two individuals, Humáyun and Shír Shah; it was between two different races, the Túrks and Afgháns. When the Emperor and his family were expelled, there was no longer any safety in that country for his countrymen and adherents. Some accounts make the number of persons of every age and sex, who now joined the camp, amount to two hundred thousand, which has an air of exaggeration.* The influx of a very great multitude, however, into a country not extensively fertile or well cultivated, and the measures resorted to by Shah Husein for destroying the grain, or preventing its transport to the army, joined to a bad season, soon aggravated the scarcity, which had prevailed from the first, into a famine, so that, all around Bheker, numbers began to perish of hunger.† The Emperor opened his treasury to supply the wants of his followers, but every thing speedily rose to an exorbitant price.

Humáyun had wasted much valuable time, in hopes of procuring a favourable answer from Shah Husein. His brother Hindal Mírza had repeatedly asked his permission to attack and occupy the rich province of Sehwán, but was not allowed, that no interruption might be offered to the success of the negociation, which the Emperor had so much at heart. That obstacle being now removed, Hindal was at length authorized to reduce the district, and informed that the Emperor himself would soon visit his camp. Shah Husein, pursuing the same policy as he had done in regard to Bheker, had fortified the town of Sehwán, and now ordered the whole surrounding country to be laid waste. Humáyun, alarmed by some intimations that had reached him, of Hindal's having a design to desert from him, and march to Kandahár, quitted for a short

Humáyun at the camp of Hindal.

* Tar. Sind, f. 156.

† A single loaf is said to have cost a mithkal.

BOOK V. A. D. 1541.

time the gardens of Báberlú, in which he had now spent five or six months, and leaving his army to continue the blockade of Bheker, proceeded by Dárbila, where he visited the camp of his cousin, Yádgár Násir Mírza, and stayed two days. Three days afterwards he reached Páter, which lies about twenty miles west of the Indus, and was met by his brother Hindal.

His marriage to Akber's mother.

This visit to Páter is chiefly remarkable for Humáyun's marriage at that place to the mother of the illustrious Akber. During the festivities that attended the Emperor's arrival, Hindal's mother, Dildár Begum, gave a grand entertainment, to which all the ladies of the court were invited; and among them was Hamída, then only fourteen, the daughter of Sheikh Ali Akber Jámi, Hindal's preceptor. Humáyun, captivated with her appearance, inquired if she was yet betrothed; and being told that she had been promised, but that the ceremony of betrothment had not yet taken place; "Then," said the Emperor, "I will marry her." Hindal, much offended, observed to his brother, that he had supposed that his Majesty's visit to Páter had been to do him honour, and not to look out for a young bride; but that, if the Emperor persisted in doing any thing so unbecoming, he must quit his Majesty's service. Dildár Begum, who overheard this altercation, interposed, reproved her son, and attempted to settle the dispute. But, as Hindal refused to apologise for the unseemly language he had used, Humáyun left the house in high displeasure, and went on board of a boat. Dildár, however, followed the Emperor, prevailed upon him to return back, made up the quarrel between the brothers, and next day gave a nuptial banquet, when the young lady* was married, and delivered to the Emperor, with

Early in A. H. 948, in the summer of A. D. 1541.

* Hamída was of the family of Zhindeh-fil Ahmed Jám, a celebrated saint; Kholaset-ul-Towáríkh, f. 261. Her style after her marriage was Hazret Mariam-makáni, Hamída Bánu Begum; Tar. Niz. f. 189.

her blessing. A few days after this event, Hindal's camp having become unhealthy, and a great mortality prevailing, Humáyun left it with his suite, and proceeded to the Indus, where he embarked, and sailed up the river to Bheker.* He returns to his camp.

He found his army in great distress; but the evil did not terminate there. The signs of ruin and desolation which appeared on every side, joined to the recent quarrel, determined Hindal, who had long ceased to serve his brother with much zeal, to come to the resolution of separating from him. For some time past Hindal Mírza had been urged by Kerácha Khan, Kámrán's governor of Kandahár, to repair to that capital, and to assume the sovereignty in the kingdom.† In these views he was encouraged by Yádgár Násir Mírza, his cousin and brother-in-law, his great adviser, who agreed to follow him in the adventure. Accordingly, Hindal having collected all his force, decamped, and took the road to Kandahár; at the same time writing to Yádgár that he would wait for him on the route, and entreating him to lose no time in forming a junction. Intended desertion of Hindal,

The news of this movement of Hindal, with information of the designs of Yádgár, reached Humáyun on the 8th of September 1541, and led him to apprehend the total ruin of his affairs. He hurried, in alarm, to the house of Mír Abul Baká, his intimate friend, a man of science, and of great weight and influence, both from his personal character, and as being descended of a holy family; and, after a long conference, despatched him to use his endeavours to bring to an accommodation Yádgár Násir, who was at that moment encamped Jemádi I. 17. Sept. 8.

* Tar. Niz. f. 189.; Jouher, c. 9.; Tar. Sind, ff. 156, 157.

† Nizám-ed-dín Ahmed, the author of the Tabakát-e Akberi, f. 152., represents Humáyun's visit to Páter as having for its object to prevent Hindal from accepting Kerácha's offers, of which the Emperor had obtained notice.

BOOK V. A. D. 1541. prevented by the Emperor's concessions. about ten kos off, on the opposite bank of the river.* Abul Baká was successful, and concluded a treaty with the Mírza, who agreed to recross the river, and wait upon Humáyun; to remain steady to his interests; and, thenceforward, to do him faithful and active service. The return he was to receive, for thus adhering to his allegiance, shows the difficulties to which Humáyun was reduced; when the Emperor reached Kábul, he was to give up to Yádgár, Ghazni, Chirkh, and the district of Lohger, territories which Báber had assigned to the Mírza's mother, for her support; and, when Hindustán was once again recovered, one third of it was to be Jemádi I. 18 Hindal's portion. Next day the Mír, having completed his mission, was crossing the river on his way back to Rohri, when the Bheker men†, informed of his mission, and desirous to intercept him, sent out a vessel manned with a strong party, who discharged showers of arrows into his boat. The Mír received Jemádi I. 19. Sept. 10. several mortal wounds, of which he expired on the following day. Humáyun was deeply affected by this misfortune, and gave loud vent to his sorrow, declaring that neither the ingratitude of his brothers, nor the treachery of his adherents, nor any of the numerous calamities that had assailed him, had ever unmanned him so much as the loss of this faithful friend. Yádgár Sept. 17. Násir Mírza crossed the river about a week after, and having ratified the agreement, returned back to his camp.

Dismissal of Shah Husein's envoy. At the same time Humáyun dismissed Sheikh Mírak, Shah Husein's envoy, with directions to inform his master that the Emperor agreed to all his proposals, but expected that he would evince his duty and allegiance, by repairing to the presence ‡; a test to which,

* Tar. Bed. f. 179.

† They are said to have been Doulat-sháhis and Barghdáis.

‡ Akbernáma, f. 49.; Tab. Akberi, f. 152.; Tar. Niz. f. 189.; Taríkh-e Sind, ff. 157, 158.; Jouher, p. 30.; Tar. Bed. ff. 178, 179.

in spite of numerous promises, the wary Arghún had no intention of submitting. CHAP. I. SECT. I.

The Emperor's affairs were now in such a situation that his ruin seemed inevitable, unless something decisive could be achieved; and nothing appeared so likely to afford relief as an attack on Tatta. Leaving Yádgár Násir in the government of Upper Sind, therefore, with directions to prosecute the blockade of Bheker, Humáyun proceeded down the river about the end of September. He had not advanced far, when numbers of his people left him, and went to the camp of Yádgár, who showed no disposition to send them back. Humáyun, however, held on in his course along the Indus, and on the 6th of November reached the vicinity of Sehwán.

Humáyun advances to Sehwán.

Jemádi II. 1. Sept. 22.

Rejeb 17, Nov. 6.

The province of Sehwán, which by historians is often called also Síwí and Síwístán, is bounded on the east by the Indus, on the west by the Balúch mountains, and on the south by the Lakki range, which runs in upon the Indus. It is watered in its whole extent by a branch of that river, called the Aral, which comes down to it from Lárkhána. Canals from this branch water the fields, intersecting the country in all directions, while, on the west, many streams descend from the hills. It is consequently a well watered, fertile, and prosperous little province. The town of Sehwán, which also, like the province, is often called Síwí and Síwístán, stands on a rising ground, close to the Lakki hills, on the banks of the Aral, somewhat above where it rejoins the Indus. It is commanded by a castle, built on an artificial mound of earth about sixty feet high, surrounded by a strong brick wall that rises from the level of the ground below. The Lakki hills, which exclude the refreshing breezes from the ocean, render the climate extremely sultry.*

Description of Sehwán.

When Humáyun arrived near Sehwán, a party of his

* See Burnes's Travels, vol. i. pp. 47. 50. 231.

BOOK V. A.D. 1541.

troops attacked a body of the enemy, who had issued from the fort, defeated them, and drove them back within the walls. Flushed with success, the victors came on board of the Emperor's ship, and represented to him that it would be an easy matter to take the town, which would give them the command of all the surrounding country. With too great facility he entered into their views, suspending the march against Tatta, and immediately laid siege to Sehwán. He probably imagined that it would occasion a delay of but a few days; but here Shah Husein had pursued the same wise policy as elsewhere. He had placed a strong garrison, and a number of his ablest officers, in the fort. The country around was reduced to a waste, and the inhabitants and cattle driven away. Even before the Emperor's arrival, the garrison had unsparingly destroyed all the gardens, garden-houses and other buildings, in the suburbs or near the place. Batteries were, however, constructed by the invaders, and operations begun and carried on with such vigour that the garrison began to be straitened.*

*to which he lays siege.*

*Approach of Shah Husein.*

Mírza Shah Husein, who had watched the danger as it approached his capital, thought it now time to commence active operations, and marched from Tatta to Sen †, a town on the right bank of the river, not far from the imperial camp; where he entrenched himself and collected a flotilla of ships and boats. He nominated Mír Alíka Arghún, a tribesman of his own, to the command of Sehwán, and ordered him to proceed to strengthen the garrison. Mír Alíka, seizing a favourable opportunity, passed with his men through the camp of the besiegers, near the bazár, and was not discovered to be an enemy till he had safely entered the place. Humáyun upon this ordered a mine to be run,

*Difficulties of the siege.*

* Akbernáma and Tar. Nizámi, and Jouher, as above.

† Burnes speaks of Sen as a town having at present a population of about 2000. Burnes, i. p. 250.

and approaches made with more vigour than ever.* In a short time, the mine being fired, a portion of the wall was thrown down; but, to the disappointment of the besiegers, as they were preparing to mount the breach, it was found that a new wall had been run up behind it. Shah Husein, meanwhile, completely hindered all provisions from reaching the imperial camp, either by the river or by land. Parties of his troops ranged the country on every side; and want, despondency, and discomfiture seemed everywhere to attend the invaders. They found the Arghúns brave, and well equipped, and plentifully supplied with all the munitions of war, while their own store of gunpowder began to fail, and they were unable to command the implements necessary for carrying on a siege which, contrary to their expectation, was protracted for some months. To add to their misery, the country was overflowed as the river rose; and disease began to rage. The soldiers, who were without bread, were supported chiefly on the flesh of the camp cattle, which they were forced to kill in order to supply their necessities; but, seeing no end to their sufferings, they lost heart, and deserted in numbers. Such was the pressure of misery, that their example was gradually followed by several officers; and, ere long, not a few even of the more eminent of the nobles absconded, among whom Mír Táher is specified; some of them joining Shah Husein, who gave them a favourable reception, while others found their way back to Bheker to Yádgár Násir Mírza, whom they instigated to set out without delay to Kandahár, representing affairs in Sind as utterly desperate.

Desertions from the imperial camp.

Some time before matters had reached this pass, one Ali Beg Jeláir, an old Túrki noble, had offered, if allowed only five hundred horse, to fall upon Shah Husein by a forced march, and surprise him where he lay, con-

* Akbernáma, f. 50.; Tab. Akb. f. 153.; Tar. Sind, f. 159.

BOOK V. A. D. 1541.

fident that by such an attack he could discomfit his army. But daring enterprises do not suit dispirited troops; and the Emperor found none of his chiefs disposed to join in the adventure.

Progress of the siege of Bheker.

Yádgár Násir Mírza, when left to continue the blockade of Bheker, had crossed over from the right bank of the river, and taken up his quarters in Rohri. The harvest that year suffered from the severity of the season, and from the ravages of hostile troops; yet his army had increased in strength. The fort of Bheker, as we have seen, is placed on an island in the Indus, where it occupies a very picturesque and a very important situation. It has opposite to it the town of Rohri, on the left bank of the river, and what is now the town of Sakar on the right bank. The river, which is here eight hundred yards wide, rolls past the island in two streams; the one four hundred, the other three hundred-and-fifty yards broad. "The waters lash the rocks which confine them, with noise and violence." "The town of Rori, which faces Bakkar, stands on a precipice of flint forty feet high; and some of its houses, which are lofty, overhang the Indus. The inhabitants of these can draw up water from their windows; but a road cut in the rock supplies the citizens with this necessary of life, without risking their lives. The opposite bank of Sakkar is not precipitous like that of Rori." * The garrison of Bheker, who were not disposed to be cooped up without making some active efforts to annoy the besiegers, made two different sallies upon Yádgár Násir Mírza, and twice surprised and cut off a number of his troops. A third time they landed from their boats, but were met by the Mírza's men, and a regular action ensued in the sandy plain by the river side, not far from the town. The advantage remained with the besiegers. Three or four hundred of the assailants were left dead

* Burnes's Travels, vol. i. p. 62, 63.

on the field; some were driven into the river, where they perished, while others succeeded in reaching their boats, and regained the fort. This repulse put an end to these sallies.*

Humáyun urges Hindal to act against Shah Husein.

When Humáyun found that his difficulties were increasing, and that he was hemmed in on every side by Shah Husein's operations, he had written to Hindal, earnestly entreating him to make a diversion in his favour, by marching down towards that prince, who would not dare to face him in the field; he added, that he was himself prevented from making such a movement, by the certainty that the fort, during his absence, would receive all manner of supplies, so that the whole labour of the siege would be thrown away. In consequence of this demand, Yádgár despatched a trifling body of 150 horse, under Terdi Beg, to his assistance. But it was too late for such a force to be of any service.

Defection of Yádgár Násir Mírza.

Yádgár Násir Mírza had, before this, begun to play a double part. Shah Husein, who was no stranger to his ambitious views, seized upon the present crisis, when the affairs of Humáyun were depressed, and those of Yádgár in some degree prosperous, as holding out a favourable opportunity for withdrawing him from his allegiance to his sovereign. He had for some time engaged Yádgár in a private correspondence, and now deputed Bába-kuli, his seal-bearer, to complete the negociation. Shah Husein offered to acknowledge Yádgár as Emperor, to read the khutba in his name, to give him his daughter in marriage, with all his treasure, which was supposed to be very great, and, to complete the whole, the succession to the throne of Sind, as her dower. It was artfully represented to the Mírza, that though Shah Husein, who was now aged, had no near relation left to soothe and comfort his de-

* Akbernáma, ff. 49, 50.; Tab. Akb. f. 158.; Tar. Sind, f. 158.

BOOK V. A.D. 1541. clining years, he was not, however, disposed to resign the reins of government while he lived: but that it was not necessary for Yádgár to wait the uncertain period of his death, before he ascended a throne: that, with the assistance of his father-in-law, he might easily conquer Gujrát, of which he should be put in immediate possession: while the whole territory of Tatta would fall to him in the course of nature, on the demise of the Mírza. Yádgár's constancy was not proof against these magnificent offers, and he joyfully acceded to the conditions proposed to him. But as he was not yet ready openly to declare himself, and as it was of consequence to amuse the Emperor, he sent forward his camp equipage one march from Rohri, as if he were preparing instantly to set out to join him.

Meanwhile, Humáyun, whose difficulties were daily increasing, despatched Abdal Ghafúr, an officer of his household *, to hasten Yádgár Mírza's motions. But the Mírza, having learned from the envoy the disabled state of the Emperor's army, and believing that he had now nothing to dread from his resentment, ordered the tents back to the city. It was at this crisis that, at the desire of the Arghún prince, he seized a ship that was on its way down the river, loaded with grain and provisions for the supply of the famished camp, and delivered it into the hands of Shah Husein, who put the crew to death.

Shah Husein seizes the Emperor's flotilla.

Shah Husein, relieved from the fear of any troublesome diversion, by his understanding with Yádgár Mírza, was now enabled to bend his undivided force against the Emperor: and news soon reached the camp of Humáyun, that the Arghún was on his way up the river with a fleet of boats, in which was embarked a large body of troops, for the purpose of cutting off the Zikádeh 17 March 3. A.D. 1542. Emperor's retreat. This intelligence was speedily followed by the astounding information, that the enemy

* He was Mír-Mál.

CHAP. I. SECT. I.

had seized by surprise the whole of the Emperor's fleet which lay close by the camp, and contained the scanty provision of stores still left for the supply of the army; and so suddenly had this been effected, that some females who were on board, had only time to make their escape, half naked, into the camp. The siege was immediately raised, and the army retreated, or rather fled with precipitation, towards Bheker, leaving their whole tents, camp equipage, and baggage behind.*

Humáyun retreats from Sehwán with the loss of his baggage;

A short time before these events, an ambassador who had been sent by Shah Husein to the Emperor, having been plundered by some persons belonging to the camp, Humáyun now sent Monaim Beg, an officer of rank, to offer explanations, and at the same time to urge Shah Husein to cease from the pursuit, and to show some sympathy to his sovereign in distress. But the Arghún, who was highly irritated, refused to admit the envoy into his presence, asking what benefits the Emperor had ever conferred on him or his family, that he should now mind his distress. Meanwhile, the Emperor continued his retreat, which was hurried and disorderly, every one thinking only of himself, or his own safety. Many fell behind, and were slaughtered by the pursuing enemy; others deserted, so that, by the time the Emperor came opposite to Bheker, few of his followers remained with him.

Here a new difficulty occurred. Humáyun had sent off expresses before him, to desire Yádgár Násir to have boats in readiness to transport his troops, when they arrived, across the river, to Rohri. But, on his arrival,

reaches Rohri.

* Akbernáma, f. 50.; Tar. Sind, f. 160.; Jouher, c. 9. The Tabakát-e Akberi, f. 158.; Tar. Niz. f. 190., says that the siege lasted seven months. If the dates are correct, it could have lasted only four. The Tar. Bed. f. 179. makes the siege last eighty days. The waters, however, generally rise in the end of April, from the melting of the snows in the mountains. (See Burnes.) The account in the text supposes that they rose in February, so that the Tabakát is probably correct, in which case the siege was raised in the course of April.

BOOK V.

A.D. 1542.

no boats were to be found. Yádgár had sent privately to invite the Arghúns to come by night, and seize all the boats near Bheker, which they had done. To obviate the difficulty and danger of attempting a passage across to the left bank, with the imperfect and uncertain means that he could hastily command, his chief officers advised Humáyun at once to turn off for Kandahár; but he declared that nothing but dire necessity would induce him to approach his undutiful and unfriendly brothers, or take refuge in their territories. He despatched a party under Roushen Beg, with orders to drive in all cows and buffaloes from the villages for ten or twelve kos around, and of their skins to construct rafts and vessels for crossing the river. These orders were speedily obeyed; and in addition to the conveyances which they afforded, a few boats, which had been sunk in the Indus, were pointed out by two neighbouring zemíndárs, and raised. These operations detained Humáyun on the right bank for several days. All this while, Shah Husein's fleet was known to be advancing upwards; but, fortunately for the fugitives, the course of the Indus below Bheker is extremely tortuous, and, from the rapidity of the current, the progress of vessels ascending is proportionally slow.

Before the rafts could be properly constructed, on the inflated skins of the cattle that had been slain, Shah Husein Mírza had arrived within two kos of the Emperor's shattered party. Numbers of the first detachment that crossed over, fell into the hands of the enemy, who took most of their rafts. This added to the confusion and alarm. The Emperor's followers found difficulty in crossing. Terdi Beg had taken possession of a boat that was lying at the ghát, or creek, on the river side, to convey his people over. One of the Emperor's Ishek-Aghas, or chamberlains, coming up, desired him to quit the boat, and clear it of his goods, as it was required for the use of his Majesty's wives and children. Terdi Beg, offended at the insolence of his manner, called him a contemptible fellow.* "Not more so than yourself," retorted the chamberlain; on which the Beg raised his horsewhip, and struck him. The chamberlain instantly drew his sword, and aimed a stroke, which luckily fell on the pummel of the Beg's saddle; when the bystanders interposed. What followed is illustrative of oriental manners. The Emperor, on being informed of this occurrence, was much concerned. But as Terdi Beg was a man of high rank and consideration, he made the offending Agha be taken to that nobleman, his hands tied with a kerchief. Terdi Beg, on seeing this proof of the Emperor's attention to his feelings, immediately untied the kerchief, seated the Agha, in the most respectful and courteous manner, beside him, presented him with a rich dress and a horse, and apologised for what had passed.† (CHAP. I. SECT. I.)

(Crosses the Indus.) The Emperor gained the left bank of the Indus in safety, but his dangers were not yet over. Yádgár Násir, distressed and alarmed at his unwished-for return, before he was ready for open revolt, in order to make a show of fidelity, pushed on against a party of Shah Husein's men, who had landed on the bank of the river not far below, killed some, made others prisoners, and forced the rest to take refuge in their boats. He then returned in triumph to the Emperor, and laid the heads of the slain at his feet. Shah Husein now halted by the river, and quietly watched the progress of events.

(Conduct of Yádgár.) Though Yádgár treated the Emperor with every external demonstration of respect, Humáyun, though he made no complaints to him of what was past, could not help perceiving the change that had taken place in his

* Merdek.

† Akbernáma, ff. 49, 50. Tab. Akb. f. 153.; Tar. Niz. f. 190.; Jouher, c. 9.; Tar. Sind, ff. 157—160.; Tar. Bed. f. 180.

BOOK V. A.D. 1542.

conduct. The Mírza still continued his secret correspondence with Shah Husein, who insisted that he should give up the two zemíndárs, who had pointed out the boats, in which the Emperor crossed. These men, getting some intimation of their danger, fled to Humáyun's camp. Yádgár requested him to deliver them up, under pretence that he had to settle accounts with them for the revenue of their lands, which lay in his district, and were in arrear. The Emperor sent them with a guard, who had orders to bring them back, as soon as their accounts were arranged. But no sooner had they arrived, than Yádgár took them by force from the guards, and delivered them up to Shah Husein.* Soon after this outrage, he openly assumed a hostile countenance, and never afterwards returned to his allegiance.

Humáyun, who by the late events was deprived of such stores as he had previously possessed, and who was in a country where famine raged, procured, with much difficulty, from Yádgár Násir a scanty supply of grain, which was soon consumed. In this exigency, compelled by want, he sent an application by Terdi Beg and some others of his chief officers, to Sultan Mahmúd Bhekeri, the enemy whom he was besieging. Mahmúd received the deputation with every honour, presented them with dresses, and gave each of them a sum of money, and a portion of grain. He then called a council, at which various opinions were given, but, in conclusion, he sent the Emperor three hundred loads of grain for the use of his household.

Disorganization of Humáyun's force.

But this small provision was soon expended. The camp followers and people of the bazar, seeing this universal distress, gradually went off, and such of Humáyun's troops as did not desert to Yádgár were com-

* Tab. Akb. f. 154.; Tar. Niz. f. 190. The zemíndárs appear, in the first instance, to have been sent into the castle of Bheker.

pelled, from the increasing destitution, to separate, and scatter themselves in small parties over the country, in every direction, in search of food; in which disorganized state they were attacked, and numbers of them put to death by the inhabitants. Wherever they had any opportunity of coming to action, they uniformly maintained their superiority: but with hunger and want it was impossible to contend; and the brave veterans whitened the plains of Bheker with their bones.* Some of them were fortunate enough to make good their way to the surrounding countries, and even the highest of the Emperor's officers, such as Kásim Husein Sultan Uzbek, went over to Yádgár, who spared neither promises nor threats to induce Humáyun's remaining followers to abandon their master. When he saw them reduced to the last extremity, he sent them an express and open invitation to desert, adding that, as for such as remained in the camp till morning, their "blood must be on their own heads."

"After this," says the narrative of the ewer-bearer, "news was brought that Fazáel Beg (who had deserted the day before), intended to seduce his brother Monaim Beg to leave the camp. The Emperor, hearing of this, said, 'Let him come, and he shall meet with his deserts.' Having, however, heard that Monaim Beg and Terdi Beg wished to escape, the Emperor sat up the whole night, watching, while these two attended him. When it was morning, his Majesty went to the bath, and desired them to wait his return. No sooner was he gone than the two Begs ran to their horses. Roushen Beg, the wardrobe-keeper†, hastened to inform the Emperor that they were going away. He was sent to call them back, but they did not mind him; so that the Emperor was himself compelled to run and recall them. Seeing no remedy, they came back. Monaim

* Tar. Sind, f. 160.

† Toshak Begi.

BOOK V.

A. D. 1542.

Beg was ordered into custody, and Terdi Beg found himself obliged to remain."*

Threatened attack of Yádgár.

It was impossible for Humáyun long to exist under such painful circumstances. He daily discovered new instances of Yádgár's hostility; but such were the difficulties of his situation, that his only chance of accomplishing any thing depended on the junction of the Mírza's forces with his own few and exhausted followers. The Mírza, however, who cherished very different views, had no disposition to meet his wishes. He even, at one time, issued out of Rohri, of which he retained possession, intending to attack the imperial camp, and thus finish the contest at one blow. Humáyun no sooner heard of his hostile approach than he drew up his remaining adherents, resolved to sell his life dear. In the meanwhile, however, Háshem Beg, a trusty and faithful officer of the Mírza, over whom he had great influence, hearing of his intentions, galloped out of the town after him, seized the reins of his horse, reproaching him with his guilty and impolitic proceedings, and succeeded in making him return back to Rohri.*

Despondency of Humáyun.

Worn out with fatigue, disappointment, and uncertainty, and deprived even of hope, the mind of Humáyun began to sink under the pressure, and he spoke of making the pilgrimage of Mekka, and of adopting a life of piety and seclusion. From this purpose he was diverted by the persuasions and entreaties of the few servants who had followed him in all his changes of fortune, who still continued attached to him, and even now clung to the hope of gaining rank and riches through his means. With tears they entreated him to resign all such thoughts, and to make one more attempt

* Jouher's Mem. c. 9. See also Tab. Akb. f. 154., and Tar. Bed. f. 180.

† Tabak. Akberi, f. 154.

to bring back fortune to his banners, by marching into the territories of Maldeo, the Rái of Júdpúr or Márwár. CHAP. I. SECT. I.

He retreats to the Desert of Márwár.

Maldeo was, at this time, the most powerful of all the Rájpút sovereigns. He was possessed of great wealth and a very large army, and had added to his hereditary dominions by extending his sway over several of the neighbouring states. He had repeatedly sent to invite Humáyun into his country*, professing the most devoted attachment, and offering to support his cause with an army of twenty thousand Rájpúts. The Emperor's followers flattered him with the belief that Maldeo would be delighted at such an opportunity of meriting his Majesty's gratitude, and that his affairs might still take a favourable turn. Yielding to their entreaties, and indeed at a loss what else to do, he finally determined to follow their advice. He made a last effort, however, to work upon Yádgár to join him, but found all his endeavours ineffectual. With a heavy heart, he, therefore, resolved to abandon Sind, and to try his fortune in the deserts of Rájputána.†

* The Taríkh-e Sind states that at this very time, Humáyun received a letter of invitation from Maldeo himself, f. 161., and Nizám-ed-dín affirms that he promised to assist him in the conquest of Hindustán, Tar. Niz. f. 191., and Tar. Bed. f. 180.

† For the later transactions in Sind, see Akbernáma, f. 50. Tabakát-e Akberi, ff. 153, 154.; Tar. Nizámi, ff. 189—192.; Tar. Sind, ff. 157—161.; Tar. Bedáuni, f. 179, 180.; Kholáset-ul Towáríkh, f. 261.; Jouher's 8th and 9th chapters.

# CHAPTER I.

HUMÁYUN'S RESIDENCE IN SIND.

## SECTION II.

HUMÁYUN IN THE DESERTS OF MÁRWÁR AND IN SIND, A SECOND TIME.

MARCH OF HUMÁYUN FROM BHEKER TO UCH. — OBSTRUCTED BY BAKHSHUI LANGA. — MARCH TO DERÁWAL. — TO THE BIKANÍR AND JÚDPÚR TERRITORY. — MALDEO AND HUMÁYUN SEND SPIES TO EACH OTHER'S HEAD-QUARTERS. — INSINCERITY OF MALDEO. — RETREAT OF HUMÁYUN. — A COVERING PARTY FORMED, AND SUCCESSFUL SKIRMISH OF CAVALRY. — HOSTILE EMBASSY FROM JESELMÍR. — HUMÁYUN ARRIVES AT THAT TOWN. — PROCEEDS TO THE GREATER DESERT. — EXTREME WANT OF WATER. — SECOND EMBASSY FROM JESELMÍR. — CONTINUED DISTRESS FOR WATER. — THEY REACH AMERKOT. — FRIENDLY CONDUCT OF THE RÁNA. — ANECDOTES OF HUMÁYUN. — STAY AT AMERKOT. — RECENT EVENTS IN SIND, AND PROCEEDINGS OF SHAH HUSEIN. — FLIGHT OF YÁDGÁR MÍRZA TO KANDAHÁR. — RESOLUTION OF HUMÁYUN TO INVADE JÚN. — BIRTH OF AKBER. — DESCRIPTION OF JÚN. — HUMÁYUN'S STAY THERE. — INCREASE OF HIS FORCE. — APPROACH OF SHAH HUSEIN. — DISGUST AND DEFECTION OF THE HINDU ALLIES OF HUMÁYUN. — SHAH HUSEIN ATTACKS HIM UNSUCCESSFULLY. — BIRAM KHAN JOINS HUMÁYUN. — HIS HISTORY. — RENEWED SCARCITY IN THE IMPERIAL CAMP. — DESTRUCTION OF THE FORAGING DETACHMENT. — SHAH HUSEIN PROPOSES TERMS. — HUMÁYUN AGREES TO QUIT SIND.

BOOK V.

A. D. 1542. March of Humáyun from Bheker to Uch.

WHEN Humáyun found that he could no longer remain in Sind with safety, he determined to accept the invitation that had repeatedly been sent him by Maldeo, and set out, with the intention of marching to Júdpúr. But as the direct road from Bheker to that place, through the desert, was too dangerous and difficult to be attempted, he resolved to take the more circuitous but practicable road by Uch. With this purpose, leaving Rohri on the 7th of May, he marched up the left bank of the Indus, and soon reached the village of Aru. This was on the route of the caravans, and grain and other articles passed through it, to and from Jeselmír and the neighbouring countries. No sooner did the merchants hear of Humáyun's approach, than, dreading the pillage that must follow the arrival of a famishing army, they loaded their camels, and pushed away into the desert, with such of their property as they were able to remove. But a sufficient quantity of grain and other provisions remained, and was seized, to enable the little camp to pass their time at Aru in what to them had become a great novelty and enjoyment, an abundance of the common necessaries of life.* Setting off again in the

CHAP. I. SECT. II.

A.H. 949, Moharrem 21. May 7.

* Some anecdotes related by the Emperor's ewer-bearer throw as much light on his character as the more important events of his reign, and do not represent it unfavourably. "On one occasion," says he, "his Majesty's water-bottle was empty. He, therefore, asked his humble servant Jouher Aftábchi, if he had any water in the ewer. His humble servant replied, 'There is water.' The Emperor said, 'Pour it into my bottle.' What water I had, I poured into the bottle, adding, 'What a horrid country this is, where one cannot get even water, and as we are now travelling at night, should I be separated from your Majesty, I shall perish for want of something to drink.' I then poured a small quantity of the water back into the ewer. The Emperor signified his approbation, saying, 'That will be enough for you.'

"In the morning, we fortunately came to a small lake, and encamped. It so happened that I had gone to the other side of it, when a deer was roused from the jungle, and ran through the camp. Although many persons struck at it, it passed them and entered the lake. When his Majesty was told, he came out, with an intention of following the animal, and said, 'I would be glad if it could be taken.' He then happened to observe me, and said, 'There is a man on the other side of the water: call out to him and say, the deer is gone hence, take it if you can.' They did so. When the humble Jouher saw the deer coming, he quickly threw himself into the water, exclaiming, 'One leg for me.' His Majesty said, 'It is well,' the other three he claimed for himself. The deer was swimming, and its strength failed. I seized and kept hold of it, till Sheikh Ata Beg was ordered to kill it. Fateh Ata (or Allah) came up, and cut its throat, as ordered. They carried it to the Emperor, who ordered one of the fore quarters to be given to me; and I accordingly received it, as he

BOOK V. A. D. 1542.

afternoon, they were exposed to considerable privations before they reached Mhow, where the Bheker territory ended. The same was the case after leaving that town, while they continued their route upwards, through a parched and barren tract, in which they had much to endure from want of every description, but especially from want of water. After a few days' march, however, they arrived at Uch, where they halted and spent about six weeks.

Obstructed by Bakhshui Langa

The ruler of that country, Bakhshui Langa, on whom the Emperor, on his former passage through his dominions, had bestowed the sounding title of Khan-Jchán, or Lord of the World, when now called upon to wait on the Emperor, or to send provisions for the supply of the camp, little pleased with the return of his uninvited guests, not only refused to render any assistance, but offered every obstruction to the people sent out to purchase supplies, so that whatever was procured was taken by force. Such was the general distress that the Emperor's followers went out into the jungle, to gather the berries of such trees and shrubs as were in bearing, to assist in sustaining life. What was the number of persons that remained with Humáyun at this time, we are not informed.*

March to Deráwal.

But this state of suffering could not be supported for ever. Even the scanty supply of fruits and seeds from the forest failed, and it was necessary to move.† At

directed. Other two of the quarters were sent to the imperial kitchen, and the remaining one to the lady exalted as Maríam, Hamída Bánu Begum, who at that time was seven months gone with child of Akber." Jouher, c. 9. See Stewart's Jouher, pp. 35, 36., which I have altered to bring it closer to the original text.

* Jouher, c. 9. Jouher particularizes the sanker, or sanger, and the ber trees as chiefly supplying them with sustenance. The latter is a wild plum. With the former I am unacquainted.

† An incident, recorded by Jouher as occurring at this time, more resembles the cruel and tyrannical mockery of the princes of Europe in the middle ages, towards their Jewish subjects, than the usual generosity of Humáyun. Those who had been sent out to bring in the stragglers, "returned, and reported that a Moghul, to whom the Emperor was in debt, had fallen down

this moment, a wandering derwísh, who had just arrived from Jeselmír, mentioned his having recently passed the fort of Deráwal, which belonged to Maldeo, and where he had seen abundance of everything. Humáyun immediately issued orders to march into the desert in that direction, and on arriving in the neighbourhood of the fort, was fortunate enough to meet with an ample supply both of grain and water. Here he halted for three days, and Sheikh Ali, one of his Amírs, who had much influence with him, proposed to take the fort by surprise; a treacherous and impolitic proposition, which Humáyun had the wisdom to reject, the more readily as it would have offended Maldeo.

Rebi I. 8. June 22.

Rebi I. 14. June 28.

Leaving Deráwal about noon, after filling their water-bags, Humáyun proceeded in the desert tract, in the direction of Ajmír and Bekanír, and travelled till noon next day; when, finding water, they halted for the night. On the day following, they again set out at midday, travelled all that day and the night after, and next day till three in the afternoon, without coming to water. About afternoon prayers, however, a pond of water was discovered to their great joy, when Humáyun alighted, returned grateful thanks to God Almighty for

Rebi I. 17, July 1.

Rebi I 18.

Rebi I. 19.

Rebi 20. July 4.

from thirst, and was lying at the point of death, with his son standing by him. His Majesty went up to him, and said, 'If you give up my debt, I will give you a pitcher of water.' The Moghul answered, 'Let me preserve my life. I give up the debt for a pitcher of water.' Upon this the Emperor took Monaim Beg as one witness of the agreement, Mozeffer Beg Turkomán as the second, and Roushen Koka as the third. After they had declared themselves witnesses, the Emperor gave him his fill of water; and the Moghul drank, and went on to the camp." c. 10. The Moghul was a subject of Humáyun; his distress and danger arose from the fidelity with which he remained attached to his fallen fortunes; and the power which the Emperor employed, as a prince, to the poor man's injury, was given to be exercised for his advantage. The cool mockery of taking three men to witness, in conformity to the musulman law, renders the incident only more disgusting. It required all the selfishness generated by early indulgence and servility, to reconcile the most common mind to so mean an abuse of power. Yet honest Jouher relates it with glee as a good story, and the Emperor himself certainly thought it so.

BOOK V. A.D. 1542.

his merciful protection, and halted. He ordered the water-bags to be filled, and sent back on his own horses to afford relief to such as had fallen behind, and were perishing for thirst, and to bring them into the camp. Such as were still alive were supplied with water, and brought in. The dead they buried. This station seems to have been near Wásilpúr, in the Bikanír territory.*

Rebi II. 17. July 31. To the Bikanír and Júdpúr territory.

By the 31st of July, Humáyun had advanced within twelve kos of Bikanír. Here he was joined by some of the stragglers of his army, who had contrived to reach Bikanír, where they found the inhabitants very ill disposed towards them. As it was of the utmost consequence to ascertain the sentiments of Maldeo, Mír Samander †, in whose judgment the Emperor reposed entire confidence, was despatched to Júdpúr, to Maldeo's court. Meanwhile, the camp moved on to Filúdi ‡, about thirty kos from Júdpúr, where it halted, and where the troops procured an abundant supply of grain, and of every thing that could recruit them after their toils and sufferings.

Maldeo sends spies to the camp.

The report made by Mír Samander on his return, was by no means favourable. He said that, whatever show and professions of attachment Maldeo might have made, it was plain that they were totally insincere. About this time, a few trifling presents of fruit were sent to the camp by the Rájpút prince. But new causes of suspicion were discovered. The Emperor's little party approached the capital by short stages. A merchant had arrived in the camp, and, among other articles, exhibited for sale a large and valuable diamond. This excited inquiry. The man was found to be Sangái Nagóri, one of the Maldeo's confidential officers. Humáyun, who had no doubts of the real character of the

* Akbernáma, f. 50. Tab. Akb. f. 154.; Tar. Niz. f. 191.; Jouher, c. 10.

† Abulfazl and Jouher both make Mír Samander the envoy. Nizám-ed-dín Ahmed says it was Atka Khan; the Taríkhe Bedáuni, Anka Khan.

‡ Or Pehlúdi.

seller, made him be told that such a diamond was fit only for a prince, and was to be gained by the sword, not purchased with money.

CHAP. I. SECT. II.

Humáyun deputes a secret agent to watch him.

Humáyun, more dubious than ever of the disposition of Maldeo, now deputed Shems-ed-dín Muhammed Atkeh, to his court. But as there was a certainty that, in the present state of affairs, all his acts would be narrowly watched, he, at the same time, despatched secretly into the city one Rái-mal Soni, a goldsmith, and a man of observation. He was desired to mingle with the Ráj-púts, and to use every endeavour to gain a farther insight into the Rái's intentions. He was directed to send back his remarks in writing if he found it safe to do so. But, if it appeared to be dangerous to commit them to writing, he was to communicate the result by a sign. If he thought Maldeo faithful, the messenger whom he sent back was to deliver his message, by taking hold of all the fingers of one hand with the other; if treacherous, the messenger was to grasp the little finger only.

Insincerity of Maldeo.

As it happened, these precautions were not unnecessary. The imperial camp had moved slowly two or three marches onward from Filúdi towards Júdpúr, Maldeo's capital, and the Rái had announced that a body of troops had left that city to meet the Emperor, and do him honour. Humáyun was encamped on the banks of the Juki tank, when Rái-mal Soni's messenger arrived. Being questioned what message he brought, he held up and grasped the little finger only. From this it was concluded that Maldeo was acting perfidiously; and the report of spies led to the conclusion, that the real object of the troops sent to meet them, was very different from the professed one. This view of matters was confirmed by a letter which reached the camp from one of the Emperor's librarians, who, during the dispersion that had taken place when the Emperor was driven from Hindustán, had sought refuge with

BOOK V.
A. D. 1542.

the Rái, and now wrote, advising the Emperor to hasten without delay out of his territory. Atkeh, the Emperor's envoy to Maldeo, had been carefully watched, so as to prevent his communicating any information to his master, and was, in reality, in a sort of free custody. Suspecting something wrong, however, and displeased with what he saw, he secretly left the city without taking leave, reached the camp, and confirmed the Emperor in the belief of his danger. There was now no time for hesitation.* The Emperor, believing that Maldeo was bent upon his destruction, commanded a retrograde movement, and resolved instantly to proceed to Amerkot, by the route of Jeselmír.

Retreat of Humáyun.

"The real intentions of Maldeo," says Abulfazl, "remain a matter of uncertainty. Some contend that he was, at first, really well inclined towards the Emperor; while others are as decided that his professions of service, and his humble letters were, from the first, wholly deceitful and false." But the observations of Nizám ed-dín Ahmed, perhaps the best historian of the period, seem to afford the real explanation of his conduct. When Humáyun was expelled from Hindustán, and, Shír Shah extended his conquests on every side, the Afghán and Rájpút princes were brought into a state of collision. Maldeo, anxious to gain support against his powerful rival, invited Humáyun to his aid, as the most formidable enemy whom he could oppose to Shír Shah. But when the Rájpút prince saw the Emperor arrive in his dominions with only a small number of followers, and they in the most destitute and miserable condition, and quite unfit to render him any succour; at the same time that Shír Shah, a body of whose troops were in the Nagór district, and threatened his frontier, had sent him ambassadors requiring him to seize and

* Akbernáma, f. 51.; Tabak. Akberi, f. 154.; Tar. Niz. f. 191.; Jouher, c. 10.; Tar. Bed. f. 180.; Ferishta, vol. ii. p. 92.; Kholáset-ul Towáríkh, f. 261.

deliver up Humáyun; urged by the promises and threats of the Afghán, and looking upon the affairs of the Emperor as totally ruined, he departed from his original intentions, and altering his conduct, resolved to give him up to his mortal foe. *

When the camp was once more in motion to return back, the Emperor sent out Roushen Beg and Shems-ed-dín Muhammed Atkeh, to seize and bring in some of the inhabitants of the country, to act as guides. They accordingly brought in two men † with their camels; the camels his Majesty ordered to be picketed with his own cattle, and the men to be placed in custody, and their swords taken from them. He made a Kázi, who was with him in camp, and knew their language, explain to them, that no harm was meant them, and that they would be well rewarded for acting as guides to the camp. The men remonstrated, and said that they were poor villagers, and totally ignorant of the road to Amerkot. They were, however, detained, and, as is usual enough in such cases, treated as being spies, or as men who stubbornly and perversely concealed what they knew; and they were threatened to be put to death. Driven to despair, the men contrived to free themselves from custody, snatched a dagger and a knife from two of the bystanders, and before any one was aware of danger, attacked and killed Tersún Beg, who had charge of them, and then rushing to where their own cattle were tied up, stabbed them, as well as the other animals picketed along with them, among which were a riding horse and mule of the Emperor's; and so desperately did these wretched men use their weapons, that they killed or mortally wounded a number of men, women, and horses ‡,

* Tar. Nizámi, f. 191.

† The Tabakát says that these men were spies seized in the camp, and that one of them was directed to be put to death to intimidate the other, f. 155. The Tar. Bed. f. 180., also calls them spies.

‡ They are said to have killed seventeen living beings, men, women, and cattle.

BOOK V. A. D. 1542.

before the imperial attendants, who at length surounded them, could put them to death.

This incident spread so much confusion and alarm over the camp, that several of the Emperor's immediate servants spoke of retiring; several did secretly desert, and he had some trouble in keeping the great body of his followers from dispersing. The little camp was, however, at last put in motion. As most of the Emperor's cattle had been slain *, and among the rest his riding horse, by these unfortunate men, his grooms went, and demanded several horses and camels of Terdi Beg, who gave a surly refusal. The Emperor, therefore, mounting on a camel, began his march. As soon as Nadím Koka, who was on foot, leading a horse on which his mother was riding, observed the Emperor's distress, he made his mother dismount, presented her horse to the Emperor, and seated her on the Emperor's camel.

A covering party formed.

As the road they now took was over a loose moving sand, where no water was to be found, they endured much distress; and, to add to their sufferings, reports were constantly brought in, that Maldeo was in pursuit, and his troops close at hand. Humáyun, the better to cover his retreat, ordered Ishán Taimur Sultan, Terdi Beg, and Monaim Khan to take a party, and bring up the rear slowly and deliberately; but if the enemy came near, then to attack them without hesitation. In this manner the whole moved on, and having passed Felúdi, reached Setelmír, in the Jeselmír territory. But during the darkness of the night, the covering party lost the road, and separated from the main body; and when morning broke, a suspicious body of men was descried at a distance, following in the track † of the retiring camp.

* Jouher says, he had only two horses and a mule left.

† Tab. Akb. f. 155; Tar. Bed. 181.; according to Jouher they consisted of three bodies of five hundred men each. He is the only writer who guesses at numbers.

CHAP. I. SECT. II

Successful skirmish of cavalry.

When it was ascertained that they were enemies, such measures were adopted for warding off the danger as circumstances allowed. The horses that were loaded, had their burdens transferred to camels; the ladies were dismounted, and their horses given to such soldiers as were marching on foot; so that a small troop of cavalry was hastily formed. It consisted of Sheikh Ali Beg, Derwísh Koka and Ahmed, the father of the historian Nizám-ed-dín, with twenty-two others, who, riding back, were fortunate enough to encounter the enemy as they were issuing through a narrow valley or defile. Sheikh Ali, at the first shot, struck the leader of the enemy, who dropped lifeless on the ground; and most of the arrows discharged by his little troop happening to take effect, and to wound some of their chief men, the enemy hastily turned, and rode off; but were pursued, many of them slain, and several camels taken very opportunely for the wanderers. Sheikh Ali now desired Behbúd Chobdár (a mace-bearer) to return, and inform the Emperor of their success. Behbúd, having cut off the heads of two of the enemy who had fallen, tied them to his saddle-girths, and, riding back, threw them down exultingly before the Emperor, who received them as a fortunate omen, prostrated himself in thanksgiving and praise, and despatched him to recal the party. Sheikh Ali was desired still to bring up the rear, and, in a short time, the weary wanderers reached a well in which there was some water, and halted.*

At the same time the party, that had lost their way during the night, made their appearance, and joined them, bringing in a number of cows and buffaloes, which they had seized in the Jeselmír country. This, with the other favourable events of the day, renewed the drooping spirits of the fugitives, and they passed the night more comfortably than usual.

* Akbernáma and Tar. Nizámi, as above.

BOOK V.

A. D. 1542.

Hostile embassy from Jeselmír.

At this station two messengers, sent by the Raja of Jeselmír, met them. They complained, that the Emperor had come into his country, with an armed force uninvited, and that, though no cows were allowed to be killed within his dominions, the Emperor's people were seizing and slaughtering these sacred animals, an act most abhorrent from the religion and feelings of Hindus. They added that this could not be permitted, and that his subjects would obstruct the passage of the imperial camp, wherever it moved. A consultation was held, when it was resolved to detain the envoys without returning an answer, and, having taken a supply of water, to march forward on their dreary journey.

Humáyun arrives at that town. Jemádi I. 1. Augt. 13.

They reached the neighbourhood of Jeselmír on the 13th of August. The Raja, Rái Lankern, who was little pleased with their visit, had placed a body of men to keep them off from the tank, which lay without the walls of the town. Many of Humáyun's followers had already dropped down, worn out and exhausted by thirst and fatigue, in passing over the sandy desert. But, as the rest came up, they attacked the enemy, and after a contest of some hours, drove them away, but not without considerable loss on their own part. The natives retreated into the fort.

Advancing about five kos, they came upon a village, where they found abundance of grain and water, but no inhabitants.

Proceeds to the greater Desert.

After this, they entered a country where the oases were fewer, and the desert more dry and desolate than any they had yet passed. To add to their distress, the Rái had ordered his son, Maldeo *, to precede their march, and fill up the wells with sand, which he had done. They seem now to have gone on for three days before they met with water. At the end of their first

* The name of the Raja of Júdpúr, as well as of the son of the Rái of Jeselmír, was Maldeo, a circumstance that seems to have produced confusion in the narrative of some historians of these transactions.

march, about noon, they reached some wells. But no water came up in any of the buckets that were let down. It was found, to their dismay, that they had been filled up. Compelled by necessity, they again moved forward. Towards evening prayers, they found a well, and orders were issued that they should halt and rest, whether water was found in it, or not. The camels were ranged around the little camp, as a defence, and, to guard against surprise, some men were appointed to make the rounds all night, on the outside of the enclosure. Humáyun himself joined them in their watch, till Sheikh Ali besought him to take repose, and supplied his place. He was prevailed upon to consent to the exchange, and having lain down, went to sleep. On waking in the morning he found his sword half drawn from the scabbard, but was unable to discover by whom it had been done.*

Extreme want of water.

That day they, once more, proceeded on their toilsome journey, and, on the fourth day, at last reached four wells, one of which, however, was found to contain no water. The remaining three were given in charge to the chief Amírs. As the buckets had been removed, and none were to be found, an iron kettle was let down to supply the want. In this desert region, water is found only at a very great depth †, often six hundred feet from the surface. The rope which is fastened to the water-bag or bucket, is drawn by a camel, or by bullocks, which are of course at a great distance from the well, before the bucket comes to the top. In this instance, the distance was too great for the voice to be heard, so that it was necessary to strike a small drum, to give the camel driver notice to halt and ease the rope, when the kettle came within reach. As soon as the first bucket was seen at the top of the well, there was a rush to seize it, and four or five persons, mad

* Jouher, . c10.

† See Tod's Rajasthan.

BOOK V.

A. D. 1542.

with thirst, threw themselves at the same time upon it, so that the rope broke, and the vessel fell down into the well. On seeing this, the perishing expectants raised a shout of despair, and some in their agony plunged in after it. When the water at length began to be brought up, the crowds around strove and fought for it, and there was not found enough to supply them all. One well had been reserved for the imperial household, but the artisans of the court, who could not be supplied, went in a body and complained to Humáyun, that Terdi Beg was supplying his horses and camels with water from his well, while they were dying of thirst.* The Emperor, riding up to the Beg, addressed him in Túrki, his native tongue, and requested that he would allow his servants to draw water for themselves for one hour, to which the Beg agreed. The distress was, however, unspeakable; many fell down and died, before they could get a drop to quench their burning thirst.

Second Embassy from Jeselmír.

At this time a son of the Rái made his appearance, bearing a white flag. When admitted to an audience, he complained that Humáyun had entered his father's dominions in a hostile manner, but assured him that, had his coming been known, the Rái would have received him with every mark of hospitality. He complained of the excesses of the Emperor's followers, and of the confinement of the two messengers. He added that, if the Emperor would halt a short time where he was, a sufficient number of bullocks and buckets should be sent, to enable him to draw up the water. By the advice of Terdi Beg, the two envoys were released.

Continued distress for water.

Having ascertained that, at the next stage, there was only one well, the Emperor divided his little camp into three divisions, which he ordered to move forward on three successive days, so as to have the benefit of the water in turns. The first division was led by the Em-

* Tar. Niz. f. 192.; Ferishta, vol. ii. p. 95.; Jouher, c. 10.

peror, attended by Terdi Beg and Ishán Taimur Sultan; the next by Monaim Beg; the third by Sheikh Ali. Yet, in spite of this precaution, the scarcity of water was severely felt, and numbers perished of thirst. We are told that, at this time, a part of the royal army, probably one of the three divisions, about mid-day, reached a pool of water, when the horses and camels, which for some days had had little or no water, could not be restrained from rushing into it, to appease their thirst, and drank to such excess, that many of them died.

CHAP. SECT. I

They reach Amerkot

The Emperor had now arrived within ten kos of Amerkot*, but the nature of his reception there was probably still uncertain. Meanwhile, protracted misery had levelled all distinctions of rank, and, in some minds, had destroyed even the feelings of common courtesy. The horse of Roushen Beg having broken down on the march, he went and asked the Begum for the horse which he had given her. When notice of this was carried to Humáyun, he alighted, sent his own horse to his wife, and after marching for some distance on foot, mounted a camel belonging to the ewer-department. After he had ridden in this way a couple of miles, Khalíd Beg, the son of Khwája Khalífa, hearing what had occurred, rode up and presented his horse to Humáyun, who continued on his course, and the same day entered Amerkot, accompanied by only seven horsemen. Most of his followers dropped in, singly or by twos and threes, in the course of the day.

Jemádi I 10. Aug 22.

Friendly conduct of the Rána

The Rána†, from various circumstances, was well disposed towards Humáyun. As soon as the Emperor arrived, he sent his brother to wait upon him, to apologise for his not himself appearing that day, it not being a lucky one, but promising to attend him on

* The Tabakát calls Amerkot a hundred kos from Tatta.

† The ruler of Amerkot is usually called Rána, by the writers who speak of him.

BOOK V. A.D. 1542.

the day following. Next day the Rána accordingly visited the Emperor, and explained to him his situation. He said that his principality was small and barren, but that he had two thousand horsemen of his own tribe of Sodhas, and that to them five thousand Samícha horse of his allies could be added, all ready to follow his Majesty, and devoted, heart and hand, to his service; and that, assisted by these, the Emperor might conquer both Tatta and Bheker. The Emperor thanked the Rána for his ready zeal, and gave him to understand that, though unfortunately he did not himself at that moment possess the means of fitting out and paying his allies, he did not despair of speedily falling upon a method of acquiring them.

Anecdotes of Humáyun.

The minute details of the Emperor's conduct at this period have much in them that is curious and interesting, as exhibiting his sanguine and thoughtless temper. When the Rána retired, as Humáyun possessed no change of apparel, he was compelled to undress that he might give his clothes to be washed, and, in the meanwhile, sat down in his bathing-gown. A bird happened to fly into his tent. Struck with its appearance, he caused the door to be shut, and the bird was taken. He called for a pair of scissors, and having cut its wing, made a painter take its likeness, after which he let it off into the desert.

The historians of his reign tell us, that at this time, he borrowed a sum of money from Terdi Beg and some others of his followers. The mode in which this loan was effected, is not mentioned by these historians, but is described in all its particulars by his ewer-bearer with graphic simplicity, and is highly characteristic of the shifts to which Humáyun, in his difficulties, thought himself entitled to resort.* When he had told the

* Abulfazl launches into an exclamation against Terdi Beg and the Amírs, whose avarice compelled him to resort to force. Nizám-ed-dín Ahmed, with more moderation, merely says that Humáyun levied a

Rána that he had no money to pay mercenaries, though he believed that his Amírs had, one of his servants, Shah Muhammed Khorásáni, had hinted to him, that he knew perfectly well where the Amírs hid their valuables. To facilitate the search which he proposed making, Humáyun called a meeting of all his Amírs in his tent. When they were convened, he found some pretence for keeping them waiting, and in the meanwhile privately despatched his servants along with Shah Muhammed, directing them to repair to the tents of the Amírs, to search for, and bring to him, all the money, and valuables, with every kind of plate or vessels that were found there, the cooking kettles and dishes only excepted. They accordingly went, and broke open the portmanteaus and boxes of the Amírs, tore up the harness and stuffing of the travelling furniture of their camels, took out all the money, jewels, and costly clothes found in them, and brought them to his Majesty. Of the money and valuables so found, he restored one half to the owners, the other half he gave to his own servants and others. Of the clothes, two-thirds were restored to the owners, the remaining third being retained for the use of the imperial household. In this rather unprincely way, so disparaging to his nobles, he was enabled to make presents of richly ornamented daggers, and of some money, to the Rána and his sons.*

benevolence (masaadet) from them. Terdi Beg seems to have been a hardy old soldier, not much pleased with the mode in which he saw affairs managed, and probably not very conciliating in his manners. From the constant demands made upon him when distress occurred, and the collisions thereby occasioned, it may be inferred that, by foresight and attention, he kept his own immediate followers and their cattle in tolerable order, and was little satisfied with the unceremonious requisitions made upon him, in trying circumstances, to correct, at his risk and at his expense, the negligence and oversights of such as had not been equally provident. Such a man could hardly be in favour with the retainers of a thoughtless court.

* For the transactions in the desert, see Akbernáma, ff. 50, 51.; Tabakát-e Akberi, ff. 164, 165.; Tar. Niz. f. 190—2 ; Jouher, c. 10,

BOOK V.

A.D. 1542.

Stay at Amerkot.

Humáyun remained about seven weeks at Amerkot, to recruit and refresh himself and his exhausted followers. During this time, he received every assistance from the Rána that his limited means allowed, and got some information of the transactions that had taken place in Sind, after his departure from Rohri.

Recent events in Sind.

We have seen that Shah Husein Mírza, after forcing the Emperor to raise the siege of Sehwán, had failed in his attempt to intercept him in his retreat. As long as he had any apprehensions of Humáyun, he continued to court Yádgár Násir Mírza, and to buoy up his mind with the hopes of succeeding him in Sind, as his son-in-law, and even of placing him on the throne of Gujrát and of Delhi itself. Yádgár, lured by these promises, had treacherously renounced his allegiance to Humáyun, and, about the middle or end of April, had crossed over to Saker on the right bank of the river, and sent some of the cannon and guns belonging to his division into the fort of Bheker. Humáyun had been compelled to leave Rhori on the 7th of May, and, on the 10th, Shah Husein, having ascertained that he was really on his way to Uch, repaired to Bheker in person. The keen and sagacious, but stern and cruel, Arghún examined every department, and the condition of every thing, with his own eyes. He sharply reprehended the governor, Sultan Mahmúd Bhekeri, for the waste committed on the corn in the granaries, and especially for having employed it, to feed his own enemy. Determined to make an example, though unwilling to punish that nobleman personally, he impaled the probably innocent storekeeper before Mahmúd's gate. Malek and Umer, the two chiefs who had assisted Humáyun to cross the river, by discovering to him where some boats were sunk, and whom Yádgár had basely seized and delivered up, he commanded to be flayed alive before the

Beginning of Moharrem.

Moharrem 21—24.

Proceedings of Shah Husein.

11.; Tarikh-e Sind, ff. 161—3.; Ferishta, vol. ii. p. 92—95.; Tar. Bedáuni, ff. 180, 181.; Kholáset-ul Towárikh, f.

gates of Saker. After Humáyun's departure, the camp followers, and men of every class, who had been unable to accompany the Emperor in his flight, scattered in consternation and despair over the surrounding country. Yádgár, whose importance was destroyed by the departure of the Emperor, shared the fate of traitors who cease to be necessary; he saw every promise made to him broken; and hardly two months had elapsed after Humáyun's departure, before he was glad to flee from Sind *, and to take the road to Kandahár. He arrived near that city when Kámrán was besieging Hindal, and had reduced it to extremity. Yádgár accompanied Kámrán to Kábul, whence that prince despatched ambassadors to Shah Husein, to request that he would send back his sister Shehr-Bánu Begum, Yádgár's wife, with her son Mírza Sanjer. The Arghún instantly complied, and sent them forward by the barren wastes and wild passes between Sind and Kandahár, with every outward mark of honour; accompanied by a number of the stragglers and others who had separated from the Emperor in Sind, and still survived in that territory. But, says Abulfazl, he committed an error, intentional or not, in sending them through that desert tract, which is destitute both of water and forage, unprovided with sufficient supplies, so that numbers perished; and those who reached the town of Shál, in addition to all their other sufferings, were seized with malignant fever, by which, among others, the princess was carried off, so that, of two or three thousand persons who were in the caravan, very few survived to reach Kandahár Shah Husein, having remained near Rohri till the middle of July, and put every thing in order, went down to Sehwán †, where he staid a week, to see that the

CHAP. I. SECT. II.

Flight of Yádgár Mirza to Kandahár.

Beginning of Rebi II.

* Jouher says, he was not allowed to leave Sind till he had paid a sháhrukhi for every man, seven for every camel, and five for every horse that accompanied him; probably as if he had been a common traveller or merchant; Tar. Sind, f. 163.; Jouher, c. 13.

† Akbernáma, f. 56.

BOOK V. A. D. 1542. breaches and damage done to the walls were properly repaired, and then went on to Sen.

Resolution of Humáyun to invade Jún. While Humáyun remained at Amerkot, he held consultations as to the course which it was most expedient for him to follow. It would appear that the Raja, Rána Parsád, had not been long in possession of his principality, and looked to the Emperor for assistance in maintaining himself against Jáni Beg, the chief who had been dispossessed, as well as for taking revenge on Shah Husein, who had put his father to death. The Rána strongly recommended an invasion of Lower Sind, and, as the first step towards that attempt, an inroad into Jún, the inhabitants of which, being ill-affected to the Arghúns, would certainly join the invaders. The small and barren district of Amerkot was not a fit place for the lengthened residence of a prince like Humáyun. It was accordingly resolved to march towards Jún with their united forces. And the Raja, having been prevailed upon to withdraw his people from the castle of Amerkot, the Emperor, on the 11th of October, placed in it Hamída Bánu Begum and the rest of his family, with such attendants as he could spare, under the charge of Khwája Moazem, Hamída's brother, and himself set out on his expedition. Four days after, on Sunday the 15th of October, in this solitary castle, surrounded on every side by sandy deserts, Hamída Bánu Begum gave birth to a prince, who was afterwards to be the Emperor Akber, the ornament of his line and family.*

Rejeb 1. Oct. 11.

Rejeb 5. Oct. 15. Birth of Akber.

The Emperor learned the joyful tidings from Terdi Beg Khan, at the first stage, about twelve kos from Amerkot, where he was still encamped. "As soon," says one who attended him, "as the Emperor had finished his thanksgivings to God, the Amírs were introduced, and offered their congratulations. He then

* Akbernáma, f. 51.

called Jouher, and asked, what he had committed to his charge. Jouher answered, two hundred Sháhrukies, a silver wristlet, and a musk-bag; adding that the two former had been restored to their owners. His Majesty inquired the reason of this, as they had been given to him to keep. Jouher said, that, in doing so, he had obeyed his Majesty's orders. On this, the Emperor ordered the musk-bag to be brought, which was done. Having broken it on a china plate, he called his nobles, and divided it among them, as the royal present in honour of his son's birth. They offered their congratulations, with prayers and good wishes for his prosperity, and that of the imperial infant. At that station they continued the rest of the day, and had such rejoicings as circumstances allowed. This event diffused its fragrance over the whole habitable world."* So unpromising were the circumstances that attended the birth of one, who was to become the most magnificent Sovereign of his age.

CHAP. I.
SECT. II.

The same day, after evening prayers, the Emperor decamped, attended by his own faithful Chaghatáis, and a number of the Amerkot Rána's men, and in five marches arrived near Jún.

Description of Jún.

The district of Jún lies to the north-west of the Ran, on the western limit of Cháchkán, near the eastern branch of the Indus, which, after traversing the desert, forms the western boundary of Kach. The territory of Jún is intersected by numerous smaller branches of the river, that divide it into many islands and districts, which, at that time, were highly cultivated. It abounded with all the necessaries of life, and for the beauty of its gardens, and the excellence of its fruits and vegetable productions, excelled every other part of Sind. The nature of the ground, broken and defended by so many streams and artificial canals, joined to the bravery

* Jouher, c. 12.

BOOK V.

A. D. 1542.

of the inhabitants, seems long to have secured to its population the same blessings of independence that were enjoyed by their neighbours, the inhabitants of the wilder and more barren portion of Cháchkán.

Skirmish of cavalry.

When Humáyun arrived in this quarter, he found Jáni Beg, the former possessor of Amerkot, and a noted marauder, lying in the neighbourhood of the chief town of Jún, with a formidable body of horse. He sent forward Sheikh Ali Beg with a hundred of his old adherents, and a party of five hundred of the Rána's Sodha horse, and himself followed with his remaining troops. Sheikh Ali, naturally bold, and trusting to be supported, charged the enemy as soon as he came near them, and entirely broke and dispersed them, before the arrival of the Emperor, who ordered all the prisoners to be put to death. From the field of battle Humáyun moved on to the town of Jún *, where he pitched his tent in a large garden, beside which the zemíndárs or chiefs, who had joined him, encamped. He dug a deep trench round the whole, so as to form a respectable fortified camp. In this position he remained for nearly nine months, during which time he invited all the neighbouring Rajas, or chiefs, to join him; and, in consequence of this invitation, the Ráis from the country of the Sodhas, the Samíchas from Kach, and the tribesmen of the Jám, who formerly were rulers of Bheker, waited upon him; so that his army at one time consisted of no less than

Humáyun at Jún.

Increase of his forces.

* When Jún was taken, two rather noted persons fell into his hands. "During the period that the Emperor besieged Sehwán, there was a musqueteer in the fort, who never missed his aim. H. M. said, 'I hope I shall one day get hold of that fellow.' He sometimes also used to say, 'I wish I could catch the man who drew the sword from under me, half way out of the scabbard.' It happened that both of these men were in Jún, when we took it; and having met in a búzeh-shop, were boasting of their feats of bravery. Their conversation being overheard, they were seized, and brought before the Emperor, who, after inquiry, ordered the musqueteer to be put to death, but forgave the thief, and made him a handsome present." Stewart's Jouher, p. 46., a little altered. Many will differ from the Emperor in his ideas of distributive justice.

fifteen or sixteen thousand horse. And here, about the beginning of December, he was joined by the infant Akber, and the whole party from Amerkot.*

End of Shábán, beginning of Dec.

As soon as Shah Husein heard of this new approach of Humáyun to his dominions in one quarter, hardly six months after he had left them in another, he hastened to meet the coming danger; and soon appeared with a formidable army on the branch of the Indus that was nearest to Jún, and pitched his camp on the opposite bank, four kos from that place.

Approach of Shah Husein.

While the two armies lay in this situation, skirmishes daily occurred. But the contest was an unequal one. Mírza Shah Husein had all the resources of his kingdom behind him; while, to Humáyun, the loss of any one of his old adherents, in whom his real strength consisted, was irreparable.

The Mírza added artifice to force. He made an attempt to detach from the Emperor's interest such allies as had joined him. To the Rána of Amerkot he privately sent a complimentary and flattering message, with a dress of honour, a rich dagger, and other presents, inviting him to abandon the Emperor's interest. These the Rána carried to Humáyun, who directed his ally, in proof of his contempt of the donor, to employ them in dressing up a dog, by Musulmans held to be an unclean animal, which he did. Shah Husein felt deeply hurt by the insult.

Disgust and defection of the Hindu allies of Humáyun.

But the cause of Shah Husein was soon more effectually served by the habitual and uncontrollable arrogance of Musulmans towards Hindus of every rank. One of them, Khwája Gházi, insulted the Rána of Amerkot, who, meeting with no redress, left the camp in disgust with all his followers, declaring that to attempt to please Moghuls † was only labour lost. This

* Akbernáma, f. 51.; Tar. Sind, f. 164.; Jouher, c. 12. The Empress's party left Amerkot, Shábán 11 (Nov. 20).

† Here we see that the term Moghul was already used to denote all northern men.

BOOK V.

A.D. 1542.

defection was instantly followed by that of all the native chiefs, whom the Emperor in vain attempted to soothe; and Humáyun was once more reduced to his own few, though brave, adherents, some of whom, and among the rest Monaim Khan, (who at a future time was destined to be prime minister of the empire) in despair deserted from his camp, and joined the Mírza.

Shah Husein attacks him unsuccessfully.

The news of the desertion of the Emperor's allies encouraged the Mírza to make an attempt to surprise, or to force his position: but Humáyun, having received intimation of the design, had taken such effectual precautions, and so completely defended the camp by new trenches, that the attempt was defeated, though not without serious loss on the Emperor's side.

Biram Khan joins Humáyun. Moharrem 7. A. H. 950, April 12. A. D. 1543. His history.

It was at this season of growing distress, that the celebrated Biram Khan arrived, very unexpectedly, in the imperial camp. After the disastrous battle of Kanáuj, which had finally ruined the fortunes of Humáyun in India, that nobleman, escaping from the field of carnage, found refuge in Sambhal with Raja Matter-Sín, one of the chieftains of the country. Shír Shah, hearing of this, sent to demand that he should be given up, to which the Raja, unwilling to incur the weight of that prince's resentment, was obliged to assent. Biram Khan was, accordingly, conducted to the royal camp, during Shír Shah's campaign in Malwa. The King treated him with marked distinction, rose when he was brought in, embraced, and addressed him in the most flattering manner. In the course of conversation, Shír Shah happening to observe that where attachment to a master is real, and proceeds from the heart, it never alters its course; Biram Khan rather emphatically replied, "Your Majesty's observation is just; real attachment can never change." With much difficulty he effected his escape, near Berhánpúr, in company with Abulkásim, who had been governor of Guáliár under Humáyun, and they took the road to Gujrát. As they travelled along, an ambassador of Shír Shah's, who was on his way back from that country, having heard of Biram Khan's escape, and that some person of distinction was lurking in the neighbourhood, sent a party of his escort, who seized Abulkásim, a nobleman remarkable for his fine countenance and noble deportment. Biram Khan, seeing their mistake, with his usual high spirit and honourable feeling exclaimed, "I am Biram Khan." But Abulkásim, eager to preserve his friend, with much presence of mind interposed, and coolly observed; "See how my faithful servant, to save me, is willing thus to run into danger! Do him no injury, poor fellow! Let him go." Biram Khan was accordingly turned away, and reached Gujrát, where he was well received by Sultan Mahmúd, who then filled the throne. Abulkásim was carried before Shír Shah, who, insensible to the noble devotedness of his friendship, put him to death. Shír Shah often remarked, that from the tone in which Biram Khan assented to his observation that genuine attachment never changes, he felt persuaded he never could gain him. Sultan Mahmúd in vain endeavoured to retain Biram in Gujrát. He obtained leave to make the pilgrimage of Mekka, repaired to Surat, as if for that purpose, passed over into Kattiawár, and thence, soon after, joined Humáyun at Jún. The Emperor was much delighted on hearing of the approach of so eminent a person, at a moment of such difficulty, and made all the leading men in his camp go out to receive and welcome him.*

Renewed scarcity in the imperial camp.

But Humáyun felt daily, more and more, that while the position of his camp made it nearly unassailable, it at the same time made it easier for the enemy to cut off his supplies. This difficulty was not felt as long as he had the tribes of the desert for his friends. But since they had abandoned him, he was compelled to send out

* Akbernáma, f. 52.; Jouher, c. 12.

BOOK V. A. D. 1543.

his own retainers in greater numbers, and to greater distances than before, in order to secure the needful provision of grain and other necessaries. In a short time, all the nearer sources of supply had failed. In this exigency, hearing that there was a castle in the Thari, which contained an ample store of corn and other necessaries, and that it could be reduced with no great force, he detached Sheikh Ali Beg Jeláir on the service; and that officer succeeded so far as to send back considerable supplies to the camp. But Shah Husein, having been informed of his motions, ordered Isa Terkhan, one of his generals, to march and attack the detachment, and cut off all supplies of grain from the imperial camp. That officer showing some hesitation, the duty was committed to Sultan Mahmúd Khan Bhekeri, who till now had remained in disgrace, and who, anxious for an opportunity of recovering the prince's favour, gladly accepted the command, and marched to the relief of the castle; while Shah Husein, to divert and occupy the Emperor's attention, pressed upon the imperial army more closely than ever, both by land and water, and engaged it in daily skirmishes. The Emperor, however, having heard of the march of the detachment that was sent against Sheikh Ali, despatched Ishán Taimur Sultan with a reinforcement to his assistance. As Sheikh Ali was superseded in the command by Ishán Taimur's arrival, he was much offended, and the circumstance produced a very unseasonable quarrel between these two officers. Sheikh Ali, it would appear, was desirous of avoiding a regular conflict.

Humáyun, meanwhile, tired of being shut up more closely than ever within his intrenchments, and seeing no prospect of effecting any thing by the defensive plan of operations to which he was reduced, had determined to hazard a battle. "At this time," says Jouher, "H. M. said, Shah Husein has advanced three or four times in battle-array, to fight. If he comes back to-morrow morning, I will march out and attack him." With this intention he repeated the Fátehi *, and changed the unfit for better horses. His resolution was to fight on the morrow. It was the holy month of Ramzán, and after breaking his fast (at sunset), one watch of the night had passed, when a person came from the river-side, and said, "There is some one on the other bank who calls for a boat." H. M. said, "Ask his name, who calls for a boat at so untimely an hour." They asked, "Who are you, that want a boat?" He answered, "I am Ishán Taimur Sultan." This was reported to the Emperor, who said, "God grant that all may be well!" A boat was sent across, and Ishán came before the throne, where he told of the death of Sheikh Ali Beg, and his own defeat." †

Destruction of the foraging detachment.

It would appear that Sultan Mahmúd Khan, having been joined by some of the neighbouring tribes, watching his opportunity, one morning about sunrise, made an unexpected attack upon the imperial detachment. The combat was desperate, and bloody. It is insinuated that Terdi Beg ‡, who probably commanded in the name of Ishán Taimur, acted but remissly. Sheikh Ali, with his sons and retainers, stood firm, and fell fighting bravely. The loss was great on both sides, but especially on that of Humáyun.

* This is a solemn prayer from the Koran, and is generally repeated when danger is apprehended.

† Jouher, c. 12.

‡ Tar. Sind, f. 164. Terdi Beg is repeatedly mentioned as behaving ill, especially by Abulfazl, who writes of him with great bitterness. But, as he was put to death by Biram Khan, whose panegyrist that writer is, some doubts may be entertained of the historian's impartiality: especially as Terdi Beg, on many occasions of danger and difficulty, is represented as comporting himself bravely, and bearing the brunt of the action. He was one of the oldest of the Chaghatái nobles, and perhaps next in importance to the Emperor. He stood in the way of the able and ambitious Biram Khan's power, the Transoxian chiefs looking up to him, as those from Persia did to Biram Khan. The consequences were seen in the next reign. It was a favourable circumstance for Biram's fame, great and undoubted as his merits were, that the historians of the age were, in general, Persians, or the immediate descendants of Persians.

BOOK V. A.D. 1543.

On learning these events, and especially the death of Sheikh Ali, the Emperor was affected, and agitated beyond measure. Shah Husein Mírza, on his part, had, like the Emperor, been preparing for a battle on the following morning. His troops had buckled on their armour, and his men were ready to mount, when a deserter from the Emperor's camp arrived with information that Ishán Taimur had been defeated, Sheikh Ali slain, and that Humáyun had resolved to lead out his troops and attack the Mírza in the field, that very day. The Mírza, apprehensive of the efforts of men driven to despair, and hoping that the Emperor would now at length be disposed to make peace, did not, for the three following days, draw out his troops as usual.

Shah Husein proposes terms.

At the end of that time, Shah Husein sent Báber Kuli, one of his chief officers, on a mission to the Emperor's camp. Humáyun, as the Mírza had foreseen, was now determined to quit Sind. An agreement was speedily concluded. The Emperor, on the one hand, agreed to quit the territories of Shah Husein, while Shah Husein, on the other, consented to supply him with thirty boats to convey his effects from the present camp, and with 100,000 mithkals in money*, 2000 loads of grain, and 300 camels, to be delivered to him at the village of Runái, when he had crossed the Indus, to enable him to proceed on his route to Kandahár. These terms being arranged, the Mírza gladly furnished him with a bridge of boats to cross the arm of the Indus at Júm. And, accordingly, on the 10th of July, Humáyun marched with his whole army from the camp which they had so long occupied, and crossed the river in two days. The conditions agreed upon were faithfully and joyfully observed by Shah Husein. The provisions and cattle for transport were brought to Runái, and divided among the troops; and from thence the

Humáyun agrees to quit Sind.

Rebi II. 7. July 10.

* Some historians omit the money, which is mentioned in the Tarikh-e Sind.

camp moved on to Sehwán, where Humáyun made every thing ready for leaving Sind, after having, on the whole, tarried two years and a half in it and the adjoining country.* CHAP. I. SECT. II.

* The transactions in Sind and the Rájpút desert are recorded by Abulfazl, Akbernáma, ff. 50—2. in the Tarikh-e Akberi, ff. 154—6. Tar. Niz. f. 192. Ferishta follows briefly, vol. ii. p. 91—5., and the Tar. Bedáuni, ff. 179—182.; Jouher, who was with the Emperor, records them in his 8, 9, 10, 11, and 12th chapters. His account, however, being written from memory at the distance of many years, though lively, does not furnish dates, and perhaps sometimes transposes events. Abulfazl, who wrote from excellent reports, though able, is laudatory, and too desirous to conceal the faults of his patron's father. The Tarikh-e Sind, ff. 161—165. is valuable, as occasionally giving the Sindian Story.

# CHAPTER I.

## HUMÁYUN'S RESIDENCE IN SIND.

---

## SECTION III.

### HUMÁYUN'S ROUTE FROM SIND TO SÍSTÁN.

RECENT STATE OF AFGHÁNISTÁN. — KÁMRÁN IN KÁBUL. — ASKERI IN GHAZNI. — KÁMRÁN'S EXPEDITION TO BADAKHSHÁN. — HINDAL IN KANDAHÁR. —EMBASSY OF KÁMRÁN TO SHAH HUSEIN — MET BY HUMÁYUN. — DIFFICULTIES OF HIS ADVANCE TO KANDAHÁR. — HOSTILE PREPARATIONS OF ASKERI. — HE ADVANCES TO TAKE HUMÁYUN. — HASTY FLIGHT OF THE EMPEROR. — ARRIVAL OF ASKERI. — AKBER TAKEN, AND SENT TO KANDAHÁR.—HUMÁYUN FLIES TOWARDS SÍSTÁN. —TEMPORARILY DETAINED BY A PARTY OF BELÚCHES. — PROCEEDS THROUGH THE GERMSÍR. — ENTERS SÍSTÁN.

BOOK V.

A.D. 1543, A.H. 950

Recent state of Afghánistán.

Kámrán in Kábul.

WHEN Humáyun gave up all thought of re-entering Hindustán at the head of an army, by effecting the conquest of Sind, he unwillingly turned his thoughts towards Kandahár, which was part of the dominions of his brother Kámrán. That prince, after separating from the Emperor at Khusháb, when compelled to abandon the Penjáb to Shír Shah, had retired to Kábul, where he assumed all the insignia of an absolute and independent king, and made the prayer for the prince be recited, and the coin struck, in his own name, thus renouncing even the nominal supremacy of Humáyun. He bestowed the government of Ghazni on his brother Askeri, who accompanied him in his flight; the government of Kandahár was held by Kerácha Khan.

Askeri in Ghazni.

CHAP. I. SECT. III.

Kámrán's expedition to Badakhshán.

Mírza Kámrán, not long after his return to Kábul, marched across the Hindu-kúsh mountains, to chastise Mírza Suleimán, the ruler of Badakhshán, who refused to acknowledge him, or to renounce his allegiance to the Emperor, defeated him in battle, compelled him to submit, and deprived him of a portion of his territory.

Hindal in Kandahár.

On his return, finding that Kerácha Khan had invited Hindal Mírza from Sind, and had delivered up to him the country of Kandahár, he raised an army, and marched towards that capital, which he besieged for six months, when Hindal, finding that resistance was vain, agreed to surrender the place, and coming out to meet his brother, resigned himself into his hands. Kámrán bestowed the government of Kandahár on Mírza Askeri, and carried Hindal Mírza to Kábul as a prisoner; but after sometime bestowed on him the district of Júi-Sháhi, now Jelálábád, in jágír.*

Embassy of Kámrán to Shah Husein;

Mírza Kámrán, eager to draw still closer the bonds of union between himself and the ruler of Sind, who had acknowledged him as his superior Lord, sent Mír Alla-dost a man eminent for his piety, and Abdal Wáháb, who belonged to the family of Sheikh Púran, the great Saint of Sind, as ambassadors, to ask the daughter of Shah Husein in marriage. After Humáyun had crossed the Indus, and begun his march towards Kandahár, he heard, when near Sehwán, that these ambassadors were not far off; and they also, hearing of his approach, threw themselves into that town. Humáyun sent a message to Alla-dost, asking to see him; but the envoy returned an excuse, pretending that the people among whom he was would not suffer him to quit it. Leaving the banks of the Indus, Humáyun and his followers now proceeded towards Fatehpúr-Gandava. After leaving that place, their route lay through a

met by Humáyun.

Difficulties of his ad-

* Akbernáma, ff. 55, 56. The Tar. Bedáuni says, that he gave him Ghazni (probably a mistake), but afterwards took it from him, and made him reside in Mouza-Derwishán, f. 181.

BOOK V.

A. D. 1543.

vance towards Kandahár.

tract of country, for some days' march desert and waste, and afterwards rugged and mountainous. The guides given them by Shah Husein, who had no desire that he should become acquainted with the country, were careful not to conduct them to the best springs or wells *, and the troops suffered much from having only brackish water, or none. To add to their distress, the road was infested by banditti, as it has been in all ages; they were chiefly Balúches, who, singly or in bands, hovered around, and plundered, without mercy, all that fell behind in the line of march. Jouher tells us that, having fallen somewhat behind, he was attacked and wounded, and the water vessels under his charge carried off, almost in presence of the Emperor. The plunder and distress were general; and, as much time had been spent on the march, and the year was on its decline, the country, which in summer is exposed to the Simúm, and the blasting winds of the desert, was now subject to such excessive cold, that the travellers' broth, we are told, was hardly poured out of the kettle, when it became a plate of ice. Even the men of most note were ill provided with clothing, to resist the severity of the cold, to which they were here exposed. As an example of their unprovided condition, the Emperor, who happened to have a fur cloak, made it be divided, giving the outside, as a most acceptable gift, to Biram Khan, and the inside, or lining, to an officer of the household. After a toilsome journey, most probably through the Bolán Pass, they reached the district of Shál-Mustung, near the northern limit of Baluchistán, and about a hundred and fifty miles from Kandahár, on which it was dependent.

Hostile preparations of Askeri.

Here they encountered difficulties of a different de-

* Such is the account of the contemporary writers, and from the Mírza's character it is not improbable. But the difficulty of the march through such a country might, of itself, account for many of the hardships endured by the Emperor.

scription. Two of the Emperor's servants, who preceded the camp, were carried off from a spring at which they had alighted, by scouts sent out by Jilál-ed-dín Beg, an officer of Kámrán's, who was stationed in that quarter. One of the two, however, contrived to make his escape, and, rejoining the Emperor, related both his own adventures, and such circumstances as he had learnt from the conversation of the party that had taken him. By this accident, Humáyun discovered that his brothers were aware of his approach, that their hostility was unabated, and that Askeri was not far off. Renouncing, therefore, his intention of proceeding to Kandahár, he turned off towards Mustung. Some of his followers, however, asked permission to go on to Kandahár, which he granted; and, at the same time, wrote a letter of remonstrance and advice to his brother, which he entrusted to one of them to deliver.

When Humáyun was leaving Sind to march against Kandahár, Shah Husein, desirous of counteracting his plans for retrieving his affairs, had despatched expresses to Kámrán and Askeri, to inform them of his movements. Kámrán instantly sent orders to Askeri at Kandahár, to put that city in a state of defence, and himself to waylay and seize Humáyun, at whatever risk. Askeri Mírza, having executed the one part of his instructions, had now advanced considerably on his way to execute the other. The Amírs, who formed his court, were, however, far from being unanimous in their opinions. Kásim Husein Sultan Uzbek, Mehdi Kásim Khan, and others, advised him not to move against the Emperor, lest that prince, driven to desperation, should take refuge in Persia, a step which might be followed by the most ruinous consequences. Abulkhair was of a different opinion, and enforced the necessity of seizing Humáyun, and to this opinion Askeri inclined. In the morning after the consultation, therefore, the Mírza marched forward on his route towards Shál-Mustung,

He advances to take Humáyun.

BOOK V.

A. D. 1543.

(in which direction he learned that the Emperor, who was not far off, had proceeded,) in hopes of surprising him. After advancing a kos or two, having by this time got into a waste and intricate country, he inquired if any of his followers was acquainted with the road. One Chupi Behâder, an Uzbek, who had been in Kásim Husein Sultan's service, but in this expedition had joined the troops immediately under the Mírza, said that he knew it thoroughly, having often travelled it back and forward. "True," said the Mírza, "you had a jágír in this quarter," and ordered him to ride forward, to reconnoitre along the road, and report what he saw. The man remarking to the Mírza that he rode but a sorry pony*, the Mírza directed Tersún Birlás, one of his attendants, to dismount and lend him his horse, which was stout and swift; and Tersún obeying very reluctantly, was sharply chidden by the prince.

Chupi, who had formerly served under Humáyun in Hindustán, having mounted his fleet steed, rode for some time at a moderate pace, till he had reached the pass of Pekh, in a valley formed by the hills, when, being out of sight, he set off at full speed, and did not halt till he reached the imperial camp, when he alighted at the door of Biram Khan's tent, and at once informed him of the danger that was at hand. Biram Khan, without delay, hastened, by a private road, to the Emperor's pavilion; and speaking from behind the kanáts or screen, informed him of the imminent danger with which he was threatened. Humáyun starting up, proposed, with his usual spirit, to meet the attack in arms: but the Khan at once convinced him that, from Askeri's overpowering superiority in numbers, there was no hope but in retreat. The Emperor upon this, indignantly exclaiming, "Are Kandahár and Kábul for ever to be the cause of contention between me and my un-

* Yábú.

worthy brothers?" despatched Khwája Moazem and Biram Khan, instantly to bring the Empress Hamída Begum, and her son, the infant Akber, who soon arrived. A hasty requisition for horses was addressed to Terdi Beg and some other Amírs, who made difficulties. But no time was to be lost; the foe would soon be upon them. Hamída Begum was hurriedly placed on horseback. It was decided that Akber, who was only a year old, would be unable to support a rapid journey in inclement weather, through a desert and waterless waste, and he was left behind under the care of his usual attendants. Humáyun then hurried away, accompanied by only forty men, twenty-two of them persons of note, and two ladies. All the rest of the party, with the whole tents and baggage, were left behind.*

Hasty flight of the Emperor.

* Akbernáma, f. 53.; Tab. Akb. f. 156.; Tar. Niz. f. 193. Such is the account given by Abulfazl and followed in the Tab. Akberi. The narrative of Jouher is somewhat different. The night before, when Humáyun reached Shál-Mustung, he took up his quarters in a garden, where a man accosted him, and asked if he knew any thing of Mírza Askeri. The Emperor said, that he did not, but would be glad if he would communicate any information he possessed. The stranger desired to speak to him alone, and all the imperial attendants, except Jouher, being removed, informed Humáyun that his son, one of the Mírza's servants, had just arrived alone; that he had left the prince in the hills, at the pass of Pekh, only five kos off, and that, before two watches of the morning were over, Askeri would arrive, for the purpose of seizing his Majesty. This information induced the Emperor to leave the garden and rejoin the camp.

Humáyun, having breakfasted on whatever was at hand, said his morning prayers, and being much fatigued with his long journey, lay down, and fell fast asleep. His people dispersed on various employments. "At noon," says Jouher, "a man came full speed from the wilds, and asked for H. M. He was in great haste. The servant said, 'Leave your horse here, and go in.' He would not leave it, but twisting the bridle round his hand, entered the tent. H. M. was asleep. He was waked, and asked the man, 'Do you bring any message?' The man answered, 'No,' but added, that Mírza Askeri was coming in a hostile manner. H. M. asked 'What is your name?' He answered, 'Chupi Behåder, by tribe an Uzbek, and I am sent by Kásim Husein Sultan.' His Majesty said, 'It is true,' sent for Biram Khan, and asked his advice. He advised H. M. to set off instantly. H. M. said, 'We must fight them.' Biram Khan answered, 'We are few: they are

BOOK V.

A. D. 1543.

Just as Humáyun was setting out, Mír Abul Hasan, the Sadr, who had been sent forward by Askeri to attempt to detain the Emperor, by engaging him in conversation, arrived, and proceeded to deliver some complimentary messages on the part of the Mírza. Humáyun, however, set off, without paying them any attention. Askeri came in sight some time after, and pushed forward a body of troops to surround the camp, intending to cut off all communication with it on every side, and to prevent any one from escaping. But he soon learned, with regret, that Chupi Beháder had brought news of his approach, and that the Emperor had already escaped, and fled into the desert. He placed a guard, to cut off all intercourse between the two camps. Mír Ghaznevi (afterwards Atkeh Khan), under whose care the young prince had been left, presented himself, and was graciously received, the Mírza expressing his regret that Humáyun had gone away; loudly professing that his sole object in coming was to wait upon the Emperor, and to do him every service. He, at the same time, sent a camel with fruit for Akber's use. But he repaired the same evening to the imperial tents, and, throwing aside all shame, took possession of the baggage, all of which he narrowly examined, causing a list of the articles to be made in his own presence. He, at first, received with civility Terdi Beg and Humáyun's other Amírs, when they waited on him; but next day, they were delivered into custody, and soon after subjected to heavy exactions, many of them perishing in the tortures inflicted on them to extort a discovery of their real or supposed wealth. The young prince was received with every mark of affection and tenderness, and carried to Kandahár by Askeri, who delivered him to the charge of his wife Sultánum Begum; but without taking him from the

Arrival of Askeri.

Akber sent to Kandahár.

coming in great force," &c. Abulfazl had seen Jouher's narrative. It does not appear whether Nizám-ed-dín Ahmed had. It carries with it an air of probability.

immediate care of Máham Anka, Jiji Anka, and Atkeh Khan, who had been appointed by his parents to nurse and watch over him. Sultánum Begum's affection for him was sincere, and like that of a mother. The young Akber was brought to the Bála-Ark, or Citadel of Kandahár, on 15th of December, A.D. 1543.* Ramzán 18. Dec. 15.

Humáyun flies towards Sístán.

Meanwhile Humáyun, and the small party of fugitives that accompanied him, after galloping off from their camp, soon reached the desert waste. Day failing, was succeeded by a night of uncommon darkness. Biram Khan, it is said, proposed to Humáyun to take advantage of it, to turn back, and come upon the camp by surprise; adding that, from his knowledge of Askeri's frivolous and selfish character, he was assured that they would find him sitting in the midst of his clerks, busy in examining the contents of the chests and packages, which the Emperor had left behind: that the probability was, that the troops would make little resistance, or would even join them. Humáyun acknowledged that the enterprise was a feasible one, but said that he was now cured of ambition, and had made up his mind to proceed, through Persia, to the holy city of Mekka.

But, though they do not seem to have been pursued by Askeri, their danger was not yet over. They kept on their course towards Sístán. One night, after a long march, the barking of a dog was heard. The Emperor had hardly time to observe, that some habitations† must be at hand, when a party of Balúches met, and stopped them. They spoke in their own language, which was not understood: but fortunately one of the ladies, who was with the Emperor's suite, was herself a Balúch‡, the wife of an officer in his service. She was employed to interpret, and it appeared that they were followers

* Akbernáma, ff. 53, 54.; Tab. Akb. f. 157.; Tar. Niz. ff. 193, 194.; Jouher, c. 13. It does not appear that Terdi Beg and the other Amírs were asked to attend Humáyun in his flight into Sístán.

† Nizám-ed-dín calls this fort, Kila Háji Bába, f. 194.

‡ She was the wife of Hasan Ali, Ishek-agha (chamberlain).

BOOK V.

A. D. 1543.

Temporarily detained by a party of Balúches.

of Malek Khati, a Balúch chief, whom Abulfazl styles the Captain-General of the banditti of the desert. This leader being at that moment absent, his people, on finding that it was the Emperor, insisted that the little troop should not pass onward without their master's leave.

The Emperor was obliged to comply, and entering the fort, the freebooters salaamed to him respectfully, spread a carpet on which he and Hamída Begum sat down, and supplied the wants of the party with all the hospitality of the desert. When day began to dawn, as the Emperor was engaged in his morning prayers, Malek Khati, who had been sent for, returned.

The Emperor's peaceable entrance into the fort, which gave him the character of a guest, had roused the robber's sense of honour. Saluting the Emperor, and making the usual polite inquiries after his health, the chief informed him, that three days before, an order from Kámrán Mírza had reached him, commanding him not, on any account, to suffer the Emperor Humáyun to pass that way, but to seize, and make him prisoner. "But," added he, "now that your Majesty has visited me, on my head and eyes be it. Yet it is better that you should ride on, and I will myself conduct you to the borders." Humáyun gladly assented. The party was again put in motion, and proceeded about fifteen kos, guided and accompanied to the confine of his territory by the Malek, who there took his leave.

Proceeds through the Germsír.

On losing the escort of his robber host, Humáyun entered the Germsír *, which lies between Kandahár and Khorásán, and at that time depended on Mírza Kámrán. Though a very unwelcome guest to Abdal Hai, the governor of the country, who remained faithful to the Mírza, and even punished some of his servants who assisted the Emperor, he was, however, received with a certain degree of respect, and supplied, though scantily,

* Germsír signifies warm country, and here denotes the low tract of land lying on the Helmend.

with such necessaries as the country afforded. It happened that Khwája Jilál-ed-dín Mahmúd had been sent into the district by Askeri to collect the revenue. Humáyun opened a communication with him, and succeeded in bringing him over to his interest; so that the Khwája waited upon him, and presented his Majesty with a large set of tents, besides horses, camels and mules, and such sum of money as he had collected; a most seasonable and acceptable supply, in his present distressed circumstances, to the Emperor, who bestowed on him what was then little more than a title, the office of Mír Sámán, Sirkár Kháseh (keeper of the imperial stores). CHAP. I. SECT. III.

The Germsír of Kandahár, in which Humáyun lingered for some days, was subject to that country, but lay close upon Sístán, a province that belonged to the King of Persia, and into which, by merely passing the Helmend, he could easily fly. His unhappy and destitute condition preyed upon his mind. Worn out by his sufferings, feeling the vanity of past enjoyments, which had vanished from his grasp, and left behind nothing but regret, and willing to turn his eyes from the deary prospect before him; with a feeling common to Musulmans in adversity, he talked of devoting the remains of his life, in some sequestered solitude, to meditation and prayer. But the remonstrances of his adherents, powerfully supported no doubt by his hankering after the enjoyments of that world, which he believed that he was desirous of abandoning, soon recalled him to more active exertions. Desirous of ascertaining the sentiments of the King of Persia, the hereditary friend of his family, he addressed to him a letter, in which he explained his situation and his wishes, and despatched it by the hands of Chupi Behâder. He would willingly have remained in the Germsír, till an answer arrived, but Abdal Hai sent to announce to him, that Mírza Kámrán had despatched a large body of men Shawál 1. Dec. 28.

BOOK V. A. D. 1543.

from Kandahár, in quest of him; that, if he remained, nothing could prevent his falling into their hands, and that his only hope of safety lay in passing into the adjoining province of Sístán, where, under the protection of the King of Persia, he would be free from danger. Seeing, therefore, that he could nowhere be safe in the wide-spreading dominions of his father, Humáyun unwillingly crossed the Helmend, and encamped in the Persian territory, by the side of the lake into which that river empties itself. He was hospitably and honourably received and entertained by Ahmed Sultan Shamlu, the governor.*

Enters Sístán.

Humáyun did not willingly abandon the territory which he considered as his own, to enter that of the Shah of Persia, a bigot, who was the chief of another sect of Musulmans from that to which he and his forefathers had adhered. But he had not a spot on which he could safely place his foot. Kámrán seemed to have come in his place, and by the extent of his dominions to have become the representative of the Chaghatái dynasty. He was master of Kábul and Ghazni, of Kandahár, Khutlán and Badakhshán. Shír Shah ruled, with absolute power and acknowledged talent, the empire that had formerly been his, and, in addition to it, the Penjáb, and the countries beyond the Indus, which he had wrested from Kámrán. In Upper and Lower Sind, Shah Husein Arghún was absolute master. Driven from every spot of which he had lately called himself master, and viewing, with the deepest dread, the possibility of falling into the hands of his brother, he resolved to abandon the kingdoms of his father, and threw himself on the dubious and untried generosity of a stranger.

* Akbernáma, f. 53.; Tabak. Akberi, ff. 156, 157.; Tar. Niz. f. 194.; Jouher, c. 13. On the few adherents who accompanied Humáyun in his flight from Mustung to Germsír, Humáyun seems to have bestowed the name of *Chuli*, men of the desert, and to have always treated them with special regard.

# CHAPTER II.

## HUMÁYUN IN PERSIA.

HUMÁYUN'S RELUCTANCE TO ENTER PERSIA. — HIS RECEPTION AND OCCUPATIONS IN SÍSTÁN. — SETS OUT FOR HERÁT AND MESHHÍD. — REGAL ENTERTAINMENT BY THE SHAH'S ORDERS. — STAY AT HERÁT AND MESHHÍD. — PROCEEDS TO JOIN THE SHAH. — SENDS FORWARD BIRAM KHAN AS ENVOY. — TREATMENT OF THE AMBASSADOR AT KAZVÍN. — HUMÁYUN AT KAZVÍN. — DEPUTATION FROM THE SHAH. — INTERVIEW OF THE SOVEREIGNS. — HUMÁYUN AT THE PERSIAN COURT. — INTOLERANCE OF TAHMASP. — GRAND HUNTING PARTY. — INTRIGUES AGAINST HUMÁYUN. — JEALOUSIES OF THE SOVEREIGNS. — ATTEMPTS TO CONVERT HUMÁYUN TO THE SHÍA SECT. — LEAGUE BETWEEN HUMÁYUN AND TAHMASP. — PARTING FESTIVITIES. — HUMÁYUN PREPARES TO SET OUT FOR KANDAHÁR. — REMARKS ON HIS TREATMENT BY THE SHAH — AND HIS OWN BEHAVIOUR.

CHAP. II.

A. D. 1544, A. H. 950.

Humáyun's reluctance to enter Persia

It was not without great reluctance that Humáyun came to the determination of abandoning his own dominions, and trusting himself in the power of a foreign prince, who had pretensions to some part of his territory, and was a bigoted adherent to a sect of Moslemism, different from that to which he himself adhered. But he had only a choice of evils left, and he submitted to what he deemed the least.

His reception and occupations in Sístán.

On entering Sístán, he was received with the greatest respect and hospitality by Ahmed Sultan Shamlu, the governor. Humáyun, at first spent much of his time in the amusements of hunting and hawking, waiting till an answer should be returned to the letter which he had addressed to the Shah. He afterwards advanced farther into the province, when the governor brought his mother and wives to entertain the empress. Many of Humáyun's late followers, who had been carried to Kandahár, escaped, and, by degrees, joined him in

BOOK V. A. D. 1544.

Sístán. Many visitors of note waited upon him out of respect, or from curiosity. Among those most acceptable to him, was Husein Kuli Sultan, the governor's brother, who had come from Meshhíd, to visit his mother and brother, before setting out on a pilgrimage to Mekka. As he was a man of piety, of learning, and of speculation, Humáyun questioned him minutely as to the tenets of the religious sects that then divided Persia, and especially as to the grand division into Shías and Sunnis, a subject which had become of the deepest importance to the fugitive prince. Having one day asked him, what was his own opinion as to the difference between the sects, Husein Kuli answered, evasively but with address, that he had for a long time meditated on the conflicting tenets of these sects, and, during the last five years, had read all the books written by both parties; that the Shías maintain that to curse and ban the three first Khalífs, is an act of piety, and agreeable to God; while the Sunnis hold, that such conduct is the mark of an infidel: but that, for his part, he conceived that, if a man conscientiously believed that by doing a certain act, he was meriting the favour of God, this never could mark him out as an infidel. Humáyun was pleased with the argument, and with the whole style of Husein Kuli's conversation, and pressed him to enter his service; but Husein Kuli excused himself, on the plea of having made all his arrangements for setting out on the great pilgrimage, though he promised to join him on his return from the Holy cities.*

Among those who joined Humáyun from Kandahár, were Háji Muhammed Bába Kushkeh and Hasan Koka, both foster brothers of Kámrán, who strongly urged him to march into Zemín-dáwer—at that time a province of Kandahár—assuring him that Amír Beg, the

* Akbernáma, ff. 57, 58.; Tar. Niz. f. 194.; Mem. of Bayezíd, ff. 2, 3.

governor, would join him, as well as the governor of Bíst and many others, and that the defection was likely to be so general that in a short time he would certainly be master of Kandahár itself. But Ahmed Sultan, the Persian governor of Sístán, who had not yet received orders from his court, in what manner he was to conduct himself towards the Emperor, seems to have taken an alarm on receiving some hint of this plan, and instantly waited on Humáyun to remonstrate with him on the subject, advising him to reject the proposal as in many respects objectionable, and offering to proceed with him at once to Irák and the Persian court. To this proposition, perhaps equivalent to a command, Humáyun signified a modified assent, and, to quiet the suspicion of the governor, excluded for some time from his presence Háji Muhammed, the author of the project that had given so much offence. Instead, however, of proceeding post with Ahmed Sultan by the direct but desert road of Tabas, Humáyun expressed a wish to visit Herát, of the magnificence of which he had heard much, as well as the holy shrine of Meshhíd. This being agreed to, he set out, attended by Ahmed Sultan, for Herát, and proceeded, by the fort of Awek in Sístán, to the town of Farra.

Sets out for Herát and Meshhíd.

Here news were at last received from the Court of Persia. When Humáyun's letter reached Shah Tahmasp, the son of Shah Ismáel, a young man then about twenty-seven years of age, an event so honourable to the new dynasty of the Sefis as the arrival of the Emperor of India, the representative of the great Taimur, to seek refuge at the foot of the throne of the king of kings, was hailed with delight. The kettle-drum was beat for three days at the royal residence at Kazvín; and a gracious answer was returned to Humáyun by the Shah, containing some complimentary verses from the royal pen to respond to those in the Emperor's letter. Firmáns were addressed to all governors and

His regal entertainment by the Shah's orders.

BOOK V. A. D. 1544.

other chief officers of the provinces and cities through which the Emperor was likely to pass, commanding them to receive and entertain the imperial guest with every mark of honour, and to furnish him and his retinue with provisions, wines, fruits, and whatever else could contribute to their comfort from stage to stage in the whole progress of their journey. In the firmán directed to the governor of Herát, he is enjoined to prepare, for the Emperor's use, five hundred trays of meat of different kinds, besides sweetmeats; and the total number of trays of every description for him and his suite was never to be less than fifteen hundred daily. A thousand men on horseback were always to attend him, who were strictly enjoined to prevent all collisions between the natives of the country and the Emperor's servants.*

From Farra, where he was rejoined by his own messengers, and by the Shah's ambassadors, who had attended them back from the court, his advance to Herát resembled a triumphal procession. For the space of twelve or fifteen miles before he reached the capital, the whole inhabitants of the nearest towns and villages had been commanded to attend, and line the road; and as he approached Herát, the whole population of the town poured out, and covered the hills and plains, the

* Akbernáma, ff. 57—9.; Bayezíd's Mem. ff. 3—5. The Shah's letter to the Governor of Herát is curious, but is illustrative of the state of Persia rather than of India. It describes the presents for the Emperor, consisting of horses, daggers, ornamented swords, housings of cloth of gold, brocades, &c., as well as directions for his entertainment. Everything is specified: loaves of white bread, baked with milk and butter, tents, table-linen, sheets, changes of wearing apparel, plate, and utensils of all kinds, sherbets cooled in ice and water, fruits, grapes, rose-water, amber, and perfumes; the number of trays of meat. The young prince was to make the Hazáras and Nukderis of the adjoining mountains come down, to the number of 30,000, and attend the Emperor on his route to Herát. On every subject, the minutest directions are given. Akbernáma, No. 1. ff. 57—59.; No. 2. f. 119. and seqq. Also Bayezíd's Mem. MS. ff. 3—10., from which Abulfazl probably copied it.

trees and house tops, as he passed along. The Amír al omra, Muhammed Khan Sherf-ed-dín Oghli Taklu, the young prince's Atálík or guardian, and the chief officers of the government, received him at the Púlmálán river, and conducted him towards the city; where the young prince himself, Sultan Muhammed Mírza, the Shah's eldest son, and nominal governor of Herát, received him in state, and accompanied him to the palace in the Jehán-árá gardens, where he found a magnificent entertainment prepared for him.*

CHAP. II.

Zikádeh 1. Jan. 26.

Having visited the palaces, mosques, colleges, monasteries, tombs, and gardens of Herát, then one of the finest cities in the world, and lingered there about a month, he proceeded towards Meshhíd, by the route of Jám, where he visited with reverence the mausoleum † of his Empress Hamída-Bánu's ancestor, Zhindah-fíl Ahmed Jám, a holy man, to whose tomb pilgrimages were made, as to a place of great sanctity. From Jám he went on to Meshhíd, where he was received with the usual procession and demonstrations of respect, by Shah-kuli Sultan Istajlu. Here he remained forty days, and visited the sacred tomb of the Imám Ali

Stay at Herát,

Zilhajeh 5. Feb. 29.

and Meshhíd. A. H. 951, Moharrem 15. April 8.

* Akbernáma, ff. 59, 60.; Tab. Akb. f. 157.

† "As he visited this tomb by night, the gate was shut. The door-keeper attempted to open it, but the chain was closed, and the Emperor was informed by him that it was impossible to remove the chain. He retired a few steps, but returning; 'O Imám,' said he, 'every person who has ever offered up his vows at your shrine has obtained the object of his wishes; your slave has also come with similar hopes to your tomb, in expectation of succeeding in his request?' Having said this, he laid his hand on the door, when, instantly, the chain was unlocked: it might even be said it was cut in two: on which his Majesty entered the holy tomb, walked round it, and offered up his prayers; after which, he sat down at an appointed place, and began to read the Koran. The superintendant of the tomb then said to the Emperor, 'If you like, you may snuff the lamp.' His Majesty replied, 'If not too great a liberty, I will do so.' The officer said, 'You have leave.' The Emperor, therefore, took up the scissors, and cut off the snuff of the lamp; after which, having said his prayers, he came out, but commanded that one of the royal bows should be suspended at the gate as an offering." Stewart's Jouher, p. 6.

BOOK V. A. D. 1544.

Reza, which, being a Sunni, he was obliged to do privately: and here he appears to have received the first direct invitation from the Shah to repair to Kazvín. Advancing therefore by Nishabúr, he visited the turquoise mines in the neighbourhood, and then went on to Sebzáwár. Having halted there forty days he resumed his progress, proceeding by Damghán, Bostám, Semnán, and Sefiábád, receiving from time to time as he went along, expresses, which brought him presents of fruit from the court.

Proceeds to join the Shah.

The real circumstances of Humáyun's intercourse with Shah Tahmasp cannot be satisfactorily ascertained. Abulfazl, whom historians in general copy, jealous of the honour of the imperial family, merely hints at, or altogether conceals, or perverts, any circumstances which were painful or humiliating to the exiled prince. Succeeding historians, following his authority, have accordingly been loud in their praises of the magnificent hospitality with which he was received. It was not until the publication of the translation of the Memoirs of Jouher *, who attended the Emperor as a domestic servant during his exile, and who tells his plain unvarnished tale, with the unconscious frankness of an aged gossip, on the minutest circumstances of incidents, to which the elegant, but cautious, historian hardly ventures to allude, that it was discovered that Humáyun had much to suffer, and many humiliations to endure. Indeed, even the proud parade of his entry into the chief towns, was less fitted to please a man, however vain, by the borrowed pomp and show with which he was surrounded, than to humble one of a proud spirit, by a public exhibition of his own misery, and his patron's grandeur.

Sends forward Biram

When Humáyun reached Kila Ders near Rei, a

* The Tezkereh al Vákiát, or private Memoirs of the Mogul Emperor Humáyun, written in the Persian language by Jouher, translated by Major Charles Stewart, H. E. I. C. S. Lond. 1832. (Printed for the Oriental Translation Fund.)

CHAP. II.

Khan as envoy.

letter arrived from the Shah, to inform him that he was at Kazvín, at that time the royal residence, and that the Emperor might now send forward Biram Beg as his ambassador. That able man was a Turkomán, originally a subject of Persia, and had accompanied the army of Najm Sáni, sent by Shah Ismáel to assist Báber in the conquest of Bokhára. He had survived the discomfiture of that army, and had ever since remained in the service of Báber and his son, in which he had risen to high distinction by his bravery, and his sound and practical talents. When Humáyun thought of entering the Persian territory, Biram Beg appears to have become the principal adviser of that monarch. He was, accordingly, despatched to court, with an escort of ten horsemen.

Treatment of the Ambassador at Kazvín.

A few days after Biram Beg's arrival at Kazvín, the Shah, a despotic prince and a bigoted Shía, desired him to cut off his hair, and assume the Táj or Persian cap, which was considered as a symbol of adherence to the Shía doctrines. This, Biram Beg, faithful to his duty, firmly, but delicately, declined, alleging that, as he was now the servant and representative of another prince, he was bound to be regulated by his master's wishes. The Shah, who had earnestly desired to gratify at once his vanity and bigotry, by making the ambassador of the sovereign of India assume the badge of his own service and religion, was much offended, but told the Beg that he was at liberty to do as he pleased. Yet to show him his danger, and shake his firmness, the Shah commanded some Chirágh-kúsh heretics, who belonged to a sect that was equally calumniated and hated by the orthodox Musulmans, and who had been long in prison, to be brought out and executed in his presence.*

* The Chirágh-kúsh, or lamp extinguishers, are heretics of the Ismáliah sect, who are much disliked, and their doctrines much misrepre-

BOOK V.

A. D. 1544.

It is usual for the kings of Persia, during the warm season of the year, to leave their palaces in the cities on the plain, and to retire to cool summer quarters, high up among the lofty mountains which are so common in that country. Those of the Shah were, this year, between Sultanía and Surlik. When Tahmasp set out from Kazvín, he sent directions to Humáyun to remain where he was, till further notice. But he, soon after, sent Babek Beg, to act as the Emperor's Mehmándár; and instructions followed that he should advance to Kazvín, where he was to rest three days, and then proceed on to the camp of the Shah.*

Humáyun at Kazvín.

Jemádi I. July or Augt. (It begins July 21.)

During the three days that Humáyun resided at Kazvín, he was lodged in one of the royal palaces, and entertained with much splendour. On the fourth day, he set out to join the royal camp, which lay between Abher and Sultanía, and travelled all night. In the latter part of the night, he desired his people to look out for water, that he might halt. While they were so employed, news was brought that Biram Beg was at hand. That nobleman soon after arrived, and observed to Humáyun, that he had advanced rather far; but the Emperor said, he could not go back. The Emperor, having said his morning prayers, then went to sleep, but was soon after wakened by the singing of the Persian pioneers, who had begun to work in repairing the road. Having bathed, and dressed himself, he took his seat in his diwán-khána, or presence chamber, as Biram Beg informed him that a large honorary procession was on its way to meet him. Here he received the vakils of the Sultans, the Khans, the Mírzas, and the great Syeds in succession, who were all presented; and then setting out, the Emperor

Deputation from the Shah.

sented by all orthodox Musulmans. They are occasionally severely persecuted. They have been already mentioned, vol. i. p. 287, *note*.

* Akbernáma, ff. 57, 58.; Tar. Niz. f. 194.; Tab. Akb. f. 157.; Jouher, c. 14, 15.; Bayezíd, ff. 2—12.

met the Sultans, Khans, Mírzas and Syeds themselves as he advanced along the road. When the King's brothers met the Emperor, Behrám Mírza presented him with a complete dress of honour, and a fiery unbroken steed, the latter, with the polite arrogance characteristic of Persians, for the purpose of putting to the test his skill in horsemanship, on which they pique themselves so much. Humáyun put on the whole of the proffered dress, except the *táj*, or cap, which, bearing the symbol of the twelve Imáms, was considered as indicating an adoption of the Shía faith. He then mounted the horse, which fortunately, to their disappointment, proved very manageable in his hands. The Emperor now again moved on, and was met by the korchi-báshi (or commander of the guards), who adressed him with a "salám-aleikum" (on you be peace), a salutation used among equals, and passed on. After him, "a number of inferior people mounted on Kermanian horses came, and made their salute: the object of their being introduced was to prove that all the Persians, whether of high or of low rank, were on a footing with our (Emperor)."*

CHAP. II.

Interview of the Sovereigns. Jemádi, July, and August.

The Shah received Humáyun with honour, and placed him on a cushion on his right hand. But his religious zeal was not long of betraying itself. "After making some inquiries concerning his health and the fatigues of the journey, he said, 'You will put on the táj' (or Persian cap). Humáyun (taking advantage of the ambiguity of the term) answered, 'The táj (crown) is a mark of greatness. I will put it on.' The Shah, with his own royal hands, then placed the cap on the Emperor's head, on which the Shah, and all the Khans and Sultans raised a shout, calling out, 'Alla! Alla!' and bending down their heads, as in prayer, according to their custom. The Emperor then asked that the

* Stewart's Jouher, p. 64.

BOOK V. A.D. 1544.

Mírzas might be allowed to be seated, but was told by the Shah that such was not the etiquette." An entertainment, served by the Emperor's butler, followed. The two sovereigns ate together. When it was finished, there was another general shout, and prostration, in honour of the coming of so great a potentate to the foot of the royal throne.* To the spectators in general, it must have appeared as if the Indian prince had conformed to the Persian usages and faith.

Humáyun at the Persian Court.

Humáyun, on leaving the presence, had quarters assigned to him between those of Behrám Mírza and Beder Khan, and was attended home by the Mírza. After enjoying the warm bath, he made his hair be cut off, apparently to conform to the Persian costume; and having received three honorary dresses, he put on one of them, and, conforming himself to circumstances with the easy elasticity of his character, passed the rest of the night in jollity and pleasure.

Next day, as the Shah marched for Sultanía, Humáyun, having gone out to salute him, was treated with cold neglect and insult. The Persian's arrogance is never displayed more conspicuously than in the advantages which he attempts to gain over an antagonist in the combat of forms, an important part in their diplomacy. Humáyun, much hurt at the slight thus put upon him, as soon as he arrived at Sultanía, went straight to the dome of the shrine of Sultan Muhammed Khodábendeh†, the grand prop of the Shía faith, and there gave vent to feelings of the deepest regret and self-reproach, for having put himself in the power of a

* Jouher, c. 14.

† Sultan Muhammed Khodábendeh (originally called Aljaptu or Uljáitu), was the son of Arghún and brother of Eazan, whom he succeeded as Emperor of the Moghuls. He was a zealous Musulman, having been converted to that religion, when he took the surname of Khodabendeh, or servant of God. He founded Sultanía, A. H. 704 (A. D. 1304), and was celebrated for his justice.

prince who could make so ungenerous a use of an accidental superiority.

Intolerance of Tahmasp.

Humáyun now found that he had placed himself in the power of a keen religious bigot, who was determined to avail himself of the advantage he had gained, to convert at all events his Indian Sunni refugees to the true Shía faith. The means he adopted were generally more marked by violence than conciliation. A large quantity of firewood being one day sent for the Emperor's use, Shah Tahmasp accompanied it with a message, that if he adopted the Shía faith, the Shah would protect and cherish him, but that, otherwise, he would set the fuel on fire, and consume him and his heretical followers in the flames. To this intolerant and insolent message, Humáyun calmly replied that they had come, firmly attached to their religion, and would maintain it: that empire was nothing, for whatever is, is by the will of the Almighty, on whom he had fixed his trust, and to whose pleasure he would submit, whatever it might be. He asked leave to proceed on the pilgrimage of Mekka. The Shah, in reply, sent to tell the Emperor that he was on the point of marching to exterminate the Sunni Osmanlis, and that it did not become him, even had he leisure, to engage in altercation, or to retaliate complaints; that Humáyun had come into his dominions voluntarily, and that he, as sovereign, would not be doing his duty, were he to suffer him to continue to hold his present false and impious doctrines.

It was not easy for Humáyun to decide how he could act with a due regard to his personal safety, in the dangerous position in which he now felt himself placed. While he was in this state of perplexity, Kázi Jehán Kazvíni, a divine of great note, and the Shah's Diwán or minister, waited upon him, and in the course of a long conversation earnestly besought him, as a matter of policy, to comply with the Shah's request.

BOOK V.
A. D. 1544.

He represented to him, that he was not a solitary being, for that the consequences of his fruitless obstinacy would affect, not himself only, but the lives of nearly seven hundred helpless Sunnis, his followers, who must share his fate: that the circumstances in which he was placed imposed it upon him as a duty, should he find himself driven to extremity, to intimate his acquiescence, on the reasonable ground that, as he was no longer master of his own actions, he must submit. "But what am I expected to do?" said the Emperor. "Let the specific demands be brought in writing."*

The Díwán was not long of returning, when he brought three papers from Shah Tahmasp. Humáyun read two of them, which he put aside. He was perusing the third, when the Shah himself, burning with impatience, came to one side of the pavilion, and called out something with a loud voice. The Diwán upon this, addressing the Emperor in a soothing tone, told him that there was no going back, and beseeched him to have regard to the circumstances in which he stood. The Shah himself presented him with the third paper, with his own hand, and read it in his presence. Humáyun would seem to have signed it, though the nature and extent of his forced acquiescence are not very clear.†

G and hunting party.

For his own royal amusement, and to exhibit to the Emperor his power and greatness, the Shah ordered a grand hunting match near the Takht-e Suleimán‡, one

* Tab. Akb. f. 158.; Jouher, c. 14.

† Jouher, c. 14., but the account is very confused in the only copy of the original which I have seen, and I am uncertain if I have always caught the sense.

‡ An interesting account of Takht-e Suleimán may be found in Major Rawlinson's notes of his journey to the ruins of that place. Journey of the Royal Geographical Society, vol. x. pp. 46—57. "In the spring and summer," says that inquisitive and intelligent traveller (p. 56.), "the neighbourhood of Takhti Suleimán is represented as a perfect paradise. The country all around is carpeted with the richest verdure: the climate is delightful,

of the most beautiful spots in Persia. The game, for several days' journey round about, was driven to a central point by the inhabitants of the country, assisted by the troops, and confined by fences or bodies of armed men. The collection of wild animals thus brought together is described as being immense. When all was ready, the Shah and the Emperor first entered to a convenient spot within the ring, and when satiated with the easy slaughter of some of the innumerable animals thus presented to them, the royal Mírzas were next admitted; and after them the chief nobles, among whom were Biram Beg and Háji Muhammed Koka, and some others of the suite of the Emperor. In the end, persons of every rank were admitted indiscriminately, and the soldiers were allowed to kill and carry off at pleasure. A second ring was formed, some days after, near the Houz-e- Suleimán (Suleimán's Lake); and after the hunt or slaughter, there were games of chou-ghán-bázi and kebk-endázi, a kind of horse-shinty, and shooting at a mark, generally a bason, or bird, placed on the top of a high pole, while riding at full speed. After some days had been passed in these amusements*, Humáyun, desirous of conciliating the Persian monarch, made up a present, consisting of the largest diamond which he possessed, "worth kingdoms,"† and of two hundred and fifty fine Badakhshi rubies, which he sent by Biram Beg, as an offering to the Shah, with a message, that the latter had been brought from

and myriads of wild flowers impregnate the air with fragrance. Indeed, there is not considered a more agreeable yailak, or summer pasture, in all Persia."

* A circumstance which occurred at one of these hunts illustrates the lax morality of the Mírzas and the servility of the court. Behrám Mírza, the king's brother was on bad terms with Abul-kásim Khalfa, a Persian nobleman of rank. Seizing a favourable opportunity, the Mírza took a deliberate aim, and shot him with an arrow, during the chase, he died upon the spot. No one dared to mention this murder to the King.

† This diamond is said to have weighed 4 miskals and 4 dangs, Akbernáma, f. 60.; Alem-arái Abási, f. 43.

BOOK V. A. D. 1544.

Badakhshán expressly for the purpose. The royal jewellers having declared these precious stones to be above all price, Shah Tahmasp signified his satisfaction, and bestowed on Biram Beg the title of Khan, with the alem-standard and kettle-drum; while Háji Muhammed Koka, who had been successful at the play of kebk-endázi, was honoured with the title of Sultan. These titles, bestowed by one sovereign on the servants of another, were, at least, of an ambiguous nature, and marked an assumption of superiority on the part of the Persian monarch.*

Intrigues against Humáyun.

For nearly two months after these events, all intercourse, whether personal or in writing, between the two monarchs, was suspended. For this, various reasons are assigned. It seems that Roushen Beg Koka, and some other Amírs who had been in Humáyun's service, but had afterwards joined Kámrán, returning about this time from the pilgrimage of Mekka, were introduced to the king of Persia. Most of them had quarrelled with Humáyun, who had charged Roushen Beg in particular with embezzling some jewels committed to his charge. In the course of their intercourse with the Shah, they represented Humáyun as quite devoid of the talents required in a king, and affirmed that, had he behaved properly to his brothers, he never need have left his own kingdom. They farther offered, if Humáyun were imprisoned, to lead a Persian army to Kandahár, which they undertook to deliver over to the Shah. A second cause is said to have been the unwillingness of the Persian Turkomán and Túrki officers to serve under Humáyun, whose father Báber, they alleged, had, by his treachery, caused the death of Mír Najm, their countryman and his army, when sent to assist him; and they apprehended that the same fate

* Akbernáma, f. 60.; Jouher, c. 14.; Tar. Niz. f. 195.; Kháfi Khan, f. 134., says that Biram got the title of Arjemend Khan, Khan-Khánán. The Alem-arái mentions that of Khan-Khánán.

might probably await themselves if they attended the Emperor. A third reason, more personal to the Shah, is also mentioned. When Humáyun, sixteen years before, after having defeated Behádor Shah of Gujrát, returned to Agra, he had, on some occasion, amused himself with the trial of divining arrows, on twelve of the first class of which he inscribed his own name, while on eleven of an inferior sort he put that of Shah Tahmasp; a circumstance which had been repeated to the Persian prince, who, some time before this, had charged him with the offence. Humáyun acknowledged the fact, but accounted for it by saying that, in what he had done, he had looked only to the relative extent of the dominions of the two princes; his being, at that moment, twice as extensive as those of Persia. "Yes," said Tahmasp, much piqued, "and one consequence of this foolish conceit has been, that you could not govern these your extensive dominions, but have suffered yourself to be driven from them by a set of clowns, leaving your children and family prisoners behind you."—"We are all in the hand of God," said the Emperor, "and must submit to the decrees of the Almighty."

Jealousies of the sovereigns.

This was not the only occasion on which Humáyun's expulsion from his dominions had formed the subject of conversation between the two princes. At an early period of their intercourse, Shah Tahmasp, when consoling his guest, who sat at dinner with him, had encouraged him to hope, in his oriental phraseology, that the sword of the Shah would be the key to open for him once more the doors of the kingdoms subdued by his father Báber; but added, that the real source of all his misfortunes lay in the injudicious way in which he had treated his brothers, whom he had rendered independent: that, for his part, he made it a fundamental point of his policy to keep his brothers weak and in subjection to him, and that, unless Humáyun adopted a similar principle, his kingdoms never would enjoy

BOOK V.
A. D. 1544.

repose. After dinner, Behrám Mírza, the Shah's brother, having advanced, according to custom, to present the basin and ewer, Tahmasp observed, "This is the way in which you ought to have treated your brothers;" a remark in which Humáyun, warm from the recent conversation, heartily and pointedly concurred. The Mírza, offended with the tone of Humáyun's assent, never forgave him, became his bitter enemy, and did all in his power to injure him with the Shah, which was rendered the easier by that prince's religious bigotry, and by the virulent feelings, generated by his unsuccessful attempt to convert the Emperor, clearly and decidedly, to his opinions.

Attempts to convert Humáyun to the Shía sect.

Humáyun certainly seems for a time to have been in danger of spending the remainder of his life as a prisoner in Persia, even if his life was safe. Tahmasp is reported at one time to have given instructions to Behrám Mírza to remove out of the way the obstinate Emperor, who was relieved from the dangers that surrounded him, chiefly by the generous intercession of Shah Tahmasp's sister, Sultánum Khánum, who strongly represented to her brother the impolicy, as well as injustice, of using any severity towards an exiled prince who had sought his protection and hospitality; and flattered him with the hopes of removing in due time the stranger's religious errors, and of gaining a royal convert. Humáyun is said to have encouraged these efforts of the friendly princess, by assuring her that he had always been privately well disposed to the Shía faith, a circumstance from which much of the animosity of his brothers towards him had proceeded. The Sultánum was effectively aided in all her endeavours by Kázi Jehán, the minister, whose piety was purer and more enlightened than that of his master, and who did all in his power to awaken generous feelings in his mind. They found an useful auxiliary in the Shah's physician, Hakím Núr-ed-dín Muhammed*, who was

* Or Muharrem.

much with the Shah, and had great influence on his mind, and whose benevolent efforts to assist the unfortunate monarch were never relaxed. Humáyun is said to have completed the favourable impressions made by the princess and her friends on the mind of the Shah, by some complimentary verses addressed to him, the concluding couplet of which, playing upon Humáyun's name, bore that other princes placed their glory in having been under the shadow of the Huma, but that the Shah, greater than all, had the Huma under his. The Huma is an imaginary bird, and the Orientals believe that, on whomsoever its shadow falls, that person is destined to sovereignty.*

League between Humáyun and Tahmasp.

Certain it is that, whatever was the cause, Shah Tahmasp, in the end, changed his conduct. He sent for Humáyun, to meet him at his summer camp. Humáyun went, and had a private conference of several hours, in which it seems to have been agreed, that the Shah was to assist him in recovering Kandahár, Kábul, and Badakhshán; that Kandahár, when taken, was to be restored to Persia, and that the Emperor and his suite were to listen to the instructions of Kázi Jehán on the subject of their religious differences. The Emperor, on returning to his quarters, took a favourable opportunity of assembling his Hindustáni followers, informed them of Shah Tahmasp's promises, which held out to them an early prospect of revisiting their native country. He added that Kázi Jehán would speak to them "on a certain subject." They were all delighted at this change, and lifted up their hands in thanksgiving. As, by the result of the negociations, which had been probably conducted, on the Emperor's side, by Biram Khan, the temporal interests of the two monarchs were become the same, a compromise seems to have taken place. Humáyun professed to favour

* Tar. Bed. f. 182.; Khol. ul Tow. f. 265.; Tab. Akb. f. 158.; Ferishta, vol. ii. p. 154—6.

BOOK V.

A.D. 1544.

the Shía partialities of the Shah, and the Shah affected to believe that Humáyun and his followers were sincere in their professions. In the whole of this difficult negociation, Humáyun was much assisted by Kázi Jehán, and the royal physician, Núr-ed-dín Hakím. The Shía divines wrote out the articles of their faith, all of which Humáyun read and assented to, and agreed that the khutba, or prayer for the Sovereign, should be recited in the Shía form.*

This reconciliation was followed by a grand ring-hunt, and a magnificent entertainment given to Humáyun near the Takht-e-Suleimán. To prove the sincerity of the new alliance, Roushen Beg and the other officers who had tendered their services to put the Shah in possession of Kandahár, were seized and brought before Tahmasp. Being no longer useful, they were sacrificed as traitors to this union of kings. The Shah gave orders that, their tent-ropes being cut and tied round their waists, they should be lowered down into the deep subterraneous prison in the Diwán of Mehter Suleimán†, there to perish miserably. Roushen Koka, who was the Emperor's foster-brother, found means to write him a letter, imploring him, by the memory of his mother, whose milk they had both sucked, to pardon and intercede for him. Humáyun, with his usual humanity, instantly wrote, beseeching the Shah, in the strongest terms, by the tomb of his father Shah Ismáel, to remit the punishment. "Doubtless," said the Shah, on reading the letter, "Muhammed Humáyun is a man of singular good nature and benevolence thus to intercede for wretches who have attempted to do him the greatest injury;" and ordered the prisoners to be delivered over to him.‡

Parting festivities.

The whole conditions of this treaty being finally

* Tar. Bed. f. 183.

† Zindán-e-Mehter-Suleimán. See Major Rawlinson's Journal as quoted.

‡ Stewart's Jouher, p. 72.

arranged, Shah Tahmasp gave the Emperor a parting entertainment. It was celebrated with great splendour, and lasted three days. Nearly six hundred awnings, and twelve bands of music, were prepared, and the whole ground was covered with carpets. The first day there was a magnificent banquet, and dresses of honour, and sabres enriched with jewels were largely distributed. On the second day, the Shah placed the Emperor by his side, and pointing to the extensive field covered with a spreading camp, told him, that all that he saw, tents, horses, camels, carpets and every thing else, was his, with whatever besides he required: adding that he would send his son, with twelve thousand horse, to recover his dominions. When the whole train and cavalcade had passed in review, in splendid array, the Shah standing up and laying his hand on his breast, said, "O King Humáyun, if there is any defect, let your generosity excuse it." CHAP. II.

The third day was devoted to a contest of shooting at the kebek. The night was devoted to a jovial party. Various liquors were put down, and bottles and goblets placed before each guest. No cupbearer was present. Every one filled his cup at his own pleasure. It was morning when the party broke up.

A little incident that occurred on the fourth day, when the camp was about to be broken up, and the two monarchs to separate, is extremely illustrative of the anxiety with which the Persians embrace every opportunity, in their mutual intercourse, to gain an advantage in point of form or etiquette. As Humáyun was completely in Shah Tahmasp's power, any show of respect to him would naturally rather have been ascribed to the Shah's generosity, than interpreted into a concession to the pretensions of the Indian prince. Yet when Humáyun, on this occasion, before setting out, went to take leave of Tahmasp, he found him seated on a small carpet folded up threefold under him,

BOOK V. A.D. 1544.

so as to prevent the possibility of any one sharing a portion of it. Humáyun, when he alighted, seeing that there was no place for him, was about to seat himself on the ground. Háji Muhammed Kushkeh, a Moghul, observing this, took off the ornamented cover of his quiver, tore it open, and spread it out for his Majesty to sit on. Humáyun, pleased with this attention, asked him who he was. He answered, "A Moghul." "You will come into my service," said the Emperor. "I am unworthy of that honour," replied the Moghul. "My master is now in your Majesty's service. Who am I? When he is promoted, I may hope to come in his place. Till then, I am dust." He afterwards became a distinguished officer.*

The twelve thousand cavalry that were to be placed under the nominal command of Sultan Murád Mírza, the Shah's third son, then an infant, were Kizelbáshes of the Túrki tribes. Bidágh Khan Kajar was named his Atálík† or Protector. Shah-kuli Sultan Afshár, the governor of Kermán, Ahmed Sultan Shamlu, the governor of Sístán, his brother Husein-kuli, and a number of other officers and Amírs, were ordered to co-operate. The Shah told Humáyun that he would add three hundred Korchi Khásch ‡ (of his own body-guard cuirassiers), ready to obey any order of his Majesty, as if he had been their religious guide. Meanwhile, the whole auxiliary force were allowed to go to their homes, in order to prepare themselves for meeting

* Jouher, p. 72.

† Sáleh va Atálík.

‡ Tar. Alim-arái Abási, f. 43. These Korchi were "beh rísh-sefídi Kachel Shah, va Bírdi Istájlo," i. e. had Kachel Shah and Bírdi Istájlo for their grey-beards (or commanders). The chiefs of the Túrki and Afghán tribes are called Rísh-sefíd, or Grey-beards. These troops being from Túrki tribes, their commanders went by this national title. The Osmanli troops are still divided into *kettles* or companies, because originally when they were fractions of tribes, each company had one kettle for cooking their food in common, a custom which they still observe: and they attach the same point of honour to preserving their kettle, that regular troops do to preserving their colours.

the Emperor, in due time, on the banks of the Helmend. The Emperor, having intimated a wish to visit Tabríz, and Ardebíl, and their Holy Places, before setting out, sent back the Empress and family, and his camp, under the command of Háji Muhammed Khan Koka, towards Sebzáwár, on their way to Sístán, while he himself, with a few attendants, made a march of about four kos from Takht-e-Suleimán, on the route to Tabríz.



The Shah, who had now regained his good humour, asked the Emperor to give him an entertainment in his quarters in the Indian fashion, and to use the Indian cookery. A royal banquet was accordingly prepared, which seems to have begun with music, and strong drinks were early sent round. This was followed by a presentation of presents.* The Shah, having asked who should divide them, the Emperor told him, whoever he might name. The Shah imposed that task on Khwája Moazem, the Empress Hamída's brother, who placed one tray of rare and valuable curiosities before the Shah, and another before the Emperor; the rest he divided to each according to his rank. The dinner followed, at which we are told that the Indian dish, kicheri †, unknown in Persia, was honoured with particular approbation. After dinner, the camp moved on to Miána ‡, while the Emperor accompanied the Shah, whose camp also moved forward, and after reaching his pavilion, remained there about an hour, to avoid a heavy fall of rain. When the rain ceased, Shah Tahmasp rose, and bidding God bless him, presented him with two apples and a knife, desired his brother Behrám Mírza to attend him to his camp, and, taking a ring off his finger, and putting it on Hu-

* Sachek.

† "Among these foods," says Jouher, "the Hindustáni rice-pilau mixed with dál, was approved of; for in that country they make their pilau with hens' eggs bruised." Jouher.

‡ At Ardebíl, a nephew (sister's son) of Tahmasp was betrothed to a daughter of Maasum Beg. Was this Khwája Moazem?

BOOK V. A. D. 1541.

máyun's, they parted. Humáyun and the Mírza, followed by a large suite, rode on. The Emperor, cutting one of the apples in two with the knife, presented one half to Behrám, in token of unceasing regard, and himself ate the other. When they came in sight of the Emperor's tent, the Mírza drew in his reins, and took leave. Humáyun presented him with a diamond ring, telling him it was a keepsake which he had got from his mother, and added many expressions of regard and esteem.*

Humáyun prepares to set out for Kandahár.

The Emperor, now left to himself, travelled onwards, and visited Tabríz, Ardebíl, the cradle of the Sefvi family, and its tombs and holy places, especially the tombs of Sheikh Sefi, the ancestor of the race, and of Sheikh Ismáel the Shah's father; after which he returned back nearly to Kazvín. Here the Shah, who was on his way to that city from his summer quarters, observing his tents, inquired whose they were. Being told, he expressed his surprise that the Emperor was not yet gone, and sent to desire that he would make a march of twelve farsangs, about forty-five miles, without delay.

Humáyun rejoined his main camp at Sebzáwár, where he found that his wife Hamída Begum had given birth to a daughter. Having given directions for taking the Begum, with the camp and heavy baggage, by the direct road through the desert, by Tabas, he himself proceeded to revisit Meshhíd, where he again

* The state of moral feeling in Persia is strongly marked by an incident that occurred at Kila-Ders. Four horsemen who were seen to come from the desert, openly attacked and murdered Yákúb Seferchi, the Emperor's butler. Being pursued and overtaken, they turned round and asked, "Why do you follow us? What we did was by orders of the Shah." It appears that the Shah having made the Emperor a present of some swords, Hasan Ali, an Ishek-Agha, chamberlain, abstracted one of them. Yákúb, having discovered this, informed the Emperor. Hasan Ali, in revenge, told the Shah, that Yákúb had spoken contemptuously of the Persian *táj* or cap. Hence the order to murder him.

circumambulated the hallowed tomb of Imám Ali Reza, and received back the bow and bowstring that he had left suspended on the gates of the shrine, a circumstance which afforded him much delight, as a proof that the holy Imám was favourable to him. At Meshhíd he was detained about a week by a continued fall of snow, when he went on to Tabas, whence he proceeded to Sístán, where he found the young prince, Sultan Murád Mírza, and the royal troops assembled, and ready for action.*

Remarks on his treatment by the Shah.

Here Humáyun must have seen, with no small pleasure, his dependence on the court of Persia about to cease. The real circumstances of his reception in that country were very different from the representations of them that have been given by the official and general historians of Persia and India. "The reign of Tahmasp owes much of its celebrity," says the late historian of Persia, "to the truly royal and hospitable reception he gave to the Emperor Humáyun, when that monarch was forced to fly from India, and take shelter in his dominions. The Persians have, in all ages, boasted of their hospitality, and the vanity of every individual is concerned in supporting the pretensions of the country to a superiority over others, in the exercise of this national virtue. The arrival of the fugitive Humáyun presented an opportunity of a very singular nature for the display of this noble quality; and we know no example of a distressed monarch being so royally welcomed, so generously treated, and so effectually relieved. All the means of the kingdom were called forth to do honour to the royal guest; and they were liberally furnished to replace him upon his throne.

* Akbernáma, ff. 56 – 61.; Tab. Akb. f.157.; Tar. Niz. f. 195.; Jouher, c. 15. 16.; Bayezíd, ff. 10—12. Ferishta, vol. ii. pp. 154—6.; Kháfi Khan. The narrative of the author of the Tar. Alim-Arái Abási, adds few circumstances to the narrative of the Indian historians, and chiefly adopts the views of Abulfazl, ff. 42, 43.

BOOK V.
A. D. 1544.

Tahmasp merited the praise which his conduct upon this occasion obtained him from distant nations; but his own feelings must have been gratified by the applause of his subjects, every one of whom felt elevated by the munificent hospitality with which his sovereign treated the fugitive Emperor of India." *

This eulogium of the eloquent and generous historian is founded on the representations of Abulfazl, Ferishta, and the writers who follow them, all of whom, in spite of some hints and unexplained allusions of Abulfazl and Nizám-ed-dín Ahmed, agree in lauding the munificence and generosity of the Persian prince. But the simple narrative of honest Jouher at once destroys all these delusions. While it confirms the accounts of the external honour and parade with which Humáyun was received in his progress through the country, it presents a most unfavourable idea of his reception at court, and of the conduct and character of Shah Tahmasp himself. He seems to have been a haughty, narrow-minded, intolerant bigot†, intent, in every instance, on displaying, in the most ungenerous manner, his superiority over the

* Malcolm's History of Persia, vol. ii. pp. 508, 509.

† "The bigoted attachment of this prince to his religion, was shown by his conduct to an English merchant, accredited by a letter from Queen Elizabeth. That great and active Sovereign, desirous of extending the commerce of her kingdom, encouraged Mr. Anthony Jenkinson to visit the distant Court of Persia. An English writer states, that a pair of the king's slippers were sent to the envoy, lest his Christian feet should pollute the sacred carpet of the holy monarch; and that after he came to the presence, the first inquiry Tamasp made was, not regarding the object of the mission, but the belief of the ambassador, whether he was a Gaur, or unbeliever, or a Mahomedan? The Englishman replied, he was neither an unbeliever, nor a Mahomedan, but a Christian; and added that he held Christ to be the greatest of prophets. The monarch, to whom he was deputed, said, that he was in no need of the aid of infidels, and bade him depart. He did so; and a man followed him from the hall of audience, till he was beyond the precincts of the court, sprinkling sand on the path he walked over: an action which could only be meant to mark the sense which the Mahomedan prince had of the uncleanness of the person that he had suffered to approach him."—Malcolm's Persia, vol. i. pp. 511—513.

unfortunate prince who was his guest, and on persecuting him into a conformity with his own religious opinions. And, in so far as he was not influenced by the intercession of his generous sister, he finally decided on restoring the exiled prince to his kingdom, merely by a calculation of the immediate benefits he was himself promised in return. Nor need this surprise us. The picture of pure and splendid generosity which the contemporary historian of Akber would gladly exhibit, to smooth the humiliation and elevate the importance of the father of his patron, is one which we should in vain expect to see realized in a court so little refined, so selfish, and in many respects so barbarous as, with all its pomp and splendour, that of Persia then was. Indeed it was not likely to be realized either in a country like Persia, or under a prince like Shah Tahmasp. The narrative of Jouher, incorrect and artificial as it is, is one of many instances of the inestimable value, for historical truth, of even the meanest contemporary record.

And his own behaviour.

The exact extent of the concessions made by Humáyun to the Shía prejudices of his patron we cannot ascertain; neither he nor the historians of his reign were anxious to dwell upon them; but they were, evidently, considerable, and appear to have shed a doubt over the purity of his Sunni principles for the rest of his life. He had adopted the bonnet of the Shías; he acknowledged that he had made approximations towards the doctrines of that sect. He had heard the reasonings of its doctors; he affected to be convinced, in certain points, by their arguments; and if he did not, as is probable, sign his assent to the leading articles of their faith, he had certainly read in public the formula of their belief. In later times he employed many Shías in his service, among others Biram Khan. We find him sometimes taunted by his brothers, as one tainted with the Shía heresy; and, after his death, the same charge was brought against his memory. The proba-

BOOK V. A.D. 1544.

bility is, that the circumstances in which he was placed in Persia led him, at that time, to affect an approbation of the Shía tenets, that he did not feel; and, in aftertimes, his pride may have prevented him from making such an explicit avowal of his religious sentiments, as was expected by the bigoted Sunnis, among whom the latter part of his life was chiefly spent.

The proceedings of Humáyun in Sind and Persia may perhaps appear to have been detailed at too great length. But as some of them have been misunderstood, and others misrepresented by former writers, I have ventured to dwell upon them, for the purpose of giving what seemed to me a fairer and more correct idea of their real nature.

# CHAPTER III.

## HUMÁYUN IN AFGHÁNISTÁN.

---

## SECTION I.

### HUMÁYUN'S CONQUEST OF KANDAHÁR AND KÁBUL. — EXPEDITION TO BADAKHSHÁN.

HUMÁYUN INVADES KANDAHÁR. — AFFAIRS OF HIS BROTHERS. — THE GERMSÍR SURRENDERED TO HUMÁYUN. — CAPTURE OF BÍST. — PREPARATIONS OF KÁMRÁN. — AKBER REMOVED TO KÁBUL. — SKIRMISH NEAR KANDAHÁR — WHICH IS BESIEGED BY HUMÁYUN. — MISSION OF BIRAM KHAN TO KÁBUL. — IRRESOLUTION OF KÁMRÁN. — PROGRESS OF THE SIEGE OF KANDAHÁR. — DEFECTION OF KÁMRÁN'S CHIEF NOBLES. — DISTRESS AND DESERTIONS IN THE GARRISON. — SURRENDER OF THE TOWN, WHICH IS GIVEN OVER TO THE SHAH'S OFFICERS. — PERPLEXITY OF KÁMRÁN. — AFFAIRS OF BADAKHSHÁN. — ESCAPE OF YÁDGÁR AND HINDAL. — ISOLATION OF KÁMRÁN. — DISSENSIONS BETWEEN THE PERSIANS AND IMPERIALISTS. — HUMÁYUN SUPPLIES HIMSELF WITH HORSES BY PLUNDER. — UNCERTAINTY OF HIS COUNSELS. — HE SEIZES KANDAHÁR. — DIVIDES THE DISTRICT AMONG HIS NOBLES. — SETS OUT FOR KÁBUL. — IS JOINED BY HINDAL, YÁDGÁR, AND OTHERS. — ADVANCE OF KÁMRÁN. — DESERTIONS TO HUMÁYUN. — KÁMRÁN SENDS AN EMBASSY — ESCAPES TO GHAZNI. — HUMÁYUN OCCUPIES KÁBUL — AND RECOVERS AKBER. — KÁMRÁN FLIES TO SIND. — CONGRATULATORY EMBASSIES TO HUMÁYUN. — YÁDGÁR MÍRZA IMPRISONED. — HUMÁYUN SETS OUT FOR BADAKHSHÁN. — YÁDGÁR MÍRZA PUT TO DEATH. — THE ARMY OF BADAKHSHÁN DEFEATED BY HUMÁYUN. — THE COUNTRY SUBMITS. — DANGEROUS ILLNESS OF HUMÁYUN. — KÁMRÁN RECOVERS KÁBUL. — HUMÁYUN MARCHES ONCE MORE AGAINST IT.

WHEN Humáyun arrived in the province of Sístán, he found the Persian troops that had been sent to his assistance, cantoned over the country. They were

CHAP. III. SECT. I.

A.D. 1545. Humáyun

BOOK V. A.D. 1545. Invades Kandahár.

nominally under the command of Murád Mírza, the third son of the king of Persia, and an infant of two or three years of age; but were in reality commanded by Bidágh Khan, of the Túrki tribe of Kajar, from which the present royal family of Persia is descended. Humáyun, in compliance with the wish of Shah Tahmasp, as soon as he arrived, collected and reviewed the troops. He found them in high order, and instead of 12,000 cavalry, and 300 korchis, or royal horse-guards, that had been promised, the muster proved that they amounted to at least 14,000 horse. After remaining about a fortnight in Sístán, he put his troops in motion, and entered the dominions of his brother.*

Affairs of his brothers.

It will be recollected that, at this time, Mírza Kámrán held the undisputed possession of Kábul, Ghazni and Kandahár, on one side of the mountains, as well as of Badakhshán, Kunduz, Kishem and other provinces, beyond them. His brother Askeri was governor of Kandahár. Hindal, another of his brothers, who, after abandoning Humáyun in Sind, had been besieged and made prisoner in Kandahár, though nominally, perhaps, governor of Júi-Sháhi, was now under surveillance or free custody, and lived privately at the palace of his mother, Dildár Begum, at Kábul. Yádgár Násir Mírza, his cousin, who, as we have seen, had been compelled to leave Sind, was now also at Kábul, but suspected, and carefully watched.

It has been mentioned that Kámrán, after his return from Hindustán, had marched to Badakhshán against Mírza Suleimán, who refused to acknowledge his authority; had defeated him, and deprived him of part of his dominions. No sooner, however, did Suleimán learn that Kámrán had marched to besiege Hindal in Kábul, than he collected a force, and recovered the districts which had been separated from his princi-

* Akbernáma, f. 61.; Jouher, c. 16.

pality. This compelled Kámrán, on his return from Kandahár, to cross the Hindu-kúsh mountains a second time. The hostile armies met at Anderáb. Suleimán was again defeated, and took refuge in Kila-Zefer, in which he was blockaded by Kámrán, to whom a great part of the territories of Badakhshán submitted. After a brave defence, Suleimán was compelled by famine to surrender. He was thrown into prison, along with his son Mírza Ibráhím. Kámrán appointed Kásim Birlás to be governor of Badakhshán; and, leaving with him a force supposed to be sufficient to maintain it in tranquillity, returned to Kábul, carrying with him the captive Mírzas. For a whole month after his arrival, the city was in a state of continual festivity; and, from this period, he is said to have given himself up to indolence and voluptuous indulgence, paying little attention to the concerns of government, or to the complaints of his subjects.*

A. H. 949, A. D. 1542. Jemádi II. 17. Sept. 28.

Nor were these the only royal personages whom he held in custody. We have seen that when he parted from Humáyun near Khusháb, on the Jelem, he was joined at Dínkot, on his way to the Indus, by Muhammed Sultan Mírza, the grandson of the great Sultan Husein of Herát, and by his sons, Ulugh Mírza and Shah Mírza. As these princes had also become objects of suspicion, they had been kept out of employment, and now dragged on an idle life at Kábul.

Nothing, therefore, could, to appearance, be more prosperous than the situation of Kámrán. But his power was unsocial, guarded by suspicion and jealousy, not by the affection even of those nearest to him. He was a sovereign in whose success none of them felt a pleasure and a pride, as if it were their own; and it rested, therefore, on a narrow and a sandy foundation.

The Germsír surrendered.

As Humáyun, advancing from Sístán, entered the

* Akbernáma, ff. 55, 56.; Tab. Akb. f. 154.

BOOK V. dominions of Kámrán, he was met near Laki, a fort on the right bank of the Helmend, by Abdal Hai, the governor of the Germsír, who approached him as a suppliant, wrapped in his winding sheet, with his quiver hanging from his neck; asked forgiveness for his former undutiful conduct, and surrendered the province into his hands. He was graciously received, and honoured with a command.

Capture of Bíst.

A detachment was now sent, under Ali Sultan Taklu, one of the auxiliary chiefs, to reduce the important city and fort of Bíst, which lies near the confluence of the Arghandáb with the Helmend, and is the chief city and the key of the Zemín-dáwer. The Persian general having been killed by a matchlock shot soon after the siege began, his followers, who were Túrks of the Taklu tribe, placed his son, a boy of twelve years of age, in the command, and carried on the siege with renewed vigour. The place was soon compelled to surrender, when the principal officers, and most of the soldiers of the garrison, joined Humáyun.

Preparations of Kámrán.

Kámrán, who had long dreaded an invasion from the territories of Persia, had placed all his frontier fortresses in a state of defence. On hearing of the Emperor's return towards Sístán, his first concern was to remove the infant Akber, Humáyun's only son, from Kandahár, where he still remained under the care of Askeri's wife, and of the nurses and household appointed by his father, and to bring him to Kábul.

He removes Akber to Kábul.

For that purpose he despatched one of his confidential officers, accompanied by a brother of Khizer Khan, the great Hazára chief, to bring the young prince from the castle of Kandahár. When they reached that place, and had explained the object of their mission, they found Mírza Askeri's ministers divided in opinion as to the policy of giving him up. Some advised that the child, attended by an honourable retinue, should be sent back to his father, who had now arrived on the

CHAP. III. SECT. I.

frontier, as being the best means of conciliating the injured and offended Emperor; while others maintained that things had gone too far for Askeri to think of obtaining any sincere forgiveness, and that, therefore, the great object now was not to throw away the favour of Kámrán. This advice prevailed, and though it was already the depth of winter, which in that country is particularly severe, the infant prince, and his sister, Bakhshi-bánu Begum, were sent off for Kábul, in the midst of rain and snow.*

Kámrán was apprehensive of a rescue, on which account he had selected a chief of the Hazáras to conduct the party, as the road between Kandahár and Ghazni was partly inhabited, and had always been infested, by robbers of that tribe. That the princes might not be known on the road, Akber was addressed as Mírak, the princess as Bacheh.† On reaching Kilát, the party passed the night at the house of a Hazára. But the prince's rank was not easily concealed by attendants, who adored him; and, next morning, the master of the house expressed his persuasion that the child under his roof must be the young Akber. Khizer Khan's brother, on hearing these suspicions of his host, lost no time in resuming his journey, and hurried on to Ghazni, whence, without delay, the infant prince was conveyed to Kábul, where he was lodged with his grand-aunt Khanzáda Begum, the favourite sister of

* The nurses and other personal attendants who were with the young prince at this time, continued in his service for some years, and, in the next reign, both they and their children rose to high distinction. The two nurses were Mahum Anka, the mother of Adam Khan, and Jiji Anka, the mother of Mír Azíz Kokiltash. The whole household was under the superintendence of Shems-ed-dín Muhammed Ghaznevi, the husband of Jiji Anka, and a man of talent, who afterwards made a figure in history, by the title of Atka Khan. It was he who helped to save Humáyun from the Ganges, after his defeat near Kanáuj. "Anka" signifies a nurse; "Atka" a nurse's husband. Their children are "kokiltashes."

† These terms signify "the young Mír," and "the child."

BOOK V. Báber, by whom he was watched with the tenderest care.*

A. D. 1545.

Skirmish near Kandahár;

Meanwhile a report having reached Humáyun on the Helmend, that Mírza Askeri was about to leave Kandahár, and to flee with all his treasure to Kábul, he pushed forward a strong party, composed partly of his Persian auxiliaries, partly of his own adherents, that he might either prevent his leaving the place, or overtake him, should he have escaped. The news proved to be false; but the party, having vauntingly approached too near the town, were received with a discharge of artillery by which many of them were killed and wounded. Mír Jemíl, one of the chief officers of the garrison, and brother of Bápus, a chief of great distinction, sallied out to improve this advantage, and was so successful, that he sent back to assure Askeri, that if he would lead out to his assistance the remaining force that was in the castle, the enemy must be completely routed. Askeri, however, supposing that the confusion was only a feint on the part of the invaders to lead him into an ambuscade, declined to move, so that the allied troops were enabled to draw off and effect their retreat, though with very considerable loss.

Moharrem 2. March 16.

which is besieged by Humáyun. Moharrem 7. March 21.

Five days after this affair, the Emperor reached the vicinity of Kandahár. He immediately proceeded to mark out the ground for the trenches and batteries, the charge of which he assigned to different officers. As the garrison was very strong, there were daily skirmishes and single combats, in sight of the two armies, and severe losses were sustained on both sides. The siege drew out into length, and the imperial camp began to suffer from scarcity of provisions. Just at that time they received intelligence that Rafía, a foster-brother of Kámrán, was encamped behind a hill that

* Akbernáma, f. 62.

† Akbernáma, f. 63.; Tar. Nizámi, ff. 195, 196.; Tar. Bed. f. 183.; Jouher, c. 17.

lay on the banks of the Argandáb, towards Zemíndáwer, with a large body of Hazáras and Nukderis, whom he had collected. Biram Khan, having marched with a detachment of Persian auxiliaries and of the Emperor's adherents, came upon them by surprise; and, after a short action, in which Rafía was taken and his force dispersed, gained possession of the camp, and returned back in triumph, with a large provision of stores, arms, grain and cattle found in it. This, for a time, restored abundance within their own lines.

Mission of Biram Khan to Kábul.

As, however, the garrison still held out obstinately, Humáyun, apprehensive of the result, and anxious to bring Kámrán to any reasonable terms, resolved to despatch Biram Khan as his ambassador to Kábul. When that brave and able man reached the pass of Roghni and Abistáda, on his way to Ghazni, he was assailed towards nightfall by a band of Hazáras who blocked up the road. He attacked them without hesitation, and, after a sharp combat, forced a passage, and slew several of their number. As he approached Kábul, he was met with much ceremony by a procession of men of note, and Kámrám gave him an entertainment at the Chárbágh palace, where he delivered his credentials. He was allowed to see the young Akber, at the palace of Khanzáda Begum. This was natural; but he was also permitted to visit Hindal Mírza, who was in a kind of free custody at his mother Dildár Begum's house; and Suleimán Mírza, the prince of Badakhshán, and his son Ibráhím Mírza, though detained as prisoners outside of the fort, were brought to the Shehr-árá gardens to meet him. He also waited upon Yádgár Násir Mírza and Ulugh Mírza, attended indeed, as in the former instances, by confidential persons appointed by Kámrán to watch him. Yet he contrived not only to deliver letters, presents and messages from the Emperor to most of them, but was able to remove their apprehensions, and to prepare

BOOK V.

A.D. 1545.

them for attempting to escape, and to return to their allegiance to Humáyun. He, in like manner, employed his insinuating eloquence with many of the chief nobles about the court, and led them not only to expect pardon, but to indulge in hopes very favourable to their future fortunes, if they joined the Emperor. During all this time, Kámrán was agitated by contending passions, and quite unable to make up his mind to any decided line of action. He saw that he was unable to bring into the field an army that could cope with that of Humáyun, supported as he was by his Persian auxiliaries; but he continued to procrastinate, not resolute to resist his brother, but, at the same time, not willing to resign his own power. At last, after having detained Biram Khan six weeks in Kandahár, he consented to his taking leave, and sent under his escort Khanzáda Begum, professedly to prevail upon Askeri to give up Kandahár, as it was pretended that that prince would not obey Kámrán's order, but really to encourage him in his defence by the hope of relief; or, should he fall into the hands of his offended sovereign, at least to secure his pardon by her influence with the Emperor.*

Irresolution of Kámrán.

Progress of the siege of Kandahár.

The siege of Kandahár, meanwhile, went on but slowly. The place was strong, and Mírza Askeri was indefatigable in his exertions. The danger reasonably to be apprehended from treachery in such a civil war he obviated by constantly shifting the posts of the garrison, and keeping all on the alert. At the beginning of the siege, the confederate army had attacked the place with much ardour. But the siege had been long, and their losses considerable. The Kizelbáshes had entertained hopes that, as soon as Humáyun, the son and heir of the great Báber, entered the territory of his father, the whole of the Cahghatái nobles and tribesmen would flock to his standard. They now found themselves disappointed, as not a man of note

* Akbernáma, f. 64.; Tar. Niz. f. 196.

had yet repaired to his camp, and there was no appearance of revolt in his favour in any part of the country. They saw no prospect of final success; so that the Persian leaders, disgusted with the service, and serving unwillingly under a foreign general, began to talk of returning home, as from a fruitless enterprise. Alarmed at a state of feeling so fatal to all his hopes, Humáyun made some desperate efforts, and one night, by a resolute advance from head-quarters, effected a lodgment, and erected a battery within a stone cast of the old town. The Kizelbáshes, roused by this able and gallant operation, pushed forward on their side, and nearer approaches were made everywhere. Askeri, filled with apprehension, asked for a cessation of hostilities, till the arrival of Khanzáda Begum, who was known to be then on her way to Kandahár, and in whose mediation he professed to place great reliance.

In consequence of these negociations, Humáyun, rather imprudently, relaxed his operations for some days, which Askeri employed, with unabating industry, in repairing the works that had been injured, and in adding new ones. On Biram Khan's arrival, Khanzáda Begum was allowed to enter the fort, that she might prevail upon her nephew to surrender. But this he refused to do, and she was not, or pretended that she was not, permitted to leave the castle. The siege was resumed with redoubled vigour.

Defection of Kámrán's chief nobles.

At this crisis, however, the affairs of Humáyun began to assume a more favourable aspect. Intelligence arrived that Kámrán, who had advanced to relieve the place, had retreated, and the effects of Biram Khan's residence at Kábul also became manifest. Ulugh Mírza, the son of Muhammed Sultan Mírza, has been mentioned as one of the princes whom Kámrán kept in a kind of state custody at Kábul, for more security changing his keeper weekly. In the

BOOK V. A.D. 1545.

course of these changes the Mírza came into the custody of Shír-efken Beg, who himself had some reason to be displeased with Kámrán. A plan for escape was formed between the prisoner and his keeper, in which Fazil Beg, Monaim Beg's brother, Kásim Husein Sultan Uzbek, and other chiefs of distinction, were led to take a part. They set out together privately from Kábul, and after many fatigues they all joined Humáyun, except Kásim Husein, who, having separated from them in a dark night, had lost his way among the hills, and fell into the hands of some Hazára banditti. But he also came in, a few days afterwards, on foot, weary, plundered and half naked. All the fugitives were heartily welcomed, and placed in commands. Not long after, Dawa Beg, a Hazára chief, declared for Humáyun, and joined him with a part of his tribe; and, ere long, letters were received from many of the leading men of Kábul, full of protestations of attachment. These events spread joy over the camp, and re-animated the wavering Kizelbáshes, who now redoubled their exertions against the beleaguered town.

Distress and desertions in the garrison.

In proportion as the spirits of the besiegers rose, the hopes of the besieged declined. Regular information of what passed in the town was obtained by means of letters fixed to arrows, which were daily shot into the camp. By them the besiegers were encouraged to go on, the garrison being represented as reduced to extremity. Such, indeed, was at length the general distress, that many of the garrison, not only soldiers and artillerymen, but even officers and men of rank, began to desert, letting themselves down from the walls by ropes. Khizer Khan, the great Hazára chief, among others, despairing of a successful resistance, leaped from one of the battlements, and was received below by some of his faithful tribesmen, and carried off on their shoulders to a hill in the neighbourhood.* The escape

* Koh-lika.

of a man of so much importance was known in the camp early next morning, and he was pursued. He hid himself in the hole of a rock, close to which his pursuers passed. One of them laid hold of the skirt of his cloak, which was probably made of the skin of some animal. He drew it in, retaining his breath; and his pursuers, thinking it had been the tail of some wild beast, passed on. On the approach of night, he crept from under his rock, and succeeded in gaining a place of safety.* CHAP. III. SECT. I.

Deserted by his garrison, his officers, and even his nobles, Askeri could no longer hope to preserve Kandahár, and, therefore, began to take measures for his personal safety. He sent his aunt Khanzáda to Humáyun, and through her, after the siege had lasted upwards of five † months, a surrender was negotiated. On the 3rd of September, A. D. 1545, he left the fort in the train of the Begum, on foot, attired as a suppliant and, according to the custom of the time, having a sword suspended from his neck; and was conducted by Biram Khan into the presence of the Emperor, who received him sitting in state in his Derbár, surrounded by his Chaghatáis and Kizelbáshes. The Emperor, from respect to the intercession of the Begum, and the near relationship of the offender, desired the sword to be taken from his neck; and, after Askeri had made his submission, commanded him to be seated. He was followed by Kámrán's chief Amírs and officers, to the number of thirty, who were brought in with their swords and quivers hanging from their necks, and their winding-sheets in their hands. Some were consigned to prison, others were released. A grand feast succeeded; in which the occurrences of the siege were talked over, and, with the usual appliances of music Surrender of the town, Thursday Jemádi II. 25. Sept. 3.

* Akbernáma, ff. 64, 65.; Tab. Akb. f. 158.; Tar. Bed. f. 183.

† The Tar. Bedáuni has three months.

BOOK V. A.D. 1545. and wine, the party was prolonged till the morning light. When the general enjoyment was at its height, and even the Mírza had forgotten his care, one of Humáyun's attendants placed some papers before him. In a moment the Mírza's countenance changed; his gaiety was gone. They were the letters which he had addressed to the chiefs of the Balúches, and of the other tribes, when the Emperor was crossing the desert; and their contents left no doubt of the full extent of his evil disposition. The wretched prince was ordered to be detained in custody, but to be brought to court from time to time, that he might visit the Emperor.*

Jemádí II. 26. Sept. 4. Next day Humáyun, accompanied by the chief Persian officers, entered the fort. Bidágh Khan claimed that the fort and all that it contained, especially Askeri Mírza and the treasure, should be made over to his master, in terms of the treaty. The Emperor expressed his readiness to give up the fort and its stores, but refused to surrender Askēri, and denied the Shah's right to the treasure; but, at the same time, expressed his readiness to present it to the Persian monarch, as a gift. He waited to see the treasure-chests brought out and examined; and after they had been closed and sealed with his seal, and that of the chief Persian commanders, he returned to the camp. Even already, mutual jealousies and fears had begun to prevail. Under the influence of these, the Kizelbáshes lost no time in sending off the treasure to prevent any attempt to sieze it. They persisted in demanding that Askeri Mírza should be given up to them, as a hostage for their safe return, and even threatened to seize him by force. The Emperor, alarmed at a pretension which might have been fatal to his repose, at once to secure his prisoner, and to make a demonstration of his own force, collected

* Akbernáma, f. 65.; Briggs's Ferishta, pp. 157, 158.; Tab. Akb. f. 158.; Tar. Bed. f. 183.

the whole of his old followers, and the adherents by whom he had been recently joined, divided them into troops, and reviewed them under arms. This alarmed the Persians, who saw his rising power with suspicion and dread, but they no longer persisted in their demand. The Chaghatáis, and such of the towns-people as chose to leave the place, had three days allowed them in terms of the capitulation, during which they could leave it uninjured, with their wives and families. On the fourth, it was given up by Humáyun to the prince Muhammed Murád Mírza, in conformity to his treaty with the Shah; while the Emperor himself moved to some distance, and took up his head-quarters at the Chárbágh of Báber*, on the banks of the Arghandáb, where he enjoyed himself for some time after his fatigues, receiving daily accessions of number from the adjoining provinces.†

*It is given over to the Shah's officers.*

The news of the fall of Kandahár, and the probability of the speedy approach of the imperial army to attack Kábul, distressed and confounded Kámrán. He ordered the young prince Akber to be removed from the palace of Khanzáda Begum to his own, and committed him to the care of Kuch Kilán, throwing into prison the former faithful guardian of his infancy, Shems-ed-dín Muhammed Ghaznevi, better known as Atka Khan. He held a council to concert the measures of precaution required by the crisis, especially as to Badakhshán, in which quarter he was apprehensive of troubles. Abdal Khálik, who had been his tutor, and Bápus, a nobleman who seems, at this time, to have been his chief minister, advised him to conciliate Suleimán Mírza, the late ruler of that country, now his prisoner, and to restore him to his government, by which means he might secure both his friendship and co-operation. Fortunately for Suleimán, Mír Nazer Ali, and some

*Perplexity of Kámrán.*

*Affairs of Badakhshán.*

* The Khulja Bágh. Jouher.

† Akbernáma, f. 65.; Jouher, c. 17.

BOOK V. A. D. 1545.

other nobles of Badakhshán, who were discontented with the existing government, had, a short time before, formed a conspiracy, and succeeded in surprising Kila-Zefer. They had also taken prisoners Kásim Birlás, Kámrán's governor, and the other officers left by him in charge of the country, of whose conduct they loudly complained. At the same time, however, they wrote to inform Kámrán, that they had no wish to renounce his authority; that, if he would send back Mírza Suleimán, they would place the country in his hands; but, should he refuse, that they would put their prisoners to death, and surrender the kingdom to the Uzbeks. Kámrán, alarmed at this danger, thought it prudent to comply with their request; and accordingly released the Mírza, who, soon after, set out to return home, accompanied by his son Ibráhím Mírza, and his mother, Khurram Begum. But they had only reached Pái-Minár, a populous village not far from Kábul, at the bottom of the hills, when Kámrán, repenting the step he had taken, despatched a messenger to recall the Mírza, pretending that he had some important information to communicate at a personal interview, after which he might resume his journey. Suleimán, justly suspicious of the object of this sudden recall, returned for answer; that as he had taken leave in what the stars had indicated as a propitious moment, he was unwilling, by any retrograde movement, to destroy the efficacy of this fortunate conjunction; but that, whatever commands the king might be pleased to honour him with, should receive the most implicit obedience. Without loss of time, he then hurried forward to Badakhshán, where he seized the reins of government, and speedily forgot his treaty and his promises.*

Escape of Yádgar and Hindal.

During the distraction caused by these proceedings, Yádgár Násir Mírza found means to escape from the

* Akbernáma, f. 65.

custody in which he was detained; so that of all the Mírzas, his relations, who had lately been in Kámrán's court, none was left, but his brother Hindal Mírza alone. Him he now found it convenient to flatter and soothe; and he was not sparing of promises to bring him over heartily to his interest. Hindal, dissembling, appeared to be the dupe of all his protestations. It was settled that he was to be admitted into a partnership in the kingdom; and that one-third of all that Kámrán then possessed, or that the princes might thereafter, by their joint efforts, acquire, was to be assigned to him. This agreement being concluded, Hindal was sent after Yádgár, with whom he had always been intimately connected, that he might compel, or prevail upon him, to return back. But no sooner had he reached Pái-Minár, than, finding himself safe among the mountains and defiles of the Hindu-kúsh range, he turned away to the west-ward, and like those who had preceded him, set out to join Humáyun.



*Isolation of Kámrán.*

The desertion of the last prince of the imperial blood who had been left with him, and of so many Amírs as accompanied them, threw Kámrán, for a time, into a state of deep dejection. The apparent facility with which so many princes, who had been guarded as prisoners with so much jealousy, effected their escape, is inexplicable, except on the supposition that Kámrán had become unpopular with his Amírs. He now complained that he felt himself forsaken, and had not one being in the world, in whose counsel he could trust, or on whose fidelity he could rely. His temper was not such as to invite frank or unpleasant communications. In his prosperity, he had been surrounded by flatterers, who had cherished his self-conceit by their base and selfish adulation. In his adversity, in spite of the change of circumstances, he listened with such impatience to a different language, that it was dangerous to use it: and those who were disposed to offer

BOOK V.

A.D. 1545.

him sound counsel, were deterred, no less by the immediate danger of the task, than by their want of confidence in his ultimate firmness and prudence in acting on their advice. He was thus left without any safe or honest friend; and, committing error after error, the numbers of his adherents daily diminished, and the moral influence of his government was totally gone.*

Dissensions between the Persians and Imperialists.

Humáyun, after the surrender of Kandahár, was desirous to have pursued his success, and at once to have marched against Kábul, but found his army too weak to venture on such an enterprise. The Persians considered the whole object of the expedition to have been attained, with the occupation of Kandahár. By that event a new kingdom was conquered for the Shah. The Turkomán and Kizelbásh Amírs, fatigued with the long campaign so far from their own country, had returned home, some with, others without leave, so that hardly any but Bidágh Khan, Abul Fateh Sultan Afshár, and Súfi Wáli Sultan, were left to support the young prince Murád; and they showed no disposition to march farther, in support of a foreign prince. With a total want of good faith, and an entire blindness to the future, they displayed, however, sufficient activity in harassing their new subjects, who hated them as foreigners and oppressors, and detested them as heretics. Complaints from persons of every rank were daily brought to the Emperor, who was unable to afford any redress. He had left the immediate vicinity of Kandahár, and advanced first to Hasan-Abdál, and next to the Gumbez-Sufeid. The Kizelbáshes, now as jealous of their allies as of Kámrán, and desirous that they should move away to a still greater distance, took measures to cut off their supply of provisions. In spite of the season, for winter was at hand, and the Chaghatáis complained loudly of the severity of the cold, it became necessary again to move, and the Persians

* Akbernáma, f. 65.

refused to allow them either to winter in the town, or to hut themselves in the vicinity of Kandahár. But no movement could be made without horses or draught cattle, which they did not possess.*

Humáyun supplies himself with horses by plunder.

About this time, a certain proportion of the Persian troops having been placed in garrison in the fort, their horses were sold to some merchants, who intended to convey them to India, and were then picketed on the outside of the town. These Humáyun, urged by his necessities, resolved to seize. Leaving his camp at Sufeid Gumbez, he himself moved to Bába Hasan Abdál, whence, after mid-day prayers, he pushed forward a strong detachment, who, before afternoon prayers, reached Kandahár, came upon the merchants by surprise, and carried off to his camp seventeen hundred horses; which, after supplying the wants of himself and of his household, he divided among his followers. The merchants to whom they belonged, waiting upon the Emperor with their complaints, could get no redress or compensation, but his bond for the full price, to be paid when the state of his affairs allowed; a security not likely to be negotiable in the bazar, either at Kandahár or Delhi.

Still, however, it was difficult to put the army in motion, as the season was severe, and Humáyun possessed no place of strength, in which the wives and families of himself and his followers could be left in safety. To obviate this difficulty, he besought Bidágh Khan to appropriate a few houses in Kandahár for their reception; a request, however, with which the Khan declined to comply.

Uncertainty of his counsels.

This delay was attended with disagreeable consequences. The confidence in Humáyun's fortune, which his troops had entertained, began to fail. Several of Kámrán's officers, who had been in Kandahár, but had subsequently entered the Emperor's service, escaped

* Tar. Bed. f. 183.

BOOK V. A. D. 1545.

from the camp, and fled to Kábul.* The scarcity went on increasing. It was now seriously proposed by some of Humáyun's Amírs, to hazard every thing; to make an attempt to surprise Kandahár; and, if successful, to justify their conduct to the Shah in the best way they could, and engage to restore it to him as soon as the Emperor had gained possession of Kábul and Badakhshán. From following this plan he was diverted by some of his council, who argued that, should the attempt be made and fail, he lost both Kandahár and the Shah, whom he thus converted into an open enemy; in which case he would be left without one ally, or place of refuge, in the world. Another proposal made at this trying moment was, to pass over into Badakhshán and there join Suleimán Mírza. But the difficulty of a winter march among the mountains and defiles of the Hazáras and Aimáks, in crossing the Paropamisan range, joined to the total want of a place of security, in which to lodge their families and baggage which they must leave behind, made them abandon that idea as quite hopeless.

He seizes Kandahár.

Just at this crisis, Muhammed Murád Mírza, the young Persian prince, died. Those who had charge of him being desirous to conceal this event, no notice of it was sent to Humáyun, to whom, however, the news was secretly conveyed. As, by this change of circumstances, the co-operation of the Persian auxiliaries seemed to become more doubtful than ever, while one obstacle of delicacy was removed, Humáyun, in despair, returned to the idea of gaining Kandahár in any way, trusting to be able to justify the act to the Shah after it was done.

This plan was warmly supported by Háji Muhammed Khan Koka.† The Emperor, while he objected to any

* Among these were Abdalla Khan and Jamíl Beg.

† He was the son of Bába Kushkeh, a man who made a figure in Báber's time.

open attack, was willing to get possession of the town, could it be carried by stratagem. This Háji Muhammed undertook to effect. Accordingly, in furtherance of the plan, notice was sent to Bidágh Khan, that the army was on the point of marching for Kábul, but that, as the Emperor wished to be free from the trouble and risk of carrying Askeri Mírza along with him, he was desirous of leaving him in safe custody in Kandahár. Bidágh Khan, who had all along earnestly desired to have the Mírza in his power, agreed without hesitation. This preliminary step being arranged, various parties were sent from the camp by night to different sides of the town, especially to three of the principal gates. About dawn, Háji Muhammed, who led the first division, leaving his ambuscade, attended by a few servants only, contrived to enter one of the gates, along with a string of camels, that were carrying hay and provender, at that early hour, into the town. The officer at the gate challenged them, and insisted on turning them back, no Chaghatái having for some days been allowed to enter. Háji Muhammed maintained that he came by Bidágh Khan's permission, to bring into the fort Askeri Mírza, who was to be left there. This story produced no effect on the officer, who proceeded to shut the gate and turn him out: upon which Háji Muhammed, drawing his sword, attacked him, and cut off his arm. The Háji's followers, who were close at hand, now rushed in, but were bravely opposed by such of the Persians as ran to the spot on hearing the uproar, and a sharp conflict ensued, which continued till Ulugh Mírza and Biram Khan, having effected an entrance at another gate, came to the assistance of their friends. The Kizelbáshes, overpowered, retreated into the citadel. Such as remained behind in the town were pursued, and put to death by the enraged citizens. About noon, Humáyun himself made his entry into the city, and was received with shouts of joy. He sent

BOOK V. A. D. 1545.

to inform Bidágh Khan, that the measures, which he had unwillingly taken, had been rendered necessary by that nobleman's unjustifiable conduct in concealing the death of the young prince Murád Mírza, who, Humáyun alleged, had been entrusted to his care, and by other unfriendly acts. Bidágh Khan, who was not prepared to sustain a siege, having, in the course of the night, thrown down a part of the back wall of the citadel, marched off unmolested towards his own country, loudly expressing his indignation at the treachery and ingratitude of his allies. Biram Khan was appointed governor of Kandahár, and ambassadors were sent to Shah Tahmasp, to assure him that, though Bidágh Khan, having acted contrary to his Majesty's intention, had been dismissed from the command, his faithful subject Biram Khan, who had succeeded him, was ready to obey all the orders of his master, the Shah. Tahmasp seems to have found it prudent to acquiesce in this arrangement, and a number of the regular Persian troops, especially the Korchis, continued in the Emperor's service.*

Divides the district among his nobles.

Humáyun, thus master of the kingdom of Kandahár, proceeded to divide its different provinces among his adherents. The Zemín-dáwer he bestowed on Ismáel Beg; Kilát, on Shír-efken Beg; Shál, on Haider Sultan, who died soon after; the district of Tírí, which lies among the Hazára hills on the Helmend, on Ulugh Mírza, except some districts of it, the revenues of which he bestowed, by way of pension, on Háji Muhammed.† To some of his followers he gave jágírs; to others, according to a custom of the times, he gave up some of the richest and most obnoxious of his prisoners,

* Akbernáma, f. 66. Tar. Níz. ff. 196, 197. Tar. Bed. ff. 183, 184.; Jouher, c. 17, 18.; Bayezíd, ff. 16—18.; Ferishta, vol. ii. pp. 157—159.

† Some of these assignments would appear to have been made at rather a later period.

from whom he allowed them to extort such sums as they could; which was often done by cruel severities. CHAP. III. SECT. I.

While the minds of the Emperor and his chief officers were engrossed by these proceedings, Askeri Mírza contrived to escape. A few days afterwards an Afghán arrived in the city, and gave secret notice that the Mírza was concealed in his house; but, with that regard to external appearances which, with some of the Afghán tribes, seems to constitute their point of honour, far more than substantial fidelity, besought the Emperor to seize the fugitive prince in such a way that the informer might not be compromised, as privy to his being retaken. The Emperor accordingly sent Shah Mírza, and Khwája Amber, his steward, who took the unhappy Mírza from under a mattress, beneath which he was hidden, and brought him to the presence. Humáyun spared his life, we are told, from his desire to conform to the dying advice of his father Báber, to be merciful to all, but especially to his brothers; and gave him into the custody of Nadím Kokiltash, one of the confidential servants of his household.*

Sets out for Kábul.

The Emperor, now possessed of a place of strength, had become master of his movements, and was eager that no time should be lost. Leaving his own family, and the families of his followers, in the citadel of Kandahár, though winter had arrived, he set out for Kábul; but, instead of taking the more open road of Kilát and Ghazni, these towns not having yet come into his power, he followed the course of the Helmend, which, penetrating through the hill-country, leads to the high mountains of the Koh-Bába, close upon Kábul. When

* Akbernáma, &c. as above. Abulfazl places the acquisition of the Turkomán horses at this time, and makes the heads of the caravan, afraid of being plundered, voluntarily offer them, on condition of getting bonds to be paid, when the Emperor conquered Hindustán, to which he consented. This, no doubt, is a sort of official representation. The ewer-bearer's account, however, is the more probable one, and he was, at the time, with the Emperor.

BOOK V.

A. D. 1545.

the army arrived near Tírí, Dawa Beg, the Hazára chief who had lately acknowledged him, and whose clan inhabited the neighbouring districts, met him with his tribe, all the headmen bringing horses and cattle, which they presented to the Emperor; and, as the country around had many fine straths and valleys, a halt of some days was made, to restore the health of the army, which had suffered in the unhealty climate of Kandahár. Here Khanzáda Begum, his aunt, and Báber's favourite sister paid the debt of nature. Here also Yádgár Násir Mírza, with Monaim Beg, and soon after Hindal Mírza and Terdi Beg, who had escaped from Kábul, as has been mentioned, joined the Emperor. Their arrival excited much joy, and was followed by that of many others, both Amírs and soldiers, who now hastened to return to their allegiance.

Is joined by Hindal, Yádgár and others.

The army once more moved forward, but, in the course of its march, was again attacked with sickness, and numbers died. This induced Hindal to propose in council, that the army should return to Kandahár for the winter, and that early in the spring, when all the necessary stores and munitions of war were in readiness, it should commence its march in full strength upon Kábul. The Emperor made no remark while the council was sitting; but having, probably, become sensible that, in the former part of his reign, he had given too much license to his brothers, after it was over, he sent him a verbal message, through Mír Syed Birkeh, to intimate that he had begun his march for Kábul before he had heard of the escape of Yádgár Násir Mírza, or of Hindal's intention to join him; that he had since seen nothing to make him change his plan, for, as to hardships, they were inseparable from war; that if the Mírza needed repose, the Zemín-dáwer was at his service for the winter, and that, in the spring, he might join the imperial array, after the war was over. The Mírza apologized for his indiscretion, and promised in future to be more guarded, both as to the time and manner in which he offered his advice. CHAP. III. SECT. I.

Among those who now waited upon the Emperor, as the camp again advanced, was Jamíl Beg, the brother of Bápus, whom Kámrán had selected as Atálík or Guardian for his son-in-law, Ak Sultan, the governor of Ghazni. He brought Ak Sultan along with him, and was graciously received; his desertion from Kandahár was easily forgiven, and he privately negociated a pardon for his brother Bápus. Many of the Amírs of Kábul had sent to invite the Emperor to push on. When the army, emerging from the mountains, reached Yúret Sheikh Ali in the territory of Pughman and Arkendi, near Kábul, Mírza Kámrán, informed of their approach, sent Kásim Birlás, with a body of troops, to impede their advance; and Kásim Mokhlis, his Master of the Ordnance *, was ordered to carry forward the artillery, and plant them in the Julga-douri, to be ready for action. At the same time, all the inhabitants of the adjoining country, with their families, were ordered to be brought into Kábul. Kámrán, having repaired the fortifications, and strengthened the garrison of that city, marched from his capital, full of confidence in his army which was numerous †, one portion of it consisting of a body of four or five thousand horse, completely appointed and clad in armour, while Humáyun's force was comparatively small and ill-provided. Kámrán took his ground ‡, not far from the body which he had sent in advance, and there exercised and reviewed his troops. When Humáyun heard that Kásim Birlás had occupied the Khimár pass, which lay directly in his line of march, he sent on Háji Muhammed Khan, with a strong detachment, who attacked him with vigour, dislodged him, and cleared the pass.

Advance of Kámrán.

* Mír-Atesh.

† The army of Kámrán is said to have amounted to 18,000 or 20,000 men; that of Humáyun to 4000 or 5000.

‡ Bágh-e-Guzergáh.

BOOK V. A.D. 1545.

As there was now the near prospect of a battle, Mírza Hindal asked, and got permission, to lead the van.

Desertions to Humáyun.

The imperial army, having cleared the defile of Khwája Pushteh, halted in the territory of Arkendi. Here Bápus, one of the chief Amírs of Kábul, was brought by his brother Jamíl; and Shah-berdi Khan, who held the districts of Gurdíz, Bangash, and Naghz, also arrived and joined the imperial camp. They were joyfully received. Every night parties deserted from the Mírza's army, and joined the Emperor. Bápus strongly urged Humáyun to push on without delay, while the general sentiment was so strong in his favour, and the enemy, from the daily desertions, knew not whom to trust.

Kámrán sends an Embassy.

Kámrán Mírza, now equally alarmed at the hostile demonstrations of the enemy, and the defection of his own followers, found himself compelled to devise means to gain time. He sent forward two men, respectable for their sacred character, who were instructed to make humble offers of submission on his part, and to entreat the Emperor to cease from active operations. They met Humáyun, when he was scarcely a mile from the enemy's camp, and prevailed upon him to halt. But soon after, suspecting that Kámrán's sole object in opening this negociation, was to gain time for effecting his escape, he advanced towards the Mírza's camp with seven hundred lancers. As he rode along, he was met by Mosáhib Beg, the son of Khwája Kilán Beg, Kámrán's Amír-al-omra, at the head of a procession of all the other Amírs of Kámrán Mírza, who came to make his own submission, and to offer their's. Their submission was accepted; but, as it was so tardy, they were not admitted to the presence, and were subjected to fines.

Escapes to Ghazni.

On reaching the camp, Humáyun found that Kámrán had escaped into the citadel of Kábul; that his

* Ním-kos, half a kos.

troops were in confusion, and beginning to break up; and that numbers had already fled. Kámrán did not venture to remain long in the citadel, but some hours after sun-set, when it was dark, taking along with him his son Mírza Ibráhím, his wives and family, made his escape, and took the Pani-Hissár road towards Ghazni. Humáyun sent Bápus, with a body of his most trusty men, to occupy Kábul, and to preserve it from pillage; and, when afterwards informed of Kámrán's flight, he despatched Mírza Hindal to pursue him. He himself entered Kábul on the evening on the 10th of Ramzán* (Nov. 15th), in the midst of a general illumination, and was delighted once more to embrace his son Akber, now about three years of age, whom he found in perfect health. The Bála-Hissár, or Citadel, made

CHAP. III. SECT. I.

Humáyun occupies Kábul.

Ramzán 10. Nov. 15.

And recovers Akber.

* There is some difference as to this date. Abulfazl has, the eve of Wednesday, Ramzán 12. A. H. 952.; but the Tar. Bed. and Ferishta make it Ramzán 10. A. H. 952. Bayezíd has Ramzán 10. A. H. 953. The Tabakát-e Akberi has "Ramzán 10. A. H. 952. or 953., God knows which." Jouher gives a lively account of Humáyun's proceedings on entering the Bála Hissár, and arriving at the palace of Kámrán. "As one watch of the night was past, and his Majesty had not yet broken his fast, he desired Wásil, the keeper of the wardrobe*, to make a plate of warm soup (ash) be brought; but soon recollecting himself, he bid him go to the palace of the Bíbí, as Baike Begum was called, and bring him some broth, if there was any. Mehter Wásil, and the humble Jouher, went; and, after paying their respects, delivered the message, that, as his Majesty had yet eaten nothing, he requested that some food might be sent him, if there was any. That lady gave a curry of beef, and a sirawal of cow's tripe that happened to be ready dressed. No sooner did his Majesty put his spoon into the dishes, and see that they were beef-curry and cow's tripe, than, laying down the spoon, and sighing, he burst into a complaint, exclaiming, 'O Mírza Kámrán! and had you indeed come to such a length, as to make the fare of Bíbí Jin, that asylum of chastity, to be only cow's flesh, and cow's stomach? Could you not have reserved one single sheep for her in your kitchen? And yet this asylum of chastity is the very person who brought here the bones of our venerated father, and placed them in his tomb.' ' not we, four sons of him whose abode is in heaven, have done something better among us?' In a word, he drank a single cup of sherbet, and put off breaking his fast till the morrow." Jouher, c. 19. Burnes informs us that, in Turkistán, none but the lower classes eat beef. Burnes's Travels, vol. iii. p. 159.

* Toshákji Begi, chief wardrobe-keeper.

BOOK V.

A. D. 1545.

no resistance; and Kábul, and all its provinces south of the Hindu-kúsh range, submitted to him. He published a general amnesty, and spent the winter in the citadel, busily engaged in settling the civil and financial affairs of the country, and in administering justice. The mother of Akber having arrived in the spring from Kandahár, under the escort of Yádgár Násir Mírza, the circumcision of Akber was celebrated by a magnificent festival, at the conclusion of which the Emperor bestowed khiláts and rewards on the most distinguished of his adherents. The government of Ghazni was conferred on Hindal; and Ulugh Mírza, who had returned from the pursuit of Kámrán, was confirmed in that of Zemín-dáwer, which had been given him in addition to Tírí and the adjoining districts.

Kámrán flies to Sind.

Meanwhile Kámrán, having escaped from the pursuit of Hindal who was not anxious to seize him, approached Ghazni, but was refused admittance into the town. He now threw himself on the protection of Khizer Khan Hazára, who carried him, first to Tírí, and then to Zemín-dáwer, whence, after some vain efforts to fix himself in that country, he was finally compelled so take refuge in Sind.†

Congratulatory embassies to Humáyun.

During this period of tranquillity, the Emperor received the congratulations of several of the neighbouring princes, on his having recovered his father's throne. An embassy from Shah Tahmasp, at the head of which was Valad Beg, was magnificently entertained, though i ade little progress in the grand object for which it was sent — the restoration of Kandahár to the Shah. A similar embassy from Mírza Suleimán, the prince of Badakhshán, was less favourably received, as the Mírza declined the Emperor's invitation to wait upon him, or, in other words, declined acknowledging his immediate authority. Mír Syed Ali, a chief whose influence was

* Akbernáma, f. 66—70.; Tab. Akb. ff. 158—160.; Tar. Niz. ff. 197, 198.; Bayezíd, ff. 17—22.; Jouher, c. 18, 19.; Ferishta, vol. ii. pp. 158—160.; Tar. Bed. ff. 184, 185.

great and extensive among the Afgháns and Balúches, also waited upon the Emperor at this period, and received the government of Duki *, dependant on Hindustán on which it borders, and not far from his own residence. Lawang Balúch, another of the principal Balúch chiefs, having also acknowledged the Emperor, was rewarded with the country of Shál and Mustung. These chiefs, we are told, no sooner received these honours, than they took their leave, fearing that the air of the city, and the habits of city life might affect the health of their followers, accustomed only to their own wastes and wilds.

CHAP. III. SECT. I.

Yádgár Mírza imprisoned.

Yádgár Násir Mírza, Humáyun's cousin, had not been long returned from escorting the imperial household from Kandahár, when he was charged with entering into new intrigues and cabals, with Askeri Mírza and others, against the Emperor. Humáyun had probably brought with him from Persia a resolution to beat down all who could be his rivals, and, in particular, to reduce the power of the princes of the blood, which, in the former part of his reign, had been productive of so many mischiefs. But he seems to have proceeded with unusual caution, probably to carry along with him the approbation of the old and powerful nobles connected with his family, and of his followers in general. Thirty distinct articles of accusation were brought against Yádgár, some of them for instances of disrespect to his Majesty; but the leading one was that, when in Sind, Shah Husein Mírza had offered him Bheker on condition of his deserting the Emperor, to which he had agreed, whereby the Emperor had been obliged to retire into Irák. On the present occasion, witnesses were examined, and evidences taken, in a manner, of which we find few examples in Asiatic history; and he is said to have been convicted by the testimony of

* Duki was probably dependant on Multán.

BOOK V.

A. D. 1546.

impartial men of veracity, as well as of his own accomplices. Some parts of the accusation he denied; as to others he was silent. He was found guilty; and Humáyun informed him, through Kerácha Khan, that since, after being so often pardoned, he had engaged anew in rebellious intrigues, he must expect no farther favour. He was accordingly thrown into prison in the Bála-Hissár, in a house near that in which Askeri was confined.

Humáyun sets out for Badakhshán.

Humáyun, being now the undisputed sovereign of the countries to the south of the Hindu-kúsh range, turned his attention to such provinces, on the north of these mountains, as still acknowledged the supremacy of Kábul. These, besides Badakhshán, consisted of Kunduz, Khost, Anderáb, and some other districts lying between the mountains and the Amu. Not content with Badakhshán, Mírza Suleimán had wrested from Kámrán these provinces, which formed no part of that principality, and seemed little disposed to part with them on the requisition of the Emperor. In the spring of 1546, therefore, Humáyun, resolving to chastise him, marched out of Kábul, and encamped in the Yúret-Chálák. To prevent intrigues in his absence, he resolved to carry Askeri along with him. But after he had proceeded as far as the valley of Kárábágh, aware of the danger of leaving behind him so restless and turbulent a spirit as Yádgár Násir Mírza, he resolved, in the words of his historian, 'to release the body of that prince from the pains of existence, and to put himself at ease.' He sent an order to that effect to Muhammed Ali Taghái, whom he had left governor of Kábul. "How should I put to death the Mírza," said that good man, "I, who never killed a sparrow?" The Emperor, upon this, devolved the duty upon Muhammed Kásim Mochi, who strangled the Mírza with a bowstring. He was buried on a rising ground opposite to the gate of the citadel, near a piece of water; and, after a time, his remains

Beginning of A. H. 953.

Yádgár Mírza put to death.

were taken up and carried to Kazvín, where they were deposited in his father, Násir Mírza's, tomb.*

CHAP. III. SECT. I.

The army of Badakhshán defeated by Humáyun.

Humáyun†, having crossed the mountains, reached Anderáb, where, at the village of Tírkerán, he found Mírza Suleimán with a considerable army, strongly entrenched, and prepared to check his advance. The Emperor, determined to force his position, sent on Mírza Hindal, with Háji Muhammed Khan, Kerácha Khan, and a strong body of troops, himself following to support them. The advance made a gallant attack on the fortified camp, as soon as they reached it; but the Badakhshán archers, who were posted behind the trenches, did great execution, and killed or dismounted numbers of the assailants. Among those who most distinguished themselves on this occasion, were a party of the Persian Korchi, or cuirassier body-guard, who accompanied the ambassador, and took a part in the action. The contest was long doubtful, till a party of hardy veterans, by a desperate effort, forced their way across the ditch, surmounted the trench, and sabred the archers behind it, who had done such execution. In a short time after this success, the whole army of Badakhshán was broken and put to flight. Suleimán, abandoning his new territory, fled along the Bángi river and by Nárín, Ishkemish and Talikán, towards the broken glens of Khost. Mírza Beg Birlás, who had commanded his archers, and some others of his principal chiefs, surrendered to Humáyun. The Aimáks who were made prisoners were dismissed, uninjured. Hindal

* Akbernáma, f. 69.; Bayezíd, f. 22.; Tab. Akberi, f. 160.

‡ Sometime before setting out on this expedition, on leaving a drinking party after midnight, Humáyun happened to stumble. His butler (Mír Sámán) Khwája Jilál-ed-dín Mahmúd, expressed his regret that his Majesty should have taken any thing that exposed him to such accidents. Struck with the observation, he renounced the use of intoxicating mixtures (hashia), and sent to tell the Sadr, and other chief men of the law, who had been of the party, that the advice should have come from them. He is said to have adhered to this resolution to the end of his life. Bayezíd, ff. 22, 23.

BOOK V. A.D. 1546.

Mírza was sent in pursuit of the fugitives; while Humáyun himself advanced by the pass of Sháshán into the valley of Khost, where he spent some days in the amusements of fishing and fowling, for which the place is celebrated, as well as for its fruits. The country around submitted, and Suleimán was compelled to seek shelter beyond the Amu, in Kuláb, and the upper districts of Khutlán.*

The country submits.

Affairs being in this prosperous state, Humáyun moved to Kishem, where he spent three or four months, and divided among the Amírs his late conquests. Badakhshán and Kunduz he gave to Mírza Hindal; the collectorate of Khost was given to Monaim Beg, and that of Talikán to Bápus. The more effectually to settle the country of Badakhshán, to secure the quiet of the peasantry, and to rest the army, Humáyun resolved to pass the winter in Kila Zefer, towards which he directed his march. But on arriving at the village of Sháhdán, between Kishem and that town, he was seized with a violent illness, which, for two months, prevented him from leaving the place. At the beginning of the disease he was for four days insensible. Reports of his death, or of its near approach, were, in consequence, spread and believed. Officers of every rank left their posts, and consulted together as to the line of their future conduct. Among the rest, Mírza Hindal himself left his government of Kunduz, and advanced from Rostak, where he had been, up the Kokcha river, one of the chief branches of the Amu, on which Kila-Zefer stands, prepared to assert his right to the vacant throne. Signs of disorder and insubordination appeared on every side. The Amírs of Suleimán, who had fled into the higher districts of the mountains, gaining confidence, began to descend, and overrun the country. At this trying crisis Kerácha Khan, the prime minister, con-

Dangerous illness of Humáyun.

* Akbernáma, f. 69.; Bayezíd, ff. 25, 26.; Tar. Niz. f. 197.

ducted himself with great decision. Mírza Askeri, from whom most immediate danger was apprehended, he removed into his own tent, and placed him there in custody. He himself, and the Amírs most devoted to Humáyun, pitched their tents close to the imperial pavilion, from which all persons were excluded except the wife of the Emperor, the royal physicians, and one or two confidential servants of the household. Kerácha was indefatigable in his attentions. The disease reached its crisis on the fifth day. While the Begum*, who watched by his sickbed, was engaged in pouring into his mouth the juice of pomegranates, which she squeezed from the fruit, to her surprise and delight he opened his eyes, and asked her, how affairs were going on. Being informed that all was in a state of perturbation and alarm, he sent for Kerácha Khan, and desired him to make haste and let it be known, that he was now convalescent. At the same time letters were despatched to Kábul by Fazil Beg, to announce the amendment of his health, so as to prevent any commotions there; and fortunately that officer reached the capital early in the morning, a few hours after the news of the Emperor's illness had arrived. In the camp, as soon as the Emperor's recovery was known, Mírza Hindal hurried back to Kunduz, and all the other officers returned to the stations which they had left. The partizans of Mírza Suleimán dispersed, and returned home. When Humáyun was well enough to bear the motion, he was carried in a covered litter to Kila Zefer, where his health and strength were rapidly recruited. Here he bestowed on Shír-efken, the son of Kuch Beg, the districts of Kahmerd, Zohák, and Bámián, and sent him to take possession of them; promising that, when he returned

* Jouher, c. 19. says that it was Chuchak Begum, who watched by his bedside: Bíbi Fatima, the Urdui-Begi of the Harem is represented by Bayezíd, f. 27. as having been most useful. Abulfazl makes Mír Birkeh the person who was with him, and who received his orders, f. 69.

BOOK V. A.D. 1546. to Kábul, Ghurbend should be added to his jágír. In a short time, the Emperor was so far recovered as to resume his favourite amusement of hunting. His protracted residence beyond the mountains, however, alarmed the Uzbeks, who possessed Bálkh and the countries on the west; and they employed themselves in preparation to repel the attack, which they believed was meditated.*

Kámrán recovers Kábul.

But while every thing seemed to proceed so prosperously, the equally unexpected and unwelcome news arrived, that Kámrán, assisted with troops and money by his father-in-law, Shah Husein Arghún, had once more returned into the territory of Kábul, had gained possession of the capital and of the young prince, and that, among other noblemen who had joined him, was Shír-efken, who had so lately profited by the Emperor's liberality.

This news was a severe blow to Humáyun. It put an end to the hopes he had fondly cherished, of at once marching into Hindustán, and promised another long and doubtful war with his brother, whose power and means of offence were much increased, by his having in his possession, not only the Emperor's son Akber and the rest of his family, but the wives and families of all his principal Amírs, who had been left at Kábul as a place of security. To add to Humáyun's other difficulties, it was then the depth of winter, and the lofty Hindu-kúsh mountains, difficult to be crossed even in summer, but then covered with snow, were interposed between him and Kábul. He instantly concluded a treaty with Mírza Suleimán, by which the kingdom of Badakhshán was restored to him, as he had enjoyed it under Báber; and leaving Mírza Hindal governor of all the other provinces beyond the mountains, Kunduz, Anderáb, Khost, Kahmerd, Ghuri, and their dependencies,

* Akbernáma, ff. 69, 70.; Tab. Akb. f. 160.; Jouher, c. 19.; Bayezíd, f. 27.

he set out from Kila-Zefer to march for Kábul. At Talikán, on the Ferkhar river, he was detained several days by the violence of the rain and snow. As soon as they abated, he went on to Kunduz, where he was hospitably entertained by Hindal, in the garden of Khosrou Shah. Several of his Amírs, however, anxious for the fate of their families in Kábul, deserted from the camp; so that Humáyun himself and his remaining officers, seeing that the troops desponded, and were wavering, were compelled to go about among them to confirm them in their allegiance, by re-animating their hopes, and by promises of reward.* After the Muhammedan festival of the Korbán, he again set out, and proceeding by Chehárder, a town on the road to Khulm, began to ascend the hills, though the quantity of snow that had fallen was such, that the roads were blocked up, and they were compelled to make a path by ramming in down, so that the horses and camels could move over it. In spite of every difficulty they surmounted the defiles of Shibertu and the pass of Rakík, and halted at Khwája Syaran, ready soon to attack Kábul itself.

CHAP. III. SECT. 1.

Humáyun marches against it once more.

Zilkaújeh 10. Feb. 1. A.D. 1547.

* Akbernáma, f. 71.; Tab. Akb. f. 161.; Jouher, c. 20.

# CHAPTER III.

## HUMÁYUN IN AFGHÁNISTÁN.

---

## SECTION II.

### CAPTURE AND LOSS OF KÁBUL BY KÁMRÁN. HIS SUBMISSION.

KÁMRÁN IN SIND.—LEAVES SIND ON HUMÁYUN'S ILLNESS.—SURPRISES GHAZNI AND KÁBUL.—HIS CRUELTIES.—HUMÁYUN ADVANCES AGAINST HIM.—IS DESERTED BY MANY NOBLES.—RESOLVES TO ATTACK KÁBUL. DEFEAT OF KÁMRÁN'S GENERAL.—HUMÁYUN TAKES THE OUTER FORTIFICATIONS.—PROGRESS OF THE SIEGE.—BRUTAL CONDUCT OF KÁMRÁN.—HIS DISTRESS AND SUBMISSIVE APPLICATIONS.—HE ESCAPES. FLIES TO BADAKSHÁN, AND THENCE TO THE UZBEKS.—HUMÁYUN ENTERS KÁBUL, WHICH IS PLUNDERED.—SENDS IN PURSUIT OF KÁMRÁN. WHO RETURNS WITH AN ARMY FROM BÁLKH.—AND ATTACKS BADAKHSHÁN.—HUMÁYUN MOVES TO MEET HIM.—REVOLT IN HIS CAMP.—THE REBELS ESCAPE TO KÁMRÁN.—THE GOVERNOR OF BADAKHSHÁN DECLARES FOR HUMÁYUN.—HIS ADVANCE.—REPULSE NEAR TALIKÁN.—THE FORT INVESTED.—SUBMISSIVE OFFERS OF KÁMRÁN.—HE SURRENDERS.—HIS RECEPTION BY HUMÁYUN.—HUMÁYUN SETTLES HIS NORTHERN DOMINIONS, AND RETURNS TO KÁBUL.

BOOK V.

A. D. 1547.
A. H. 953.
Kámrán in Sind.

BUT it is now necessary to explain by what means Mírza Kámrán had been able to effect so great a change in his circumstances. We have seen that, when formerly compelled to abandon his capital by night, he attempted to seize Ghazni. Being disappointed by the vigilance of the garrison, he had taken refuge with Khizer Khan Hazára*, who received him with every mark of distinction, and conducted him first to Tírí, among the Hazára

* Kámrán had given his daughter to Khizer Khan's son.

mountains, and next into the low country of Zemíndáwer. That province was then governed by Hisám-ed-dín Ali, a son of Mír Khalífa, who not only defended the forts against the invaders, but was successful in harassing them in the open country. Humáyun, as soon as he learned that Kámrán had appeared on the Helmend, having bestowed the government of Zemíndáwer on Ulugh Mírza, despatched him and Yádgár Násir Mírza to that province, at the same time issuing orders to Biram Khan, who was at Kandahár, to join the two Mírzas, and to pursue Kámrán without loss of time. These orders were ably executed; and the Hazáras no sooner heard of the approach of the Mírzas and the governor of Kandahár, than they abandoned the low country, and retreated into their highland wilds. Kámrán, thus left without farther hopes of success, was glad to fly, through the country of the Balúches, to Bheker, where he was well received by Shah Husein Arghún, whose daughter had for some time been betrothed to him. Shah Husein assigned him a residence at Páter; and he soon after married Chuchak Begum, who continued faithful and attached to him in all the vicissitudes of his future life. CHAP. III. SECT. II.

Kámrán had been little more than three months settled at Páter, when, the news of Humáyun's expedition against Badakhshán, followed by the report of his illness, having reached him, he resolved to try his fortune in the country of Kábul. His father-in-law, who was not displeased at the departure of so restless and ambitious a prince, afforded him every aid that he could desire; and Kámrán soon set out from Sind accompanied by a thousand chosen horse. After he had passed through the Balúch country, and arrived near Kilát, he fell in with a party of Afghán horsedealers, whom he plundered; and, seizing the horses, distributed them among his followers, most of whom thus became Leaves Sind on Humáyun's illness.

BOOK V.

A.D. 1547.

possessed of a led horse. This enabled him to advance rapidly on Ghazni, which he entered by surprise, having had a previous understanding with some of the inhabitants. The governor, Záhid Beg, he put to death, and carefully cut off all communication with Kábul. Emboldened by success, he pressed on for that city, accompanied by his Sindi troops, and, preceding the news of his own return, reached it early in the morning. On taking possession of the gates, he found that the governor Muhammed Ali Taghái was gone out to take the warm bath. The Mírza made him be brought forth, undressed as he was, and sabred him on the spot. The city and citadel, with all the Emperor's family, fell into his hands without resistance. He went to reside in the Bála-Ark or Bála-Hissár. The young prince, Akber, who had already been exposed to so many changes of fortune, he treated with tenderness, but again removed him from the care of Mír Atka, and placed him under the charge of his own servants.

Surprises Ghazni, and Kábul

His cruelties.

Whether from irritation of temper or from policy, he now indulged in acts of extreme severity and cruelty. He blinded Fazail Beg and Mehter Vakíla, whom Humáyun had sent to forward the preparations for his intended expedition against Hindustán. He put to death, or imprisoned, many others of Humáyun's most faithful adherents. Hisám-ed-dín Ali, the son of Mír Khalífa, chancing about this time to return from Zemíndáwer, the government of which he had resigned to Ulugh Beg, was seized by the Mírza, who, in revenge for the repulse he had received from him in that province, ordered him to be torn limb from limb. By great exertions he succeeded in detaching many of the chief men of the country, and among others Shír-efken, from their allegiance to Humáyun. He spared no efforts to collect an army and every munition of war; and in a short time he was once more acknowledged in all the districts dependant on Kábul and Ghazni as the lawful sovereign.* CHAP. III. SECT. II.

Humáyun, meanwhile, informed of what was passing, having pursued his painful march over the snow and through the defiles of the mountains, proceeded for the Abdereh pass. Shír Ali, one of Kámrán's most active officers, crossing by Zohák and Ghurbend, had taken possession of the Abdereh defile, which he had fortified to check the Emperor's approach, but, unable to oppose Mírza Hindal and Kerácha, who led the advance, retreated, when they marched towards Zohák to attack him. As soon as the Emperor's army had passed the defile, however, he returned by a circuitous road, and, hanging on their rear, took such baggage, stores, and stragglers as fell behind. When the Emperor reached Charikárán, in his descent towards Kábul, a new desertion took place. Many of his followers, filled with apprehension for their families in Kábul, and among them some men of rank, such as Iskander Sultan and Mírza Senjer Birlás, Báber's nephew, making their escape from the camp, found their way into the town. Humáyun, seeing the danger to which he was exposed if this spirit continued, called a council, and invited all his officers to deliver their opinions with unlimited freedom. It was there agreed that, as Kámrán had shut himself up in Kábul, and did not seem disposed to hazard a battle, it was advisable to march past the town to Bori and Khwája Pushteh, where the army would be better off, and could have supplies in abundance. In pursuance of this plan, every thing was ready for the march, and the Emperor was about to mount his horse, when it occurred to him, that if he passed the city as proposed, it would be imagined that he intended to leave it behind, and go on to Kandahár; in which case the greater part of his men, who

Humáyun advances against him:

and is deserted by many nobles.

* Akbernáma, f. 70.; Taríkh-e Sind, f. 167.; Tab. Akberi, f. 160.

BOOK V. A. D. 1547.

had families in Kábul, would take that opportunity of deserting; and that, therefore, it was better at once to attack the town. If the Mírza hazarded a battle to preserve it, 'twas well; if not, that, at least, desertion would be prevented, and the troops placed under cover.

Resolves to attack Kábul.

Háji Muhammed was, therefore, sent on, with the advance, by the Minár pass, while the Emperor took the Páyán pass, on the direct road to the city.

Defeat of Kámrán's general.

When Mírza Hindal came near Deh-Afghánán, one of the suburbs of Kábul, he was met by Shír-efken at the head of a body of Kámrán's best troops, and an action ensued, bravely supported on both sides. Some of the Emperor's men, however, broken by the impetuosity of the attack, at last turned and fled. Humáyun, who was at a little distance, observing this, and seeing Mírza Hindal still gallantly maintaining his ground with the handful of men left with him, was on the point of galloping to his succour, when Kerácha Khan begged to be allowed to lead the reinforcement. The Khan charged with much vigour, and himself engaged Shír-efken hand to hand. Shír-efken, who was a distinguished swordsman, discharged upon him three furious blows in quick succession, all of which he warded off with his sabre. Shír-efken then let fall a fourth, but missing his aim, was thrown forward on his horse; upon which Kerácha, pushing on his charger, unhorsed him, and took him prisoner.* Háji Muhammed, mean-

* This is related differently by different writers. Bayezíd says, that when Shír-efken heard of Humáyun's approach, he was in the bath, and drunk; that, without informing Kámrán, he set out to engage the enemy: that near Bába Shesh-per he met the enemy's pickets: that Syed Ali, a Korchi, there attacked him, seized him by the waist, made him prisoner, and carried him to the Emperor: that Kerácha Khan insisted he should be put to death; that a quarrel arose between Shah Mírza, Ulugh Mírza's brother, and Jemíl Beg, the brother of Bápus, as to which of them had made him prisoner; and that, upon the testimony of the soldiers, the prize was given to Jemíl Beg. Probably these commanders claimed a right to whatever was gained by their retainers. Bayezíd, f. 30.

CHAP. III. SECT. II.

while, arriving with his division by a different road, and attacking the enemy in flank, they fled in every direction. Humáyun showed a disposition to have spared Shír-efken; but Kerácha and other officers remonstrating upon the bad example of pardoning a deserter and rebel of such rank, his head was struck off on the spot, in the Emperor's presence. Without loss of time, Humáyun followed the retreating troops towards Kábul, and advancing by the Khiábán, an avenue and pleasure-ground leading to the Iron-Gate*, a part of his troops pressed on the fugitives with so much ardour, that they entered the outer inclosure along with them. Mírza Khizer Khan, the Hazára, and the Arghún auxiliaries, believing all to be over, rode off, and took refuge among the neighbouring Hazáras, so that the outer enclosure of the city was taken without farther resistance, Shír Ali retiring into the fortified town. Most of the prisoners taken in this action were put to death.†

Humáyun takes the outer fortifications.

The Emperor, having established his head-quarters at the Koh-Aakabein (Eagles' Hill), which commanded the town, planted his artillery, and commenced a cannonade upon it. Kámrán, who, for some time, had expected to be besieged, had placed both the town and citadel in the best posture of defence, and had a strong garrison within the walls. This enabled him to make daily sallies, for the purpose of interrupting the operations of the besiegers, which led to many desperate rencounters. In one of these, Háji Muhammed Khan, while engaged in marking out ground for trenches, was attacked by Shír Ali, and severely wounded in the right arm. He was rescued by his own men, and, being unable to walk, was carried to his quarters, where for some time he remained dangerously ill. A

Progress of the siege.

* Derwáza-Aheneín.

† Akbernáma, ff. 70, 71.; Tab. Akb. 160, 161.; Tar. Niz. ff. 197, 198.; Jouher, c. 20.; Bayezíd, ff. 18—20.

BOOK V. A. D. 1547.

report of his death reaching the Emperor, an officer was sent to take charge of his portion of the trenches. This so much hurt the old veteran that, ill as he was, he ordered his horse, and rode out to visit them, in consequence of which over-exertion he had a severe relapse. Mírza Sanjer, who had so lately deserted from Humáyun, was run off with, during a sally, by his horse, which carried its rider to the Bágh-e-Benefsheh*, where its former owner had lived. He was taken, and carried before the Emperor, who sent him to prison.

The town and citadel were too extensive to admit of their being fully blockaded by the besiegers. Even at an early period of the siege, a few men of rank deserted from Kámrán; but as it continued, and scarcity began to prevail, numbers, seeing no prospect of relief, made their escape, and for the most part joined the Emperor. When the siege had lasted for some time, a large caravan from the north reached Charikárán, bringing about five hundred horses and much valuable property. Kámrán, informed of its arrival, directed Shír Ali to take a detachment and plunder it. Some of his officers objected to this, as Humáyun, they said, would not fail to send a party to pursue them; so that, either the detachment would be unable to reach the caravan, or, if it did, would be unable to get back to the town, in which case no benefit could be derived from the sally. Kámrán, however, persisting, the detachment set out, surprised the caravan, and bore off the booty. Humáyun got notice of their march and its object. But as several hours had already elapsed since they left the fort, instead of making a vain attempt to overtake them, he put his whole troops in motion to block up the roads and guard the fords, so as to prevent their regaining the town. This was done so vigorously and successfully, that Shír Ali, when he returned, found it impossible to effect an entry in any quarter; so that

* Violet garden.

he was compelled to retire to a distance, and wait for an opportunity of throwing himself into the place by surprise. A grand sally from the fort was at length concerted, under cover of which a way might be opened for his troops to regain the fort. But, after desperate efforts, the besieged were repulsed, chiefly by the steadiness of a small body of matchlock-men, and forced to fall back, with a great loss in killed and wounded. Shír Ali, after this repulse, losing all hope of being able to enter the town, made for Ghazni, but was pursued, overtaken, and defeated at the Sejáwend pass, his followers dispersed, a considerable part of the merchandise and horses plundered from the caravan, recovered, and a number of prisoners taken. When the pursuing party returned to the camp, Humáyun sent for the merchants who had been plundered, and delivered up to them whatever they could identify as having belonged to them: an act of justice which, in those times of rapine, made a most favourable impression, and was afterwards very beneficial to his affairs. This act of generosity was accompanied by one of a very different description. The prisoners that had been taken, about thirty in number, were led out in front of the trenches, opposite to the city gate, and there put to death, in presence of the besieging army and of the garrison. This act of cruelty marks the decided turn that had taken place in the spirit of the war, which, from various causes, as is but too common in civil wars, had, for some time past, been gradually assuming a character of great ferocity.

Brutal conduct of Kámrán.

The relations of such as had suffered in this execution hastened to Kámrán, and loudly demanded retaliation for the blood that had been spilt. Though he had himself been the aggressor, and shown the example, the demand was in accordance with his irritated feelings. The relations of such as had been employed in the transaction were seized, and subjected to a cruel

BOOK V. A. D. 1547.

revenge. Bápus had been ordered by the Emperor to superintend the late execution. Kámrán, under pretence of retaliation, gave over that nobleman's wife to the rabble in the bazar, to be dishonoured, and murdered his three sons, who were between the age of three and eight years, throwing their dead bodies over the walls, towards that part of the trenches where Kerácha Khan and Mosáhib Beg commanded. The sons of these two last mentioned Amírs he caused to be tied to stakes, and exposed suspended by ropes from the castle wall, at the same time intimating to their unhappy parents that they must either join him, or make the Emperor raise the siege, or at least open for him through their lines a passage, by which he might leave the fort, otherwise that their children should be treated as those of Bápus had been. Kerácha, who was then Humáyun's prime minister, made answer aloud in hearing of the troops, to Kámrán's men who were on the battlements — that his children must all meet death in the course of nature, and in the allotted time: that they could not fall better than in the path of duty to their benefactor: that his own life belonged to his sovereign, from his allegiance to whom nothing should make him swerve; "but," added the minister, "if Kámrán will return to his allegiance, my life, which at any time I would gladly give for that of my children, shall be gratefully devoted to his service." Humáyun gave his brother to know that, should he carry his threat into execution, he and his son must expect the same fate, as soon as the city fell. Kámrán, however, made the wife of Muhammed Kásim Khan Mochi, with some other females, be suspended by the breasts from the battlements, and continued to rage, with odious brutality, against the helpless and unoffending children and wives of his enemies.

As the cannonade still continued, Kámrán, to check the fire of the besiegers, is said to have ordered the young prince, Akber, to be exposed on that part of the wall where the fire of cannon and musquetry was hottest. If we do not, with Abulfazl, allow that Sambal Khan, the Emperor's master of artillery, wondered from what unknown cause the hands of his artillery and matchlock-men trembled; why the bullets took a crooked course, and why their matches did not communicate their usual fire, yet we must detest the being who closed a scene of dastardly cruelty towards his innocent prisoners, by exposing his infant nephew to such a risk. The firing, however, ceased.* CHAP. III. SECT. II.

The siege had now continued so long, that the chiefs, who were in the Emperor's interest, began to join his camp from a distance, from Zemín-dáwer, Kandahár, Kilát, and Badakhshán. They all had stations assigned to them, so that the blockade was completed all around, and every day became closer. Kámrán, now much straitened, began to feel apprehensions for his own safety. He sent the humblest and most submissive confession of his past errors to Kerácha Khan, beseeching him to intercede with his offended brother, whom it was now his supreme wish faithfully to serve; and

His distress and submissive applications.

* It is difficult anywhere to find instances of flattery so gross as the greater part of Abulfazl's account of the infant years of Akber. Akbernáma *passim*. The Emperor, who wished to be thought invested with a supernatural character, did not discourage such representations, but rather favoured any artifice that could add weight to the belief. The story of Akber's being actually exposed on the walls is related by Abulfazl, as well as by Nizám-ed-dín Ahmed, Tar. Niz. f. 199., who mentions that Máhum Anka interposed her body to preserve him from danger, in which he is followed by the Tar. Bedáuni, Ferishta, and in general all subsequent writers. Yet the fact seems doubtful. Bayezíd, a contemporary, and on the spot, though he minutely describes the other atrocities, takes no notice of this, ff. 31, 32.; and Jouher, who was also in the camp, only says, in mentioning the cannonade which which was opened from the Koh-Aákabein and returned from the fort, "Mírza Kámrán upon this *threatened* to expose his Majesty's son, Muhammed Akber, to the fire of the battery. When information of this reached the Emperor, he ordered the cannonade to cease, but his troops to remain in the trenches on every side, and to guard them well." — End of cap. 20.

BOOK V. A. D. 1547.

offering, in proof of his sincerity, to put his life and fortune in the Emperor's hands. Humáyun, with his usual easy good nature, was disposed to forgive him. But Kerácha Khan and Mosáhib Beg,—whether they only foresaw new trouble and fresh intrigues from the Mírza's residence in his brother's court; or whether, according to others, they were alarmed lest their own importance should be gone, were Humáyun to reign supreme, without a rival,—are accused of having privately filled the mind of Kámrán with dread of the danger that awaited him should he surrender to his brother; and, at the same time, terrified him by the information that the Emperor's army was every day growing in strength. As friends, therefore, they are said to have advised Kámrán to make his escape, offering secretly to assist him in passing through the lines.

Thursday, Rebi, I. 7. A. H. 954. April 27. He escapes.

At all events, the Mírza, on the 27th day of April, the night being very dark, left the citadel by a breach opened in the wall, was conducted through the trenches, and made the best of his way for the mountains on foot. Humáyun, on hearing of his escape, sent Mírza Hindal to pursue him. The Mírza overtook him after he had reached the hills, which he found him ascending, mounted on the back of a man. Hindal was about to seize him, but desisted on the earnest prayers of his brother, not to force him back to certain death; and being affected at his deplorable and destitute situation, presented him with a horse, and turned back.*

* Akbernáma, ff. 71—73.; Tar. Akb. ff. 160, 161.; Tar. Niz. ff. 198, 199.; Jouher, c. 20. and 21.; Bayezíd, ff. 30—32.; Tar. Bed. f. 185.; Ferishta, vol. ii. pp. 161—163.; Bayezíd affirms that Hindal allowed Kámrán to pass through his lines, that he was recognised and seized, but a sign taken from him, after which he was allowed to go on. Other authorities affirm that Háji Muhammed was sent in pursuit and overtook him, when Kámrán exclaiming in Túrki, "Go and say to your father, Bába Kushkeh, it was I that slew him." Háji Muhammed, who was an old soldier and a Moghul, did not push on, but turned back and let him go; Tar. Bed. f. 185. and Tab. Akb. He probably also knew him as a child, being Kokildash to one of the imperial family.

Flies to Badakhshán, and thence to the Uzbeks.

Kámrán had concerted with his adherents, that they should meet him at the hill of Istálíf, in the Kohdaman, north of Kábul, where he was to collect an army, and make a new attempt; but, on his arrival, seeing nothing in readiness, he set out again by night attended only by Ali-kuli, a Korchi, and proceeded onward by the valley of Senjed. He was met on the way by a party of Hazáras, who robbed him of the little he had left. One of them, however, recognizing the Mírza, he was carried to their chief, who took him to Zohák and Bámián, where he was joined by Mírza Beg, Shír Alí, and a few more, who still adhered to his interest. In the course of a week, they collected about a hundred and fifty horse, with which they went down to Ghuri, which they summoned to surrender. But Mírza Beg Birlás, the governor, declaring his determination to hold the place for Humáyun, the party had begun to pass on, when one of their number, a man of no note, in a rude and blustering manner, abusing the privilege allowed to companions in misfortune, began to rail at Kámrán, exclaiming that, if he was really the son of Báber, and had any sense of honour, he would not allow the governor to escape so easily. Kámrán explained to his restive adherent, that he had neither stores nor implements for conducting a siege, nor were his people in a humour for it. But, at length, stung by the renewed reproaches of the man, he turned back, and by a piece of fortunate temerity, defeated Mírza Beg, who had with him a thousand foot and three hundred horse, and took the place; in which was found a large supply of stores, besides the horses, arms and accoutrements of the troops. Leaving Shír Ali to defend this important acquisition, he pushed on towards Badakhshán, in the hope of prevailing upon Mírza Suleimán, and his son Mírza Ibráhím, to join him. But these princes, who had no attachment to any of the brothers, and were wholly bent on making themselves independent,

BOOK V. A.D. 1547.

and on securing their country from foreign invasion, declared their determination to adhere to the treaty lately concluded with Humáyun: so that Kámrán, finding no prospect of success in that quarter, was compelled to turn for succour to the Uzbeks, the grand enemies of his race, and marched down to Bálkh, in hopes that Pír Muhammed Khan, the Uzbek chief of that province, might espouse his cause.*

Humáyun enters Kábul which is plundered.

Meanwhile, Humáyun, having entered Kábul, had the satisfaction of embracing his son Abker, whom, as well as all the ladies of his family, he found safe. He, however, gave up the town to be plundered for one whole night by his troops, as a punishment on the inhabitants for allowing their town to be surprised. This, had it been the real cause, was punishing them for the fault of a governor chosen by himself, and for all the subsequent misery which, through his negligence, they had endured. But the real motive was, probably, his inability to remunerate his troops in any other way for their long-suffering and privations, before and during the siege. He put to death some Múllas, who had encouraged Kámrán in his rebellion and misdeeds.

Sends in pursuit of Kámrán.

Being apprehensive that the Mírza might establish himself in Badakhshán, he despatched Kerácha Khan across the mountains, to chase him out of his dominions. That general, accordingly, descending on the northern face of the range, laid siege to Ghuri, which he took, after it had been long defended with gallantry by Shír Ali, who, when it was no longer defensible, effected his escape, carrying the garrison along with him.

Kámrán returns with an army from Bálkh.

Kámrán had not been long at Bálkh, before he succeeded in engaging the governor, Pír Muhammed Khan, in his interest. That chief, and indeed the whole Uzbek confederacy, had seen with jealousy and alarm,

* Akbernáma, f. 73.; Tab. Akb. ff. 161, 162.; Tar. Niz. ff. 199, 200.; Jouher, c. 21.; Bayezíd, f. 32.; Khol-ul Towáríkh, f. 267. This last calls Pír Muhammed Khan, Wali of Turán.

the late visit of Humáyun to the provinces on the Amu. When he heard, therefore, of Kámrán's approach, to ask succour against his brother, he considered the occasion as a most favourable one for fomenting that discord among the sons of Báber, which hitherto had been so advantageous to the Uzbeks. He received the Mírza with every mark of distinction, lodged him in his own palace, and soon accompanied him back into the country which acknowledged the sovereign of Kábul, at the head of a powerful force. With his aid, Kámrán recovered Ghuri, and took Baklán; and adventurers flocked to his standard from every quarter. Hindal Mírza, who with the troops of Kunduz, had formed a junction with Kerácha Khan and Suleimán Mírza, was unable to resist such an invasion. His army, therefore, soon broke up; he threw himself into Kunduz; Kerácha Khan recrossed the mountains, to bring an adequate reinforcement from Kábul, while the Badakhshán Mírzas hastened back to defend the narrow passes of their own mountains. Pír Muhammed Khan, seeing his ally, Kámrán Mírza, undisputed master of the open country, returned home to Bálkh, leaving with him a strong body of Uzbek auxiliaries.*

Attacks Badakhshán.

The Mírza, availing himself of his good fortune, resolved to make his first attack on the dominions of Suleimán. For that purpose, he advanced to Kishem and Talikán, whence he detached a body of his Chaghatái and Uzbek troops, under Rafík Koka, to occupy Rostak, a town and district situated on the Kokcha river, within the territory of Badakhshán. Suleimán, collecting the militia of the adjoining highland district of Kuláb or Khutlán, marched suddenly into Rostak, and made a sharp attack upon Rafík, with whom he came up near Kila Zefer. He was, however, repulsed, and compelled once more to take refuge among his

* Akbernáma, f. 74.

BOOK V. A. D. 1547.

mountains. Such an effect had the news of Kámrán's success on his old followers and soldiers at Kábul, that nearly 3,000 of them left that place, and joined him in his new adventure.*

Humáyun moves to meet him.

No sooner did the Emperor hear of the dangers that threatened him on the side of Bálkh, than he left his capital, and marched to place himself at the head of his troops in the north. He had only reached Ghurbend, in the Koh-daman of Kábul, when he met Kerácha Khan on his way back from his unfortunate expedition. Kerácha, as he crossed the hills, had been plundered of all his baggage by the Aimáks, who, with the Hazáras and other hill-tribes, were the only gainers by these intestine wars. The destitute condition, to which he was thus reduced, made it indispensable for Kerácha to go on to Kábul, there to refit, so as to enable him to take the field; and Humáyun moved from Ghurbend to Gulbehár, where he halted to enjoy the pleasures of the chase, and to await his minister's return. As soon as Kerácha rejoined the camp, the Emperor, intent on his original purpose, again moved on. But, through this ill-timed delay, the season for passing the hills was lost, and in attempting to surmount the passes of the Hindu-kúsh mountains, when they were covered with deep snow, the difficulties and dangers were found to be such, that, after much disorder and loss among the troops and cattle, which plunged, and stumbled, and sank in the snow, the attempt was abandoned, and the army returned to Kábul, to await the return of spring.*

Revolt in his camp.

When the season arrived, in which it was practicable to cross the mountains, Humáyun, as he was about to set out, was prevented by an unexpected revolt.† The real nature of the intrigues which produced so many revolutions, for a long series of years, in the family of

* Khol. ul Towáríkh, f. 267. † Akbernáma, f. 74.

Taimur, it is impossible, at this distance of time, to discover, even were it of much importance. Some observations are obvious enough. Though much respect was paid to the members of the imperial family, as descendants of Taimur, or of Báber, no one individual of them was viewed with exclusive veneration as the eldest, or legal representative of the dynasty. Any one of them who could command success, could command obedience. The throne of the individual was always, therefore, unsteady. Possession, within the range of the family, brought right along with it. There were no great bodies, of the nobles, of the law, or of the church; no corporations, living beyond the life of man, and maintaining, while they existed, the same uniform spirit and character, that could be opposed to a spirit of change. The towns, though they had wishes and interests of their own, having no municipal government, no correspondence with each other, no central point or council, by which their common interest could be known or pursued, were without power, or influence in affairs of state, and could only show their uneasy feelings by riot or revolt. A few Amírs, with their followers, decided the question, who was to rule. Even among them, there were nobles, but no body of nobility. There was no Senate, or States-General, or Parliament, in which they had a right to take their seat, and where they could consult in common. The king's court was the centre of union, and from the crown all honour flowed to the individual; for dignity was not hereditary. The possession of the ear, or even of the person, of the sovereign was the great object of the ambitious. The great Amírs strengthened themselves, for influence at court, by adding to the number of their retainers; and all in the lower stations who aspired to rise, connected themselves with some powerful noble. The consequence was, that a few of these grand Amírs, by a combination among themselves, or by a sudden *coup d'état*, could

BOOK V. A. D. 1548.

make and unmake the sovereign. Princes of talent could overrule, and give an useful direction to the power thus accumulated in a few hands; while such as were deficient in political skill, became the instruments, and too often the victims, of this unregulated power. As there were few steady checks to the exercise of power, every governor, as well as every sovereign, was nearly despotic in his own government. In such a state of things, discontent and collision were inevitable.

Some discontent would appear to have prevailed at the court of Kábul among the leading nobles, though we are ignorant of its exact nature and extent. Kerácha Khan was Prime Minister, an office which he had earned by important services. It is probable that in this high station, encouraged by the easy humour and indolence of Humáyun, he may have arrogated too much to himself, and carried matters with too high a hand; and the Emperor could hardly fail occasionally to feel the engrossing spirit of his minister; while, on the other hand, Kerácha was easily inflamed at any obstacle to his authority. The possession of the purse is always the most important part of a minister's power, and any interruption in that power is most sensibly felt. It happened that Kerácha, who had got the Emperor's consent to bestow a trifling sum of ten tumáns * on a particular officer, had himself written the order on the treasury to carry it into effect. When it was presented, Khwája Gházi of Tabríz, the Diwán or Minister of Finance, who had returned from Persia during the late siege, and been appointed to that important office, refused to pay it, and at the same time represented to the Emperor that as he, by the nature of his office, was answerable for the expenses of the army, he could not allow any other person to interfere in his department. The order, when refused, was carried back to Kerácha, who took

* In that age this sum might be equal to 80*l.* or 100*l.*

fire, and hastened to complain to the Emperor, but received no satisfaction. This produced a coolness, and the offended Prime Minister, resolved to carry his point, went so far as to form a party among the Amírs, who demanded that Khwája Gházi should be dismissed. This demand being refused, the cabal were so much offended, as to talk of revolting to Kámrán. To prevent matters reaching so serious a length, the Emperor sent to Kerácha, to assure him of his regard, to attempt to conciliate him, and to desire that matters should go on on their former footing. But Kerácha haughtily insisted as a preliminary, that Khwája Gházi should be given up to him in bonds, to be treated at his discretion, and his office bestowed on Kásim Husein Sultan. To this demand, not more unjust and alarming to a faithful servant than degrading to his master, an answer was returned, not rejecting it with scorn, but, rather jesuitically, reminding Kerácha that he was Vizír, that the Diwán was under his control, and that he might, therefore, easily contrive some future opportunity on which he could call him to account. But even this dereliction of imperial duty and of honour, did not satisfy the incensed Vizír, who, finding that he could not bend his sovereign, resolved to renounce his allegiance; and, in concert with a number of the leading men of the court, among whom were Bápus, Mosáhib Beg, Ismáel Beg Duldi and others, attended by three thousand veteran horse fully equipped, left Kábul by the Pái-Minár pass, seized the imperial herd or stud which was at Khwája Riwáj, drove it before them, and took their course through the Koh-daman.

Humáyun, utterly unprepared for such a defection, sent orders to the troops that were nearest at hand to hasten to Kábul; and as they arrived, they were sent off in pursuit of the rebels, with orders to impede their progress. Terdi Beg, Monaim Khan, Muhammed Kuli Birlás, and other officers, who adhered to the Emperor,

BOOK V. A. D. 1548.

were successively despatched in this manner in the course of the day; and at noon, when the hour was at length declared to be fortunate, the Emperor himself set out, and at length overtook and attacked the rear-guard of the fugitives near Kárá-bágh. Having pushed them before him, he had got close upon Korácha Khan, towards the close of the day, on the banks of the Múri, when night interposed. The fugitives, continuing their flight, passed the bridge of Ghurbend, which they broke down behind them; whereupon a detachment, that had followed them up to that time, returned back to Humáyun at Kárábágh. That prince, finding that they had escaped his immediate pursuit, hastened back to Kábul, to prepare for a campaign on the Badakhshán side of the hills, which he now saw would be more necessary, and the event more doubtful than he had expected. Kerácha, on his part, leaving Temir Shagháli in the district of Penjshír, to collect and forward all the intelligence he could procure from Kábul, proceeded by the Upper Hindu-kúsh pass, and joined Kámrán in Kishem.*

The rebels escape to Kámrán.

Humáyun, on his return to Kábul, despatched orders to his Amírs in every quarter, to furnish their quotas to the army he was preparing to lead against Kámrán. Among others he invited Háji Muhammed Khan to join him from Ghazni. In the course of about a month, on the 12th of June A. D. 1548, he left Kábul and proceeded to Kárábágh, where he halted ten or twelve days, waiting for his stores and field equipage. Here, to the general surprise, he was joined by Háji Muhammed, whose fidelity seems to have been suspected. Kásim Husein Sultan Uzbek also arrived from Bangash, and was gladly welcomed.

Humáyun collects his forces.

A. H. 955, Jemádi I. 5. June 12.

It was while they were still at this station that Mírza Ibráhím, Suleimán's son, arrived from Badakhshán.

The Governor of Badakhshán declares for him.

* Akbernáma, f. 74.; Tab. Akb. f. 162.; Tar. Niz. 200, 201.; Ferishta, vol. ii. p. 163.; Jouher, c. 21.; Bayezíd, f. 33, 34.

CHAP. III. SECT. II.

This was an important event for Humáyun. His anxiety to meet the Emperor had made him venture to leave home without escort, and expose himself to the peril of passing through a hostile country. Advancing by way of Perián, when he arrived at the Penjshír territory, he found Temir Shagháli in possession of all the passes. Malek Ali Penjshíri, however, one of the hill-chiefs, having joined the Mírza with his tribe and family, they engaged Temir Shagháli, who was killed in the action. Malek Ali, after this, guarded the Mírza through the passes, but could not be prevailed upon to accompany him into the imperial camp. The Emperor, however, sent to express his obligations to him. Mírza Ibráhím was soon after sent back, to inform his father of the Emperor's motions, and to concert with him a plan for co-operating with the army on its arrival at Talikán.

His advance.

Humáyun, marching from Kárábágh, proceeded by Gulbehár, whence he sent back Akber and his mother to Kábul, the command of which he entrusted to Muhammed Kásim Khan Mochi. He next advanced through the beautiful valley of Penjshír, which lies in a high situation, close upon the country of the Siáhposh Káfirs, and is famous for its fruits and delightful climate. From Bazárak, a village in the valley, he sent forward some of his officers to ascertain the state of the northern provinces; and, following with his army, surmounted the passes of the Hindu-kúsh, and descended to the banks of the Bángi, one of the chief rivers that rise in the mountains. He found that Kámrán's generals had abandoned Anderáb, on hearing of his approach. He therefore made Terdi Beg push on, that he might seize the families of the rebels, which had been left in Khost. This, if accomplished, would have been a decisive blow in Humáyun's favour; but Kerácha Khan, foreseeing that such an attempt might be made, had despatched Mosáhib Beg to remove them; and just as Terdi Beg

BOOK V. A.D. 1548.

reached the Khost territory, Mosáhib succeeded in conveying them safe to Talikán.

On reaching the low country, Humáyun was joined from Kunduz by his brother Hindal, who brought with him a prisoner of considerable importance, Shír Ali. This chief had long possessed much influence in the court of Kámrán, whom he had often urged to attack Kunduz, representing it as an easy conquest. He was, at length, entrusted with a force to make the attempt, and had reached the town. But a party from the fort having one night surrounded the house in which he was, and come upon him by surprise, Shír Ali, in trying to escape, threw himself into the river, but broke one of his arms, and was taken. Humáyun received him with distinction, gave him a dress of honour, and restored him to the government of Ghuri. He was a man of great vigour, foresight and activity; but it is not very easy to discover the principle on which officers, at this distracted period, the moment they passed, by desertion or the fortune of war, from one army to another, were entrusted with commands of importance. There seems to have been little steady fidelity, or honour, among the adherents on either side.*

The important conflict between the Emperor and Kámrán, who had received so large an accession of strength by the revolt of the Amírs, was now about to take place. When rather more than the half of July 1548 was passed, Humáyun, encamped in the Aleng Kazan of Anderáb, was joined by the Kázi of Anderáb, with a number of the neighbouring tribesmen†, and others, who had been followers of Mosáhib Beg. He lost no time, but resolved to attack the enemy while still divided. Putting his troops in motion, and giving Hindal the advance, he marched to lay siege to Talikán, at that time garrisoned by Kerácha Khan and

* Akbernáma, f. 75.; Tab. Akb. f. 162.

† The Tukba, Simchi, and Balúch are specified. Akbernáma.

the rebel Amírs, with a party of Kámrán's troops under Mírza Abdalla, who were making every preparation to place it in a condition to sustain a long siege. Kámrán himself, with the main body of his army, was lying at a distance near Kishem and Kila Zefer.

Repulse near Talikán.

Humáyun, trusting to this division of the enemy's force, had ordered Mírza Hindal and the advance to cross the Bángi above Talikán*, and to take up ground on the other side of the river. But the rebel Amírs, aware of the Emperor's movements, had, by express, informed Kámrán of their danger, and added that Hindal and his division could with ease be cut off by a sudden attack. Kámrán had, in consequence, made a forced march of nearly fifty miles†, had arrived near Talikán, and already occupied a rising ground not far from the fort. No sooner, therefore, had Hindal's division passed the river, than Kámrán attacked and broke it, while unsupported by the main body, plundering their baggage, and driving them back in confusion to the side from which they had come.

The Emperor, who reached the river just when this discomfiture occurred, was eager to cross at once, in face of the enemy. But finding that to be dangerous, the bed of the river being full of loose rolling stones, which rendered footing insecure, he was compelled to march about a mile farther up, where the bottom was of firm rock, and there he crossed. Without delay he again moved downwards, to drive Kámrán from the rising ground which he had occupied. As he approached it, he found that a strong party which he had pushed forward had been vigorously assailed and driven back; but, as soon as the imperial standard was seen advancing, Kámrán, convinced that the main body was

* Talikán stands upon the Ferkhar river, which joins the Bángi. Both branches, however, seem to be occasionally called Bángi. Below Talikán the river generally gets the name of the Talikán river.

† 25 kos.

BOOK V. A.D. 1548. now at hand, hurriedly deserted his position, and retired into the town with the loss of his own baggage as well as of that which he had taken. Humáyun now plundered and laid waste the surrounding country, and sat down before the fort. Such prisoners as he had taken were put to death. Being anxious, however, to put an end to hostilities, he wrote to his brother*, making an overture for an accommodation, but it was rejected. Batteries were, therefore, erected, and operations begun.

The fort invested.

The siege went on for about a month, during which time the Emperor was joined by Mírza Suleimán and his son, with large reinforcements, as well as by Chaker Khan, the son of the late Sultan Weis Kipchak, with a force from Kuláb. Kámrán, meanwhile, finding that he had no prospect of relief from any quarter, as the Uzbeks, rejoiced to see the princes of Kábul destroying each other, refused him any farther assistance, became most eager to open the negociation which he had so lately rejected. For this purpose he shot into the camp of the besiegers, arrows having attached to them letters addressed to the Emperor, in which, by the humblest confession of his offences, and by promises of a change of conduct, he attempted to propitiate his resentment, and proposed Mír Arab Mekki as his mediator. The Emperor having agreed to receive his submission, the Mír was sent into the fort, and, after some conferences, finally concluded a capitulation by which the Mírza,

Submissive offers of Kámrán.

* Hardly any letters passed in that age between princes in which quotations from favourite poets are not to be found. Humáyun wrote to Kámrán, "O my unkind brother, what are you doing? For every murder that is committed on either side, you will have to answer at the day of judgment. Come and make peace, that mankind may no longer be oppressed by our quarrels." The letter was sent by Nesíb, a diviner, (rammál). Kámrán, having read the letter, was silent; and when the diviner requested an answer, the Mírza only repeated the well-known verse, "He that would obtain sovereignty for his bride, must woo her across the edge of the sharp sword." Nesíb, considering this as his answer, bowed and returned to Humáyun.

renouncing his claim to independence, agreed that the Khutba should be read in the Emperor's name, that the revolted Amírs should be delivered up in chains, while he himself was to be permitted to retire to Mekka. Accordingly the Emperor's Sadr entered Talikán, and on Friday, the 17th day of August, recited the prayer for the prince in his name, in the Grand Mosque. Kámrán, with his family, having come out of the town, was conducted by Háji Muhammed to the limits of the imperial territory. He requested that Bápus might be one of the Amírs who were to accompany him in his exile, because, he said, he was his *protègé*, and he wished to have an opportunity of atoning for the sore injury he had done him. The revolted Amírs were brought as prisoners into the Emperor's presence, and pardoned, probably on a private understanding under the treaty.*

CHAP. III. Sect. II.

Rejeb. 12, August 17.

He surrenders.

The army was still encamped in a valley on the banks of the Talikán river, when, on the 22nd of August, the Emperor was surprised to learn that Kámrán was not far off, and on his way back to throw himself on his mercy. When Kámrán left Talikán, he was under the deepest apprehension for his personal safety. But when he had gone a few stages, and heard of the generous reception, which Humáyun and given to the revolted nobles,—as he had no real wish to go to

Rejeb. 17, August 22.

* The first who was brought in was Kerácha Khan, with his scymetar hanging from his neck. The Emperor made it be taken off, permitted him to make his obeisance, addressed some conciliatory words to him, and then desired him to be seated on his left, below Terdi Beg Khan. The same ceremony was gone through with the others, who had all places assigned them. When Korbán Keráwal, who had been a personal servant of Humáyun's came in, and bowed down with shame, performed the *kornish*, "And you too," said the Emperor, "What cause of offence could you have?" Korbán answered, "What can those do, whose face God has blackened?" On which Hasan-kuli quoted the couplet, "He who puffs at the lamp which God has lighted, singes his beard." All the rebel lords, says Abulfazl, but especially Kerácha Khan, who had a very long beard, felt much ashamed. Akbernama, ff. 75, 76.; Tab. Akb. ff. 162, 163.; Jouher, c. 22.; Bayezíd, ff. 33—37.

BOOK V. A.D. 1548. the Holy Cities,—he began to imagine that he might still have something to expect from his brother's clemency; an idea that was encouraged by Mírza Abdalla, and others who accompanied him, to whom the pilgrimage was as little pleasing as to himself. After he had travelled about forty miles*, therefore, he turned back, and sent on Bápus to wait upon Humáyun, and communicate to him his most humble petition to be received under his protection. Humáyun at once acceded to his wishes, made every preparation for his honourable reception, and sent out Hindal and Askeri, his brothers, the latter of whom he released from bonds on the occasion, with Mírza Suleimán, and many great Amírs, as an honorary procession, or Istakbál, to meet and conduct him to the presence, with the sound of kettle-drums and trumpets.

His reception by Humáyun.

When Kámrán approached the Emperor, who was sitting in state in the pavilion of public audience, he took a whip from the girdle of Monaim Khan, who stood by, and passing it round his neck, presented himself as a criminal. "Alas! alas! exclaimed the Emperor, there is no need of this; throw it away." The Mírza made three obeisances, according to the usual etiquette of the court, after which the Emperor gave him the formal embrace, and commanded him to be seated. Kámrán began to make excuses for his past conduct, and to express his regret. "What is past is past," said the Emperor. "Thus far we have conformed to ceremony. Let us now meet as brothers." They then rose, and clasped each other to their breasts, in the most affectionate manner, and both burst into tears, sobbing aloud, so as to affect all who were present. Humáyun, on resuming his seat, desired his brother to sit next to him on the left, the place of honour, adding kindly in Túrki, the language of their family, "Sit close

* 10 Farsukh or farsangs, Tab. Akberi.

to me." A cup of sherbet was brought, of which the Emperor having drunk the one half, handed it to his brother, who drank the other. A grand entertainment followed, at which the four brothers, who now met for the first time, after a long separation, sat on the same carpet and dined, or, to use the words of the historian, eat salt together. The festival was prolonged for two days, in the midst of universal rejoicing. As Kámrán, from the rapidity and hurried nature of his return, had left his tents behind on the road, the Emperor ordered him to be supplied with a set pitched close to his own, and, at his desire, consented to Askerí's going to stay with him.*

CHAP. III. SECT. II.

A council was now held about the expediency of an attack on Bálkh. There was considerable diversity of opinion. The army was, therefore, ordered to march on to Nárín, where the road divides, one branch leading to Bálkh, the other to Kábul. The Emperor, meanwhile, turned off with his three brothers to the fountain of Bend-kushá, near Ishkemish, where he spent some days in a party of pleasure. Báber was encamped at this spot, when his cousin Khan Mírza and his brother Jehángír Mírza, came and submitted to him. This event, with the date, Báber had commemorated by an inscription on a flat slab of rock. Humáyun now made an addition to it, to record the meeting and reconciliation of all the brothers.†

Humáyun settles his northern dominions.

On leaving this spot, he proceeded to Nárín, where it was resolved to defer the expedition against Bálkh till the following year. He, therefore, in the meanwhile, applied himself to the settlement of his northern dominions. Khutlán, a province beyond the Amu, at that time, as now, generally called Kuláb‡, as far as the

* Akbernáma, f. 76.; Tabakát-e-Akberi, f. 163.; Jouher, c. 23.; Bayezíd, ff. 35—39.

† Ibid.

‡ Kuláb lies beyond the Amu, between Derwáz and Shughnán. Burnes's Travels, vol. iii. p. 275. It is the old Khutlán, or a portion of it.

BOOK V.

A.D. 1548.

frontier of Muk and Karatigín, he allotted to Kámrán Mírza, giving him Chaker Ali Beg Kulábi, the son of Sultan Weis Beg, as Amir-ul-omra to accompany him to his province. He permitted Mírza Askeri to go with Kámrán, bestowing on him the district of Karatigín. These assignments were little more than nominal. Kuláb was considered as dependant on Badakhshán; Karatigín probably was not. Chaker Ali was governor of Kuláb; but, at the same time, was a sort of independent chief, who did not owe much submission either to Humáyun or Suleimán. The Emperor's seal-bearer presented Kámrán, when near Nárín, with the perwána, or grant of his new territory, and congratulated him on his appointment. It gave Kámrán but little satisfaction. What "said he," have I not been sovereign of Kábul and of Badakhshán? And is not Kuláb a mere pergana, or district, of the latter? "How can I serve in it?" "I have heard that you are wise," said the keeper of the seals, "and I know you to be so. May I be permitted respectfully to observe, that, after all that has passed, the wonder rather may be, that you have got even this, or any thing." The justice of the observation was felt by Kámrán. He, next day, waited upon the Emperor, was honoured with a khilát, and the investiture of Kuláb, and, accompanied by Askeri and Chaker Khan, set out for his government. Many of Chaker Khan's followers left him, and attached themselves to Kámrán. They army broke up. Suleimán Mírza and his son Ibráhím continued to hold the government of Badakhshán, to which Talikán was added, with Kishem and some other districts. Mírza Hindal retained Kunduz with Ghuri, Kahmerd, Baklán, Ishkemish and Nárín. Shír Ali remained with him as Minister. They all repaired to their governments, while Humáyun proceeded to Khost, and thence to Perián, on his route to the Penjshír pass.*

* Bayezíd, f. 39—41.; Akbernáma, &c., as above.

Perián was a fort, which the great Taimúr had built, when he chastised the infidels of Kittúr. Humáyun, who found it in ruins, resolved to restore it. For that purpose, when the army came up, he divided the work among all his Amírs, each having a particular portion allotted to him to build or repair; and so effectively did the work proceed, that in the course of the ten days that the army tarried there, the fort, with its walls, gateways and defences, was completely restored. The name of the place he changed to Islámábád, the "City of the True Faith." He also made enquiries as to the silver mines in the vicinity, but found that they would not repay the expense of working. Having crossed the mountains, and descending by the banks of the Penjshír river, he halted some time at the Ashterkeram pass; so that it was the beginning of winter before he reached Kábul, and the ground was already covered with snow. After waiting some time for a lucky day, he made his entry into the town on the 5th day of October A.D. 1548.*

CHAP. III. SECT. II.

Returns to Kábul.

Ramzán 2. October 5.

* Akbernáma, f. 77.; Tar. Nizámi, ff. 200, 201.; Jouher, c. 23.

# CHAPTER III.

## HUMÁYUN IN AFGHÁNISTÁN.

## SECTION III.

### STATE OF KASHMÍR. — EXPEDITION TOWARDS BÁLKH. — REVOLT AND DEFEAT OF KÁMRÁN.

STATE OF HUMÁYUN'S COURT. — EMBASSIES FROM KÁSHGAR, AND TO PERSIA. — EMBASSY FROM KASHMÍR. — RECENT HISTORY OF THAT COUNTRY — AND OF HAIDER MÍRZA. — HE INVITES HUMÁYUN TO KASHMÍR, AND THE INVASION OF INDIA. — HIS CHARACTER AND ADMINISTRATION. — POSITION OF KÁMRÁN. — HUMÁYUN'S EXPEDITION AGAINST BÁLKH. — KÁMRÁN FAILS TO JOIN HIM. — SIEGE AND SURRENDER OF EIBEK. — DELAYS OF HUMÁYUN. — SUDDEN ATTACK BY THE UZBEKS. — CONTINUED ABSENCE OF KÁMRÁN. — REPULSE OF THE UZBEK ADVANCE. — HUMÁYUN RESOLVES TO RETREAT. — PANIC IN HIS ARMY, ROUT, AND FLIGHT TOWARDS KÁBUL. — HUMÁYUN WINTERS IN KÁBUL. — PROCEEDINGS OF KÁMRÁN. — HIS ATTEMPT ON BADAKHSHÁN AND KUNDUZ. — RETURNS TO KULÁB. — IS DEFEATED BY THE UZBEKS. — EXCITES A REVOLT IN KÁBUL. — HUMÁYUN PREPARES TO SEIZE HIM. — IS SURPRISED BY KÁMRÁN. — WANT OF ZEAL AMONG HUMÁYUN'S CHIEFS. — FLIGHT AND WOUND OF HUMÁYUN. — HE IS JOINED BY A REINFORCEMENT. — PROCEEDS TO THE NORTH, AND PREPARES TO RETURN TO KÁBUL. — CONDUCT OF KÁMRÁN. — HE OCCUPIES KÁBUL. — ADVANCE OF HUMÁYUN. — HIS COMPACT WITH HIS CHIEFS. — THE ARMIES OF HUMÁYUN AND KÁMRÁN MEET. — HUMÁYUN ENDEAVOURS UNSUCCESSFULLY TO NEGOTIATE. — ORDERS AN ATTACK. — DEFEAT AND FLIGHT OF KÁMRÁN. — HUMÁYUN RE-OCCUPIES KÁBUL.

BOOK V.

A. D. 1548. A. H. 955. State of Humáyun's court.

DURING the following winter Humáyun had a short interval of leisure, which he employed in settling the internal affairs of his dominions. His greatest danger evidently lay in the unsettled temper and tendency to intrigue of his great Amírs.

Kámrán had long governed Kábul with absolute

power; and the nobles and the people whom he had ruled, probably regarded his right to the crown as at least equal to that of his elder brother. He felt himself by no means secure, even in his own court. In some degree, at least, to guard against the dangers by which he was surrounded, he resolved to remove to a distance Kerácha Khan and Mosáhib Beg; the former of whom had been Minister to Kámrán and to himself; the latter the son of the late Khwája Kilán; both of them men of sufficient influence and talents, and who, from recent experience, he believed, did not want the disposition to be dangerous leaders in any revolt that should break out. He, therefore, intimated to them that they had his permission to leave his service for a time, and proceed on a pilgrimage to Mekka. They, accordingly, set out on this unwished-for act of religious duty, but lingered in the Hazára country, and in the end, through the mediation of their numerous friends, found means to work on the easy good nature of the Emperor, who forgot their rebellion, and permitted them to return. We have seen that Humáyun, in the earlier part of his reign, had repeatedly suffered from the rebellion of Muhammed Sultan Mírza and his sons. One of them, Ulugh Mírza, in coming from his government of Zemín-dáwer to join the Emperor (while yet beyond the mountains), being accompanied by Khwája Moazem, the brother of Hamída Begum — a rash, wrong-headed man, who had recently fled from court in consequence of an assassination of which he had been guilty — had been induced by the Khwája to make an attack upon some Hazáras who lay near the road towards Ghazni, in the course of which the Mírza was cut off. Not long afterwards his brother, Shah Mírza, was waylaid and slain near the Minár pass, by a brother of Háji Muhammed, in consequence of some old family quarrel-of-blood. This removed two unquiet and dangerous spirits of high name and pretension.

BOOK V.

A.D. 1548.

Embassies from Káshghar and to Persia.

At this time he received an embassy from Abdal-Reshíd Khan, the son of Sultan Saíd Khan, the chief of Káshgar; and he despatched one to Shah Tahmasp, most probably to deprecate his resentment for still continuing to keep possession of Kandahár, and to keep alive his hopes of its being restored at no distant period.

Embassy from Kashmír.

Recent history of that country.

A. H. 947, A.D. 1540.

But the embassy which most interested him was one that arrived from Kashmír from his cousin Haider Mírza Doghlat. It will be recollected that when Humáyun was defeated, and compelled to abandon first Delhi, and afterwards Láhúr, he had resolved to accompany Haider Mírza and Khwája Kilán, in an attempt to conquer Kashmír. When every thing was arranged for that purpose, and the Mírza was waiting for him at the entrance into the mountains of that country, the sudden approach of Shír Shah had spread a general alarm, in consequence of which Khwája Kilán had fled towards Kámrán on the Jelem, and, either faithless to his engagements with Humáyun, or seized and carried off against his will by Kámrán, as was pretended, had accompanied him to Kábul. Humáyun, thus cut off from communication with Haider Mírza, and fearing a design on the part of Kámrán to deprive him of his personal liberty, had proceeded through the desert, and joining Hindal and Yádgár Násir Mírza, marched on in hopes of gaining possession of Bheker and Tatta. Mírza Haider, thus deprived of the reinforcements he had reckoned upon, as well as of the advantage of the Emperor's name, determined to proceed in his enterprise, with such imperfect means as he possessed.

The beautiful region of Kashmír had long been a prey to intestine commotions, chiefly occasioned by the two rival families of Chak and Makri, which contended for the office of Prime Minister under princes, who, whether from nonage or other incapacity, were quite unfit to direct the affairs of such a kingdom. In the course of these contentions, the party of Abdal Makri having been expelled, had, through the medium of Haider Mírza, applied for assistance, first from Kámrán, and afterwards from Humáyun, while he yet filled the throne of Delhi. The Mírza, who was Báber's cousin-german, was not a stranger to Kashmír. About eight years before, Saíd Khan, the sovereign of Káshghar, encouraged by the distracted state of the country, had sent his son Sekander Sultan, accompanied by Haider Mírza, at the head of an army of 12,000 men, which advanced from the north by the valley of Lár, and took possession of the capital. This Tartar force committed the devastation usual to barbarous troops, and was soon loaded with booty. Muhammed Shah, the king of Kashmír, and his chiefs, with numbers of the inhabitants, fled to recesses in the surrounding mountains, whence they descended to harass and attack the invaders. Haider, after being nearly three months in possession of the country, made a treaty with the Kashmírian lords, and their nominal king, by which it was agreed, that Sekander Sultan should marry that monarch's daughter, and that the Tartar army should return back to Káshghar.

CHAP. III. SECT. III.

A. H. 939, A. D. 1533.

Shábán 9. March 6.

End of Shawál, about May 20.

Haider Mírza, after his return to Káshghar, had an eventful life. He was finally obliged to quit the country, and, passing through Badakhshán, repaired, as we have seen in an earlier part of this history, first to the court of Kámrán, and afterwards to that of Humáyun, whom he attended in his disastrous campaign of Kanáuj, and afterwards in his flight to Láhúr, where he prevailed upon him to attempt the conquest of Kashmír. When he found, however, that Humáyun had taken the route of Bheker, and so abandoned his enterprize of Kashmír, he resolved to prosecute it himself with such means as were in his power, trusting for success to the distracted state of the kingdom, and the assistance of the refugee chiefs and their partizans, by whom he had been invited. He, accordingly, put in motion his troops, which

and of Haider Mírza.

BOOK V. amounted to about 4,000 men. Malek Achi Chak, who then governed the kingdom in the name of Názúk, the nominal king, collected an army of 3,000 horse, and a large body of infantry to oppose him, and took possession of the Karmal pass, to obstruct his entrance into the country. But Haider Mírza, proceeding unobserved by unfrequented routes, after overcoming great difficulties, surmounted, on the twenty-second day of November, the steep pass of Panúj, which Malek Achi had neglected, thinking it impracticable to cavalry; descended on Srínagar, the capital of Kashmír, and without bloodshed or opposition, took possession of it, and of the country. Malek Achi's army, filled with consternation, disbanded, and he himself, seeing no hopes of regaining his ascendency by the strength of his own party, repaired to the court of Shír Shah, carrying with him a daughter of the late king, whom he gave in marriage to the Afghán prince. Aided by Shír Shah, he was enabled to re-enter Kashmír at the head of 2,000 horse. He was soon joined by his adherents, and his force rose to 5,000 cavalry. But Haider Mírza and the Kashmírian chiefs in his interest, attacked, and completely routed the invaders; and the Mírza, in spite of numerous intrigues and factions, beame the ruler of the whole of Kashmír.

A. H. 947, Rejeb 22. A. D. 1540. Nov. 22.

A. H. 948, Rebi II. 20. A. D. 1541. August 13.

Mírza Haider had now ruled Kashmír seven or eight years with all the authority of an absolute prince, though he administered the government at first under the name of Názúk Shah, the native king, and, after the return of Humáyun to Kábul, in the name of that prince, when, anxious to form a still closer connection with the Emperor in his future plans, he deputed Mír Samander on a mission to Kábul. The envoy met Humáyun soon after his return from Talikán. The Mírza in his letters, with every profession of loyalty and attachment, invited his majesty to Kashmír, and gave a glowing description of the charms of its climate, of its

A. H. 955, A. D. 1548. He invites Humáyun to Kashmír, and the invasion of India.

spring and autumn, with their flowers and fruits, and of all the delights of that favoured region. But the grand recommendation which he pointed out, was that it would serve as an impregnable position from which His Majesty could pour down his troops for the conquest of Hindustán, an enterprize which he urged him to attempt without delay.

Nothing could have been more in accordance with the wishes of Humáyun. The invasion of that country, and the expulsion of the Afghán dynasty, had long been the favourite dream of his ambition. But to march across the Indus at that moment was to endanger his kingdom of Kábul and his own existence. Every thing had been arranged for an attack on Bálkh; and as it was of the first importance to settle his territories beyond the mountains, and to secure his other dominions from the intestine dangers to which they were so subject, before he ventured to engage in distant expeditions, he resolved to proceed with the expedition he had undertaken. He, however, returned a favourable answer to Haider Mírza's invitation, of which he assured him he was determined to avail himself as soon as his expedition against Bálkh was over, and his troops ready to take the field for a new enterprise. Such, undoubtedly, was Humáyun's intention. But it was long before he could carry it into effect. He had still many reverses to undergo; nor was Haider Mírza doomed to aid him in its execution. That eminent man continued for some time longer to rule in Kashmír. He added Great and Little Tibet, Rájuri * and Pakheli to his dominions. He was a prince of distinguished talent. Finding the country which he had conquered to be in a very wretched condition, he devoted himself assiduously to its improvement, and attempted to restore the industry of his subjects. He encouraged agriculture, invited mechanics and artizans from a distance, and employed them in the construction of public and

His character and administration.

* Rájour.

BOOK V. private works. Under his care, says Abulfazl, the country became a garden, and the ornament of the world. That historian blames him for the excessive attention he paid to the fine arts, and especially to music, as having occupied so much of his time as to interfere with his attention to public affairs. He was finally slain, about two or three years after the period of which we treat, in a night attack of some native chiefs who had conspired against him, and surrounded the house in which he slept. He was a man of worth, of talent and of learning, and the Taríkh-e Reshídi, a History of his own Times, which he left behind him, is one of the most valuable works of that age.*

A. H. 958, A. D. 1551.

Position of Kámrán.

The state of affairs at Kábul was not certainly such as would have justified Humáyun in undertaking new and distant adventures. The allegiance of his brother Kámrán was far from being assured, and that prince, who had so long governed Kábul, might be supposed still to have partizans in that country, who could create trouble, should the Emperor march towards Hindustán. Kámrán had already quarrelled with Chaker Khan, and they had come to open hostilities. When invited to repair to Kábul, on the promise of Humáyun to provide him with another principality, the Mírza had declined the invitation. The Emperor had resolved to make a campaign against Bálkh, which he seems to have promised to Kámrán, as his government.

Humáyun's expedition against Bálkh. A. H. 956, A. D. 1549.

As soon, therefore, in the following year as the weather permitted, Humáyun summoned his troops to attend him, and left Kábul. The object of the expedition, though probably carefully concealed, was Bálkh. That country had been wrested from the Persians by the Uzbeks, and was held by Pír Muhammed Khan, a young Uzbek prince, who had received and assisted Kámrán when driven from Kábul. Humáyun probably considered the assistance so rendered to his

* Akbernáma, f. 55.

brother, as a sufficient excuse for the attack which he meditated; while the possession of a rich and extensive territory, that would have given him the command of the whole of the left bank of the Amu down to the desert, was probably his most powerful motive. He sent to warn Kámrán and the other Mírzas in the North, to be ready to co-operate with him, as had been arranged at the end of the preceding campaign. He was detained about a month at Yúret Chálák, not far from Kábul, waiting for Háji Muhammed Khan from Ghazni; and by other business of importance; and while yet at that station, he was joined by Mírza Ibráhím from Badakhshán. The army at length moved to Istálif, were Abás Sultan, an Uzbek prince who had just married Humáyun's youngest sister*, probably suspecting that the expedition was directed against his countrymen, disappeared without taking leave. Humáyun advanced deliberately by the Penjshír route, waiting to hear that the Mírzas were in motion: and immediately on learning that they were in the field, he marched down to Anderáb, and thence by Talikán to Nári †; and crossing the high grounds between the Bángi and Ghuri rivers by the pass of Nári, halted in the Nílber valley, celebrated, beyond all the valleys of that region, for its beauty in the spring. Here he was joined by Mírza Hindal from Kunduz, and by Mírza Suleimán from Badakhshán, but Kámrán did not make his appearance. Kámrán, though he had quarrelled with Chaker Ali Beg Kulábi, the son of Sultan Weis Beg, the chief of the country, and the minister assigned him by Humáyun, and though he had even driven him out of Kuláb, had, however, kept up a correspondence with the Emperor, assuring him of his fidelity, and of his being prepared to co-operate with him. Trusting to these assurances, Humáyun had marched on, expecting

Kámrán fails to join him.

* Gulchehreh-Begum.

† Or Nárín.

BOOK V.

A.D. 1549.

to be joined by his brother. When he at length found that Kámrán failed to appear, both he and the Mírzas began to feel considerable anxiety. Mírza Ibráhím was sent back, at Mírza Suleimán's request, to provide for the safety of Badakhshán, and to embody a force in that country.

Siege and surrender of Eibek.

Having arrived at Baghlán *, the Emperor pushed forward the Mírzas Hindal and Suleimán with a strong force to Eibek, a fertile and populous district in the territory of Bálkh, defended by a strong fort. As the detachment approached the chief town, it met Pír Muhammed Khan's Atálík or Minister, who, hearing of the Emperor's approach to the Uzbek territory, had hastened, attended by the chief officers of his government and a large body of troops, to place Eibek and the frontier in a state of defence, and to check the invaders. On his arrival near that town, however, he unexpectedly encountered the Emperor's troops, and, contrary to his intention, was compelled to throw himself into the castle of Eibek, unprovided as it was. Humáyun instantly sat down before the place, and pushed on his approaches with such vigour, that in a few days the besieged, who had neither water nor provisions, asked quarter, which was granted, and the city surrendered. †

Delays of Humáyun.

At an entertainment given by Humáyun on this occasion, when the cup had gone round, he is said to have asked Khwája Bagh, the Atálík, what were the best steps to be taken to ensure the conquest of Bálkh. The Uzbek, surprised at the question, after reflecting a little, answered, that being an enemy, he was not perhaps the safest person to consult. The Emperor replied, that Uzbeks were downright honest men, and he knew him to be the frankest of the Uzbeks. The Atálík rising up said, "If you would conquer Bálkh, cut off our heads,

* Or Baklán.

† Akbernáma, f. 77.; Bayezíd, f. 42.

hasten on to the capital, and it will be yours." "You are Musulmans," said the Emperor, "how can I put so many believers to death?" "If you will not do this," said the Atálík, "I have another proposal to suggest. Pír Muhammed Khan is much directed by me. I will undertake that all the country on your side of Khulm shall be ceded to you; that the Khutba shall be used in your name; and that he will send a thousand chosen men to attend you when you march against Hindustán." This proposal, too, the Emperor rejected. It was generally believed that, had he pushed on at once to Bálkh, after taking Eibek, Pír Muhammed, who was filled with consternation by the blow he had received from the loss of all his best troops and officers, who was himself unprepared, and had received no assistance from the Uzbeks beyond the river, must have submitted at discretion to any terms proposed. Humáyun sent the Uzbek Sultans, Amírs and Bís, or chiefs of tribes, whom he had taken, to Kábul, keeping with him only the Atálík.*

Sudden attack of the Uzbeks.

The Emperor halted several days at Eibek, chiefly in consequence of his anxiety at the non-arrival of Kámrán. At length, however, he again put his army in motion, and advanced towards Bálkh, by the way of Khulm. When they reached Astáneh, the shrine of Shah Aulía, the ground for the camp was taken near a stream that flowed hard by; the Audience Hall had not yet been put in order; the people of the bazar were just come up, and were busy arranging their loads; and the Emperor, who had been on a visit to the holy shrine, was in his private tent, quite unconscious of the vicinity of an enemy, when a loud shouting and uproar was heard in the direction of the camp-bazar. An attack had been unexpectedly made in that quarter. Kabuli, an officer of rank, who had hastened to the rescue, had fallen; and his head was cut off and carried to Bálkh.

* Bayezíd, ff. 42, 43.; Akbernáma, f. 78

BOOK V. A.D. 1549. An Uzbek, Khan Behåder, who had been disabled by a sabre cut and made prisoner, was brought before the Emperor. Humáyun asked him who it was that had made this attack on the camp. The prisoner answered that it was Shah Muhammed Sultan, of Hissár, the son of Berendúk Sultan. The Emperor asked if he was mad. "Sire," said the Uzbek, "he is a young man of high spirit and full of confidence. Since leaving Hissár he has not yet seen Pír Muhammed Khan, and is anxious to signalize himself before entering Bálkh." Humáyun thus learned that the Uzbeks from beyond the Amu were beginning to arrive.

Continued absence of Kámrán. The army, however, continued its march, and next morning advanced towards the numerous canals* and streams that intersect the country near Bálkh. Though the progress of the army had been slow, expecting the arrival of Kámrán, it had now reached Bálkh, and he had not yet arrived. It seemed evident that he had no intention of coming, and a general apprehension was diffused among the troops that he intended, while they were engaged in the siege of Bálkh, to give them the slip, and march once more to Kábul. So that, says Bayezíd, who was then in the camp, they were more afraid of the Mírza than of the Uzbeks.†

Repulse of the Uzbek advance. In the course of the day, about afternoon prayers, Mírza Suleimán, Mírza Hindal, and Háji Muhammed Sultan Koka, who had the advance, attacked the advance of the Uzbeks, commanded by Abdalla Sultan and Khosrou Sultan, sons of Sekander Sultan, near the Takhteh-pul, and drove them across the bridge, which they also passed to the Bálkh side of the stream. For his exertions on this occasion Háji Muhammed was honoured with the patent of Khan. The whole army advanced by the canals of Bálkh to within about half a kos from the town, and encamped for the night. A

* Júibárha.

† Bayezíd, ff. 33, 34.

council was now called. The general opinion was, that as Kámrán had not joined, he either had marched, or would march, to Kábul; that the disastrous consequences which would result from his occupation of that city must be prevented at all hazards; and that the present was the proper time for retreat, while Abdal-azíz, the son of Obeid-Khan, the grand Khan of the Uzbeks, who was now on his march from Bokhára, had not yet crossed the Amu. The danger of Kábul affected all, from the Emperor to the lowest soldier, who had families in that city. It was resolved to retreat, and to take up a position near the entrance of the hills at Dera-Gez, a valley with narrow defiles, which were easily to be defended. From that position they could either march on Kábul, should Kamrán have moved in that direction; or, if he had not, they could there remain encamped; reinforce the army by assistance from the Aimák tribes, or by recruits from other quarters; and, as soon as the Uzbek auxiliaries had recrossed the Amu and returned home, march down with renewed vigour and superior advantages to the conquest of Bálkh, and perhaps of all Máwerannaher. At midnight the council broke up, orders were issued for a retreat, and it instantly commenced. The rear was entrusted to Mírza Hindal, Suleimán Mírza, and Husein Kuli Sultan, the keeper of the seal.*

Humáyun resolves to retreat.

It was morning when the army reached the broken

* In this account of the proceedings at Bálkh, the account of Bayezíd is chiefly followed; it is a very probable one, and he was in the camp, and had the means of being well informed. Abulfazl, (ff. 78, 79), who is followed by Ferishta and others, makes Abdal-azíz join before the retreat, and a general action is described, in which the Uzbeks had 30,000 men (Tar. Niz. f. 201.), but were defeated, and driven into the town. Abulfazl says that Humáyun proposed to improve the advantage by an immediate attack, which was not done; while Jouher ascribes the proposal to Hindal, adding that the Emperor would not allow the place to be attacked that night. This proposal might have followed the success of the advance described in the text, when the kochekhend, or outer fortified enclosure of the town, was entered.

BOOK V. A. D. 1549.

ground on the banks of the river that flows through the Dera-Gez. In the course of the night the Uzbeks had been apprised of the retreat of their enemy, and issued out in force to pursue them. To retreat in order and with coolness in the face of an enemy, is one of the most difficult achievements even of veteran regular troops, but with an irregular army is hardly possible. The imperial soldiers no sooner found that they were on their march for the Dera-Gez, with their faces turned towards Kábul, than, believing that Kámrán was already master of that place and of their families, they were seized with consternation, and numbers of them, separating from the army, made the best of their way home across the hills, in bands or singly. All attempts to arrest or bring them back were fruitless. The panic had become complete. The Uzbeks, who went in pursuit of the retreating army, were not long of overtaking the rear-guard in the morning, when it had reached the Dera-Gez. The Uzbeks charged, and met with a short and slight resistance. It soon gave way and dispersed, the Uzbeks killing or unhorsing all whom they overtook. Humáyun was at the time not far off, standing on the other side of the river with a body of his servants. News was brought to him that the Uzbeks were close upon Mírza Hindal, and that Malek Mírza had been taken. He was much distressed. "Mírza Hindal," said the keeper of the seal, "is no child, but a soldier, and will come on the best way he can." Humáyun ordered an officer who was standing by, to go and get word of Hindal. He was himself preparing to cross, when a party of Uzbeks, who reached the opposite bank, discharged an arrow at the Emperor, from an eminence. Bayezíd, who was present, tells us that he held up his shield to protect his Majesty's person; but the arrow struck the Emperor's horse in the breast. It was a favourite horse, which he had got, when at Herát, from the minister of the

Panic in his army.

Rout.

CHAP. III. SECT. III.

Flight towards Kábul.

young prince. The Uzbeks were, however, driven off, and the Emperor pursued his retreat. Having advanced a little way, he ordered Husein Kuli Sultan to rally the men and form them, so as to resist the Uzbeks. He answered that it would be better to allow those who were now with his Majesty to go on, as they would be unwilling to turn and leave him. "Not a man of them," continued he, "will at this moment mind my orders." "You yourself," said the Emperor, "do not now heed my orders." "Emperor of the world," answered Husein Kuli, "pardon me;" and turned back, saying to the author, "Come you along with me, and let the other servants attend his Majesty." As the fugitives came up, such as Khizer Khwája Khan, Mosáhib Beg, Muhammed Kásim Mochi, Shahem Beg Jeláir and others, Husein Kuli called upon them to turn and fight. But nothing he could say, could induce any of them to stand and help him. "All were striving," continues Bayezíd*, each to get the other's horse, pulling it to themselves. At last the Muhrdár (keeper of the seal) was compelled also to draw off." He overtook Humáyun about noon, who received him most kindly, and praised him in the most cordial manner. The Emperor's adventures for some succeeding days, when he sought to repass the mountains by unknown or little-frequented roads, a prey to thirst, hunger and fatigue, and guided by the barbarous inhabitants, are related in the liveliest and most picturesque manner by Bayezíd†, who was a sharer in his flight. At length, by the route of Kahmerd and Ghurbend, he reached the vicinity of Kábul, which he entered on the first day of the fast of Ramzán. In the midst of the general rout and panic that took place in the Dera-Gez, some chiefs are mentioned as having distinguished themselves; Hindal Mírza, Terdi Beg,

Ramzán 1. Sept. 23.

* Bayezíd, f. 45.

† Bayezíd, ff. 45—50.

BOOK V.

A.D. 1550.

Monaim Khan, Shah Bidágh and Tulik Khan Kochín are particularly named. When the rout was seen to be irreparable, the leaders dispersed, taking different roads. Mírza Suleimán returned to Badakhshán. Hindal, attended by Monaim Khan, found his way to Kunduz. Many of the Emperor's Amírs and officers, among whom was Shah Bidágh, fell into the hands of the enemy. The Atálík and other Uzbeks, who had been made prisoners at Eibek, having been allowed to return to Bálkh, made so favourable a report of the handsome treatment which they had met with, that Pír Muhammed, to show his sense of this conduct, sent back all his prisoners to Kábul, in the most humane manner; a striking instance, when contrasted with the consequences of the recent cruelties exercised at Kábul, how in war generosity produces generosity, while retaliation of injury generates the darkest passions that disgrace human nature.

Humáyun winters in Kábul.

Humáyun, on reaching Kábul, found everything safe, and that Kámrán had never in reality attempted to cross the mountains. He passed the winter in the Bála Hissár of Kábul. Kámrán, meanwhile, whose failure to join his brother had been the real cause of the late discomfiture, resolved to take advantage of the Emperor's misfortunes, to increase his own power. We have seen that he was but little satisfied with the allotment of Kuláb, which had been made to him when he was reconciled to his brother; that he had very soon become embroiled with Chaker Ali Beg, the Minister assigned him by Humáyun, and had expelled him from his province. He, nevertheless, made every profession of allegiance to the Emperor, who, confiding in his promises, had marched to Bálkh, when Kámrán's breach of promise led to the most disastrous consequences. No sooner had Humáyun recrossed the mountains, than Kámrán, who is said, for some time before, to have been carrying on a secret correspondence with several

Proceeding of Kámrán.

of his brother's chief Ministers, hastened to improve the opportunity for his own advantage. Leaving Askeri Mírza, therefore, in Kuláb, he marched to seize the dominions of Suleimán Mírza.* CHAP. III. SECT. III.

Suleimán, unable to oppose him, retired from Talikán without fighting, and fell back upon Kila-Zefer. Kámrán entered Talikán, which he gave to Bápus Beg, and advanced to Kila-Zefer. Suleimán, placing Ishak Sultan in that fortress, the principal one of Badakhshán, withdrew to the highlands and narrow valleys of the upper country, and waited at the village of Jurm, in an inaccessible position, to see what turn affairs would take in the country below. His attempt on Badakhshán,

Kámrán, finding that nothing could be effected by any operations against Suleimán in Badakhshán, marched down to Kunduz. He there attempted to work upon Hindal Mírza by professions of friendship, and by representing their interests as being the same, to enter into an alliance with him, and to desert Humáyun. Hindal, however, did not listen to his proposals, but remained faithful to his allegiance. Upon this, Kámrán laid siege to the place, and pushed on his operations with vigour, while Hindal omitted no exertion in its defence. Kámrán, seeing himself baffled in all his attempts, at last asked assistance from the Usbeks, with whom he entered into a treaty; and a large auxiliary force was soon sent to assist him in the siege. Hindal, being hard pushed by this new and active enemy, had recourse to a stratagem, which seems to be a standing one in Eastern wars. He caused a letter to be written in Kámrán's name, addressed to himself, proceeding on the supposition that the two Mírzas had made up their differences, and entering into details as to the best plan for overreaching the Uzbeks. The letter was entrusted to a kásid, or messenger, who, it and on Kunduz.

* Akbernáma, ff. 78, 79.; Tab. Akb. ff. 163, 164.; Tar. Niz. ff. 200, 201.; Jouher, c. 24.; Ferishta, vol. ii. pp. 165, 166.; Khol: ul Towáríkh, f. 267.; above all Bayezid, f. 42–50. He is very minute.

BOOK V.

A. D. 1550.

was contrived, fell into the hands of the Uzbeks. He was searched, and the letter discovered. The Uzbeks, concluding that the brothers had made a reconciliation to which they were to be sacrificed, alarmed and disgusted, abandoned the siege, and returned home. In consequence of this defection, the operations made little progress.

Returns to Kuláb.

It was about this time that news reached Kámrán, that Chaker Ali Beg had descended from the mountainous country into which he had been driven, and was plundering and laying waste the territory of Kuláb. Askeri, who had marched out to chastise him, was defeated, and compelled to take shelter in the town. By Kámrán's orders, Askeri marched out against him a second time, and was a second time routed. This compelled Kámrán to raise the siege of Kunduz; the rather as he learned that Suleimán Mírza had descended from his mountain retreat, and had formed a junction with Ishak Sultan at Kila-Zefer, of which he had taken possession. Kámrán, detaching a body of troops to check the advance of Suleimán, himself hastened to Kuláb. On his approach, Chaker Beg hurriedly raised the siege, and Askeri marched out and joined his brother.

Is defeated by the Uzbeks.

Kámrán, taking Askeri along with him, now marched back to meet Mírza Suleimán. He had reached Rostak*, near which he was encamped, when a large body of Uzbeks under Saíd, who had gone out on a foray, observing a camp at a distance. fell upon it, without inquiring whose it was, and completely plundered it. Kámrán, Askeri and Mírza Abdalla Moghul, with a few of their men, escaped to Talikán. Saíd, on learning the real state of matters, sent back the prisoners and plunder that had fallen into his hands, excusing himself to the Mírza for having, by mistake, carried off his baggage. But the mischief done was irreparable. Kámrán's army was broken and dispersed. Suleimán

* Rostak lies on the Kokcha branch of the Amu.

and Hindal, taking advantage of the mischance, advanced in conjunction against him; while he, seeing that his strength was broken, and that all hope of effecting any thing on the Amu had vanished, made the best of his way to Khost, intending to proceed from thence, over the hills, by the route of Zohák and Bámián, as that on which there was least snow, so as to reach the Hazára country, where he could learn the true state of Kábul; and either try his fate there once more, or retire to Bheker, as circumstances might dictate.*

Excites a revolt in Kábul.

It is asserted that, all this time, there was a party in Humáyun's court favourable to Kámrán. It was headed by Kerácha Khan, Mosáhib Beg, Kásim Husein Sultan Uzbek and other Amírs of the very first rank, and was in general composed of those who had already rebelled, who had joined Kámrán, and had finally surrendered along with him at Talikán. Though they had been pardoned, and had accompanied Humáyun in his Bálkh expedition, and now attended him in his court, they had never been restored to favour, and were still in disgrace. They are said to have carried on a private correspondence with Kámrán, inviting him to advance, and assuring him that, from the general disaffection towards Humáyun which now prevailed, they would undertake to restore him to his throne. Of the truth of these assertions, and indeed of the real causes and nature of the intrigues and discontents that produced the many revolutions at Kábul at this era, very little is, with certainty, known. The events of the times have been recorded chiefly by the servants of Humáyun and his son, who are disposed to represent every thing in

* Akbernáma, ff. 79, 80.; Tab. ff. 163, 164.; Tar. Niz. ff. 201, 202.; Ferishta, vol. ii. pp. 166, 167.; Ferishta says that Humáyun wrote to Ali Shír Khan, one of Kámrán's officers, making him great promises, to seize his master, and send him prisoner to court. Bayezíd, f. 50. gives the command of the Uzbeks to Mír Taulon Uzbek, not to Said.

BOOK V. A. D. 1550. the most favourable light for that prince, who, with many high and agreeable qualities, was evidently very thoughtless and very impolitic. We may sometimes, from the course of events, infer that suspicions of treachery are alleged to save the credit of the prince. At the same time, that treachery was common, and left little imputation on the character of the traitor, is no less evident from the whole history of the times.

When Kámrán, after his disaster on the Amu, was crossing the mountains, he received communications from the discontented Amírs, urging him to march at once upon Kábul, where they would join him. To lull the suspicions of Humáyun, the Mírza sent him envoys to announce his coming, the object of which he pretended was to ask forgiveness for his late offences, and to submit himself in every respect to the Emperor's orders, relying solely on his never-failing clemency. Humáyun is said to have listened with favour to these pretences, till reminded by his counsellors how little A. H. 957, faith could be placed in his brother's representations; and that any new indulgence which the Emperor might grant him, might be ascribed rather to weakness than generosity. Humáyun prepares to seize him. Humáyun, therefore, made preparations for intercepting the Mírza, and leaving Kábul to the nominal charge of Akber, under the direction of Muhammed Kásim Khan Birlás, he marched for the hills by Kárábágh and Charikárán, and halted for a time at Ab-Bárán.*

Divides his forces. Here Kerácha and the Emperor's other advisers,—for Kerácha seems still to have had influence,—recommended that the different passes in the mountainous country should be occupied, so as to prevent the Mírza's escape. Abulfazl asserts that this advice was given for the purpose of weakening the Emperor's force. But, if Kámrán was suspected of attempting, with his broken

* Abulfazl says he left Kábul in the middle of 957.

bands, to reach the Hazáras, it was only by some such operation that he could have been intercepted. Accordingly Háji Muhammed Khan was sent towards Zohák and Bámián with one strong division, and Monaim Khan towards Sal-Auleng with another. It is affirmed that at this time, Kerácha Khan and the conspirators sent daily reports to Kámrán of all that passed in the imperial camp; and that, when every thing was prepared for the Mírza's success, by the dispersion of the army, he was instructed to turn away from Zohák and Bámián which he had reached, and hastening by forced marches towards the Dera Kipchák, a dependency of Ghurbend, where Humáyun lay with his diminished force, to fall upon him by surprise. It is said that the Emperor's suspicions were lulled asleep by the constant asseverations of those about him, that Kámrán's only anxiety was to throw himself at the Emperor's feet. But the division of the troops for the purpose of intercepting him, shows that this was not altogether relied upon; and it seems clear that Humáyun was not only ill-informed of his brother's movements, but supposed his force to be much less than it really was.

Is surprised by Kámrán.

The Emperor had passed up the defile of Kipchák, and was encamped at the upper end of it, when, about nine in the morning, a servant of Mír Asghar Munshi, one of the officers appointed to guard the pass, arrived full speed and out of breath, calling out, "The Mírza is coming," which spread an alarm among the men. Humáyun, being angry, ordered the man's head to be struck off. The troops were instantly armed, and marched for the Dera, or valley. They soon came within sight of the Mírza's advance. When Humáyun had got a bowshot within the valley, a hill was seen another bowshot farther off, behind a projection of which the Mírza's advance, under his son-in-law Ak Sultan, had taken their station. The ground in front of this projection was broken and rocky. Hussein

BOOK V.
A. D. 1550.

Kuli Sultan, the Keeper of the Seal, Kunduk Sultan brother of Biram Ughlan, Mírza Kuli Choli, Pír Muhammed Akhteh and others bravely pushed on to drive them from their position; but, the ground being steep and difficult, they did not succeed. Pír Muhammed was slain by an arrow. Mírza Kuli's horse fell and broke his rider's leg. His son, who was with the guards, while charging to remount and carry off his father, was also slain. The Muhrdár's horse was wounded, and threw him. Bayezíd, who attended him, brought another horse, and succeeded in remounting him, and in carrying him off to the Emperor's lines.

Want of zeal among Humáyun's chiefs.

The Emperor himself now advanced. When he reached the spot where the slain were lying, Kámrán made his appearance on the projecting hill with his wives and daughters, followed by the rest of his troops. The Emperor's matchlock-men, says Bayezíd, did not load their pieces with ball, most of them having been in the service of the Mírza at Kábul. The Mírza's people keeping up an uninterrupted discharge of arrows, most of the horses and men of His Majesty's party were soon wounded. At this period, continues Bayezíd, Kásim Husein Khan was on the other side of the river, and had before him a good way by which he might have reached the Mírza's advance, but he made no onset, and stood still. None other of the Sirdars ventured to charge the Mírza. Kámrán, perceiving that they were shaken, marched down the declivity, and pushed on straight for the standards. The standard-bearers, not thinking themselves able to keep their ground, turned and fled: and Kásim Husein Khan with his force fled also.

Flight, and wound of Humáyun.

The rout was now general, and Humáyun joined in the flight, returning back the road by which he had come. One Babái of Kuláb, overtaking him,—whether he knew who he was is uncertain,—struck him a heavy blow on his cap * which wounded him behind the ear, and

* Táj.

had raised his sword to repeat the blow, when Humáyun, turning round, and looking his assailant sternly in the face, exclaimed, "Wretched rebel!" Babái, from surprise, suspended his blow for a moment, when Mehter Sagái, the wardrobe keeper, afterwards known as Ferkhat Khan, interposed, and Babái drew off. Humáyun was supported, and born away on horse-back. Muhammed Amír and Abdal Wáháb protected his retreat. Humáyun, however, was so severely wounded, and so faint from loss of blood, that, in the course of his flight, he threw off his jabba, a quilted or padded corselet, which he gave to one of his servants to carry. The man, being pursued, soon afterwards threw it away, to lighten himself in his flight; an incident that was afterwards followed by very important consequences.

Humáyun now resolved to push for Zohák and Bámián, where he expected to find Háji Muhammed and his division, who had gone up by the Sirtán pass. As he had become faint, and was unable to bear the motion of his own spirited horse, he exchanged it for a small ambling pye-bald one, offered him by Mír Syed Birkeh, on which he was lifted, and the Mír and Khwája Khizer, riding on each side of him, supported him as he went along. Towards the end of the night, he reached the entrance of the Sirtán pass, having been joined by a few of the fugitives. The cold air and fatigue had by this time much affected him, and he again felt faint from his wound. Mír Birkeh took off his cloak, and threw it over him. It was morning when he gained the top of the pass, where he soon began to feel the heat of the morning sun, and halted by the side of a stream, where he had his wound washed and dressed, and said his orisons: and, not long after, Háji Muhammed Khan arrived with three hundred well equipped veteran horse. This placed Humáyun in comparative security.* He is joined by a reinforcement.

* The spirit of defection was still in operation. He one day sent out Shah Bidágh Khan, Tulik Kochín, Majnún and others to the number

BOOK. V.

A.D. 1550.

As he still suffered much from his wound, he remained for some days in the hills about Zohák and Bámián. Meanwhile, however, he consulted with his Amírs, what steps were most advisable to be taken. Háji Muhammed advised going to Kandahár; others were for pushing on for Kábul, while some were for retiring upon the provinces on the Amu. Shah Muhammed, Háji's brother, was sent down with Háji's men to pass through Kábul, and to proceed to secure Ghazni. Humáyun wrote by him to Akber, to announce at once his defeat, and his safety. Having himself finally resolved to proceed to the northern provinces, he went on to Kahmerd.* On his route, he was entertained by the wandering Aimáks, according to their notions of hospitality. While with them, he learned the approach, first, of one caravan with 300 horses, and afterwards of another with 1700, on their way from the west of Hindustán. Of these Humáyun seized as many as suited his purpose, giving his bond for the amount. From Kahmerd he proceeded by Alenjek, where he halted a week, and then went on, and encamped on the banks of the Bángi. Here, as they were mistaken for a caravan, a voice was heard from the other side of the river, inquiring, what news they had of the Emperor. Humáyun ordered that no answer should be given, but that in return they should ask, Who the enquirer was, —by whom sent,—and what he had heard of the Em-

Proceeds to the north.

of ten, on a reconnaissance towards Kábul. Of the whole number Tulik Kochín only returned.

* The ewer-bearer relates several amusing anecdotes chiefly regarding the difficulties to which Humáyun was reduced, and to his want of clothing. It was long before they could get for him, wounded as he was, a samiána, or awning fit to cover one person; his coat being clotted with blood, he was glad to get back a cast off coat, which he had given a domestic, by whom it had been worn; his trowsers being spotted with blood, an old woman brought and presented to him a pair of her own silk drawers. "These," said he, "were never intended for man to wear, but necessity has no law;" and he drew them on. He gave the woman a present, with a certificate relieving her from all taxes. Jouher, c. 24.

peror? The man informed them that he was of the Meshi tribe; and had been sent by Nazeri Sal-Alengi to get news of the Emperor, as a report had reached them that His Majesty had been defeated, had left the field of battle wounded, and had never since been heard of; but that the quilted cuirass, which he wore in the fight, had been found, covered with blood, and carried to Kámrán, who was overjoyed, believing that the Emperor had perished. The man was desired to come over, brought into the Emperor's presence, and asked if he knew who it was. "Can the Grace of God be obscured?" said he;* on which he was dismissed, and ordered to spread the news as widely as he could; and to desire his master to meet the Emperor when he returned that way.

And prepares to returns to Kábul.

At Khinjan the Emperor met Mírza Hindal who accompanied him to Anderáb, where he was joined by Mírza Suleimán and his son Ibráhím Mírza; as well as by all the detachments which had been sent out before the action to intercept Mírza Kámrán; and every preparation was now made for recrossing the mountains to Kábul.†

Conduct of Kámrán.

But it is time to return to Kámrán, whom we left on the field of battle at the Dera Kipchák. When told that Humáyun was entirely defeated and had fled, he could hardly believe his own good fortune. The defeated troops fled by three different roads; by that of Ghurbend; by the direct road to Kábul, and by the road to Istálif. Parties were sent in pursuit of them all. Numbers were overtaken and slain, or stript of whatever they possessed. The Hazáras too, ever ready for indiscriminate plunder, infested the ways, stopped

* This answer is that recorded by Abulfazl. The ewer-bearer merely says that the man did recognize him.

† Akbernáma, ff. 80, 81.; Tar. Nizámí, ff. 201, 202.; Tab. Akberi, 164, 165.; Jouher, c. 24.; Bayezíd, ff. 50—53.; Kholáset-ul-Towáríkh, f. 267. Both Jouher and Bayezíd were in the action.

BOOK V. A.D. 1550.

all whom they met, and robbed them of their horses, arms, and clothing. Kámrán's flatterers soon restored him to his accustomed presumption. Before he left the ground, Bába Saíd brought in Kerácha, who was wounded. The Mírza addressed him courteously, inquiring if his wound was severe, and soon restored him to his wonted favour and authority. Soon after, Husein-kuli Sultan, the keeper of the seal, a man much esteemed both by Humáyun and his father, was brought in as a prisoner: when Kámrán himself struck him with his sabre, and commanded him to be hewn to pieces in his own presence. Takhjí Beg, another old and respected Amír, shared the same fate. Bába Kulábi arrived with information that the Emperor was wounded; immediately upon which, Yasan Doulat was despatched with a party to attempt to overtake him in his flight. Kásim Husein Sultan, who had taken little part in the action, retired when it was over to a neighbouring hill; from which he was soon after induced to descend, and enter the Mírza's service.

The Mírza proceeded, without loss of time, to Charikár, where a man arrived bringing the Emperor's bloody cuirass, which completed the Mírza's satisfaction. He hastened on to Kábul, and at once sat down before it. Kásim Khan Birlás who commanded in the place, though formerly a servant of Kámrán, determined to hold out faithfully for the Emperor, unmoved by the reports which universally prevailed; till they were confirmed by the bold assertions of the Mírza, and by a sight of the bloody cuirass, which was sent in for him to examine. Convinced by the statements that were made, and by this melancholy confirmation of them, and believing resistance to be now fruitless, he surrendered the town, and Akber became a third time a prisoner in the hands of his uncle.*

He occupies Kábul.

* Akbernáma, &c. as above.

Kámrán now lost no time in increasing his army, and in dividing the different governments of Kábul among his partizans. His prime adviser was Kerácha. He gave Júi-Sháhi (now Jelálábád) to Askeri, Ghazni to Kerácha, and Ghurbend to Yasan Doulat. He seized all Humáyun's treasures, and, having imprisoned his Diwán, extorted large sums from him. He drew to himself whatever he could, by all kinds of tyranny and extortion; so that, if he enriched his treasury, he impoverished his kingdom.



Advance of Humáyun.

But he was not left long to carry on these operations in peace. Three months had not passed when news was brought to Kábul that Humáyun still lived, and was marching from Anderáb, at the head of a formidable army. Kámrán immediately concentrated his army, and being joined by a number of Hazáras and other mountaineers, moved forward to meet him, before he could descend to the low country.

His compact with his chiefs.

By the time Humáyun had lain about six weeks at Anderáb, he had been joined by many detached bodies of his army, and had collected such a force, that, his wound being now cured, he resolved once more to march over the hills to Kábul; and, it being still summer, to take the direct route of Hindu-koh. There had recently been so many instances of defection and desertion, even among Amírs of the highest rank, that, apprehensive of being again abandoned in trying circumstances, as he alleged that he had already been, he resolved to administer to them a test-oath, to secure their fidelity by superstition, as Abulfazl insinuates, since true religion and a sense of duty had been insufficient to retain them in their allegiance. This oath was to be administered to each body of men in the way supposed by them to be most binding upon their consciences; and, by the terms of it, they engaged to follow and obey him, as their prince and leader, faithfully, sincerely and honestly. By this solemn act, he pro-

BOOK V. A.D. 1550.

posed not only to influence such as took the oath, but to inspire all his friends and followers with confidence. To carry this design into effect, he assembled the Mírzas, Amírs and chief men, who were with the army, and explained to them his purpose. Háji Muhammed Khan Koka, who, says Abulfazl, was deficient both in respect and fidelity, observed that when all had taken the oath as required, it might be proper for his Majesty to take an oath on his part, engaging "that whatever we, his well-wishers, recommend with a view to his interest, and deem indispensable for that purpose, he will consent to, and perform." Mírza Hindal, firing at this suggestion, exclaimed, "Háji Muhammed! what means all this? What are you saying? Never surely did servants address a master, or slaves their lord, in language like this!" Humáyun, however, interposed; "Let it be," said the Emperor, "as Háji Muhammed and the other chiefs desire. Whatever they shall advise for my interest and with good intent, that will I execute." *

When this mutual agreement, unparalleled perhaps in Asiatic history, had been ratified and confirmed, the army marched on. On the part of Humáyun it was an attempt to secure the fidelity of the army and its leaders, under all circumstances. The singular demand of Háji Muhammed, imperfectly explained by contemporary writers, seems to indicate a general want of confidence in the judgment and steadiness of the Emperor, which indeed, if we consider the whole previous course of his history, is not wonderful. Háji Muhammed was a foster-brother in the family, and may, therefore, be supposed to have been sincerely attached to it. But his freedom on this occasion was not grateful to royal ears, and was probably never forgiven. Abulfazl, the Minister of Humáyun's son, always speaks

* Akbernáma, f. 82. Jouher also, c. 25. mentions the incident with some slight variation.

of him with distrust and dislike, though he seems to have been one of the Emperor's most efficient servants. CHAP. III. SECT. III.

"Could any limits have been imposed upon the absolute power of the prince, the present was not, perhaps, an unfavourable crisis. It, in many respects, resembled those situations in which the barons of England extorted charters and concessions from the King. A civil war raged. The monarch had been eminently unsuccessful in his enterprises, had suffered many defeats, and been repeatedly driven from his throne. His talents for government were not of a high class; and his popularity was, probably, not great in his new kingdom. His nobles, who were powerful, had been sufferers by his repeated failures, yet on them was placed his only hope of restoration. They had still much of the Tartar independence, and exercised the right of transferring their allegiance from one competitor to another, as their private interest seemed to require. It was in their power at any time, if not to raise, at least to pull down their monarch. All this made it easy to humble the crown. But when that was done, the result was little favourable to liberty, or to any settled government. The power, which the Sovereign lost, the nobility did not gain. They had no principle of cohesion among themselves. There was no body connected as a peerage, no hereditary rank, nor great ancestral possessions, that secured to certain families a large and regular dependence of followers. There was no Great Council in which they could meet and deliberate, and take common measures for the benefit of their order. Nor was this defect of concert and stability confined to the nobles. In like manner, there was no church. There were many revered Khwájas and Múllas, whose fame and influence was extensive; but it was confined to the individual. There were no assemblies of the church or of churchmen, interposed between the King and the nobles, or between the nobles and the people, acting, by turns, as a pro-

BOOK V. A. D. 1550.

tection, or a check, to them all. The popular, or municipal, power had no existence. There were no large towns, governed by their own magistrates, and asserting particular privileges,—no corporations, that united large bodies of the lower classes in a common interest, and gave them the means of a common defence. There, was, in reality, no common-weal at all,—no foundation for free institutions. The people had nothing to do with law or authority, but to obey them. Nothing was fixed or stable, but despotism. All power was in the Sovereign, and in the irregular and, as short-lived, so, generally rapacious power of the Amírs, derived from him, founded on his grant, and personal to the individual from whom it could at any time be withdrawn. There were, therefore, no materials, out of which the fabric of liberty could be built. Any power taken from the Sovereign went to particular nobles, and continued equally despotic in their hands. A regular body of laws, free institutions, or permanent protection against misrule, was never dreamt of. The prince was the shadow and representative of God upon earth. If, for any cause, he was deposed, another was substituted in his place, everything else remaining unchanged. The great peculiarity, in the present instance, was, that the great Amírs did not displace the monarch, but placed restraints upon his power. This led, necessarily, to a standing council, which, had not everything else been adverse, might have proved the first step, one element of a better government; for any permanent institution, whatever it may be, that acts as a check upon absolute power, must in its tendency be favourable to liberty, by setting limits to oppression.

The armies of Humáyun and Kámrán meet.

Humáyun, having surmounted the northern slope of Hindu-kúsh, descended on the south into the valleys of Penjshír and Ashterkerám. On arriving near Shutergerden, he saw the army of Kámrán drawn up on a hill right in the line of march. CHAP. III SECT. III.

Humáyun endeavours unsuccessfully to negociate.

The two armies being now close upon each other, Humáyun, desirous to save the effusion of human blood, sent Mírza Shah Sultan *, of the family of the Syeds of Termiz, to the camp of Kámrán to propose a pacification. The men of these holy families were the great negociators of the time, and the respect paid to the sanctity of their character, in the midst of the ravage and rapine that prevailed, often enabled them to alleviate the mischiefs of war. The Mírza was, besides, related to the imperial family. The proposals which he carried were, that Kámrán should acknowledge the supremacy of his elder brother; and that they should unite their armies, and in conjunction undertake the conquest of Hindustán. To this Kámrán consented, but on condition that he should keep Kábul, while Humáyun retained Kandahár. Humáyun sent back his envoy a second time, accompanied by his Sadr, to propose by way of compromise, that the young Prince Akber should be left in the government of Kábul, which, as well as their conquests in Hindustán, should be common to both. Kámrán, it is said, was disposed to have acceded to these terms, but was dissuaded by Kerácha Khan, who insisted on not giving up Kábul, exclaiming, "My head and Kábul;" meaning death or Kábul. A battle, therefore, became inevitable. Humáyun issued orders that the whole army should be ready for action next morning, four hours before sunrise.

Kámrán's astrologers declared that day to him unfavourable for an engagement, and he, in consequence, sought to gain time. While the armies lay thus opposed to each other, Khwája Abdal Simd, and several officers who had been separated from the Emperor at

* He is called the brother of Mír Birkeh.

BOOK V. A. D. 1550.

the surprize of Kipchák, and had taken service with Kámrán, deserted and went back to him, carrying information that there was considerable perturbation and alarm in the enemy's camp. In the course of the day, Humáyun put his troops in motion. He himself took the centre, Suleimán Mírza had the right wing, Hindal the left, Mírza Ibráhím the advance, and Háji Muhammed with some veteran officers, the reserve. Kámrán drew out his troops to meet him, himself taking the centre, and assigning the right to Askeri Mírza, the left to Ak Sultan, his son-in-law, and the advance to Kerácha Khan. "When they came near the enemy," says Jouher, "and there was but a slight space between the two armies, Háji Muhammed Khan advised that the troops should be brought to a halt, and that no fight should take place that day. As there was a compact between the Emperor and his Amírs, he saw no remedy, but ordered Beg Mirek to make the troops halt. At this moment the Mírzas came up and said, that "they were not for encamping; that the battle must be fought that day; that it was not prudent to wait to be attacked, but better for them to attack Kámrán, and to conquer or die." The orders had been issued, but difficulties occurred; the troops were not prepared to encamp. Abdal Wáháb came, and represented to His Majesty, "The army is now face to face to the enemy. We have no tents to enable us to encamp." His Majesty said, "Let us advance in order. If we are opposed, it is well. If not, we shall take up a position on the banks of the river." The army, therefore, again moved forward." *

Orders an attack.

Kámrán was posted on a lofty eminence, having the rest of his army hard by. Mírza Ibráhím, who commanded the Emperor's advance, by a desperate attack, seized the heights. He was followed by the Emperor,

* Jouher, c. 25.

who ordered the matchlock-men by whom he was attended, to open a fire on the lower ground. Kerácha, moving forward with a body of cavalry, attacked and broke the Emperor's left, and wheeling round, proceeded to charge the right wing, when he was wounded by a matchlock bullet, and soon after dismounted and made prisoner, by a man of inferior rank. As they were leading him from the field, one Kamber Ali, whose brother Kerácha had put to death at Kandahár, coming behind him and taking off his steel-cap, cleft his skull with a blow of his sabre, and cutting off his head, presented it to the Emperor, who afterwards directed it to be placed over the Iron Gate of Kábul, to verify the Khan's words, "My head and Kábul." In Kerácha the Emperor lost a formidable enemy. After a well contested battle, Kámrán, seeing the imperialists victorious on every side, abandoned the field, and fled, by the pass of Bádbáj, towards the Afghán country. A party under Hindal and Háji Muhammed, which was sent to pursue him, soon returned, having used but little diligence in the attempt to overtake him. Mírza Askeri was taken prisoner. The victors plundered the enemy's camp, and slew numbers of them. Many, who surrendered, were received into the Emperor's service. The victory was complete, and most opportune for his affairs. But what above all delighted him was the arrival of the young Akber, who was brought by Hasan Akhteh, to whose care he had been entrusted, after his father had had reason to fear that Kámrán had carried him off. He affectionately embraced his son, engaged himself by vow to make certain pious and charitable donations, and resolved on no future expedition to separate from him more.

Defeat and flight of Kámrán.

We are told that the Emperor soon after observed two camels loaded with trunks, wandering without drivers on the field of battle. "Let every man take what booty he can find," said the Emperor, "these two

BOOK V. A. D. 1550.

camels are my share." When the boxes were opened, he was alike surprised and gratified to find that they contained the very books which he had lost at the rout of Kipchák. Some of the most flagrant offenders were put to death. In the evening, the Emperor had a grand entertainment in the Garden-palace of Charikárán, to celebrate his victory; after which he lost no time in proceeding to Kábul, which he entered next day without resistance.*

Humáyun re-occupies Kábul.

The first days after his arrival in that city were spent in rewarding his friends, and punishing his enemies, some of them capitally. Mírza Suleimán, who with his son, had rendered distinguished service, was sent back to Badakhshán, loaded with rewards. Mírza Ibráhím remained some time longer, and, before his departure, was betrothed to Bakhshi Bánu Begum, the Emperor's daughter. Akber got the district of Chirkh in Lohger, as a jágír: and Háji Muhammed Khan was appointed his Minister, with the care of his education. Humáyun spent about a year in Kábul, at this time.

A. H. 958, A. D. 1551.

* Akbernáma, ff. 82, 83. Tab. Akb. ff. 164, 165.; Tar. Nizámi, f. 202.; Jouher, c. 26.; Bayezíd, ff. 53, 54.; Ferishta, vol. ii. pp. 166, 167.; Khol. ul-Tow. f. 269.

# CHAPTER III.

## HUMÁYUN IN AFGHÁNISTÁN.

---

## SECTION IV.

### SUBSEQUENT HISTORY OF KÁMRÁN. DETERMINATION OF HUMÁYUN TO RECOVER INDIA.

WANDERINGS OF KÁMRÁN. — REPOSE OF HUMÁYUN. — NEW ATTEMPTS OF KÁMRÁN. — MEASURES TO SEIZE HIM. — HE FLIES TOWARDS THE INDUS. — CHANGE IN THE POLICY OF HUMÁYUN. — TRANQUILLIZATION OF AFGHÁNISTÁN. — HUMÁYUN MARCHES AGAINST KÁMRÁN. — NIGHT ATTACK ON THE IMPERIAL CAMP. — DEATH OF HINDAL. — THE CAMP OF KÁMRÁN SURPRISED. — HE FLIES TO SELÍM SHAH. — HUMÁYUN LAYS WASTE BANGASH. — THE GAKERS OFFER TO SURRENDER KÁMRÁN. — HIS VISIT TO THE CAMP OF SELÍM SHAH. — HIS HUMILIATING RECEPTION, ESCAPE, SUBSEQUENT WANDERINGS, AND DETENTION BY THE GAKERS. — SURRENDERS TO HUMÁYUN. — IS DEPRIVED OF HIS EYESIGHT. — REMAINING INCIDENTS OF HIS LIFE. — HIS INTERVIEW WITH HUMÁYUN. — IS DESERTED BY HIS ATTENDANTS. — PROCEEDS TO SIND AND MEKKA. — DEVOTION OF HIS WIFE. — THEIR DEATHS. — HUMÁYUN PLUNDERS THE COUNTRY. — DEFECTION AMONG HIS TROOPS. — HE RECROSSES THE INDUS. — REBUILDS AND PROVISIONS PESHÁWER. RETURNS TO KÁBUL. — FAVOURABLE STATE OF HIS AFFAIRS. — HE RESOLVES TO RECONQUER INDIA.

CHAP. III. SECT. IV.

A. D. 1551. A. H. 958

Wanderings of Kámrán.

MEANWHILE Kámrán, after his defeat at Ashterkerám, having made his escape from the field, fled, attended by only eight followers, and found his way through many difficulties and dangers, towards Deh Sebz, a district in the midst of the country of the Afgháns. It is to be recollected that, at this time, the Afgháns consisted of a set of independent tribes; or, if they owned

BOOK V. A.D. 1551.

any submission to Kábul, it was only nominal. They lay chiefly in the tract to the east of Kábul and Ghazni. The wild Afgháns, through whose country Kámrán passed, met him as he fled, and plundered him and his followers of the little they had left. He found himself compelled to cut off his hair and beard; and wandering in the disguise of a Kalender, or religious mendicant, found his way through the hills to Melek Muhammed of Mandráwer, the most distinguished chief of the Lamghánát, to whom he discovered himself, who, out of consideration for the Mírza's former rank and greatness, took a warm interest in his affairs. The reverses of fortune which he had endured, did not deter the Mírza from still indulging in schemes of ambition. He was soon joined by a party of soldiers of fortune, who had escaped from the late defeat, and collected a number of adventurers from the neighbouring country, and from the wandering tribes, so that his force amounted to fifteen hundred men. He was supposed to have extended his intrigues into the court of Humáyun, a suspicion which gave that prince, still but insecurely settled on his throne, no small degree of uneasiness. It so happened that, at this very moment, Háji Muhammed Khan suddenly left the court of Humáyun without leave, and withdrew to his government of Ghazni; a step which the Emperor suspected to be connected with designs in favour of Kámrán; though he affected to talk of this insult as merely a piece of humour. He, however, despatched a considerable force to defeat the new efforts of Kámrán, who, unable to resist, fled from Mandráwer to the upper part of the valleys of Alankár and Alisheng. Being pursued thither also, he next fled eastward into the county of the Khalíl, Mehmend and Daúd-zái Afgháns, among whom he arrived in a most destitute situation. The few followers, who had attended him thus far, there dispersed, and scattered over the country. His pursuers, having followed him as far as Ghaz and Shahidán, returned home. CHAP. III. SECT. IV.

Repose of Humáyun.

Humáyun had now a short period of repose, during which, still farther to confirm Suleimán Mírza in his interest, he asked Shahzáda Khánum the Mírza's daughter in marriage, and she was betrothed to him. Mírza Askeri, still his prisoner, he sent to be guarded in Badakhshán, whence he had permission, which was equivalent to a command, to proceed to Mekka. That prince survived nearly seven years, and died at last between Damascus and the holy city.* A. H. 965, A. A. 1558.

New attempts of Kámrán.

No reverses could damp the ardour with which Kámrán strove to regain his throne. He again began to collect a new body of adventurers around him. They consisted chiefly of the Khalíl and Mehmend Afgháns, joined by numbers of soldiers of fortune of every description, who flocked to his standard in hopes of plunder or of place, should he regain the crown. With these he soon infested the whole eastern borders of Kábul, and, occasionally, pushed his plundering excursions into the heart of the more level country, retiring with his marauders, when pursued, into the narrow glens and mountain recesses which encompass the greater part of Kábul. Humáyun saw the necessity of putting a speedy and final stop to these incursions, and was sensible that the only effectual mode of doing so was to follow his enemy into the country that afforded him refuge, wherever that might be. He sent, therefore, to invite Háji Muhammed to join him in this expedition with the troops of Ghazni. But, hearing in the meanwhile that Kámrán had laid siege to a fort near the Chárbágh, not far from Júi-Sháhi (now Jelálábád), he set out in that direction with the few troops he had with him, without waiting for the reinforcement from Ghazni. Kámrán, hearing of his rapid approach,

* Akbernáma, ff. 83, 84.; Khol. ul Towáríkh, f. 270.

BOOK V. A.D. 1551.

raised the siege, and retreated downwards to Pesháwer; whence, making a circuit by Bangash and Gardíz, he proceeded towards Kábul, giving out that it was for the purpose of forming a junction with Háji Muhammed. Abulfazl affirms that that Amír was now entirely in Kámrán's interest, and had invited him to unite their forces for an attack upon the capital. However that may be, at that very time Biram Khan arrived at Ghazni, on his way from Kandahár to Kábul. He was an old friend of the governor's, who received him with much honour, and invited him to a grand entertainment within the fort, intending, says Abulfazl, to have seized him. Biram Khan, who got some intimation of evil designs, feigning an excuse, waived the invitation, and encamped by a stream near the town; where he was visited by Háji Muhammed, whom by his superior art and address, he prevailed upon to accompany him to Kábul. Humáyun, meanwhile, no sooner heard of Kámrán's movements, than he hurried back to defend his capital. The Mírza, after he had arrived within one march of Kábul, hearing that Biram Khan and Háji Muhammed were not far off on their march to join the Emperor, seeing all chance of success gone, turned back, to wander some time longer in the straths and hills of Lamghán.*

* Akbernáma, f. 84.; Nizám-ed-dín Ahmed) Tab. Akb. f. 165. and Tar. Niz. f. 203.) makes Humáyun write to Kandahár to request Biram Khan to visit Háji Muhammed and seize him. He also affirms that Haji wrote to Kámrán inviting him to come to Ghazni, when he was ready to acknowledge him as king. From whatever cause, it is clear that the ruin of Háji Muhammed was resolved upon. Perhaps his conduct in the matter of the test-oath was not forgotten. Abulfazl is so much a partizan of the Emperor and of Biram Khan, that we can hardly expect from him an impartial account of transactions in which that great man was concerned. Háji Muhammed probably stood a little in Biram's way. He had been Prime Minister, and seems to have been laid aside, first for Kerácha, and now for Biram Khan. Whether the disaffection laid to his charge was real, or only a pretext for superseding him, it is hard to determine. If real, it seems strange that he should twice have been induced to go to Kábul. He evidently at this time did not consider his life to be safe.

After Biram Khan and Háji Muhammed had reached Kábul, the latter, when one day entering the city, was stopped at the gate and turned back, with rather a pointed message from the governor. This, added to the manifest jealousy which the Emperor had shown, naturally roused his suspicion that something was in agitation against him. He, therefore, resolved to escape before the Emperor arrived; and, to prevent being detained, instead of proceeding straight to Ghazni, he set out for Kárábágh on the north, under pretence of a hunting party; passed the defile of Minár, and made his way through the hills to Bába Kochkár, whence he hastened, by the Damankoh of Behzadi and Alinder, towards Ghazni. CHAP. III. SECT. IV.

Measures to seize Kámrán.

When Humáyun soon after reached Siah-sang near Kábul, on his way back to oppose Kámrán, he was met by Biram Khan. Finding that Kámrán had retreated, and resolved to follow him wherever he was to be found, that an end might be put to those eternal alarms of which he was the cause,—he issued orders that not a man should leave the camp, or enter Kábul. As he was not at his ease in regard to Háji Muhammed, he despatched Biram Khan to prevail upon him once more to return to the camp, if possible amicably, but at all events to bring him. The Khan, by his prudent and conciliating management, and by engaging for certain conditions which he confirmed by oath, succeeded in mollifying and reassuring the Háji, and finally conducted him to the presence when all the forms of a reconciliation took place.

A few days after this event, the Emperor marched back to the Lamghánát in pursuit of Kámrán. By the time he reached Júi-Sháhi, the Mírza fled through the passes of Kuner Nurgil higher up the Kama River, while his followers dispersed. Biram Khan, now honoured with the title of Khan-Khánán, was sent with a body of troops to pursue him, which he did with so much vigour

BOOK V. A. D. 1551. Who flies towards the Indus.

that the Mírza, not finding himself safe in the territory of Kuner Nurgil, went off towards the Indus. Biram Khan rejoined the Emperor at Daka, between Júi-Sháhi and the Khaiber Pass.

It was at this time that the Emperor caused Háji Muhammed Khan and his brother Shah Muhammed to be seized. They were charged with turbulent and rebellious designs, and after the forms of a regular investigation, were found guilty, stript of all their honours and possessions, and when they had been kept a short time in prison, were put to death. Indeed, in the condition in which the countries under Humáyun then were, it was not safe for the prince, after quarrelling with any subject, to leave him powerful. It would have been only affording him the means of aiding a rival with greater effect. Humáyun, influenced probably by the stern, but successful, policy of Biram Khan, seems, at length, to have resolved to quell rebellion, and to punish disaffection with unsparing severity, in every one, from the prince to the peasant. Ghazni and the other jágírs of the two brothers, were divided among the Emperor's adherents.*

Change in the policy of Humáyun

The winter Humáyun spent in hunting and festivity, and in settling the neighbouring country. Early in the spring he had the satisfaction of receiving deputations from different tribes of Afgháns, with acknowledgements of submission and tributary offerings. The flight of Kámrán allowed things to assume a better form than they had done for a long period. Biram Khan returned to Kandahár. The countries of Ghazni, Gurdíz, Bangash and Lohger were entrusted to Hindal; Kunduz, which the Mírza had held, was given to Mír Birkeh; Júi-Sháhi to Khizer Khwája Khan. When these arrangements were made, Hindal, leaving Kunduz, repaired to Ghazni. But before Mír Birkeh arrived at

Tranquillization of Afghánistán.

* Akbernáma, f. 84.; Tab. Akb. f. 165.; Tar. Niz. f. 202, 203.; Jouher, c. 26.

Kunduz to supply his place, Mírza Ibráhím contrived to get possession of it, and it was allowed, if not by secret treaty, at least by connivance, to remain in his hands.

It was about this time that Shah Abul-Maali entered Humáyun's service. He was a Pírzáda, or son of a Pír or saintly personage, and claimed to be descended of the Syeds of Turmez who were connected with the imperial family. He was a man of decision and talent, by which, and by the unbounded influence he gained over the Emperor's mind, in spite of his presumptuous and overbearing temper, he rose to high rank and estimation.

Humáyun marches against Kámrán.

But Kámrán, meanwhile, had not been idle. In the course of his wanderings, he had contrived to collect about him a new and considerable body of adventurers, with whom he advanced, and once more entered Júi-Sháhi, the middle point between the upper and lower country. The Emperor immediately summoned Hindal and the Jágírdárs nearest to the capital, to join his array. They obeyed, and he marched against Kámrán, who, without meeting him, retreated into his usual mountain recesses. When the camp reached Surkháb, however, Kámrán, descending from the hills, made a fierce attack by night on the advance, which lay at the Siah-áb between that town and Gandemak. The troops, though surprised, defended themselves bravely, and maintained their ground; but lost many men, and a great part of their baggage.

Humáyun proceeded on his march, through a broken mountainous country, so close on the hills, and so beset with steep lowering cliffs, ravines, valleys and hill passes, that he was in constant danger of being surprised, or of having the different divisions of his army separated from each other, and cut off by the sudden attacks of an unseen foe. Passing Júi-Sháhi, he advanced as far as Jirbár, a township in the territory of

BOOK V. A. D. 1551.

Nanginhár, beyond Behsúd, guarding his camp and march with watchful care. On his arrival, he ordered the camp to be surrounded with trenches to prevent surprise, and erected a temporary fort on a rising ground.

Night attack on the Imperial camp. Zekáda 21. eve of Nov. 20.

Two Afgháns brought a report that the Mírza intended, that same night, to attack the camp with a body of Khalíl and Mehmend Afgháns. It was the eve of the 20th of November. The guards were ordered to watch in the trenches, and to be on the alert. About the end of the first watch of the night, an attack was made accordingly. The Emperor was on the rising ground; Hindal in the camp below. The onset was furious, and the contest continued hot for some time, each officer defending his own portion of the works, some part of which, however, the enemy succeeded in scaling, and entered the enclosure. Some men of note were slain; all was confusion and uncertainty, friend and foe being mixed together and covered by the darkness of the night; when the rising of the moon showed the real state of things, and the imperialists recovered their superiority.

Death of Hindal.

The assailants took to flight, but Mírza Hindal had fallen in the fray. "When the affair was over," says Jouher, "and his Majesty inquired for his brother Hindal, no one had the courage to tell him. He then called out aloud from the height; but, although surrounded by at least three hundred persons, none answered. He ordered Abdal Wáháb to go and bring news of the prince. He went, but, in returning, was shot by one of our own matchlock-men, who mistook him for an Afghán, and thus was he added to the number of martyrs. Mír Abdal-Hai was next sent, and brought back the melancholy intelligence, which he communicated by repeating two verses of a poet. The Emperor instantly retreated to his pavilion, where he was overwhelmed with grief, till his Amírs came and consoled him, saying that his brother was blest, in having thus fallen a martyr in the service of his Majesty."*

It appears that Mírza Hindal, on hearing of the intended night-attack, had carefully visited all his trenches, after which he had thrown himself down in his tent to take some rest, when he was roused by the uproar and alarm occasioned by the onset of the Afgháns. They had attacked the works on every side on foot, with shouts and war-cries; and a body had succeded in getting over the Mírza's trenches. The night was dark. The Mírza started up, and hastened to meet and repel the assailants, having only his bow and arrow in his hand. His men had hurried away in confusion, to protect their horses from being plundered, so that none of his immediate servants were with him. He soon met an Afghán face to face, and so near that it was necessary to close with him. By main strength he had gained the upper hand, when his antagonist's brother, Tirenda, a Mehmend Afghán, came to his assistance, and slew the Mírza without knowing him. When the battle was over, the Afghán brought the Mírza's ornamented quiver and arrows, unconscious to whom they belonged, and presented them to Kámrán, as the spoils of a man of rank. Kámrán no sooner saw the quiver than he recognised it as his brother's, and, dashed his turban on the ground in an agony of grief. The Mírza's body was left for some time unnoticed, where it fell. After the first confusion, when the troops began to collect, and were returning to assail the Afgháns, Khwája Ibráhím, one of his servants, as the troops which he had joined were passing near the Mírza's tent, saw, in the darkness of the night, a man

* Jouher, c. 26.; Bayezíd, who was in Monaim Khan's service, relates that the Khan, during the alarm, rode up to the rising ground, and found the Emperor in tears. Having asked the cause, "Have you not heard," said he, "of the martyrdom of Mírza Hindal?" Monaim replied, "You lament your own gain. You have one enemy less." His Majesty checked his lamentation. Bayezíd, f. 59.

BOOK V.

A. D. 1551.

in black armour lying on the ground. He did not at first stop, but pushed on towards the Afgháns, till he recollected that Hindal had that evening put on a black cuirass. Turning back, he examined the body, and found that it was the Mírza's. His right hand had been cut off, and some fingers of his left, apparently in an attempt to defend his head; and a cross blow, that had fallen on his mouth, had nearly separated the head from the one ear to the other. With great presence of mind, he lifted up the body, and carried it into the Mírza's pavilion, where he laid it down and covered it with a cloak, ordering the porters to admit no one, as the Mírza was fatigued with his exertions, and had received a trifling wound; and desired that no noise or bustle should be allowed, that could disturb him. When the enemy was finally repulsed, the Khwája mounted a rising ground, and in the Mírza's name returned thanks to the troops for their exertions which had secured the victory. His conduct was warmly applauded by the Emperor. Hindal's remains were conveyed first to Júi-Sháhi, and, after a time, to Kábul, where they were interred at the feet of his father Báber. He was thirty-two years of age at the time of his death. Ghazni, the jágír of Hindal, was given to Akber, to whom were also transferred the Mírza's adherents, and the daughter of the deceased prince was betrothed to him.*

* Akbernáma, f. 85; Jouher, c. 26.; Bayezíd, ff. 59, 60.; Tab. Akb. f. 165.; Khol-ul-Tow. f. 270.; Jouher mentions an incident connected with the death of Hindal, which is highly illustrative of that tenderness to animal life, that is common with pious Musulmans. Two days before the night attack, when the Emperor and his brother were returning from chasing a strong position for a fortified camp, they met three deer; "one, Hindal pursued; another Shah Abu-Maali; the third escaped. When Hindal was over against the deer, he shot it with an arrow in such a way that it never moved, but raising its face thrice towards heaven, yielded up its life to God. All who were present were filled with wonder, (it seeming) as if the deer had lifted up its complaint to the Almighty Creator." Jouher, c. 26. Two days after, the Mírza was slain by the Afgháns, "having no other arms to oppose to the enemy but his bow and arrow." He was born in A. H. 925, and slain 958, being about 33 lunar years of age.

CHAP. III. SECT. IV.

The day after this attack, Humáyun fell back to Behsúd, where he constructed a fort, and remained all the winter, watching the proceedings of Kámrán, who wandered from one tribe of Afgháns to another, attempting to rouse them to espouse his cause. In this position, surrounded by mountains on every side, he was beset by the Afgháns, who prowled round his camp, which they dared not attack, and harassed his troops, plundering and putting to death such of his men as fell into their hands. They often came up close to the works, and upbraided their enemy with cowardice, for not daring to come out, and fight on even ground. These insults Humáyun appears to have borne with a patience not usual to him: but his Amírs and officers, at length, began to murmur aloud. It is not improbable that he was unwilling to risk a winter retreat through the passes between Behsúd and Kábul, and perhaps he had suffered more in the late attack than his historians admit. When the spring returned, and it was possible once more to act in the wild country of the Afgháns, he thought it best to anticipate any attack they might meditate; and learning that Kámrán lay, at no great distance, with a body of troops that he had collected, he resolved, by a bold attack, to beat up his quarters, and, if possible, to secure his person. With this intent, he set out from Behsúd, and marched the whole night, in the supposed direction of the Mírza's camp. The road was long, and the weather was still piercingly cold. Kámrán had been entertained by all the neighbouring tribes in succession, staying seven or eight days with each. This rambling mode of life rendered it uncertain among whom he might be found. At the end of the night, Humáyun halted to rest his troops, and mounted again at peep of dawn. At that early hour, he was fortunate enough to fall in with two of Kámrán's followers, charged with a mission to Malek Muhammed of Mandráwer. From them he

A. H. 959, A. D. 1552.

The camp of Kámrán surprised.

BOOK V.

A. D. 1552.

was directed to the encampment of the tribe with which the Mírza was to be found, and, hastening on, reached it as the sun rose. They rushed in ere the Afgháns, who amounted to 14,000 fighting men, could recover from their surprise, and put to death all the men whom they met, making prisoners of the women and children, whom they afterwards sold as slaves.* Kámrán made a narrow escape, the assailants entering his tent at one side, while he escaped by the other; but Maksúd, his favourite, who slept in it was taken prisoner. The surprise was complete; the resistance feeble; the booty, especially in sheep and cattle, very large. This disaster was decisive of the Mírza's fate among the Afgháns, who were seized with general dismay, and did not afterwards dare to protect him. He, therefore, fled; but meeting with no succour from the Afghán tribes, crossed the Indus, and, compelled by the extremity to which he was reduced, sought refuge with Selím Shah, the Afghán King of Delhi. Humáyun, no longer apprehensive of any attack from the Afgháns, left his fortified camp of Behsúd, and returned in triumph to Kábul.†

He flies to Selím Shah.

End of A. H. 959, and of A. D. 1552. Humáyun lays waste Bangash.

Towards the end of the year, the Emperor moved down into Bangash to chastise the Afgháns in that quarter, who had sheltered and assisted Kámrán. As Bangash lies on a far lower level than Kábul, and the winter is consequently much less severe, he was able to carry on hostile operations in that country, while the grounds above were covered with snow. While he himself moved down from the capital, he ordered a second division from Ghazni, under Akber, to co-operate with him by marching on Bangash by the route of Gurdíz. The invaders spread, plundering and laying waste the country on every side, seizing the effects, and driving off the sheep and cattle of the different tribes,

* Jouher makes the prisoners, male and female, amount to 12,000.

† Akbernáma, ff. 84—87.; Jouher, c. 27.

into whose territory they came, and especially of the Abdal-Rahmáni and Bermzídi Afgháns. Monaim Khan, with a third division of the Emperor's troops, advancing from his jágír of Nanginhár by way of Tíra, attacked the habitations of Fateh Shah, an Afghán chief, who was accused of belonging to the hated sect of Chirágh-kúsh, and destroyed or plundered his whole property, he himself narrowly escaping, but severely wounded *. To complete the satisfaction which Humáyun enjoyed from these successful operations, which wasted the territory of his enemy in every direction, he was met by ambassadors from Sultan Adam Gaker, the head of the Gaker race, who brought the important intelligence that Kámrán had wandered into his territories, and that, if the Emperor would visit him, he was ready to acknowledge his Majesty, and to deliver his brother into his hands. Along with the ambassadors came Jogi Khan, a servant of Kámrán's, bearing a letter from that prince, in which he made every protestation of attachment, with expressions of regret for the past, and promises of submission for the future. This was an opportunity not to be neglected. Humáyun was convinced, from long and painful experience, that he never could be personally safe, or secure of executing any of his plans, while Kámrán was at large. Without delay, therefore, he bent his march towards the Indus, which he crossed near Dínkót, on his way to the country of the Gakers.

The Gakers offer to surrender Kámrán.

We have seen that Kámrán, after his camp had been surprised in the night-attack, and his allies routed and dispersed, finding that no more assistance could be gained from the Afgháns, who were confounded by the

Kámrán visits the camp of Selím Shah.

* Jouher tells us (c. 27.) that Humáyun, while in Bangash, heard one Pekh Mazhabi had made a place for himself in the Bangash territory, and was misleading men: on which he sent a party to punish him, who made his wives and children prisoners. He may probably be the person mentioned in the text, Mazhabi merely signifying "sectary."

BOOK V.

A.D. 1553.

blow inflicted on some of their tribes, hastened towards the Penjáb, resolved, as a last resource, to court succour from Selím Shah, the Afghán sovereign of Delhi, and the hereditary enemy of his family and race. That prince was then at Bín, a township of the Penjáb, and engaged in operations against the chief of Jámu when Kámrán's envoy arrived. Instantly perceiving the advantage to be derived from this incident, he joyfully invited him to his court, and, as he approached, sent an honorary procession to receive him. Kámrán saw with disappointment, however, that it was composed of persons of inferior rank, and, that on entering the camp, he was not met by the King. The unhappy prince soon discovered that he was no longer a sovereign, and endured all the painful feelings of degraded majesty, heightened by a sense of his own imprudence, in having thrown himself into the hands of a bitter enemy. When introduced to the presence, he found Selím seated in state, with much pomp, on his throne. Having, either intentionally or by accident, made some delay in approaching the king, he was thrice loudly reminded by the master of ceremonies *, before the whole Court, that he was in the presence of the Lord of the World. As he approached the throne without making his obeisance, the officer who introduced him, seized him rudely by the neck, and made him bend to perform the kornish, proclaiming at the same time that the son of the Makadam, or head-man, of Kábul, had come to make a petition to his Majesty. To add to his vexation, Selím for some time affected not to notice him, and when he did, looking haughtily his way, only half rose from his seat, gave him a passing welcome, directed that his tent should be placed among those of the Mír-zádas, and gave orders to present him with a caparisoned horse, a dress of honour, a female slave and an eunuch. The

His humiliating reception.

* Mír Tuzúk.

late powerful sovereign of Kábul, Kandahár, Badakhshán and the Penjáb, felt indignant and humbled, at receiving such treatment from an upstart Afghán. He was permitted to go at large, but was watched as a prisoner. Selím, who had some tincture of learning, and piqued himself on his skill in composing extempore verses, often sent for the Mírza, who was an elegant poet and an accomplished scholar, and contended with him chiefly in metrical composition, an intercourse which invariably terminated in disgust. Kámrán was not long of discovering that the promises made to him were never meant to be kept, and that he had humbled himself to become the mere dependant of an Afghán, whom he hated, and who was his mortal foe. Worn out with petty annoyances also, he became tired of life, and resolved to attempt, at whatsoever risk, to effect his escape.

His escape.

When Selím had concluded his business in the Penjáb, he set out to return to Hindustán, carrying along with him the Mírza, whom he continued to flatter with hopes of assistance, which he never meant to render. His intention was to have sent him as a prisoner to some hill-fort, to be reserved as a check upon Humáyun. As the camp approached the Satlej, Kámrán saw that no time was to be lost, and privately despatched Jogi Khan, a trusty servant, to Raja Kambhu, a hill chieftain, whose country was only twelve kos from Máchiwárá, the grand pass over the river, to ascertain if that chief would afford him protection. The Raja promised to receive him: and as soon as the camp had crossed the river at Máchiwárá, the Mírza effected his escape. Having dressed one of his servants in his own sleeping robe, and, in order the more effectually to lull the vigilance of the guards and spies by whom he was surrounded, made Bába Saíd a nobleman of his household sit up reading aloud by his bedside, as if he had lain down to go to rest, he proceeded to disguise him-

BOOK V. A. D. 1553.

self in female attire, and throwing over him the robe or veil used by Musulman women, which covers the whole body and conceals the shape, having only a small aperture left for the eyes, he walked out of the female tents unsuspected, and having at a convenient place mounted a fleet horse, found his way to the concerted place of refuge among the hills.*

His subsequent wanderings,

The Raja received him as he had promised, and entertained him hospitably for some time; till, learning that a force was on its march to demand that the Mírza should be given up, unable to resist the power of Delhi, he sent off the prince to another hill-chief, the Raja of Kalúr †, who possessed the strongest place in that quarter, but who soon after, from a similar apprehension of incurring the resentment of Selím, sent him on to Jámu. The Raja of that territory, however, afraid of once more drawing on himself the hostility of the Afghán, from which he had before suffered, would not grant permission to the Mírza to enter his dominions. Kámrán, finding himself thus situated, set out for Mánkót ‡, where he very narrowly escaped being made a prisoner. He was compelled once more, therefore, to disguise himself as a female, and set out on horseback with an Afghán horse-dealer, who was returning to Kábul. In passing through the Gaker country, he discovered himself to the Sultan, and claimed his assistance to regain his throne. That chief, who had been an ally of Báber's, detained the Mírza as a prisoner at large, at the same time giving information to Humáyun, as has been mentioned, that the Mírza was in his power. Kámrán, finding himself in this desperate situation,

and detention by the Gakers.

* The Kholáset-ul-Towáríkh says, at Rájeghát 20 kos from Sirkend, f. 283.

† The present capital of Kalúr is Belláspúr on the Satlej. Forster's Travels, vol. i. p. 240. 8vo. ed. The Kholáset calls it Kehlut, and makes him go thence to Nagerkót and thence to Jámu. Ferishta, vol. ii. p. 169. says that he took refuge with the Raja of Nagerkót.

‡ Mánkót lies in the hills between the Rávi and Chenáb.

sent Jogi Khan along with the Sultan's envoys, with conciliatory letters to his brother, to attempt to soothe him.

We have seen that Humáyun received these letters while on his expedition into Bangash, and that he immediately resolved to march into the country of the Gakers, and to spare no exertion to get into his hands an enemy, who for many years, had thwarted all his plans, and made a battle-field of his dominions. Having also some views on Kashmír, he sent back from his camp Khwája Jilál-ed-dín Mahmúd, to take charge of Kábul during his absence, and carrying Akber with himself*, to initiate him into business and the art of war, crossed the Indus near Dínkót, and soon entered the territories of Sultan Adam, who, on his approach, began to entertain some fear of the guest whom he had invited, as well as some apprehensions for his own safety and independence. The Emperor sent on Monaim Khan to quiet his fears, as well as those of the Mírza; and, after some delay and evasion, the Sultan at length came, and waited upon the Emperor in the territory of Pírhála, where the Mírza soon after found himself, most unwillingly, constrained to submit to his brother, and to join him in his camp.

Surrenders to Humáyun.

After some days spent in entertainments and festivity, Sultan Adam †, having received a dress of honour, a

* Abulfazl makes Humáyun carry Akber with himself. Akbernáma, f. 89. Other authorities make him accompany the Khwája back to Kábul.

† Abulfazl (Akbernáma f. 88.), gives a short account of the succession to the chiefship of the Gakers. He observes that the Gakers consist of many tribes who inhabit between the Sind and Behat (or Jelem). Their country once belonged to the Kashmíris. In the reign of Sultan Zein-ed-dín Kashmíri, Malek Kad, an Amír of Ghazni, who was connected with the ruler (Hákim) of Kábul, invaded the country, and wrested it from the Kashmíris. Malek Kad was succeeded by his son Malek Kilán, whose son Malek Pír became chief of the tribe (úlús). After him Tátár was the director (Názim) of the family (kabíleh). This chieftain was always in a state of hostility with Shír Shah, the Afghán king of Delhi, and with his son Selím Shah, considering himself to be connected with the im-

BOOK V. A. D. 1553.

standard, and kettle-drum and some rich presents, the reward of his important, but dishonourable, service, took his leave. Consultations were now held as to the disposal of the Mírza. The Emperor's councillors were unanimously of opinion, that there could be no hope of tranquillity for his dominions while the Mírza was in life; and that his death was due no less to the Emperor himself, than to the quiet and peace of his subjects.

Discussions as to his fate.

Humáyun, both from his own natural disposition and the impressive parting advice of his father, was very averse to proceed to extremities. Upon this his Amírs, the Muftis, Doctors of the Law and other men of note who accompanied the army, presented a petition, advice and remonstrance under their seals, praying that capital punishment might be inflicted on Kámrán, as an act required by justice, and indispensable to the public peace. This paper Humáyun sent to Kámrán, who was much agitated on reading it. He sent a message in return to say, that those whose seals were affixed to this paper asking for his death, were the very persons, who had urged him on to the extremities, that had brought him to his present misery.

Is deprived of his eyesight.

Though strongly urged on every side, Humáyun obstinately persisted in refusing to imbrue his hands in his brother's blood; but he resolved, by depriving him of his eyesight, to render him unfit for public life. For this purpose, he ordered the Mírza's servants to be removed from about his person, and supplied their place by some of his own. He instructed his ewer-bearer, Jouher, from whom we have the detailed particulars of this event, to watch the interior of the tent, and on no

perial family. For when Báber invaded Hindustán, Tátár entered his service and served him faithfully. He fell in the war with Rána Sánga, leaving two sons, Sultan Sarang and Sultan Adam. On the death of Sarang, the chieftainship of the tribe came to Sultan Adam, who at this time continued to hold it; though the two sons of Sarang, Kemál Khan and Saíd Khan Gaker, laid claim to the dignity, and were their uncle's enemies.

account to yield to sleep for a moment. Jouher went on duty about afternoon prayers, when the unhappy prince asked for a prayer carpet, and on receiving it, prostrated himself in prayer. His evening prayers he also said within the tent. Entering into conversation with the ewer-bearer, he made him champoo him, asking him several questions, such as, his name, how long he had served the Emperor, and if he had ever been in Mírza Askeri's service. It was then Ramzán, and he told his attendant that he had fasted six days *, asking him if he would be his substitute, to fast in his stead. What followed may be best given in Jouher's own words. "I replied, 'I will fast for you; but the Mírzá himself will yet be able to keep his fast. Be bold, and let not melancholy take possession of your heart.' He then inquired, 'Do you know what is to be done with me.' I replied, 'Kings know the revenues of kings; but this is clear to me, that no man breaks his own arm; and, moreover, his Majesty the Emperor Muhammed Humáyun is most merciful and beneficent.' In this manner the night passed away." CHAP. III. SECT. IV.

Next morning, the army marched and the Emperor gave orders that the Mírza's eyes should be lanced. He then set out. The orders, when communicated to the servants who had been sent to attend the Mírza, produced disputes who was to do the deed, each shifting it from himself. Sultan Ali Bakhshi, the paymaster, who brought the instructions, directed Ali Dost, a chamberlain, one of the persons to whom the charge of the Mírza's person had been committed, to proceed to execute the duty enjoined. This he absolutely refused to do, without the Emperor's direct commands. "You," said he, "addressing the paymaster," will not pay out a single Sháhrukhi without his Majesty's direc- A. H. 960. Ramzán 7. August 17

* This would mark the time as being the 6th day of Ramzán, supposing that Kámrán had fasted that and the five preceding days (16th August A. D. 1553.)

BOOK V. A. D. 1553.

tions. How can I do such a deed as this without his Majesty's personal orders? Should he to-morrow ask me, 'What made you do this deed, and disable my brother?' Am I to answer, 'I did it because Sultan Ali Dost bid me?' No, I cannot do it." Thus they disputed together. At length, the humble Jouher said, "I will go and inform his Majesty." Ali Dost, Sultan Baríki, Gholám Ali Sheshangusht *, the Darogha of the Feráshkhána, and I, the humble Jouher, galloped after his Majesty, and addressed him. Ali Dost, among the rest, spoke to him in the Túrki language, saying, "Nobody will do this deed." The Emperor, in the same language, called him names, and said, "Thou, what has come over thee? Do thou go and do it." What followed, as perhaps the most faithful account of such a scene that is on record, may best be described in the words of an eye-witness and agent. †

"Having received this order, we returned to Kámrán, and Gholám Ali said to the Mírza, 'O Mírza! would that Almighty God tore my tongue from the roots, rather than that the words I speak should come from my mouth. But for the commands of princes there is no remedy. Our orders are to lance your eyes.' 'Kill me at once,' said the Mírza. Gholám Ali replied, 'None dare so far overpass his orders as to kill you.' He then proceeded to execute the work. Having folded a handkerchief which he had in his hand into a ball, to serve for a gag, the Ferásh ‡ thrust it into the Mírza's mouth as he struggled. They then held his hands, dragged him out of the pavilion, laid him on the ground, and struck the lancet into his eyes, such was the will of God! fifty times more or less. Like a brave man he did not utter a single groan. But when a man sat down on his knees, he said to him, 'Why do you sit on my knees?

* The sixfingered.

† Jouher, c. 27.

‡ An inferior servant who takes up and lays down the carpets, assists in pitching the tents, &c.

Will you not leave off till you have had your will of me?' Except this expression, he breathed not a complaint, but maintained a perfect manly firmness, till they poured some lemon juice and salt into his eyes. Being then tortured beyond endurance, calling on the name of God, he exclaimed aloud, 'O Lord! for the offences which I have committed in this world, surely I have suffered retribution. I may now entertain hopes of my future salvation." CHAP. III. SECT. IV.

"The Mírza after this was placed on horseback, and we rode on after the army, till we came to a grove planted by Sultan Fírúz Shah, where, the weather being hot, we alighted. After resting, he was again mounted on horseback and brought on to the camp, where he alighted at the tent of Mír Kásim Kohbur, which was already pitched.

"As I saw the Mírza restless and suffering much, I could not stay beside him, but returned to my own quarters, where I was sitting with my head bent down in sadness, when his Majesty's eye fell upon me. He sent Ján Muhammed, his librarian, to ask what had been done in the affair on which I had been sent, and how I had succeeded. I answered, 'Everything has been completed as ordered.' His Majesty then said, "You need not return thither. Get ready water for my bath."*

Remaining incidents of his life.

Thus was a termination put to the public life of this unhappy prince, who had contributed so much, by his unquiet ambition, to injure the interests of his family, and to restore the Afghán ascendency in India. The remaining incidents of his life are but few. Soon after reaching the camp, he sent a message to Monaim Beg to request that Beg Múlúk, his favourite, might be sent to wait upon him as usual. The Emperor at once complied with his desire. On the Beg's arrival, the Mírza,

* Jouher, c. 27.

BOOK V. A. D. 1553.

in the fulness of his heart, seizing his hands, pressed them to his eyes with many tears, and exclaimed,

> "Though a veil is drawn over the eye of my body;
> I see thee still with that inward eye, that so oft has pictured thy countenance."

He continued to accompany the camp, until it arrived on the banks of the Indus, on its return to Kábul. Here he sent for Monaim Beg. "You know," said the Mírza, "in what splendor I have lived in Kábul. How then can I endure to be carried to it, such a spectacle as I now am." He asked leave to go to Mekka, without passing through his old dominions; adding that, if refused, he would kill himself by the way, when his blood would rest on his brother's head. The Emperor, for a whole day, refused to grant this request. How could he set him at large, he said, after having reduced him to blindness. At length, however, Monaim and some others of his Amírs prevailed on the Emperor to let him set out, and also to have a meeting with him; to which he agreed on one condition, — that the Mírza should place a check upon his feelings, and not allow himself to break out into complaint or lamentation. At midnight, the Emperor, lighted by a lantern, and attended by five or six men of distinction, repaired to his tent. Monaim sent in a person to apprise the Mírza that his Majesty was come. Yúsef, the Mírza's Korchi (armour-bearer), taking his blind master by the arm, led him out as far as the tent-ropes. When Humáyun's eyes fell on the handkerchief that the Mírza had tied over his eyes, he burst into an involuntary flood of tears, while Kámrán, observant of his promise, maintained a silent composure. The Emperor entered the tent, and having thrown off his shoes, sat down close by the entrance, and made a sign to Yúsef, who led in the Mírza, and, in consequence, took him to the higher place, opposite to the Emperor. When those who attended his

His interview with Humáyun.

Majesty had followed and entered the tent, he made them a sign to sit down where they stood. The Emperor continuing to sob aloud, the Mírza repeated a couplet from a popular poem; CHAP. III. SECT. IV.

"The cowl of the solitary hermit is exalted to the skies,
When the shadow of a monarch like thee falls upon it."

adding soon after this other;

"Whatever falls on my soul from thee is subject of thanksgiving,
Be it the shaft of ruin, or the dagger of tyranny."

Humáyun, taking no notice of the reproach which the latter part of the quotation implied, loaded him with kind expressions; calling God to witness how little things had turned out according to his wishes, and how deeply and tenderly he sympathized with his brother's sufferings. The Mírza inquired of Yúsef, "Who were in the tent?" He was told, Mír Terdi Beg, Monaim Beg, Bápus Beg and some others; on which he addressed them and said, "Be all of you witnesses, that whatever has happened to me, has proceeded from my own misconduct and fault. If it be known that his Majesty has shown favour to me, let it also be known how little I have deserved it." Humáyun, much affected, and wishing to put an end to the scene, his voice interrupted by convulsive sorrow, faltered out, "Let us now repeat the Fateheh" (a prayer). The Mírza upon this earnestly recommended his children and dependants to the Emperor's care, who said, "Set yourself at ease on that subject: they are my own children." The prayer being over, Humáyun rose to depart, on which Yúsef, taking the Mírza's hand, led him out to the same spot where he had gone to receive the Emperor, when he came and there took leave of him. As soon as the Emperor was gone and at a little distance, Kámrán, no longer under restraint, groaning aloud, gave vent to his smothered emotions, and burst out into heart-rending

BOOK V.

A. D. 1553.

lamentations; so that the sound of his cries and of his wailing was heard in the tents all around.

He is deserted by his attendants.

Next day it was publicly intimated, that all such of the Mírza's former servants as were inclined might accompany him; but none were found disposed to share his present miserable condition. "Those who lately had boasted of his friendship," says Abulfazl, "now denied his acquaintance." In this situation, Humáyun asked Chilmeh Koka, one of his household, who happened to be standing by, "Whether he would remain in his service or go to Mekka with the Mírza." The generous man replied, that highly as he was honoured by being in his Majesty's service, a sense of duty called upon him to attend the Mírza, that, to the best of his power, he might cheer his dreary nights, and his dark and solitary days. "Blessings be upon you," said Humáyun. To his faithful management the care of the funds destined for the Mírza's support in his pilgrimage was entrusted, and this worthy man rose to high rank in the succeeding reign. Beg Múlúk, the favourite of his prosperity, deserted the Mírza after accompanying him a few stages, and returned to the camp. The Emperor was much incensed on hearing of his conduct, and this heartless desertion, says Bayezíd, made him abhorred of small and great.*

He proceeds to Sind and Mekka.

Kámrán travelled down the Indus to Tatta, where Shah Husein, his father-in-law, allotted him a palace for his residence, and an estate for his support. He persisted, however, in proceeding on his pilgrimage. His Arghún wife, Chuchak Begum, in spite of every remonstrance, resolved to accompany him, and having embarked without her father's knowledge, was discovered before the ship set sail, but refused to return with the persons whom he sent to bring her on shore. He

* Akbernáma, ff. 88—90.; Jouher, c. 27.; Bayezíd, 63—65.; Tab. Akberi, ff. 165, 166.; Tar. Niz. ff. 203, 204.; Ferishta, vol. ii. pp. 169, 170.

himself in consequence went on board to fetch her. But the lady nobly remonstrated with him. "You gave me to my husband," she said, "when he was a king and happy; and would take me from him now that he is fallen, and blind, and miserable. No; I will attend and watch him faithfully, wherever he goes." Shah Husein, compelled to admire her generous spirit and to yield to her determination, sent on board of the vessel whatever could contribute to the comfort of the voyage.* She attended her husband with unwearied affection till his death, which happened about four years after (on the 5th of October, A. D. 1557). She survived him only seven months.

CHAP. III. SECT. IV.

Devotion of his wife.

Their deaths. A. H. 964, Zilhajeh 11.

But to return to Humáyun's proceedings in the Gaker country. After the Mírza was thus given up and deprived of sight, the Emperor marched against Píraneh, a chief of the Janúha tribe, who possessed a strong fort in the Bhíra country. He gave himself up after a stout resistance, but Sultan Adam having asked that he and his country should be delivered into his hands, his request was complied with. The Emperor now ravaged the neighbouring districts, destroying many villages, while the army gained much booty.†

Humáyun plunders the country.

Thus far successful, Humáyun resolved to improve his advantage and to march on to Kashmír, to the conquest of which he had been so long and so urgently invited by Sultan Haider Doghlat. But his Amírs and their followers, who had left their families behind in Kábul, were extremely averse to the expedition. He persisted obstinately, however, and orders were given for advancing by way of Bimber. In the morning, when the march was to begin, a great part of the troops, instead of taking the route pointed out, turned away

Defection among his troops.

* Taríkh-e-Sind, 168.

† There is some diversity in the accounts of different authors as to the series of events in this campaign. I follow what, from a comparison of authorities, seems the most probable.

BOOK V. A.D. 1553.

towards Kábul. Abul Maali, the Emperor's favourite, and a violent man, rode up and shot with his arrow one of the refractory leaders. The Emperor wished to pursue and chastise them, but the chief Amírs represented to him, that the defection was too general to be stopped, and they renewed their representations, in which they were joined by Sultan Adam, that the present was not a favourable time for such an expedition; that the Afgháns of Delhi, who had not long before crossed the Jelem from Rhotas and returned into the Penjáb, were now assembling in great force, and should he march to Kashmír, would occupy the hill pass by which he had gone, and shut up the only route by which he could return; that he had not force enough to meet them in the field, so that Kashmír would become his prison. Besides this, intelligence had arrived that Shah Selím himself was on his way back from Delhi with an overpowering force.

He recrosses the Indus.

Humáyun, though deeply wounded by the conduct of his troops, was compelled to yield, and soon after marched for the Indus. To prevent his being followed into the Gaker and Bhíra country, a report was circulated, and believed in the Afghán camp, that he was on his march to besiege Rhotas. This prevented their moving, so that he was enabled to pursue his course, and cross the river without being followed by the Afgháns.

Rebuilds and provisions Pesháwer.

On reaching Bekrám, now Pesháwer, he found that the fort had been destroyed by the neighbouring Afgháns; and sensible of its great importance for his meditated invasion of Hindustán, as well as for keeping the Afgháns in order, he resolved to rebuild it on a more extensive plan. The delay which this occasioned was far from being agreeable to the Amírs, who were all eager to return to Kábul. Having, however, issued his orders, he made the different portions of the works be distributed to the different Amírs; and leaving Terdi Beg and Monaim Beg to see it finished under the imme-

CHAP. III. SECT. IV.

diate superintendence of the master of the works, the fortifications were completed in a very short time, and a strong garrison placed in it under the command of Sekander Khan Uzbek. The harvests of the Dilázák Afgháns being still on the ground, the grain was cut down, and served to provision the fort It was soon after attacked by the neighbouring Afgháns, but Sekander made a successful defence, and repelled them.

Beginning of A. H. 960. End of A. D. 1554. Returns to Kábul.

Humáyun returned to Kábul in the end of the year. One of his first employments was to justify himself in regard to his treatment of Kámrán. We are told that he deplored to the ladies of the harem the cruel necessity in which he had been placed; and that he wrote at great length to Abdal Reshíd of Káshghar, a friend and relation of the family, explaining in detail the facts of his intercourse with his brother. Indeed it must be allowed that, in this whole unhappy affair, Humáyun seems to have offered violence to his own feelings, and to have departed from his usual character.*

Favourable state of his affairs.

But, however that may be, Humáyun now found himself in a situation very different from what he had been at any previous portion of his reign. He had earned much dear-bought experience. His brothers, who had so often interfered with his views and thwarted his designs, were all removed; Kámrán was deprived of sight, and in banishment; Hindal had fallen in fight; and Askeri was in a far distant land, whence he was not likely to return, and where he could not be dangerous. The other Mírzas, his relations, had either been removed by the arm of justice, or by various accidents; or lived, dependant on his will. The more factious and powerful of the great Amírs, such as Kerácha Khan and Háji Muhammed Khan, had fallen by the sword of his authority. There was now no rival to the throne; no noble behind and above the throne. The most

* Akbernáma, f. 90. and other authorities as above.

BOOK V. A. D. 1554.

powerful of them, Biram Khan the Amír-al-omra, being a Persian Túrk without local connection, and a Shía, was, in spite of his great talents, less formidable to the sovereign than much inferior men: since, as it was through the sovereign that he must govern, it was his interest to increase the power of the crown, his only support.

He resolves to reconquer India.

Encouraged by this state of affairs, and by the peace that prevailed in every part of his dominions, Humáyun now determined to attempt the conquest of Hindustán, which had so long been the object of his ambition. And the circumstances in which that country was placed at this crisis were in every respect most favourable to his design. But it is necessary to return to that country, from which we have been so long absent, and to take a view of the events that followed the expulsion of Humáyun from Delhi and the Penjáb, about thirteen years before this period, when the superior energy and conduct of Shír Shah established for a time the ascendency of the Afghán over the Chaghatái dynasty.

# BOOK SIXTH.

THE SÚR DYNASTY IN INDIA.

## CHAPTER I.

### SULTAN SHÍR SHAH SÚR.

SHÍR SHAH OCCUPIES THE PENJÁB ON THE FLIGHT OF HUMÁYUN AND KÁMRÁN. — THE GAKERS REFUSE TO SUBMIT TO HIM. — THEY DEFEAT HIS DETACHMENTS. — HE ERECTS THE STRONG FORTRESS OF RHOTAS. — AND RETURNS TO DELHI AND AGRA. — QUELLS A REVOLT IN BENGAL. RESOLVES TO REDUCE MALWA. — GUÁLIÁR SURRENDERS. — RECENT STATE OF MALWA. — KÁDER SHAH ASSUMES THE SOVEREIGNTY. — QUARRELS WITH SHÍR SHAH — WHO MARCHES AGAINST HIM. — APPARENT RECONCILIATION BETWEEN THEM. — ARTIFICE OF SHÍR SHAH. — FLIGHT OF KÁDER SHAH TO GUJRÁT. — ATTEMPT TO SEIZE THE NOBLES IN MALWA. — KÁDER SHAH RETURNS, AND IS DEFEATED. — RÁNTAMBÓR SURRENDERED TO SHÍR SHAH, WHO RETURNS TO AGRA. — MULTÁN OCCUPIED IN HIS NAME. — HIS ADMINISTRATION. — HE RETURNS TO MALWA. — CAPITULATION OF RÁISEN. — TREACHERY OF SHÍR SHAH AND MASSACRE OF THE GARRISON. — HIS SCHEMES ON MÁRWÁR. — HE INVADES IT WITH A LARGE ARMY. — IS MET BY THE ARMY OF MÁRWÁR. — EXCITES DISSENSION AMONG THE RÁJPÚTS. — DESPERATE ATTACK ON HIS CAMP. — RETREAT OF MALDEO. — SHÍR SHAH TURNS OFF TOWARDS CHEITÚR — AND THENCE TO KALINJER. — CAPTURE OF THAT FORT, AND DEATH OF SHÍR SHAH. — HIS CHARACTER, ABILITIES AND GREAT DESIGNS. — SCANTY RECORDS OF HIS CIVIL ADMINISTRATION.

CHAP. I.

A. D. 1540.
A. H. 947.
Shír Shah occupies the Penjáb on the flight of Humáyun and Kámrán.

When Shír Shah entered the Penjáb on the invitation of Kámrán's envoy, his successes had so far exceeded his expectations, that he could hardly believe his own good fortune, and was apprehensive that the total want of opposition which he experienced might be a stratagem to draw him on into danger. After crossing the Satlej and the Biáh, as he came near the capital of the

BOOK VI. A. D. 1540.

Penjáb, and still found himself unopposed by any effective force, his suspicions were further confirmed that this system of retreat was a mere feint; and that Kámrán and his brothers had withdrawn all their troops, and retired for a moment, only to return with their united force, and enclose him on every side with greater certainty, when he should have incautiously advanced into a country, where it would be easy to cut off his communication with that through which he had passed. He, therefore, proceeded slowly, sending a strong column in advance, and followed, cautiously, with the rest of his army and his artillery, which he brought forward ready for action. But, in a few days, hearing from all quarters of the discord among the brothers, he became persuaded that the baseness of Kámrán in negociating a secret treaty with him was not affected, and saw that he might prudently venture on bolder measures. He, therefore, pushed on for Láhúr. His sudden approach, as we have seen, dispersed the brothers: and not content with occupying the capital of Kámrán, he pursued them in their flight. On reaching the Chenáb, he detached one party to pursue Humáyun and such of the Mírzas as had taken the Multán road, and another to follow Kámrán to the Niláb or Indus, whilst he himself proceeded to Khusháb on the Jelem. Thence he proceeded to Bhíra, where he halted for some time, to cover the troops which he sent out to take possession of every part of the Penjáb. The Balúches, a barbarous and daring tribe, had long been settled in great numbers in the lower part of that country. Ismael Khan, Ghází Khan and Fateh Khan Balúch Dudai, who were chiefs of various clans or districts, acknowledged Shír Shah; and the whole of the rich and extensive country between the Jelem and the Satlej submitted to him without a blow.*

* Akbernáma, f. 54.; Tar. Nizámi, f. 215.

CHAP. I.

The Gakers refuse to submit,

While encamped at Bhíra, Shír Shah sent to invite Sultan Sarang and Sultan Adam to visit his camp, or, in other words, to submit to his authority. They were the chieftains of the Gakers, and ruled the greater part of the rough hilly country lying between the Jelem and the Indus. But these chiefs, who had long been on friendly terms with Báber and his family, declined the invitation. The Gakers are a numerous tribe. Their country lies to the north of the Penjáb, though they seem, in earlier times, to have extended as far down as Multán. Their present territory, the same that they occupied in Shír Shah's time, extends over the greater part of the tract of country that lies to the north of the Júd hills, or Salt Range, between the Indus and the mountains. It is a table-land buttressed by the Salt Range, rising eight hundred feet above the plains of the Penjáb. The Gakers are famed for their beauty, and claim a Rájpút origin. Their country is rugged, mountainous, and intersected by rugged ravines and precipitous dells, which make it easily defensible; and, in all ages, they have bravely defended it.*

and defeat his detachments.

Shír Shah, who was eager to reduce the Gakers to obedience, penetrated into their country as far as Hatía †, one of their chief places; whence he sent out strong detachments to scour the neighbourhood. But the Gakers, with undaunted courage, attacked and defeated his troops, took a number of them prisoners and sold them for slaves. The King proposed to revenge this affront by attacking them in person, and mentioned his design in council; but his nobles unanimously

* See Elphinstone's Caubul, and Burnes's Travels. "From Rotas," says the last-named traveller, "we entered a mountainous and rugged country of great strength, and our road lay in ravines. The chaos of rocks, their vertical strata, terminating in needles from decomposition, the round pebbles that lay imbedded in the sand-stone, and the wild scenery, made this an interesting neighbourhood." Burnes's Travels, vol. ii. p. 55.

† In Báber's Memoirs mention is made of a Hati Gaker, from whom probably the place was named.

BOOK VI. A.D. 1540.

joined in advising him to lay aside all thoughts of such an undertaking, which, from the bravery of the enemy, and the broken and difficult nature of their country, would require, not only a strong force, but much time and great circumspection. They justly remarked that, to subjugate such a race effectually, it was necessary to possess, in their vicinity, some strong hold, which could serve as a place of arms, in which a strong force could be permanently stationed: that this would not only bridle their incursions into his territory, but that detachments could be sent out from it to waste the country and harass the inhabitants, so as to compel them to abandon their most troublesome fastnesses: that this could only be the work of time, which he could little spare, as the rich and extensive empire of Hindustán called for all his vigilance. These considerations decided Shír Shah to suspend the proposed attack, but he determined to erect on the borders of their country a strong fortress, on the grand line of road between Kábul and India, that might at once be a formidable barrier against invasions from the north, and enable him to penetrate at will into the Gaker country. Having surveyed the hills of Nander*, and in the vicinity of Balnáth, he selected a spot; and to the north of the Jelem, on the border of the Gaker territory, he began to build, on one of them, a fortress of singular strength which he called Rhotas, after his favourite castle of that name in Behár. It was completed in the course of some years, in a style of massy grandeur, that excited the wonder of his own times, as well as the admiration of succeeding ages. Eager to return to his dominions in the south, he appointed his favourite general Khowás Khan, Sipáhsalár, or commander-in-chief of all the Penjáb, with an allowance of a tenth part of the revenue of the province, and committing to Haibat Khan

He erects the strong fortress of Rhotas,

* The Tar. Akberi, f, 166. has Nandina or Tanda: the Tar. Nizámi, f. 215. has Nandina: the Tilch Nisábnáma, Nandana.

Niázi the charge of the building of Rhotas, with the command of a special force in the north-west, he returned to Delhi, whence he soon after proceeded on towards Agra.*

CHAP. I.

and returns to Delhi and Agra.

* Akbernáma, f. 54.; Tab. Akberi, f. 166.; Tar. Nizámi, f. 215.; Ferishta II. p. 118. The ruins of Rhotas were visited by Burnes in 1832, "On the 1st of March," says he, "we reached the celebrated fort of Rhotas, considered to be one of the great bulwarks between Tartary and India. As we wound through the dismal defiles, and might be ruminating on the various expeditions which had traversed this very road, the fort burst upon our view, like the scene of a magic lantern. It had been hidden from us by towering precipices. We approached its ponderous walls by a straggling path, which time had chiselled in the rock, and soon reached its lofty gateway. The black hoary aspect of the fort, and the arid sterility of the surrounding rocks, inspired us with no favourable view of the neighbourhood, which has been the resort of many a desperate band." "Shere Shah was its founder. Twelve years and some millions of rupees are said to have been wasted in its construction." When Humáyun returned from his exile, "he commanded that the fort of Rhotas should be levelled; but so massy are its walls, and so strong is the whole edifice, that his Ameers and Oomrahs ventured to ask his Majesty, whether he came to recover his throne or destroy a single fort, since the one undertaking would require as much energy as the other. Humáyun contented himself with levelling a palace and a gateway as the monument of his conquest, and prudently marched to Delhi. We examined its walls and outworks, its gates and bastions, and the people pointed out to us the orifices for pouring oil on the besiegers. We viewed with admiration the elaborate loopholes for the matchlock, the deep wells cut in the live rock, and the bomb-proof magazines of the fortification." Travels, vol. ii. pp. 53, 54.

According to the Afghán accounts, the difficulties attending the erection of Rhotas were not small. They say that Shír Shah, before beginning to build, invited the Gaker Chiefs to come and acknowledge him. They sent him in answer a péshkesh of some quivers full of arrows, and two maces, with a message, that, being soldiers, they had nothing else to give. Shír Shah, enraged at the insult, replied that they might rest assured, that, God willing, he would drive such a nail into their breasts as should not be removed till the day of judgment. He then selected one Toder Kehtri to build the castle, supplying him plentifully with money, and returned to Agra.

The Gaker chiefs, in alarm, engaged by oaths to each other, not to assist in the work; and issued an injunction prohibiting all their dependants from serving at it as labourers, under pain of banishment. For sometime Toder was unable to procure a single stonemason, and the work was at a stand. This state of things he reported to Shír Shah, who answered, "I selected you from among many, to execute this work, thinking you a man of sense and experience. You have been supplied with money. Go on, at any expense, to fulfil my object, and draw

BOOK VI.

A. D. 1542.

It was his intention to have made arrangements for the good government of that city, now his capital, and of the various districts dependant upon it; and he seems now to have struck coin, and made the prayer for the sovereign be read there in his name, as King of Hindustán. But news having arrived, that Khizer Khan Sirwáni, to whom he had entrusted the government of Bengal, had married the daughter of Mahmúd Shah Púrabi, the late king of that country, and had assumed the state of a sovereign prince, Shír Shah deemed it prudent, before engaging in any other enterprise, to check this incipient defection in the bud. Without loss of time, therefore, he marched into Bengal.* Khizer Khan, unable to offer any resistance, came out in istakbál to meet him, and was seized and thrown into prison. Shír Shah then proceeded to divide the provinces of that rich kingdom among a number of officers wholly independent of each other; and leaving Kázi Fazílat, better known by the name of Kázi Fazíhat, a man eminent for his learning as well as his talents, to superintend the whole with the title of Amín, hurried back to Agra, where he now found leisure to settle everything according to his wishes.†

Quells a revolt in Bengal.

Resolves to reduce Malwa. A. H. 949.

As soon as the affairs of the capital were arranged, Shír Shah turned his eyes to the neighbouring provinces, some of which had not yet yielded to his arms.

on my treasury for the amount, whatever it may be." Toder, it is added, on receiving this order, on the first day offered such workmen as would engage, an ashrefi for every stone; and every one who brought a stone received a yellow ashrefi. The Gakers, hearing this, disregarding the prohibition, came down in such numbers that, in a very short time, the rate was reduced by competition to one rupee each stone; and by and by to ten takkas; till at last it came to one behlúli. In this manner, it is added, by dint of expense, was the fort completed. When a report of what was doing was made to Shír Shah, he entirely approved of what had been done, and praised the conduct of Toder most highly. Nisábnáma-e Afghánán, ff. 94, 95.

* Khol. ul Towáríkh, f. 276. Some authors defer this till his subsequent return to Agra.

† Tar. Niz. f. 215.; Tab. Akberi, f. 166.; Tar. Bed. 189.

His first object seems to have been to reduce the extensive and populous country of Malwa; for which purpose he led his army towards the fort of Guáliár, which was still held for Humáyun by Abul Kásim Beg. Guáliár, which was reckoned impregnable to open force, had for some time been blockaded by Shujaa Khan, one of Shír Shah's Amírs; and the garrison was already reduced to the greatest distress for want of provisions. In consequence of this, the King, as he approached the place, had the satisfaction of being met by the besieging general, and by the governor of the castle, who surrendered that important fortress into his hands.*

CHAP. I.

Guáliár surrenders.

The victorious Afghán now continued his march into Malwa. It was by no means in a settled condition. When Humáyun, six years before, after his return from Gujrát, had hastily quitted the kingdom, that he might counteract the ambitious designs of his brother Askeri and reduce the growing power of Shír Khan, Malu Khan, one of the principal officers of the late Khilji government, assisted by the good wishes of the Zemíndárs and natives, attacked the imperial generals, who had been left behind with very inadequate means of resistance; and being attended with an almost invariable course of success, in about a year reduced the whole of Malwa from Gujrát to Bhilsa under his power. Malu Khan was thus encouraged to assume the ensigns of sovereignty; and he accordingly mounted the throne at Mándu, under the title of Káder Shah of Malwa. About the same time Bhopat and Puran-Mal, the sons of the late Raja Siláh-ed-dín or Silhádi, who had possessed such extensive dominions in that kingdom, returned from Cheitúr, to which they had fled on their father's death, and recovered their family possessions of Ráisen, and Chandéri, acknowledging the new king as their superior lord.†

Recent state of Malwa.

A. H. 944.

Káder Shah assumes the sovereignty.

* Ibid.

† Ferishta, vol. ii. p. 271.; Malu Khan is described in the Tabakát, f. 166. and in the Tar. Niz. f. 115.,

BOOK VI.

A. D. 1542.

Quarrels with Shír Shah,

Scarcely was Káder Shah seated on his throne, when he received a letter from Shír Shah, then only King of Bengal, inviting him to make a diversion on the side of Agra, so as to distract the attention of Humáyun, their common enemy, who was then once more on his march to attack the Afghán prince. This letter, or firmán, was sealed at the top, a form used in addressing an inferior. The new king, offended at what he held to be an insult, returned his answer by a similar letter or firmán, sealed in like manner at the top. On receiving it Shír Shah, filled with indignation, tore off the seal, which he placed on the point of his sword, at the same time exclaiming, that if he was ever fortunate enough to meet with Káder Shah, he should know in what way to remind him of this indignity.*

who marches against him. A. H. 949.

When Shír Shah now at length entered Malwa, Káder Shah, unable to cope with him in the field, retired before him. The Afghán advanced into the very heart of the new king's dominions. When he had reached Sarangpúr on the Kali-Sind, Káder Shah, probably seeing little prospect of being able to make a successful resistance, to the great surprise of Shír Shah's officers, though probably by a private understanding with that prince himself, made his appearance one morning at the King of Delhi's Derbár. The two princes retiring, conferred together; after which Káder Shah was introduced with the greatest ceremony and honours, received a present of an hundred and one horses, was presented with the dress worn by Shír Shah when they met, and invited to sleep in the royal tents. Next day, the army marched on to Ujein, where the Afghán caused his minister and relative, Shujaa

Apparent reconciliation between them.

and by Ferishta, p. 274. as one of the officers of the late Khilji government. Bedáuni, f. 149. says that he was one of the slaves of the Khilji Sultans, and was entrusted with absolute power in the kingdom. By Behádur Shah he was treated with great distinction, probably as the Prime Minister of Malwa.

* Ibid.

Khan, to perform obeisance to Káder Shah, as King of Malwa. But this deference was of short duration, and only assumed to serve a purpose; for, the day after, Shír Shah informed the King of Malwa, that he had been graciously pleased to confer on him the government of Laknou, to which he must remove with his family without loss of time. This was language not to be misunderstood; and we may well wonder that, after this resolution had been communicated to him, Káder Shah should still have found means to effect his escape; which he did, disguised as a slave, and with his family retired into Gujrát.* Shír Shah, being thus left in the undisturbed possession of the country, appointed Shujaa Khan to the command of Sivás, and in general of the eastern portion of Malwa; giving Háji Khan Sultan charge of Dhár and the western districts of his new conquest; after which, he himself marched to the northward to secure the possession of Rántambór.†

CHAP. I.

Artifice of Shír Shah,

and flight of Káder Shah to Gujrát.

But Malwa, although conquered, was far from being settled. For many years past it had been almost entirely divided among a number of great local chiefs who were nearly independent. The direct power of the kings had, therefore, been extremely limited. The first step towards establishing absolute power in the person of Shír Shah, which was called securing the peace of the country, seemed to be to get possession of the persons of the most distinguished of these chieftains; and this Shujaa Khan resolved to effect. In pursuance of this policy, Moyín Khan of Sivás, one of the most powerful of them, who was at the time in Shujaa's camp, was taken into custody by his orders.

Attempt to seize the Nobles at Malwa.

* The Nisábnáma-e Afghánán, f. 96. gives a somewhat different account of these transactions.

† Tabak. Akb. f. 166.; Tar. Niz. f. 215.; Ferishta IV. 270—273. and II. p. 110.; Bedáuni, f. 140. There are some discrepancies of little moment, concerning the powers of these Amírs.

BOOK VI. A. D. 1542.

On hearing of this outrage, Moyín's son Nasír Khan immediately collected all the force of his principality, and marched as far as Sarangpúr to his father's rescue. But Shujaa Khan, being joined by the Raja of Guáliár, who had lost his capital, defeated Nasír Khan in battle, and forced him to take refuge in the wild mountains of Gondwána.*

Káder Shah returns, and is defeated.

Meanwhile, Káder Shah, having had time to breathe after his expulsion, collected a body of adherents on the borders of Gujrát, and advanced from Bhanswára to attack Háji Khan. Shujaa Khan, informed of his motions and that a battle was likely to take place in two days, threw himself into his palankeen, and proceeding with all possible speed for forty-eight hours, joined Háji Khan in the evening, where he lay in sight of the enemy. He was still in time to make arrangements for anticipating the enemy by a night attack, which fully succeeded, Káder's army being dispersed, and his camp taken. Shír Shah, admiring the talents and activity of his general, soon after recalled Háji Khan, and nominated Shujaa Khan sole Governor of Malwa. From this period we hear no more of Káder Shah.†

Rántambór surrendered to Shír Shah.

Shír Shah, on leaving Malwa, marched for Rántambór, which was still held by the adherents of Sultan Mahmúd Khilji. But that strong place being soon yielded up by capitulation, he once more returned to Agra, where he was allowed to spend nearly a year in arranging the civil and military administration of his dominions, now so extensive in Hindustán, in Malwa, in Bengal and the Penjáb. In this last province, Haibat Khan had

He returns to Agra. A. H. 950. A. D. 1543. Multán occupied in his name.

* Ut supra.

† Ferishta as above. Ferishta II. 119. says that Rántambór was still held for Prince Muhammed Lodi, probably meaning Mahmúd Shah Lodi, the son of Sultan Sekander Lodi. But that prince seems to have died some time before. The Tabakát and Taríkh-e Nizámi, as well as the Nisábnáma, f. 96, affirm that it was held by the servants of Sultan Mahmúd Khilji, which is most probable. The governor, according to Bedáuni, f. 149, was Khan Khánán Sirwáni.

conducted his operations with success. The kingdom of Multán, during the confusions that had recently prevailed, had come into the possession of the Balúches, under one of their chiefs Fateh Khan. Shír Shah was desirous to have the direct possession of the country; and though Fateh Khan had acknowledged Shír Shah, it was easy to contrive a pretext for hostilities. Haibat Khan marched his army into the Multán territory, defeated Fateh Khan who came to oppose him, and was soon in possession of the whole kingdom of Multán. Shír Shah, much satisfied with this important service, bestowed on Haibat Khan the lofty title of Azím Humáyun.*

His administration.

While Shír Shah remained at Agra, he applied the whole powers of his active mind to the settlement of his dominions. He is said to have divided all Hindustán, of which Bengal never was considered as forming a part, into forty-seven districts, and to have appointed proper officers for the government and protection of each. "He introduced," says Abulfazl, who is not partial to him, "some of the many plans of Sultan Alá-ed-dín, of which he had heard as they are detailed in the Taríkh-Firúzsháhi." It may be observed that many of the laws of that prince were made to remedy a disorganization in the state of society, similar to what, in the beginning of Shír Shah's reign, prevailed in India; and cruel and capricious in his general conduct as was the prince who imposed them, to a considerable extent, they did produce a favourable effect. "Robbery and theft, formerly so common," says Ferishta, speaking of Alá-ed-dín's reign, "were not heard of in the land. The traveller slept secure on the highway, and the merchant carried his commodities in safety from the sea of Bengal to the mountains of Kábul, and from Telingána to Kashmír." †

* Tar. Niz. f. 215.; Tab. Akberi, f. 166.

† Briggs's Ferishta, vol. i. p. 345.

BOOK VI.

A. D. 1543.

He returns to Malwa.

As soon as affairs admitted of his absence from the capital, he resolved to turn his arms once more against Malwa. Though the greater part of that kingdom had submitted to him, Puran-Mal, the son of Silhádi Purebi the late powerful Rájpút chieftain, still maintained himself in Ráisen, Chandéri and the surrounding districts, in great force. To give his operations the appearance of a Holy War, and to excite the enthusiasm of his Muhammedan soldiers, Shír Shah gave out, that his chief reason for the war was to punish Puran-Mal, a Hindu infidel, who, among the two thousand women shut up in his harem, had dared to detain many Moslem females as concubines. The fort of Ráisen was blockaded, and attacked for a long time without success, the Rájpúts making a vigorous resistance. At length, when both parties were worn out, terms were proposed by the mediation of Prince Adel Khan and of Kutb Khan Náib, and a capitulation was entered into, by which Puran-Mal agreed to surrender the fort; while Shír Shah, on his part, undertook to allow the Rájpút prince to retreat uninjured, with his whole family, women and followers, and all their effects and property. On the faith of this treaty, solemnly ratified, Puran-Mal marched out, and encamped, attended by about four thousand Rájpút horse. This escape of their heathen enemy filled with indignation Shír Shah's divines and spiritual advisers, particularly Mír Syed Rafía-ed-dín, all of whom, not ignorant of their master's wishes, signed and presented to him a regular fetwa, or opinion, declaring that such an agreement made with infidels was contrary to religion, and was not binding; and that the king's duty was to visit his unbelieving foe with indiscriminate slaughter. Shír Shah, basely acting on their base decree, after taking possession of the fort, surrounded the Raja's camp with all his army, and poured in showers of arrows upon them. Thus treacherously assailed, the Rájpút and his followers de-

Capitulation of Ráisen.

Treachery of Shír Shah,

termined to sell their lives dearly. They, therefore, according to the custom of their race, first put to death all their women and children. After this, to disappoint the avarice of their relentless enemies, they heaped up their rich stuffs, jewels and all the valuable property which they possessed, and setting fire to their tents and pavilions, consumed the whole in the flames. They then proceeded in a body to meet death, and, each tying himself to his neighbour by his skirt or girdle, they charged the army of the King with desperate valour, cut to pieces a number of their enemies, till, surrounded and assailed by overwhelming numbers, they fell, fighting to the last man. In this massacre, about ten thousand of every age and sex are said to have fallen.*

*And massacre of the garrison.*

After this unworthy success, Shír Shah returned once more to Agra, where he remained several months, being detained, part of the time, by a dangerous illness. Here his ambition led him to meditate new conquests on the side of the Rájpút country. The death of Rána Sánga and the minorities that followed had introduced much discord and disorder into the government of Chaitúr or Mewár; and the repeated attacks made on their territory by the King of Gujrát and the Emperor of Delhi, with the defeats sustained by the Rána in the wars with these princes, had reduced the extent of the dominions, no less than the political influence of that prince, the ancient head of the Rájpúts. Maldeo, who was at this time the chief of the rival principality of Nagór and Júdpúr (or Márwár), in this decline of the acknowledged head of their race, strained every nerve to raise himself to the high eminence, from which the

*A. H. 951. His schemes on Márwár.*

* Tar. Niz. ff. 215, 210.; Tabakát-e Akberi; Akbernáma, ff. 54, 53.; Nisábnáma-e Afgh. ff. 96, 97.; Kholáset ul Towárikh, f. 277.; Tar. Bedáuni, f. 149. The Nisábnáma says that two only were found alive after this massacre, both female children; one of them the daughter of Maldeo, whom Shír Shah consigned to be brought up as a dancing girl: the other he gave up to a party of jugglers, or bázigars. This, if true, would be an additional stain on his character.

BOOK VI. A.D. 1544.

Rána seemed to be falling; a station which he deemed to be due to him, at least from his power. Maldeo appears to have possessed great talents, as well as the bravery common to all his family. According to the historian of the Rájpúts, the prince of Márwár, in the course of ten years, by reducing many local hereditary chieftains under his sway, had extended his territories on every side, so that they comprehended all the present country of Márwár, including Merta, Nagór and Filúdi, much of Bikanír and Bikampúr, Ajmír with several other smaller districts, and a large portion of Ambér or Jeipúr, which brought him close on the limits of Agra and Delhi. Several of the petty princes in that quarter, who had formerly acknowledged the Lodi Kings of Delhi, had now submitted to him. The immediate cause or pretext of the quarrel between Maldeo and Shír Shah is not explained: but in the state of confusion to which the country to the west of the Jamna was reduced, by the destruction of the House of Lodi, the expulsion of the House of Taimur, and the breaking up of the overruling influence of that of Rána Sánga, there could hardly fail to be disputes between two princes of equal ambition, for the possession of the numerous towns and districts, which had been recently conquered by these powerful dynasties, but which, now deprived of their support, were looking round for some powerful protector. Whatever the cause, Shír Shah resolved to invade Maldeo's territories of Ajmír and Nagór, of which the Raja had but recently gained possession.

Invades it with a large army.

Well aware of the difficulty of the enterprise, he took the field with an army of no less than eighty thousand men *, and advanced towards Márwár, with a caution unusual in Indian wars. Wherever the army was to pass the night, he caused a trench and rampart to be

* The Kholáset gives him 50,000 horse.

thrown up round the camp, and guarded it with the utmost care and vigilance. On reaching the sandy desert, when it was impossible to throw up works, he made bags be filled with sand, and ranged them as a defensive wall. He was not long of seeing his enemy. On the frontiers of Ajmír, Maldeo met him at the head of fifty thousand Rájpút horse, and the two armies lay for a month in sight of each other, daily engaging in sharp skirmishes. The Rájpúts were, at that time, as formidable as any enemy in the East. Shír Shah, met by this powerful array of warriors, constrained in his movements and straitened in his supplies, would willingly have retreated. But, besides the loss of reputation, the danger of a backward movement in the sight of such a force was much to be dreaded.

Is met by the army of Márwár.

In this exigency, finding it necessary to attempt something, the artful Afghán at length resorted to a stratagem suggested, it is said, by some petty Rájpút chiefs, who had joined his camp. They knew that many of the Rajas who had attended Maldeo in the field had, like themselves, been deprived of a great part of their territory by that prince, so that they still bore him a grudge, and were not disinclined to shake off his yoke. Shír Shah made letters be written in the name of some of the principal disaffected Rajas who followed Maldeo. In these letters which were addressed to himself, he made them affirm that, though they fought under Maldeo, they detested his sway; that, if the Afghán King would engage to reinstate them in their former possesions, they would gladly desert Maldeo in the approaching battle, and serve Shír Shah as faithful subjects; and that even Maldeo's oldest dependants, tired of his pretensions, would join them in the revolt. Shír Shah wrote a few words on these letters, acquiescing in the demands which they contained, and contrived that they should appear to be intercepted, and thus fall into the Raja's hands. Maldeo, not unaware of

Excites dissension among the Rájpúts.

BOOK VI.

A. D. 1544.

the sentiments of many of his chiefs, believed the correspondence to be genuine, and put off the battle, which was to have been fought that very day. The more that his gallant Rájpúts, who confidently anticipated a victory, urged him to an instant attack, the more was he convinced of their treachery, and he soon after ordered a retreat. The cause of this movement came to the knowledge of his chieftains, who felt their high sense of national honour wounded by the imputation with which they were unjustly charged; at the same time that their pride and high-raised expectations were disappointed by a retreat in the face of an enemy, whom they regarded as already in their power. In vain did they with oaths assert their innocence. One of them, Kumbha, the head of a Rájpút principality, declared to Maldeo, that he was resolved to wipe off the aspersion thrown on the Rájpút name by attacking the enemy, though he should be followed only by his own tribesmen.

Desperate attack on Shír Shah's camp.

Accordingly, as Maldeo with the army commenced his retreat, during the night, Kumbha, with eight or ten thousand men chiefly of his immediate followers, turned back, and marched to surprise the Afgháns. As their route lay over rough and broken ground, they were divided, and the greater number lost their way, so that only about four thousand at daybreak reached the hostile camp. Still, however, with the reckless intrepidity of their tribe, they rushed in with a furious onset, pushing for Shír Shah's tents. Dismounting, and using only their daggers and short swords, they bore down all opposition, and scattered dismay and death over the camp. Numbers of the Afgháns soon lay dead on the ground, and the bold daring and desperate valour of a handful of Rájpúts seemed about to be rewarded by the rout and total discomfiture of their foes; when Jilál Khan Jilwáni, an Afghán general, came up with a fresh body of troops in compact order.

Under cover of this timely succour, Shír Shah rallied his men; and the wearied Rájpúts were surrounded, and assailed on every side by showers of arrows, which rapidly took effect. The Rájpút ranks were soon thinned. Kumbha, with his most devoted followers, who had entered the fight determined not to retreat, fell, bravely fighting, to the number of two thousand. Shír Shah, after the battle was over, seeing the havock that had been made in his army, and how nearly the fate of the day had been balanced, is said to have exclaimed, "How nearly had I thrown away the empire of Delhi in seeking for a handful of bájri." Bájri, a poor and coarse grain, is the chief produce of the sandy and sterile plains of Márwár. Maldeo, meanwhile, continued his retreat into the hill-country of Júdpúr; but soon discovered, with grief and self-reproach, the artifice to which he had sacrificed the success of his campaign, and the glory of his arms; as well as the injustice he had done to his gallant countrymen.*

Retreat of Maldeo.

Shír Shah had already suffered too much in this expedition to venture to follow up his success against Maldeo and his Rájpúts of Márwár; but, turning south, marched into Mewár, for the professed purpose of reducing Cheitúr. The Rána, whose power had been much reduced since the reign of Rána Sánga, desirous to avert his arms, sent ambassadors, offering to acknowledge him as his superior lord. Shír Shah accepted this submission, and continued his march through the heart of the country of Dhandina, now Jeipúr, towards Rántambór, the jágír of his eldest son Ádel Khan, who asked leave of absence from the Derbár, for a short time, to enable him to put the castle in order, and to

Shír Shah turns off towards Cheitúr.

* See Tab. Akb. ff. 186, 187.; Tar. Nizámi, f. 216.; Tar. Bedáuni, ff. 149, 150.; Kholáset ul Towáríkh, ff. 277, 278.; Ferishta II. pp. 121, 122.; Kháfi Khan, Tod's Rajasthan, vol. ii. pp. 24—27. The name of the brave Rájpút chief is variously given, Kumbha, Kanba, Gobna, Goya, and Goind. I have followed Colonel Tod and Ferishta. Bedáuni calls him the Vakíl and Vazír of Maldeo.

BOOK VI. A. D. 1545. and thence to Kálinjer.

provision it; having done which, he promised to rejoin his father.*

The King now turned his arms against the Raja of Kálinjer, a fort which was considered as the key of Bandélkand, and a most important position as regarded both Behár and Malwa. It "resembles in its situation," we are told, "and exceeds, in its size and natural strength, the fortess of Guáliár, being built on a high rock of great extent, which forms one of the hills in the range of mountains extending from Rhotas, or Sahsarám, to the confines of Ajmír."† The Raja, admonished by the fate of Puran-Mal, refused to listen to any terms of accommodation.

Capture of that fort, and death of Shír Shah.

Batteries were raised against the fort, mines run and approaches made, but the siege was long. The works, however, were, at length, brought close to the place; a breach was effected, and an assault ready to be made, under a heavy cannonade; when, as Shír Shah was actively directing the operations, a rocket ‡, discharged probably for the purpose of assisting to clear the breach, rebounded from the wall, and bursting, fell among, and blew up, the whole magazine or tumbril of these fireworks, so that the King, and several noblemen and divines who were along with him ||, were dreadfully burnt by the explosion. In spite of the excruciating

* The Tar. Nizámi does not mention the approach to Cheitúr, but leads him at once to Rántambór, f. 216. The Nisábnáma leads him straight to Kálinjer, Adel Khan taking leave for Rántambór by the way. The Akbernáma makes the chiefs of Cheitúr "and Rántambór" send him the keys of their forts: Ferishta II. p. 123. makes Cheitúr surrender by capitulation.

† Hamilton's Gazetteer, in the Article "Callinger."

‡ Briggs's Ferishta, vol. ii., p. 123. has, "a shell thrown against the fort burst in the battery, and communicating to a powder magazine," &c. produced this catastrophe. It may be doubted if bomb-shells were then in use. The Tabakát, which has been followed by other authorities, has *huqqa-hái pur dárue tefeng*, pipes full of gunpowder; a description which would apply, either to rockets or grenades.

|| Among these were the celebrated Sheikh Khalíl, Shír Shah's spiritual guide, Múlla Nizám Dánishmend, and Deria Khan Sirwáni.

CHAP. I.

pain which he suffered, he had fortitude enough to walk to the trenches, and directed that the accident should be concealed from his troops. Here he remained, and as, from time to time, new storming parties advanced to the assault, he cheered them on with his voice, issued occasional orders with astonishing composure, and sent away such of his officers as came about him, to join the action. The attack was continued with unremitted vigour. As the cry to evening prayers was heard, news were brought to the King, that the fort had fallen. "Thanks be to Almighty God," he said, and quietly expired. This event happened on the 24th of May, 1545.*

A. H. 952. Rebi. I. 12.

His character, abilities, and great designs.

Shír Shah reigned rather more than five years over Hindustán†, besides the time he had previously reigned over Behár and Bengal. He rose to the throne by his own talents, and showed himself worthy of the high elevation which he attained. In intelligence, in sound sense and experience, in his civil and financial arrangements, and in military skill, he is acknowledged to have been by far the most eminent of his nation, who ever ruled in India. He is reported to have divided his time into four equal parts, one of which he appropriated to the administration of public justice, one to regulating

* Tabakát-e Akb. ff. 186, 187.; Tar. Niz. f. 216.; Tar. Bedáuni, f. 152.; Kholáset ul Towáríkh, f. 279. Abulfazl, Akbernáma, f. 55. makes the date of the accident A. H. 952, Moharrem 10., which would be A. D. 1545, March 24; but, f. 91. he makes it Rebi I, 11 (May 23.) Ferishta, vol. ii. p. 124. makes it Rebi I, 12. (May 24), and the Nisábnáma, the 17th (May 29).

The Afgháns, who honoured and lamented Shír Shah, affirmed that mysterious warriors of surpassing form and bravery were seen in the front of the assault, but had disappeared, and could not be found when it was over. Shír Shah always encouraged superstitious belief; and by his liberality was careful to have the fakírs, as well as the Musulman doctors, in his interest.

† Shír Shah is by all allowed to have been for fifteen years an Amír of high rank before mounting the throne. The Tar. Niz. and Tar. Bedáuni make his reign over Hindustán five years; the Kholáset ul Towáríkh, five years and two months: Abulfazl gives him five years two months and thirteen days. Akbernáma, ff. 54 and 92.

the discipline and concerns of his army, one to his religious observances, and the remainder to rest and recreation. In his military character there was a rare union of caution and enterprise. He was remarkable for the care with which he never failed to defend his camp by trenches; and he paid more attention to his commissariat and his artillery, than any prince of his time. He received into his service the numerous adventurers who swarmed over India, marked or branded their horses to prevent frauds, and allowed them pay. He often attended in person, when the troops were to be paid, to receive any complaints, and to secure them against any undue deductions. His temper appears to have been generous: he was a lover of justice, and intimately acquainted with the revenue and agricultural system of India; a knowledge without which no ruler in that country, whatever his abilities may be, can hope to do justice to his subjects. He was anxious to restore, and to open the communication between the different parts of his dominions, which had been grievously interrupted by the wars and revolutions of twenty preceding years. For this purpose, and in order to facilitate the safe and early transmission of intelligence, he built a line of seráis*, or hostelries, at short, regular distances, on the whole road from the farther extremity of Bengal to the Indus, through the entire length of his empire, and a similar line from Agra to Mándu, the high road by which the foreign trade from Gujrát to the interior of Hindustán passed in those days. These seráis were open to strangers of every rank and religion, and were entrusted to servants, who, at the public expense, furnished travellers with water and victuals, as they arrived; at one door of the serái supplying victuals, dressed or undressed, to Musulmans, at another undressed victuals to Hindus. Every Serái

* Abulfazl says that he erected these Serâis, "after the fashion of the Hákims of Bengal." Akbernáma, f. 55.

had a doasp-bam, or post-house, called by the Hindus Dákchóki, so that news even from the Niláb was conveyed in a few days to the court, wherever it might be; and this system of post houses he extended in different directions over the principal roads in his dominions; enlarging the number of horses, so as to answer not only the purpose of conveying intelligence to the government, but also the demands of private trade and correspondence. The system was not a new one, but had fallen into disuse, and was by him much improved and extended. One other object which he had in forming the great line of posts was to prevent the influx of Chaghatáis into his kingdom; and to afford the earliest notice of any invasion or movement from Kábul, whence he dreaded the return of the exiled family. On each side of the grand roads were planted rows of mango and other fruit trees, affording both shelter and refreshment to the tired and thirsty passenger: and wells, supported by solid masonry, were dug at short distances. At all the chief halting-places, he built mosques, and provided for them an adequate establishment of Imáms, Moazzins and servants. He appears also to have made provision for the care of the indigent sick.* The police, which he established, was strict and vigilant. So safe were the highways, we are told, that the most helpless person might carry a bason of gold, and sleep in the open country, without need of a watchman.

He seems to have had more of the spirit of a legislator and of a guardian of his people, than any prince

* A great part of this establishment still remained in Bedáuni's time, after the lapse of fifty-two years, f. 148. and Kháfi Khan, f. 59. at a still later period, remarks, "It is said that the class of persons, who are now to be found in the various seráis of Hindustán, generally known by the name of Bhatiárahs, and whose employment it is to kindle fires and perform other menial offices for travellers, are the descendants of the people originally placed there by Shír Shah." Perhaps, however, this establishment may be found to date from a still earlier period.

BOOK VI. A.D. 1545.

before Akber. By his enemies, he is accused of perfidy, and facts seem to justify the charge. But it is to be remembered that his history has been transmitted to us by his enemies chiefly: and the charge, unfortunately, is not confined to him individually, but extends to nearly all the princes who were his contemporaries. When we consider the confusion, approaching to anarchy, which prevailed all over Hindustán at the moment of his accession to the throne, and the incessant wars that he carried on during his short reign, we must feel surprise that, with all his habitual activity, he was able to effect so much as he did, and that, in so limited a time, he so entirely acquired and so long retained, the affection of his subjects. He himself, when contemplating the disorder that prevailed at his accession, the plans of reform which he meditated, and his own advanced period of life, was heard to exclaim, "Alas, that I should have attained power, only at the close of the day." His memory was long cherished by his subjects with fond admiration and regret.*

Some incidents related of him may serve to illustrate his character. He was eminently distinguished for the impartiality with which he administered justice, without respect of persons. One day, his eldest son Adel Khan, riding on an elephant through a street of Agra, in passing a house the walls round which were in disrepair, observed the wife of the inhabitant, a shop-

* Tab. Akb. f. 178.; Tar. Niz. f. 217.; Tar. Bed. f. 148.; Briggs's Ferishta, vol. ii. p. 125.; Dow's Ferishta, vol. ii. p. 265.; Akbernáma, f. 54, 55.; Kholáset ul Towáríkh, ff. 278, 279.; Kháfi Khan, ff. 57—59.

Shír Shah seems, in several instances, to have destroyed older towns, and rebuilt them elsewhere. In the first year of his reign, he destroyed old Kanáuj, and built, says Bedáuni, f. 147, "what is now called Shír-ghar on the banks of the Ganges." In like manner, he destroyed Shemsábád, and restored it in another place. At Delhi, he destroyed the old fort, and began a new one on a larger scale, which he left unfinished. Tabak. Akberi. He is also said to have meditated the destruction of Láhúr, that it might not serve as a *place d'armes* to the Chaghatái princes, in any future attack on India.

keeper, undressed and bathing herself. Strúck with her beauty, he fixed his eyes upon her, threw her a *bíra-pán*, and passed on. The woman, who considered that, by this freedom, he treated her as a wanton, feeling her honour wounded, resolved not to survive the affront. Her husband, when informed of the incident, had great difficulty in preventing her intention. He went straight to the levée of Shír Shah, and, among other suitors, preferred his complaint. The King, having investigated the circumstances, pronounced judgment ordering the law of retaliation to be enforced; and that the shopkeeper, mounted on an elephant, should in his turn throw a *bíra-pán* to the prince's wife, when undressed and preparing for the bath. Great influence was exerted to mollify the King, but in vain. Such, he said, was the law of their religion, and, in administering justice, he knew no difference between prince and peasant: that it should not be said that a man, because his son, could injure a subject whom he was bound to protect. The complainant, in delight, withdrew his complaint, saying that now that he had gained his right, his character was restored and he was satisfied; and, at his entreaty, the matter was ended.*

At the battle on the Chonsa, Háji Begum, Humáyun's wife, was taken prisoner. Shír Shah treated her with every mark of courtesy and respect; and on Humáyun's return from Persia to Kábul, she was sent back to her husband in the most honourable manner.

The day that he made his entrance into Delhi, a woman, who sold vegetables, called out to her neighbour, as he passed: "Delhi, truly, has got a master, but he is an old one." She was overheard by the King, who, on this, made his horse caper and show off: and

* Khol. ul Tow., f. 278.

BOOK VI. A. D. 1545.

Shír Shah was diverted when he heard the old woman add, "Well, old though he be, he is an active one."*

Shír Shah was buried in his family estate at Sahsarám, in a very magnificent mausoleum, erected in his lifetime, and which still exists. It stands in the centre of a small lake about a mile in circumference, bounded by masonry, with a descent by a flight of steps to the water.

Scanty records of his civil administration.

It is impossible to conclude the history of such a prince, without regretting that so few materials remain for affording a view of the internal administration of his dominions. Many of his revenue regulations were retained or renewed by Akber, and seem to have made a part of Toder-Mal's improved system of finance. But Shír Shah was soon succeeded in the throne by a hostile family, whose partizans were not disposed to see any merit in the virtues of an enemy.†

* Ibid. f. 279.

† The chief authorities for this reign are the Tabakát-e Akberi, the Tar. Bedáuni, the Khol. ul Towáríkh, Ferishta, the Akbernáma and Kháfi Khan. Ferishta does justice to the Afgháns: Abulfazl views all their proceedings with a prejudiced eye.

# CHAPTER II.

## SULTAN ISLÁM, OR SELÍM SHAH SÚR.

SHÍR SHAH'S SECOND SON PLACED ON THE THRONE. — WEAKNESS AND PROFLIGACY OF HIS ELDER BROTHER. — MEETING OF THE BROTHERS, WHO PROCEED TOGETHER TO THE CAPITAL. — ISLÁM'S SCHEME FOR SEIZING HIS BROTHER FAILS. — FORMAL SUBMISSION OF ADEL KHAN, WHO RETIRES TO BIÁNA. — FURTHER ATTEMPT TO SEIZE HIM. — HE FLIES TO KHOWÁS KHAN IN MEWÁT. — THEY ARE JOINED BY SOME OF THE CHIEF AMÍRS, AND MARCH ON AGRA. — ALARM OF ISLÁM AT THEIR APPROACH. — HE MOVES OUT TO MEET THEM. — DEFEAT, FLIGHT AND DISAPPEARANCE OF ADEL KHAN. — ISLÁM SECURES HIS FATHER'S TREASURES IN CHUNÁR. — PROCURES THE DEATHS OF THE HOSTILE CHIEFS. — EXTENT OF HIS DOMINIONS. — HIS JEALOUSY OF THE GOVERNORS OF MALWA AND GUJRÁT. — THREATENED REVOLT IN THE PENJÁB. — NEW WORKS AT AGRA AND DELHI. — THE ARMIES OF HINDUSTÁN AND THE PENJÁB MEET AT AMBÁLA. — DEFEAT OF THE REBELS. — ISLÁM OCCUPIES THE PENJÁB. — AND REPAIRS TO GUÁLIÁR. — FATE OF KHOWÁS KHAN. — POWER OF THE AFGHÁN NOBLES UNDER THE SÚR DYNASTY. — SHUJAA KHAN OF MALWA. — ATTEMPT ON HIS LIFE BY AN AFGHÁN. — HIS QUARREL WITH ISLÁM — WHO INVADES MALWA. — FLIGHT AND RESTORATION OF SHUJAA KHAN. — TEMPORARY SUCCESS, AND FINAL DEFEAT OF AZÚN HUMÁYUN IN THE PENJÁB. — DISGRACEFUL CONDUCT OF ISLÁM AFTER THE VICTORY. — HE ADVANCES TO RHOTAS. — CONTESTS WITH THE GAKERS. — DISCONTENTS IN HIS CAMP. — HE MAKES PEACE WITH THE GAKERS, ON THEIR EXPELLING THE REBELS — WHO RETREAT TOWARDS KASHMÍR — AND ARE EXTERMINATED IN THE DEFILES. — ISLÁM BUILDS MÁNKÓT. — HIS NARROW ESCAPE FROM ASSASSINATION. — KÁMRÁN VISITS HIS CAMP. — ADVANCE AND RETREAT OF HUMÁYUN. — MEDITATED DESTRUCTION OF LÁHÚR, AND REMOVAL OF THE CAPITAL TO MÁNKÓT. — MUTUAL SUSPICIONS OF ISLÁM AND HIS NOBLES. — DEATH OF ISLÁM SHAH. — HIS CHARACTER AND POLICY. — ADMINISTRATION OF JUSTICE. ACCOUNT OF SHEIKH ALÁI, AND THE MEHDEVIS.

CHAP. II.

A. D. 1545.
A. H. 952.

Shír Shah's second son placed on the throne.

On the occurrence of the melancholy event which arrested Shír Shah in the midst of his successful career, the Afghán chiefs, who were in the camp, assembled and consulted together. None of the late

BOOK VI. A. D. 1545.

King's sons was on the spot. Adel Khan, the eldest, was still at Rántambór. Jilál Khan, his next brother, who was then not far off, at Rewah*, a town in the Pergana of Kalinjer, got immediate notice of his father's death; and being favoured by a strong party of the principal Amírs, arrived in the camp in three days. There, chiefly through the influence of Isa Khan Hijáb, he was proclaimed King, and ascended the throne, in the fort of Kalinjer, under the name of Sultan Islám Shah, though by the natives of India he was generally called Selím Shah, and, by the northern or Chaghatái soldiers, Selím Khan.

A. H. 952. Rebi. I. 15. May 27.

Weakness and profligacy of his elder brother.

The ostensible reason assigned by the Afghán Amírs for thus passing over the heir-apparent was the distance from the army at which he happened to be at that crisis, and the necessity, in order to prevent rebellion or any ambitious pretensions to the succession, that the vacant throne should be filled without delay. It would appear, however, that Adel Khan, who was of a depraved character, was very unpopular among at least one portion of the Afgháns, and that he was in reality set aside, even more on account of the weakness of his character than for his hopeless depravity and profligacy.†

Immediately on his accession, Islám wrote to his brother, Adel Khan, telling him that he had been constrained, against his will, in order to prevent any commotions and from other public considerations, to assume for a time the title of sovereign; but that he was about to repair to the capital, where he hoped to meet him, and to have an opportunity of manifesting all the

* The village of Rewah, near Panna. Panna is south of Kalinjer, Rewa south-east in Bogilkand. The Tar. Niz. f. 217. has Ayún; the Tab. Akb. Riún a dependancy of Bhal; the Nisábnáma, f. 165. Diún a dependancy of Panna. Different authors make the enthronement three, five, and eight days after the late King's death. Bedáuni says he was called from Tahía.

† Tar. Niz. f. 217.; Tab. Akb. f. 178.; Akbernama, f. 91.; Nisábnáma, f. 165.; Ferishta, vol. ii. p. 126.

attachment and obedience due to him as his elder brother. He then set out for Agra. On reaching Kora in the Doáb, he was met by Khowás Khan, the commander-in-chief, a nobleman of great influence, who arrived from his jágír of Sirhend; and the ceremony of enthronement was once more gone through, submissions made, and offerings presented, with much pomp and festivity; after which, Islám again wrote to his brother, calling upon him, in conciliating and humble terms, to hasten to meet him.

Adel Khan, justly jealous of Islám or Selím's intentions, wrote to Kutb Khan Náib, Khowás Khan, Isa Khan Niázi and Jilál Khan Jilwáni, who were regarded as the principal Afghán nobles, to ascertain whether, if he complied with his brother's invitation, he could depend on their protection. He, at the same time, wrote to inform his brother that, if these four noblemen came to conduct him and guaranteed his safety, he was ready to accompany them to Agra.

To this proposal Selím agreed, and the four great Amírs accordingly proceeded to wait upon Adel Khan; reassured him as to his personal security; promised that he should be put in possession of whatever jágír in Hindustán he might choose; and, after the first interview with the King, should be at liberty to repair to it, freely and without impediment. On the faith of these assurances Adel Khan set out; and Selím, who had proceeded as far as Síkri* on a hunting party, hearing of his approach, went and received him in a field near Shikárpúr, where rich cloths were spread on the ground, on which the two princes took their seat with much state. The two brothers, at this meeting, showed every sign of mutual affection; Selím repeating his excuses for the part which necessity had compelled him to act. After sitting and conversing together for some time in

Meeting of the brothers, who proceed together to the capital.

* Afterwards Fatehpúr-Síkri.

BOOK VI. the most friendly manner, they rose and set out for Agra. On reaching the citadel, although Selím had given strict orders to the guard that only two or three attendants should be allowed to enter along with his brother, yet the Amírs by whom Adel Khan was accompanied, being by no means satisfied what the King's intentions were, in spite of all opposition, pushed forward after him with their followers and adherents in considerable numbers, into the hall of public audience, and thus defeated the plan that Selím had formed of seizing his brother's person.

A.D. 1545. Islám's scheme for seizing his brother fails.

The King, not disconcerted by this failure, heaped every mark of honour and distinction upon his brother, overwhelmed him with flattery, and renewed his assurances of respect and obedience. He repeated his former assertions that he had assumed power only to keep his turbulent countrymen in order, and to retain the sovereignty in their father's family; but added, that the happy moment was at length arrived when he could follow the dictates of his heart and duty, and resign both the command of the army and the possession of the throne to the legitimate heir. So saying, he approached Adel Khan and, taking hold of his hands, placed him on the throne. Adel Khan was not deceived by the apparent warmth of his brother's professions, but, being more of a boon companion and a lover of ease than a man of action, had not the courage nor the presence of mind to take advantage of them. He saw their insincerity, and he believed himself in danger. He, therefore, immediately rose from the throne, and in his turn, seated Selím Shah upon it, at the same time saluting him as his sovereign lord, and offering the customary congratulations. His example was instantly followed by all the nobles of the court, who presented their offerings, and tendered their homage, as is usual at the commencement of a new reign. Selím Shah, if defeated in his original purpose, thus at least effected a great object,

Formal submission of Adel Khan.

by seducing his brother to make a solemn and public renunciation of his rights. Adel Khan fixed upon Biána as his jágír, and when the first interview was over, was allowed, according to agreement and by the intervention of the four great Amírs, to retire to that place, attended by Isa Khan Niázi and Khowás Khan.* who retires to Biána.

But, hardly had two months elapsed, during which time Selím Shah was everywhere acknowledged as King, when he despatched Ghazi Mahali†, one of the chief officers of his household, to Biána with a pair of golden fetters, and with orders to seize Adel Khan and bring him as a prisoner to court. Adel Khan, informed of his approach and intention, hastened from Biána to Mewát, where Khowás Khan then was, and complained to him bitterly of his brother's breach of faith. The hardy veteran, attached to the family of Shír Shah, in which he had risen to dignity from the rank of a slave, and hurt by the insult offered to himself by this open infraction of a solemn agreement to which he was a party, gave orders for seizing Ghází Mahali, and placed on his feet the fetters which he had brought for Adel Khan.‡ This was an insult that could have been offered to royalty, only by one who was prepared to go all lengths. Khowás Khan followed it up by writing to the principal Amírs who were with Selím Shah, several of whom were already much offended with that prince's conduct, and privately brought them over to his plans. Being joined by Isa Khan Niázi, he set out along with him and the prince for Agra, at the head of a considerable army. On the road he received letters from Kutb Khan and Jilál Khan Jilwáni, who, like them, had guaranteed the safety of Adel Khan, de-

Further attempt to seize him.

He flies to Khowás Khan in Mewát.

They are joined by some of the chief Amírs,

and march on Agra.

* Ut suprà, Add Tar. Bedáuni, f. 153, and Kháfi Khan.

† The Tar. Niz., the Nisábnáma and other authorities call him Ghází Khan; the Tar. Niz. adds, az Moharramán va mokarrabán, e. o. (Sultán) Ferishta calls him "an eunuch."

‡ Ferishta says that Khowás sent back Ghází to the court with his feet in the golden fetters.

BOOK VI. A. D. 1545.

claring their willingness to support the faith which they had pledged to Adel, and to join him; but they required, in compliance with a point of Afghán honour, an instance of which we have already met with, that the army should reach Agra before sunrise, when their troops, unseen by the eye of day, would abandon the King, and move over into the ranks of his rival.

The rebels, proceeding on their march, reached Síkri, twelve kos from Agra, where Khowás Khan, who was celebrated for his piety, waited upon Sheikh Selím Chishti, a holy man, who then resided at that place; and as it happened to be the eve of a great Muhammedan religious festival*, unwisely suffered himself to be so long delayed by attending the prayers and service employed on that occasion, that he did not reach the capital till breakfast time† next day, when the sun was high in the firmament.

Alarm of Islám at their approach.

Selím, when informed of his brother's approach, was in the utmost consternation; and addressing Kutb Khan and some other nobles, whom he knew or suspected to be engaged in this revolt, told them, that, even allowing that he had acted rashly in regard to Adel Khan, he thought he had a right to expect that Khowás Khan and Isa Khan would have written to him to remonstrate, before proceeding to such extremities. The Amírs, seeing his alarm, told him that even now it was not too late to avert the evil; and Kutb Khan offered his services to effect a reconciliation. Upon this, Selím Shah empowered Kutb Khan and the other Amírs who were in Adel Khan's interest, instantly to proceed to the camp to meet and negociate with that prince. His motive for this measure, apparently so pregnant with danger, was to remove from his person men with whom he did not think himself safe; intending, as soon as they were gone, to

* The festival was the Sheb-e Berát.

† Chásht.

set out for Chunár, where his father's treasures were kept,—to take possession of them,—to raise an army,—and then return to combat his brother whom, at the present moment, he was unable to meet in the field. From following this plan he was diverted by the remonstrances of another Isa Khan, the Mír-Hájib, or Chief Chamberlain, who represented to him, that it was a most dangerous policy in a prince to resign his capital, and abandon his friends and the force of which he was in possession, that he might set out, with the purpose of throwing himself on the loyalty of others who were at a distance: that much depended on first impressions; that he had with him a firm and hardy band of two or three thousand chosen and attached followers, who had been in his service before he mounted the throne, besides many other troops *; that he should boldly march out with this force, and might rest secure that none who bore the name of Afghán, whatever might be his inward wishes, would dare to desert him in the plain and in the light of day.

Selím, abandoning his first intentions, was prevailed upon to follow this advice; recalled the Khans who had just left him; told them, that he was resolved not to trust such faithful friends in the hands of the enemy; and ordered the troops to march out, and form in the plain of Agra. The Afghán chiefs who had engaged to revolt to Adel Khan, when they saw Selím Shah lead them openly into the field, gave up their intention of deserting, and took their station in the line; so that Adel Khan's army, as it advanced, was opposed by the whole force in the capital. A battle ensued in sight of Agra, in which, in spite of the exertions of Khowás Khan, who was disappointed and disconcerted at finding the two great Khans, on whom he had reckoned as auxiliaries, ranged against him as enemies, the victory declared for Selím. Adel Khan fled from the field,

He moves out to meet them.

* Ten thousand Firmuli Afgháns.

BOOK VI.

A. D. 1545.

Defeat, flight, and disappearance of Adel Khan.

and escaped down the country to Tahía *, where he disappeared, and seems never to have been heard of more. Khowás Khan and Isa Khan Niázi retreated to Mewát; where they for some time maintained themselves, and even defeated, at Firúzpúr in that province, an army sent against them by the King. But, the royal army having been reinforced, the Khans were compelled to quit Mewát, and sought refuge with the native Rajas in the mountains of Kemáun. Selím sent Kutb Khan with a detachment in pursuit of them. He took post for some time on the skirt of the Kemáun hills, and plundered the hill-country, but did nothing effectual.†

Islám secures his father's treasures in Chunár,

Selím Shah, thus relieved from his danger, marched down to Chunár that he might secure the treasures of his father. Having by degrees clearly ascertained the truth and extent of the secret correspondence which had been carried on between the nobles in his own service and Khowás Khan before the battle, he determined on revenge. Jilál Khan Jilwáni ‡ was a chief of great power, and one of the four who had become security for Adel Khan's safety. He had entered into the conspiracy, but Selím, though aware of the fact, feared to attack him by open force. What he dared not attempt openly, he accomplished by strategem.

and procures the death of the hostile chiefs.

The camp having reached the town of Kóra §, the King invited Jilál to play a match at chougán; lured him from his quarters, and then seized both him and his brother Khodáidád. To avoid the odium of himself putting to death two Amírs of such distinction he gave them over into the custody of an Afghán, with whom

* Ferishta has Patna; the Tar. Akb. f. 180., and Tar. Bed. f. 154. have Tahía, probably rightly. The Nisábnáma has Panna, which accords as to situation with Tahía. The difference is chiefly from the diacritical points.

† Tar. Nizámi, f. 219. and other authorities as above.

‡ Or Jiláw.

§ Some say, on his return from Chunár; the Nisábnáma, on going thither.

they had a blood-feud, by whom, under pretence of legal retaliation, they were slain. The treasures which the King removed from Chunár were conveyed to Guáliár, which, probably as being nearer the capital, he resolved to make his stronghold. He himself returned to Agra.

Selím Shah now sought out, and pursued with unrelenting severity, all who had taken part with his brother, or who were suspected of being in his interest, "sweeping them off," says Bedáuni, "like men from a chessboard." Kutb Khan, who had been a principal in all the intrigues, alarmed at these proceedings and especially at the death of Jilál Khan Jilwáni, fled from the low country of Kemáun, where he was in command of the army, and retired to the Penjáb. Haibat Khan Niázi, the governor of that great province, on whom the late King had bestowed the title of Azím Humáyun, received him courteously; but having been called upon by Selím to deliver him up, and the ascendency of the royal arms being at this period too decided to admit of opposition, Kutb Khan was surrendered to the King, and along with Sháhbáz Khan Niázi, who had married the King's sister, and twelve other Amírs of note, was sent to Guáliár, where most of them perished in prison.

Extent of Islám's dominions.

All the dominions that had been conquered by Shír Shah were now in the possession of his son, and were for some time ruled by him in peace. His kingdom was of great extent, reaching from Pesháwer to the sea of Bengal, and from the Himaláya mountains to the confines of Gujrát. He was however jealous of some of his father's great Amírs, who administered the government in several of the more important provinces, with nearly despotic power. Shujaa Khan *, the governor of Malwa, was one of these. Since he had had the sole command in that kingdom, he had employed himself with much activity in reducing the numerous jágírdárs who possessed the chief part of the country,

His jealousy of the governor of Malwa.

* Also often called Sazáwal Khan.

BOOK VI. A. D. 1545.

and had succeeded in establishing his ascendency over the whole of it. His very success, however, had excited the suspicions of his jealous master, who summoned him to court. He obeyed the call, and having satisfied Islám of his fidelity, was allowed to resume his station.

and of the governor of Multán.

Azím Humáyun, the governor of the rich and extensive provinces of the Penjáb, fell under similar suspicions, and was in like manner called to the presence. Unwilling to place himself in the power of a sovereign, in whose eyes his power and prosperity were crimes, he feigned various excuses, but sent in his place his brother Saíd Khan, a nobleman of great talent and bravery, who was well received by the King, and treated with every external distinction, and much apparent regard. Islám easily saw through the pretences alleged by the ambassador for his brother's conduct, and, by those who knew him best, was supposed to be only waiting for a convenient time to cut him off. One day the King took Saíd into the interior of the harem, where he pointed to a number of heads that were ranged on the wall, and asked him, as if casually, if he knew any of them. Some time before, Islám had given orders for blowing up by gunpowder a chamber in which were lodged many of the most distinguished prisoners in the fort of Guáliár.* Their ghastly heads were now ranged around, elevated on the points of spears. Saíd examined them without betraying any emotion, and mentioned the names of several whom he had known, the first men of the state. In their fate, however, he seemed to read his own.

Threatened revolt in the Penjáb.

Having arranged his affairs at Agra, Islám now resolved to march by Chunár to Rhotas in Behár, to bring from these strong fortresses a farther portion of the

* We are told that among the persons blown up on this occasion was Kemál Gaker, the son of a Gaker chief, who escaped in a way so extraordinary that it was deemed miraculous, and the incident was reported to the King for his instructions. He commanded his life to be spared, and at a future time sent him into the Penjáb to accompany the army employed against his countrymen the Gakers.

hoarded wealth of his father. Saíd Khán, who foresaw that he could not long remain in the royal camp with safety, made his escape while the army was on this route, and having caused horses to be posted all along the road, reached Láhúr. This circumstance, joined to the delays of the viceroy of the Penjáb, and the news which at the same time reached Court that Khowás Khan was marching to meet Azím Humáyun, made the King suspect that a rebellion, supported by a confederacy of the leading nobles of the empire, was in agitation. He, therefore, halted; measured back his way to Agra; and called upon Shujaa Khan to join him from Malwa with the forces of that province.

New works at Agra and Delhi.

As Agra and Delhi were now once more become the capital cities of the Afghâns in India, Islám, before leaving Agra, employed his troops in surrounding it with a wall. Here having been joined by Shujaa Khan with troops from Malwa, he sent back that nobleman, after conferring with him, and soon after proceeded towards Delhi with all the forces that he could collect. There he remained for some time, awaiting the arrival of the more distant forces. The interval of leisure thus afforded he employed in surrounding with a strong wall of stone and lime the new town of Humáyun, which that Emperor had enclosed with one of stone and clay. Islám caused many new edifices to be built hard by, on the banks of the Jamna; and on them and the space which he had enclosed, bestowed the name of Selímgarh, which now forms, says Kháfi Khan, the southern suburb of Delhi.* The name given to it, of Selímgarh, would seem to show, that Islám did not disdain to use the appellation by which he was vulgarly called.

The armies of Hindustán and the Penjáb meet at Ambála.

Islám now advanced towards the Penjáb; while, on the other side, Azím Humáyun, Khowás Khan and Isa Khan with their united forces, amounting, it is said, to

* Tar. Niz. f. 219.; Tab. Akb. f. 180.; Tar. Bed. f. 155.; Ferishta, vol. ii. p. 132.; Kháfi Khan.

BOOK VI. A.D. 1546. A. H. 953. more than double the royal army, marched to encounter him. The two armies came in sight of each other near the town of Ambála, south-east of Sirhend. Selím, on coming near the hostile army, ascended a rising ground with some of his Amírs, to reconnoitre the array of the enemy. Having for a while surveyed them, he suddenly turned round, exclaimed that it would ill become his dignity to encamp in sight of rebels, and ordered his troops to be instantly formed in battle order, and to advance to the attack.

Defeat of the rebels. It so happened that, the very night before, a misunderstanding had arisen between the two principal leaders of the malcontents, on a subject of fundamental consequence. Khowás Khan, who had been brought up and elevated to high rank in the very household of Shír Shah, retained his attachment to his patron's family, and insisted that the royal dignity should be kept in that line, and conferred upon Adel Khan, his eldest son, under whose banner they should fight, and whom they should spare no exertion to find out, and to place on his throne. Azím Humáyun on the other hand, with the independent spirit of an Afghán and the ambition of an adventurer, quoting some well-known lines of a Persian poet, insisted that there was no hereditary descent in sovereignty, which followed the longest sword. This ill-timed dispute was still unadjusted, when the army of the King appeared in sight. Khowás Khan, in disgust, refused to lend his aid to minister to the pretension of Azím Humáyun, and, with his friend Isa Khan, withdrew his forces from the field. Such a movement, at such a time, was decisive of the fate of the battle and of the campaign. The victory, however, was not bloodless. In spite of the defection of so great a part of the confederate force, the onset of Islám's troops was valiantly opposed by the army of the viceroy of Láhúr, the strength of which consisted in the Niázis of his own tribe. Numbers of them were, however, slain, and the rest driven from the field. In the midst of the confusion caused by the conflict and the rout, while the officers of the victorious army were crowding around the King to congratulate him on his success, that prince narrowly escaped from an imminent danger. Saíd Khan, who had so lately fled from the camp to join his brother, taking advantage of the bustle that prevailed, and being perfectly familiar with the composition and arrangement of Islám's army, mixed with the royal troops, and being in complete armour so that he could not be known, accompanied by two or three* of his followers, rode towards the King, as if to join in the general congratulation, intending to have gone up to him and slain him in the very midst of his triumph. He had got near the person of the prince, when one of Islám's elephant-drivers, recognising him by his voice as he inquired whereabouts the King was, discharged a lance at him. Saíd, however, nothing daunted by the discovery, cutting his way through the troops immediately around him, plunged among the horses and elephants that crowded in confusion near the spot, and by his valour and presence of mind effected his escape. Numbers of the rebels in their flight were drowned in the water-courses round Ambála; many were plundered or slain by the peasants. The remainder fled to Dínkót near the Indus.† Islám pursued them, and marched through the Penjáb as far as Rhotas, receiving the submission of the local authorities as he went along. Having settled the country as far as time permitted, he left a strong force under Khwája Veis Sirwáni to keep the Niázis from regaining their ground, and himself returned to Agra, whence he soon after

Islám occupies the Penjáb,

and repairs to Guáliár.

* Two, Tab. Akb. and Nisáb-náma. Some have *ten*.

† The Tar. Niz. makes the defeated Niázis flee to Dínkót near Roh, and is followed by Ferishta and Bedáuni, &c. The term "Roh" is applied not only to the district of Kohat, but to the whole Kohistán, or highlands, along the right bank of the Indus.

BOOK VI. A. D. 1546. repaired to Guáliár, where he was fond of residing, and which he in some measure made his capital.*

Fate of Khowás Khan.

When, at the battle of Ambála, Khowás Khan and Isa Khan separated from Azím Humáyun and the army of the Niázis, the latter retired to the mountains, while the former, attended by five or six thousand men, hastened to attack the city of Láhúr, hoping to make himself master of it during the general confusion. But, hearing that he was closely pursued, he crossed the Rávi, and at the village of Miáni was overtaken by Yahía Salwái who had been sent after him. Khowás Khan, though at the time suffering from the effects of a recent wound, left his litter; and mounting on horseback, engaged and repelled the enemy, after which he continued his route. Escaping by the foot of the Sewálik mountains, he remained among them for some time. At length Islám Shah wrote to Táj Khan Keráni, the governor of Sambhal, enjoining him to draw Khowás Khan by any means from his retreat. On the invitation of Táj Khan, who owed him his preferment, he left his mountain retreat, and came down to Sambhal. But Táj Khan, forgetful of what he owed the illustrious refugee and anxious to secure the royal favour, treacherously put his benefactor to death, and having cut off his head, sent it as an offering to Islám Shah, who was then at Bín in the Penjáb. Khowás Khan was one of the most distinguished men of his time. His liberality, especially to religious men, was unbounded. Abulfazl represents his character, as he does that of all connected with the Súr dynasty, in an unfavourable light. "He was," says that writer, "originally one of the slaves of Shír Khan, and by downright fraud and cunning, by seizing the property of the learned and good and bestowing it on the ignorant and low-minded, gained a certain degree of credit among the lower classes of his own country-

* Tar. Nizámi, f. 220.; Tab. Akb. 131.; Tar. Bed. ff. 155, 156.; Ferishta, vol. ii. pp. 133, 134.; Khol. ul Towáríkh, f. 281.

men." "His corpse was conveyed to Delhi," says Ferishta*, "where it was interred: and such is the veneration in which the name of Khowás Khan is held, even at the present day, that his tomb is frequented by devotees, and the common people, considering him as a saint, go there to offer prayers for the success of their undertakings."† "And to this day," says a still later author, "his name is celebrated in Hindustán, in poetry and song."‡

Power of the Afghán nobles under the Súr Dynasty.

While Selím resided at Guáliár, an incident occurred which had nearly shaken his throne. It must have been visible in the progress of the narrative, that the Súr dynasty of Shír Shah was entirely military. It was supported solely by the Afghâns, a rough and uncivilized people, who cherished strong notions of independence and equality; and who, if they could not be called republican in their principles, were at least led by a number of their own hereditary chiefs, a sort of native oligarchy, all of whom regarded the grand officers of the empire with some jealousy, as placed above them only by accident. The greater chiefs regarded the sovereign himself with much the same eye. They had been the equals of Shír Khan, his father, and it was by their exertions that he sat on the throne. The governors of provinces, though nominally servants of the crown, and removable at will, were often in reality so powerful, each in his own government, that they considered themselves as individually holding their power by much the same right as the King held his throne. They were in fact, in general, removable only by assassination or by war. Shujaa Khan, as we have seen, had reduced nearly the whole of the former kingdom of Malwa under his authority. He maintained the pomp and parade of a prince, like the other governors of the

Shujaa Khan of Malwa. A. H. 954.

* Akbernáma, f. 91.

† Ferishta, vol. ii., p. 137.

‡ Khol. ul Towáríkh. f. 276.

more extensive provinces, and, like some of them, was suspected by Selím of aiming at independent power. The viceroy of the Penjáb being now humbled, Shujaa was now become the greatest subject of the empire.

Attempt on his life by an Afghán.

It happened one day that an Afghán, of the name of Othman*, came intoxicated into Shujaa's hall of audience, and as his countrymen are noted in India for their rude and unpolished manners, began to spit about him on the cushions and carpets. The servants remonstrated with him, but in vain; and on their insisting that he should leave the presence-chamber, he struck one of them a blow on the face. Shujaa Khan, informed of this outrage, ordered the offender's hands to be cut off. Othman, thus mutilated, repaired to Selím Shah at Guáliár, and, having gained access to him, demanded justice upon his Majesty's lieutenant, who had treated him thus cruelly. Selím, whether merely to get rid of the man's importunity, or with any more remote object, answered, "What, are not you too an Afghán? Go, and take your revenge." This expression was repeated to Shujaa, who only remarked, that it was a very idle way of talking. And though one of his servants told him that he had seen Othman sitting in a cutler's shop, whetting his knife, and using threatening expressions, still he took no precautions.

Some time afterwards Shujaa Khan, having gone to Guáliár to wait upon the King, in passing through the streets of the town on his way to the royal derbár, saw Othman, who had long been watching his opportunity, sitting in a shop, wrapped up in an old mantle. Shujaa made his palankeen stop, and desired some assistance to be given to the wretched man, whose face he recollected. Othman, seizing the favourable moment, approached him, and with the blade of a short sword which he had

* Ferishta calls him Othman Khan, probably erroneously: others designate him as Othman *merdi*, one Othman.

CHAP. II.

fastened to the stump of his mutilated arm, and concealed under his cloak, attacked Shujaa, and inflicted a wound on his side. The viceroy's followers, rushing on the assassin, put him to death.* This occurrence, connected with the known jealousy of Selím Shah and the expression he had let fall, naturally alarmed Shujaa Khan, who, though he afterwards appeared at court and received rich presents, took the earliest opportunity that offered to withdraw from Guáliár with all his followers, without taking leave, and retreated hurriedly to Malwa. Selím, offended at this act of insubordination, as well as by his slighting expressions, sent a strong detachment to pursue, and bring him back, and soon after himself marched into Malwa with the rest of his army, that he might seize Shujaa; "although," says Nizám-ed-dín, "that nobleman was one of thirty-five† persons who were personally engaged in placing his father, Shír Shah, on the throne." When Selím had advanced as far as Mándu, Shujaa Khan fled to Bhánswára, on the borders of Gujrát, declaring that he would never draw his sword against the son of his old master. All opposition being thus at an end, Islám Shah placed Isa Khan Súr in the government of Malwa, leaving him at Ujein with twenty thousand horse‡, and returned to Guáliár. Soon afterwards, however, when Islám was compelled once more to return to the Penjáb, Shujaa Khan, from what motives we are not informed, but probably from his tried talents and the difficulty of governing Malwa without his aid, was restored to the government of that kingdom, which he, and his son after him, enjoyed for many years.§

His quarrel with Islám, who invades Malwa. Flight and restoration of Shujaa Khan.

A. H. 954, or 955.

While Islám Shah was thus successful in Malwa, his

* Some accounts say that the assassin made his escape.

† Ferishta says, thirty-six.

‡ Bedáuni, 30,000.

§ Tab. Akb. f. 463.; Tar. Niz. f. 220,; Ferishta, vol. iv. pp. 273, 274. and ii. p. 134.; Tar. Bed. f. 156.

BOOK VI.

A. D. 1547.

arms suffered a reverse in the Penjáb.* Azím Humáyun, who had so long governed that country, though expelled, had still a strong influence within it, and was attended beyond the Jelem by a considerable body of brave and determined adherents. Having collected his force, Azím Humáyun attacked near Dínkót, and defeated, Khwája Veis Sirwáni, the general whom Islám had left to keep him in check; and, pursuing his advantage, extended his inroads as far as Sirhend. His predatory troops spread themselves all over the Penjáb, carrying off not only the cattle, but the inhabitants, and throwing the whole country into confusion. To redress this evil, Islám lost no time in sending a large army to the assistance of his general, who compelled the rebels to retreat once more towards Dínkót. A general action was soon after fought at Sambala near that place, in which Azím Humáyun, who had now an army of twenty thousand horse, was totally defeated, and numbers of Niázi women, falling into the hands of the conquerors, were sent to Islám Shah. That monarch's treatment of them is disgraceful to his character. The helpless females were sent to Guáliár, and there given up to be dishonoured. He also exhibited a scurrilous pageantry in his camp. Selecting from the rabble some wretches whom he called by the names of Azím Humáyun, Saíd Khan, Sháhbáz Khan and others, he dressed them up in tawdry finery, and bestowed on them lofty titles, made the vilest creatures in the camp carry pompously before them the standards, regal umbrella and other symbols of royalty and state, that had fallen into his hands in the late battle, and paraded them with insulting mockery. The bands of music performed before their doors at the usual stated times, the most noted blackguards in the bazar being selected for the duty. These marks of contempt shown to men of rank and family, with the dishonour of the Niázi ladies, were much felt

Temporary success and final defeat of Azím Humáyun in the Penjáb.

Disgraceful conduct of Islám after the victory.

* "In 954. or 955," says Bedáuni, f. 157, "God knows which."

and resented by the Afgháns in general, most of whom are in some way connected together, and who, at all events, have a profound respect for the honour of their tribes.* CHAP. II.

After this defeat the Niázis, unable to keep their ground at Dínkót, fled for protection among the Gakers beyond the Salt Range, and also spread among the hills on the outskirts of Kashmír. Islám, sensible that, to ensure the tranquillity of his other dominions, it was necessary to extinguish the embers of rebellion in the Penjáb, and especially to crush the power of the Niázi chiefs, marched into that country at the head of a powerful army. He advanced as far as Rhotas, the completion of which he urged forward with much earnestness, and used every effort to reduce the Gakers, who were at once proud of their independence and attached to the family of Báber. The building of Rhotas was a work of immense toil and difficulty. The Gakers did everything in their power to impede the progress of a fort, which was placed chiefly as a check upon them. Islám Shah employed one portion of his troops in building the fortifications on a magnificent scale, and the other portion of them not so employed were sent against the Gakers, who kept them busy with daily combats. By day the Gakers met them hand to hand in fight, and at night crept like banditti round the camp, and by sudden attacks where least expected, carried off men and women, bond and free, all of whom they kept in shameful captivity, and sold as slaves indiscriminately. For two years, while the works were going on, Islám kept his Afgháns employed with stone and mortar, or in constant skirmishing, and all the time kept back their pay. Their hatred to him became extreme, and vented itself in reproaches and abuse; for such was their terror of him, and the ascendency that he had

He advances to Rhotas.

A. H. 955.
A. D. 1548.

Contests with the Gakers.

Discontents in his camp.

* Ut suprà. Some make this ill-judged pageantry occur after the first defeat.

BOOK VI. A. D. 1548.

acquired over their minds, that none dared to remonstrate. At length Shah Muhammed Firmuli, a nobleman whose wit and humour sometimes enabled him to tell bold truths, informed the King that, the night before, he had had a singular dream. "My King," said he, "methought I saw three bags fall from the sky; one was filled with earth, one with gold, and one with paper. The earth fell on the soldiers, the gold on the Hindu clerks of office, the paper on the royal treasury." Islám Shah, who saw at once the tendency of the fable, was diverted, and promised that as soon as he returned to Guáliár he would make the accountants write out the bills for the two years' arrears, and pay the amount. "It so happened," says the historian, "that this never was performed, as he was carried off before it was effected."*

He makes peace with the Gakers on their expelling the Niázis,

But, brave as was the defence of the Gakers in their wild country, and successful as they were, sheltered by their glens, ravines and jungles, in repelling the attacks of the royal army, they at length clearly saw that they could expect no quiet while they continued to shelter Azím Humáyun or his followers. Sultan Adam having sued for peace, it was granted on condition that Azím Humáyun and his followers should leave the country. This being agreed to, the Niázis, now more distressed than ever, determined to attempt Kashmír. They seem to have been invited by a party, who offered them the government, it is said, with treacherous views.

who retreat towards Kashmír,

At all events, Islám Shah put the mountain tribes of Kashmír on their guard, and urged them to avert the approaching danger. Misled, it is said, by their guides, though no such treachery is necessary to account for what followed, the Niázis entered the passes of that mountainous region, and soon found themselves cut off from all retreat or advance. The precipices above were occupied by armed men. In vain did the Niázis

* Tar. Bed. f. 158.

CHAP. II.

do all that courage could effect, the very women, among whom were the mother and wife of Azím Humáyun, arming themselves to defend their honour. A shower of stones from hands unseen poured down upon them, and not an individual escaped. In this defile Azím Humáyun and his brothers Saíd Khan and Sháhbáz Khan, the King's brother-in-law, were slain, and their heads cut off and sent to Islám Shah.*

and are exterminated in the defiles.

While Islám's forces were engaged against the Gakers and the tribe of Jenjúha, who occupied the strong country on the banks of the Jelem, not content with the works still carried on at Rhotas, he began to construct another fort at Mánghar or Mánkót, on the farthest outskirts of the Sewálik mountains. It was on a most extensive scale, and was composed of four or five forts, on as many eminences, but all connected together. Abulfazl says that Islám Shah founded it in consequence of some bad omen that had affected his imagination, and as a place of refuge against the impending evil. It was while encamped at Bín, superintending the building of this fort, that he made a narrow escape from being assassinated. As he was ascending a confined pass on his way to the fort, a man, who had concealed himself, rushed upon him with a naked sword, and aimed a blow which Islám skilfully warded off with the end of his whip, which, however, being cut through, his face was somewhat wounded. When the assassin was raising his arm for a second stroke, the King, who was a powerful man and versed in athletic exercises, leaping from his horse and clasping the assassin's arms, called upon some Amírs who had galloped up to his aid, to put the man to death. "Let us inquire," they said, "who instigated him to such a deed." "No," said Islám Shah, "the wretch may be

Islám builds Mánkót.

His narrow escape from assassination.

* Tar. Niz. f. 221.; Akbernáma, f. 91.; Tar. Bed. f. 158.; Khol. ul Tow. f. 282.; Ferishta II. p. 135. One may suspect that the guides were unjustly accused of treachery. The catastrophe was a natural one, where the natives were prepared.

BOOK VI. A.D. 1548.

the ruin of many houses. Put him instantly to death." This act of generosity does not appear to be much in unison with Islám's habitual conduct. He observed, however, that the villain's sword was one which he had himself presented to Ekbál Khan, a man whom he had raised from the lowest rank, had elevated to situations of dignity in his court, and honoured with his particular favour. Islám now deprived him of his rank, and restored him to his original meanness. But though the Afghán Amírs, by whom he was detested, urged the King to put him to death, Islám Shah refused, saying that, however much he was ashamed of the patronage which he had afforded to one so unworthy, he would not utterly destroy what he had once cherished.*

Kámrán visits his camp. A. H. 959, A. D. 1552.

Having settled the Penjáb and strengthened his frontier, Islám, who had now been two years beyond the Satlej, set out on his march back to Delhi. It was at this time that Kámrán Mírza, who, driven from Kábul, and afterwards from the Afghán country, had come to his camp some time before, disappointed in his expectations of succour, made his escape, and fled first to the Sewálik † mountains and afterwards to the Gakers. Islám continued his march, and had arrived at Delhi, when news were brought that the Emperor Humáyun had reached the Indus with an army, on his way to invade Hindustán. The King was then ill, and, at the moment, had a number of leeches on his neck. He instantly shook them off, and without even washing away the blood, tied a handkerchief round his neck, ordered his horse, mounted, and the same day was encamped three kos from the town. The troops, who

Advance of Humáyun.

* Tar. Niz. f. 220.; Tar. Bed. f. 168.

† Kámrán, as he approached Islám's camp, was received by Hímú Bakál, who was sent out to meet him. This supposes Hímú to have already attained considerable rank, and he is accordingly said to have been in high favour. Tar. Bed. f. 158.

had already suffered so much from want, were driven distracted by this new movement; so that some of his Ministers ventured to represent to him that, as a powerful enemy was marching to meet him, and the troops were in distress and murmuring, it would be a gracious act and befitting his royal dignity, to discharge their arrears of pay. Islám told them in reply that, if he paid the troops at that time, they would ascribe the concession to his necessities and to compulsion, and would act upon that supposition on future occasions; but he assured them that, after he had returned victorious from this campaign, he would order the whole arrears of the last two years to be paid all in one sum. The soldiers, stifling their feelings and seeing no remedy, repaired to the camp. The draught-bullocks, employed for moving the cannon, had all been sent to pasture at great distances. Determined that no time should be lost, the King commanded the foot-soldiers to drag them along; which they did for several days, some of the larger guns requiring each one or two thousand men to move them. Without loss of time he thus reached the Penjáb. Humáyun, having secured his brother Kámrán, and failed in an attempt to reach Kashmír, aware of Islám's approach, returned to Kábul. Upon which Islám, worn out with sickness and disease, retraced his steps from Láhúr, and soon after repaired to Guáliár.*

His retreat to Kábul.

It was during this and his former residence at Láhúr that Islám Shah, following up in some measure his father's ideas, is said to have seriously meditated the destruction of that capital. It was a large and flourishing city, the centre of a rich trade, and amply furnished with every useful and costly production of the times. It had a numerous and warlike population, and large manufactories of arms, offensive and defensive, of mili-

Meditated destruction of Láhúr, and removal of the capital to Mánkót.

* Tar. Niz. f. 221.; Tar. Bed. f. 169.

BOOK VI. A.D. 1552.

tary accoutrements, and of every warlike store. If recovered and occupied by the exiled family, or by any invaders from the North, it would become, he imagined, a most convenient station, both for arming their troops, and for invading India. His plan was to have razed this noble town from the foundation, and to have removed the capital of the Penjáb to Mánkót, which was more remote from the country of the Afgháns, and from the desert along the left bank of the Indus, while, from its position in the Siálkot range, it was less liable to invasion, and more capable of defence. But this truly oriental plan, so pregnant with misery and ruin to thousands of his subjects, was never carried into effect.

Mutual suspicions of Islám and his nobles.

Shír Shah, during his short reign, had placed his kingdom in so formidable a position, that the reign of his successor was disturbed by no foreign invasion; but it was troubled, first by civil wars, and afterwards by repeated conspiracies. Whether these were owing to the jealous temper of Islám, or were a consequence of the insubordinate and independent habits of his Afghán nobles, is not very clear, in the scanty and unsatisfactory accounts that have been transmitted to us of the history of his reign. But it would rather appear that Islám, fretted by finding them constantly in his way, when he wished to rule as an absolute prince, attempted systematically to weed out the more powerful Afghán chiefs*, without being sufficiently aware that, while he got free of a temporary annoyance, he was destroying the real strength of his dynasty and race. We have seen that attempts upon his life, probably produced by this severity, were made at different times, though they failed. Even in his favourite retreat of Guáliár, to

* Bedáuni tells us that his suspicions of the designs of the Afghán chiefs had produced in his mind the most inveterate hatred; that he mixed opium in his drink, eat serpents and drank poison, probably as antidotes while he thirsted for the blood of his Afghán subjects, f. 169.

CHAP. II.

which he retired as a place of security from these attempts, he was not safe from the assassin's arm. One day while he was out hunting at Anteri in that neighbourhood, a band of men, instigated by persons of note, lay in wait, for the purpose of putting him to death as he returned. It so happened that he came back by a different road from that which he was accustomed to take, and thus the plot failed. But the king was soon informed of what had passed, and put to death those who were convicted as the leaders of the conspiracy, or supposed to be so. But he did not stop there; and it is alleged that there was hardly any Amír distinguished for power or influence, on whom his suspicions did not fall, and whom he did not put to death, or imprison.*

Death of Islám Shah

The latter part of the life of Islám Shah was rendered wretched by bad health and bodily suffering. His disease, whether a fistula or piles, was attended with tumours all over his loins, occasioned much pain, and baffled the efforts of his physicians. These and other bodily infirmities brought him to the grave, after a reign of between eight and nine years.†

A. H. 960. A. D. 1553.

His character.

His character, as given by historians, is not exactly what one would expect from the public transactions of his reign. All allow that, in person, he was handsome, and that his bodily strength, which was naturally great, had been cultivated by constant activity and exercise. He is said to have had a competent degree of learning, and to have treasured up in his memory the chief works of some of the best Persian poets. He was intelligent, acute, fond of the society of learned men and of pious

* Tar. Niz. f. 222.

† Abulfazl makes him die 22. Zikádah, A. H. 960. (Oct. 30, A. D. 1553), after a reign of eight years two months and eight days; the Nisábnáma, 26.; Zihajeh (Dec. 3rd), after a reign of eight years nine months and seven days; the Taríkh-e Nizámi gives him nine years, and is followed by Ferishta; Tab. Akb. f. 182.; Tar. Nizámi, f. 221.; Akbernáma, f. 91.; Khol. ul Towárikh, pp. 279—281.; Ferishta, vol. ii. pp. 134—138.; Nisábnáma, f. 114.

BOOK VI. A. D. 1553. divines, and remarkable for his skill in extempore poetical composition, as well as for his wit and ready repartee. He always maintained a powerful army, abundantly supplied with horses, elephants, artillery and stores; and subjected it to strict discipline. "Though he vexed his soldiers extremely," says Abulfazl, "yet he conducted himself with justice to his other subjects."* "He adopted," says another writer, "the same principles of justice and policy as his able father: the strong were not permitted to oppress the weak. His internal administration was excellent. The Kanúngoes, who keep the revenue accounts of perganas, he employed to watch over and report on the condition of the ryots, and the state of cultivation of the soil, on the crops, and the extent of offences and crime. Few princes on record," he adds, "in military skill, in policy, justice and good government, have ever equalled these two."† He is represented as magnificent in his state, and as liberal in his donations to public works and to holy men. He preserved all lands granted for religious or charitable purposes inviolate. He kept up his father's seráis in their whole extent, and the distribution of food to travellers, and for that purpose carefully protected all the lands that had been given them. In addition, he ordered a serái to be built between each two of his father's; adding a mosque, a reader, a well, and a water-carrier to each. He also gave the post-houses so many additional horses as to enable them to convey intelligence with increased speed from place to place over every portion of his extensive empire.‡

The great objects of his reign seem to have been to establish himself on the throne to the prejudice of his elder brother; and, after that was accomplished, to reduce the power of the great nobles, who almost over-

* Akbernáma, f. 91.

† Khol. ul Tow. f. 284.

‡ Tar. Niz. f. 221.; Akbernáma, f. 91.; Ferishta, vol. ii. p. 130.; Kháfi Khan, ff. 59—61.; Nisábnáma-e Afghánán, f. 111.

shadowed the throne. His father, adopting a different policy from his, turned the power and talents of his nobles to account, and preserved their affection and his own superiority, by the ascendency of his talents. CHAP. II.

Islám, before he mounted the throne, had conducted many military expeditions; and, if we may judge from the success of all his measures after he became king, though unfeeling and cruel, he must have been a prince of no ordinary sagacity and talent.

Indeed, even Abulfazl, though, in writing the life of the two first monarchs of the Súr dynasty, he loads them with reproaches and speaks of them with aversion and contempt, is compelled, in a later part of his work, when writing the history of Mobárez or Muhammed Shah Adel, to do them more justice. "From the time that Mobárez Khan came to the throne," says he, "the affairs of Hindustán went backwards; for, in truth, the father and son, his predecessors, were men of talent, and skilful in the administration of affairs. Alas! that they should have spent their lives in ingratitude and rebellion. Had these two persons been servants of the imperial family, the one might have shone at the court, the other in charge of the frontier, to the benefit of their lawful sovereign as well as to their own happiness. The direction of the council might have been entrusted to the father, the protection of the frontier to the son: at all events, loaded with the favour of their lord, in return for faithful service, they would have enjoyed that life which the truly wise regard as life indeed. Such servants would have deserved such a master. But even the enjoyment of supreme power founded on ingratitude, men of superior intellect hold as worse than death. The Great Being that regulates the world soon scatters it abroad."* The doctrine of legitimacy is here applied with some boldness. The Tartars had been only five years masters of Delhi when Humáyun mounted

* Akbernáma, f. 92. No. 3. f. 206.

BOOK VI. A.D. 1553.

the throne, which, for a long course of years preceding, had been in the possession of the Afgháns. But such is the spirit of adulation. The family which happens to fill the throne when the author writes holds it by divine appointment; and all opposition to them, at whatever previous time, is treated as revolt, contumacy, or rebellion.

Islám Shah made an attempt to settle all the affairs of his kingdom on a regular systematic plan.* He endeavoured to concentrate all power in his own person. "He deprived the Amírs of all their war elephants," says Abdal Káder, "leaving them perhaps only a bad female one for carriage." His tents and the screens enclosing them were of a red colour. He appropriated to himself the whole revenues of his kingdom instead of scattering them by assignations; and paid his soldiers wholly in money, instead of keeping up the practice of the *dagh*, or giving them horses furnished by government and branded with a stamp to distinguish them, a mode which Shír Shah had employed. Reports came in to him regularly from every part of his territories; and in return, he wrote mandates concerning every matter and thing, whether relating to religion, civil government or revenue, descending to the minutest details in all that concerned the army or cultivators, tribesmen or merchants. To these mandates, whether agreeable to the law or not, it was necessary to conform in their minutest particulars. No reference to Kázi or Mufti was allowed.

Early in his reign, he stationed large bodies of troops, consisting generally of five thousand horse each, in different parts of his dominions. He seems to have kept up something like a standing army, which his plan of bringing all revenue directly into the public treasury must have assisted him in doing. He was anxious to keep the dread of his power unceasingly before his great

* Tar. Bed. f. 156.

officers: and justice in civil cases was administered not by the Mufti or Kázi, but by a Munsif or Amín. "Every Friday," says Abdal Káder, "the great Amírs of five thousand, ten thousand and twenty thousand horse, pitched a lofty tent with eight balls*, and placed on a throne a slipper of Selím Shah's, with a quiver which he had given to the Sirdár. First of all the commander of the army, then the Civil Judge†, called Amín, and afterwards all others in turn, offered obeisance to it, by bowing towards it with the utmost reverence; after which, every one went and seated himself in his place. A secretary‡ then came forward and read distinctly and fully, a code of regulations extending to eighty sections§ of paper, more or less. In this code was found a direction for every case of difficulty; and all were obliged to conform rigidly to its injunctions. If it happened that any Amír acted contrary to them, the secretary sent a report of the circumstance to the Court, and an answer was forthwith received, with orders for the death or ruin of the offender as a punishment. These forms continued to be observed till the end of Selím Shah's reign. The author of this work, in the year H. 956, being young, and in the country of Bijwárah, a dependency of Biána, went with his maternal grandfather, on whom be the mercy of the Almighty, to the camp of Feríd Táran, a commander of five thousand, and saw this form and ceremony observed." ‖

Administration of Justice.

There seems to have been a considerable degree of religious ebullition at this time in Hindustán, as often happens in disturbed periods. An instance of it is recorded, in which Islám Shah had some concern. One Sheikh Hasan, a favourite scholar or disciple of the celebrated Sheikh Selím Chishti of Síkri, having at-

Account of Sheikh Aláí and the Mehdevis.

* Hesht sargheh.
† Munsif.
‡ Dabír.
§ Band.
‖ Tar. Bedáuni, ff. 156, 157.

BOOK VI. tained great distinction, himself undertook the office of training aspirants in the road of spiritual knowledge in the city of Biána. On his death, he was succeeded in his saintly influence by his son Sheikh Alái, a man of great attainments in learning and in the knowledge of spiritual things, who continued to draw many followers around him, and sustained the reputation of the school.

It so happened that Sheikh Abdalla Niázi, an Afghán, and also favourite scholar of Sheikh Selím Chishti, having returned from the pilgrimage of Mekka, came and settled in Biána. In the course of his travels, which had extended into Arabia, Persia, Khorásán and Transoxiana, he had imbibed the opinions of the sect of Mehdevis *, which at that period appear to have been extensively diffused. Sheikh Alái, who met him, was delighted with his manners and conversation; and gradually adopted, in their full extent, the new doctrines, which in many respects agree with those of the Sufis, renouncing those of his father and former religious teachers.

The founder of this sect, which added another to the many that have divided the Musulmans, was Syed Muhammed, a native of Juánpúr, born about A. H. 847;
A. D. 1482, to 1505. but whose religious mission extended from 887 to 910, when he died at Farra in Khorásán.† He professed to be the Mehdi, the Comforter or Paraclete, promised alike by the Christian and Muhammedan religions; and his followers pretended that the truth of his mission was proved by numerous miracles. The leading articles of their faith were, that he was indeed the promised Mehdi, whom it was necessary to love and follow; all who did not being infidels; that his inspiration, like that

* This sect extended into the Dekhan. Ismael Nizám Shah of Ahmednagar was led by his Minister Jemál Khan to join it. Ferishta, vol. iii. p. 277. This was in Ferishta's own time. The progress of the sect even gave rise to a kind of religious war. Ibid. pp. 277, 278.

† A. H. 910.; Zikádeh, 19. (A.D. 1505, April 23.)

of Moses, was derived directly from God, without the intermediate agency of angels; that the Mehdi and Muhammed were equal in authority; and that none of the Hadís, or traditional sayings of Muhammed, were true, unless confirmed by the Koran or by the Mehdi, to whom alone was committed the task of admitting souls into bliss, or consigning them to misery. The mission of Muhammed and of the Mehdi were for purposes quite distinct from each other; that of the former being to preach the laws of faith; that of the latter, the commands and rules for the practice of good works. The Koran revealed to Muhammed was to be explained by the Mehdi. He taught that it was possible to see God even in this world—by a total oblivion of self in holy meditation, followed, in the progress of pious abstraction, by a moral or spiritual death. In this progress towards the Divine or Beatific vision they marked out several stages, in the last of which the successful devotee, losing his identity, became united with the Deity. In the course of this progress, he ceased reading the Koran, which, with every other study, became superfluous as the mystic vision advanced; he passed or raised the seventy thousand veils that obscure the view of things as they really exist; was blest with the sight of heaven and of hell—of the souls of the just and of the prophets, before being absorbed into the being of God. Such were their chief articles of faith. Those relating to works flow naturally from them. As they held that worldly wealth or possessions were the root of all evil, and that attachment to wives, children, relations, or any thing earthly, by diverting the mind from things divine, produced infidelity and led to hell, the chief of their practical doctrines were the renunciation of all the world and its gifts, houses, land, women, children, silver and gold; when persecuted, the only alternative offered, was to desert their country or to have recourse to arms: their conversation was to

BOOK VI. be only with the virtuous: they were as they advanced to quit all society, the better to enjoy uninterrupted meditation on God, thereby in the end to attain the longed-for vision: they were to fight for the Word of God, either with the sword of poverty or of prayer, or with that of war. To kill an infidel they deemed no crime; and they might lawfully take ample license in retaliation, or revenge, of such as molested their sect. Such as had only begun their heavenly course were enjoined to read the Koran, and to observe the five stated times of prayer. The more advanced seem to have been exempted from all external observances.*

Sheikh Abdalla, on his return from the Hejáz, following out the precepts of his new faith, had taken up his residence in a garden near Biána at the Mhár Tank, a neighbourhood frequented by persons of the lowest class, and was accustomed himself to repair to it, to draw water, and carry it away on his head with unaffected humility. When prayer-time came, he collected a number of individuals of the lowest class, water-drawers, carriers of wood and grass-cutters, who lived around. Them he instructed with the honest zeal of a missionary, and with the eloquence and knowledge of a man of letters. His preaching was successful, and his patience and unremitting fervour brought in many to his fold.

Sheikh Alái, who was struck with the fervour and unction of his teaching soon became persuaded of the truth of his doctrines; confessed that this was indeed true religion; recommended it to his followers; renounced his own tenets; and having humbly joined the new sect, deserted his monastery, the rents attached to it and his dwelling, and invited his family to follow him to share his poverty and humble living; but offering, if they were unwilling to do this, to divide his property with

* See Colonel Miles's interesting Account of Muhammed Mehdi; Transactions of Literary Society of Bombay, vol. ii. pp. 281—294.

them according to the law, and then let them go, in God's name. Having removed to the neighbourhood, and placed himself under the spiritual guidance of Sheikh Abdalla, he continued his study of the new creed, conformed to the rules of the sect, and divided all he possessed among the poor. Many of his former disciples followed him, and embraced the new doctrines. He daily, at the hours of morning and afternoon prayer, expounded the Holy Koran in presence of assembled multitudes with such persuasive eloquence, that his hearers, catching his enthusiasm, inevitably became converts; and hundreds, abandoning their wives and families, their goods and possessions, and all that tied them to the world, renounced their sins and all evil courses, and ranged themselves among the disciples of the Mehdevis. All that they possessed they enjoyed in common; or, if any, such as agriculturists or merchants, continued in their occupations, they made a vow to devote a tenth of their income to charity and the service of God. In every thing they trusted to God. They used no cooking vessels, but when they received a handful of flour mixed it up, just as it was, with salt and water, and used it while it lasted. In some instances, where they happened to get nothing, they were known to fast for two or three days with perfect resignation, without venting a complaint or manifesting any indication of suffering. But in spite of their destitute condition, they always went armed, carrying a sword and shield or other arms, that they might repel their enemies. And, wherever they saw any person do what was contrary to their notions of right, they, in the first instance, mildly warned him to desist; but if he persisted, they proceeded to compel him by force and violence to alter his conduct. Such of the magistrates as had adopted the Mehdevi opinions gave their sanction to these proceedings; so that those

BOOK VI. of them who disapproved of this outrageous conduct, were unable to afford a remedy.

Sheikh Abdalla, seeing to what lengths the unregulated zeal of Sheikh Alái was hurrying him, admonished and chid him gently, and suggested to him the propriety of making a pilgrimage to Mekka. Sheikh Alái, in deference to this advice of his spiritual guide, but without abating any thing of his usual proceedings, set out attended by a retinue of six or seven hundred followers.* In passing Khowáspúr, which lies in the Júdpúr territory, Khowás Khan, the celebrated Afghán chief, who was then stationed on that frontier, came out with an honorary procession to meet him, listened to his teaching, and became a convert to his opinions. But that nobleman, displeased with the violence of some of his acts and doctrines, and dreading the consequence of his principles on the troops, soon gave him up; and Alái, disconcerted by this defection, and influenced by various other circumstances, returned to Biána, just about the time when Islám Shah mounted
A. H. 959. the throne in Agra. The Sheikh was summoned to Court among other religious men of the time. But there, in defiance of the usage and etiquette of Courts, and following the levelling principles of his sect, instead of the usual salutation to the sovereign, he pronounced only the ordinary and familiar greeting to an equal.† This departure from rule was eagerly seized by the King's Ministers, who charged the obnoxious innovator at once with want of reverence to his Majesty, and with heresy: and Múlla Abdalla Sultánpúri, who at that time enjoyed the title of Makhdúm-al-mulk, after having various conferences with him, went so far as to issue a fetwa or opinion, declaring him guilty of a capital offence. Islám Shah ordered a trial to take place in

* Ferishta gives him 370.; the Taríkh-e Nizámi. 600 or 700; the Tabakát, 700 or 800; the Nisáb-náma, 900.

† Alik-is-salám.

his presence, and before such as were considered to be the chief doctors and múllas of the age. In the course of the investigation that ensued, Sheikh Alái maintained his cause with such superiority of talent over them all, and, when he proceeded to explain the mysteries of the Koran, produced such an effect on Islám Shah himself, that he exclaimed, "Nay, now, Sheikh, give up your peculiar and heterodox fancies, and you shall be made Mohtesib* of all my kingdom. Hitherto you have exercised judgment without permission from me; henceforward do so under my authority." But the Sheikh, true to his principles, refused to consent. Islám Shah, softening the severity of Múlla Abdalla's decree, ordered him to be banished to Hindía.†

Here, such was the extraordinary influence of the eloquence and persuasive powers of Alái, that he soon gained over Behár Khan Sirwáni, the governor, and the greater part of his troops to his opinions; so that his guards became his followers. Makhdúm-al-mulk, on learning these tidings, filled with saintly rage, besought and prevailed upon the King to order him back to Delhi, where a council was convened to try him once more for the crimes laid to his charge. Before this council Makhdúm-al-mulk appeared as his accuser. "This man," said he, "pretends to be the promised Mehdi; he would be king of all the earth. Your army is attached to him: your subjects, in the social relations of life, deserting their duties as parents, husbands, and children, cling to his novelties. The kingdom is in danger of falling into the utmost confusion." Still, however, Islám Shah would not yield to the severe conclusions of his Ulema; and directed that Alái should be sent into Behár to Sheikh Badeh Tyeb Dánishmend, by

* The Mohtesib is the great Censor morum.

† The Nisábnáma says, to the Dekhan, f. 113, and that he stopped at Hindía on his road

BOOK VI. whose fetwa he professed that he would be guided; and himself set out for the Penjáb.

Sheikh Badeh, to whom Alái was thus committed, had been much followed as a religious guide by Shír Shah, the king's father, who held him in such reverence that he was accustomed, when the holy man was going out, to place the shoes before his feet. Sheikh Badeh, long and deeply versed in the theology of his age and religion, entirely coincided in opinion with Makhdúm-al-mulk, and to that effect wrote his fetwa or decree, which was forthwith forwarded by express to Islám Shah, who commanded the personal attendance of the prisoner. At this period Sheikh Alái was seized with a pestilential disease then raging. This malady was farther irritated by the fatigue of his long journey to the Penjáb; so that, when he reached the presence of the King, he was unable to speak. Islám Shah, still desirous to save him, standing by his side, gently addressed him: "Only whisper in my ear," said the prince, "the promised Mehdi is not come, and be free." Sheikh Alái, absorbed in a meditative trance, did not heed his words, and Islám, driven to extremity by his unrelenting divines, commanded him to be scourged. At the third stroke of the lash, says the historian, he resigned his soul to his Creator. Islám Shah directed that his body should be interred in the tomb of his forefathers.*

* The account of this transaction is taken from the Tabak. Akberi, f. 182.; Tar. Nizámi, ff. 221—223.; Ferishta, vol. ii. pp. 138—141. See also the Taríkh-e Bedáuni, ff. 161—163. The author Abdal Kader, then very young, was carried by his father to see Alái when he passed Besáwer, on his route to Mekka. See also the Nisábnáma-e Afghánán, ff. 111—114. Some authors place Alái's death in A. H. 955.; Bedáuni, with more probability, in A. H. 957.; Tar. Bed. f. 167.

# CHAPTER III.

## SULTAN FIRÚZ SHAH SÚR, OFTEN CALLED THE SHAH-ZÁDA FIRÚZ KHAN.

### ACCESSION AND MURDER OF FIRÚZ SHAH. — ACCOUNT OF HIS UNCLE AND MURDERER, MOBÁREZ KHAN.

CHAP. III.

A. D. 1553, A. H. 960. Accession of Firúz Shah.

On the death of Islám, or Selím, Shah, the Afghán chiefs who were with him at Guáliár acknowledged his son Firúz Khan, then only twelve years of age, as their sovereign, and placed him on the throne. Coin was struck, and the prayer for the reigning prince offered, in his name. But his reign was short. Mobárez Khan, his maternal uncle (the son of Nizám Khan Súr, Shír Shah's younger brother), hardened by a guilty ambition, on the third day after the death of his cousin Islám Shah, entered the private apartments of the palace, with the intention of putting to death the young King. Firúz's mother, Bíbí Bái*, was the sister of Mobárez Khan. On hearing that her brother was forcing his way into the harem attended by armed men, alarmed at the danger which threatened her son, she rushed out, and seizing the hem of his robe, with prayers and tears besought him to spare his sister's boy; offering to convey the youth to some far distant land where he would live as a private person, and never aspire to be king: or, if that was not allowed her, she prayed her brother at least to spare her son's life, though doomed to imprisonment, however severe. But Mobárez, throwing her off, seized the young King, and barbarously murdered him in his mother's arms.

His murder.

* This lady is by different writers called Bíbí Bánu, Bíbí Bái, and Bíbí Máhi, the last probably by mistake.

BOOK VI.

A.D. 1553.

This sad event was an unhappy consequence of the affectionate temper of the Queen. Islám Shah, her late husband, who had formed the most unfavourable opinion of Mobárez Khan, and feared his attempts on the life of his son, had repeatedly resolved to put him to death, and was as often prevented only by her intervention and tears. After he had taken to his death-bed, the King again told Bíbí Bái that she must choose between her brother and her son; that if she valued her son's life, she must suffer her brother to be taken out of the way; that there was no other security for the prince. But Bíbí Bái, who thought Islám's suspicions unfounded, and that Mobárez was too much of a voluptuary, and too much devoted to idle amusement to be ambitious, finally prevailed upon her husband to spare the future murderer of their son.

Account of his uncle and murderer Mobárez Khan.

Abul-fazl remarks that Nizám Khan Súr, the younger brother of Shír Shah, left one son and three daughters, and that this son, as well as the husbands of all the three daughters, attained the regal dignity. The son of Mobárez Khan now became king by his crime; one of the daughters had married the late King Islám Shah; another married Ahmed Khan Súr, the viceroy of the Penjáb; and the third, Ibráhím Khan Súr, both of whom, in their turns, we shall see proclaimed Kings of Delhi.*

* The authorities to be consulted for this short reign are the Tar. Niz. ff. 222, 223.; Akbernáma, f. 91.; Tar. Bedáuni, f. 170.; Ferishta, vol. ii. p. 141.; Khol. ul Tow. f. 284.; Kháfi Khan, f. 61.

# CHAPTER IV.

## SULTAN MUHAMMED SHAH ADEL SÚR, OFTEN CALLED ADELI.

ACCESSION OF MOBÁREZ KHAN, OR SULTAN MUHAMMED SHAH. — HIS CHARACTER. — DEATH OF SEKANDER KHAN FIRMULI AT THE DERBÁR. — REVOLT AND DEFEAT OF TÁJ KHAN. — CHARACTER OF THE MINISTER HÍMÚ. — SPREAD OF DISAFFECTION. — REVOLT OF IBRÁHÍM KHAN IN BIÁNA. — HE TAKES DELHI AND AGRA, AND ASSUMES THE SOVEREIGNTY. — DISTRACTED STATE OF THE EMPIRE. — REVOLT OF AHMED KHAN IN THE PENJÁB — OPPOSED AT FARRA BY IBRÁHÍM KHAN, WHOM HE DEFEATS. — OCCUPIES AGRA AND DELHI. — DECLARED EMPEROR BY THE AFGHÁN NOBLES. — HUMÁYUN ENTERS THE PENJÁB. — HIS GENERAL BIRAM KHAN DEFEATS THE AFGHÁNS ON THE SATLEJ. — HUMÁYUN DEFEATS AND EXPELS AHMED KHAN. — IBRÁHÍM AGAIN TAKES THE FIELD. — ADVANCE OF MUHAMMED SHAH'S FORCES UNDER HÍMÚ — WHO DEFEATS IBRÁHÍM, AND BESIEGES HIM IN BIÁNA. — REVOLT OF MUHAMMED KHAN IN BENGAL. — RETREAT OF HÍMÚ FROM BIÁNA TOWARDS BEHÁR. — FLIGHT, AND FATE OF IBRÁHÍM KHAN. — HÍMÚ JOINS MUHAMMED SHAH NEAR KALPI. — DEFEATS AND DESTROYS THE ARMY OF BENGAL. — HUMÁYUN AT DELHI. — HIS DEATH. — HÍMÚ SENT AGAINST AKBER. — HE OCCUPIES AGRA AND DELHI. — IS DEFEATED, AND KILLED AT PÁNIPAT. — SUBVERSION OF THE AFGHÁN DYNASTY. — DEFEAT, AND DEATH OF MUHAMMED SHAH IN BEHÁR. — HIS CHARACTER. — HIS SON SHÍR SHAH. — REMARKS ON THE AFGHÁN DYNASTY IN INDIA. — COMPETITORS FOR THE SOVEREIGNTY AT THE TIME OF HUMÁYUN'S RESTORATION.

CHAP. IV.

A.D. 1553, A.H. 960. Accession of Mobárez Khan, or Sultan Muhammed Shah.

AFTER this detestable murder, Mobárez Khan mounted the throne, with the consent of the nobles and vazírs who were on the spot, under the title of Sultan Muhammed Shah Adel, or the Just, an epithet which the common people changed into Adeli; or, by a farther corruption, into Andli, or "the Blind."

His character.

Sultan Muhammed possessed no qualities fitted to

BOOK VI. A.D. 1553.

make him a good king or a good man. He was grossly ignorant, and hated learning. He paid little attention to public affairs, spending the greater part of his time in the recesses of the harem, wholly given up to sensual indulgence and debauchery, varied only by the amusements of music and dancing. In music he is said to have acquired uncommon proficiency; and we hardly discover another commendable trait in his character. He was fond of low pleasures and of low companions, who flattered him and confirmed him in his vices.

In his expenditure he was childishly profuse. Having heard tales of the magnificence and generosity of Sultan Muhammed Toghlak, he became ambitious of rivalling him, and several times threw open the doors of his treasury, when he bestowed largesses lavishly on the common people, in the vain hope of gaining their affection. With a similar object he made a practice, in going through the streets of a town, to shoot golden-headed arrows; and the person into whose house they fell or who found them, on bringing them back, was presented with the sum of five hundred tangas* in money. But these practices he did not long persist in.

On his accession he bestowed the office of vasír and lieutenant of the palace, with the chief management of affairs, on Shemshír Khan, who had been a slave of Shír Shah, and was the younger brother of the celebrated Khowás Khan; Doulat Khan Nouháni, a new convert and his protégé, was raised to rank, and got charge of the Nouhánis; and Hímú Bakál, a Hindu, was raised to offices of high trust, and soon became the Minister who exercised the most commanding authority.

Such appointments were not likely to conciliate the haughty Afghán chiefs who were near the throne, and thought themselves not much below it. Discontent spread on every side. Sultan Muhammed was hated,

* About 50*l*.

and, what for a king was more dangerous, he was despised. The government had lost the vigorous hand that directed it during the two late reigns. The general discontent was attended by its natural concomitant, a spirit of insubordination; and a disposition to revolt began to show itself from the very first month of his reign, and spread extensively, more especially among the King's own nearest connections of the Súr family; insomuch that, ere long, the kingdom was in reality broken down into a variety of different states. That discord which had always been the bane of the Afgháns in India reappeared in full operation.*

Death of Sekander Khan Firmuli in the Derbár. A. H. 961, A. D. 1554.

An incident which occurred in the palace soon after the accession of the Sultan to the throne marked the crisis of this spirit. Sultan Muhammed, who did not often appear in public, having one day held a public derbár in the fort of Guáliár, proceeded, in presence of his most distinguished nobles, to make a distribution of various jágírs. Among the rest, the government of Kanáuj, which was held by Shah Muhammed Firmuli, a nobleman of an eminent Afghán family, was taken from him, and conferred on Sirmast Khan Sirpani, also an Afghán, but of inferior note.† Sekander Khan, Firmuli's son, a youth of handsome mein, but of a lofty and impatient temper, who, as well as his father, was present when this arrangement was announced, exclaimed, "What, are things come to such a pass, that our estate is to be given to a set of Sirpani dog-merchants?" at the same time audibly hinting something about the field of battle. His father, who was unwell, chid him for indulging in such language, and attempted to restrain his impetuosity, but in vain. Turning on his father, he asked him if he had forgotten that Shír Shah, intending to put him to death, had

* Tar. Niz. f. 223.; Tab. Akb. f. 184.: Tar. Bed. f. 171.; Akbernáma, f. 92.

† Kháfi Khan says, one who had made a trade of selling dogs, which does not seem probable.

BOOK VI. A. D. 1554.

kept him in an iron cage, from which he had been released only at the intercession of Selím Shah? Did he not see that it was now once more the plan of the Súr family to bring ruin on them and their race? Was he blind, or was he so dastardly as tamely to submit to such contemptuous treatment? This violent conduct occasioned considerable confusion in the Derbár. Sirmast Khan, a tall and powerful man, approached Sekander in a conciliating manner, saying, "My son, why all these hard words?" at the same time laying his hand soothingly on the young man's shoulder, but intending to secure him and make him prisoner. Sekander, aware of his object, drew his dagger, and plunged it into the breast of Sirmast, who fell lifeless on the ground. The uproar and confusion upon this became extreme. Sekander, infuriated with passion, drew his sword and attacked those nobles near him who attempted to secure his person, killing some, and wounding others. The King, availing himself of the disorder that prevailed, made his escape into the harem, when the doors were barred behind him. He was followed by Sekander, who made an attempt to force his way in, but it was too late. Several Amírs, drawing their swords, prevented Sekander's escape, while he continued for some time to slash around him like a mad man. At last Ibráhím Khan Súr, who had married Adeli's sister, wounded him with his sword, and other Amírs rushing on, overpowered him and put him to death. Doulat Khan Nouháni, at the same time, with one blow of his sabre, slew Shah Muhammed Firmuli, the unhappy and innocent father. The whole affair lasted upwards of half an hour.*

Revolt and defeat of Táj Khan.

It is said that Táj Khan Keráni, the brother of that Suleimán Khan Keráni who afterwards ruled Bengal under the name of Ali Shah†, as he was coming out of

* Tab. Akb. f. 185.; Tar. Niz. ff. 171, 172.; Nisábnáma, f. 116.

† Rather perhaps of Hazrat Ali, for he seems to have declined the name of king.

the fort of Guáliár that morning after having attended the levee, happened to meet Shah Muhammed Khan Firmuli, who was then on his way to the Derbár, and as they entered into conversation, told him, that affairs were going on so ill, and were managed by such contemptible agents, that he was resolved to return no more to the Court, but to set out and see what could be done elsewhere; and he invited Firmuli to go along with him and join him in the adventure. This Shah Muhammed declined, and went on to the fatal meeting—while Táj Khan, hearing in the course of the day what had occurred, made his escape from Guáliár the same evening, and took the road of Bengal with his followers. As soon as it was known that he had left the city, Adeli sent a strong force to pursue him, and himself followed soon after, and overtook the Khan at Chibra-Mow*, where he defeated him; but Táj Khan, effecting his escape, retreated to Chunár. As he marched through the country, he seized such of Adeli's collectors of the revenue as fell in his way, and took possession of all the public money and other property on which he could lay his hands, with an hundred elephants. He was soon joined by his brothers Imád, Suleimán and Khwája Elías, who held perganas on the banks of the Ganges, and in Khowáspur-Tánda; and no longer concealed his views, but appeared in open rebellion.†



Meanwhile Adeli, who had moved from Guáliár to Chunár, advanced to chastise the Keránis. The two armies met on the opposite banks of the Ganges, and faced each other for some time, but without engaging. At last Hímú, who was now high in the King's confi-

* Chibra-Mow, which is not in the maps, is a town of the Doáb; Briggs reads eight, Dow, eighty miles from Agra. Another copy of Ferishta, reads eighty miles from Agra, and sixty from Laknou; the Tab. Akb. f. 185, has forty kos from Agra, and thirty from Kanáuj, which is probably correct. It is a dependency of Kanáuj, and was the birthplace of the author of the Inshá-e Medhárám, Tar. Bed. ff. 171, 172.

† As above.

BOOK VI. A.D. 1554.

dence, made a proposal, that if he were allowed to take a few elephants*, he would undertake to cross the river, to attack the enemy, and to destroy them. The King acceded to his request; and Hímú having led his troops over the river, engaged the Keránis in a battle, which, though desperately contested, ended in a complete victory. Táj Khan was fortunate enough to escape into Bengal, where, at no very distant period, he gained possession of the throne.

Character of the Minister Hímú.

Hímú, the Minister of Adeli, who was thus successful, was a Hindu, and in spite of the prejudiced and partial representations of the historians of the house of Taimur, must have been a man of extraordinary capacity. He is represented, indeed, by Abulfazl as having owed his rise to the vices of Adeli, and as being one of those low time-servers and flatterers, whose elevation is gained by indulging that love of gossip, slander, and scandal, in which the great too often delight; and his elevation is given as a proof, what mean creatures can rise to the highest dignity, by studying the humours of those above them. He was, we are told, totally devoid of the ordinary qualities that lead to fortune. He had to struggle against the disadvantages of low birth, a mean person, and want of address; being originally a shopkeeper† in Rewári, a town of Mewát; and, by extraction, of the caste of Dhúsir, the meanest class of Hindu shopkeepers. By his low wit and pleasantry, says the unfriendly historian, he rose from obscurely selling his worthless wares in a narrow lane among his wretched companions, to be employed as a purveyor‡ by Selím Shah; and having attracted his notice by his activity and his knowledge of business, he was taken into the royal service, gradually came to enjoy a share of the

* Ek halqeh fil ra, keh chand zinjír bashed; Tar. Bed.

† Baqál.

‡ The Kholáset ul Towáríkh says he was made Modi-e-Sirkár, an office, probably, nearly corresponding to that of purveyor, f. 28½.

royal confidence, and was employed in many important transactions, in both the political and revenue departments. In the offices which he filled when so promoted, he is accused of bringing numbers to misery, while he pretended to be acting only from zeal for his master's service, though in truth he was busy all the while enriching himself from the property of the oppressed, and by his misdeeds was whetting the axe against his master and himself. His pains and assiduity as a spy and an informer, a set of men too dangerously encouraged by those in power, is said to have gained him the favour of the late king, Selím Shah, by whom, among other offices of trust, he was raised to that of Superintendent of Bazars*, which includes an extensive exercise of police duties.

When Sultan Muhammed Shah Adeli usurped the throne, being altogether ignorant of business, Hímú, who, from his office, had frequent access to him, by his address and insinuation, and by relieving him from the drudgery of business, contrived to become so useful, and to gain so complete an ascendency over the king's mind, that he was soon elevated to the highest rank, became Prime Minister, and the whole duties of government gradually devolved upon him, Adeli, in reality, retaining only the name of king. Hímú placed and displaced officers, gave and resumed jágírs at pleasure, with absolute power. He got possession of the royal elephants, as well as of the treasures which had been accumulated by the last two kings, and he freely expended what they had collected. In this way, it is affirmed, he gained for himself a number of low and sordid adherents, who looked up to and worshipped him as their only hope and reliance. He bore for some time the title of Basant Rái, and afterwards assumed that of Raja, vainly decking himself with the lofty title of Raja Vikramájít.

* Sheikhji-Bazár, Tar. Bed.

BOOK VI.
A. D. 1554.

In all this, there is certainly much prejudice and misrepresentation; for even Abulfazl is forced to give unwilling testimony, that in the Cabinet he directed affairs of state and the business of the country with singular success; and that though his frame was so feeble that he could not ride on horseback, and even in the field was forced to be carried about in a litter or on an elephant, yet such was his spirit that he maintained stout contests with the enemies of his King, and, by his determined courage, was victorious in many battles, and achieved exploits worthy of the highest reputation. The truth is, that he was a man who had raised himself from a low rank by great and commanding talents; who was eminent both as a statesman and a general; and who sustained the throne of a worthless prince in difficult times, hated and envied by the nobles as a man of nothing, and detested by the Musulmans of all parties as an infidel and a Pagan, who stood in their way on the road to power. To add to these misfortunes, he has been harshly treated by the writers of the opposite party, the only historians of the times, for what, in his situation, was a merit,—his having long been the prop of the Afghán dynasty, and the most formidable enemy of the line of Taimur. In person, as we have said, he is represented as having been of mean deportment, hard-favoured, and of low stature. He never wore a sword, and was unable to ride on horseback. Yet, with all his disadvantages, such were his good fortune and valour that he gained two and twenty battles for the King, whose cause he espoused against the various Afghán pretenders to the throne, and secured a complete ascendency over them all, establishing, with every class of men, the highest reputation for courage and conduct in the field and ability in the Cabinet.*

* Compare Akbernáma, f. 92.; f. 184.; Tar. Bedáuni, f. 171.; Tar. Niz. ff. 223, 4.; Tab. Akb. Kholáset ul Tow. f. 284. This last

Perhaps the choice of a Hindu Minister, however odious to the Afgháns, was a measure of sound policy in a dissipated and depraved prince like Adeli. From the aspect of the times, it is clear that such a monarch could not have raised any great Afghán noble to the power enjoyed by Hímú, without exposing himself to the risk of being dethroned by his own servant. Nothing of the kind was to be apprehended from a humble and almost despised Pagan, whose consequence depended altogether on that of his patron.*

Spread of disaffection.

The timely vigour of Hímú succeeded in quelling the rebellion of Táj Khan Keráni; "but," says the historian, "rebellion had roused herself from her deep slumber, and the line of firm and well-compacted policy of Shír Shah, and of the steady and stern command of Selím Shah was snapped, so that every where things fell into disorder." Adeli was at once hated and despised. The governors of provinces were powerful, and possessed armies entirely under their controul. The suspicious temper of Adeli hastened the crisis. Having conceived doubts of the fidelity of Ibráhím Khan Súr his cousin, the son of Gházi Khan Súr, an uncle of Shír Shah, he had resolved to arrest him. Ibráhím's wife, a sister of the King's, having got intimation of this intention, communicated it to her husband, who, in consequence, fled in disguise from Chunár to his father Ghází Khan, the governor of Biána and Hindáun. Adeli despatched Isa Khan Niázi in pursuit to chastise him. They met near Kalpi; an action took place, in which Ibráhím had the advantage, and defeated Isa Khan. He now openly threw off his allegiance; and collecting an army in his father's government was soon able to march towards Delhi, of which he took possession, ascended the throne,

Revolt of Ibráhím Khan in Biána.

He takes Delhi and Agra, and

does him justice. See also Ferishta, vol. ii. who, as usual, follows Nizám-ed-dín Ahmed, and could hardly have a better guide in general.

* Tar. Niz. f. 224.

BOOK VI. A.D. 1554. assumes the sovereignty.

and assumed the title and all the ensigns of royalty. Pursuing his success, he next marched towards Agra, which also he reduced, as well as many of the adjoining districts.*

On receiving the news of this alarming revolt in the very centre of his dominions, which threatened to deprive him of his most important provinces and of the kingdom itself, Adeli, instead of following the Keránis to complete their ruin, hastily began his march from Chunár towards Agra. When he reached the Jamna, he was met by an envoy from Ibráhím, craving forgiveness, and offering to submit once more to the King, provided his Majesty would send to his camp Rái Hasan Khan Jilwáni, Behár Khan Sirwáni, who now held the title of Azím Humáyun, and some other chiefs of distinction, at once to receive his submission, and guarantee his safety. Adeli gladly agreed to this request, in which he saw an end of the contest. But the deputed nobles, whether they were from the first in concert with Ibráhím, or whether they were gained over only after reaching his camp and conferring with him, in the end joined the rebel, who stood much higher than the King in the general estimation. Adeli, thus betrayed, finding himself unable to meet his antagonist in the field, retreated, first to Panna, and then to Chunár, abandoning, for the present, Agra and the neighbouring provinces of Hindustán to his rival, who assumed the style of Sultan Ibráhím Súr. The events that rapidly followed compelled Adeli to confine his attention for some time to the task of retaining Behár and the provinces to the east of the Ganges, where he appears to have firmly established his authority.†

Distracted state of the Empire.

But the misfortunes of Adeli were not confined to the successful rebellion of Ibráhím. Disaffection and revolt had spread into all the more distant provinces.

* Tab. Akb. f. 185.; Tar. Bed. ff. 172, 173.

† Tab. Akb. ff. 172, 173.; Akbernáma, f. 92.

Three other viceroys, the governor of the Penjáb, the governor of Malwa, and the governor of Bengal, all at the same time aspired to independent power; so that, at this crisis, the dominions of Shír Shah, by the feuds among his family, were divided among five Afghán kings; Adeli possessed Behár, Juánpúr and great part of the country east of the Ganges; Sultan Ibráhím Súr held Delhi, Agra, the Doáb and the provinces west of the Jamna, as low down as Kalpi; Ahmed Khan Súr, who assumed the title of Sultan Sekander Shah, enjoyed the Penjáb; Shujaa, generally called Sazáwal Khan, the kingdom of Malwa, and Sultan Muhammed Shah Súr, the kingdom of Bengal; for which he had probably even already a competitor in Táj Khan Keráni.

Revolt of Ahmed Khan in the Penjáb. A. H. 962. A. D. 1555.

The first of these princes who now marched to invade the dominions of his neighbours, was Ahmed Khan Súr *, also a cousin of Shír Shah, and who, like Ibráhím, had married a sister of Adeli. He had for some time enjoyed the government of the Penjáb, and now, in the utterly disorganised state of the Afghán monarchy, resolved, like other members of the Súr family, to set up for himself, and not content with the possession of his own province, aspired to the throne of Delhi. Having conciliated the different nobles who possessed influence in the Penjáb, and especially Tátár Khan Kási, Haibat Khan and Nasíb Khan Taghúchi, who had been Selím Shah's chief officers in that province, all of whom regarded Adeli with contempt and disgust, he assumed the title of Sekander Shah †, and at the head of ten or twelve thousand well-appointed horse and a large attendance of less regular followers, marched towards Delhi and Agra. His cousin, Sultan Ibráhím Súr, who was now in possession of all the pro-

* According to the Kholáset ul Towáríkh, f. 286, he was brother's son to Shír Shah, and Ferishta calls him his nephew. But the Tar. Niz. f. 225.; the Tar. Bed., and the Nisábnáma, f. 117, more correctly make him his uncle's son.

† Sultan Sekander, Khol. ul Towáríkh.

BOOK VI. A.D. 1555.

vinces around these capitals, marched out to oppose him with much parade and splendour, at the head of an army of seventy or eighty thousand horse excellently equipped, in which there was a remarkable number of officers of high rank.* He is said to have bestowed on not fewer than two hundred the privilege of having rich kanáts or screens round their tents, even in the royal camp, the Alem and túgh standards, and the right of having the nakára or kettle-drum.

Is opposed at Farra by Ibráhím Khan,

The armies met at Farra, about ten kos from Agra. Sekander Shah, struck with the great superiority in numbers, as well as with the composition of the army of his rival, became desirous of entering into a negociation, and sent to propose a compromise, expressing his willingness to retire from Ibráhím's dominions; that that prince should have absolute possession of Delhi and Agra, with their dependant provinces, and whatever he could conquer to the eastward of them; and on the other hand, that Sekander Shah should be acknowledged as sovereign of the Penjáb, Multán and the neighbouring territory; and that the whole of the Afgháns should unite, and make a common cause in repelling Humáyun and his Tartars, should they pass the Indus. The two armies, composed of fellow-countrymen and relations, were delighted at the prospect of this accommodation. But difficulties were started, and Sultan Ibráhím, trusting to the superiority of his numbers, broke off the negociation, and left the quarrel to be decided by the fate of a battle. This was not long delayed. The vigorous charge of Sekander's left wing, which routed the right of the enemy and pursued them as far as Agra, decided the day. Ibráhím, seeing that the defeat of his army was complete, effected his escape to Sambhal. Sekan-

whom he defeats.

* Kháfi Khan says that there were fifty or sixty Amírs in his army. Among these were chiefs of high distinction, especially Háji Khan Sultan, the ruler of Alwar, Husein Khan Jilwáni, &c.; Tar. Niz. f. 225.; Tab. Akb. ff. 185, 186.; Akbernáma, f. 92.; Tar. Bed. ff. 174, 175.

der Shah, following up his victory, made himself master of Agra and of Delhi, and was soon in possession of the whole extent of country from the Indus to the Ganges.

He occupies Agra and Delhi,

Successful thus far, Sekander was desirous of establishing his right to the throne by the appearance at least of a free election by his countrymen. For this purpose, soon after his arrival in Agra, he prepared a magnificent banquet, to which he invited all the chiefs of the Afghán race. When assembled, he told them that he regarded himself as but one of their number, and claimed no kind of superiority over the other leaders of his countrymen. He remarked to them that among the Afgháns, Sultan Behlúl had raised his tribe of Lodi to honour and reputation; that Shír Shah had, in like manner, rendered the tribe of Súr illustrious; that these distinguished princes, by living in harmony with the tribesmen of their nation and cultivating their affection, had done great things; while their successors, Sultan Ibráhím Lodi, and Muhammed Shah Adeli, by following a different course, had involved their kingdoms in ruin and misery; that, at present, civil discord and civil war prevailed on every side among the Afgháns, circumstances the more to be deplored, as their implacable enemy Humáyun, who had now conquered Kábul and had no longer any brothers who could thwart his designs, was ready to pour down upon them with the whole force of his dominions, and to reap the fruit of their infatuation; that the only hope of the Afgháns lay in union; that if they consented to lay aside private feuds and act in concert like a band of brothers, they could still repel the son of Báber; that their interest was the same; that they had one common cause; that he had called them together to consult in common for the

and is declared Emperor by the Afghán nobles.

* Ibráhím escaped first to Etáwa, and thence to Sambhal. Different accounts of the battle are given. I follow that of Bedáuni.

BOOK VI. A.D. 1555. common good; that at such a crisis, all personal claims to superiority must cease; that he appeared among them only as a private individual, and invited them to choose, as their leader, the man who, from his talents, was best fitted to give unity to their great national efforts, and to lead them to victory; and that to such a person, whoever he might be, selected by their free choice, he was ready at once to swear allegiance, and to humble himself as his most faithful subject. The assembly, with one voice, called out that Sekander Shah, the worthy cousin of Shír Shah, was the wished-for person, and that he alone should be their leader and sovereign. They then proceeded to take a solemn oath to be faithful to him, and to live in peace and unanimity among themselves; and having seated him on the throne of Agra, they presented to him the usual congratulations and offerings, as their King. But the distribution of honours and jágírs that followed, soon put to flight all their wise and virtuous resolutions, and once more introduced discord and heart-burnings into the camp of the Afgháns.

Humáyun enters the Penjáb.

When Sekander, having settled affairs at the capital and subdued the provinces around it, was preparing to pursue still farther the advantages he had gained over Sultan Ibráhím, and had even a fair prospect of attacking Adeli, and gaining possession of the rich kingdoms of Behár and Bengal, to which he was about to direct his march, the unwelcome news arrived that Humáyun, secure in the throne of Kábul, was on his march to recover the Penjáb itself, which he had entered, and occupied a large portion of the country. It is probable that Sekander, when he set out for Agra, had removed the most efficient part of the military force of the Penjáb. To protect a country that was the seat of his power, and to check the progress of an invader whose success would be alike fatal to all the Afghán candidates for power, Sekander, without loss of time, despatched Tátár Khan and Haibat Khan with forty thousand horse. It is only necessary in this place to observe that these generals were defeated on the Satlej at Máchíwára by Biram Khan with great loss, and retreated towards Delhi. Sekander, collecting his whole force, was soon able to oppose the invaders with an army of seventy thousand men, and checked Biram's advance, near Sirhend. Here, however, Biram having been reinforced by the arrival of Humáyun in person, a great battle was fought which proved unfavourable to Sekander. That prince was forced to take refuge among the Sewálik mountains, where he maintained a position for some time, and even overran a great portion of the Penjáb in the beginning of Akber's reign. But, being again hard pressed, he was compelled to abandon that country, and found his way to Bengal, where he succeeded in seizing the reins of government, but soon after died.

His general Biram Khan defeats the Afgháns on the Satlej.

Humáyun defeats and expels Ahmed Khan.

No sooner did Sultan Ibráhím Súr ascertain that Sekander had detached the strength of his army towards the Penjáb, than, leaving his retreat in Sambhal, he crossed the Ganges, and directed his march towards Kalpi, resolved to recruit his army, and to attempt to regain the kingdom. It so happened that, at the very same time, Muhammed Shah Adeli, influenced by the same motives, and burning to recover the territory that he had lost, had detached Hímú, now his Prime Minister, from Chunár with a formidable army, five hundred elephants and a powerful train of artillery, to occupy Agra and Delhi. Hímú, on arriving near Kalpi, encountered Sultan Ibráhím, who was already once more at the head of a considerable force of Afgháns, Nouhánis and Zemíndárs of Biána, and made an attempt to surprise Hímú by night at Khanwa, about ten kos from Biána. After a severe contest, Ibráhím, being defeated, was compelled to take shelter in that fortress, in which he was immediately shut up, and besieged by Hímú. His father Gházi Khan contrived, however, to

Ibráhím again takes the field.

Advance of Muhammed Shah's forces under Hímú,

who defeats him, and besieges him in Biána.

BOOK VI.

A.D. 1555.

supply the place with provisions which he sent from Hindáun by the neighbouring hills.*

Revolt of Muhammed Khan in Bengal.

While Hímú was thus employed, Muhammed Khan Súr †,—also a near relation of Shír Shah, who had been governor of Bengal, but who during the confusion that followed the accession of Ádeli, had declared himself king of that country by the title of Sultan Jilál-ed-dín—encouraged by the insubordination and disorder that everywhere prevailed, advanced into Behár, in order to expel Adeli and to add that province to his kingdom, having aims at the same time upon Júanpúr, and his ambition extending even to Delhi itself. This invasion made Adeli hastily recall Hímú from the siege of Biána, after he had battered it for three months. His army had wasted the country on every side, and added all the disorders of rapine and pillage to the horrors of a frightful famine, which at that time raged, and carried off thousands of the population on every side. The starving inhabitants saw, with feelings of envy and anger, the five hundred elephants of Hímú regularly fed with fine rice and sugarcane; and a public table kept, to which all the Afghán Amírs and officers of note were invited, and entertained with wasteful profusion.

Retreat of Hímú from Biána towards Behár.

Hímú, abandoning the siege with reluctance, retired by the village of Mundháker ‡, followed by Ibráhím, who hung upon his rear, and attacked him near that place. But Hímú again proved victorious, and the Sultan fled to Alwar to ask succour of Háji Khan. Hímú detached his nephew with a strong force, who pursued the flying prince for two or three stages, and then returned. Háji Khan, who was little pleased with Sultan Ibráhím's visit, afforded him no assistance. Driven to extremity, therefore, he resolved to abandon

* Tar. Niz. f. 226.; Tar. Bed. ff. 175, 176.; Ferishta, vol. ii. p. 153.

† He is also called Gouria from Gour his capital; and sometimes Muhammed Khan Bengáli.

‡ Mundháker is about six kos from Agra.

that quarter: and bidding a last adieu to his father, brothers, and family whom he left in Hindáun, he took the road to the country of Panna, attended by a few faithful followers.

Flight and fate of Ibráhím Khan.

The future history of Sultan Ibráhím Súr may be given in few words. The historian Abdal Káder regrets that a man possessed of so many valuable qualities should have been unsuccessful in war. Handsome in person, polite, accomplished, generous and brave, he suffered sixteen or seventeen defeats in the course of two or three years. His father Ghási Khan was taken by capitulation in Biána by one of the Emperor's generals not long after Ibráhím's departure, and the whole family young and old put to death, so that Ibráhím himself was the only remnant of the race, whose pomp and power, says the historian, is now but a tale.*

After leaving his father, Sultan Ibráhím, who was very popular, having collected a considerable force, marched towards Bhatta †, a Hindu principality in the east of Malwa, and attacked Raja Rámchander the native chief, by whom, however, he was defeated, and taken prisoner. The Raja treated his prisoner with distinguished courtesy. He visited him in person and presented him with honorary presents, allowed him to retain all his tents and the ensigns of royalty, seated him on his throne, and attended by his native Hindus, waited upon him as his subject. Here Ibráhím remained till after the death of Shujaa or Sazáwal Khan, the Prince of Malwa, when the Afgháns of the Miána tribe, who had a quarrel with his son and successor Báz Behåder, invited Ibráhím to Ráisen where they had

* Tar. Bed. f. 175.

† Bhatta. This word is variously written in the manuscripts. Dow reads it Bhetah; Briggs, Punna; the MSS. of Kháfi Khan have Tahta or Thatta. The real reading seems to be Bhatta, which is a district of Ghara or Garrah in Malwa. See Hamilton's Hindostán, vol. i. p. 316.; and Gazetteer, *sub voce* Garrah.

BOOK VI. A. D. 1556.

established themselves, offering to raise him to the throne of Malwa in opposition to their enemy. He joined them, and Durgáwati, the Ráni of Garrah, having been associated in the confederacy, their affairs were for some time prosperous. But Báz Beháder having contrived to detach the Ráni from the league, Ibráhím, finding that all prospect of success was gone, fled to Orissa, where he remained several years, till that province was conquered by Suleimán Keráni of Bengal; (A. H. 975.) when he waited upon Suleimán, in consequence of a solemn agreement, and was treacherously put to death.*

Hímú joins Muhammed near Kalpi.

Meanwhile, Hímú, after defeating Sultan Ibráhím at Mundháker, continued his march down the Jamna with the utmost celerity, and joined Adeli. Muhammed Shah Súr, the King of Bengal, had spread his detachments over the province of Juánpúr, and he himself had advanced to Chapergháta †, fifteen kos from Kalpi. Here the hostile armies lay, divided only by the Jamna; and the Sovereign of Bengal, who had a large and highly equipped army of both horse and foot, with a number of elephants, was prepared to cross the river, and looked forward with confidence to a decisive victory. But the sudden and unexpected arrival of Hímú changed the face of affairs. The moment he came, he sent his troops across, and fording the river with his elephants, fell on the army of Bengal by surprise. The resistance made was comparatively trifling. The enemy, in the obscurity of the night, could distinguish nothing, and forsook their camp. The slaughter was great among the fugitives. Many Amírs of rank perished. Muhammed himself was never heard of more. The whole camp, and the property that it contained, became the prey of the conquerors.‡

Defeats and destroys the army of Bengal.

Having thus removed another of the competitors for

* Tar. Niz. f. 226.; Tab. Akb. f. 186.; Tar. Bed. f. 176.; Kholáset ul Towáríkh, f. 286.

† Chaper-ghát, Akb. 92. and 145.

‡ Tab. Akb. and others as above.

his throne, Adeli returned to Chunár, in order to collect a force with which to expel from Hindustán the Emperor Humáyun, who, after his victory over Sekander Shah at Sirhend, had advanced as far as Delhi, which he had occupied, while his troops which had been pushed forward had taken possession of Agra and the surrounding provinces. The death of Humáyun, which followed soon after, encreased the anxiety of Adeli to check the invaders; and in a short time Hímú was despatched with an army of fifty thousand horse and five hundred elephants towards Agra, to take advantage of this occurrence, to recover what had been lost, and to expel the invaders from his kingdom.

CHAP. IV.

Humáyun at Delhi.

His death.

Hímú sent against Akber.

The events that followed will be related more in detail in the reign of Akber. Suffice it to say that, on the approach of Hímú's army, Sekander Khan Uzbek and the other generals of the Emperor Akber, who had succeeded his father, sensible that they were unable to resist so powerful a force, retreated to Delhi. Hímú, having occupied Agra, pursued the retreating enemy. Near Delhi he was encountered by the governor of that capital, the veteran Terdi Beg, who gave him battle, but was defeated and retreated towards the Penjáb, leaving Hímú in possession of both capitals.

reoccupies Agra and Delhi.

The victorious Hímú now moved out of Delhi with all his force, and advanced to Pánipat, on the plains of which the fate of India has been so often decided. The invaders were commanded by Biram Khan, and the youthful Akber. In a well contested battle, the fate of war was at length unfavourable to Hímú, who was wounded in the eye by an arrow, taken prisoner and carried before Akber, and put to death by order of Biram Khan.

Defeated, and killed at Pánipat.

This battle was decisive of the fate of the Afghán dynasty. After the death of Hímú the fortune of Adeli rapidly declined. Before that event, Khizer Khan, the son of the late Muhammed Shah Súr, who

Subversion of the Afghán dynasty.

BOOK VI.

A. D. 1556.

had been defeated and slain at Chapargháta, having succeeded his father in Gour and assumed the title of Sultan Beháder, collected a large army, which he led against Adeli to revenge his father's death, and overran a portion of the eastern provinces that Adeli still enjoyed. In spite of his character for effeminacy, that prince took the field in person, and met the invader, whom he bravely engaged in a well-contested battle, in which, however, he was unsuccessful and was slain, after a reign of nearly three years.

Defeat and death of Muhammed Shah in Behár.

His character.

This depraved effeminate prince, while he seems to have been devoid of every moral excellence, had a refined taste, and was distinguished for his skill in music and dancing. Mían Tansín, the great master of these arts, acknowledged himself his scholar: and Báz Beháder, the King of Malwa, and one of the most gifted musicians of his age, ascribed his excellence to the instructions of Adeli. It is added, that he was scrupulously exact in all religious observances; he never omitted the prescribed prayers, and was regular in fasting, and altogether abstained from intoxicating liquors. His body was never found.

His son Shír Shah.

His son Shír Shah is said to have assumed the ensigns of royalty in the fortress of Chunár upon his death. His reign was probably short and limited in power, as he has been wholly passed over by most historians.

Remarks on the Afghán dynasty in India,

With him ended the Súr dynasty, which rose by the genius of one remarkable man, was sustained by the talents of another, and fell by the ignorance and vices of their successors. It illuminated Hindustán for a short time by its radiance; but its light, says Abulfazl, was only that of the glowworm, which shines in the darkness of the night, during the absence of the real sun, but vanishes as soon as that luminary once more ascends the firmament in its glory.

The Afghán dynasty had ruled India about a hundred

and six years, reckoning from the accession of Sultan Behlúl Lodi, without making allowance for what may be called the interregnum of Báber and Humáyun; and only twenty-six years since the accession of Shír Shah, and the Súr family.

CHAP. IV.

And the five competitors for the sovereignty at the time of Humáyun's restoration.

Of the five kings, who at the same moment contended for independence in the Afghán empire of India, we have seen, that Adeli fell in battle; that Sultan Ibráhím of Biána, after repeated defeats, fled to Malwa, and finally perished in Orissa; and that Sultan Muhammed Shah of Bengal, having been slain at Chapergháta, was succeeded by his son Sultan Behâder. Sultan Sekander of the Penjáb, the fourth competitor, having been defeated by Humáyun and Biram Khan at Sirhend, took refuge in the Himaláya mountains, as has been mentioned, and after various transactions, which belong to the reign of Akber, fled to Bengal, where he contrived to seize the reins of government; but soon after died, and was succeeded by Táj Khan Keráni and Suleimán Keráni.

Shujaa or Sazáwal Khan, the fifth, who was the ruler of Malwa, does not seem to have invaded the territories of the Delhi kingdom. On his death, which happened about this time, his son Behâder, stripping his brothers of their share of their father's dominions, mounted the throne under the name of Sultan Báz Behâder of Malwa, and held the sovereign power for many years.

Such was the fate of the five kings who were contending in the heart of the Afghán empire, when Humáyun returned into India, and whose discord paved the way for the conquest of the country. It is now necessary to retrace our steps, and to accompany Humáyun from Kábul in his successful invasion of Hindustán.*

* The chief authorities for this chapter are the Tab. Akb. ff. 182—185.; Tar. Niz. ff. 223—226.; Akbernáma, ff. 91, 92.; Tar. Bedáuni, ff. 174—176.; Ferishta, vol. ii. pp. 143—152.; iv. pp. 275, 276.; Kholáset ul Towáríkh, ff. 281—286.; Kháfi Khan, ff. 61—65.

# BOOK SEVENTH.

## HUMÁYUN'S RECONQUEST OF INDIA, AND DEATH.

HUMÁYUN RESOLVES TO ATTEMPT THE RECONQUEST OF INDIA.—HIS SUSPICIONS OF BIRAM KHAN—WHO ENTERTAINS HIM MAGNIFICENTLY AT KANDAHÁR—AND ARRANGES TO ACCOMPANY HIM ON HIS INVASION.—HUMÁYUN'S PREPARATIONS AT KÁBUL.—HE IS JOINED BY BIRAM KHAN.—SETS OUT ON HIS EXPEDITION, AND REACHES THE INDUS.—STATE OF INDIA.—HUMÁYUN CROSSES THE INDUS.—OCCUPIES RHOTAS AND THE NORTHERN PENJÁB, AND ENTERS LÁHÚR.—SUCCESSFUL PROGRESS.—OCCUPATION OF SIRHEND.—CONTINUED DISTRACTIONS IN HINDUSTÁN.—BIRAM KHAN CROSSES THE SATLEJ.—BATTLE OF MÁCHÍWÁRA.—ADVANCE OF SEKANDER SHAH.—HUMÁYUN SUPPORTS BIRAM.—BATTLE OF SIRHEND.—FLIGHT OF SEKANDER, AND DISPERSION OF HIS FORCES.—SHAH ABUL MAALI.—DECISIVE EFFECTS OF THE VICTORY AT SIRHEND.—HUMÁYUN RE-OCCUPIES DELHI.—DISTRIBUTES THE PROVINCES, WHICH ARE RAPIDLY REDUCED.—SURRENDER OF BIÁNA.—FREQUENT INSUBORDINATION OF HUMÁYUN'S OFFICERS.—REVOLT OF MÍRZA SULEIMÁN IN BADAKHSHÁN.—MISCONDUCT OF ABUL MAALI IN THE PENJÁB.—HE IS SUPERSEDED BY AKBER, WHO EXPELS SEKANDER SHAH.—ACCOUNT RECEIVED OF THE DEATH OF HUMÁYUN.—HIS PLANS FOR THE GOVERNMENT OF THE EMPIRE.—PARTICULARS OF HIS DEATH, WHICH IS FOR A TIME CONCEALED.—ALARM EXCITED BY THIS EVENT.—DANGER OF THE CRISIS.—CHARACTER OF HUMÁYUN.

BOOK VII.

A. D. 1554.

Humáyun resolves to attempt the reconquest of India.

No sooner was Humáyun released from the danger of rebellion and civil war by the blindness and banishment of Kámrán, his only surviving brother, than his mind reverted to his long-cherished wish for the recovery of the throne of Delhi. But, before venturing on such an enterprise, it was necessary to secure himself in his kingdom of Kábul and its dependencies, that, while attempting the conquest of India, he might not see himself deprived of his older dominions in the West.

Serious doubts of the fidelity of Biram Khan, his most powerful subject, had been infused into his mind. Biram had lately done him an important service, by placing Háji Muhammed in his hands. But he nevertheless stood in an ambiguous position. For several years Biram had ruled Kandahár with nearly absolute power in correspondence with Humáyun as his sovereign, though, as it would appear, he also represented himself to the Shah of Persia as *his* servant. Humáyun, after ceding Kandahár to the Persians, had surprised it by treachery; and, to pacify the Shah, pretended that he held it only for a time, and that Biram, the Shah's natural-born subject, in reality held it for both sovereigns, till it could be restored to Persia. This double relation, though recognised by both monarchs, was but too well fitted to allure a bold and ambitious man to indulge in schemes of independence; and instances of treason were in that age so common, that the insinuations against Biram seemed not improbable, and were easily believed. To advance into India, leaving behind a man so powerful and so dangerous, if hostile, would have been imprudent, and Humáyun determined to remove him from his government. His suspicions of Biram Khan,

Humáyun's chief confidence seems at this time to have been placed in Monaim Khan, an Amír of prudence and experience, who had for some time been atálik, or governor, to Akber. Eager to carry his plans against Biram into execution, though the winter was yet severe and the ground covered with snow, Humáyun set out from Kábul, attended by his Minister, and proceeded by Ghazni for Kandahár. Biram, who was not unaware of the Emperor's suspicions, but who preferred a dependance upon him to becoming the slave of the Persian King, adopted a decided line of conduct suited to his manly character. On Humáyun's approach, he advanced with a pompous cavalcade nearly forty miles from Kandahár to meet him, put himself at who entertains him magnificently at Kandahár. A. H. 961.

BOOK VII. A.D. 1554.

once into his power, professed the most unlimited devotion to his interests, and comported himself with so much submission and frankness, that he not only entirely removed the Emperor's suspicions, but, by his insinuating address and the sure influence of a strong mind over a weak one, soon regained his usual ascendency over him. Humáyun, faithful to his original plan, still offered Monaim Khan the government of Kandahár; but that honest Minister advised his master on no account to make any such change when about to set out on an expedition of so much importance; but intimated that, if successful in India, it would be in his power to act in regard to Kandahár as he might think proper, and with perfect safety. Humáyun spent the rest of the winter at Kandahár, where Biram Khan entertained him with unostentatious magnificence.*

and arranges to accompany him on his invasion.

In the spring, Humáyun set out on his return towards Kábul. He was accompanied as far as Mukur by Biram Khan, now once more his prime adviser. Sensible, however, of the uncertain tenure by which even the most faithful subject holds his favour when at a distance from the court, and desirous, perhaps, of sharing the danger and the glory of a mighty undertaking, Biram requested that he might be allowed to leave a deputy in the government which he had so long held, and permitted in person to attend his Majesty in the expedition that he meditated. This was readily granted. He returned to Kandahár, to make arrangements for its government in his absence, and to prepare the chosen body of troops with which he was to join the invading army. He prevailed upon the Emperor to remove Terdi Beg Khan from the government of Zemíndáwer, which lay in his neighbourhood, and to

* At Kandahár, Humáyun found Khwája Ghází just returned from a mission to Persia, and restored him to the office of diwán, the duties of which he had so honestly discharged.

bestow it on a dependant of his own.* Terdi Beg, of whom Biram seems to have been already jealous, probably got at this time, in compensation, the government of Anderáb and other districts to the north of the Hindu-kúsh mountains.†

Humáyun's preparations at Kábul.

Humáyun now proceeded towards Kábul, whence he addressed letters, not only to the different parts of his own dominions, but to Samarkand, Bokhára, and the cities of the north, inviting adventurers to join him in his grand enterprise. The rest of the summer he devoted to settling and securing the territories he already possessed, and to providing arms, military stores, and other requisites for the campaign which he meditated.

He is joined by Biram Khan. Shawal 2. Augst. 31.

Biram Khan, faithful to his agreement, joined him at Kábul the day after the Id, or grand festival at the conclusion of the Muhammedan fast of Ramzán: and so delighted was Humáyun with his arrival, that, to do him honour, he commanded the whole festivities of that day of rejoicing to be repeated.

Sets out on his expedition middle of Zilhajeh,

The necessary preparations for the expedition being at length completed, Humáyun appointed his infant son, Mírza Muhammed Hakím, to be the nominal governor of Kábul, entrusting the active direction of affairs to the fidelity and experience of Monaim Khan. He himself, taking with him his eldest son Akber, then between twelve and thirteen years of age, set out, about the middle of November, at the moment selected by the astrologers of the court as presenting a most propitious aspect of the stars and the heavens. His family and harem he left behind at Kábul. He was accompanied by only three thousand horse, Biram Khan being left behind to complete the remaining arrangements, and to bring on the artillery, stores and

* Behâder Khan Sistáni, who became distinguished in Akber's reign.

† Anderáb and Ishkemish, Akbernáma, ff. 90, 91.; Tab. Akb. f. 166.; Tar. Niz. f. 204.; Tar. Bed. ff. 187, 188.; Jouher, c. 28.; Bayezíd, ff. 67—72.; Ferishta, vol. ii. pp. 171, 172.

BOOK VII. A.D. 1554. A.H. 962. end of Moharem. reinforcements which were daily arriving. Humáyun, on reaching Júi-sháhi, embarked on a raft, was floated down the Kábul river, and reached Peshávwer in the latter part of December, when he loaded Sekander Uzbek with praises for his gallant defence of the place and raised him to the rank of Khan. On the last day of the year 1554 his standard waved on the banks of the Indus, where he halted three days, and was joined by Biram Khan and the rest of the army from Kábul; at the same moment that he received with surprise the gratifying intelligence that Tátár Khan Kási, the Afghán governor of the northern part of the Penjáb, on hearing of his march, had abandoned the fort of Rhotas, the strongest in the Penjáb, of which it was regarded as the northern bulwark, and had retired with his whole force to the south.

Sefer 6, Dec. 31, and reaches the Indus.

State of India. Indeed no moment could have been more favourable for an invasion of India. Selím Shah, a vigorous prince, had now been dead about a year, and had been succeeded by Adeli, whose accession, we have seen, was the signal for general revolt and rebellion. Four competitors for the throne of Delhi had appeared among the Afgháns, each possessed of a large extent of country and of a powerful army. The whole empire of Delhi was one scene of civil war and of intestine confusion. The capital itself had been repeatedly taken and retaken. Ahmed Khan, the Afghán governor of Láhúr, who, under the title of Sekander Shah, was one of the candidates for the throne, had carried away the army of the Penjáb to Delhi; so that the province was left without troops for its defence, and the garrisons had been withdrawn or neglected while Sekander was at a distance, busily employed in playing the greater game of Delhi. The retreat of Tátár Khan from Rhotas was, therefore, probably only a measure of prudence or necessity. Humáyun crossed the Indus unopposed on the 2nd of January 1555, and pursued

Sefer 8. A.D. 1555. Jan. 2.

his march by Perhala, through the country of the Gakers. He invited Sultan Adam Gaker, the chief of that hardy tribe, to join him; but the Sultan, with many protestations of attachment, excused himself, alleging that he had most unwillingly been compelled to enter into a treaty with Sekander Shah before that prince set out on his expedition against Delhi, and had given him his son as a hostage for its due observance. Humáyun, believing that he was well disposed towards the family of Báber, and eager to push on, left him behind; with joy took possession of the fortress of Rhotas, which he found deserted; passed the Jelem and the Chenáb; and, without striking a blow, saw himself master of all the northern part of the Penjáb.

Humáyun crosses the Indus.

Occupies Rhotas and the Northern Penjáb,

On arriving at Kilánúr, between the Rávi and the Bíah, Humáyun divided his forces, despatching a strong body under Biram Khan and Terdi Beg to attack Nasíb Khan, an Afghán general who lay encamped near Harhána*; while he himself directed his march to the capital, Láhúr, which, being abandoned on his approach, he entered on the 24th of February, and was received with every demonstration of joy by the inhabitants.

and Láhúr.

Rebi II. 2.

Feb. 24.

Not long after his arrival, Humáyun, learning that a large body of Afgháns † was near Dibálpúr, despatched Shah Abul Maali with eight hundred horse to beat up

Successful progress.

* This town is variously called Harhána, Hariahána, and Hariána, and seems to have lain between Kilánúr and Jalindher.

† The Muhammedan historians in general give the command of this army to Sháhbáz Khan and Nasír Khan. Jouher represents it as led by Umer Khan Gaker, who had collected it about Multán, and was marching towards Fírúzpúr to join the Afghán army on the south of Satlej. This is not improbable, and the orthodox historians may have dropt the name of the Gaker as a semi-barbarian. In the action, Abul Maali, who had rushed into the midst of the enemy and was surrounded, was saved only by the gallant exertions of Ali Kuli Sistáni (afterwards Khan Zemán), his second in command, who penetrated the masses of the enemy, shouting out the *takeber*, or Musulman war cry, and brought him off. Akbernáma, ff. 92, 93.; Jouher, 29, 30.

BOOK VII. A.D. 1555.

their quarters. Abul Maali, a brave but arrogant and presumptuous youth, and the especial favourite of Humáyun, charged them without hesitation, though they were found, it is said, to amount to twelve thousand men, and after a short but well contested action, defeated and dispersed them, taking their whole baggage, women and families. This victory, being the first gained in the campaign, was vauntingly extolled by Abul Maali and his partizans, and served still more to feed his already inordinate vanity.

Meanwhile, Biram Khan pushed on to Harhána, which, after a slight skirmish, was given up, and much valuable plunder, as well as the wives and families of the Afgháns, fell into his hands. The prisoners were all set at liberty, and the women and children were collected and sent under the protection of an escort to Nasíb Khan, in consequence of a vow made by Humáyun, that if providence restored to him the sovereignty of India, he would allow no men who were servants of God to be made captives of man. Several of the elephants and some of the more valuable property were sent, as was the custom, to be presented to the Emperor.

Biram now advanced to Jalindher, where the Afgháns had taken up a position: but no sooner did he come near them than they again retreated: "for such," says Abdal Káder, "was the terror which the Afgháns at this time entertained of the Moghuls, that, though they were thousands in number, if they saw the approach of but half a score of big turbans, though they might perhaps belong only to Láhúris, they instantly turned and took to flight, without looking behind them.* In the present instance, the Afgháns not only escaped with their lives, but carried off their baggage. This they were enabled to do, through an altercation that occurred

* Tar. Bed. f. 188.

in the imperial camp, and the consequences of which, at a future time, were very important. Abulfazl tells us, that Terdi Beg was desirous to have pursued and brought the Afgháns to action, but that Biram Khan did not approve of that movement, and refused to give orders for carrying it into effect. Terdi Beg, believing that a pursuit would complete the destruction of the enemy, sent Baltu Khan to Biram, with instructions to leave no means untried to induce him to follow the retreating enemy. Baltu accordingly delivered his message, when Khwája Moazem Sultan, a wrong-headed man, Akber's uncle, who happened to be present, rudely interfered, and even proceeded to use insulting language, which Baltu in anger retaliated. On this the Khwája, drawing his sword, aimed a blow at Baltu, and struck him on the arm. Humáyun no sooner heard of the occurrence than he issued a firmán committing the examination of the whole affair to a confidential officer, who, hastening to Biram Khan's camp, by the use of his Majesty's name and by his own advice and conciliatory manners, succeeded in pacifying, at least in appearance, the angry Amírs. Biram, who seems to have proposed halting for some time in the Penjáb, cantoned his troops in Jalindher and the neighbourhood, and distributed the adjoining districts among his officers. But Sekander Uzbek, who commanded the advance, and was stationed at Máchíwára on the Satlej, finding what he regarded as a favourable opportunity, crossed the river, and pushing forward took possession of the important town of Sirhend. Biram, whose bravery was tempered by prudence, and who seems to have been desirous to secure the country that had been gained and to concentrate his force, highly disapproved of this movement as being too much in advance, and the event seemed to justify his views.*

Occupation of Sirhend.

* Akb. ff. 92, 93.; Tab. Akb. f. 167.; Tar. Niz. ff. 204, 205.; Tar. Bed. f. 188.; Jouher, c. 29, 30.

BOOK VII.

A. D. 1555.

Continued distractions in Hindus.

While Humáyun thus overran the Penjáb, civil war continued to rage in Hindustán, which was wasted by the armies of various pretenders, and became the scene of the wildest anarchy. Delhi, the ancient capital, and the point nearest to the invaders, had repeatedly changed masters. Sekander Shah *, the late governor of the Penjáb, was now in possession of it. He had lately defeated Sultan Ibráhím, one of his competitors, and was preparing to march from Atáwa against Sultan Adeli, another of them, when he heard of Humáyun's invasion and success. The danger was pressing. Not only was the Penjáb the province from which his troops were chiefly drawn, and on which he most relied for support, but the victorious standards of Humáyun might be expected soon to wave on the towers of Delhi itself. Sekander, therefore, was compelled to divide his army; and while, with the main body of it, he continued his operations against Adeli, he despatched a strong reinforcement to support Tátár Khan, who had now retreated out of the Penjáb in the direction of Delhi, instructing him to march back, and crush, or at least keep in check, the invading army. Tátár Khan, thus reinforced, advanced at the head of 30,000 men towards Sirhend. His approach induced Sekander Uzbek to abandon that place, and to retreat across the Satlej to Jalindher; a movement for which he was severely censured by Biram, who regarded such a retrograde motion as ill-timed, and told him that, having advanced, however improperly, he ought to have maintained his post at Sirhend to the last, and sent to him for instructions.

Biram Khan crosses the Satlej.

Without loss of time, Biram Khan now collected his troops, and proceeded against the enemy. On reaching Máchiwára, Terdi Beg and some others of the generals were against passing the Satlej at that time, as the

* Ahmed Khan Súr, the governor of the Penjáb, assumed the style of Sultan Sekander. He is also often called Sekander Shah.

rainy season was close at hand; and advised merely guarding the ferries and fords, and acting on the defensive, till the monsoon was over. Biram, on the other hand, was for crossing without delay, and he was not a man whose plans were easily to be thwarted. His high capacity, his bold and determined spirit, and his discriminating patronage of merit, had brought about him a numerous party, absolutely devoted to his interests. By great exertions, in which he was zealously assisted by his partisans, he succeeded in transporting his division across the river, and now, the safety of the whole being compromised, Terdi Beg and the others saw themselves compelled to follow, however unwillingly.*

Battle of Máchíwára

The Afghâns, who had already reached the banks of the river, and were preparing bundles of reeds to form rafts for crossing, on hearing of this operation, and finding that Biram's army was very inferior in numbers to their own, resolved to engage them. The battle began towards evening. Biram's troops, which he had drawn up near the river, remained firm on their ground, keeping up a discharge of arrows, till it grew dark, when they were forced to intermit it. But a house having taken fire in a village that formed a large portion of the Afghán lines, the conflagration spread to the surrounding huts, most of which were roofed with straw, and soon extended over the whole village. Biram's men were now enabled by the flames to see every motion of their enemies, and to take deliberate aim, so that all their arrows told, while those of the Afgháns were discharged at random into the darkness around. The Afgháns continued, nevertheless, for some time,

* Many of them were Persians or Persian Túrks, as Kásim Khan Nishapúri, Haider-kuli Beg Shámlu, &c. The motley nature of Humáyun's army may be conceived from the tribes of the four generals commanding the divisions; Biram Khan was a Persian Túrk, Khizer Khan Hazára an Afghán Hazára, Terdi Beg Khan was a Túrk of Ferghána, and Sekander Khan an Uzbek.

BOOK VII. A.D. 1555.

bravely to maintain their ground; but at length, harassed and worn out by the unequal contest, they took to flight, and resigned the field. Next day, Biram resumed his march, and soon occupied Sirhend without opposition. Humáyun, delighted with this important victory, honoured Biram Khan with the title of Khan-Khánán, Yar Vafádár (Lord of Lords, the Faithful Friend); and his army was, soon after, strengthened by reinforcements sent by the Emperor.*

Advance of Sekander Shah.

When the news of this discomfiture reached Sekander Shah, giving up every other enterprise, he collected the whole of his force, to check the progress of a torrent from which he had so much to dread. With an army of 70,000 horse, a number of war-elephants, and a strong train of artillery, he marched for the Penjáb. On hearing of his approach, Biram Khan, whose army was still far from numerous †, despatched repeated expresses to Humáyun, who still remained at Láhúr, representing to him the urgent necessity of his hastening to his relief with the rest of the troops; and, in the meantime, he raised strong entrenchments round his camp, to enable him to keep his ground at Sirhend until the reinforcements arrived.

Humáyun supports Biram.

Humáyun was confined by sickness when he received Biram's letters, but immediately despatched his son Akber, with a large body of troops, to his assistance, and, a few days after, was well enough to follow them.

Rejeb. 7.‡ May 28.

On reaching Sirhend, he found that Sekander Shah had already arrived, and had been a fortnight before the place; that he had strongly fortified his camp with ditch and parapet, "according to the practice of Shír Shah," and had made daily attacks on the imperial troops, who kept behind their trenches. Humáyun

* Akbernáma, ff. 94, 95.; Tar. Niz. ff. 204, 205.; Tar. Bed. 189.; Jouher, c. 31.; Bayezíd, ff. 79, 80.; Ferishta, vol. ii. pp. 174, 175; Khafi Khan.

† Jouher says, it consisted of only 700 or 800 men, meaning, perhaps, northern men or Persians.

‡ The night of the 7th Rejeb, may have been the night of the 27th May.

established his head-quarters in a garden near the town, and, for some time, skirmishes and single combats daily took place, conducted with much bravery and more courtesy than was usual in that age and country, the wounded and the slain being given up to their friends. Great apprehensions of the result were, however, entertained in Humáyun's camp, the number of fighting men in which is represented as amounting to only five thousand.

Seeing that it was necessary to supply defect of numbers by increased activity and energy, Humáyun resolved to attempt cutting off the supplies of the Afghán camp; a system of annoyance which he had so successfully employed against Beháder Shah of Gujrát, at Mandsúr. For carrying into effect a plan of campaign, apparently so unsuitable to his diminutive force, he must have trusted to the great superiority of his Túrks, Moghuls, and other northern men over the troops of his adversary, whether in forays or in combating man to man. Terdi Beg was appointed to execute the details. He soon interrupted their communications, intercepted a large convoy of provisions, defeating a detachment under one of Sekander Shah's brothers, whom he slew, and brought back to the camp his banner and the insignia of his dignity. This action seems to have drawn the enemy from their trenches, to support and bring off the detachment; and, the engagement spreading from one division to another, brought on a general battle of the whole line sooner than was anticipated. The Afgháns directed the violence of their attack against Biram Khan's division, hoping that if it, which was understood to be the strongest, was defeated, they would more easily break the others. But Biram, when attacked, retired into the works which he had thrown up in front of his encampment, and stood on the defensive, and the enemy were unable to force his position. Meanwhile

**Battle of Sirhend.**

BOOK VII.

A.D. 1555.

Humáyun, seeing that Biram was able to maintain his ground, ordered the division under Shah Abul Maali and Terdi Beg to charge the attacking enemy in flank and rear, which was done with such effect that their whole army, now said to amount to nearly an hundred thousand men, soon became a mass of confusion, dispersed and fled from the field, leaving behind their whole baggage, field equipage and artillery. The battle was fought on the 22nd day of June, the summer solstice, during the rainy monsoon. The wind and rain, which happened then to be excessive, soon relaxed the pursuit. Sekander Shah escaped from the field of battle, and, with much personal danger, found his way to that part of the Sewálik mountains that skirts the Penjáb.*

Shában 2. June 22.

Flight of Sekander and dispersion of his forces.

Shah Abul Maali.

Hardly was the din of battle over, when a contest arose between Shah Abul Maali and Biram Khan upon the question to whom, in the official account, the honour of the victory should be ascribed. The young man who thus put forward his pretensions in opposition to the Khan Khánán, had been introduced to Humáyun only four years before, but had suddenly risen to the highest place in his favour. He was from Káshghar, but claimed descent from the celebrated saintly family of the Syeds of Turmez, was brave, enterprising and accomplished, but presumptuous and insolent. A striking instance of his bold contempt of authority had lately occurred at Kandahár. Shír Ali Khan had, without leave, quitted the service of Shah Tahmasp, in which he was Mír shikári, or grand huntsman, and entered that of Humáyun. Abul Maali, a keen Shía, intoxicated with religious zeal, and desirous of gratifying the Persian king, descended, like himself, of a religious family, boasted publicly, and even in the Emperor's presence, that he would put the

* Ut supra, and Khol. ul Tow. ff. 286, 287.

traitor to death wherever he met him. The Emperor, regarding this threat as a mere idle bravado, took no measures to protect the fugitive. One night, however, the boaster did execute his threat, and assassinated the Khan. Humáyun, though he felt his authority insulted, yet, seduced by his partiality for the criminal, not only did not bring him to punishment, but soon after raised him to offices of the highest trust, made him the chosen partner of all his pleasures, and familiarly addressed him as, "My son." On the present occasion, the young favourite, confident in his master's partiality, demanded that his name should occupy the most conspicuous place in the official announcement of the victory, under pretence that he had not only gained the first success in the campaign, but had had the most share in the present battle. The veteran Biram Khan, on the other hand, claimed that honour, as having had the management of the whole plan of the campaign, as well as having been the first to invade the enemy's country, which he had overrun and occupied. Any formal decision of the question was evaded by bestowing the distinction contended for upon Akber, whose claim neither of the competitors was likely to dispute.

Decisive effects of the victory.

The battle was quite decisive. No enemy any longer appeared in the field. A pillar of heads was erected. The Emperor despatched Sekander Uzbek towards Delhi, to clear the road to the capital, and himself followed, with the main body of the army, as far as Samana, where, finding that Sultan Sekander had not retreated towards Hindustán, but had taken shelter in the highlands of Sewálik, whence he might threaten the low country of the Penjáb, he halted, and sent back Shah Abul Maali with a strong detachment to Jalindher, to keep him in check, and to hinder him from raising his old province in the rear of the advancing

BOOK VII. A. D. 1555.

army. The whole resources of the Penjáb were placed at Abul Maali's disposal.

Humáyun had not remained long at Samana to find shelter from the heavy rains which were falling, and to rest and refresh his troops, when despatches reached him from Sekander Uzbek, who had advanced to Delhi without opposition, earnestly urging him to pursue his advantages, and to repair to the capital without loss of time. He accordingly put his troops in motion, and on the 23rd of July once more ascended the throne of Delhi, in the imperial city.*

Humáyun reoccupies Delhi, Ramzán, 4. July 23.

Distributes the provinces.

The first act of his government was to distribute the provinces among his retainers. Hissár Firúza, though not yet reduced, he reserved to the crown, but assigned to Akber, as being the province which he himself had received from Báber, when he first entered India. Sirhend and some other districts were granted to Biram Khan, in addition to Kandahár, which he still held; Shah Abul Maali got the Penjáb; Terdi Beg Khan had Mewát, which was not yet conquered; Sekander Uzbek was sent forward to occupy Agra; Ali Kuli Sistáni was despatched to reduce Mirat and Sambhal, and Haider Muhammed Khan, akhteh-begi (grand-marshal) was sent against Biána. The Emperor himself remained stationary at head-quarters in the fort of Delhi, to watch over the progress of his arms, and the general settlement of the country.

Rapid reduction of the provinces.

The different provinces fell rapidly into his hands. Hisár-Firúza surrendered after a short siege. Agra made no resistance. Bedáun was conquered and occupied by one Kamber Diwána, a man of low birth and singular habits, but brave and of popular talents, who acknowledged the Emperor, and appears to have been recognized by him as Governor. Ali Kuli Sistáni, after taking possession of Mirat and Sambhal, which had been

* Akbernáma, ff. 91—95.; Tab. Akb. ff. 167, 168.; Jouher, c. 32.

assigned to him, attacked Kamber, who was hated by the Amírs of family, and having taken Bedáun by stratagem and treachery, put him to death, and pretending ignorance of the Emperor's wishes, sent his head to Humáyun, who, though he felt and professed much displeasure, left the culprit unpunished.*

While these events were passing to the eastward, Haider Muhammed marched to reduce Biána, his new government. That important fort had long been in possession of Gházi Khan Súr, one of the most eminent and powerful of the Afghán chiefs, whose son Ibráhím Shah was one of the five princes who, at the same moment, were contending for the sovereign authority in this distracted country. We have seen that Ibráhím was defeated, and expelled from Delhi and Agra by Sultan Sekander; after which, he was defeated at Kalpi, and blockaded for three months in Biána itself, by Hímú, the Hindu Minister of Adeli. When relieved from this danger by the retreat of Hímú, who was called away to Behár to oppose an invasion of the King of Bengal, Ibráhím, having made an attack upon Bhatta in Malwa, was defeated and taken prisoner, and now remained in captivity in the hands of the Raja of that country. His father, Gházi Khan, did not attempt to resist Haider Muhammed in the field, but retired into his strong fortress, where for some time he successfully defended himself; but finally entered into a capitulation, and surrendered the fort, under the most solemn

**Surrender of Biána.**

* The history of Kamber Diwána is related at considerable length by the contemporary historians. Ali Kuli was entirely devoted to Biram, and the whole proceedings against Kamber have much the appearance of one of the violent acts of Biram, who probably, considering his occupation of the country and eccentric doings to be inconsistent with regular government, contrived to effect his ruin, without appearing directly to thwart the Emperor. Kamber was buried in Bedáun, and his tomb was frequented as a place of pilgrimage down to a late period, by the lower classes, among whom his reputation and popularity were very great. See Akbernáma, f. 96.; Tab. Akb. f. 168.; Tar. Bedáuni, f. 191.; Briggs's, Ferishta, vol. ii. p. 177.

BOOK VII. A. D. 1555.

assurances of personal safety. No sooner, however, had Gházi Khan marched out, than Haider, burning with eagerness to possess the wealth which Biána was known to contain, shamefully violated his agreement, and put him to death with all his family, even to the children at the breast. Humáyun, incensed at this act of perfidious cruelty, which he justly ascribed to avarice, instantly commissioned an officer of his household, known in the next reign as Shehâb-ed-dín Ahmed Khan, to proceed to Biána, to supersede Haider Muhammed in his government, and to place all his property under sequestration, which was done, but not before Haider had succeeded in embezzling some of the most valuable of Gházi Khan's jewels, substituting inferior ones in their place. It must be allowed that the return of Humáyun into India was marked by many instances of insubordination and rapacity on the part of his officers. They seem to have come back, thirsting after the riches of the land from which they had so long been banished, and eager to retrieve the time they had lost. A stronger arm and a firmer purpose than Humáyun's were necessary, to restore the discipline of his hardy, but rapacious, followers.

Frequent insubordination of Humáyun's officers.

While Humáyun was thus making extensive conquests in Hindustán, he suffered some loss of territory in the north. We have seen that when he finally regained Kábul by the aid of Mírza Suleimán, that prince, by grant or by connivance, had added Kunduz, and several other provinces beyond the mountains, to his own principality of Badakhshán. The neighbouring districts of Anderáb and Ishkemish were the jágír of Terdi Beg, for whom they were held by Mokím Khan, as his lieutenant. They lay temptingly for the Mírza, who endeavoured to add them to his dominions by corrupting the fidelity of Mokím. Failing in this attempt, he threw off the mask, and besieged him in Anderáb. Unprepared for such an attack, Mokím contrived, nevertheless, to escape from

Revolt of Mírza Suleimán in Badakhshán.

the fort which he could not defend, and succeeded in fighting his way to the hills, whence he returned to Kábul.

Misconduct of Abul Maali in the Penjáb.

But the most important transactions of this period were those of the Penjáb. When the Emperor marched from Láhúr to oppose Sultan Sekander, he committed the management of the province to Ferkhat Khan as hákim or governor, with suitable officers to support him.* After the battle of Sirhend, when Sultan Sekander was threatening the Penjáb from the Sewálik hills, to which he had fled, Humáyun, as we have seen, sent Shah Abul Maali to command the army opposed to him, with orders to proceed to Jalindher, and there to establish his head-quarters, to watch the Sultan's motions, and to prevent his entering the low country. Scarcely, however, had Abul Maali reached the Penjáb, when his native arrogance exceeded even its usual bounds. He assumed the deportment and pomp of a prince, acted in every respect like an absolute sovereign, and so despotically, as to disgust and alarm all the officers of government. Instead of remaining at Jalindher, as he had been ordered, he proceeded to Láhúr. The Emperor's officers in authority there, having consulted together, agreed not to admit him into the city: but this resolution was not acted upon, and he speedily usurped all

* Bapús Khan was made foujdár or military collector, Mírza Shah Sultan, Amín or civil administrator, and Mehter Jouher (the Memoir-writer, and lately Humáyun's ewer-bearer), treasurer of the Penjáb and Multán. Some time before this, Humáyun had appointed Jouher to be collector of Haibatpúr-pati. The circumstances attending his introduction, when taking leave on setting out for his district, are illustrative both of the character of Humáyun, and of the state of the public service. "My lad," said Humáyun, "listen to what I say,—A Moghul having been sent from the camp on a duty similar to yours, took two blankets from a Ját, and seeing the man's surprise, exclaimed, 'What, you rascal, am I not come *to collect?*'" On hearing this insinuation, continues the ewer-bearer, I replied, that having had the advantage of pouring water on his Majesty's hands, for so many years, I would acquit myself with credit and honour. The Emperor replied, "Good comes of good, and evil of evil." Jouher's Mem. c. 29.

BOOK VII. A.D. 1555. the powers of the government. Humáyun, however, partial to his favorite, for a long time would listen to none of the complaints preferred against him, till he found that he had gone so far as to displace Ferkhat Khan, the Emperor's governor of Láhúr, and to put a creature of his own in his place; and that he was squandering, with the wildest extravagance, the imperial treasure, and the revenues of the country. At length, the Emperor was plainly told that Abul Maali undoubtedly aimed at independence, an imputation in that turbulent age by no means improbable. To add to the other evils, Sultan Sekander, who hitherto had remained at Mánkót, collecting an army and taking into his pay all the mercenaries that were to be found, finding every check withdrawn, poured down his whole force into the Penjáb. Yet such was Humáyun's delicacy to the feelings of his favorite, that he superseded him only by giving the Penjáb to Akber, under the pretence that, as the imperial harem was about to pass through that country, he was the most proper person to be in command. Abul Maali was nominated to the charge of the imperial domain of Hissár Firúza, which had been held by Akber, so that he seemed merely to have exchanged governments with the prince.

He is superseded by Prince Akber.

But while the nominal authority in the Penjáb was given to the youthful Akber, the efficient power was vested in the stern Biram Khan, who attended him as his atálík or protector. It was about the end of the year when the prince and his governor set out. On reaching Sirhend, the object of Akber's coming being well understood, he was joined not only by the troops from Hissár, but by many imperial officers of the highest rank, serving in the Penjáb under Abul Maali, who came uncalled and without leave, the prince's approach being hailed as a fortunate relief from the extremities to which they were driven by the favorite's overbearing and tyrannical conduct. They were all graciously received;

Beginning of A. H. 963. End of A. D. 1555.

and the army being increased by the arrival of several bodies of troops from the neighbouring districts, proceeded across the Satlej to Sultánpúr on the Bíah.

The unmilitary movement of Abul Maali from Jalindher to Láhúr having left the low country along the hills defenceless, Sultan Sekander, having descended into the plains, was enabled to occupy, and collect the revenues of the perganas, to a considerable distance around. Abul Maali, never deficient in bravery or in spirit, assembled the troops that were nearest Láhúr, and advanced towards the enemy by slow marches, to give time to those at a distance to join him. He gained some advantages in the field; but as soon as Akber's approach was known, he was deserted by his principal officers, to whom he had become odious. He, therefore, retreated to Láhúr, whence being summoned to attend the prince, he found himself compelled, most unwillingly, to wait upon him at Sultánpúr, not long after his arrival. He was coldly received, but, humbled as he was, his presumption did not desert him. Akber, from consideration for his father's partiality to the Syed, invited him to dinner, graciously pointed out to him his seat, and treated him, as his guest, with all politeness and attention. On his return home from the party, he had the insolence to send a message to Akber, to say, that the prince was no stranger to the relation in which he stood to Humáyun; reminding him that when he dined publicly with the Emperor at the ring-hunt of Júi-Sháhi, the prince himself had seen that he sat on the same cushion, and eat out of the same dish with the Emperor, while the prince waited by, and dined afterwards on a portion sent to him: whereas at the recent dinner, he had been placed on an ordinary rug, and served from a separate tray. The prince, smiling, bad the messenger go back, and express his surprise that Abul Maali could not distinguish between the becoming etiquette of princes, and the familiarity of private attachment; and

BOOK VII. A.D. 1556.

that, moreover, his pretensions betrayed an extreme ignorance of their relative situations. Abul Maali's mortification was extreme. Akber, soon after, put his army in motion, and attempted to come up with Sultan Sekander, who, on hearing of his approach, retreated into his mountain recesses, and once more pitched his camp at Mánkót.

Who expels Sekander Shah.

Account received of the death of Humáyun.

The army had reached Hariána in its advance, when it was overtaken by a messenger bringing Biram Khan information of an alarming accident that had befallen the Emperor, which rendered it inexpedient to move farther onward, or to commence active operations: and the march of the army was directed on Kilánúr, to await the result. As they approached that place, another express arrived bringing a despatch, said to be written by orders of the Emperor himself immediately after his accident, and giving good hopes of his speedy recovery. But a third followed close after, with the authentic accounts of his death.

Humáyun's plans for the government of the empire.

From the time when Humáyun arrived in Delhi, he devoted himself to a general superintendence of the affairs of his kingdom, and to watching the progress of the armies which he had sent in various directions to reduce different provinces. He saw clearly that there were great defects in the system of government of the empire, and set himself to devising means of improving it. The plan which he projected was to separate the empire into several great divisions, each of them to have a local capital, and a board of administration for directing local affairs. Delhi, Agra, Kanáuj, Juánpúr, Mándu, and Láhúr were among the capitals pitched upon. To each of them was to be assigned a considerable military force, under an able general, so as to render it independent of assistance from the others; while the Emperor was to give unity to the whole, by visiting them in turn with an army of about twelve thousand horse, which were to be under his own immediate command, and at all times ready to move in any direction. This plan, however, he never had time, had he even possessed sufficient steadiness, to carry into execution.

Particulars of his death.

Having in some degree arranged affairs at Delhi, he was about to proceed to Agra; had conferred the government of Delhi on Terdi Beg, in public derbár; and had even sent forward his péshkhána *, or advanced set of tents, preparatory to his setting out. On Friday the 20th of January, 1556, in the evening, some of his old officers who had just returned from the pilgrimage of Mekka, as well as some who had come from Gujrát, were introduced to him, and he inquired with much interest into the news which they brought. He also received despatches from Monaim Khan in Kábul, with accounts of his family and harem that were still in that quarter. At the close of the day he went up to the terrace-roof of his library, in his palace in the Dín-panáh fort of Delhi, attended by such persons as happened to be with him, and presented himself as usual to the crowds assembled round the Grand Mosque close by, who made the customary obeisance or salutation: after which he went on with the inquiries in which he had been engaged. When it began to grow dark, he sent for some of his astronomers to observe the rising of Venus, it being his intention to hold a grand public audience, and to promote several of his Amírs, exactly at the propitious moment of the rising of that planet. As he was about to descend, and had reached the second step of the stairs, he heard the moizzin, or cryer from the minaret of the mosque, summoning the

* In India, persons travelling at their ease have two sets of tents, one of which is sent in advance and pitched, so as to be ready for the traveller on his arrival on the ground; the tents which he quits being immediately packed up, and sent forward to be ready in like manner, in their turn. The tents so sent in advance are called the péshkhána.

BOOK VII. A.D. 1556.

faithful to evening prayer, and was preparing to sit down, out of respect, till the call was over, when his foot became entangled in the skirt of his mantle*, and the marble steps being smooth and slippery†, his staff slid, so that he lost his footing, was precipitated forward, and lighted on his head on the ground below. He was taken up insensible, was found to have received many bruises on his body, but in particular a violent contusion on the right temple, and a quantity of blood was observed to have oozed from his right ear. According to some accounts, he for a time recovered his speech. He lingered four days, being the greater part, or the whole of the time, in a state of insensibility, and expired on the evening of the 24th of January, in the forty-eighth year of his age, after a reign of rather more than twenty-five years.‡

Rebi I. 11. Jan. 24. ..

Which is for a time concealed.

The heir apparent being at a distance, the great Amírs who possessed the chief influence very much dispersed, and the army still surrounded by formidable enemies, it was resolved by the nobles who were on the spot, to conceal this event till the suitable arrangements could be made. Expresses were immediately despatched to inform Akber of his father's death, and to call a meeting of the principal officers. The more effectually to lull suspicion, one Múlla Bekasi was dressed up in the imperial vestments, and presented to the public at the usual times, in an open gallery of the palace on the side next the river, which had been the late Emperor's

* *Postin.*

† "The stairs" we are told by Mr. Elphinstone (History of India, vol. ii. p. 175.), "in such situations are narrow steps on the *outside* of the building, and only guarded by an ornamental parapet about a foot high," — "so that the King fell headlong over the parapet."

‡ Abulfazl, Jouher, and Ferishta make his death happen on the 11th Rebi I.: the Tabakát-e Akberi, followed by the Taríkh-e Bedáuni, on the 15th. Abulfazl (f. 98.) says that the Emperor, after his accident, sent a letter to Akber by Názir Sheikh Juli to inform him that he was doing well: but this was probably a mere official intimation, issued for political purposes by those about his person.

favourite seat, and where he was accustomed to receive the salutations of his subjects, who assembled in crowds below. For seventeen days the truth was unknown in Delhi. At last, on the tenth day of February, Terdi Beg, who officiated on the occasion as Amír-al-omra, a dignity to which he aspired, throwing off the mask, and attended by all the Amírs of the surrounding districts who had repaired to head-quarters, proceeded to the Grand Mosque, and caused the prayer for the Emperor to be recited in the name of Akber. Rebi I. 28. Feb. 10.

Alarm excited by this event.

The announcement of the Emperor's death, circumstanced as affairs then were, produced great alarm and excitement all over the country, which the nobles, assembled at Delhi, used every means in their power to allay. When the rites and ceremonies attending the sepulture and mourning for the Emperor were over, the leading Amírs hastened, each to his own government, to watch over the current of events, and to confirm the minds both of their own followers and of the natives of the country in their adherence to the new government. Terdi Beg Khan, as the most eminent of the ancient nobility and governor of Delhi, by a kind of election or recognition of the Amírs who were on the spot, assumed the general direction of affairs. One of his first acts was to send the insignia of empire with the crown jewels to the young Emperor, accompanied by the officers of the household, the imperial guards, and Mírza Abul-Kásím, the son of the late Kámrán Mírza, whose close alliance to the throne now made him an object of jealousy. The crisis was one of the deepest importance, for at that moment the conquest of India could be considered as only begun: and three formidable rivals contended with the youthful Akber for the throne of Delhi.*

Danger of the crisis.

* Akbernáma, ff. 98, 99.; Tar. Nizámi, ff. 205, 206.; Jouher, c. 33.; Ferishta, vol. ii. pp. 177, 178.; Tar. Bedáuni, ff. 189—192.; Kholáset ul Towáríkh, f. 288., Kháfi Khan.

BOOK VII. A. D. 1556.

Character of Humáyun.

The real character of Humáyun may be better gleaned from the events of his reign than from the representations of his historians, whose judgment was influenced, not only by that reverence with which Orientals regard the sovereign authority, but by a natural respect for the princes, his descendants, under whom they wrote. He was a man of great quickness of parts, but volatile, thoughtless and unsteady. Personally of distinguished bravery, he was occasionally successful in war, without possessing the higher talents of a general. In the earlier part of his reign, seconded by the veteran officers and well-trained army which his father had left him, he overran, first, the kingdoms of Malwa and Gujrát, and next those of Behár and Bengal, very important and glorious acquisitions; but, destitute of those powers of combination which are as necessary for consolidating and retaining a conquest as bravery and a well-disciplined army are for making it, he was compelled to abandon them all; and the greater part of his reign presented a series of reverses, rebellions and anarchy, the fruit of his want of political firmness and determination. His disposition was naturally generous, friendly and affectionate; his manners polite, frank and winning. He had a ready wit, excelled in repartee, and, from the anecdotes recorded by his ewer-bearer and other writers, seems to have been considerate to his servants, and popular in his intercourse with the lower classes. But, though Haider Mírza, an excellent judge, speaks with much respect of his accomplishments, and of his talents and deportment as a prince, yet his generosity, guarded by no resolute sense of duty or steady feelings of self-respect, degenerated into prodigality, his attachments into weakness; and hence, down to the day of his death, he was the prey of flatterers and favourites. From his father he inherited a fondness for literature and the arts, and he delighted in the society of literary and scientific men. Like many of the eminent personages of his age, he was not only an admirer of poetry, but himself a writer of verses; and Abulfazl mentions that a complete diwán of his composition was in the library of his son.* He is also said to have made no inconsiderable progress in mathematics and astronomy. He liberally patronised such as were eminent in these sciences, and promoted several of them to offices of trust. At the time of his death he was about to construct an observatory, and had collected the necessary instruments for that purpose.† But a fatality seemed to attend even his merits. His astronomical knowledge was directed chiefly to the frivolous or pernicious doctrines of astrology and the occult sciences; and the course of his policy, as well as the actions of his ordinary life, was too often regulated by an absurd and childish attention to signs, omens and superstitious observances.‡

An incident that occurred in his early years exercised a considerable influence on his mind. Going one day a-hunting with his tutor, Humáyun proposed to take an omen as to the fortune of his future life, from the names of the three first persons he should meet. The tutor suggested that he might content himself with the first alone; but the prince kept to his purpose. It happened, we are told, whether accidentally or by pre-arrangement, that the first was a decrepid old man called Murád (Desire); the second, a man driving an ass loaded with firewood, was Doulat (Dominion); the third, who was found tending some cattle, was Saadet

* Specimens of his poetry are given by Ferishta and Kháfi Khan, and may be found scattered over the works of other historians.

† Akbernáma, f. 100.

‡ He never, in entering or leaving house or mosque, put his left foot first; and if he observed any of his attendants do so, he called him left-handed, and made him go back, and advance again. Tar. Bed.

BOOK VII. A. D. 1556.

(Good Fortune, or Success); a coincidence which delighted the prince, and from which he was led confidently to augur the accomplishment of his aspirations for extended sovereignty. The impression thus made on him induced him, when on the throne, to institute an arbitrary classification of his whole court and household under three heads. His brothers and other near relations, his Amírs and officers of State, with all the military, he classed as Ahil-e-doulat, or men of dominion, their aid being necessary for the attainment and exercise of power. Doctors and men learned in the law, divines, syeds and religious men, múllas, poets, and such as were skilled in the sciences and arts, were ranked as Ahil-e-saadet, men of good fortune, as their presence was supposed to bring as well as to intimate the existence of prosperity; while the beautiful and elegant females of his domestic establishment, singers, musicians, dancers and other ministers of enjoyment, were the Ahil-e-murád, the objects of desire, as affording the means of elegant and sensual gratification.

These arrangements he mingled with his astrological fancies.* He constructed an extensive pavilion, in the principal hall of which the revolutions of the spheres, the place of each constellation, especially the signs of the Zodiac and the course of the planets, were represented. It contained also seven spacious apartments, each called by the name of one of the days of the week and of its presiding planet. These were richly fitted up with carpets and hangings, of the colour which custom had appropriated to the presiding star of each day; two of these apartments, with two days of the week, being devoted to each of the three before-

* The astrological fancies entertained by Humáyun, and the doctrines regarding the chapels of the planets, and the corresponding dresses, mansions, days and seasons, are very ancient. See Pocock's Specimen Hist. Arabum, pp. 143—150.; Oxon. 1806. See also the Dabistáne Mozáhib, and the Desátír.

mentioned classes; and Humáyun gave public audience in them, occupying the apartment corresponding to the day of the week on which the audience was held. On these occasions the Emperor himself, the princes, the officers of state, and the whole court appeared dressed in the colour of the day. The details on this subject, as well as of a number of other artificial arrangements in which he delighted, — the drawing of the three golden arrows of the three classes; the twelve arrows of another of his divisions, founded on the twelve celestial signs, by which both political enterprises and promotions were often decided; and the arrangement of his household into four branches, corresponding to the four elements, — are given at great length by some historians of his reign, especially by Abulfazl, himself a believer in astrology and in omens. The observances are so minute, and must have been so inconvenient, that we can hardly believe they were ever long or very scrupulously adhered to, though in some important and not very creditable transactions of his reign we find traces of their existence. The astrology with which they were connected was then, indeed, a prevailing folly; but a powerful mind, though it might have yielded to the general impressions of the time, would not have suffered itself to be so deeply entangled in the idle and puerile observances of the art, nor accepted them as a substitute for rational and substantial knowledge.

The drum of justice was another of his institutions, borrowed from ancient tradition. A huge drum being placed near the imperial tent or pavilion, any one who suffered from injustice might claim redress by striking it according to certain rules, and the Emperor himself attended to the appeal. In early times, where law was very imperfectly and arbitrarily administered, and where complaints did not easily reach the ear of the despot, such an institution, rude as it is, or indeed any

BOOK VII. A.D. 1556.

other professing to forward the means of redress, was commendable, and might be useful. But its revival in a more advanced age betrays an extreme want of legislative skill; and it must be confessed that in this, as in many other of Humáyun's regulations that have been noticed, there is a great want of plain practical sense, a pedantic application of inapplicable learning, and too great an appearance of playing at kings.

He was a good Mussulman, rigid in the observance of the stated prayers and ceremonial of the law. He was, however, strongly suspected of leaning to the Shía sect, partly from his patronage of many Persians, or Shías, of distinction, such as Biram Khan, Abul Maali, and others; partly, perhaps, from the show of adherence to it which his political situation induced him to manifest when in exile in Persia.*

A floating palace several stories in height, with a garden and a bazar, or market, which he constructed at Agra on ships linked together and connected by platforms, and floated down the Jamna, has been celebrated, and, as well as several other of his contrivances, evinces his fondness for the mechanical arts.

But though Humáyun was brave and good-tempered, liberal and fond of learning, his virtues all bordered

* Such, we are told, was his reverence for the name of God, that he never pronounced it till he had performed the stated ablutions (wázu). One day he was observed to address Mír Abdalla Hai, the Sadr, or Chief Judge, by the abbreviated name of Mír Abdal. Having subsequently performed the legal purifications, "Excuse me, Mír," said he to the Sadr, "for not having a little ago given you your full name; but Hai being one of the names of God, I could not, situated as I then was, pronounce it."

Kámrán Mírza, who was a Sunni, and fond of religious disputation, had frequent arguments with his brother on the differences between the two sects. The Sunnis treat the Shías as being heterodox. One day, as they were riding together, they observed a dog, an unclean animal, lift its leg irreverently against a tomb-stone. "The man who lies there must be a heretic" (rafzi) said Kámrán. "Yes," said the Emperor; "and the dog an orthodox brute." Briggs's Ferishta, vol. ii. p. 179. We have seen that he was himself occasionally a persecutor of such as he called heretics.

on neighbouring defects, and produced little fruit. There seems to have been a frivolity in his mind that neutralized his good qualities; and it is probable that, had he continued to fill his father's throne, he might have been the last emperor of India of his race. The bold, determined policy of Biram Khan, so different from the weak and vacillating conduct of Humáyun, had its full sway after that prince's death, and, aided by the rising genius of Akber, established the empire of the family of Taimur on the foundation which it has maintained, with more or less splendour, down to our own times.*

* Akbern. ff. 97—100.; Tab. Akb. ff. 168, 169.; Tar. Niz. ff. 205, 206.; Tar. Bedáuni, ff. 191, 192.; Briggs's Ferishta, vol. ii. pp. 177—180. Humáyun had deeply studied the religious and mystical poetry of the Persians, to which his warm feelings, and lively imagination, gave him a natural partiality. This bias may account for an incident related by historians who are willing to believe that he had some supernatural presentiment of his death. They tell us that though, through life, he could not bear to hear death spoken of, and even forbad its being mentioned in his presence; yet that, just before his last accident, he frequently started the subject himself, and took pleasure in listening to conversations upon it. He mentioned an occurrence that befel him at that time, and by which he was much affected. "I lately rose," said he, "after midnight to say the stated prayers, and afterwards retired again to rest; when, just before dawn, as I was lying, my eyes shut but my heart awake, I heard a supernatural voice clearly repeat these verses:

"O Lord! of thine infinite goodness make me thine own:
Make me a partaker of the knowledge of thy attributes:
I am broken-hearted from the cares and sorrows of life;
O call to thee thy poor madman (lover)! O grant me my release!"

He is said often afterwards to have repeated these mysterious lines with deep emotion, while the tears gushed from his eyes.

# SUPPLEMENTARY REMARKS

## ON THE STATE OF GOVERNMENT AND MANNERS IN KÁBUL AND THE SURROUNDING COUNTRIES DURING THE REIGNS OF BÁBER AND HUMÁYUN.

As the course of events has brought us to the reign of Akber, when the Chaghatái government was finally established in India, and took a form which, with little change, it retained for nearly two centuries, it may be proper to take a slight review of the state of government and manners during the two preceding reigns in Kábul and the surrounding countries, where Báber and Humáyun spent most of their time. Though a space of more than fifty years, it was in general a period of war and confusion, leaving little leisure for any legislative efforts, or for the cultivation of the arts of peace.

Government and regal etiquette.

The government was such as might be expected from a body of foreigners settling themselves by force in a country, with the inhabitants of which they had no sympathy but that of a common religion, and was necessarily military. Everything was directed by the will of the King, who was surrounded by his Amírs and great officers. He was nominally absolute, as in all Asiatic states. His court exhibited, or affected, a great appearance of splendour, and had nearly the same establishment of officers that had existed under the powerful princes of Samarkand and Khorásán. We find the Master of the Household, Master of the Horse, Grand Huntsman, Master of Requests and Chamberlains, with body and night guards—besides all the officers of the harem and female apartments. The prince, whether in the capital or the camp, held daily levees—in the one case, in the Great Hall; in the other, in the Pavilion or Tent of Audience, at which the Amírs and men of note, and all such as were desirous of favour and attention, presented themselves. The Sovereign generally sat at the further end on cushions, or, on more ceremonious occasions, on a throne placed on a platform raised some steps above the rest of the hall or tent; and the places to be occupied by his sons and brothers, by his near relations, by foreign ambassadors, by his Amírs, by men of saintly reputation, by men of letters, and by all the various classes of his subjects, were fixed by the Master of Ceremonies with a most scrupulous nicety, according to their supposed rank or importance. The upper classes were in general allowed to be seated; the inferior remained standing. All, on entering, made their obeisance to the prince; but such as were introduced for the first time, or after an absence from court, were attended by the Master of Ceremonies, made their obeisance, first at a considerable distance, and afterwards nearer to the throne, according to their supposed dignity. This obeisance, among all the greater Oriental nations, was originally the act of prostration before the Monarch, to which the Mongol tribe added the ceremony of beating the head upon the ground nine times; but this had been softened, in the course of time, and by the progress of civilisation, into a grave and respectful inclination of the body, and a slight kneeling or bending of the knee. The court etiquette was loaded with forms, which, in quiet times, were strictly observed. On some festivals, and on grand occasions, there were magnificent banquets. The feast consisted of many courses of numerous dishes of all kinds: soups, roast, pillau, sometimes of animals dressed entire (stuffed with almonds, raisins and currants, and smothered in rice), stews, meat and game of every sort, carved and sent about on trays, fruits, preserves and sweetmeats, with sherbet, but no wine—a forbidden enjoyment which was indulged only in private, but, where enjoyed, indulged in to excess. The attendants were often arrayed in rich and showy dresses. During the dinner, the guests were entertained by music, vocal and instrumental, by wrestlers, posture makers and jugglers; rarely perhaps, if ever, at that period to the west of the Indus, by dancers. It was usual, on such grand occasions, to invest with khiláts those who had performed important public services, or whom it was meant to distinguish by the royal favour. These khiláts generally consisted of a dress of honour, sometimes made of rich stuffs, of satin, velvet, cloth of gold, or adorned with embroidery; sometimes even of dresses that had been worn by the Sovereign himself, with various additions according to circumstances; shawls, sabres of fine workmanship with enamelled hilts, often enriched with jewels and precious stones, daggers, coats of armour, horses, and, occasionally, sums of money.

The charm which the courts of happier countries derive from the presence of female society, was of course entirely wanting to that of Kábul. The ladies of every rank were kept strictly to private apartments, which were accessible only to females, and eunuchs, and, at times, to very near relations.

The court. The court was composed chiefly of the Amírs and Begs, who held the different provinces and districts of the kingdom, and of the officers of state and of the household. Though the usual and official language was that of unreserved obedience to the prince, yet they formed a real check upon his power. The army which had effected the conquest was composed of many bodies of men of different races, who each followed a particular leader, generally the chief person of a tribe or family. They were all soldiers of fortune, and regarded themselves as entitled to their share in the success. Many of them had joined the King voluntarily with their tribe or followers, and considered themselves at liberty to withdraw, or to shift their allegiance, when displeased. By means of combinations among themselves, they were even able, on occasion, to overpower the monarch, who found it convenient, and indeed necessary, to keep them in good humour. Much, therefore, depended on the talents of the Sovereign. But even the romantic bravery and generous temper of Báber were not always sufficient to keep within the limits of duty haughty and ambitious tribesmen, who set a high, sometimes an inordinate, value on their own services; and dangerous revolts and rebellions occurred under both him and his son. There existed no hereditary nobility except in the heads of tribes; all was personal, and proceeded from the monarch. And even the men of tribes, when they had left their wilds, and, for a series of years, had lived in towns, or followed their individual pursuits, scattered over the country, felt less connection with their chief, who was compelled to look to local influence of another description for the support of his consequence. The power possessed by the leader of the tribe was thus gradually exchanged for that of governor of a province. This change was, of course, extremely favourable to the royal authority. But, though nobility was not hereditary, it generally continued to run very much in the same families; for the sons of Amírs and officers of note were generally, early in life, introduced at court by their fathers, and gradually promoted to situations of trust and influence.

The information we possess concerning the state of the provinces under the Kábul government is but scanty. State of the provinces. They would seem to have been governed very much according to the form ascribed to the early feudal states. The leading men in the conquering army, or at court, were sent to the various provinces, attended by their old followers, and districts were assigned to them. Of the state of landed property we have few details. The former inhabitants were not expelled from their lands. The labour and skill of the peasant and farmer are necessary under every government; there were no capitalists who farmed on a large scale. Every village had probably, as in Persia, a kilanter or head man, and some village counsellors, who afforded a certain degree of protection and succour. The person appointed to the jágír settled himself on the spot, took possession of the forts and public buildings, and placed his immediate retainers in offices of trust within his government; probably, at the same time, assigning to them some allotments of land. Through them, though rarely by them, he collected the rents, or, more properly speaking, a share of the produce of the lands, and the public taxes, the measure and extent of which were often much at his discretion. As all powers, military, civil, and criminal, were vested in his person, the comfort, or misery, of the inhabitants was in his power, and was essentially influenced by his character. The complaint of a despised boor did not easily reach the court, and, if it did, was not likely, except in cases of crying and flagrant injustice, to be much attended to: and woe to the unhappy wretch who made a complaint, and afterwards returned under the power of his oppressor! Every governor was like an absolute prince while his power lasted. His chief danger arose from intrigues at court, where he was constantly obliged, either by his personal presence or through his friends, to maintain his influence. He was liable to be removed at any time at the pleasure of the King. It is plain that this system exposed the inhabitants to great extortions, and was, in many ways, unfavourable to the prosperity and improvement of the country. The governor, who held his office by an uncertain, and probably a short tenure, was anxious to make the most of his time, and apt to regard the possessions and property of the governed merely as the means of enriching himself and his dependents. The hen was too often killed for the golden egg.

The army. The army did not resemble that of European governments, divided into regular regiments and troops, with officers each commanding and exercising a certain number of men dressed in a national uniform and paid by the state. It was composed of the immediate followers of the King, and of those of the great chiefs, attached to them from various considerations of family, or hope, or gratitude; and of portions of the tribes, as the Aimáks, Moghuls, Hazáras, under their native chiefs. Almost every man of rank had retainers, who attached themselves to him to share his good fortune, and his consequence depended on their bravery and number. Every leader had his standard, which marked his rank, the highest being that of the *túgh*, a standard surmounted by the flowing tail of the mountain cow, an object of great ambition, and granted only to a few. Round these standards they marched to battle, and round them they rallied, if broken. They had no uniform dress. Each wore that of his tribe or country, or such as he fancied.

Besides these greater leaders, there were independent warriors (Ekkeha) who joined the service, either alone, or with a few followers, as volunteer soldiers of fortune, some of whom rose to eminence.

The fighting men were in general Tartars, chiefly belonging to Túrki tribes, or descended of tribesmen, with some Persians and Aimáks. They consisted almost entirely of cavalry. The old inhabitants of Kábul, whether of the cities or plains, seldom adopted the trade of arms, but remained shopkeepers or peasants. A Tájik is sometimes, but rarely, mentioned as engaged in war.

The army gradually changed its form in progress of time. When the first generation of conquerors died away, local levies became common, and regular bands of mercenaries were formed. The earlier troops, having little or no pay, depended for their support chiefly on plunder, and the leaders looked to the command of districts. There was nothing like a standing force. The army was composed of local troops, with a few mercenaries raised on the spur of the occasion.

When the royal army took the field, it was generally arranged in three divisions; centre, right wing, and left; with an advanced guard and reserve, and some flying pickets around. The household troops were generally placed in the centre, and officers of experience named to the command of each division. Their arms were the sabre and dagger, sometimes the bow and arrow, and the spear or mace. There were already some companies of matchlock-men in the army, who seem always to have been trained mercenaries. Cannon had also begun to be used; but they were heavy and unmanagable, used chiefly in sieges or in distant cannonades. Shír Shah seems to have been one of the first who brought them with effect into the field. In regular battles, the guns were frequently connected together by chains, or ropes of bulls' hides, which served as breast-works, behind which archers and matchlock-men were placed, to prevent the irruption of cavalry between the guns, especially during the rather long intervals between the discharge and re-loading of the ponderous ordnance.

The fate of an action being generally decided by the sabre, plate and chain armour, and shields, were in use, with helmets, and sometimes chain-cloth coverings for the horse.

Fortresses. Their fortresses derived their strength from their situation on steep hills or grounds difficult of access, and from the height and thickness of their walls. They were sometimes regularly attacked by sap and battery, sometimes by mines, and defended by countermines. Night surprises, however, and assaults by scaling-ladders, were the most common modes of attack. Sometimes blockade was resorted to, and lines of circumvallation drawn round the place.

The country had few large cities; Kábul, Kandahár, Ghazni and Pesháwer were the chief. The amount of their population is uncertain. The smaller towns and villages were numerous, as the peasantry did not live in scattered dwellings, but in villages surrounded by walls; as a refuge for themselves and their cattle, in case of any sudden attack, or against the rapacity of marauders. The larger towns were inhabited by tradesmen and artisans, merchants, shopkeepers, the guardians of mosques and religious foundations and their dependents, public and private teachers, and labourers. The streets were narrow and dirty; the exterior of the houses mean, any attempt at elegance being reserved for the interior. The houses of the more wealthy were built in one or more squares, opening within into a court or parterre surrounded by piazzas. Large cities.

The principal buildings were the mosques and the tombs of the kings or holy men, and probably a few of the palaces of the kings. Some of the bazars were built at considerable expense, and with some elegance, and were frequently arched over, and closed at night by gates. There were also caravanserais, of which the large court within was surrounded by small apartments, usually with an upper story, and sometimes having a flat roof, in which merchants and traders could be accommodated, with their goods and cattle, on arriving from foreign parts.

The kingdom of Kábul was inhabited by many different races of men, and was composed chiefly of hill-country, with some rich plains. The greater part of the inhabitants of the hills were tribesmen, in a great measure independent and supported by their flocks. The peasantry and shepherds of the lowlands were in general Tájiks, the descendants of the old inhabitants of the country, and used the Persian tongue. They cultivated various grains, and reared some cattle, but Inhabitants.

were much exposed to be plundered by the tribes of the surrounding hills.

Administration of justice.

As to the administration of justice, there was, properly speaking, no regular court of justice in the country, except that of the Kázi could be considered as such, which, however, was confined to questions of marriage, dowry and others arising out of the Muhammedan law. The jágírdárs, and under them their collectors, and, in the royal domains, the collectors or other officers of government, decided in all questions, civil and criminal. There was little form. The parties appeared in person to state their own cases; and inquiries followed, liable to much partiality and corruption. The lower officers could fine and inflict corporal punishment to a certain extent. The powers of life and death, and of inflicting larger fines, were reserved to the higher officers alone.

But while the officers of government administered equity, according to usage or their ideas of right (for laws of enactment, except those of the Koran, there were none), in the plains or what may be called the conquered country, the tribes that wandered over and pastured the large mountain tracts, or partially cultivated the richer valleys and cattle lands, were little visited by the Sovereign's officers, but maintained, in a great degree, their independence. They made some annual payments as tribute, and preserved their ancient usages and customs. Each had its acknowledged chief, and a council of the principal men of the leading families, who managed its affairs and decided controversies.

The most difficult cases were such as related to blood-feuds, which, however, were left to the revenge of the injured family, according to the principle of retaliation of the Muhammedan law; and when the price of blood could not be fixed, or was refused, the prosecution of private revenge frequently occasioned assassinations and feuds for several generations.

The religion of the country west of the Indus was the Musulman. This may be called the legal religion of the country, though, properly speaking, there was no establishment. The Muhammedans have no state-establishment of their religion, which, however, they consider as the only true faith, and as not given to them only, but to the whole world. They have no order of priesthood; as in patriarchal times, every father of a family is its priest. Everywhere, indeed, mosques, often of great magnificence, have been built for public use, and endowed often with extensive lands for their support, and that of the servants of the mosque. But this has been done by private piety, and not by the state, which makes no general provision for the celebration of religious services, or the extension, or purity of religious instruction. Yet, in no country does religion present itself more to the eye of the observer, or seem more deeply and habitually to influence individuals of every rank. Every mosque has its guardian, generally some descendant of the founder. The faithful are daily summoned five times to prayer by the voice of the moizzin from the minaret of the mosque. Some Múlla, or man of supposed piety, acts as Péshnamáz, by reciting the stated prayers, the congregation repeating them along with, or after him, and carefully following him in all the bendings and humble prostrations which he makes at the proper parts of the service, towards the kibleh, which marks the position of Mekka. He is qualified for his office by no imposition of hands, or other ceremony, but owes the preference he enjoys, to his piety, the favour of the guardian of the foundation, or the silent adherence of the people. His office confers, or implies, no supernatural effusion of sanctity, or of spiritual gifts. He may quit his situation at will, and return, like any other man, to the business of the world. Religion.

Men of learning and piety.

I recollect no mention of any colleges founded in Kábul for the instruction of students in the sacred or profane sciences, though such were common, and often very magnificent, in Máwerannaher, in Khorásán and in India. But there were always men of learning and piety, who devoted themselves, as private guides, to the teaching of others; and when they acquired reputation, numbers flocked to them for the benefit of their lessons. The ordinary schools taught the pupils who frequented them, to read and write the Arabic and Persian languages, with something of accounts. Men often read the Koran in Arabic, and recited their prayers in the same tongue, without knowing one word of the meaning, but, in so doing, they performed a religious duty. The superior instructors devoted themselves to various employments, such as teaching the artificial mode of reading the Koran, with its sacred intonations, delivering lectures on its import, and expositions of the hidden or recondite meaning of its texts, and the mystical sense of its facts and doctrines. The various teachers and various schools, of course, took different views of God and nature, some leading to the wildest enthusiasm and bigotry, others to the humblest piety. The mystical tendency of their speculations, directed to the annihilation of self and the exaltation of the Deity, often ended with a long course of metaphysical meditations on the doctrine of the non-existence of matter, and the non-entity of everything, except the Divinity. One of the most remarkable of these schools is that of the Sufis, which seems to terminate in a refined philosophical deism or pantheism, yet has produced volumes of the most beautiful poetry. The disciples of these meditative schools, whom research and reflection had rendered tolerant, lived retired, and mixed little in the world. But the men destined for public life, who had studied only the Koran and its observances, with the traditions of the prophet, were distinguished above all others for their intolerant

bigotry, and for their detestation and persecution of every other religion.

To some it may appear singular that of no religion are the followers more penetrated with a feeling of its truth and superiority to all others, or more distinguished for their inflexible adherence to it under every trial, than those of the Mahomedan, a religion which yet has no regular priesthood, and no state establishment. But, at the same time, it must be remembered, that, though it has no regular state establishment, it has innumerable foundations, and lands of greater or less extent belonging to mosques, tombs, colleges and religious institutions, and supporting great numbers of zealous and active dependents in every part of the country, and that the influence of the wandering mendicants and derwíshes is very great. But still the real secret of this heart-felt adherence must be sought for in a different quarter, in something inherent in the doctrines and practical observances of the religion itself, which strike the imagination and affect the heart, joined to the narrow spirit of an exclusive sect, that looks with contempt and pity on every other, and breeds up every Musulman, even in his early days, to regard himself as a partizan, and a warrior of the faith.

But, even among Musulmans, there were differences of belief, and the grand division between Sunnis and Shías occasioned controversies, and persecutions and wars. The Sunnis adhered to the four first Khalifs, as the legal successors of Muhammed; while the Shias, regarding Ali, the cousin and son-in-law of the Prophet, as his lawful heir, considered the three first Khalifs as usurpers, and cursed them in the public prayers of their mosques, and often in their private orisons and ejaculations, as traitors. In early times, the inhabitants of Máwerannaher, Khorásán and Kábul, had followed the Sunni faith, which was still adhered to by the natives of the kingdom of Kábul, some of the hill tribes excepted. The doctrines of the Shías were introduced from Arabia, and diffused chiefly in Persia, and by the Persian conquests in Khorásán and elsewhere. There were some Kizelbásh, or Persian Shías in Kábul. The hatred of the partizans of the two sects towards each other was often extreme.

Almost every man had his spiritual guide, whom he consulted in his difficulties and doubts, and by whom he was much influenced in his conduct. Men eminently distinguished for piety were supposed to be sometimes visited by gleams of divine light; and though the Mahomedans are unitarians of the strictest kind, admitting of no partner to God, yet such men were reverenced after death, and pilgrimages were made to their tombs.

Literature. Kábul could not be said to have any native literature or science. It appropriated, and imitated, that of the Persians. The poems of Ferdausi, Háfez, Sádi, Jámi and the other great Persian poets, were familiar to every man of education. But though the country produced no great poet, many individuals, some of the highest rank, wrote agreeable verses, and a taste for poetry was fashionable with every class. The subjects were generally love and religion. One is sometimes surprised to see so much tenderness and respectful delicacy of feeling, flowing from the pen of sturdy warriors, and addressed to females, who were shut up, and guarded, as prisoners and slaves. But war, which calls out and exercises many of the higher parts of our nature, is not necessarily hostile to the gentler affections, and, in every situation of life, nature vindicates her rights. This was the age of the great historians, Mír Khwánd and Khwánd Amír, who wrote chiefly in Khorásán; but, except Báber's own Commentaries, we know of no historical work produced in Kábul.

Sciences. The sciences, like the literature, of Kábul were borrowed from those of the Arabs and Persians, but little proficiency and no improvement was made in them. Some few studied mathematics and astronomy chiefly as subservient to astrology, in which all were believers; and the marches of armies, and the movements of kings were directed by the conjunctions of the heavenly bodies. No journey or march was undertaken, no great work begun, but at the hour fixed by the astrologer.

Their medicine, where it was not empirical, they borrowed from the Arabs; and they, probably from constant experience, possessed considerable knowledge in the treatment of wounds.

Architecture.

Of their architecture we learn little. It was probably borrowed from Herát and Samarkand. Some of the tombs still remaining are said to possess considerable elegance. The times were too turbulent to admit of attempting many of the works of peace: and means were not found to restore even the noble reservoirs and water-courses, constructed in earlier times for irrigating and enriching the country, but which had fallen into decay.

State of morals.

To estimate the condition of morals, and the degree of happiness or comfort existing in such a state of society, is never an easy task. The practice of polygamy, accompanied, as a necessary consequence, by the seclusion of women, and the existence of slavery, which are common to all Musulman countries, have always a powerful and demoralizing influence on manners. But the plurality of wives and concubines is nearly confined to the upper ranks, and the more wealthy; and though the evil consequences of the practice are felt, in the undue importance and the prominence given to the sensual passions, in the debasing effects of jealousy and mistrust on the character, in the mischief of entrusting the education of the rising generation, the young of both sexes, to the nurture of women, totally strangers to the business and the virtues of active life; and in addition to this, in the endless discords and enmities, which the claims of rival mothers introduce into the bosom of families; yet, being avowed and sanctioned by the law, it is attended with none of that degradation of feeling and character that attends the pursuit of promiscuous debauchery, or of unlawful concubinage, when the sense of duty is overpowered by the influence of a passion acknowledged to be guilty, and the indulgence is pursued with the feelings of a criminal, who is conscious that he is breaking the law. The connection of wife and concubine are equally lawful, and alike recognized by the Musulman religion, and the issue of both have their shares in the succession. The practice of slavery appears to have been confined to domestic slavery, a condition, in the East, in which the slave is generally treated as a favoured and confidential servant, often as a child of the family. We find no traces of agricultural servitude. The lower ranks seem all to have been free. Their wives were more fortunate than those of their superiors, since their duties required them to move about, and probably sometimes to assist in field-labour.

Condition of the higher ranks,

The higher ranks, who lived in the possession of comparative wealth and plenty, seem to have had the usual and almost necessary virtues of their station — bravery and liberality towards the dependents and followers who formed their strength. They were generally hardy, and with some skill in war, which was their trade, but was practised rather in the way of foray and skirmish than of regular tactics. Having the virtues and the vices of adventurers, they were not uniformly steady in their allegiance and fidelity to their Sovereign; their adherence to whom they considered as a matter to be regulated by considerations of mutual convenience, in which they were too often directed by notions of mere temporary expediency. Some of them we have seen were men of talent and generosity, and many had some taste for liberal studies, and delighted in the Persian and Túrki poets and moralists.

The great body of the inhabitants, agricultural and pastoral, were probably a good deal oppressed. The exactions of government, joined to the constant march and devastation of armies, and the plundering incursions of the hill tribes, must have left them little that they could call their own. There was indeed, generally, some castle, or walled town, to which they could, in such cases, retire. But they were, nevertheless, often taken by surprise, when their families and cattle, and hoards of grain were liable to be carried away, and their standing corn trampled down, or consumed by the horses of the invaders. But, even in the most unfavourable circumstances, there is an elasticity and spring in the human mind, that long resist the pressure of the heaviest calamity. Oppression is never, indeed, directly favourable to the moral habits. Where force cannot be opposed to it, it calls up artifice and cunning. But it also sometimes calls up the nobler passions. The bonds of union between the members of communities and the members of families, are drawn closer by their sufferings, and by their exertions to avert them. The generous affections are brought actively into play; united efforts are made to oppose the common enemy; great sacrifices are submitted to for the sake of one another; the disinterested and domestic affections daily gain strength in the midst of suffering, and through the very agency of suffering. Men become more affectionate parents, more attached children and friends, and better members of the little community. There are little numberless pleasures that the eye of oppression cannot detect, or its hand interrupt. History in general gives little information as to the daily employment, and feelings of the great body of the lower classes, but, in this instance, what little can be gleaned, is not unfavourable. and of the people.

These remarks of course apply chiefly to the inhabitants of the plains; the inhabitants of the hills and mountains preserved their old independence unchanged.

Revenue. As to the revenue, its extent and nature, we know little. The principal was probably a land-tax, which from the mountaineers was levied in the form of tribute. Báber informs us that the revenue of Kábul from both these sources was only eight laks of Sháhrukhis, or about 33,333*l.* 6*s.* 8*d.* In addition to this, there were the tumgha, or custom duties, on all cattle, sheep and other articles brought into the country, and probably some transit duties and shop duties. There were, besides, the péshkeshes, and other offerings made to the prince on festivals and other great occasions. These consisted in money, horses, rich cloths and other rarities; and, though part of them went out again in the form of khiláts and gratifications to favourite servants, the surplus in the king's favour was probably considerable. At the same time the revenue of Kábul was never great. Báber, soon after he conquered Kábul, levied on Kábul and another district, a contribution of thirty thousand loads of grain (kharwar) to distribute among the tribes who had accompanied him in his conquest, but the burden was found to be too great, he tells us, and the country suffered extremely.

Absence of free institutions. The fixed and stationary condition of all large Asiatic kingdoms, which, from the first traces of history to the latest times, exhibit only the purely despotic form of government, has naturally excited the attention of all readers of history. No progress seems ever to have been made towards free or liberal institutions, or if any liberal laws or regulations were made under a good or great monarch, they totally disappear in the reign of his successor. Nothing is stable, but the absolute will of the sovereign. The great difficulty of obtaining anything like free or permanent institutions lies in this very absolute power, and in the great extent of the kingdom. In a small district of hill country, separated by natural limits from other similar or different districts, the whole, or a great proportion, of the inhabitants can meet and confer about their concerns. They can agree about the acquisition of certain benefits, or the removal of certain wrongs, which affect them as a body. They can appoint the most powerful or popular man among them to watch over their rights, with certain powers conferred for what they conceive to be the general benefit. If no powerful chief or king is near, who has strength enough to subdue them, they may, for a greater or less time, preserve a certain degree of self-government. The same is the case in towns, especially in commercial or trading towns. Their common interest and the direction of men of substance, of experience and knowledge, draw and knit them together. They engage in fraternities; every trade, or craft, or profession, forms unions, and draws together numerous bodies, who work for their own, or the common good, and, in process of time, acquire a corporation-spirit, that makes them ready to do and suffer much for a common cause. From governing their own little society, they acquire the habits that fit them for taking a share in the government of the town. Something of a representative constitution is the consequence. Their wealth enables them to fortify their town, and, in a country where many such towns exist, they can command troops, can employ their wealth, and form leagues or combinations, so as even to be a check upon the government, or to attain independence. Such were the free towns of Italy, of the Low Countries, and of Germany. In England, the towns, after obtaining the right of governing themselves, by joining with the crown or the great barons, became an important part of the political system. It is only by checks that any authority can be limited, and institutions are necessary to support and maintain these checks. Thus, in England, the power of the nobles never could have been brought as an effective check upon the power of the king, had they not been of hereditary rank, and accustomed to meet together in parliament and elsewhere, as a recognized body; in a word, to consider themselves as a political corporation, having rights. They might, otherwise, have formed combinations and leagues, and engaged in rebellions and commotions; but these, if successful, would have terminated to the advantage of one or two of the chief leaders, not of the nobles as a body opposed to the king. Their rank, being hereditary, gave them both permanence and cohesion, and enabled them to act in concert for the common interest. But in the East, nobility is only personal. Except where there are tribes, the personal influence of any individual is small. The nobles hold no assemblies as a separate body, and have no duties to perform as such. They cannot, therefore, combine or act in union, but by rebellion. There are no public institutions (not religious), in which they, or any other subjects of the state, meet for deliberation on ministerial or any other public purposes; no county meetings, no boards of justices, no juries, no town meetings. The means of combining, or of coming to a common understanding, are, therefore, limited. Absolute princes never favour the growth of privileges to nobles, or cities, or districts; they are more willing to destroy these rights. They centralize every thing, and make every thing depend on their own will and pleasure. Thus, were a movement to take place, even for the most beneficial objects, no hereditary leader can be found, no political body to assist, no permanent institution to give security to the object if attained. It is a rebellion which, if successful for the moment, falls away of itself, like a house built on sand, and leaves not a trace behind. Thus such despotic governments do not afford the fulcrum to support the political lever, and the force is applied in vain. Inferior, internal political institutions, scattered over the country, or means of consultation and combination among powerful hereditary chiefs, are necessary, as checks to absolute power. They cannot long exist, without bringing a considerable degree of freedom in their train. Counties, and the public meetings they produce, towns, parishes, corporations, and, at a later period, courts of law and juries, are the great elements of liberty. They bring men together, make them reason, and accustom them to act with foresight, with moderation, and in concert. The Mahomedan governments of the East have only two checks, the dangerous one of rebellion —and the power of religion and popular opinion, or custom, represented, sometimes successfully, sometimes without effect, by the Ulema, the heads of the religion and law. But revolution produces a change of governors, not of government. Any effectual change must go deeper, and begin with the fundamental elements of civil and political society. Yet, now that the Janissaries are gone, the Ulema is perhaps the nearest approach to a corporation of any body in Turkey.

# INDEX

TO THE

## SECOND VOLUME.

---

END OF THE SECOND VOLUME.